MVFCL

Eitelsbacher
Kronenberg
1973er Kabinett
Produce of Germany

Karthäuser Hofberger
Erzeugerabfüllung
Werner Tyrell, vorm. H.W. Rautenstrauch

Denominazione di Origine Controllata

Classico Superiore

BOTTLED IN ZONE OF PRODUCTION
BY A.V.F.F. S.n.c. Sona—VERONA

SOLE AGENTS: PATERNO IMPORTS LTD - CHICAGO - ILL.

PRODUCT OF ITALY

5060 VR

P
APPELLAT

BA
B
N

MIS EN BOUTEILLES A LA PROPRIÉTÉ

Médaille d'Or   Paris 1962

CHAMBERTIN

CLOS DE BÊZE

APPELLATION CONTROLÉE

PIERRE GELIN
PROPRIETAIRE A FIXIN ET GEVREY-CHAMBERTIN (COTE-D'OR)

QUALITÄTSWEIN · RHEINGAU

Freiherrlich Langwerth von Simmern'sche
Kellerei
Eltviller   Eltville   Sonnenberg
Riesling   1970er   Riesling

GESETZLICH GESCHÜTZT

B

co

adriatica

PRODUCT OF YUGOSLAVIA

1972

CABERNET

RED WINE
FROM ISTRIA

ALCOHOL BY VOLUME 12% CONTENTS 1 PT. 8 FL. OZ.

The Rothbury Estate

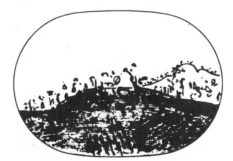

HUNTER VALLEY
PRODUCE OF AUSTRALIA   750ml

SIMI
SINCE 1876

château
MONDE
GAZI

TES DE B
1971

shipped by

D1506010

THE INTERNATIONAL ALBUM OF WINE

THE INTERNATIONAL ALBUM OF

WINE

Your Personal Record of Wine Labels and Tastes

STEVEN J. SCHNEIDER

designed by

PAUL BACON

HOLT, RINEHART AND WINSTON

NEW YORK

COPYRIGHT © 1977 BY VINEYARD BOOKS, INC.
PREPARED BY VINEYARD BOOKS, INC.,
159 EAST 64TH STREET, NEW YORK, N.Y. 10021.
ALL RIGHTS RESERVED, INCLUDING THE RIGHT TO REPRODUCE
THIS BOOK OR PORTIONS THEREOF IN ANY FORM.

PUBLISHED SIMULTANEOUSLY IN CANADA BY HOLT, RINEHART
AND WINSTON OF CANADA, LIMITED.

LIBRARY OF CONGRESS CATALOGING IN PUBLICATION DATA
SCHNEIDER, STEVEN J.
THE INTERNATIONAL ALBUM OF WINE.
INCLUDES INDEX.
1. WINE AND WINE MAKING.   I. TITLE.
TP548.S458   641.2′2   75-21474
ISBN 0-03-014641-0

FIRST EDITION

MAPS BY JILL WEBER
ILLUSTRATIONS BY PAUL BACON

PRINTED IN THE UNITED STATES OF AMERICA
10 9 8 7 6 5 4 3 2 1

Contents

Acknowledgments

In assembling a book such as this, it is impossible to remember all one's debts for information and assistance and to thank all who have added to one's understanding of wines over the years. In addition to those named below, others have aided in providing information about particular growing areas and regulations and in supplying labels. Friends have generously read through the text, making corrections and supplying updated information.

I am particularly grateful to Peter M. F. Sichel and his firm, H. Sichel Sonne; Serena Sutcliffe; Alexis Bespaloff; and to my patient partner and friend, William Bolter. Extra thanks go to Darrell Corti, who kindly consented to collaborate in describing the wines of his native California. Among friends in the French wine trade I mention gratefully Jean-Pierre Moueix, Jean François and Cristian Moueix, Patrick Danglade, Jean Delmas, François Samazeuilh, and Peter A. Sichel; and I am indebted to many more. In the English trade kind assistance was offered by John Grant, Cyril Ray, Lionel Frumkin, and Loeb and Co. Ltd. Alexander C. McNally of Heublein in the United States made helpful corrections relating to Hungary, Frederick Ek gave his informed time to several questions, and the late Frank Schoonmaker characteristically gave information and most generous encouragement. The Enology Department of the University of California at Davis reviewed and criticized the chapters on tasting and grape growing and wine making.

The Australian Wine Board and their outpost, the Australian Wine Center in London, have given information and patient replies to many questions.

I dedicate the tasting chapter to Leon Grinberg and Michael Train. Neither requires assistance in matters of taste; it is rather that I have benefited so often from their acuity.

Paul Bacon has designed this book with his irrepressible talent and inventiveness, and I am most appreciative of his contribution. *The International Album of Wine* originated in the offices of Vineyard Books, and its format was set out by Julie Colmore and the late, much missed Albert Leventhal. Thanks are extended to Peter Dworkin, my Vineyard editor, in direct proportion to his long labors to accommodate my original texts to a general Anglo-American audience. His persistent attentiveness to this task is reflected throughout the finished book.

Thanks are one matter; apologies are no less in order. First and last, it is too bad that lack of space caused so many hundreds of fine wines to be passed over in silence, wines as worthy as those included, along with the people whose labor and perseverance account for their quality. Space also forced the elimination of chapters on other wine-producing countries. And each time I have gone back over the manuscript some understatement, overstatement, or error has leaped out of a page; I cannot believe they have all been caught and tamed, and those that remain are to be laid to my door. Finally, the accidents of tasting experience have surely drawn me into unjust praise, blame, or characterization of some wine. It could not be otherwise, and so, as François Villon suggested,

Au fort, pour éviter riotes
Je crie à toutes gens mercis.

To Serena
Remembering a year of grace
With thanks beyond count

Preface

Some wonderfully entertaining books have been written by amateurs of fine wines, books full of anecdotes and personal appreciations in which the pleasures of quality wine are vividly expressed. Other excellent books are more scientific, dealing with vine culture, wine production, and chemistry. A trader in fine wines (and that is what I am) flounders between these extremes. He is an emissary shuttling to and fro between wine makers (with their knowledge, talents, pretensions, and illusions) and consumers (with their desires, illusions, appreciation—or lack of it—curiosity, and sometimes vanity). What use can his professionalism be to a candid and interested consumer? Certainly he cannot command the consumer to enjoy one wine or scold him (or her) for preferring another.

Too often I open the mail or put down the telephone wishing that the fine wine trade really had all the glamour, luxury, and fakery that many imagine. Quick fame or at least early retirement could be hoped for. But humdrum reality shows its plain face morning, noon, and night. Trading fine wines in fact resembles dealing in antique furniture, thoroughbred horses, quality teas, precious stones, and the like. Quality standards do exist, though they may be a bit subjective, a bit elusive, for the value arises from a confusing mixture of natural materials and the human skills used to shape these materials into a final product. Professionals, makers and traders alike, play a part in determining standards of taste, yet the consumer, whether beginner or connoisseur, ultimately accepts or rejects the final product at its price.

Quality wines are made in certain places, from certain grape varieties, and in certain ways with the intention of obtaining certain tasting characteristics in the finished wine. The question "What did the wine maker intend?" is important in understanding a wine. It is also a key question in appreciating a wine, if by appreciation we mean something more than eating when hungry, drinking when dry, or swallowing alcohol when anxious or tired. And right here is the nitty-gritty of our story. A fine wine is not fully enjoyed without some notion of what it is—you might even say "who" it is—and where it came from.

Fine wines are made purposefully to canons or standards of taste. These ideals or preconceptions in the mind of the wine maker may derive from old traditions, as in Europe's established vineyard regions, or they may be new ideas, as in the pioneer vineyards in California or Australia. But it is not too much to say that fine wine falls into families or groups according to the canons or intentions by which it was made. This book aims to introduce wine drinkers to the main families of fine wines, illustrating each family with outstanding examples.

Most of these wines are available at moderate prices in major British and American markets. For the wines of regions such as Burgundy or Piedmont, which often bear the labels of diverse shippers and small growers, these examples must stand for many individual wines. The particular wine selected to represent its wine type may not be carried in your area, and you may of course substitute the labels of other producers to fit your situation and preferences. Space for labels and notes on other wines, or for your second or third notation on a favorite wine, is provided at the end of the book.

The aim of the book explains its design, with its representative wine labels matched with space on the facing page in which readers can record their impressions. It also explains why the book is devoted almost entirely to fine wines that have identity rather than common beverage wines that could be produced nearly anywhere that grapes can grow. And it explains why a trader rather than a wine chemist wrote the text. As I said a moment ago, the trader is an emissary, an interpreter between producer and consumer. His business is characterizing and evaluating wine in terms of its tasting qualities and the relation of those tasting qualities to the wine's origin—the region, individual vineyard, and vintage year from which it came. This book, an introduction to fine wine families, is an extension of that business function.

The conventional descriptive language of the fine wine trade differs from a wine chemist's language much as a jeweler's vocabulary departs from that of a crystallographer's or a music critic's from that of a physicist studying sound. Trade language, like traders, is meant to organize and introduce information and experience to wine drinkers and succeeds when interested consumers discover and enjoy more as a result.

Muddling the differences between professionals and amateurs (consumers) is silly at best, harmful at worst. We in the international wine trade have the job and the obligation to characterize, evaluate, and transmit fine wines to amateurs for their enjoyment. Not surprisingly, it takes ten years' business experience to do this reasonably accurately, ignoring one's personal preferences—or so I found. Among amateurs, whose sensible goals are personal appreciation of wines and cultivation of *their own* tastes, are many who feel that their stature is enhanced by striking a professional posture, by characterizing and evaluating a whole crop of wine or predicting the future development of certain wines, for example. Horrible illustrations can be found of amateur pomposity and professional incompetence. When you open and drink a bottle of fine wine from a major producing region, I hope that the language and information in this book will suggest to you conventional, expected tasting qualities of that region's family of fine wines. You have a right to receive these qualities for your money, and so have a vested interest in reading and knowing about them.

Money gives access to fine wines. So does information. Neither substitutes for appreciation of fine wines. Fine wine is an "individual" with a personality and ancestry of its own, and its full excitement can be felt only when you meet it halfway, bringing to it your curiosity, perceptions, and knowledge. If you use this book to organize, record, and remember one of the most innocent, varied, and sociable pleasures in the world—and one of the few that the twentieth century not only has allowed to survive but also has ameliorated and distributed within easy reach—then this book will have succeeded. Above all, taste and drink, for the wines will tell more about themselves than I, or anyone else, can do.

Steven J. Schneider

BORDEAUX, LONDON, BOSTON
DECEMBER 1974–MARCH 1976

Tasting Wine: An Attitude and a Vocabulary

That part of humanity rich enough to afford continuing scientific exploration is gradually beginning to observe that pleasure may not be a luxury but a necessity. We do not know if primitive man decorated the walls of his caves out of needs any more or less urgent than those with which he pursued the deer and bison so vividly sketched there. We do know that later eras separated human activities into those necessary to sustain biological life and those considered luxuries. Yet observation challenges the simple opposition of necessity and luxury (pleasure). Perhaps it is a luxury to have one's back rubbed, particularly by the right person. But newborn infants who are not coddled, held, touched, and caressed do not simply lead less pleasant infancies. They can literally die for lack of this "luxury." Perhaps a hot shower after a cold afternoon of winter sport follows one "luxury" with another. But humans suspended in a liquid environment the same temperature as their body and otherwise deprived of external physical stimulation can go mad. What we think of as pleasure seems also to be a necessary condition of human existence.

Wine happens to be a beverage. Water better serves the need to replace body fluid, yet no Western civilization has omitted wine. It may not be demonstrable that wine is a necessity. But this chapter, and this book, is dedicated to a demonstrable necessity, the necessity to enjoy life, in which wine is one enhancement.

I would like to draw your attention to some other pleasures in perhaps more familiar circumstances, so as to situate wine among them. Suppose that you play the piano, or indulge in a sport such as tennis. Consider what happens to you during a great recital or at a tennis match between two world-class professionals. Moments of musical performance and interpretation give rise to a sense of exhilaration and wonder. Similarly, extraordinary tennis play sweeps us away with excitement, admiration, and a sort of aesthetic thrill. What is common to these arousing performances? First, we are generous in spirit; the performance is so splendid that we are beyond envy. We spontaneously praise, cheer, or applaud from the heart. Yet, had we not struggled with the keyboard or racket for many frustrating hours, could we appreciate fully what was taking place before us?

We were not born with a concept of virtuoso performances of Mozart or of daring net play at match point. Humdrum things are readily learned—to set the handbrake before leaving the automobile, to take the umbrella when clouds lower. But it is the long, painstaking learning of sights, sounds, and skills that prepare us for some of our happiest and most aesthetic experiences. It is as possible merely to quaff wine as a beverage as it is to enjoy watching two athletes bash a ball about without knowing how the game is scored. Cultivating a taste for fine wine, "learning the game," is another matter. Music and painting are composed in certain traditions; games are played to cer-

tain rules; and wines are made in certain styles. The success of fine wines is achieved against certain odds, and their expression involves preconceived qualities of taste and reveals novel ones.

While remembering the piano concert and tennis match, it is a good occasion to mention a disagreeable experience we have all lived through. At the concert or tennis match, someone cannot refrain from saying something like, "You should have heard so-and-so play that," or, "So-and-so would make these fellows look sick." How many variations there are to such a remark! By the tone of voice they all attempt to say, *My* experience is greater than yours." Translation: "I am better than you." Cultivating a taste for wine will bring occasions for many self-important remarks to come your way; they probably have already. It is amazing how vanity is injected into wine conversations. My defense, and you too may find it helpful, is to cultivate a maximum personal interest in fine wine itself. In this spirit one can readily shrug off whatever boasting some silly ass insists upon parading. In wine as in other subjects, well-informed people share their thoughts and information gracefully.

Wine is a sensual experience, but its full enjoyment is helped by some knowledge of what to expect. This in turn requires a language to express, record, and communicate the experience. This chapter introduces wine terms and a vocabulary of taste. The purpose is to assist tasting; the terms have evolved to give points of reference and suggest physical realities that cause different taste sensations. They come at the beginning of this book rather than the end because these terms are indispensable. Just as the language of horsemanship, of the ballet, of the guitar allows amateurs of those skills to communicate, so the language of wine is the means of sharing wine experiences. As we shall shortly see, the tasting note that records our impressions is nearly as important as our senses; it marks our perception of what a wine offers and is a building block in both present and future pleasure in the world's rich variety of fine wines.

Wine is fermented juice of wine grapes. Substances in this ripe fruit remain in the wine made from it. The fermentation that converts sugar into alcohol also creates substances that were not in the grape. We are able to sense quite a number of them. Still other qualities are contributed by the wine maker, such as maturation of wine in oak barrels. In a glass bottle, secured by a cork and left to age, substances react with each other to form still different compounds that can be sensed. When exposed to the air, a few more changes can take place in the last moments before we actually sniff, sip, and drink the wine.

So much for the wine; what about the taster? The taster is an animal that walks upright, has money to spend on wine, and can perceive stimuli. This person usually has not thought much about what goes on inside his mouth to make up the sensations that we call taste. Scientists are able to distinguish three classes of taste sensations. First, gustatory sensations are primary tastes we can distinguish with the tongue. Sweetness is detected at the tip of the tongue, saltiness at the front and sides, sourness or acidity also along the sides, and bitterness at the center and back. The second class, tactile sensation, is possible in the mouth because of receptors in the tongue and other soft tissue. The oiliness of a substance can be sensed here, as can viscosity and puckering sensations. The third aspect of our sensations of wine is perceived in the upper nasal cavity, behind the mouth and above the palate. Stimuli carried in vapor form are received by a sensitive organ, the olfactory region. Perceptions are carried to the olfactory bulb in the brain, and the sensations pass to higher brain functions such as memory and reason. At this point we begin to think *about* what we are experiencing.

To taste ideally, each stimulus should reach all sensitive organs. We sniff wine vigorously before tasting it to enable aroma-producing compounds to reach the olfactory region. We take a mouthful and let it contact the tongue and mouth. Then, to help the olfactory system along further, we take a little air into the mouth and inhale slightly, in fact slurping the wine and drawing all the impressions possible in vapor form up to the olfactory region. Swallowing gives wine a last exposure to the olfactory receptors.

Suppose we are tasting a sparkling Italian wine called Asti Spumante, made from a fragrant grape variety called Muscat and produced so as to contain some unfermented grape sugars. It is visibly sparkling, white, and denser than water. Our nose first collects certain floral odors. In our mouth, the tongue senses sweetness; the mouth surfaces register a prickling, bubbling tactile sensation and will notice that this is a rich, heavy liquid more like honey than water. Many substances, both from the grape and the fermentation, will stimulate olfactory receptors. If we have ever eaten Muscat grapes, their strong flavor may be remembered. If we were to try to verbalize this to another person, experience and reasoning would have to be exercised. We might choose words such as smoky, pungent, sweet, luscious, or cloying, or primitive expressions such as yummy or icky, depending on personal taste. Some would be good wine terms, some would not. An experienced taster would detect Muscat on the first whiff and a well-read taster would already know that Asti Spumante is based on Muscat.

At a professional tasting, a wine would be spat out, since many wines are tasted and getting drunk makes for bad judgment. At a social or ceremonial occasion, objectives are more mixed; slurping and spitting and note taking are not in order. The value of intoxication at such affairs, however, can be tangible.

Ideal wine tasting aims at getting the maximum number of sensations out of the wine. A clean white surface, good side illumination, and a room as odorless as possible are desirable. The taster can judge appearance and color, evaluate wine odors, taste and spit out the wine, making notes along the way, from appearance, to smell, to mouth and olfactory impressions. The most significant tasting rule that amateurs can learn from professionals is not to comment on wines until everyone has tasted and made his notes. However difficult a rule to obey, its common sense is crystal clear. Inevitably, outside comments about some feature of a wine influence our own perception of it.

The illustration at the end of this chapter shows glass shapes traditional to different wines and a "universal" glass. Most have a space in which vapors can collect and be approached by the nose. Most shapes curve in to contain this space, concentrating odors for the benefit of the taster. Therefore, a glass should be filled to only one-third or even less of its volume. In formal testings showing many wines, many tasters prefer to smell all the wines before tasting any. As a rule, notes follow visual inspection, smelling, and tasting.

The COLOR, its shade or intensity (degree of lightness or darkness), and its hues (purple as opposed to red) suggest tasting attributes. Color, and its degree of brilliance, is itself a feature of a wine's style. Another visible feature is viscosity: Is it a heavy, oily liquid or a thin, mobile fluid? Various wine terms describe and grade appearance.

AROMA is a collection of attributes that come from the grape and its skin. BOUQUET is the collection of attributes arising from the production of wine, its fermentation and treatment up to bottling, and from maturation, or aging. Both aroma and bouquet are perceived by sniffing and while the wine is in the mouth, but these terms are commonly linked with smelling, on the understanding that olfactory perception continues throughout tasting.

From here, most tasters proceed to attributes associated with wine's CONSTITUTION, including BODY and BALANCE. These terms apply to basic features such as alcoholic strength, acidity, sweetness, dryness, astringency, and the presence or absence of important flavors. Then, as wine is smelled, warmed, and savored in the mouth, a somewhat different experience is registered—a progression of sensations through tasting, one succeeding the other. The French use a term, *épanouissement,* which suggests the opening or blooming of a flower. In English, this process might be called the wine's DEVELOPMENT to one's senses. Attention is on the quality and clarity of different sensations and to the harmony among them. At last an elusive phase of tasting appraises the FINESSE and AFTERTASTE of wine. Description now dwells on more subtle overall impressions; attention is given to aftertastes that complete and reflect the whole tasting experience.

Terms for aroma and finesse tend to be fanciful, for the impressions they treat are fleeting and elusive, and thus are hard to verbalize. Terms for constitution and development, more straightforward attributes, are more oriented toward qualities that chemical analysis can measure. Terms for bouquet can be chemically oriented or relate to conditions of storage and degree of maturation.

Reflect a moment on these aspects of wine, and you will imagine quite a range of "tasting" activity. We are asking a great deal of our sensory apparatus: to perceive different things at the same time, to be open to suggestion at one instant and to concentrate on something quite precise at the next. The taster clearly must keep an alert mind, with memory poised to help recognize different sensations and imagination ready to become active. But the taster also tries to maintain a prudent, objective attitude, cross-examining himself or herself about impressions real or fancied. We begin to see why the tasting note is a prelude to concentration as it draws our attention to the separate departments of wine's anatomy. As we return to it at a later time, the tasting note becomes basic to our experience and memory. By taking on the discipline of answering separate points about wine, seeking terms to note them down, we actually assist ourselves to taste better and remember more.

Common sense now begins to explain some rituals of wine tasting. If the purpose of sniffing a specially shaped wineglass one-third full of a red wine is to detect combinations of odors identifying a certain grape variety, then a standard, complete procedure makes sense. First, smell the wine undisturbed. Second, swirl the liquid to assist substances into vapor form where the nose can "get at them." (To swirl it, we hold the glass by its base.) Third, agitate the glass violently and smell again. A complete declaration of odors ensues. We taste dry wines before sweet ones because the senses get fatigued by sugar and do not accurately register, for example, the acidity of a wine. If I tell someone to take his cigar out of the tasting room immediately, I am not being prissy. I am only defending my hopes of sensing the aroma of a particular wine and noting down an evaluation of it.

Some pages ago it was said that advance information about wine production, grape variety, and normal tasting features helps enjoyment of a wine. Such advance information, it can be seen now, leads something of a double life. Expectation and some prior knowledge of wine types alert us to a wine's qualities. Unfortunately, it may also suggest them to our imagination when they are not there. The rule of silence during formal tastings at least keeps notions from spreading. A tendency to fancy explains also why tasting without knowledge of the wine tasted, or "blind" tasting, is so useful.

The cardinal purpose of formal tasting, however, is to group wines of one type or genus. When these are tasted with some preparatory knowledge, a sense of their qualities sets in the mind. Repeat this experience a few times, and the taster will commence to discover wines as individuals of a family and to perceive them almost as persons. Great enjoyment of wine, many of its aesthetic values and excitement, begins with this discovery. Recall the excitement and pleasure of that great performance, musical or otherwise. From color to aroma, bouquet, body, development on the senses, and finesse, a wine gives our senses a performance. And when we relate that performance to the family of wine in question, it can leap out at our senses and minds, dazzling and delighting them.

Wine vocabulary is one means of educating ourselves to perceive wine qualities. The tasting note is a sort of snapshot of ourselves in the act of tasting. Along with notes, most professionals and many amateurs use numerical ratings for wine. Neither as a professional whose business is to buy and sell wines nor as an after-hours amateur whose business is to enjoy them have I found numerical ratings helpful. The effort of putting sensations into words, however, helps me to remember a wine and helps to taste it too. Qualities of a wine in relation to vintage year, the property from which it came, its type, and its region are better noted for me by words than numbers. However, the enology department of the University of California at Davis has created a model of a tasting scorecard that exemplifies numerical systems. Of a maximum 20 points, they allot the following maximum number of points for each factor.

FACTOR	POINTS
Clarity and freedom from sediment	2
Color (depth and tint and appropriateness, for type)	2
Aroma and bouquet	4
Freedom from acetic odor	2
Total acid to the taste	2
Tannin (astringency)	2
Extract (body)	1
Sugar	1
General taste (the mouth's impression of flavor)	2
Overall impression	2

Simpler scoring systems can be found or devised. A 7-point system gives 1 point for color, 2 points for odors, 3 points for impressions in the mouth, and 1 point for aftertaste. Charts that rate vintage years often give numerical values. These I attack on logical grounds. Scor-

ing cards for individual wines may be a matter of personal preference, but anyone interested in differences between vintages searches for information about wine styles, ranges, extremes, and norms. This, numbers cannot truly give. Numbers serve only when used with statistical rigor. Two vintages of opposite character could both be rated 16 out of 20. To say a vintage uniformly produced dark red wines rich in alcohol and flavor but coarse, while another produced variable light red wines with subtle but not strong aroma and delicious aftertaste, is at least to inform someone what they are likely to find in the bottle. To rate both of these 16 out of 20 is more subjective than words alone might be.

A vocabulary, or glossary, of wine terms usefully groups itself around the major wine features: color, aroma, bouquet, constitution, development to the senses, and finesse. Some terms repeat themselves in a new context. An aroma may be "pungent"; so might an aftertaste.

Fanciful words should be avoided in principle, but some have passed thoroughly into wine vocabulary. "Dumb," in the sense of mute, is an example. It is an accepted term for a wine that does not develop well or clearly to the senses. Fanciful words often note exceptional wines, either for quality or defect. People come up with some peculiar formulas under stress. Groping to praise an old sweet white wine from Sauternes, someone might conclude that it is "an amber jewel melting in the mouth." The phrase is downright nonsense and bad wine description, and it ignores the fact that amber originates in pitch from evergreen trees and if it could be tasted would probably be unpleasant. Some private purpose of fixing that experience in memory may be served by extreme language. Still, the best tasting note remains one that captures perception of a wine with an apt selection and juxtaposition of accepted wine terms. Such a note is of use to ourselves and others.

The reader may have realized that, over time, tasting notes will chart the evolution of his own appreciation for wine. Most fine wine drinkers commence by preferring bland features, progress to admiring and enjoying wines with very assertive characteristics, and evolve further toward wines stressing finesse, aftertaste, and harmony. As notes become complimentary and perceptive about wines of one family or type, and more curt and disinterested in those of another, a periodic review becomes a prudent excursion into possible taste preferences that may lie ahead of us.

A Wine Taster's Vocabulary

COLOR, APPEARANCE It is helpful to look at wines in pairs. Three viewpoints give our visual impressions. The first one is straight through the wine at eye level, preferably with a light source some distance behind the glass. Then the taster agitates the wine, looking at the physical behavior of the liquid in the glass. Finally, the taster looks down through the wine, with the glass tilted over a plain white surface. In the first maneuver we notice attributes of color and clarity. In the second we discern a wine's viscosity, thick and oily or watery. Do the "legs" of the alcohol run or creep down the sides of the glass? In the third exercise we analyze color. As we tilt it, a lighter color at the rim is disclosed. The wider this whitish rim, the less pigmentation.

Pigments are extracted from grape skin. The darkness of a wine, the pigment content, therefore indicates the degree to which a wine has been in contact with and received substances from its skin. White wines are not usually steeped in skins; their juice is pressed away immediately after crushing with such pigment as it has absorbed. Rosé wines are pigmented by red skins but are left in contact only briefly with the skins. The substances received from skins include many contributors to gustatory and olfactory impressions. Dark wines with much pigment are often wines with intense or more abundant impressions.

Color and brilliance are points of wine style and merits in themselves. Clarity is expected of all wines. Limpidity, the quality of being clear, may range from *cloudy*, in the case of sick wines, and progress through *opalescent*, *shaded* or *troubled* or *veiled*, to *clear*, *limpid*, and then to degrees of brilliance described by terms such as *fiery*, *lustrous*, *glittering*, *radiant*, *brilliant*, and *crystalline*. Brilliance and acidity are related; insufficiently acidic wines often lack luster. Old wines may deposit sediment that fouls their appearance when stirred, but inherently cloudy wines are unhealthy.

Color has two main attributes. Intensity or shade is the lightness or darkness of the color. Hue distinguishes red or yellow from brown. Hue may be elaborated by tints. A basically medium red wine may show purple tints; medium yellow wine may show green tints.

Hue in red wines may be derived precisely by a color chart or evoked in more general terms. Among good wine terms are *purple red* (e.g., young wines), *ruby*, *red* or *medium* or *clear red*, *red brown*, or *brick red*. Hue then progresses increasingly to *brown* with terms such as *mahogany*, *coffee*, *amber*, and *tawny*.

White wines are described as *yellow green* or *greenish yellow*, *straw yellow*, *yellow*, *gold yellow* or *golden*, *yellow brown* or *brownish yellow*, and finally *amber* or *brown* or *maderized*. White wines can be so pale as to be called *greenish white*, *pallid*, *watery* in appearance, *colorless*, none of which is complimentary.

Rosé wines are *light red* or *rosé*, *orange*, and *pink*. Redness is a virtue in rosé wines. Orange suggests oxidation. Pale pink suggests wines with little flavor. For both red and yellow, the appearance of brown hues is associated with oxidation, or maderization, as it is also called. Oxidized wine shows stale, unclean, or "turned" flavors and odors. Slight oxidation accompanies degrees of maturity in old wines, especially in red wines, but strongly oxidized brown wines are defective. Brick red or tawny are not damning descriptions for old red wine when they complement brilliance. "A tawny-colored, fiery old Bordeaux" is red wine being described, not denigrated, but "brownish yellow color" is a condemnation of a young white wine.

A taster may note color objectively and stop there, or note color objectively and relate it to the type of wine being described. Thus two notes—"a clear, medium red hue" and "medium red hue, clear, but dark for young Beaujolais and without violet tints"—are two valid notes. The second stresses surprising intensity, hue, and tints for that wine type.

AROMA

AROMA In smelling wine we sense elements of both aroma and bouquet. Typically the aroma of young wines dominates their bouquet. The reverse is generally true of mature wines, though exceptions abound.

Qualities contributed by grapes and skins include odors associated with flowers, fruits, spices, or some minerals. Major grape varieties, such as Gewürztraminer or Riesling, can have flagrant odor combinations. Some odors, such as that of Muscat, come clear across the room. Other varietal odors, typically those of lesser grapes such as Chasselas, a common white grape that varies according to growing conditions, can be muted and evade even experienced tasters. Detection and characterization of varietal aroma are essential beginnings to sensory evaluation of red and white wines. Rosés can be distinctive but rarely are. Grape varieties fare differently in different localities, and few have a universal aroma.

Grape aromas are variously *spicy*, *peppery*, *fruity* (an overworked term but unavoidably so), *grapy*, *flowery*, *perfumed*, *smoky*, *musky*, or, when odors evoke stems or grape condition, *stemmy*, *stalky*, *woody*, *vegetal*, or *moldy*. But aromas reflect three main classes of odors: *spicy*, like cinnamon; *flowery*, like lilac; or *fruitlike*, resembling essence of lemon or the odors released when the skin of an orange is bruised. Wine types made both from single grape varieties and traditional grape mixtures have characteristic aromas.

Recognition of aromas is developed in systematic tasting. Occasionally odors can be pinpointed. The grape combination used in the Châteauneuf-du-Pape wines of southern France often simulates cinnamon, chocolate, and vanilla. Characteristic odors may include bouquet as well as aroma elements.

It is useful to describe the intensity of a quality in an aroma and the aroma's immediacy or reluctance. The aroma of grape varieties is one of the more elusive experiences for the beginning wine taster. Comparing wines of single varieties (varietal wines) from different regions can be helpful. Sauvignon Blanc from Bordeaux and the Loire Valley, Pinot Noir from California and Europe, and Riesling from Alsace and the Mosel in Germany are some examples. When varietal aromas are confidently recognized and confirmed by blind tasting (and only then), a wine taster may legitimately abbreviate his tasting note by simply using the varietal name, as in "strong Sauvignon aroma."

BOUQUET

BOUQUET A variety of substances are produced by fermentation of grape juice (must) into wine. Others accumulate as wines mature. Ethyl alcohol, a product of fermentation, is perceived by smelling. Wines with much alcohol tend to have strong bouquet, for alcohol dissolves many substances well and makes them accessible to our olfactory sense. The important term *vinosity*, the wineyness of wine, describes both alcohol content and the collection of odors—tart, astringent, fresh, piquant, acid, or mineral—that are present in wine but not, for example, in vodka. This winey sensation is seconded by other odors, some associated with resins, some with burning, and others linked with earthy, woody, metallic or mineral substances, or with vegetable or fruit matter. Some suggest animal smells such as leather or skinlike odors. Different wine styles arrange odors differently. Red Burgundy wines, for example, have bouquet in which the sense of alcohol usually precedes earthy or fruity sensations; here bouquet is often touched by animal odors or takes a spicy direction. Red Bordeaux wines can have a distinct bouquet that begins by reflecting oak and advances to reveal a collection of wine odors. These are all accepted qualities and make for style of bouquet.

Certain substances give sweetish odors to wines. Other odors, the smell of oak among them, foreshadow an astringent impact. Rich odors suggest nuts, bruised bark, and tobacco. The taster should cultivate a general sense of these and other elements of style. When we come to defects, however, more precise knowledge is useful. The sour smell of vinegar points to acetic acid; when palpable, such wine is termed acetic—sick—and should be rejected. The acrid smell of sulphur dioxide is a frequent defect. Wine with decayed wood odors and moldy smells may come from unclean barrels said to be "barrel-smelling" (in France) or "off-barrel" (in California). A beerlike smell and sensation of mold and vegetation may come from continuing yeast activity in wine termed yeasty, or "working." Oxidation, or maderization, browns color and creates a stale odor sometimes characterized as "dead leaves." Such wine is said to be maderized, or oxidized. Other faults have other symptoms.

A bouquet with defects is not "clean," though it may be vinous and defective. Clean bouquet may be found in wines with different vinosity, alcoholic impressions, and odors. These odors may be *acid, spicy, flowery, fruity, resinous, aromatic, grapy, sweet, nutty, woody* (in its acceptable sense, not that suggesting rotted wood), or *perfumed* (in a natural sense of musky, flowery or spicy). An unclean bouquet is not acceptable. A taster should try to identify the defect, using such technical knowledge as he may have, but at least a clear memory of the off-odor should remain.

Mature red wines acquire bouquet that we associate with terms such as *spicy, earthy, oak, mature, smoky,* or *musky.* Each of these will vary in intensity. The bouquet of white wines tends toward flowery or fruity impressions or toward sweetness, nuttiness, or earthiness (often a prelude to staleness). The intensity of a bouquet in mature wines, its immediacy, duration, and complexity, normally exceeds that of young wines. The term *mature* for bouquet suggests these values, particularly those of complexity. Certain wine types are appreciated for their youthful qualities. Their vinosity must be noted, but the praise extended to them often follows their aroma rather than bouquet.

Volatile elements pass into vapor more readily at warmer temperatures. Temperatures below 50 degrees F. do not favor proper tasting. In red wines extreme cold will render bouquet impossible to appreciate. Many red wines lack flavor and seem acetic at temperatures above 75 degrees F.

The balance of a bouquet in young and old wines is a tasting conception. A harmonious or balanced bouquet would include the influence of adequate alcohol, generous vinosity, and more specific features of the wine. These might be spicy, earthy, or aromatic, but would be clear and distinctive and would complete the bouquet. The balanced bouquet of an older wine might add more components. But a wine that gave nothing to the nose but a powerful odor of grape skin and stem, or of earthiness, or of dirty woodiness suggesting only the wooden tub in which it was fermented, would have a coarse, poor bouquet. A scent of one grape variety pervasive enough to muffle other impressions would be, in wine terms, vulgar. This is the case of aroma overpowering bouquet. Some varieties have this defect; some American grapes, the Concord, for example, become virtual caricatures of forceful aroma.

Clearly the bouquet is a statement about the skill with which the wine was made and the quality of ingredients available to the wine maker. Its merits and defects announce what can be expected of the wine. Balance or the lack of it among the elements of bouquet usually show up in the mouth impressions that follow. Cleanness and vinosity are minimal virtues. The presence of other, more distinctive characteristics elevates a bouquet in esteem as these are harmonious, balanced, clear, and of course pleasurable to start with. Marginal defects, a hint of woodiness, a suggestion of some acetic quality in mature wine can be tolerated. But firmly noting unclean bouquet is a first duty of the taster.

CONSTITUTION   Most wines we taste are young. Most wines remembered for their dramatic quality are old. The constitution of young and old wines changes as substances break down and others form. Our starting point is the constitution of young wines. Their appearance, aroma, and bouquet have been inspected. Olfactory impressions have already "scouted" the wines. We proceed to taste.

Some principal substances, such as alcohol, acidity, sugar, and tannin, have an impact on taste. But impressions associated with them are not exclusively due to these substances. Substances other than sugar give a sense of sweetness. A complicated collection of compounds is responsible for the sense of fruit in a wine, yet fruit is a good tasting term.

Alcohol has a palpable impact in the mouth, a warm or hot feeling. It also gives sweetish impressions, masks acid, and contributes to a sense of body. Alcohol must be balanced by acid, by fruit, and in most red wines by some degree of tannin, giving astringency felt in the mouth. Its proportion is not easily judged; wines of 13 percent can taste insipid, wines of 10.5 percent can feel balanced. But without sugar, generous alcohol is noticeable, as a mouthful of vodka or some other nearly flavorless but alcoholic beverage quickly demonstrates. Alcohol acts quickly in the mouth.

Sugar in proportions greater than one-half of one percent gives wine very different impressions than might be registered without it. It moderates perception of acidity and high alcohol content. Other flavors may be masked by sugar. Not all "sweet" impressions are sugar, and a species of sweetness that we intuitively identify as natural in wine is really a collection of compounds including aldehydes, some acids, and amino acids that give a sensation of fruit. Our notions of fruit, sweetness, and other flavors intertwine. It is sufficient in evaluating wine constitution to notice the difference between sugar and the extended impressions we may call fruit and flavor, as exemplified in a grape or a cherry.

Acids, of which tartaric is the most important, give sour primary tastes. Their presence in wine is essential. They are responsible for the tart, refreshing, vigorous qualities required of wine. If they are lacking, the wine gives an insipid, unclear, or flabby impression.

There is a difference between the tart taste of acids and the bitter one of tannin, with its tactile, puckering, astringent effect on gums, palate, and tongue. Tannin precipitates in time, as do some acids, and this reduction in tartness and astringency is one difference between young and old red wines. Tannin, which can be masked by abundant flavor, by alcohol, or by sugar (as in fortified wines), is one element of wine evaluation. The two common errors in judging the future of fine red Bordeaux are to consider as promising wine with much tannin but lacking other constitutional elements, or to reject as unpromising wine with abundant flavor, fruit, and other qualities including adequate acidity because its tannic impression is not strong. Constitution relates to balance.

Tasting terms for constitution are numerous, but a taster who has distinguished alcohol, acidity, tannin (astringency), sugar (or lack of it), fruit, and intensity of flavor will use the terms well and will intuit something of a wine's future maturation.

Terms associated with alcohol are: *hot, warm, big, heavy, full, generous, solid, strong, vinous, balanced, light, thin, weak, short, feeble, paltry.*

Terms associated with acidity are: *harsh, hard, flat, raw, green, acid, tart, sour, firm, balanced, piquant, lively, fresh, sound, with bite, healthy, solid, clean, light, supple, soft, dumb, dull, short, small, weak, flabby, lifeless, insipid, dead, empty.*

Clearly catchall terms, such as *round, mellow, soft,* and *dry,* may combine appraisals of alcohol, acidity, and sugar.

Terms associated with tannin unfortunately overlap with those identified with acidity. This is acceptable shorthand, but an effort to discriminate is worthwhile. Usual expressions include *puckering, astringent, rough, harsh, bitter, stemmy, woody, dry, green, hard, tannic* (preferred with adjectives stating degree), *balanced, bland, smooth, silky, round, supple.* Terms following *balanced* are not well employed here and indicate little or no tannic impression.

Terms associated with sugar include its effects on texture—for example, *mellow, rich, heavy, viscous.* More strictly, however, sugar is evaluated in terms of its primal taste. *Liquoreux* is a sweet (dessert) wine tasting term combining appreciation of sweetness, vinosity, flavor, and finesse as understood among French tasters.

Words such as *very sweet, syrupy, sweet, medium sweet* are all found with remarkable inconsistency. A careful evaluation could be entirely satisfied with the terms *very sweet, medium sweet, sweet, slightly sweet,* and *dry,* or *fermented dry* (to express a wine that might show much fruit but contained no noticeable unfermented sugar).

Terms associated with fruit and flavor are necessarily more fanciful. The presence of these qualities in the mouth has been described as *fruity, richly flavored, rich, lush, luscious, intensely fruity, chewy, meaty, grapy, zestful* (often confused with acidity), or with specific references to fruits such as cherries or apples. An indication of balance is always preferred, as in "an alcoholic hot wine with some acidity but inadequate fruit and flavor to balance."

Acetic identifies a defect of too much acetic acid, which is to say enough to notice its presence. *Acescent* also identifies a sick impression arising from excess acetic acids, ethyl acetate, or both. Defects noted in bouquet include acetic, yeasty, rotted, moldy, stalky, woody, or other tainting impressions. Turbid wines typically suffer from chemical rather than bacterial spoilage. Constitutional terms mainly concern sound wines.

DEVELOPMENT TO THE SENSES

Up to now we have been asking what is in wine that can be perceived. This starts out being difficult but yields to effort. Having several times sensed a strong defect such as sulphur dioxide, we can identify it when sensed again. Having tasted both Vouvray and California Chenin Blanc, we may recognize the aroma of Chenin Blanc when it recurs.

At some point in beginning tasting experience, in addition to noting astringency or lack of it, or other physical facts in isolation, we are going to notice a progression. Immediate sensations of alcohol and tartness give way to fruit; some odors of the aroma return as flavors; and various impressions dart about the mouth and nasal geography, suggesting images of spices, flowers, and fruits. Sensations arrive, retreat, and return. There are any number of possibilities; the progression is the key. This development of wine to the senses is instinctively pleasurable.

In becoming confident and perceptive enough to characterize the development of different wines, one bright day we experience a "rightness" in some wine's development. We have passed to another level of evaluating and appreciating wine. Not surprisingly, finding terms for a complicated set of sensations is more difficult than finding them for some one substance. By this time some potential terms may already lurk in the reader's brain. The French or Italians, with their tendency to personalize all experiences, might indignantly characterize a wine as having a coarse, nasty development. They are not speaking some incomprehensible language but struggling to tell us something, much as we might struggle to tell them that a performance of an American folksong contained all the notes but was sung in a sense-

less way that did not capture the meaning, and we wish they could hear a "correct" performance.

Up to now we have identified, or tried to. Now we are praising or blaming. This is no surprise. Physical reality is giving way to a different reality, that of our aesthetic judgment. How should a wine develop to our senses? Reading a book is not going to bring this aesthetic appreciation. That will come with tasting many sorts of wines and arranging them into patterns of experience. But we have read enough about wine tasting to realize that a remark such as "I am not in the mood for white Burgundy" is no more unusual than saying, "Let's not go to the football game. I'd rather go to the tennis match."

Our new concept of aesthetic judgment has a second dimension. Six families toil all year on a Sauternes vineyard trying desperately to produce a wine that will overpower our senses with its sweetness and lusciousness, from its bouquet through every tasting sensation. If we taste it and say, "This develops badly because it is sweet," our judgment is senseless. Our personal taste may not fancy sweet wines. But Sauternes is made to a traditional type, to canons of taste that demand the wine be sweet, that praise and relish this quality.

The idea of style of performance is familiar to us; it is its application to wine that is novel. All singers must be able to sing on pitch, but opera singers are not judged by the same expectations as blues singers, folk singers, jazz singers, and so on. Personal taste chooses among styles. But evaluation of performance within a style accepts the frame of reference.

Terms for the development of wine to the senses may not seem farfetched or more vague than they need be, once it is understood that they describe wine style.

Some qualities: *frank, even, firm, harmonious, robust, graceful, exciting, stimulating, interesting, subtle, charming, silky, seductive, elusive.*

Some criticisms: *dumb, erratic, hesitant, blunt, dull, insipid, weak, thin, common, coarse, vulgar, nasty, offensive.*

FINESSE AND AFTERTASTE

Just as terms arose to characterize a wine's development to the senses, other terms have arisen to characterize its departure, its finesse, and finally its aftertaste. As with terms for development, we meet words of praise and blame. Terms of development apply to ongoing sensations, successions of impressions. Terms for finesse and aftertaste carry us into the even less precise area where actual sensations have technically stopped, but the brain, the memory, is still preoccupied with them. We have had this experience elsewhere. At the end of a song, there is an instant when sound has ended but the music is "with us" still. Often this is a moment of keen pleasure and strong emotion. Fine wines provide similar moments in which sensations fade away, but some delightful awareness of a wine's whole impression remains.

Notions of finesse and aftertaste, if based on wine's physical reality, are also conditioned by expectation. Evaluations of finesse and aftertaste must refer to the canons of taste appropriate to the wine type in question. Châteauneuf-du-Pape red wines are expected to be dark-colored, richly flavored, and assertive. Such wines will not leave our taste sensations as would Bordeaux; but examples of fine Châteauneuf-du-Pape will display aftertaste consistent with the impressions that preceded it and mark the wine type.

Greater familiarity with wine types allows us a shorthand. Having observed the more objective facts about wine, we may finish a tasting note by noting the development of aftertaste as being true to type, true to expectation. If some terms for finesse seem nearly foreign, remember that they were chosen long ago, when men ignorant of wine chemistry praised wines by personalizing them. To do so they used the superlatives of their times, not of ours.

Qualities: *fine, refined, having breed or race, noble, stylish, loyal, true.**

Absence of finesse: *common, vulgar, coarse, clumsy, lacking finish.*

One can go through a lifetime of enjoyment—sensual, real enjoyment—of wines without paying attention to aspects of development and finesse and without regard for the aesthetic traditions that shape

*Terms such as these that stress pleasurable experiences have long been used in conventional European wine language. Chemists, notably at the Enology Department of the University of California at Davis, think that these terms of analogy lack precision and consider them poor wine terms. They prefer language closely related to identifiable substances in wine. Either extreme can be rendered ridiculous by any adult with some experience of what is generally called culture. The use of emotive terms where precise description is both possible and called for seems sloppy, while to discard expressions that stand for whole experiences where convention has found them useful seems to ignore a chief use of language.

those terms. Alternatively, one may consider it more enjoyable to cultivate conscious appreciation of the many sorts of fine wines that exist, each with its species of elegance and breed. For those who accept their pleasure in wine as immediate sensual enjoyment and no more, learning to taste accurately will still enhance enjoyment, for accuracy will make you conscious of what you enjoy and so guide your buying of wines. For others who wish to carry wine tasting further and seek aesthetic pleasure comparable to the appreciation of fine music, it is hardly necessary to confirm lessons learned elsewhere. Understanding and cultivation of taste for different traditions seems best approached with humility and an alert mind. Personal preference seems best exercised with decisiveness and a disregard for fashion. Wine is not the only matter in which two great follies run singly or paired: a foolish self-importance that will not understand the values others have cared to cultivate, or gullibility so foolish that something famous becomes something one must personally relish.

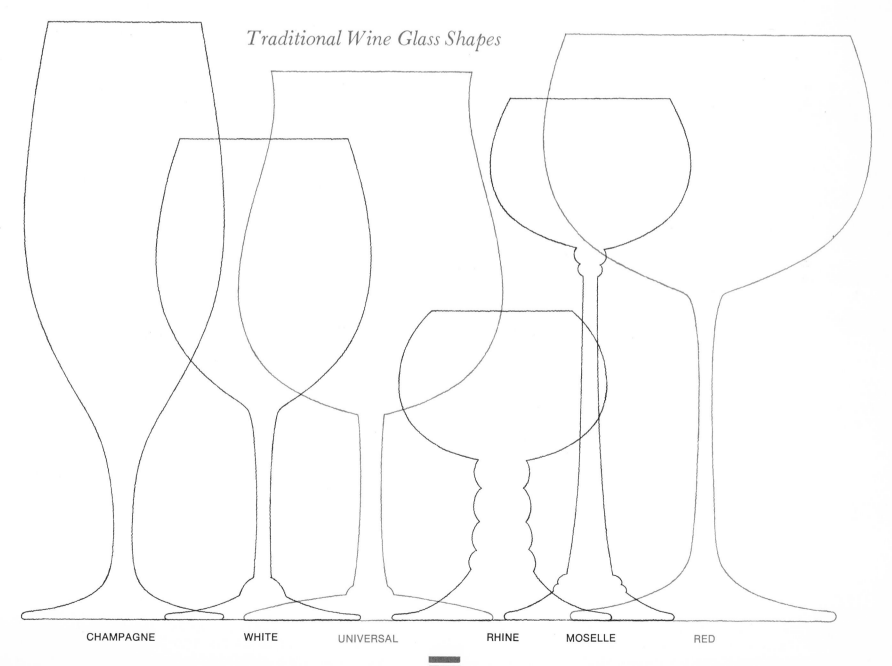

Traditional Wine Glass Shapes

CHAMPAGNE   WHITE   UNIVERSAL   RHINE   MOSELLE   RED

Grape Growing and Wine Making

Readers know, or can guess, that there is a technology of grape growing (viticulture) and wine making (vinification) and can imagine hundreds of scientific works that study these subjects and give advice to grape growers and wine makers. Viticulture and vinification cannot be condensed into a few pages. My purpose is to sketch main points of production in such a way as to give outsiders some intuition about what accounts for good quality and to conjure up a picture of what lies behind a defect or lack of quality in a wine. On the one hand, this awareness increases enjoyment of excellence in a wine. On the other hand, some idea of what facts lie behind a disaster in wine making can help one separate wine that is the result of a brave attempt in a terrible harvest from downright badly made wine that should be returned to the seller. Just as this is a question of the fairness and integrity of the grower, so will a fair-minded consumer want to distinguish an effort to make the best of a tough situation from inexcusable negligence or diseased wine.

Why, after all, are not all wines from famous wine regions excellent? If these famous European regions are so great, why isn't each of their wines delicious, balanced, and flavorful? To start with, insufficient sun and heat give insufficiently ripe grapes; fine wine cannot be made out of them. If heat during maturation is too intense, the grapes' acidity is consumed (metabolized) too rapidly, as are other substances. Therefore, the finest wine grapes can be grown only in a zone with certain average temperatures and during a frost-free period of at least 90–100 days (120 days is required for many premium varieties). In the best zones April averages at least 50 degrees F.; monthly averages climb to between 60 and 70 degrees during summer and descend to 50 degrees during October. But climate varies year to year; *average* expresses the usual condition. Any climate zone with good averages is going to experience worse conditions. Thus any zone that averages best conditions is also going to be a zone that experiences far-from-best conditions; it is a marginal zone in that sense. There is no way around this. With this perspective, we can appreciate the next point.

Wine makers do not make wine; nor do they make soil, vines, or grapes. Wine makers make sure nothing goes wrong. And when the weather goes wrong, as it *inevitably* will, wine makers make the best of the situation that results. The resulting battle that goes on in the fields and in the cellars to extract the best results is a complex one, but it boils down to people attempting to offset or minimize the effects of bad weather. The sense of what a bad vintage means can perhaps be conveyed in geographic terms. What a bad vintage means to a German winegrower is that, as far as *that* year is concerned, his vineyard might as well have been picked up and stuck inland of the Russian coast of the Baltic Sea; and he must make the best wine possible "there." Or a Rhône grower may confront July and August weather that transports his vineyard to Africa.

The winegrower wakes up in the morning and looks at his vineyard worried about three things: sugar, acidity, and rot. As grapes mature, sugar builds up and acidity declines. The buildup of sugar is accompanied by myriad changes in the grape skin that will give flavor and color to his wine. The fall in acidity brings the potential wine from extremely sour to tart. At some point, when grapes contain between 20–25 percent sugar, they will make wine with sufficient alcohol. (Half as much alcohol as sugar emerges from vinification; a grape containing 25 percent sugar would produce a wine about 12.5 percent alcohol.) At the same time, one hopes, acid will have dropped to the right proportion. But ripe fruit rots. Wet weather, above all, brings rot. Rot may be getting the better of the grapes while they are not yet ripe and are too acid. The grower can be forced to pick before rot destroys all the fruit on the vine. This is the archetype of a "bad year." There are countless variations—alterations of hot, cold, dry, damp. Some European countries allow growers to add sugar to the juice of unripe grapes to increase alcohol. But that does not replace the aroma and flavor of naturally ripe grapes. Nor does the vineyard present a single picture; one patch is wet and rotting, another is unripe, another can be picked. Grapes may be brought to the fermenting vats in any variety of conditions of sugar content, acidity, and freedom from rot.

The planting of the vineyard itself was influenced by these same preoccupations—sugar, acidity, and rot. Healthy vines give ripe grapes. The right grape variety in the right place—that phrase means little more than matching a type of plant to a piece of ground and its environment so as to get a healthy vine. Vineyard layout also respects hygiene. In cool climates slopes are preferred, for they expose each vine better to the sun and drain away water that could promote rot as well as chill the air immediately around the ripening grapes. All the treatments of soil and vine, all manner of tricks such as controlling the foliage or the pebble content of the surface are nothing more than efforts to reach a condition of sufficient sugar and proper acid in grapes that are clean from the wine-making point of view.

Thin, sour-tasting wines without generous flavor are consequences of unripe grapes. Unripe because the vine and site were badly matched, unripe because of weather that year, unripe because rot was spreading faster than grapes were ripening and the grower saved the remaining clean grapes and made wine from them, or unripe because of overcropping—the results lie in the same class. At another extreme alcoholic, lifeless wines, insipid, without brilliant color, tasting "baked" or "hot," come from grapes of high sugar content but ones exposed to enough heat to lose the acidity that would have rectified their dull, flat-tasting qualities. These are characteristic of inferior regions; for such wines to come from superior zones is unusual. It is not impossible for a vineyard to be overtaken by a spell of burning weather and be unable to harvest in a timely way, but more commonly there is an error in judgment involved. Somewhere acidity can be found—in the few bunches of unripe grapes, in the last juice pressed from the skins, in the stems, in the skins. Within a few famous growing regions are hot areas whose wines chronically suffer from high alcohol and insufficient acidity—the Palatinate in Germany, areas in the southern Rhône in France, and others in Italy are examples. Some vine varieties may be mismatched with given climatic conditions so as to produce the same insipid results; the Rhine Riesling grape in Italy and Yugoslavia is perhaps an example. As for rot itself, its musty, stale, or vegetal impression is familiar to anyone who has accidentally bitten into rotted fruit.

Grape juice of proper acidity is technically expressed in France as being as acid as a liter of water containing between four and eight grams of sulphuric acid or, in California, as a liter of water containing five to ten grams of tartaric acid. On the chemist's scale of pH wine measures about three to three and one-half.

In addition to weather patterns, other vineyard facts account for insufficiently flavored wine. Vines draw sustenance from substances in the soil and manufacture ripe grapes whose flavor mainly concentrates in their skins. If too many vines are crowded onto a piece of ground, quality crashes dramatically; there is not enough nourishment to go around. Similar effects can be caused by producing exaggerated amounts of grapes per vine. The most helpful concept is *grapes per area of ground,* however the excess is created. Among fine wines it is observed that those from young vines fade and "dry out" more quickly in bottle with time. A like effect is attributed to wines from overproduced grapes.

There is a vulgar misconception that harvests reduced to small size by natural causes are automatically superb ones and those rendered above average by excellent growing conditions are poor. This is simply wrong and can be demonstrated statistically and nowhere more clearly than where this doctrinaire idea is most often applied, Bordeaux. There is quite another case in which ripe grapes are encouraged to concentrate and shrivel to produce intense white wines of which the great examples are Sauternes in Bordeaux and the high-grade German white wines. Here quality is obtained at the expense of quantity; but this reduction in grape quantity takes place *after* an excellent harvest has been matured on the vine, and that is another story. In vineyards properly planted in properly tended vines properly pruned, abundant yields result from successful growing conditions, the kind that give good wine. Poor crops come from poor weather or unhealthy vines, resulting in weak wines lacking full flavor.

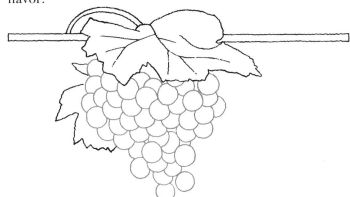

Dry White Wines

White wines are normally made by fermenting the juice alone, without skins, pips, or any stems. This makes it a little easier to follow their processing. Main steps in wine-making procedure are suggested; below these appear the hazards connected with them and any defects that may arise.

(PROCEDURE) Grapes brought speedily from the field are put through a machine (a crusher-stemmer) that strips stalks and stems away from the grapes and pumps the mass of grape and juice into a press. Press designs vary, but the aim is to extract juice quickly and separate it from the skins and other solid matter.

(HAZARDS) Grape juice, like wine, reacts with air in different ways. This oxidation can result in stale and unpleasant tastes and odors that we sense as not being fresh or clean and in darker color. The manipulations through the crusher-stemmer and then through the press give an opportunity for this contact with oxygen. The grapes are given a dose of sulphur dioxide as they go through, to reduce oxidation. If this is too heavy, yeasts (mainly on the skins) are killed, and fermentation must be begun by artificial yeasts. In California this is standard practice; wineries substitute cultivated yeast strains, fearing the "off" flavors of naturally occurring yeasts. In Europe induced fermentations are generally less favored.

●

(PROCEDURE) Juice may be fermented in vats or in small wooden barrels. Yeasts interact with sugars to begin a complex process summed up as fermentation. Sugar is converted to ethyl alcohol and carbon dioxide gas, among other things. As alcohol is formed, the fermenting juice heats up, and fermentation becomes more rapid and violent.

(HAZARDS) Fermentation is a process accelerated by a rise in temperature, but it produces "off" flavors at too high a temperature. Wines made by too hot, too rapid, and too violent a fermentation do not seem to achieve best flavor, in amount or kind. Europeans consider danger levels to be 35–40 degrees C. (95–104 degrees F.). Temperature problems can stop fermentation, a failure called "sticking." The must may require warming and new yeast strains to start again, with lost time and risk of exposure to oxygen. For all these reasons, temperatures are kept low to slow the fermentations; in Burgundy fine white wines are often vinified at between 20–28 degrees C. (68–82 degrees F.) in California at 50–55 degrees F.

The tasting defects of "hot" fermentations are often coarse wines without a full sense of fruit and wines occasionally giving a "cooked" tasting impression. Examples of inexpertly vinified white wines reach us from Italy and France from small growers who often lack adequate temperature-controlling equipment.

White

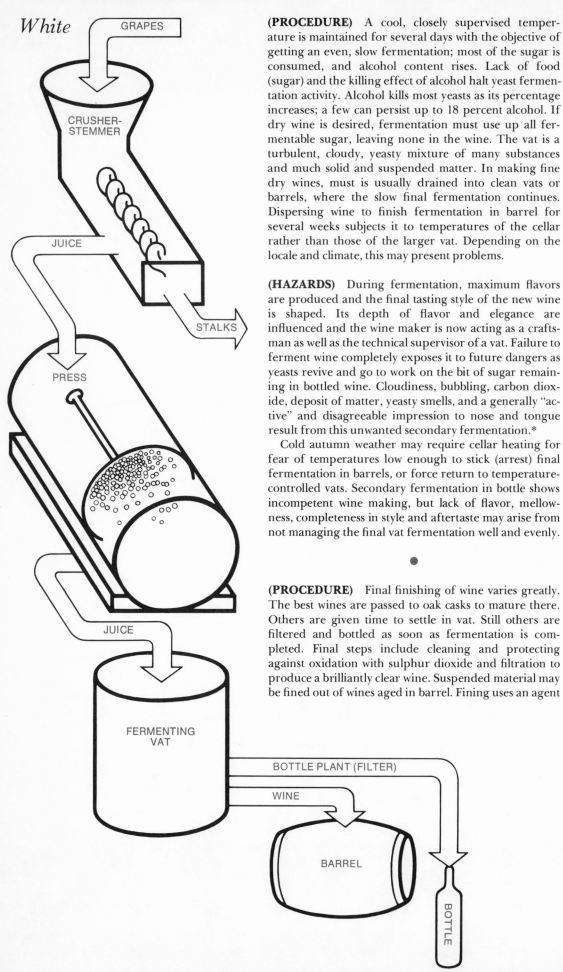

GRAPES

CRUSHER-STEMMER

JUICE

STALKS

PRESS

JUICE

FERMENTING VAT

BOTTLE PLANT (FILTER)

WINE

BARREL

BOTTLE

(PROCEDURE) A cool, closely supervised temperature is maintained for several days with the objective of getting an even, slow fermentation; most of the sugar is consumed, and alcohol content rises. Lack of food (sugar) and the killing effect of alcohol halt yeast fermentation activity. Alcohol kills most yeasts as its percentage increases; a few can persist up to 18 percent alcohol. If dry wine is desired, fermentation must use up all fermentable sugar, leaving none in the wine. The vat is a turbulent, cloudy, yeasty mixture of many substances and much solid and suspended matter. In making fine dry wines, must is usually drained into clean vats or barrels, where the slow final fermentation continues. Dispersing wine to finish fermentation in barrel for several weeks subjects it to temperatures of the cellar rather than those of the larger vat. Depending on the locale and climate, this may present problems.

(HAZARDS) During fermentation, maximum flavors are produced and the final tasting style of the new wine is shaped. Its depth of flavor and elegance are influenced and the wine maker is now acting as a craftsman as well as the technical supervisor of a vat. Failure to ferment wine completely exposes it to future dangers as yeasts revive and go to work on the bit of sugar remaining in bottled wine. Cloudiness, bubbling, carbon dioxide, deposit of matter, yeasty smells, and a generally "active" and disagreeable impression to nose and tongue result from this unwanted secondary fermentation.*

Cold autumn weather may require cellar heating for fear of temperatures low enough to stick (arrest) final fermentation in barrels, or force return to temperature-controlled vats. Secondary fermentation in bottle shows incompetent wine making, but lack of flavor, mellowness, completeness in style and aftertaste may arise from not managing the final vat fermentation well and evenly.

•

(PROCEDURE) Final finishing of wine varies greatly. The best wines are passed to oak casks to mature there. Others are given time to settle in vat. Still others are filtered and bottled as soon as fermentation is completed. Final steps include cleaning and protecting against oxidation with sulphur dioxide and filtration to produce a brilliantly clear wine. Suspended material may be fined out of wines aged in barrel. Fining uses an agent

such as egg white; this is stirred into the wine, and it settles slowly in a maze of filmy matter, dragging down particles with it. Fining is usual for red wines, unusual for white wines. Tartaric acid, wine's most important acid, can form potassium tartrate salt, which may precipitate in the bottle as clear, flaky crystals. All manner of physical and chemical steps may be taken to deal with high concentrations of this tartrate salt to prevent the future precipitate from forming.

(HAZARDS) Some steps taken to forestall precipitation from tartaric acid combinations cause a loss in acidity, reducing the wine's liveliness. Cold stabilization to force precipitates before wine is bottled is much debated, with proponents claiming no blunting of the full range of wine flavors and odors by subjection to extreme cold and others claiming such effects.

While wine must be cleared bright and protected by some sulphur dioxide against oxidation, it is possible to be negligent during filtering and bottling, exposing the wine to air, to unclean equipment or unclean bottles. These defects, resulting in off tastes, in serious chemical reactions, or in oxidation, are becoming rare. Nevertheless, excessive use of sulphur dioxide at this stage, as in others, is not so rare, and many wines bear the marks of it.

Maturation of wine in oak barrels contributes flavors and odors to the wine. While some producers consider this an interference with natural grape flavors, the majority consider its palpable heightening of odor and taste indispensable to the finest white wines, particularly of Chardonnay (White Burgundy) style. Unclean oak can taint wine. Airspace atop the barrel promotes oxidation. If held too long in oak, fruity qualities are diminished and replaced by overpowering woody and coarse tasting qualities. In Italy and South America white wines are frequently stored in barrel too long; dull, charmless, oxidized white wines result. The proper contribution of oak maturation is usually considered to be a heightening of bouquet by an aromatic, slightly woody odor; more depth of taste and aftertaste; and other tasting qualities extracted during a wine's stay in barrel. Oak maturation involves both canons of taste for a class of wine and judgment on the part of the cellar master, or *éleveur,* concerning each individual wine. For fine white wines, such tempering is done in one-third to one-half the time required for reds.

---

*Future yeast activity in the bottle can be forestalled by killing yeasts, by bottling with an anti-microbic agent, by fine filtering, or by fermenting until the wine is dry so as to eliminate the food that might permit future yeast growth. Heating (pasteurizing) the wine is the oldest method, however. Some fine wine makers claim this results in flabby, dull wines that evolve poorly in bottle. It is one thing for a scientist to have proved that only after six to nine months do dead yeasts release the ultimate flavor qualities of Champagne. It is another to wonder about the importance of residual yeast cells to the flavor of still white wine. I have certainly sampled many pasteurized wines whose tasting qualities suffered from that process. But have some excellent wines pasteurized by the new "flash" (very rapid) process escaped our detection? An experiment could be set up. Meanwhile, controversy continues. The effects of pasteurization, where detectable, are wines that lack liveliness, in which alcohol is sensed but the full range of fine wine's fruity impressions is not. This combination, described as "dead" or "rubbery," resembles dull wines from very hot climates.

Sweet White Wines

Sweet wines are those that contain unfermented sugar. Human senses can begin to detect sweetness when there is between .5 percent and 1 percent unfermented sugar. However, the wines we call semisweet would typically contain on the order of 2 percent, and sweet or dessert wines 6 percent, unfermented sugar. The most esteemed sweet wines are made from grapes concentrated by noble rot, *Botrytis cinerea*. The concentrating effect of this mold, increases in glycerine and related substances, and decreases in acidity are discussed in the Sauternes chapter (see page 78).

(PROCEDURE) Although more difficult to pick, and although initial fermentation from them may be harder to start, desiccated or concentrated grapes give juice that yeasts will ferment into alcohol just as in dry white wines. In many sweet wines, man intervenes to stop the fermentation process, leaving some residual sugar. Microfiltration can strain yeasts out of the fermenting must at some point, ending their activity. In Sauternes more often a killing agent, usually sulphur, is used when wine makers decide on a moment when the amount of remaining sugar balances the alcoholic strength attained thus far by fermentation. In many German wines, yeast activity is muted naturally by high sugar concentrations. In Port, Brandy is added to stop fermentation.

(HAZARD) It is imperative that yeast action be stopped permanently, since not merely traces but a real quantity of sugar remains, and this could produce a disastrous secondary fermentation. But this urgency suggests use of additional sulphur dioxide, which in itself is a procedure that at high levels can produce offensive wine. Pasteurization is an alternative solution for inexpensive semisweet wines of which not much quality is expected, but its suspected damaging effects rule it out for fine dessert wines. Unlike sulphur dioxide used to control oxidation by combining chemically with oxygen, use of sulphur dioxide to kill yeasts has no chemical escape route, and sulphur dioxide in free form may remain in the resulting wine. Some is tolerable; airing will reduce it. A great deal is not acceptable. Countries set different limits for sulphur dioxide content in sweet wines, and the allowance is pegged higher than for dry ones.

Red Wines

(PROCEDURE) Skins contribute flavor and taste substances to wine. Typically fine red wines are destined for long maturing in bottle, and more tannin content is expected of them. While the grape bunches are put through the same crusher-stemmer, in many regions when it is doubted that the skins contain enough tannin, tannin-rich stems and stalks are added to a part of the crop in the vat. The red wine vat thus contains not merely juice but the whole grape and even some stalk. This leads straight to a dramatic difference between red and white wine fermentation.

There is a mass of skin, pip, pulp, and even stalk that rises to the surface as vats ferment and form a cap of matter atop the fermenting mass of liquid.

(HAZARD) This cap is a menace. It can strangle yeasts of oxygen. It covers a heat-producing fermentation and so risks raising temperatures in the middle of the vat above the 40 degrees C. at which yeasts are killed (sticking the fermentation). This order of heat bakes away acidity. In this cap, a loose jumble of grape matter, acetic acid bacteria work rapidly to convert alcohol to vinegar. Before all this was well understood, it was common to have a new vat of wine spoiled as fast as it was made. The cap also contains skin from which pigment, many flavoring substances, and tannin are extracted by the fermenting wine. There are various tricks to break up, submerge, and cover the cap with wine so as to foil this potential spoilage and keep the vat cool throughout. Acetic (*piqué*) new wines are rare, but when found, the cause is usually in this elementary vinification process.

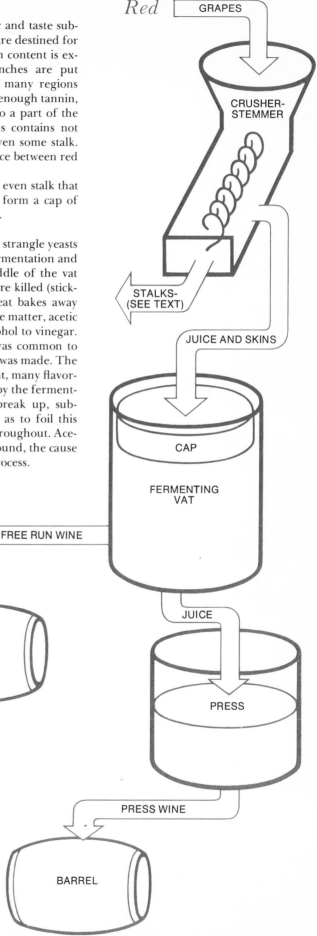

Red

GRAPES

CRUSHER-STEMMER

STALKS-(SEE TEXT)

JUICE AND SKINS

CAP

FERMENTING VAT

FREE RUN WINE

FREE RUN WINE

BARREL

BOTTLE

JUICE

PRESS

PRESS WINE

BARREL

(PROCEDURE) Although white wine vinifications are surveyed to maintain temperature and thus extract proper flavor, red wines add the complication that much of their essential character is, in most quality regions, given by contact with skins. This maceration, as it is called, is crucial to red wine. While the wine maker surveys the basic conversion from sugar to alcohol, he is also preoccupied with the length of time the fermenting juice is to remain in contact with skins. Acidity, color, tannin, intensity of taste, and degree of harshness are all involved.

(HAZARDS) Maceration time defines red wine style across the full range from rosé to dark red; it is possible to make radically different wines from the same vat of red grapes. Much of this book deals with accepted wine styles. The light, fragrant wines of Beaujolais properly receive only a short fermentation on the skins before the juice is pressed off; this shows in their pale color, relatively low tannin, and fresh qualities. A Beaujolais vinifier who left his must three weeks on the skins would pull out a dark, astringent wine that would not show the accepted style of his region. A grower of an important red Graves property in Bordeaux who pulled his wine after two days on skins, trying to make something that consumers could drink immediately, could be accused of betraying the accepted standards of color, intensity of taste, acerbity, and long-lived wine expected of red Graves.

●

(PROCEDURE) While the cap is being broken up, submerged, or pumped over with wine, and while pigment and tannin extraction are being monitored, the wine maker is also watching the temperature of his fermenting red wines. Grapes coming into the vats with skins loaded with yeasts can provoke a more tumultuous fermentation than with white grape juice. Temperatures shoot up particularly at the center of the vat. Red wine is fermented at higher temperatures than white in most regions (70–85 degrees F.) and the agitated fermentation presents a stronger threat to quality. When extraction of color and tannin is satisfactory, the must is run off the skins and may finish its first fermentation in vat or go to barrel.

(HAZARDS) It is agreed that hot fermentations have negative effect on quality and tend to produce wines with a "baked" taste sometimes reflecting in their lack of brilliance and lack of firm taste a loss of acidity in the vat. The degree of fruitiness of wine is influenced by temperature, but higher temperatures result in quicker extraction of pigment. Other tasting qualities are influenced by the degree of maturation.

Parallel to these questions of wine style the cellar master is assuring that his red wine completes fermentation entirely, leaving no residual sugar, since red wine is commonly dry. Where red wine is to be bottled immediately after vat processes are done, sugar offers the risk of secondary fermentation in bottle. Some Italian and Iberian wines are deliberately bottled with incomplete fermentation, but fizzy red wine that smells of yeast has normally been badly vinified.

(PROCEDURE) Acidity is critical to the taste, brilliance, and conservation of wine. Tartaric acid is most important, but many red wines include some amount of malic acid. This can be attacked by bacteria, breaking it down into lactic acid and other compounds and releasing carbon dioxide gas in the process. This malolactic fermentation can be encouraged to take place in the vat, in the barrel, or not at all. (In regions of low acidity, malolactics are discouraged.) A fall in acidity results, and when it is over a red wine may be said to be finished in all its major processes. By warming vats and adding cultures from vats undergoing malolactic fermentation to those not yet started, the cellar master finishes his red wine. This requires more sophisticated chemical analysis, to be assured that it is completed.

(HAZARDS) When malolactic fermentation is not done or not finished, and when the process takes off in bottle, an unpleasant, unhealthy impression is produced. This is rarely found anymore in fine wines aged one or two years in cask; it still crops up in Beaujolais, for this red wine is often hastened into bottles the autumn it is made and shipped abroad as Beaujolais Nouveau. French authorities characterize this impression as the "dairy" odor of lactic acid. Malic acid itself has an unripe apple taste (the Latin word for apple, *Malus*, is its root).

●

(PROCEDURE) Finished red wines of quality are usually run off into barrels. Periodically the contents are drained off the lees that will have precipitated to the barrel bottom and put into fresh barrels. In the case of fine Bordeaux this may be done anywhere from three to eight times. Finally, after anywhere from a few months to two years (most common), and exceptionally four to six years, the wine is clarified (fined) and bottled. During the first year fine Bordeaux is still "working," releasing gases and kept with barrel hole upright and glass stoppered to allow gases to escape. Eventually it is sealed in a topped-up condition and matures more quietly.

(HAZARDS) During barrel age, red wines deposit some tannin, some tartrates, and protein. If the wine maker does not look after this, fouled wine or excessively heavy deposits in bottle may occur. Wines must be clarified, and barrel aging is a slow, careful way to do this. But, as discussed in white wines, oak itself contributes to flavors and odors. Red wines given too much barrel age may taste stale, virtually woody, and lack fruit. Those given too little may lack the expected tasting characteristics of their wine type, be it Bordeaux, Burgundy, or a Barolo wine from northern Italy.

If barrels are not clean moldy tastes may result. Improper ullaging (filling the barrel to the brim to exclude air) permits acetic acid formation.

In young wines there is often a healthy smell of oak quite different from the fetid impression imparted by dirty wood. This last often mixes with sour impressions or acetic ones, for dirty wood commonly houses bacteria responsible for these odors and tastes.

(PROCEDURE) Red wines may be bottle-aged before they are sold and are often aged by consumers before they are drunk.

(HAZARDS) While many wines are quite ready to drink soon after bottling, others may display all sorts of tasting defects. Fine red Bordeaux may go through a dull, tasteless period of several years after bottling. Odors develop as wines mature; young wines may disappoint those who prematurely expect mature features.

Certainly fine wines rarely taste "right" shortly after bottling; this condition is called "bottle sickness." It is most noticeable in red wines that have spent many months maturing in cask. Lesser wines are specifically vinified for prompt consumption after bottling.

The dull, expressionless set of tasting qualities associated with heat stabilization (pasteurization) has been referred to and should be remembered in drinking inexpensive wines from the south of France, Italy, Greece, and Iberia, to mention a few sources that still use this practice of assuring that no biological process takes place after bottling.

Carbonic Maceration Process

An unusual way of making red wine has been devised and is being used in France, in California, and elsewhere. It is the carbonic maceration process.

(PROCEDURE) This process separates maceration, to obtain color and taste, from fermentation to obtain alcohol and other substances. Red grapes are first put into a vat that is covered over, or "sealed," by a layer of carbon dioxide gas. This deprives the mass of grapes and the yeasts of oxygen. Extraction of color and other substances from the skins proceeds, and an internal (intracellular) fermentation occurs. When maceration has gone on long enough, the juice is run into a vat open to the air. Now normal fermentation goes to work rapidly and is soon completed. The resulting wine is exceptionally fruity with much aroma and a certain lightness of body. Its qualities are compared to the attractive, immediate ones of Beaujolais.

(HAZARDS) Carbonic maceration is difficult, costly, and dangerous by comparison with standard fermentations. No rotten grapes can be allowed in the vat, so a part of the harvest must be discarded. For if anaerobic bacteria (bacteria living independently of oxygen) get started in the oxygen-free vat, they will shoot through the entire must in no time, and the vat is lost. A special closed vat is required to maintain the carbonic atmosphere. If the maceration is insufficient, and it is more difficult to gauge in these conditions, the resulting wine is inadequate in color and tasting qualities, and one cannot "go back and try again." Sometimes it is very difficult to start the fermentation in the second vat in the absence of the skins and yeasts that have been left in the carbonic (first) vat.

Although the wine resulting from this process is deliciously ready to drink as soon as it is made, it fades quickly with age. Sometimes it is desirable, or even necessary, to blend it with more hardy wine from the standard process. Achieving this blend is not simple. The wines often shock the public at first, tasty as they may be, in that they do not resemble expected tasting qualities of the region from which they come. Further, the wines have a cloying aftertaste some find unattractive.

Rosé

By this time the reader will have guessed how rosé wines are made, and the guess is correct. Instead of holding crushed red grapes in the vat until a full red color is achieved, the juice is run off quickly. Sometimes pressing extracts enough pigment from the skin to produce the desired color. Elsewhere maceration may be necessary. Whatever the particular device, the basic notion is the same and is no more than interrupting the process of making wine from red grapes at some point when color is right and then finishing the wine as if it were white.

In Europe rosé wine is never legally made from a mixture of red and white wines. Red and white grapes are often mixed, however.

Champagne

Champagne making is discussed elsewhere (see page 156). But it is as well to notice that it would be possible to make a sparkling wine from any wine, once it was fermented. Yeasts either in the wine or introduced could be given some sugar to "feed" on, and as they fermented this sugar, carbon dioxide gas would be produced. If this gas were not allowed to escape but somehow captured in the wine, it would be bubbly or sparkling. A century ago sparkling wines were produced in areas that today we do not even dream of in connection with them, such as Bordeaux.

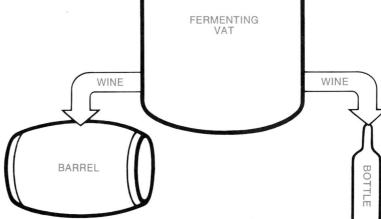

Carbonic Maceration

GRAPES

LAYER OF CO²

MACERATION VAT

JUICE

FERMENTING VAT

WINE

WINE

BARREL

BOTTLE

Buying and Serving Wine

Fine wines are expensive to produce, transport, and market. This causes them to cost anywhere from a moderate to a great amount of money. Excellent solutions to this problem may exist—such as having terribly rich friends who feel comfortable dining at home only when surrounded by good company—but they are not reliable ones. Even extreme solutions may not work. Eighteen years ago I went into the fine wine business, but I can assure readers that this did not solve the problem.

With or without a cellar in which to store younger (less expensive) wines for the future, fine wine buying is a strategy, or at least it includes tactics. Fine wine is sold through an international trade consisting of four business activities: producing wine, exporting, importing (distribution), and retailing. Were the producer to deliver wine free to a French exporter, a typical retailer would have to charge approximately $1.50 per bottle. Obviously, then, when wine is offered for $2.00 a bottle, little money is spent on the wine itself. Only starting around the figure of $2.00 can one find quality wine.

Cost of production is not the only influence on the price of wine. Branded wines will include advertising expenses in their price. The wine import duty in England approaches $1.00 per bottle. American taxes are less, but freight is higher; sparkling wines bear a steep duty of nearly $1.00 per bottle.

At prices of about $2.00 or £1.00 a fair wine is one without faults, a good one offers tasting qualities associated with the country of origin or grape variety used, and a real buy offers individual character. A German shipper's blended white wine, an Italian Lambrusco, and lesser French appellations can be good at such prices. The price structure in America for domestic wines is naturally lower.

By this time it should be clear that imported wine sold at $1.89 cannot have the tasting qualities given by limited production per area, aging in wood cask, and other expensive care. Beginning at about $3.00, quality can be expected of wines from large production areas where cost rather than scarcity determines price. Regional German wines, Chianti, regional French wines such as Côtes du Rhône or Muscadet, or property wines from lesser areas of Bordeaux are some examples.

As prices exceed roughly $4.00, young vintages of fine Bordeaux, village appellations of Burgundy, and other high-quality wines become available. These would include *classico* Chianti, varietals from good northern Italian producers, the finest examples of lesser French and Italian regions, and a great range of California wines.

At $5.00 a bottle and up, price is set more by demand than cost of production. New rules operate. Certain wines are demanded *because* they are expensive and famous—glamour wines we might call them. Elite names of Bordeaux and Burgundy; the greatest rare wines of Germany; some varietals from small California wineries; Italy's greatest Barolo and Gattinara; vintage Ports; and special Champagne bottlings all can cost a great deal. These include remarkable wines, but also wines whose intrinsic value bears no resemblance to their price. As a rule, better value is obtained by seeking the best wines of a category whose image is lower rather than the least expensive wines of a category whose image is higher.

The most enterprising buying tactic mobilizes knowledge and bargaining power to buy larger units under separately negotiated prices. A group of consumers—a wine club, in effect—can decide to buy young wines—oncoming vintages of Bordeaux and Burgundy, for example—paying in advance for case lots in return for a considerable discount. Stores normally discount 10 percent for cases. But if a wine is not yet bought by a store, and a club or group knows that it wants a specific wine, it is perfectly proper to drive a bargain with a store. The retailer is taking no commercial or financial risk; he is not being asked to hold or even display the wines, but simply to bring them in. He should charge 15 to 20 percent above his cost. A barrel of wine containing 24 cases (dozens) is the minimum wholesale purchase unit for Bordeaux wines. A group of 12, each taking two cases of wine, can in this way buy at good terms. For wine already in the retailer's inventory, however, this logic does not apply.

Cellaring quantities of wine for future maturation is exciting, worthwhile, and often economical, but the problem of protection from heat, light, and vibration cannot be avoided. Wine contains living matter and unstable substances that respond unfavorably to heat above all. Therefore wine storage for longer than a few weeks demands stable low temperatures (from 40 to 65 degrees F., or 4 to 18 degrees C.). Storage in stores and restaurants leaves much to be desired, especially in overheated America. Merchants who have solved the problem are proud to show their facilities to buyers, and purchases of expensive wines or large quantities should be made with inquiries about storage conditions. It is easier than first imagined to insulate an apartment closet or basement, keeping out heat and temperature variation. Recently introduced wine storage units do this also, but do so at a high price.

Good wine service attempts to make what we consume look and taste its best. It attends to last-minute considerations that aim at clean, bright condition, a temperature suitable for tasting, and the right amount of exposure to air. Red wines should be stood up for a day before serving. Whites should be cooled (not frozen). Dirt, which is only matter in the wrong place, gets into wine through failing to cut away sufficiently the metal capsule and clean the bottle top, or by poor decanting. If you suspect glassware is soapy or tainted, pour in a little clean water, swirl, smell, and taste; all will be revealed. Anyone who believes the lees, crust, deposit sediment, or sludge deposited by old wines is no matter for concern is invited to taste some from the heel of an old wine that has been decanted. Decanting procedure is illustrated on the next page.

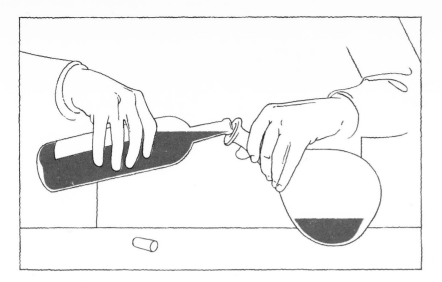

Careful decanting is born of concern for results, a concern sometimes not found in restaurants. Bad decanting is robbery; old wines are expensive, and restaurants selling them at a profit are either prepared to serve them correctly or not. Wine not limpid when held to the light has not been transported and/or decanted with adequate care. Avoid unpleasant arguments or at least win them by announcing beforehand that badly decanted wine will not be paid for. It is better to settle for young wine free of deposit than meekly stare at a glass of venerable muddied wine. By insisting on minimal standards you help wine lovers who follow you. Would you pay for a film that was out of focus, or one without a sound track?

White wines with high tartaric acid content may deposit flaky crystals that also appear on the inside surface of the cork. They settle quickly and are usually harmless. Some of the tricks for preventing this phenomenon are worse than the crystals. Do not add to public pressure for playing them by rejecting such wine before you taste it.

The smell and taste of dirty wood or cork is rare, but happens. Try nibbling a bit of old cork so that you recognize its tainting qualities when they do happen. Occasional corky wines are a fact of life. A whole series of them are also a fact of life but justify your returning the wine and the seller's returning your money.

Low temperatures diminish the possibility of wine substances reaching our sense organs. Yet cool white wines are generally regarded as more pleasant to drink than warm ones. Choosing a temperature balances off these two conflicting facts. Most tasters compromise around 50 degrees F. for white wines. Sparkling wines, naturally agitated by gas bubbles, are more readily sensed than still wines, and so are often drunk cooler. This is a matter of preference, but nearly frozen wine can hardly be sensed at all.

Sustained hot temperatures roaming toward 100 degrees F. can seriously damage wine. Red wine flavors and odors are usually more abundant and complex than those of whites. Cold reduces appreciation of these; heat vitiates the wine. On the table, in the glass, in the hand, and in the mouth, red wine has the opportunity to warm and progressively release "all it has to say" to our senses. Prudent tasters start it on its way at about 60 degrees F.

Young reds with forward tasting qualities, much aroma, and fruity character, such as Beaujolais, red Loire wines, wines made by carbonic maceration, and some light reds from northern Italy, are enjoyable at temperatures as low as those suggested for whites. Mature wines cannot declare their qualities easily at these temperatures.

Exposure to air is something of a mystery. Left long enough in oxygen, natural red wines typically form acetic acid (vinegar). Yet experience shows that airing enhances the tasting qualities of many wines, certain families of them above all. On the other side, ancient or delicate wines can "turn" or deteriorate in air with amazing speed—a dismal and costly disappointment.

Among red wines tending to blossom with as much as several hours' airing are Rhône reds, wines from Syrah grapes (Australian Hermitage, for example), the Italian Barolo wine family, and California Cabernet Sauvignon made in a tannic, powerful style. The following scheme is only approximate but suggests guidelines from which to depart when necessary:

■ Young reds showing dark red or purple color, tasting grapy, emphatic, tannic, and intense—allow one to three hours.

■ Five- to ten-year-old wines showing medium red color, strong bouquet and aroma, tasting with good grape impressions as well as vinous, and fresh—allow half an hour to two hours.

■ Faded wines with the complex, distinctive bouquet of mature reds, wines tasting very delicate, lacking in assertive grape impression—serve immediately and allow to develop in the glass. This procedure is a safe start for all old wines, those aged 20 years or more.

■ White wines releasing a whiff of sulphur dioxide when opened can be aided by airing, even by decanting for additional exposure. Fine white wines of rich style often seem to benefit from the same half an hour to an hour of air that young red wines take so well.

Different wines are served with various foods according to a cosmopolitan variety of conventions. What constitutes "matching" is either conventional (cultural) or subjective. It can be said that certain wines—for example, tart white wines or astringent reds—have strong, obvious effects on mouth and palate. An enormous literature lurks waiting for anyone interested in this subject. Unfortunately so does an extraordinary amount of talk about it, as have discovered fellow spirits whose notion of an entire evening's adult entertainment hungers, if I dare say that, for something more than a catalogue of mouth and nose impressions—a purgatory unimproved by giving everyone equal time.

Professional wine tasters seem to agree that where a succession of very fine subtle wines, especially mature ones, is a main offering of a lunch or dinner, simple food helps focus attention on the wines. And certain substances deaden one's ability to perceive wine well. Sugar, spicy, or aromatic things like cinnamon or anise, pungent things such as vinegar or cooked tomatoes, and the family of tongue-brutalizing peppers are obvious taste-killers.

When serving wine to guests, a little deference to generally accepted conventions is no more than common courtesy. Usually younger, simpler wines precede more mature, stronger ones; drier white wines introduce either reds or richer whites; dessert wines or Port end a series. When seeking one's own enjoyment there are no rules, and anyone who obeys a voice other than his own is perhaps a bigger fool than God made him.

Like special glasses designed to show wine well, proper service pays attention to the nature of wine and the nature of our perceptive organs. Anyone who learns, thinks, and cares about these two groups of facts will serve wine well.

FRANCE

Quality table wines are judged by French standards more than by any other, and French wines permeate all aspects of wine culture from grape growing to the language used to express appreciation of wine quality. This is a historical fact rather than a matter of justice or reason; in some future era other wines may serve as models, and their nuances will be canons of taste for their time. Today, however, a book intended to guide a reader toward wine appreciation must begin with France.

Five families of great wines stand atop the long list of those made in France: red Bordeaux (claret), sweet wines of Bordeaux (Sauternes and Barsac), a sparkling wine (Champagne), and both red and white wines from the several areas known collectively as Burgundy. In addition, excellent wines are made along the Loire River (mainly white), along the Rhône River in the south of France, and in the hills of Alsace, which face the Rhine River frontier with Germany. These will be introduced at length; their tasting qualities will be sketched so that the adventurer in wine may begin to build his own experience on some frame of reference. But since France produces and exports so many other lesser wines, it is helpful to have a brief idea of what to expect of these and so avoid two dangers. Tasting a wine from some lesser region with great expectations of all things French will bring disappointment and a skeptical attitude to finer, costlier wines, of which great qualities *should* be expected. Or, having tasted some of the truly remarkable Burgundies or clarets that France exports, a very high standard may be expected of simpler wines from the south or elsewhere; these hopes, too, will be dashed by the limited qualities such wines really offer.

The Romans appear to have made the first serious attempts to cultivate the *Vitis vinifera* species of wine grape in Europe, probably in the Valais region of Switzerland. During the Christian era this viticulture spread over Europe; today some thousand varieties of wine grape have evolved and have adapted to many areas, each with its topography, climate, and human preferences. But more recent events give us fine wine as we know it. During the eighteenth and nineteenth centuries the use of cork and glass bottles to conserve wine made possible new visions of wine making and allowed fine wines to mature in a stable manner in a neutral environment. Rather than pink wine or white wine drawn off large barrels and quickly consumed, a whole variety of red, white, and rosé wines could be captured and protected in glass, to be drunk in small amounts as needed or desired.

This progress was interrupted in the late nineteenth century by an aphid pest, the American plant louse phylloxera, which destroyed the roots of European vines. The initial reaction of vine growers was to cross their European varieties with one of several American vine species resistant to this pest. Many vineyards were replanted in these hybrid, or Direct Producer, vines, but the quality of wine that resulted was disappointing. A second tactic was successful, however. This con-sisted of grafting a European variety onto an American root. With few exceptions—sandy soils in which phylloxera cannot live, high altitudes (which it shuns), or geographically isolated areas where even its flying form cannot penetrate—today's vineyards are built upon grafted vines using this European/American combination. The many French wines we are about to meet, and nearly all other wines in Europe, are of this sort.

Fine wine, French and other, is an ancient tradition, radically improved during the great centuries of European economic and technological growth, and finally cast into a contemporary form by the need to defend itself against a dangerous pest. The technological understanding born of necessity has been carried forward in a way unimagined a century ago; and in France as elsewhere, fine wine making aims at traditional goals but achieves them, or tries to, by modern means.

As with its Latin neighbors, Italy and Spain, viticulture in France is a colossal affair. Some 3.2 million acres of land (1.3 million hectares) are under vine, on which a million growers harvest almost 1.6 billion gallons (60 million hectoliters) per year. The area covered is but 2.8 percent of the countryside, but 8 percent of all gross agricultural revenue arises from wine grapes, and wine is the second largest agricultural export. Approximately one-half bottle daily is consumed for every French person. Yet what interests us is only a fraction of this, the more than 260 million gallons (10 million hectoliters) of quality wine that are classed as *Appellation d'Origine Contrôlée*, or fine wine coming from designated traditional regions and made according to traditional standards. These have distinctive style, unusual tasting qualities, and cannot be replaced by plain wine from other areas. In addition to the famous wines mentioned at the beginning of this chapter, other appellation wines, less good, are exported and therefore interest all who shop for wine.

The lesser appellations of France mainly come from three zones. South and east of Bordeaux, growing conditions allow balanced red and white wines to be made in reasonable quantity. All along the Mediterranean coast and inland, wines of strong alcoholic degree can be produced regularly; but their flavor and aroma is more limited because of hot weather, and the tendency is toward large production of very simple, bland wine. In the east of France, special wines are produced in the cool climate of Savoie and the Jura. These secondary appellations are all on the peripheries of the great ones of Bordeaux, Burgundy, and the Rhône, which have proved to be the best places for highest quality.

Around Bergerac, along the Dordogne River east of Bordeaux, is a large vineyard area planted in grapes also used in finer Bordeaux wines. Appellation Bergerac red has some Bordeaux tasting qualities; it is a light, slightly astringent red wine with a good suggestion of grape to its bouquet, tasting evenly and cleanly but without the lovely finish or intensity of good Bordeaux. A still lighter red appellation, Pécharmant, also comes from this region. Both red wines should smell and taste like bland Bordeaux and give a healthy, though not long-lasting, impression on the palate; they should be consumed young. Made in the same vineyard area, from varieties used for sweet Sauternes, is Monbazillac, normally a sweet wine, though it can be made dry by picking the white grapes early, before they have accumulated much sugar. Monbazillac of a good year shows a flowery, rich odor common to sweet wines of quality and should follow on the palate with an unctuous sensation, a great deal of flavor, and definite sweetness lasting well into the aftertaste. Many growers clean this wine excessively with sulphur dioxide. Montravel and Rosette are other white wine appellations which, like dry or semidry Monbazillac or white Bergerac, are mellow and should taste clean, but lack the liveliness of fully balanced whites with lots of fruit and acidity.

Farther east along the Lot River is an ancient vineyard whose red wines take the name of its principal town, Cahors. Today two distinct sorts of red wine are sold under this name. Old-fashioned Cahors, as it might be called, is inky dark in color with a striking aroma of grape skin, with wood and earthy odors. Its effect on the palate is equally vigorous, strongly astringent, and puckering, with intense taste suggesting Bordeaux flavors, for the grapes are the same, but much coarser. It ages for decades and when old is spicy, subtle, and interesting. Young, it is harsh. Most Cahors producers, and the large cooperative cellars that exist here, cannot easily sell such traditional wines in France and instead make a much blander, lighter-colored red wine with an agreeable bouquet and a clean impression to the taste that ends with a sensation of considerable alcohol. These may be compared remotely with some California wines in general balance and taste. Since imported wines will be moderately expensive, it is only the old-fashioned, heavy, intense Cahors that offers something special to compensate for the price; and it must be sought out by trial and error. It is unmistakable and should be put away to age.

Around Pau, near the Pyrenees, a white wine called Jurançon, rather heavy and slightly bitter, and a red wine called Madiran, bearing some perfume and a curious flavor (subtle but sometimes dry, sometimes sweet and a bit stale), are made from red and white Bordeaux grapes in different mixes. North of Toulouse the appellation Gaillac covers two short dull wines, red and white. The ordinary wines of Toulouse are light in taste and have no appellation, but it is possible to make a lively, light red wine here to drink young; and a producer determined to obtain color and flavor can often do so. Unfortunately, most Toulouse ordinary wines are dressed up in Bordeaux bottles with château names or other suggestions that they are something other than ordinary wine, which both distracts and deceives. In the future, better wines may come from Toulouse. An acid sparkling wine called Blanquette de Limoux, without a great deal of flavor and without delicacy, is made to the east.

The Mediterranean coast is divided into the Languedoc-Roussillon area from the Spanish border to the Rhône and the Provence area from Marseille to Italy. Sweet aperitif wines, with much aroma and taste but of the weight of sherry or other fortified wines, are easily made in this hot landscape; Banyuls and Muscat de Frontignan are the two Languedoc names most exported. The better-known wines are red and come from the area around the Aude River, which flows from Carcassonne to the sea at Narbonne. The appellations defining these are a thorough mess and need some explaining. South of the Aude River and the town of Lézignan, in the middle of a great grape-growing plain that continues to Narbonne, is the big designation Corbières. This is not an appellation exactly but a VDQS (*Vin Délimité de Qualité Supérieure*), a second category of delimited growing area not so good as appellation but with the same general set of rules for growing and making wine. Higher up, in the hills to the south, are better patches of vineyard that have the right to an appellation called Fitou. A similar situation unfurls on the north side of the Aude. A big VDQS area called Minervois starts in the plain and runs up into the better land of the hills. Beyond, the best part of this flank of the Aude Valley has the appellation St. Chinian.

Corbières and Minervois from the hot plain are light, dull red wines with very little odor or taste of grape, bland at best, with little staying power in the bottle and lacking the acidity and character that make wines interesting rather than just drinkable. But the same names, Corbières and Minervois, can contain wines from the higher ground with good color, a pleasant, vigorous taste, and clean finish—quite nice red indeed, if not completely distinctive or fine. Such wines are equal to the bright, light red wines of the appellations St. Chinian and Fitou. This muddled situation was caused by political pressure to include the many growers of ordinary wine in the plain in some sort of distinctive geographical designation implying quality. In consequence, the wine buyer abroad is quite lost, for the designation Corbières or Minervois tells him little. Generally such wines are better if they display a darker red color, as this reflects some intensity of taste. All should be inexpensive. The best should have a grapy aroma and give a clean impression to the taste, in which the drier qualities of skin and flavors associated with pigment should not be overpowered by too much alcohol, which gives a "hot" dull effect to red wines in the absence of enough flavor.

A few other appellations are scattered around this Aude growing area. A rather cloying red wine called Banyuls Grand Cru and sweet aperitif-grade wine is made around that coastal town. Very plain white wines without much life are Clairette de Bellegarde and du Languedoc. Grand Roussillon is plain red wine rather like Corbières, tending to a good deal of alcohol for its flavor and to keep poorly in bottle. In addition to Frontignan, other Muscat wines are called Lunel and Mireval.

But the more interesting wines for the future are not any of these minor appellations but rather the sound red wines and some rosé that are made between Montpellier and Nîmes, either on large properties or by government-assisted *Caves Coopératives*. Here it is possible to obtain an inexpensive, reasonably good, and complete red wine of some 11 percent alcohol, with proper color and very pleasing to the palate. This requires a good guiding policy, either by one of the big shippers in Nîmes who know what foreign markets require or by imaginative management at the *Coopérative*. These reds are mostly sold in France as Costières du Gard, a VDQS. Again, for the buyer abroad, the depth of color will usually give a clue as to the intensity of taste that such wines will offer to the palate. Few are distinguished, none has finesse in its aftertaste, but they can be generous, clean, and truly good. The whites suffer more from the heat and are insufficiently acid or flavorful for the most part. All are wines to drink young.

Wines exported from the eastern Provence side of the sea are chiefly rosé in special long, fluted bottles, slightly sweetish and pleasant without a strong character. They are made from red grapes used for fine Rhône wines, Carignan, Grenache, and others; the rather flat, coarse whites come from Ugni Blanc, also used in the Rhône. All appellations are allowed red, white, and rosé versions and are of VDQS quality if not name. There are four: Cassis, Bandol, Bellet, and Palette. Wine drinkers will quickly decide if they have a taste for Provence rosé; after that, it is a question of selecting shippers or properties whose wines are not tainted with sulphur dioxide and have enough fruity flavors to drink agreeably.

Corsican wines are of several kinds, all tending to be expensive because of the transportation costs. Patrimonio is an appellation in the north of the island that produces very rich, ponderous, quite alcoholic wines. Grapes of Italian and north African parentage are used in this hot climate where liveliness and flavor are difficult to achieve, and alcohol gets too high. In hilly ground in the south, at Porto Vecchio, Sartène, and Ajaccio, red wines that offer a forward style can be made, but this vital development to the taste with much flavor comes only at the price of careful growing with expensive ground pipe irrigation and special vinifications. The designation "Corsican" has been reserved to such wines of appellation pretension; others—bland, dull alcoholic wines from the eastern plain—must call themselves "Wines of the Emperor's [Napoleon] Island."

Eastern France

In the higher ground between the Rhône and Switzerland, an old viticulture continues to make special wines. These are strong-flavored and light-colored, much as many Swiss wines; they are also expensive, for they are preferred locally, and production is not very large. Around Annecy, white quality grape types such as Chardonnay and Pinot Blanc are vinified into still white wine called Crépy and a sparkling white Seyssel, with the addition of three local varieties. Slightly aromatic in impression, with a fairly aggressive flavor a bit tinged with bitterness, these have limited appeal to most drinkers. Two unusual wines are made in the Jura Mountains to the north. The best-known and most typical is Château-Chalon, a so-called yellow (*jaune*) made by allowing yeasts of a particular indigenous sort to form a film on the wines in barrel, which are not topped up but are left for six years to allow this very slow fermentation to work its flavors into the wine. A heavy, rather pungent wine results, discolored by oxidation into a yellowish-orange tint, with a highly distinctive aroma and a variety of special flavors. It suggests some of the nutty but stale effects of Madeira or old sherry, and indeed the production process resembles that of these familiar fortified wines. Côtes de Jura, L'Étoile, and Arbois are other appellations in the locality producing both *jaune* wines and rather hard, thin red and flat-tasting dense white wines. *Vin de paille* (straw wine) is another specialty sold under these appellations. Made from concentrated grapes that have been dried on straw mats for two months, it is a sweetish, very alcoholic wine with pungent flavors.

At France's border with Germany in the northeast, some very light, acid white wine is made under the VDQS designation Vin de Moselle; it resembles the delicate but quite astringent white wines made in neighboring Luxembourg, also from cold vineyards. The vineyard is planted in Sylvaner, Riesling, and Auxerrois white grapes used in Alsace and Germany for white wines. The Moselle wines have fragrance and bite but little body or generosity.

The VDQS system includes some 60 designations for local wines that display character and claim enough tradition to entitle their designation to protection. The line between VDQS and lesser appellations mentioned in these few pages is more a legal distinction than one of quality. Quality ranges from definitely fine wines, such as the traditional reds of Cahors, to the blandest VDQS Minervois. In today's wine economy a clean wine, white or red, that offers distinctive taste and a perceptible balance between fruit, body, acidity, and aftertaste is worth between $2.30 and $4.00 retail in America and slightly more in England because of higher duties. Many wines from countries other than France compete in this same arena. It is appropriate to judge lesser French wines against them and to remember that lesser appellations and VDQS have been sorted out by a long process of trial and error that itself has promoted the famous, more expensive French wines to their eminent position. Such minor wines are fairly marketed to consumers at the lower end of the price scale if they are technically sound and have no faults. As prices increase, consumers should expect, and receive, some distinct character associated with the region, with the grape variety, and with the name; they should, therefore, be prepared to pay $3.00 or more.

Appellation Contrôlée and Quality Control

The laws of controlled designation, or *Appellation Contrôlée,* have spread out into the Common Market wine-producing countries and beyond. We shall meet them or their Italian or German counterparts again. Their original purpose was to stop fraudulently designated and technically bad wine from reaching commercial channels and, ultimately, consumers. It quickly became apparent that such detailed regulation could be usefully pressed further to push, cajole, and bully wine producers into improving their vines, land, and production methods. In France efforts at regulation began amid agricultural crises early in the twentieth century; major enactments came during the 1930s. These had two purposes: to guarantee authenticity of origin and to set minimum quality standards, typically by defining grape varieties permitted but also by setting chemically measurable minimum specifications for wine. The laws also prohibited substances that were dangerous, or whose use would have amounted to a confession that the wine was below appellation standards.

Today these ideas have been reorganized within the Common Market into a more general concept called VQPRD—Quality Wine Originating from a Designated Region. In Bordeaux, for example, the appellation laws insist that a wine calling itself Pomerol come from a precisely defined region by that name. It must be made from one or more of the permitted grape varieties. The appellation authorities must give permission to plant land even if such land lies within the appellation. Only a certain quantity of wine per planted area may be produced—less for the finer, more expensive appellations, such as Pomerol; more for the lesser, cheaper appellations, such as Bordeaux rouge. Vines must be four years old to produce appellation-grade wine.

When the new wine is vinified and finished, samples are passed to the authorities for chemical analysis. They must meet minimum alcohol-percentage requirements and not exceed maximum limits for components unpleasant in large proportions, such as volatile acidity, or unstable ones, such as unfermented sugar, or dangerous ones, such as free sulphur. The same procedure is in effect for every appellation in France; elsewhere, however—in Burgundy, for example—the land within an appellation may be officially divided by quality into the best plots, the less good, the even less good, and so on.

In Bordeaux a further quality control is exercised by a tasting panel made up of a grower from the appellation, a broker (*courtier*), and a shipper (*négociant*) who buys wine from growers through a broker and sells it to the world wine trade. Representatives of these three sections of the wine business form a panel (called *label*) that tastes all wines submitted for the appellation without knowing which wine is which. They may accept a wine, adjourn a wine if they agree it has temporary problems that should be looked at later, or refuse a wine if they consider it should not receive the appellation.

While the interest of the appellation authorities stops approximately here, a second enforcement bureau called the Repression of Fraud also polices wine. Mixing two vintages is a matter of indifference to the appellation authorities as long as both are of the same origin but could bring a brush with the Repression of Fraud if the vintages were not what they called themselves on the label. Detection of similar misrepresentation of commercial rather than technical significance could also result in penalties, including prison.

This is an extremely coherent scheme for controlling wine quality and origin. There is nothing wrong with it and much that is right.

But human factors have caused it to be in fact much looser and less relevant than it seems. To protect quality, output of wine per area is restricted. Under pressure from the farm lobby in France, still more important than in other countries, the Ministry of Agriculture annually accedes to requests for an increase in quantity permitted. Chemical scrutiny of wine is done effectively; the *label* tasting is less effective. A few dreadful wines are thrown out. But the panel is highly reluctant to reject a wine for an appellation, particularly a higher appellation, because the decision could ruin a farmer. The understandable but bad reason is that the differential in price between appellation Pomerol and plain Bordeaux or ordinary wine, to which grade such rejected wine would be demoted, represents a loss of money that could bankrupt a vineyard.

In all fairness, it is a nearly impossible task to sit on a *label* and judge a great number of unidentified wines with a fading palate, blurring impressions, and a mounting fear of doing an injustice. Also, the sample, drawn from one vat or one barrel, may not be valid for the entire crop. It has happened that growers have opined contemptuously on their own wines, clearly recognizable to the broker and shipper on the panel; one *label* even witnessed the comic spectacle of the shipper and broker begging the grower of a famous wine simply to adjourn rather than condemn forever a "villainous and unworthy Pauillac"—the grower's own, as it turned out—the shipper and broker tasting well that day.

The administration controls the total amount of appellation wine in a grower's cellar. But suppose, in two successive vintages, the first is pale and lacks body and the second is dark and rich? A grower may well be tempted genuinely to improve the former with 15 or 20 percent of the latter, more often than not at a financial sacrifice. This is illegal but beneficial. It is also unprovable.

What underlies all these observations is that higher levels of quality cannot be legislated; appellation laws set minimum standards and guarantee that quality wine is from the district named. After that, the wines are as excellent as weather permits, the grower's means permit, and the grower's determination dictates. The quality level at which overseas consumers begin to be interested in fine wines is well above the minimum quality that is possible to enforce—and this essential fact is true not only in Bordeaux but also throughout fine wine regions in the major producing countries.

One form of quality control most neglected outside France is that exercised by the growers themselves. Year after year, property after property isolates lesser grapes in the vineyard and wines in the vats and disposes of them separate from the better-grade château wine. Sometimes this is done by marketing the less good wine under a second name, sold more cheaply; at other times it is sold simply as wine of that appellation. (During the nineteenth century many famous châteaux made "*second vin,*" but such a proliferation of names and grades is thought too confusing for today's already crowded marketplace.) Clearly this private quality control lies entirely outside appellation laws, and only the proprietor knows for sure what he has done. But wine drinkers should realize that when something exceptional is in the glass, particularly when coming from a lesser vintage, they are benefiting from an enhanced quality achieved by financial sacrifice on the part of the grower.

France has declared an intention to modify its appellation laws. One reform limits grower options to declassify crops into lesser appellation grades representing broader regions within which vineyards fall. Until recently a Beaune grower could choose to sell part of his crop as mere red Burgundy, or a Pauillac grower might sell part of his crop as Haut Médoc, a larger region enclosing Pauillac. A second line of reform revamps yet again the legal maximum amount of wine permitted per area of vineyard. It remains to see how all this will work. The wine trade is applauding from the sidelines. I am skeptical. First, old laws were weakly enforced for the brutal reason that French farmers have more political clout than the overworked staff of government technicians attempting to enforce either old or new laws. A farm vote that can get some restrictions relaxed today can get new restrictions relaxed tomorrow. Some serious investment in research and development, and in an agricultural extension service sufficiently funded to deliver the scientists' discoveries to the farmers, would seem more germane to a government effort than a spider web of punitive legislation.

Trashy French wine cannot compete with trashy wine from lands whose production cost is lower, and to play the card of quality to the limit requires the encouragement of highest quality. How to do this is a mighty puzzle. Growers can be seduced into making large amounts of poor wine through exclusive contracts guaranteeing them a market for whatever slush they crank out; but forcing all wines to compete each year on an open market, where prices are closely related to quality and quantity, while a commendable antimonopolistic notion, is about as realistic as legislating a ceiling on the number of presents parents may give their children. In large appellations of middle or lower grade, some roughshod, anonymous grading of wine could be done. One could visualize grades A, B, and C for Bordeaux red and white wines with no more than Bordeaux appellation, much as beef is graded in the United States. Then, for example, an importer in Great Britain could affirm in provable manner that he dealt only in Grade A Bordeaux red. Two things would result—much injustice and much progress.

The problem with laws is that they fiddle with the incentives that only a marketplace can really shove in the face—and minds—of those whose work and ambition account for the quality of things. The new laws are complicated and sound virtuous. But, by and large, they repeat what the old laws said. A historian would say that repeating a law confesses one's inability to enforce it.

Château Bottling

Château bottling has clear origins. In past times, when wines circulated less widely than today, when few wine drinkers visited vineyards to taste at the source (and could therefore remember what they tasted), opportunities for fraud abounded. The rise of great vineyard estates in the eighteenth century, interrupted by the French Revolution, continued with increasing momentum in the early nineteenth century and brought the issue of authenticity to the forefront. Increasingly, important châteaux commenced to bottle at the property to protect their wines from adulteration by intermediaries. At first this special measure was considered appropriate only for the finest vintages; by the end of the nineteenth century, château or estate bottling was widely generalized. In our time, estate bottling is practiced without regard to vintage quality except for a tiny number of properties (and honor to them) and many growers who bottle only their better wine. Mobile bottling plants have put château bottling within the reach of growers incompetent or unequipped for this special task. Today we have an unprecedented variety and quantity of wine coming from individual vineyards.

Consumers should understand that a château name is a trademark and that more than one such name may be owned by a grower. Should the grower have six names to dispose of, he may distribute his wine among them as he pleases as long as he stays within the confines of appellation law. Appellation law concerns itself mainly with authenticity of origin from within a defined region and only rarely with the respective merits of properties within that region.

READING THE LABEL

COLOR

Rouge	Red.
Blanc	White.
Rosé	Rosé (pink).
Clairet	Very light red wine rapidly fermented and intended for immediate consumption.
Blanc de Blancs	White wine from white grapes as distinguished from red; a Champagne term now diffused into other regions.

BOTTLING

Mise en bouteille au (or du) château	Bottled at the vineyard property.
Mise en bouteille dans nos chais	*Chai* is a cellar; usually this means that a shipper has bottled the wine in his cellars.
No mention of bottler	French law requires that the firm or individual responsible for the wine print its business name and locale on the label. If château-bottled, the grower is the *responsable*. If there is no mention of bottling, it is the shipper (*négociant*) or *Cave Coopérative* that is the *responsable*.
Cave Coopérative	Government-supported grower cooperatives. Their name *must* normally appear as the *responsable* on their wines.
Négociant, Négociant-Éleveur	Shipper, wholesale merchant firm buying wines, usually from producers, and selling to importers. Most inexpensive wines are *négociant*-bottled.

VINTAGE

Année, Récolte, Millésime	Year, harvest, vintage; all meaning wine of that crop.

LEGAL CATEGORIES OF WINE

Appellation d'Origine Contrôlée, Appellation Contrôlée, AOC	All mean appellation wine. Whenever an appellation name is used, it must be appellation wine whether or not one of these formulations appears.
Vin Délimité de Qualité Supérieure (VDQS)	A second tier of quality below AOC.
Vin de Consommation Courante (VCC), an old designation, now Vin de Table or, if exported, Vin de France	Table wine meeting general standards for hygiene and of no special origin within France. This is commonly called *vin ordinaire*. The term has little meaning.
Vin Jaune, Vin de Paille	"Yellow wine," "Straw wine" (see page 28).
Vin Gris	White wine from red grape juice pressed immediately and fermented as if it were white wine.
Méthode Champenoise	"Champagne method." Secondary fermentation in bottle, with aging to enhance flavor. True of all Champagne and for sparkling wine from appellations requiring the process, such as Vouvray.
Vin Mousseux, Mousseux	Sparkling wine made from the bulk (Charmat) method unless appellation law restricts it, as it does in many regions, to the Champagne method.
Vin Doux Naturel	Dessert wine containing unfermented sugar; in principle over 15 percent alcohol.
Vin Nouveau, Vin Primeur	Terms traditionally used in Beaujolais for very young wines shipped as early as November 15 of the year in which they were vinified. These should be consumed within months of shipment.

Bordeaux

Bordeaux is the world's most important and greatest fine wine region. A panorama of fine reds, full-bodied white wines from Graves, and a unique family of sweet white wines from Sauternes and Barsac flow from some 300,000 acres (120,000 hectares) of growing area dispersed across 80 miles (130 kilometers). An enormous quantity and variety of lesser red and white wines is produced. Obviously Bordeaux's climate favors viticulture, but the region's extraordinary prestige comes from its unmatched variety of high-quality wines and the very large size of so many of the estates that produce them.

Fame is both cause and effect of connoisseurship pursued generation after generation. The large production of major vineyards facilitates widespread collection and accumulation of their wines. The extraordinary individual character of important wines animates this collecting passion. But great wines not only show individuality; they also commonly display generic character peculiar to their subregion or appellation, be it Médoc, Graves, Pomerol, St.-Émilion, or Fronsac, Bourg/Blaye, Pauillac, or Sauternes. They also express the features of a given vintage, no two of which are identical. These three dimensions of quality—appellation, individual château style, and vintage character—can be explored endlessly with steady improvement of taste and knowledge. A perennial infusion of new curiosities arrives as each crop comes to fruition, so there is no risk of boredom.

Some 150 world-famous properties each produce yearly between 5,000 and 25,000 cases (dozen-bottle units) of fine wine. Hundreds of others lie just behind the front rank. No professional or amateur can "know" all Bordeaux, yet much can be learned. Several years ago I lunched at a Médoc vineyard with three other Bordeaux shippers. A decanter of red Bordeaux was brought out toward the meal's end. We sniffed it, drank it, and guessed at its identity. One shipper had never tasted the particular vintage, yet he divined it exactly—Château Mouton Rothschild 1934. This was no miracle. Mouton Rothschild is a wine with marked character not resembling many others in any year. The 1934 vintage had a peculiar style, unctuous, faintly oily, and leaving a slightly burned effect. Other guesses included Château Lynch Bages 1934, a vineyard near Mouton that resembles it in savor and in rich impression, and Mouton Rothschild 1947, a vintage sharing some features with 1934.

The point of this story is that château style, local style (here a "family" group of Pauillac wines), and vintage style announce themselves in distinguished Bordeaux wines. And there are enough fine clarets to allow many of us this experience. Of course, the fellow who picked out the 1934 Mouton made crashing mistakes before and since; and certainly one should not ruin the enjoyment of fine wines by making a competition out of their appreciation.

Recently Bordeaux has been much criticized. Its prices are too high. Its prices have fallen too low. Its merchants are too clever by half, or else they are stupid. Everything is wrong with Bordeaux, it would seem, as the international wine trade suffers its first real trauma since the 1930s. One is reminded of the scene at dismissal time on the terrifying first day of primary school. Mothers wait anxiously for the exit of their children. The children pour out, each runs to his mother and begins abusing her. She should not have left him at this fearsome school. She should not have come for him so soon, interrupting his fun. One screams, another sobs, still another kicks Mother in the shins. Why, one wonders, are all these children venting their emotions on their mothers? The answer dawns slowly: They know Mother will always be there, no matter how they behave.

Bordeaux appellations are based on geographical regions, with lower appellations drawn very large and containing progressively smaller and more restricted regions, considered better. Up to 1974 wines from the better regions could be declassified and designated by the name of the larger region to which they belonged. While this "cascade" declassification has been ended, the hierarchy, geographical and qualitative, illustrates the concepts and approximate merits of the appellations. (See the map on page 35.)

RED WINES: MÉDOC

	Bordeaux	Bordeaux Supérieur	Médoc	Haut Médoc	Margaux Moulis Listrac St.-Julien Pauillac St.-Estèphe
Alcoholic degree	10°	10.5°	10°	10°	10.5°
Hectoliters per hectare	50	40	45	43	40

WHITE WINES: WINES OF LEFT BANK

	Bordeaux	Bordeaux Supérieur	Graves	Graves Supérieur	Sauternes Barsac
Alcoholic degree	10.5°	11.5°	11°	12°	13°
Hectoliters per hectare	50	40	40	40	25

These tables may appear illogical in places. Stricter requirements for Bordeaux Supérieur than for Médoc, for example, stem from the desire to distinguish between *supérieur* and ordinary Bordeaux. Sauternes is a more famous name than Barsac, so the appellation laws allow Barsac growers to fly their wine under the colors of Barsac or to sell it as Sauternes. The technical standards are the same. Distinctions between Bordeaux Supérieur and Bordeaux and Graves Supérieur and Graves are not geographical but technical, relating to alcohol content and quantity produced per vineyard area.

Bordeaux's list of appellations is long. The most important will be introduced separately: the commune appellations of the Médoc, Pomerol, St.-Émilion, Sauternes, and white and red Graves. But the following lesser appellations appear in English-speaking markets, and the interested consumer will want to identify them on the map. They have been ranked approximately in order of quality. However, the best wines of an inferior appellation systematically surpass the poorer wines of superior appellations. As the Russian proverb says (and they should know): "Where there is law there is injustice."

SECONDARY BORDEAUX APPELLATIONS

WHITE WINES

APPELLATION

Cérons
 Ste.-Croix-du-Mont
 Loupiac
 Premières Côtes de Bordeaux
     with commune name (Cadillac,
     Gabarnac, and so forth)
	Semisweet to sweet wines that should have some unfermented sugar. A few wines of very high quality.

Côtes de Bordeaux St.-Macaire **Premières Côtes de Bordeaux** **Entre-Deux-Mers**	Usually semisweet wines but also many dry ones.

RED WINES

APPELLATION

Côtes Canon Fronsac and **Côtes de Fronsac** **Lalande de Pomerol and Néac**	Good to very fine wines rivaling lesser wines of St.-Émilion and Pomerol. At best, generous and rich.
Sables-St.-Émilion **Montagne-St.-Émilion** **Lussac-St.-Émilion** **Parsac-St.-Émilion** **St.-Georges-St.-Émilion** **Puisseguin-St.-Émilion**	The satellite St.-Émilions vary in quality from harsh and dull to excellent; equal to good St.-Émilion of lesser grade.
Côtes de Blaye (Blaye, Blayais, **Premières Côtes de Blaye)** **Bourg (Côtes de Bourg, Bourgeais)** **Graves de Vayres**	Variable wines, some light and thin, at best dark, generous, a trifle coarse.

Premières Côtes de Bordeaux
     (with commune name 11.5
     percent alcohol,
     otherwise 10.5 percent)
	Good examples have fruit and character; excellent drinking when young, the best mature well.

Bordeaux—Côtes de Castillon **and Côtes de Francs** **Ste.-Foy-Bordeaux** **Bordeaux Supérieur**	Red wines with general characteristics of Bordeaux; many excellent individual properties.

Red wine style is far more varied than is commonly supposed. If a relatively small Bordeaux district such as Fronsac were situated off on its own, it would probably attract the attention given to the wines of, for example, Chablis. Traditional standards of taste, which prize finesse and delicacy above other qualities, elevate two large regions, Médoc and Graves, over all others. In modern times St.-Émilion and, above all, Pomerol have risen to equal Médoc and Graves in price and popular reputation. A second tier of red wine quality comes from the appellations Fronsac, Canon Fronsac, Graves de Vayres, Blaye, Bourg, and some wines of the Premières Côtes de Bordeaux. After this rushes a flood of appellation Bordeaux or Bordeaux Supérieur red wines; some are delicious, some good, some execrable.

Several types of red wine can be recognized, and so a few necessarily imperfect generalizations can be inflicted upon the reader. One extreme of red Bordeaux is dominated by astringency and by tannic and/or woody tastes; in youth it is assertive and harsh, to the point of being startling. Although such wines occur in the Médoc, notably in the north and west, and in Moulis and Listrac, young Graves reds are more frequently of this type and oppress the senses with a density only years of age will mollify. Leognan wines answer to this description more than those of Pessac. Some truly great wines emerge, but they are difficult to commercialize and judge in their early years.

Next, and most important, are Bordeaux red wines formed on what can only be called a classical model. Medium red and brilliant in hue, in time the color becomes ruby. With clean bouquet and aroma forcefully resonating flavors of the Cabernet grapes, their distinctive odor has been compared to black currants. Astringent, hesitant or muted for several years after bottling, tasting qualities eventually reveal a wealth of successive sensations—odors, flavors, tactile impressions endlessly mingled. This harmony, along with delicacy of aftertaste, has been defined by the Bordeaux wine trade as finesse for at least two centuries. Most classic clarets are from the Médoc and Graves. A very few wines, not always the same properties each year, appear in St.-Émilion and Pomerol. This archetypal Bordeaux red wine matures with unparalleled distinction. Its long history, not logic, has made its tasting qualities a standard for all mature red wines.

A different family of vigorous red wines, with forward and heady aroma and bouquet, comes foremost from Pomerol and St.-Émilion but includes others on the Right (east) Bank of the Gironde estuary. Right Bank wines immediately appeal to the taste; rich flavor, vinosity, mineral or earthy savors, and often fruit are all prominent—a mouth-filling impression in which finesse may often be wanting. Development in bottle is typically quicker than in classic Bordeaux, but many live to old age. Similar qualities are found at lower levels of intensity and flavor in wines from Fronsac, Blaye, Bourg, Graves de Vayres, and other locales. The popularity of Right Bank wines derives from the ease with which their tasting qualities are appreciated. Some sites in the Médoc give similarly unctuous "plushy" red wines, round and full but lacking finesse.

The wines from the fringes of St.-Émilion lack the full fruit and appeal of the best of the appellation, or of Pomerol wines, often being blunted by flavors termed "earthy, woody, stalky." This area is known as the satellite St.-Émilion appellations, for they attach St.-Émilion to their local names, as in Lussac-St.-Émilion.

The broad bottom of the quality pyramid offers a massive quantity of red Bordeaux in a supple, diminished form. Such wines balance adequate astringency to be lively and enough fruit to be charming. Age adds flavor and bouquet to their basic qualities. This is plain red

Bordeaux as it should and can be. Unfortunately, in this economically marginal class of wines the worst wines are also found in abundance.

The white wines of Bordeaux fall into two major categories, dry and sweet. Enclaved in southern Graves is the sweet-wine region, with outposts across the Garonne in Loupiac and other districts. The best Sauternes and Barsac are subtle and astonishing. Fruit, lusciousness of flavor, sufficient acidity to preserve a lively sensation on the palate, and a balance between alcohol and unfermented sugar are cardinal elements of quality. Better examples carry considerable unfermented sugar without being cloying; more modest Sauternes support less sugar. Traditional French cuisine has prized these luscious wines with heavy fish dishes, boiled lobster, *charcuterie, foie de volaille,* as well as with desserts. Today's fashions find little place for them, but anyone who dismisses without sampling the great sweet wines of Bordeaux has obstinately made up his mind that nineteenth-century gastronomy and French cuisine cannot be right.

Fine white Graves, a small class unto itself, has generous body and matures slowly. Lesser Graves wines merge into the generality of Bordeaux whites. These may be medium-bodied white wines, modern, tart, and lively whites (some coming from a single variety such as Sauvignon), or, unfortunately, plain wines often poorly vinified and smelling of sulphur dioxide.

On the Left Bank of the Gironde, Cabernet Sauvignon, Cabernet Franc, and Merlot are the major grapes, laced with some Petit Verdot (a deep-colored, late-ripening grape) and traces of Malbec; the Carmenère, a permitted variety, hardly is seen. On the Right Bank, Merlot and Bouchet (Cabernet Franc) dominate. In the sweet and dry white-wine regions, Sauvignon, Semillon, and some Muscadelle are the noble grapes used for appellation wines.

The untroubled faith of the past—that the terrain, first and last, was responsible for nuances of highest wine quality—wavers before today's belief that microclimate accounts for final quality, provided other conditions are met. No doubt Bordeaux's best vineyards are excellent terrain for viticulture. Great rivers of gravel rise up in long bands throughout the Médoc and in Sauternes. There are fine sites on the Right Bank, too. A wealth of mineral nourishment and other land features are all there. But is it really their splendid deep gravel slopes dipping toward the Gironde that make the best wines of Margaux, St.-Julien, Pauillac, and St.-Estèphe so exquisite? Or is it the particular immediate climatic environment that results from their situation, a climate broadly determined by their location leeward of sheltering forests between them and the sea, moderated by the Gironde air currents, and topped off by their disposition to sun and wind? Some wines of startling finesse certainly issue from those picture-postcard vineyards with acres of white gravel framed by the Gironde. So the debate rages on.

Classification of the Châteaux of the Gironde

Cutting across modern appellations and value as expressed by today's prices are classifications, ancient and modern, that appear on Bordeaux wine labels by such mentions as "Grand Cru Classé en 1855," "Cru Classé," "Premier Grand Cru," and similar formulas. The consumer may well be confused; even many owners do not know the background of the so-called Official Classification of 1855. Years of part-time research have given me the following view of the origins of the 1855 Classification, but different versions appear elsewhere.

From the late eighteenth to the mid-nineteenth century, important Médoc properties were periodically classified by Bordeaux brokers, then a powerful class of intermediaries between châteaux and *négociants.* The properties had no say in the classification, and no government body was involved. As vineyards improved or declined, they were periodically shifted up or down in the classification or declassified entirely. There were five grades; a price difference of 20 percent separated each of the first four grades. In 1855 Napoleon III requested a collection of Bordeaux wines for his International Exposition in Paris. He turned to the Chamber of Commerce, a commercial law court of Bordeaux. Knowing nothing about wines, the Chamber asked the brokers for their classification. They complied, but with trepidation and warnings against giving such a list an official character. For they foresaw exactly what could and did happen: one ranking, representing the merits of various wines at one point in time, received an "official" standing, became frozen, and reduced itself in time to a list of 60 odd vineyard names. The hastily drawn 1855 Classification was shorter than many predecessors; some omissions are obvious, several instances of corruption very probable.

The notice "Grand Cru Classé en 1855" that appears on claret labels is therefore not in itself a guarantee of quality in 1977. The 1855 Classification extended to Sauternes but not to the Right Bank. Since World War II, Graves and St.-Émilion growers' associations have erected classifications of their wines.

The issue of classification is clearly controversial. Eighteen years in Bordeaux have convinced me that classifications drawn by interested parties are invalid. Today growers, shippers, and brokers all have commercial allegiances to different properties. No government body is competent or has the authority to classify vineyards. Furthermore, any classification not providing for reform and renovation at five- to ten-year intervals is probably worse than none. When classifications erroneously suggest to importers and consumers a superiority or inferiority of vineyard names, they obstruct improvement of low-classified or nonclassified vineyards; by depressing their prices, bad classifications steal the means and incentive for improving quality. This neglected point is more serious than sustaining profits to a high-classified vineyard no longer worthy of its rank. To reclassify wines based on current prices would not, as some have claimed, be objective; market demand is already structured by existing classifications as much as by real qualities.

Since objective, competent periodic reclassification is impossible, the best solution would be abolition of all classifications. For human and legal reasons this is also impossible; the past will not simply go away. Anyone—importer, retailer, restaurant, or consumer—who cares about quality Bordeaux wine would do best to disregard classifications and emphasize the current tasting qualities of the many splendid wines of Bordeaux.

The traditional emphasis on finesse and elegance has been seriously modified in favor of easier tasting qualities, notably those of St.-Émilion and Pomerol, as the rising prices of these wines since 1900 so clearly show. A notable exception is the great sweet dessert wines of Sauternes and Barsac. If one compares an 1870 tasting note to one of 1970, he will find that the criteria for Sauternes have changed very little.

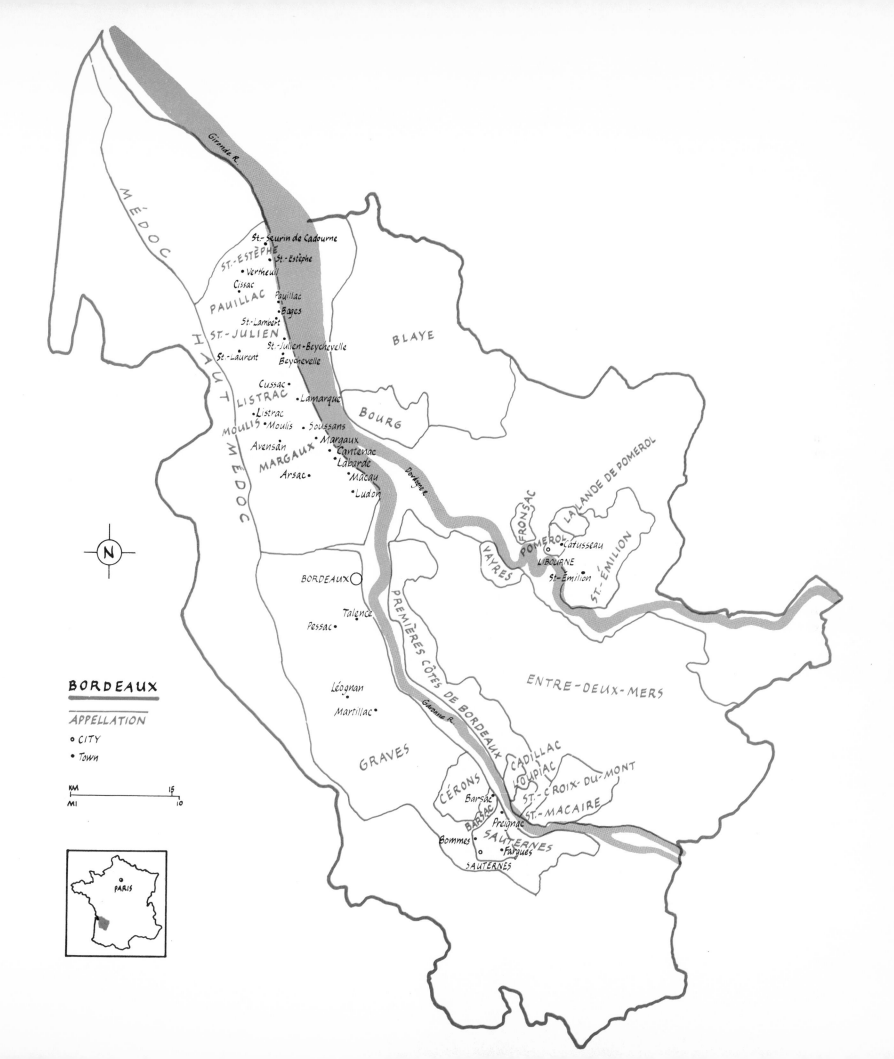

Gironde R.

MÉDOC

St.-Seurin de Cadourne

ST.-ESTÈPHE
• St.-Estèphe
• Vertheuil
Cissac
PAUILLAC
Pauillac
Bages
St.-Lambert
ST.-JULIEN
St.-Julien-Beychevelle
St.-Laurent
Beychevelle

HAUT MÉDOC

Cussac
LISTRAC
Lamarque
Listrac
MOULIS • Moulis
Soussans
Avensan
MARGAUX
Margaux
Cantenac
Labarde
Arsac
Macau
Ludon

BLAYE

BOURG

Dordogne

FRONSAC
POMEROL
LALANDE DE POMEROL
VAYRES
Catusseau
LIBOURNE
St.-Émilion
ST.-ÉMILION

N

BORDEAUX

Talence
Pessac

Léognan
Martillac

Garonne R.

PREMIÈRES CÔTES DE BORDEAUX

ENTRE-DEUX-MERS

BORDEAUX

APPELLATION
○ CITY
• Town

KM   15
MI   10

GRAVES

CÉRONS
Barsac
Barsac
CADILLAC
LOUPIAC
ST.-CROIX-DU-MONT
Preignac
ST.-MACAIRE
Bommes
SAUTERNES
Fargues
SAUTERNES

PARIS

READING THE LABEL: CLASSIFICATIONS

Médoc and Sauternes	Grand Cru Classé en 1855, also written as Grand Cru Classé (See page 34)	
Graves	Grand Cru Classé	Classified by growers in 1959 with the approval of the Ministry of Agriculture. The best vineyards are included.
St.-Émilion	Premier Grand Cru Grand Cru Classé Grand Cru	Between 1954 and 1958, the St.-Émilion growers classified themselves with government approval. These three categories form an unreliable guide to the wines.
Other traditional Médoc classifications	Cru Exceptionnel Cru Bourgeois Supérieur Cru Bourgeois Cru Artisan	Historic terms for descending grades of superior wines one notch below those châteaux classified in 1855. They include both fine and inferior properties and are functionally obsolete, but the first are accepted by the Ministry of Agriculture.

The Bordeaux Wine Market

Great château wines are either sold openly on the market or contracted to one or more *négociants* for a period of years. Brokers will negotiate prices of openly traded wines between growers and shippers during the winter after each vintage. A property making 15,000 cases may sell different amounts to several shippers who in turn may offer the wine to importers all over the world. The less famous properties either sell their wines to shippers or offer it as appellation-grade wine for blending into generic or branded wines.

Fine wines require two years' care in barrel, so that two more recent crops come along before the older vintage is bottled. The quantity and quality of these new crops naturally affect the value of wines already bought and still in barrel, and the fine wine market is therefore volatile and unpredictable; growers and shippers make gains and losses often without respect to their efforts or abilities. Exclusive contracts to *négociants* were intended in part to temper these ups and downs; like many devices that tamper with supply and demand, however, they have gravely aggravated price swings during the last five years.

Bordeaux Generic, Monopole, Varietal, and Other Shippers' Wines

Growers are responsible for the quality of château-bottled wines; the shipper is a financing, warehousing, and expediting intermediary. But most Bordeaux is "shipper's wine." Five forms are common:

1. WINE titled by its appellation of origin (Bordeaux, St.-Émilion, Sauternes), sold under the shipper's name, and governed by appellation law, of course. Whether it is good, bad, or indifferent depends upon the shipper.
2. WINE titled by a shipper's trademark or *monopole* and bearing an appellation. Mouton Cadet from La Bergerie or Roc Rouge from Cruse, both appellation-grade Bordeaux, are examples.
3. WINE without appellation, usually common (current consumption) grade. Label design, trademark, and the shipper's name may imply appellation wine, yet quality depends entirely on the shipper.
4. WINE designated by grape variety. French laws demand it be 100 percent of the variety named; the grower is held rigorously accountable. But varietal wines need *not* comply with appellation laws and can be deceptive when they come from shippers whose names or labels are associated with appellation-grade Bordeaux.
5. WINE from individual vineyards and bottled by the shipper. These wines must be from the property and are governed by their respective appellation. Enforcement is limited to total quantities once the wine is in the shipper's cellar. The shipper, accountable for the total volume of every appellation in his cellar, could mix two wines without easily being caught. Normally there is no profit in this; no juggling can produce more appellation wine than was bought to start with. He could, however, substitute 5,000 cases of lower-grade St.-Émilion for 5,000 cases of a finer property St.-Émilion and probably not be caught. As in most businesses, most people are honest and some are not.

Nearly all shipper's wine is blended *Appellation Contrôlée* grade governed more by importers' demands than shippers' ideas. Importers demand identical quality year after year at identical prices. It is unlikely that consumers the world over would rise up foaming at the mouth and lynch the importers of wines that varied in taste according to the vintage, but importers seem convinced this would happen. Thus, shippers strive for uniformity of blend. They must therefore hold and finance large stocks of wine. Their ability to blend well is hampered when a vintage year on the bottle is demanded. When prices for an appellation leap up and down by 300 percent, their lives become nightmarishly difficult. This helps explain the hard selling of branded nonappellation wines.

From the wine drinker's point of view, shippers' wines offer familiarity, but at a price. A branded product must be advertised and typically passes through more distribution levels, which raise its final price.

In the fine appellations, generic wines are a paradox. Château-bottled wines can win public recognition and command high prices. Over time, the best land and management is drawn into château-wine production. The more prestige to the appellation, the truer this is. Inexorably, what remains for appellation grade is the worst wine, especially in smaller, more famous appellations, less so in larger ones. Obtaining a quantity of good Bordeaux Rouge from the more than 25 million gallons (a million hectoliters) produced is no trick. Finding the same quantity of good generic St.-Julien is impossible, and the price of what is available is excessive.

Consumers therefore get progressively less value precisely in the prestige appellations whose higher renown and higher price lead them to expect quality.

A few lesser appellations permit shippers to blend at reasonable prices. These include Bordeaux and Bordeaux Supérieur Rouge and Blanc; Médoc and occasionally Haut Médoc; white Graves; St.-Émilion and its satellites. In better appellations, best value is logically found among lesser properties.

Summary

Bordeaux white wine falls into three groupings—fine sweet wines, white Graves of quality, and a mass of lesser white wines. Reds consist of old-fashioned clarets too dense and astringent to drink young, scores of classic clarets from great properties, a large collection of tasty Right Bank clarets ranging from great Pomerols to earthy Bourgs and Blayes, and a reservoir of red Bordeaux wine varying from very good to foul.

Appellation laws set the quality floor on Bordeaux's extensive production and guarantee wine origin. But the heights of quality are attained by grower effort and grower sacrifice, not legislation. Past and present classifications by merit are not useful for different reasons. Irreducible uncertainties in quantity and quality of successive crops combine to make Bordeaux prices unstable.

For wine lovers it remains, as always, to learn to appreciate the tasting qualities of fine Bordeaux and enjoyably to expand acquaintance with the world's largest and greatest quality red-wine and sweet-white-wine producing area. From among thousands of estates some 100 labels have been chosen here to represent the main fine wines, a mere sniff of what awaits you.

Calvet Bordeaux

Prominent among traditional shippers, Calvet has a superior position in France as well as in foreign distribution. It markets both Bordeaux generic wines and Burgundies. Throughout its life this firm has taken a strict view of its business role as *négociant* (shipper). Considering that these functions are at odds with those of a vineyard owner, Calvet has never acquired vineyards, feeling this would pose conflicts of interest. Their good Bordeaux generics are representative of expected qualities as seen by the French market and are packaged traditionally. Among old rivals doing like business are Eschenauer, Cordier, Dourthe, Schroder and Schyler, and the three firms represented on this page.

VINTAGE   DATE   PRICE

GUESTS

MENU   COMMENTS

De Luze St.-Émilion

Quite a few Bordeaux shippers would agree that De Luze is perhaps the best of the large blenders of Bordeaux generic wines, wines as good as market conditions permit. The firm is unusual in selling quantities of cognac under labels similar to those used for its wines. Members of the family own important properties, including Château Cantenac Brown in Margaux (the best), Château Paveil de Luze, and Château Malleret, also in the Médoc. Participation amounting to ownership has been taken in De Luze by a British company, but the firm continues under French management. Its U.S. marketing arrangements, albeit reorganized, make the wines expensive, but the same applies to all such firms using big foreign agents.

VINTAGE   DATE   PRICE

GUESTS

MENU   COMMENTS

Barton & Guestier Prince Noir

Originating in the late eighteenth century, this well-known shipper combines British and French family names in distinctly Bordeaux style. It was one of the first major shippers to be taken over by its own overseas agent, in this case Seagrams. In addition to generic wines B & G markets what are in effect generics by brand names of which this label is the best known. Château Leoville Barton and Langoa Barton are personal property of the Barton family, not of the company, though these wines are distributed abroad in tandem with those of B & G.

VINTAGE   DATE   PRICE

GUESTS

MENU   COMMENTS

Cruse Roc Rouge

Dating from the early nineteenth century, Cruse is a fixture of the Bordeaux wine trade whose wines are widely distributed throughout the world. The firm trades Burgundies as well and have commenced marketing varietal wines using labels similar to their traditional generic wine labels. Historically both the firm and members of the numerous family have been aggressive buyers of vineyard properties. The most famous is Château Pontet Canet, recently sold to a Cruse in-law. Château d'Issan is the most beautiful, and there is also La Dame Blanche. Roc Rouge is their standard Bordeaux red wine. A protracted trial, widely reported, has hurt the firm's position for the moment. Their generic Bordeaux wines are made to standards similar to those of other major firms and are better than the line of Burgundies. Cruse's English distributors seem to manage lower prices than their American counterparts.

VINTAGE   DATE   PRICE

GUESTS

MENU   COMMENTS

BORDEAUX

APPELLATION BORDEAUX CONTROLEE

1973

CALVET

NEGOCIANTS A BORDEAUX-GIRONDE-FRANCE

GIP LIBOURNE

RED BORDEAUX WINE	IMPORTED BY FOREIGN VINTAGES GREAT NECK N.Y.	PRODUCE OF FRANCE VINTAGES 11021 U.S.A	Alc. 11% by vol. Cont. 3/4 Quart

---

BARON ALFRED de LUZE FONDATEUR DE LA MAISON EN 1820

1971

BARON DE LUZE

SAINT-ÉMILION

Appellation Saint-Émilion Contrôlée

A. de Luze & Fils

NÉGOCIANTS A BORDEAUX (GIRONDE)

RED BORDEAUX WINE - PRODUCT OF FRANCE
PRODUCED & BOTTLED BY A. de LUZE & FILS - BORDEAUX
NET CONTENTS 1 PINT 8 FLUID OUNCES - TABLE WINE
ALCOHOLIC CONTENTS 11,8 % BY VOLUME

IMPORTED BY

SHAW-ROSS IMPORTERS, INC.

MIAMI, FLORIDA

BORDEAUX CONTENTS 1 PINT 8¼ FLUID OUNCES	**B&G** FONDÉE EN 1725	RED WINE ALCOHOL 12% BY VOLUME

PRINCE NOIR

APPELLATION BORDEAUX SUPÉRIEUR CONTROLÉE
PRODUCE OF FRANCE

BOTTLED BY

BARTON & GUESTIER

BARTON & GUESTIER — FRANCE
NÉGOCIANTS AU CHATEAU DU DEHEZ
BLANQUEFORT - GIRONDE

ÉLEVÉ DANS SES CHAIS

1969

Cruse

ROC ROUGE

APPELLATION BORDEAUX CONTROLEE

RED BORDEAUX WINE

PRODUCT OF FRANCE

MIS EN BOUTEILLES DANS NOS CHAIS

Cruse & Fils Frères

NÉGOCIANTS A BORDEAUX (GIRONDE)

SOLE DISTRIBUTORS FOR THE UNITED STATES
THE JOS. GARNEAU C° NEW-YORK N.Y.

CONTENTS 1 PINT 8 1/2 FLUID OUNCES   ALCOHOL 11% BY VOLUME

Sichel Belair Claret

This agreeable light red wine comes from an unusual wine-making installation built south of Bordeaux by Sichel & Co. It buys grapes from local growers, paying according to quality, and vinifies wines of various styles sold under its firm name. This is quite different from buying finished wine, yet the product is marketed at the price and in the way that other shippers' blended wines are treated. This approach is original. Belair Claret is a Cabernet-Merlot blend, part of which is vinified by carbonic maceration process to accentuate the fruit and immediate attraction of the wine. This is successful at some slight expense of usual Bordeaux style, but the consumer is the gainer.

VINTAGE   DATE   PRICE

GUESTS

MENU   COMMENTS

Mouton-Cadet

It is widely conceded that the extraordinary success of this label is based on its association in the public mind with the famous wines of Château Mouton Rothschild. Two things should be said in one and the same breath: this wine is a red Bordeaux blended wine like another; La Bergerie, the shipping firm owned by Philippe de Rothschild, owner of the famous château, has succeeded in translating the glory of a property into an staggering success in a commercial wine as no other château owner, past or present. Apparently the public truly wishes to identify with famous wines. A plain white Bordeaux packaged the same as the red is less successful.

VINTAGE   DATE   PRICE

GUESTS

MENU   COMMENTS

Château Mondesir Gazin, Bolter, Schneider
Château Grand Barrail, Bolter, Schneider

Here is yet another attempt to solve the problem of supplying a continuity of inexpensive Bordeaux wines. The shipper, in this case my own company, buys different crops of such minor properties as it judges to have made unusually successful wine in some particular vintage. The separate wines are cask-aged in Bordeaux and bottled there. (Wines are more economically bottled by shippers than under the high rates fixed by the châteaux.) The resulting wines necessarily vary in tasting qualities, wine by wine, year by year, but the design of each label continues, bearing new wine names in subsequent years according to what is bought. This compromise allows the shipper to choose according to his view of what are best buys but offers some continuity of appearance to remind wine buyers of their past experience with the shipper.

VINTAGE   DATE   PRICE

GUESTS

MENU   COMMENTS

Château Timberlay, Alexis Lichine & Cie.

Under this label very large quantities of wine have been shipped to America for many years, each bearing a vintage. The wines are quite standard in taste and vary hardly at all. This may resolve for the shipper the problem all shippers find in dealing with a variable agricultural product. Timberlay is not the only label of which quite similar observations could be made.

VINTAGE   DATE   PRICE

GUESTS

MENU   COMMENTS

SICHEL

VINIFIÉ A CAVE BEL·AIR · St MAIXANT (Gde)

BELAIR CLARET

APPELLATION BORDEAUX CONTROLÉE

SICHEL & FILS FRÈRES

NÉGOCIANTS A BORDEAUX (GIRONDE)

ALC. 11,5 VOL. - CONT : 730 ml - 25,8 FL. OZ - VIN, WINE

PRODUIT EN FRANCE - PRODUCT OF FRANCE

BARON PHILIPPE DE ROTHSCHILD

1972

MOUTON-CADET

MARQUE DÉPOSÉE

APPELLATION BORDEAUX CONTROLÉE

CONT. 1 PT. 8 FL. OZS
RED BORDEAUX WINE

LA BERGERIE

ALC. BY VOL. 11,5 %
PRODUCT OF FRANCE

BARON PHILIPPE DE ROTHSCHILD S.A.

NÉGOCIANTS A PAUILLAC GIRONDE

MIS EN BOUTEILLES DANS NOS CHAIS

---

château MONDESIR GAZIN

PELLATION CÔTES DE BLAYE CONTRÔLÉE

1971

shipped by

BOLTER SCHNEIDER & Cº

---

château grand barrail

APPELLATION
BORDEAUX
SUPÉRIEUR
CONTRÔLÉE

1971

mis en bouteilles par

BOLTER, SCHNEIDER & Cº

GRAND PRIX EXPOSITION NATIONALE VINS DE FRANCE MACON 1961

1893 PARIS
PRIX D'HONNEUR

1897 PARIS
MÉDAILLE D'OR

GRAND VIN DE BORDEAUX

1894 ANVERS
MÉDAILLE D'ARGENT

1910 BRUXELLES
MÉDAILLE D'ARGENT

MÉDAILLE D'OR PARIS 1962

CHATEAU TIMBERLAY

APPELLATION BORDEAUX SUPÉRIEUR CONTROLÉE

1970

R. GIRAUD

PROPRIÉTAIRE A SAINT-ANDRÉ-DE-CUBZAC (GIRONDE)

MIS EN BOUTEILLE AU CHATEAU

PRODUCE OF FRANCE
Contents 1 Pint 8 Fl. oz.

Shipped by
ALEXIS LICHINE & Cº
NÉGOCIANTS A BORDEAUX GIRONDE FRANCE

RED TABLE WINE
Alcohol by vol. 12 %

Imported by BASS CHARRINGTON VINTNERS (USA) LTD. New York, N.Y.

Château Rouet (Fronsac)

The Fronsac district produces clarets whose color, body, and forward tasting style remind a taster of those of Pomerol, though they do not have as much delicacy and fruit. The vineyards are among the steepest in Bordeaux, nestled among bluffs overlooking the Dordogne and the alluvial plain below. Not marked by any unusual characteristic, the red wines of Fronsac show the general qualities of flavor, moderate astringency, and attractive aftertaste common to quality Bordeaux wines. But, relatively neglected, they often represent exceptional bargains. Château Rouet is one of some 20 properties at the head of the list of Fronsac wines and represents well what can be expected of the area. Its clarets develop quickly in bottle and can be enjoyed young. Their bouquet improves with age, but the emphasis is on balance and completeness.

VINTAGE   *DATE*   *PRICE*

GUESTS

MENU   *COMMENTS*

Château de la Grave (Bourg)

Bourg and Blaye red wines have full-flavor, chewy texture with mouth-filling qualities, and a vigorous development to the senses. Mean years lack fruit and are astringent, and even at best the wines do not show the fruit and appeal of lesser wines from better Bordeaux regions. Their richness of tannin and body allows some to mature surprisingly in bottle; this property, for example, produced a still remarkable 1953 claret. Best values are obtained in complete vintages—1961, 1962, 1966, 1970, 1971, and probably 1975. Intensity gives these modest clarets the extra excitement that finish and fruit do not supply; price does not vary much between better and worse years. Rarely marketed as generics, single vineyard wines can be interesting bargains useful for frequent economical drinking.

VINTAGE   *DATE*   *PRICE*

GUESTS

MENU   *COMMENTS*

Château de Hartes (Entre-Deux-Mers)

The vast Entre-Deux-Mers district is a poor relation to more famous Bordeaux wines, though centuries ago its sweet wines commanded, with Sauternes, the highest prices. Traditionally an unctuous semisweet style, too often marred by excessive use of sulphur dioxide and lacking charm, is made here. More recently, growers have striven for tarter whites with more fruit to suit contemporary taste abroad. De Hartes belongs to this latter, more modern style of white and shows clean qualities, fresh aroma and aftertaste. Along with lighter whites, many growers are turning to young red wines, some made by the carbonic maceration process, others stressing Merlot, to obtain supple, appealing light red wines that can reach a market that has rejected the ponderous whites of old. Red and white are sold to the public in the $2.00 to $3.00 class. Only well-made ones, and the emphasis is alas necessary, are worth buying.

VINTAGE   *DATE*   *PRICE*

GUESTS

MENU   *COMMENTS*

Domaine de Maillard (Côtes de Bordeaux Saint-Macaire)

Clustered around the Garonne River in the vicinity of Sauternes, a once prosperous and famous sweet wine district is suffering a long decline in popularity. The best wines echo in character the succulent dessert wines of Barsac and Sauternes but do not equal them in lusciousness and finesse. Once expensive, Cérons, Cadillac, Ste.-Croix-du-Mont, and Loupiac are now names that draw little attention and low prices, for sweetness in itself is no longer held a virtue; rather the contrary. Good examples of these appellations are far from common wines, however, for they offer a flavor and balance particular to the Bordeaux combination of Semillon and Sauvignon grapes that has made Sauternes famous. Bottle age promotes fine bouquet. This St.-Macaire shows a fresh aroma, delicious flavor, and clean aftertaste, important in a region where excessive use of sulphur dioxide mars many wines.

VINTAGE   *DATE*   *PRICE*

GUESTS

MENU   *COMMENTS*

1970
CHÂTEAU ROUET
CÔTES FRONSAC
APPELLATION COTES FRONSAC CONTROLÉE

Roger Danglade
PROPRIÉTAIRE À St-GERMAIN-LA RIVIÈRE (GIRONDE)

GIP-LIBOURNE

Grand Vin   de Bordeaux

CRU EXCEPTIONNEL
CHÂTEAU DE LA GRAVE
COTES DE BOURG
APPELLATION COTES DE BOURG CONTROLÉE

R. BASSEREAU, Ingénieur Agricole, Propriétaire à Bourg-sur-Gironde

PRODUCE OF FRANCE

MIS EN BOUTEILLES AU CHATEAU

CHÂTEAU

DE HARTES

ENTRE·DEUX·MERS
APPELLATION ENTRE-DEUX-MERS CONTROLÉE

Philippe Mazeau propriétaire à Targon (Gironde)
MIS EN BOUTEILLES AU CHATEAU

1970
Grand vin de Bordeaux

Domaine de Maillard
COTES DE BORDEAUX - SAINT-MACAIRE
APPELLATION COTES DE BORDEAUX
ST-MACAIRE CONTROLEE

DUBOURG Frères, Propriétaires à St-André-du-Bois

MISE EN BOUTEILLES A LA PROPRIETE

Jung Libourne

MÉDOC AND HAUT MÉDOC

The home of the most famous, most refined, and most individual red wines begins at a little stream in the industrial suburbs of northern Bordeaux—a roughly rectangular vineyard area, tall and narrow, running north for some 45 miles (75 kilometers). Its terrain includes flatlands reclaimed in modern times from the brackish inundations of the Gironde estuary, superior outcroppings of gravel beds cultivated as long as history will reveal, wetter clay soils to the west, and good hilly vineyard slopes in its northern extremities. From at least the eighteenth century, quality wine production as we understand it today has been its main agricultural business. England and the rest of Europe have long been its customers and peopled the cosmopolitan life of Bordeaux with representatives of their commerce. An individual of cultivated taste may conceivably prefer the finest wines of Burgundy or of Germany to those of the Médoc; but great, mature Médoc has in the last two centuries become a standard of taste for fine red wines.

In delineating districts within the greater Médoc earlier in this century, the *Appellation Contrôlée* laws did no more than codify accepted designations for subregions of recognized quality and character; appellation organization begun in the 1930s was completed in the 1950s and now stands in the following form: the upper, northern quarter of the vineyard, formerly called the Bas Médoc (lower Médoc) is the appellation Médoc, considered slightly inferior to the lower three quarters, now called the Haut Médoc. In fact, better wines of the Médoc differ insignificantly from lesser wines made throughout the Haut Médoc. The Haut Médoc is carved into six local appellations embracing at least five distinct winegrowing areas and other subregions not hallowed by appellation status. These six appellations are Listrac, Moulis, which resemble each other, and Margaux, St.-Julien, Pauillac, and St.-Estèphe to the north. Just south of Margaux lie other vineyards that may claim the name Haut Médoc. Largely planted on wetter, often reclaimed land, these share some tasting qualities or family resemblances.

By any accounting, be it a slavish adherence to the 1855 Classification or a strictly contemporary evaluation, most of the finest properties lie in the confines of four great appellations that march north along the estuary—Margaux, St.-Julien, Pauillac, and St.Estèphe. It is no surprise, therefore, that most of the labels selected to represent Médoc wines are children of these four communes. Originally four Médoc appellations of equal prestige were conceived: St.-Estèphe, Pauillac, St.-Julien, and Haut Médoc, which included Margaux, Listrac, Moulis, and communes immediately south of Margaux such as Cantenac. Necessary reforms subverted that intention. After World War II, disgruntlement grew in Margaux and elsewhere, for these unhappy villages could justly point to past history and claim that their wines had always been distinguished by commune name rather than submerged in some larger appellation. In the early 1950s the wrong was righted, but in creating three new appellations—Listrac, Moulis, and a greater Margaux appellation taking in Cantenac, Labarde, Arsac, and Soussans—much of the finest land and best properties were automatically subtracted from the Haut Médoc appellation, stripping that designation of its original significance.

The zones of best-quality vineyard begin around Ludon and unfold north through St.-Estèphe with a westerly outpost in Listrac-Moulis. Interspersed within this vineyard and to the west and north are Haut Médoc and Médoc appellation areas that include numerous fine vineyard sites, some equal to the good but not the best vineyards in the six commune appellations.

The red-grape varieties used in fine Médoc wines must come from six permitted types. Carmanère is not seen; Malbec is being phased out; in fact, growers juggle four grape types in their efforts to achieve proper vineyard structure: Cabernet Sauvignon, Cabernet Franc, Merlot, and Petit Verdot. The particular savor of Médoc wines and their astringent authority of taste are generally attributed to Cabernet Sauvignon. Cabernet Franc is a generous producer of lighter wine contributing some unctuosity. Merlot, a tender bountiful grape that may have been introduced by a Swedish refugee nobleman in the eighteenth century, bears in quantity, matures early, and adds a mellow or supple quality to red wines. Most fine vineyards are composed roughly of two-thirds Cabernets and one-third Merlots. But several have also a small amount—perhaps 3, 5, or 8 percent—of Petit Verdot. This is a dark, intense, late-ripening grape that, when properly mature, can contribute much coloring matter, alcohol, and acidity to a harvest. Frequently these small additions improve a difficult vintage out of all proportion to the percentage of Petit Verdot planted.

Whether because of soil types or microclimatic conditions, certain varieties fare better in certain plots. Since it takes four years until a vine may be used for *Appellation Contrôlée* wine and eight years or more until its grapes are truly sources of fine wine, not only distribution of grape varieties but also distribution of vines of varying age is a major question of strategy for the grower. This is a complicated matter, and it is a lucky proprietor who knows the history of his entire vineyard. When plots must be torn up, being too old to bear economically, the current balance of grape varieties in the property often dictates that some other variety should be replanted in the available land. But will that variety be successful in that spot? If the agricultural foreman (*maître de vignes*) has a long memory, or remembers what his father told him about each parcel of land, or if the owner himself has this experience, so much the better. But arranging the structure of a vineyard is an intricate balancing act in which profitability (quantity), security (degree of risk of frost or rot) and quality factors (grape varieties and vine age) are all intertwined. Into this warp and woof of considerations the grower must weave the design of his property style. For example, Mouton Rothschild, a justly celebrated estate, makes powerful distinctive wines on a vineyard largely composed of Cabernet Sauvignon vines. It is perfectly conceivable that delectable wines could be produced on the same terrain with half Cabernet and half Merlot vines. Yet this would certainly produce a resentful outcry from wine lovers everywhere, for the style of this claret would be dramatically changed.

Fine wine growers the world over struggle with similar considerations. In St.-Émilion and Pomerol, where the choice of grape varieties narrows to Merlot and a type of Cabernet Franc called Bouchet, the variables are slightly reduced—but only slightly. And even where a single vine variety is employed, be it Riesling on the slopes of the Rheingau or Nebbiolo in Italy's Piedmont, growers agonize over conflicting considerations of age, quality, economic survival, risk, and vineyard style. Like Portugal's Douro, the Médoc is an exceptionally complicated wine region, for it has so many varieties and so many growing conditions. The business of making small quantities per acre of fine wine in marginal climates is difficult enough, and ungrateful enough for natural reasons, to deserve more appreciation for success and more tolerance for circumstances than it presently receives.

This is a book about wine, not money. But since there is not much to say about the sex life of the Merlot vine, the reader has a right to expect something about the "other" subject, money calculations in the business of fine wines. Again, because it is large, complex, and competitive, the Médoc serves as an example for similar considerations elsewhere in Bordeaux and the world.

There may not be much justice in the world, but there is an abundance of cause and effect, and in the long run the effect of a disastrous drop in quality of some wine is a drop in its price. Growers in the Médoc, as elsewhere, understand this, and the fine wine business begins with an assumption that quality wine is what must be sold. To detail vineyard expenses is to trace the production of wine. Planting is laborious and expensive. Economies of agricultural mechanization are more limited in fine wine than in common wine because of the attention each plant demands, but they are there; so is the increase in the cost of labor, approximately offsetting economies. While losses due to poor vinification are reduced by modern equipment, this same equipment increases capital investment. Fine wine must be aged in barrels, and 15 percent of the crop is lost in evaporation. The cost of barrels has risen from some $20 per barrel in the mid-1960s to over $100 ten years later. A barrel yields approximately 250 bottles of wine. A Médoc château of economic size requires about 400 barrels per crop, and there are usually two crops maturing in the cellar and sometimes three. Wine must be financed for the two years during which it ages in barrel, adding between 20 to 30 percent to its cost. Bottling costs will soon reach $0.50 per bottle.

A property that cut corners where it could but still made fine wine that would mature well in bottle must today receive between $1.50 and $2.00 per bottle from the shipper to make a good rate of return. A property expending all conceivable efforts on quality would have to receive nearer $3.00. These figures apply to properties producing about 10,000 cases a year at present costs of production. They imply that consumers must expect to pay about $4.00 (or £2.00) per bottle for fine Médoc of good standard and some $5.50 to $8.00 per bottle for finer wines. These calculations are based on past transport costs and present import duties and reflect the fact that wines must pass through wholesale and retail chains of supply, which in turn must show profits. In regions other than Bordeaux, cost factors vary. But it is safe to say that fine wine cannot be delivered to consumers beyond its country of origin for less than $3.00 a bottle under present world conditions, with a very few exceptions. More precisely, it cannot be delivered for very long at losing prices without the growers turning to some other more profitable crop.

Margaux, St.-Julien, Pauillac, and St.-Estèphe are the famous appellations. But what of the rest of the Médoc? Outside the four premium appellations, the most obvious and important family of clarets comes from the big cluster of vineyards in the appellations Listrac and Moulis. These lie around three villages: Listrac, Moulis, and Grand Poujeaux. In the past, wines from these quarters were astringent, often rough clarets that matured tediously and not always with good grace. Properties led a difficult life, for prices were low, and growers were too poor to invest in improving their land or wine-making equipment. The short-lived prosperity of the period from 1969 to 1972, coming after the moderate price increases of 1964 through 1969, has improved this situation. At present, over a dozen vineyards make fine wine in this sector—clarets with dark color, firm body, a vigorous attack on the palate, and balance and finesse equal to all but the finest wines from the famous communes. Of course there are always excep-

tional wines in various years, and since 1945, two or more of these so-called bourgeois growths have made crops ranking among the first dozen of the whole Médoc. Yet, overall, wines from Moulis-Listrac seem oriented to a basically firm and rather full, dry style of red Bordeaux. Efforts by the Cooperative Cellar at Listrac to make supple light wines ready for immediate drinking have been unsuccessful; what has resulted more often than not is mean wines without enough fruit or insipid clarets, dull, bland, and offering neither individual distinction nor any general merits associated with Médoc wines. Better results occur at individual properties.

A second family of wines has been mentioned already—the unctuous, rather fruity, pleasing clarets made in the southern Médoc in Ludon, Macau, and their environs. While rarely reaching heights of finesse or achieving great authority of taste, the virtues of such clarets include early maturation, a gentle tasting quality the French like to call "tender," and all the appeal this adjective suggests. Similar wines are met with throughout the Médoc; many are produced on low-lying land near the estuary and some on the estuary's damp islands.

Improvement in wine making has given growers more choice in claret style than in past times. Whether it is in the hilly vineyards of Vertheuil west of St.-Estèphe or east of St.-Christoly well to the north of St.-Yzans, one finds wines falling into three types: well-made clarets reflecting the firm tasting qualities of good Médoc; astringent, meager wines that have fallen short of this goal; and still others that have been forced into a soupy, bland artificial style without the distinctiveness expected of any Médoc appellation.

Saint-Estèphe

Largest of the Médoc commune appellations, St.-Estèphe contains many virtues and, if not a multitude, a passel of sins. Virtues and sins are both château-bottled these days, and properties here as elsewhere cluster in several wine types. But standing in the path leading to the vineyards is one of those Hydra-headed wine generalizations that owes its life to the great distance that those who peddle it scrupulously keep from the act of tasting. Its kernel of nonsense can be expressed in the following misinformation: "Clarets of St.-Estèphe are great, dark-colored, strong tannic wines, hard in youth but which mature to a great old age compared with wines from communes farther south in the Médoc." Those who pass on counterfeit money used to be considered as guilty as those who coin it. I am willing to let whoever coined this characterization of St.-Estèphe wines off lightly—a choice of 30-year-old St.-Estèphe blended from a property I will not name as his only beverage until 1995, or tap water.

With the notable exception of Calon-Ségur, until a century ago St.-Estèphe wines were considered poor cousins of communes to its south. One of its three finest wines, Montrose, is remarkable among the classed growths in that we know positively that it was created from woodland only in the early 1800s. Today St.-Estèphe is virtually one contiguous vineyard starting just north of the Shell Petroleum complex and the Lazaret drainage ditch above Lafite-Rothschild, extending westward through Cissac up to Vertheuil, rolling north along the Gironde to St.-Estèphe village and St.-Corbian, and mushrooming again around the town of St.-Seurin de Cadourne. All of it is conditioned by its terrain, often more wind exposed than farther south, and its weather, which natives claim is hotter, giving higher alcoholic degrees. Soils vary from sandy in the west to gravel and pebble nearer the Gironde; deep brown freestone subsoils alternate with calcareous and clayey understructures; parts of the surface are too fertile in nitrogenous matter, others are superb. Within these limits, the last word in St.-Estèphe wine style is had by the men who make the clarets, and in such a vast vineyard variety runs in many directions. As elsewhere in Bordeaux, some properties believe their consumers still desire traditional profound wines with great color and acidity, choose their varieties accordingly but more important vinify their wines accordingly, with longer vatting and little regard for the wine's appeal in youth. At the opposite end of the range are properties whose owners are convinced that consumers will buy wine only at 4:30 P.M. to drink at 8:00 P.M. the same day; that all wines not instantly drinkable are doomed, and their growers will surely starve to death.

Between those who strive to make old-fashioned wines and those who insist on St.-Estèphe that is drinkable at bottling lies the majority of properties annually producing claret with more or less firmness and the vigorous alcoholic style so common in the region. First we have what might be called the Light Brigade, led by vineyards such as Haut-Marbuzet and the Cave Coopérative (called Marquis de St.-Estèphe), which charges at that part of the market eager for palê wines, sweetish smelling, bland, smooth to taste with a pleasant flavor while young—which is when they should be drunk. Then comes an assembly of fine wines led by Calon-Ségur, Cos d'Estournel (whose style varies from year to year), de Marbuzet, Pomys, de Pez, Ormes de Pez, Capbern, Phélan Ségur, and led also by the now good wines produced at Lafon-Rochet, clarets of generous color, some astringency modified by a grainy, rich tasting impression, and authoritative aftertaste. Finally, one does encounter old-fashioned clarets exceedingly dark and brilliant in color, with astringency and body to match, difficult when very young and releasing their perfume and superb Cabernet tasting qualities only with time. Montrose is certainly a standard bearer of this style of St.-Estèphe, but similar clarets have been produced at Cos d'Estournel and Capbern and other good sites. Besides these clearly superior wines, the vast vineyard area of St.-Estèphe and its environs nurtures a variety of clarets, including some with stronger alcohol and body than is possible farther south in the Médoc.

St.-Estèphe wines fan out into looser, more general and less intense tasting qualities than those of the heartland of Pauillac, St.-Julien, and Margaux. The appellation's rich and assertive qualities are epitomized by its oldest vineyard, Calon-Ségur, but the character of its wines is better described as less definite, complete, and long-lived than that of classic clarets immediately to the south.

Thanks to a large planted area, generic St.Estèphe wines representing the appellation qualities can be found at reasonable prices, a statement no longer true of smaller Médoc appellations. And for the adventurer in wine, its many lesser growths offer individual clarets in abundance and variety. There seems little or no useful distinction between wines of this class that lie immediately outside the appellation borders of St.-Estèphe, such as Cissac in Cissac, or Coufran, Grandis and Bel-Orme Tronquoy de Lalande in St.-Seurin, and those, such as Beausite in St.-Corbian, that fall within the St.-Estèphe perimeter.

Pauillac

Pauillac's 6,700 acres (2,700 hectares) of vines have their southern boundary at St.-Lambert, just north of St.-Julien, and continue into Bages, spreading west and north of the town of Pauillac until, above Lafite-Rothschild, a little marsh, a sort of figurative moat, ends the appellation just beneath a large hummock marking the start of St.-Estèphe. Transitional vineyards blur the division between St.-Julien and Pauillac, unlike the spacious separation of Margaux from appellations to its north. One major property, Pichon Lalande, is as much St.-Julien as Pauillac; others run over the border, and Château Latour's vines used to reach as far south as Beychevelle.

Nevertheless, superior clarets of Pauillac have a unity of style, allowing that some dance off to the south à la St.-Julien and others tramp slightly muddily westward. Simply put, the wines are very rich, very red, and, if Médoc is a vinous throne, very regal. They lack nothing: intense bouquet, vehemently Cabernet; dark ruby color, scintillating, lustrous; heroically full constitution, acerbic and resounding with fruit; mature, intense, enveloping flavor; piquant aftertaste, long and elaborately fine. The finest vineyards have something over and beyond this, best imagined as an assertive personality. While tasting yet another vintage of Latour, Mouton, Grand-Puy-Lacoste, or Lynch Bages, it is not too fanciful to think of the letter of Mozart telling how he perceived in his mind the outline of a symphony "like some portrait of a goodly man." This feature—personality, character, style, whatever it be—persists dramatically through vintage changes among the best Pauillacs and adds to their technical virtues a pleasure familiar yet always new.

The presence of three very famous estates in a single commune—Latour, Mouton Rothschild, and Lafite-Rothschild—surely paints all its wines in brighter colors than the eye might see were identical clarets to be labeled Premières Côtes de Bordeaux. But as much could be said of any famous appellation. In fact, only some dozen names comprehend nearly all the great wine made in Pauillac. Some are gracious wines always tasting with a soft touch—Pichon Lalande, Lafite, and Haut-Batailley, for example—commonly offering opulent fruit, maturing quickly, and temptingly delicious to drink when four or six years in bottle. Mouton Rothschild, Lynch Bages, Grand-Puy-Lacoste, Croizet-Bages, and Pontet Canet form a clan of fiery clarets with exceptional mouth-filling texture, whose flavors suggest at once herb, spice, and fruit. Each is capable of finesse to match its spacious constitution; Mouton Rothschild stands at the head of the squadron in every point except color, in which it is challenged by Lacoste. A geographically more scattered company of blander wines lacks the full verve of those just mentioned: Grand-Puy-Ducasse, Haut-Bages-Libéral, Clerc-Milon, Haut-Bages-Averous, and Haut-Bages-Monpelou (like the elegant Tourteran, over the border in St.-Saveur), and, these days, Duhart-Milon, once a powerful wine. A few properties such as Lynch-Moussas are being restructured, and others have dropped off in quality beneath attention. Mouton-Baron d'Armailhacq, now called Mouton-Baron-Philippe, is owned by the proprietor of Mouton Rothschild, A few vineyards, most notably Pichon-Baron, maintain their reputation and price while making rather dry wines that develop irregularly in bottle.

It is impossible to sidestep completely the controversies surrounding two large, important estates—Château Pontet Canet and Château Lafite-Rothschild. Until 1972 Pontet Canet was bottled in Bordeaux, often without vintage, by its owners, Cruse & Fils Frères, Bordeaux shippers. The author is not the only Bordeaux wine merchant to have found in Pontet Canet a gamut of quality ranging from excellent vintage wines to usually thin, disappointing clarets not worth the price of fine Pauillac. Pontet Canet was not alone among famous wines in making nonvintage blends; during the 1960s Branaire Ducru, Cos d'Estournel, and Château Margaux all tried to dabble in what proved to be the same mirage. Pontet Canet was bought by M. Guy Tesseron in 1975; the new owner brings to Pontet Canet a good record from his rehabilitation of the dilapidated Lafon Rochet vineyard. Vintaged wine is expected to resume at Pontet Canet.

The important vineyard of Lafite, with most of its land in Pauillac but a parcel in St.-Estèphe, has kept its geographic integrity for at least a century and a half, when a plateau of land called the Carruades was bought from Mouton. Wine from Carruades used to be sold separately but became in time the second wine of Lafite. Lafite produces excellent wine. Its clarets are perfumed, enticing, elegant, and charming. Since approximately the 1962 vintage, however, and some may opine since World War II, the power, scope, and authority of taste associated with high-ranking and certainly with top-ranking Pauillacs seem absent from the wines. With the possible exception of 1966, there is not a Lafite vintage that professionals could agree contended for top place among the Médocs of these crops. This was not always the case, as a parade of glorious wines originating before 1928, many still vital and stunning in quality, testify. At any rate, consumers who find current samples of Lafite less striking than some other Pauillacs or other fine vineyards in the Médoc are not tasting any differently than a good number of the Bordeaux trade whose business is fine wines.

Château Latour, like Château Margaux in Margaux, is a standard of quality not only for Pauillac but also for Bordeaux. Latour embodies Pauillac tasting qualities but adds dimensions and distinctions of its own. While Margaux emphasizes the finesse of great Médoc wines to the point of standing alone in occasional brilliant years, Latour emphasizes the style, harmony, and scope of Médocs and in best years does so to such a degree as to become a difference in kind. These are classical virtues; and the more good Médoc claret one drinks and remembers, the greater grows appreciation, enjoyment, and esteem for the mature wines of Château Latour. This vineyard regularly makes wines well above the level expected of poor vintages, as 1940, 1944 (dazzling), 1956, 1958, 1960, and 1963 will show. The longevity attributed to Latour is also a fact, not merely in super-vintages such as 1870, 1928, or 1945, but in far less sumptuous years such as 1916, 1918, 1922, and 1924. The 1950 clarets were light and charming, but it is hard to think of another château whose 1950 one would hesitate to open today for fear it might improve still more with a few years.

In 1962 Latour was bought by Viscount Cowdray and Harveys of Bristol, the English wine merchants, with part ownership remaining with the French proprietors. Important investments in stainless-steel tanks and other equipment followed. Soon after, the cellar master, M. Meté, retired. Having seen no tribute elsewhere, I pay one now to a laconic craftsman who taught more about maturation of wine in cask and bottle to a twenty-five-year-old foreigner than anyone but the wine itself; one who persistently vinified great wines that not only are but in their classic balance and coherence look to remain the finest collection of clarets from one estate that those of us of a certain age can expect ever to drink.

A second wine of Latour is marketed under the label "Forts de Latour," and further labeling and marketing devices are apparently in the offing. These are sound Pauillac wines.

Château Mouton Rothschild has made superb wines since the nineteenth century. By 1900 its prices had risen to those of a First Growth. It is no denigration of this magnificent wine to observe that its style,

development on the palate, and aftertaste are more individual than those of Latour or Margaux. They would be difficult to imagine occurring in any claret but a Pauillac. The Ministry of Agriculture has just declared Mouton a First Growth. It seems to me the equal in finesse and quality to the other First Growths, though different. Having said this, I repeat (see the remarks on classification of Médocs on pages 34 and 36) that in the judgment of this writer the Ministry of Agriculture does *not* have the *authority* to classify wines by merit, nor the *competence* to do so, however good the intentions may be.

Saint-Julien

More than in any other Médoc commune, the land of St.-Julien is occupied by magnificent fine wine properties. Little premium growing area is devoted to generic wine production among the roughly 4,200 acres (1,700 hectares) of appellation vines. It is the most expensive and, with Pomerol, the most sought-after red wine in Bordeaux. While terrains have often changed hands dramatically between Classed Growths, the finest wines without exception are still produced by vineyards inheriting the names of estates classified in 1855. A few "bourgeois" growths market quantities of claret of which the most aggressively sold is Château Gloria.

The riverine vineyard is superb, an undulating gravel-covered strip running over subsoils of freestone and clay patches, wonderfully exposed to sun. Inland soils have more sand and silicate and their subsoils some peat, but a rectangle cut out on the south between Beychevelle and Gruaud Larose and running north to the gates of Pichon Baron and Latour would encompass some of the most favored vineland of the Médoc or indeed the world. Style of wine ranges from ultraseductive, silky perfumed wines such as Beychevelle and Léoville Poyferré, progresses through Gruaud-Larose, Ducru-Beaucaillou, and Léoville Las Cases, constituting a sort of classic middle ground, continues through denser, somewhat harder clarets made by Ronald Barton at Léoville Barton and Langoa Barton, emerges into more plushy, rounder wines such as Branaire-Ducru and St.-Pierre, and on to sometimes thick-tasting wines at Talbot and dark but less refined ones at Lagrange. This is but a generalization; nearly every one of these great estates has made a variety of styles depending on vintages and changing ideas of the wine makers.

St.-Julien unites features found separately elsewhere to a degree that accounts for the immense favor its clarets obtain and the instant appeal they exercise even to beginners. Successful crops show a good, complete constitution. They begin life with strength and harmony. Their acidity, tannic aspects, and vinosity are perfectly sufficient to father a long life. These basic ingredients are matched by a most delightful and plentiful taste of ripe noble grape with all the pleasantly distracting and appetizing sensations we sum up as fruit. Nor do these appealing qualities fade away as in less-balanced wines; they persist marvelously into middle age, joining with higher bouquets and longer tastes that harmonize with initial impressions and end evoking all of them. This is finesse.

A few châteaux epitomize the difference between St.-Julien and other Médoc clarets, or, if you prefer, best embody what is distinctive in this appellation. Léoville Poyferré, Ducru-Beaucaillou, Gruaud-Larose, and Beychevelle are such a representative group. This does not mean that the two Barton wines did not head the St.-Julien list in 1945 and 1952 (they did), or that Talbot was not remarkable in both

1948 and 1949 (it was), or that Branaire-Ducru did not make amazing 1934 in that turgid year or vital, exciting 1964 in a loose and difficult vintage (it did). It is simply that to taste the four properties named above in more than one good vintage will usefully introduce great quality as uniquely interpreted in St.-Julien.

St.-Julien is sometimes described as divided into a cluster of vineyards around the village of Beychevelle, purportedly yielding lighter wines, and another around St.-Julien-Beychevelle just north of it, whose clarets are said to be heavier and more like those of Pauillac. This north-south dichotomy is not as useful as differences of terrain between vineyards astride the gravel slopes overlooking the river and those inland. As to the color and acidity of wines, the grower's role is more telling than, say, any difference between a plot of Ducru-Beaucaillou and a parcel belonging to Langoa Barton catty-corner across the D.2 road. Finesse and bouquet decline as the riverine vineyards give way to wetter, flatter, different ground extending through Château Lagrange and across the appellation border into Haut Médocs made in St.-Laurent, notably Château Camensac, Bellegrave, Larose-Trintaudan, La Tour-Carnet, and Liversan. Subtle, unctuous wines can be made in St.-Laurent, as old vintages of La Tour Carnet show, but these do not equal the glossy, impressively fruited, and refined wines of St.-Julien at their best.

Since St.-Julien is a small vineyard area and its wines are so eagerly demanded in France and abroad, the most obvious temptation for growers is to overproduce wine on the area of their estates. The official appellation limit here as elsewhere in the Haut Médoc's better regions is 40 hectoliters per hectare (423 gallons per acre). But, as the introduction to Bordeaux pointed out, political pressures impel the Ministry of Agriculture to raise these limits regularly, allowing more wine into the system and sowing the expectation that such tolerances will continue. These expectations entice growers into vineyard practices that swell future crops. Against this it must be said that 40 hectoliters per hectare is a low figure. There is certainly a violent drop in quality at a certain point in production, a very shocking one indeed. But it does not occur at this point. And while there are few vineyards with uniformly ten-year-old vines, properties with a young vine structure should and will give more abundantly. A small yield associated with a mix of young and old plants is more to the point, consideration taken as well of the grape varieties. A vineyard with 10 percent Petit Verdot 20 years old can afford to bring in 65 hectoliters per hectare (about 700 gallons per acre) from a plot of 11-year-old Cabernet Franc and make refined wine of the two.

It is exceedingly difficult to judge such matters from outside a vineyard property, even the proximate outside of a Bordeaux shipper. Without having any concrete grounds to justify it, my guess is that, fine as they are, the following St.-Julien would be far better still if less were produced: Gloria, Beychevelle, Gruaud-Larose, Léoville Las Cases, St.-Pierre.

When important properties in St.-Julien fail to produce exciting wine, it is nearly exclusively for lack of the fruit that ripeness contributes. Naturally this is the major cause of inadequate wine over most of the world's fine districts, and to say a year is bad is usually to say it is unripe. But awkward wines seem to develop more fruit and charm in St.-Julien than elsewhere in the Médoc. The years 1954 and 1958 saw some St.-Estèphe and Margaux clarets best used as compulsory beverages for war criminals, but many flowery and attractive if short-lived St.-Juliens. The 1964 harvest was mightily rained upon, and many a thin, nasty claret staggered out of fields of rot and mold high

and low in the Médoc, but St.-Juliens of 1964 are generally accepted to be not only that year's best Médocs but excellent wines in themselves with appeal and some harmony.

In fine Médocs generally, there is a period lasting as long as five or six years after bottling when the wines either taste "dumb," without pronounced features, or taste erratically. It is inevitable that eager consumers wish to sample a new crop of clarets as it is bottled and shipped abroad, but it cannot be said too firmly or too often that impressions received at this time cannot be relied upon. Mature St.-Julien is the only worthwhile witness to its qualities and, indeed, needs no other.

Margaux

The concentration of vineyards in the southern portion of the Haut Médoc has made classification in this premier wine-producing area a long-standing problem. The renowned commune of Margaux now gives its name to a broad appellation including the communes Cantenac, Labarde, Soussans, and Arsac. Until shortly after World War II, however, this area was absorbed into the larger Haut Médoc appellation.

Farther south in the southern Médoc, Parempuyre, Blanquefort Le Pian, and Ludon make appealing wine with fruit (in youth) and generally soft tasting qualities. Château La Lagune is the best example. On Margaux's western edges a different family of wines struggles against a tendency to thin clarets. Somewhere a line had to be drawn beyond which vineyards could not share in the image of Margaux; it is enough to notice that the hard qualities of some Margaux properties from Arsac to Avensan exemplify some of the general features of wines falling between the Margaux appellation and those of Listrac and Moulis to the north and west. Villegeorge, a vineyard seen abroad, evinces many of the faults and merits of this terrain, as do Citran and Bel Air-Marquis d'Aligre in some years. Color and unctuosity are sometimes a bit limited, but they are often compensated by breed and fineness of aftertaste in ripe vintages. Such wines must be tasted with much attention and concentration if their subdued and elusive qualities are to be discerned and enjoyed. They make little impression if simply quaffed.

For the properties that commence with Cantemerle just south of the Margaux line and extend into Soussans to its northern limit, and which mostly lie on a variety of gravel, clayey, or pebbly soils, often with iron-rich subsoils beneath them, no one generalization fits well. Near the river, gravel beds end, and a fertile lowland called *palus* appears. Astraddle this, marginal properties can be found making supple, agreeable clarets somewhat deficient in both intensity and backbone; Siran and Dauzac are two well-known examples. But for the heartland of Labarde, Cantenac, Margaux, and Soussans, which ends at the long drainage ditch called the Jalle de Tiqueforte, or Tayac, it is more helpful to evoke the extreme range of superb wines than to invent geographic groupings.

At one end of the spectrum are weighty clarets whose dark color, spicy, overpowering bouquet (often blunt in youth), vigorous body, astringency, and slow development in bottle seduce the blind taster into guessing them Pauillac or wines other than Margaux. Old-fashioned in their makeup, often very noble in proportions, they offer rich qualities with age and in time a special finesse unlike that of communes farther north. Malescot-St. Exupéry shows this style more often than most of its counterparts, but like wines have been made at Giscours and Palmer and are presently made from time to time at Cantemerle, Issan, and Cantenac Brown, and more rarely elsewhere.

Occupying a middle ground are many vintages of fine properties that show lovely luminous color, a bouquet in which flowery elements seem to merge with the bloom of ripe grapes, a balanced but exciting series of tasting impressions, and above all a finesse for which Margaux has always been and should always be praised over other wines. Great vintages of Château Margaux are the apotheosis of these fragrant seductive wines, which invite the nose and palate to return again and again to the glass in search of the elusive but delightful impressions. It is not too stuffy to call such wines classic Margaux clarets and only fair to notice that they occur often in nearly all the best-rated vineyards of central Margaux. Such wines may come across slightly "dumb" in the few years following bottling, but their seeming lightness, a gift of finesse, by no means augurs a short life. Good, balanced clarets of this high class mature exquisitely, as anyone knows who has drunk vintages of the 1920s or earlier within the last generation. Château Palmer, Issan, Cantenac Brown, and Boyd-Cantenac have produced such clarets, following Château Margaux in merit and occasionally overtaking it around the hairpin bends of a particular vintage.

Another kind of Margaux claret seems to emphasize finesse and delicacy at the expense of other qualities. Such wines frequently deceive not only the buyer who tastes them in barrel before bottling but also the overseas wine drinker who sets out comparative tastings of each new crop of clarets as they are shipped in a laudable effort to acquaint himself with the new crop and lay away its wines for the future. Pale and unimpressive in color, with a faint odor, bland and undramatic and with a hesitant finish, such wines easily get dismissed with a shrug for their apparent small stature and with regret that there "is not more to them." Maturity brings out exciting qualities and unique combinations of finesse and charm. Subtly understated odors and impressions, difficult to perceive in youth, cumulate and expand delightfully in middle and old age. It is difficult to think of another Bordeaux region offering wines that are both a challenge to discern and a special treat to enjoy when fully declared in their panorama of bouquet, silky texture, and nearly ethereal finish and

aftertaste. In my experience Brane-Cantenac sometimes makes such wines, as do Bel Air-Marquis d'Aligre and La Tour de Mons. And among the best properties wines of this exceptional genus have been made from time to time, notably in 1928, 1929, 1950, and 1953. It may be wishful thinking that makes me fancy like qualities in some 1973 Margaux.

Since readers inevitably will consult a list of 1855 Classified Growths in Margaux (and should) and will collect them (and should), some miscellaneous information is useful. Several labels of classified Margaux wines are omitted from the following pages, either because it is difficult to say anything good about them or, because of vineyard reconstruction, the wines cannot be evaluated. Marquis-de-Terme's owner sells directly to the public and refuses to allow members of the wine trade to taste the wines, which therefore cannot be commented upon. Several properties now make the second wine of more famous ones, and it is expected that they will be lesser versions of the principal wines, which do receive comment. A château crop may be honestly and reasonably divided into more and less expensive parts. The following pairs, to the best of my knowledge, represent such arrangements: Brane-Cantenac (Durfort Vivens), Palmer (Desmirail), Boyd-Cantenac (Pouget), Dauzac (Siran). Malescot-St.-Exupéry and Marquis d'Alesme-Becker, and Lascombes and Ferrière, are paired in ownership or control, but the relationship is not clear.

It can be read or overheard that Lascombes and Prieuré-Lichine are paired, but this is not correct. The Prieuré in Cantenac is at least an eighteenth-century vineyard and now makes most distinctive wine based on Merlot, slightly unusual but delicious and individual. Lascombes belongs to Bass-Charrington, a brewery group that owns Alexis Lichine & Cie. Lascombes was once a small, ultrarefined vineyard perched in the heart of Margaux but is now a large-size vineyard producing even claret of a fruity style.

Nor is Château d'Angludet, as I have been told with much self-assurance in several places, a second wine of Château Palmer. Rather it belongs to Mr. and Mrs. Peter A. Sichel. Angludet's range of styles tempts me to place it between the second and third sorts of Margaux described—the very classical and the very delicate. Château d'Issan used to be bottled by Cruse & Fils Frères in Bordeaux, but since 1972 it is château-bottled.

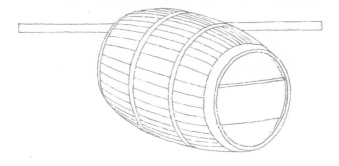

Château Fourcas Hosten

This vineyard begins at the village of Listrac and runs north a few kilometers to the hamlet of Fourcas that gives its name to this property, considered the principal one in the appellation. From 1962 to 1971 its wines were made indifferently in a firm but dry style. Since 1972 new ownership has installed the previously lacking *chai,* and new management, in which the author figures, has directed its wines, as exemplified in the 1973, toward a style emphasizing fruit and aftertaste with more careful attention to balance than former owners could afford. New Cabernet Sauvignon plantings have been added to old Petit Verdot, Merlot, and old Cabernet. It is difficult to comment on one's own efforts, but the vintages 1972–75 reflect each vintage style, show an aftertaste made possible by old vines, and offer the authoritative tasting impressions expected of the best Listrac wines.

VINTAGE   DATE   PRICE

GUESTS

MENU   COMMENTS

Château Fourcas Dupré

Clarets made at Fourcas Dupré come mainly from the large hummock of Fourcas, shared with Fourcas Hosten. They tend to darker, sterner wines than are made at Listrac vineyards south of the village, such as Fonreaud and Lestage, and they often develop awkwardly in youth. Color is a stronger point than charm; but in the past great vintages have been made here, notably the 1947, among the best of the Médoc. When mature, the wines have a long rather than an elegant impression in most years; nevertheless, they represent the appellation style in a distinctive way and make interesting contrasts to some of the drier, more powerful wines from Moulis and Grand Poujeaux.

VINTAGE   DATE   PRICE

GUESTS

MENU   COMMENTS

Château Dutruch Grand Poujeaux

This not very well-known wine is, along with Poujeaux Theil, the leader of a small family of powerful dark clarets of vibrant color, sinewy body, and remarkable attack on the palate. It is a distinguished Médoc by any standard. Its 1961 and 1962 wines only now show their scope and bouquet. Both are classical and old-fashioned wines. Gressier Grand Poujeaux, with its unusual flat, glossy texture, is neither so dramatic nor so fine in aftertaste. Other members of the family, Château Brillette and Château Moulis, have something of Dutruch's color and intensity but lack complete tasting qualities and excitement. Good vintages of Dutruch Grand Poujeaux and Poujeaux Theil should certainly be laid down, but these are among the slowest wines in the Médoc to develop.

VINTAGE   DATE   PRICE

GUESTS

MENU   COMMENTS

Château Chasse-Spleen

Like many of its neighbors in Moulis and Grand Poujeaux, Chasse-Spleen struggles between astringency in unripe years and rather overpowering style in fuller ones. Capable of majestic heights at maturity, the younger versions are difficult to appreciate, for their tannic impressions and strong effect generally mask what are often spicy and quite delicious Médoc wines. Color is typically brilliant. Chasse-Spleen averages more finesse than its more grapy and commercial neighbor Maucaillou (also a good claret) and manages a full constitution and authority of flavor sometimes lacking in equally priced wines to the south, such as Citran. Its performance lately has been more erratic than a decade ago, giving the impression that its wine maker is struggling too hard to compensate for a natural vigor and power bound to startle less experienced tasters.

VINTAGE   DATE   PRICE

GUESTS

MENU   COMMENTS

CHÂTEAU FOURCAS HOSTEN

MIS EN BOUTEILLE AU CHATEAU

LISTRAC — HAUT-MÉDOC

1970

APPELLATION LISTRAC-HAUT-MÉDOC CONTROLÉE

Sté CIVILE DU CHATEAU FOURCAS HOSTEN
PROPRIETAIRE A LISTRAC. GIRONDE

GIP - LIBOURNE

Château
Fourcas Dupré

CRU BOURGEOIS SUPÉRIEUR

LISTRAC - MÉDOC

APPELLATION LISTRAC CONTROLÉE

1970

MIS EN BOUTEILLES AU CHATEAU

Sté Cie du Château Fourcas Dupré
PROPRIETAIRE A LISTRAC - MÉDOC (GIRONDE)

© by Berthon - Libourne

1961

Grand Vin

Château Dutruch

GRAND POUJEAUX

Moulis-en-Médoc

Appellation Moulis contrôlée

MISE EN BOUTEILLE AU CHÂTEAU

GRAND VIN

CHATEAU
CHASSE-SPLEEN

1970

Moulis en Médoc

APPELLATION MOULIS EN MÉDOC CONTROLÉE

F. LAHARY, PROPRIÉTAIRE A MOULIS (GIRONDE)

Cos d'Estournel

The Oriental-style Château Cos d'Estournel overlooks a marshy meadow separating it and St.-Estèphe from Pauillac. At its east side it faces the Gironde and the vineyards it has occupied since its consolidation in the mid-nineteenth century. It is a large vineyard whose wines are habitually brilliant. Color is dark and bright; bouquet is finer than any other St.-Estèphe. Tannic young wines develop into noble clarets clean and natural in flavor if astringent. Some vintages such as 1952 and (apparently) 1961 remain disappointingly dry. Others are served well by powerful constitutions that carry them triumphantly into graceful middle age (1953, 1955). Occasionally supple wines are made somewhat out of character but are excellent (1962). Truly mean years (e.g., 1956, 1963) are quite hopeless at Cos, a regal wine but not one with reserves of fruit or charm. For these indispensables it relies upon the fine grape condition only better vintages can bring.

VINTAGE　　　　　*DATE*　　　　　*PRICE*

GUESTS

MENU　　　　　*COMMENTS*

Château Montrose

Montrose, the most recently created great Médoc property, was carved out of a wooded area in the 1820s. Traditional vinifications produce inky dark, brilliant wines of striking authority and much acerbity both in youth and in age. It is a mistake to assume that these qualities promise the longevity of a Latour, to which the wines are often compared by traveling amateurs. In fact Montrose frequently dries out in bottle earlier than wines with more charm. Exceptions are either odd years such as 1952 or vintages of the 1920s (1929!) that are no longer accessible. But at ten to 15 years of age the wines are robust, dramatic, and delicious, provided their tannic mouth-filling qualities are accepted as part of the style. Distinguished recent vintages still available are 1961, 1962, 1966, and 1970, with 1966 proving erratic.

VINTAGE　　　　　*DATE*　　　　　*PRICE*

GUESTS

MENU　　　　　*COMMENTS*

Château Calon-Ségur

The popularity of this ancient vineyard rests on disparate tasting qualities. Its broad assertive flavors approach or cross the line separating generosity from coarseness in vintages where acidity is limited (1959, 1960, 1964). But this same grainy, loose chewy style pleases simpler wine drinkers. On the other hand, in fine years and in lesser ones too, Calon finds the balance and yields dark, powerful clarets full of character that lasts long on all sensations. Their richness is integral to their style. In the end its lapses are fewer than those of most great properties and its successes superb in uniting traditional virtues of the Médoc, the St.-Estèphe wine type, and the magic touch of individuality. The vintages 1966, 1970, and 1971 join fine older wines (1928, 1929, 1934, 1945, 1947, 1948, well-stored 1949, and 1953). Philippe Gasqueton also owns Capbern Gasqueton nearby and du Tertre near Margaux.

VINTAGE　　　　　*DATE*　　　　　*PRICE*

GUESTS

MENU　　　　　*COMMENTS*

Château Lafon-Rochet

This vineyard was bought in rundown condition some 15 years ago by the current owner of Pontet Canet, Guy Tesseron, and has been restored slowly to quality rank as shown in 1966, 1967, and 1970, all of which equaled or exceeded standards of the vintage. It is not possible to define the standard of a vineyard very much in evolution, but this one will figure among the better wines of St.-Estèphe. The 1970 is a wine with fine dark color, spicy aroma, and a complete bouquet reflecting a good constitution and confirmed to the taste. This rich-flavored claret develops frankly on the palate; it is a trifle chewy as befits a young wine, but not the least coarse. Previous vintages, lacking this intensity, approached but did not equal this style. Vine age is an obvious explanation, experience in making Lafon-Rochet another.

VINTAGE　　　　　*DATE*　　　　　*PRICE*

GUESTS

MENU　　　　　*COMMENTS*

MIS EN BOUTEILLE AU CHATEAU

COS D'ESTOURNEL 1967
SAINT-ESTÈPHE
APPELLATION SAINT-ESTÈPHE CONTROLÉE
SOCIÉTÉ DES VIGNOBLES GINESTET PROPRIÉTAIRE A SAINT-ESTÈPHE

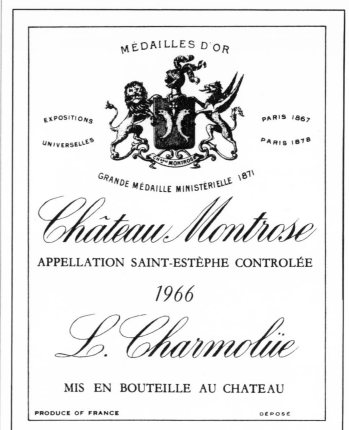

MÉDAILLES D'OR

EXPOSITIONS UNIVERSELLES

PARIS 1867
PARIS 1878

GRANDE MÉDAILLE MINISTÉRIELLE 1871

Château Montrose

APPELLATION SAINT-ESTÈPHE CONTROLÉE

1966

L. Charmolüe

MIS EN BOUTEILLE AU CHATEAU

PRODUCE OF FRANCE   DÉPOSÉ

Grand Cru Classé
en 1855

CHÂTEAU
Calon-Ségur
PREMIER CRU DE
SAINT-ESTÈPHE
MÉDOC

Récolte
1962

Mis
en Bouteille
au Château

Appellation Saint-Estèphe contrôlée

GRAND CRU CLASSÉ
EN
1855

CHATEAU
LAFON-ROCHET

1962

SAINT-ESTÈPHE-MÉDOC

APPELLATION SAINT-ESTÈPHE CONTROLÉE

STÉ CIVILE DU CHATEAU LAFON-ROCHET
ADM. GUY TESSERON. PROPRIÉTAIRE A SAINT-ESTÈPHE-MÉDOC (GDE)
MIS EN BOUTEILLES AU CHATEAU

Château Phélan Ségur

It is interesting to contrast this big vineyard, whose wines are well distributed in America and England and which certainly aims to make them drinkable soon after bottling, with Marquis de St.-Estèphe, the cooperative of this large appellation. The latter is more of a compromise and varies less than Phélan, whose extremes run from complete, fairly dark-colored clarets in 1961, 1962, and 1966 to ones with insufficient flavor and fruit. The cooperative's wines tend to lighter color and less character, and like the wines of another cooperative, La Rose Pauillac, I find them dull and not really showing consumers what the appellation tastes like. Phélan Ségur tends to full coarse wines that are drinkable quickly in bottle and often go down within a decade, but they offer generous aroma and bouquet and a finish identifiably appropriate to the appellation.

VINTAGE   DATE   PRICE

GUESTS

MENU   COMMENTS

Château Les Ormes de Pez

Owned by the proprietors of Lynch-Bages in Pauillac, this St.-Estèphe bourgeois growth is housed under the same roof in barrel and partakes of a similar style of wine making stressing aggressive aroma and tasting style. It impresses the palate quickly with body and a distinct taste in which grapy notes mix with aromatic ones that some compare to cassis and raspberries, others to licorice in very full vintages such as 1961, 1962, and 1966. Like Lynch-Bages, good success in Ormes de Pez is reserved for riper years that allow this generosity of aroma and taste to come through well to the senses; mean vintages are not redeemed easily, for fruit and charm are not strong points in the property. A Château de Pez makes wines in straightforward Médoc style that are easily confused with this wine. Ormes de Pez's eccentric tasting qualities will appeal to Americans nurtured on thick-textured California Cabernet Sauvignon.

VINTAGE   DATE   PRICE

GUESTS

MENU   COMMENTS

Château Coufran

Like other Médoc bourgeois growths, such as Sigognac, Senejac, and Grandis, this property differs from the famous classified growths in price and does not as often achieve the highest peaks of quality, but it is a truly fine wine made with ambitions and ideals quite similar to those for which we pay so much attention and money. Coufran sent out exceptional wines in odd years such as 1944, as well as in better crops in the years following World War II. Like Bel Ormes Tronquoy, its style tends to forceful tastes, some coarsensess occasionally, a grainy texture suggesting both earth and grapeskin, and higher alcoholic degree in many years. This contrasts with the lighter, supple styles of some of the wines referred to above. Its attractions are more immediate, if less refined, than nearby properties such as Grandis and de Pez.

VINTAGE   DATE   PRICE

GUESTS

MENU   COMMENTS

Château Loudenne

Bought a century ago by the enterprising brothers who founded Gilbey's distilling company, Château Loudenne is principally a wine-shipping company, Domaines du Château Loudenne, Gilbey's, though it also has its own recently planted vineyard. Its small production of white wine is the best in the Médoc, well made to offer fruit and charm to the extent obtainable in this red wine country. The red Loudenne is medium-bodied, shows good Médoc style and clean finish. It improves yearly as vines mature. This wine is selected here to represent a company whose strength lies in lesser-priced generic wines and branded ones sold also under the label Georges Maréchal. Good judgment and knowledge in selection and highest technical standards in production and blending elevate this shipper to top rank among those exporting red Bordeaux for daily economical drinking and offering authentic tasting qualities.

VINTAGE   DATE   PRICE

GUESTS

MENU   COMMENTS

Mis en bouteille au Château

1962
Grand Vin du
Château Phélan Ségur

SAINT ESTÈPHE

APPELLATION St ESTÈPHE CONTROLÉE

S^{té} Civile de Château Phélan Ségur
à St Estèphe (Gironde)

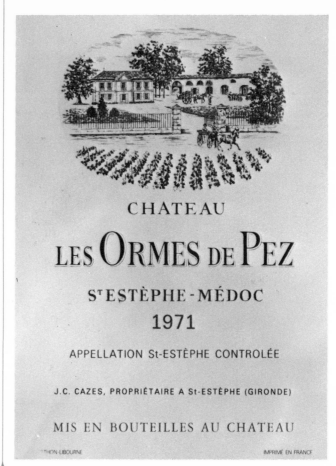

CHATEAU
LES ORMES DE PEZ
St ESTÈPHE - MÉDOC
1971

APPELLATION St-ESTÈPHE CONTROLÉE

J.C. CAZES, PROPRIÉTAIRE A St-ESTÈPHE (GIRONDE)

MIS EN BOUTEILLES AU CHATEAU

THON - LIBOURNE   IMPRIMÉ EN FRANCE

CHATEAU
COUFRAN
HAUT-MÉDOC
1955

APPELLATION
HAUT-MÉDOC
CONTROLÉE

Louis Miailhe
PROPRIÉTAIRE
St SEURIN-DE-CADOURNE (GIRONDE)

MIS EN BOUTEILLES AU CHATEAU

CRU GRAND BOURGEOIS

CHÂTEAU
Loudenne
APPELLATION MÉDOC CONTROLÉE

W. & A. Gilbey Ltd
PROPRIETAIRES A ST YZANS DE MÉDOC GIRONDE

MIS EN BOUTEILLES AU CHATEAU

MÉDAILLE D'OR
DÉCERNÉE PAR LE GOUVERNEMENT
FRANCAIS POUR LE VIGNOBLE
LE MIEUX CULTIVÉ

PRODUCE OF FRANCE

Château Latour

Brilliant and complete wines justly considered a standard of judgment not only for the Médoc and Pauillac but for Bordeaux wines generally earn Latour superlatives. With the possible exception of 1953, it has expressed its own balance and traditional finesse in every vintage and, as every fine wine should, it has captured something of the character of each vintage as well.

The staying power and even maturation of its wines are rightly praised as remarkable. The notion, often stupidly and wrongly parroted, that it is a crime to drink Bordeaux young here finds its just application. Its remarkable success in deficient vintages has been endlessly, but correctly, sung. If I had one comment to venture on its appreciation, it would be never to drink it alone but always with another Médoc as a foil.

VINTAGE   *DATE*   *PRICE*

GUESTS

MENU   *COMMENTS*

Château Pichon Baron

A family division in the nineteenth century created this property and Pichon Lalande out of a single estate bordering St.-Julien and facing Latour. In many years Pichon Baron is an astringent version of Pauillac, variable in most points such as color, amplitude of fruity impressions, and even development to the senses. Very powerful, individual, and refined wines from before and just after World War II prove the estate's potential. Vintages since the 1950s have something of this character in full years such as 1955 and 1962, but those who require charm and attraction will be disappointed in years (such as 1966) normally displaying such qualities. Its extreme, firm, and dry style of Pauillac can be compared to Château Batailley. Château Lannessan, southwest of Beychevelle—a full, florid, mouth-filling claret in good years—has the same ownership.

VINTAGE   *DATE*   *PRICE*

GUESTS

MENU   *COMMENTS*

Château Pichon Lalande

This complement and neighbor of Pichon Baron straddles Pauillac and St.-Julien. The bouquet and taste of its wines show an elegance and charm that relieve some of the sterner qualities of more conventional Pauillacs. Like many St.-Julien wines, attractive results are obtained in deficient or awkward years; the 1964 was among the best of the Médocs, 1958 was pleasing. Young wines tasted beside more powerful Pauillacs seem inadequate, but Lalande develops securely in bottle now that some planting errors have been rectified by different vine types. The style, balanced but forward in impressions, is better compared to Ducru Beaucaillou or Lafite than to Pichon Baron or weighty Pauillacs such as Lynch-Bages. It belongs in any experience of fine Médocs; bouquet and finesse are the strongest of its virtues.

VINTAGE   *DATE*   *PRICE*

GUESTS

MENU   *COMMENTS*

Château Lafite-Rothschild

This celebrated estate lies in the north of Pauillac with a large parcel over the border in St.-Estèphe. A second parcel, the Carruades, was acquired early in the nineteenth century; its wines are now integrated into those of Lafite. Old vintages of this world-famous vineyard reflect an extraordinary assembly of qualities. These objectively powerful clarets did not give an overwhelming impression, for the senses were distracted by an enormous bouquet, subtle and lingering. Similarly, taste sensations of delicacy and flavor seemed to mingle and linger endlessly. Vintages over the last 20 years or more have been elegant, supple, and fine clarets, among which 1953, 1961, and 1966 stand out best. All are expensive.

Lafite's proprietors also own Château Duhart Milon, once a powerful dark wine dominated by the Petit Verdot variety but now soft, and limited.

VINTAGE   *DATE*   *PRICE*

GUESTS

MENU   *COMMENTS*

MIS EN BOUTEILLE AU CHATEAU

GRAND VIN
DE
CHATEAU LATOUR

DÉPOSÉ

APPELLATION PAUILLAC CONTROLÉE

CHATAU LONGUEVILLE
Pauillac-Médoc

1966

au BARON de PICHON-LONGUEVILLE.
BORDEAUX
CRU CLASSÉ EN 1855

MIS EN BOUTEILLES AU CHATEAU
APPELLATION PAUILLAC CONTROLÉE
SOCIÉTÉ CIVILE DE PICHON-LONGUEVILLE
PROPRIÉTAIRE A PAUILLAC (GIRONDE)

IMPRIMÉ EN FRANCE   BERTHON-LIBOURNE

CHATEAU PICHON LALANDE
— 1966 —
APPELLATION PAUILLAC CONTRÔLÉE

FRANCE

CHATEAU PICHON LONGUEVILLE COMTESSE DE LALANDE S.C.
W·A·B·MIAILHE PRÉST-DIRECTᴿ A PAUILLAC-GIRONDE

DÉPOSÉ

MIS EN BOUTEILLES AU CHÂTEAU

MIS EN BOUTEILLES AU CHÂTEAU

CHATEAU LAFITE-ROTHSCHILD
1961

DÉPOSE

APPELLATION PAUILLAC CONTRÔLÉE

Château Mouton Rothschild

This is a superb wine and a superbly maintained vineyard. Its wines, unlike those of Latour and Margaux, do not sum up the style of whole tribes of lesser Médocs but rather are original, with their own magnificence. This character has been maintained for a very long time; 1870 Mouton is still recognizably Mouton, or was a couple of years ago. Aroma is distinctive, described as cassis or black currants, being in fact strongly Cabernet. Very dark color, nearly blackish in ripe years, refining well to lighter hues, is characteristic. Brilliance is excellent but not Mouton's stellar point. Development on the palate is overpowering and delicious, without hesitation, remarkably full of flavor and consistent with the bouquet. Its finesse is less obvious at first than other features, due to the strength of body and flavor. Both young and mature wines are harmonious. Vintage successes follow Médoc patterns with striking off-year successes (1951, 1954, 1956).

VINTAGE   DATE   PRICE

GUESTS

MENU   COMMENTS

Château Lynch Bages

Lynch Bages offers dark, chewy and impressive style, spicy, exciting aroma, and full bouquet. Its instantaneous tasting impressions have been likened to licorice and its mouth-filling effect compared to that of Mouton, great examples of Pontet Canet, and sometimes Grand Puy Lacoste (with which I disagree). In any event this habitually dark-colored, full-tasting Pauillac is always distinctive in good vintages and drinks well when young and middle-aged, provided one accepts its thick style and strong impressions as part of its character. The great years of the 1940s and 1950s were all successful; its 1962 is distinctly superior to its 1961, not alone in the Médoc; and with a lapse in 1964, it reaffirms its style and quality in each succeeding good year. Off-vintages tend to skid off the road entirely; its opulent flavor and body are virtues requiring ripe grapes.

VINTAGE   DATE   PRICE

GUESTS

MENU   COMMENTS

Château Grand-Puy-Lacoste

Among the most brilliantly colored wines in the Médoc and distinctively Pauillac, the clarets produced at Lacoste are firm, tending to hardness, develop variously in bottle in fits and starts, sometimes dry out quickly (1950, 1952, 1955), and frequently attain exciting, even brilliant peaks (1949, 1953, 1962) when aged eight, ten, and 15 years, rarely longer. It is a wonderfully chameleonlike wine and one to drink when it tastes as though it should be drunk. Its merits are intensity, finesse, indelible Pauillac character. Its bouquet and aftertaste normally reflect longer barrel aging than usual but in a favorable sense. Off-years are thin and mean, but when it succeeds it is with vitality, sparkling impressions, and a sort of dashing style that can only repeatedly be achieved by wine makers who consciously pursue an image, cost what it may.

VINTAGE   DATE   PRICE

GUESTS

MENU   COMMENTS

Château Pontet Canet

Among the largest vineyards in Pauillac, Pontet Canet is superbly exposed in the center of the appellation. The name rather than the wine is controversial, because for years the company that owned it bottled unvintaged Pontet Canet in Bordeaux. Since 1972 it is exclusively château-bottled. Great vintages of this claret, a nineteenth-century favorite, display powerful and refined characteristics, though such samples have rarely been available to the public. Imposing body, fine brilliant color, rich bouquet, distinctly Pauillac in breed, and excellent finesse gave the wines a classical type. It is to be hoped urgently that regular château bottling will make these distinguished wines available and dependable.

In 1975 the vineyard was bought by M. Guy Tesseron, owner of Lafon Rochet. The former owners, members of the Cruse family, own a lesser wine, Haut Bages Libéral, a pretty well-proportioned Pauillac, with much small production.

VINTAGE   DATE   PRICE

GUESTS

MENU   COMMENTS

ANNÉE DU CENTENAIRE

1853   1953

JAMES
DE
ROTHSCHILD
1844-1881

BARON NATHANIEL
1812-1870

HENRI
DE
ROTHSCHILD
1872-1947

1953

Je dédie cette récolte à mon
Arrière-Grand-Père le Baron Nathaniel
qui acheta le Domaine de Mouton le
11 Mai 1853, à mon Grand-Père le Baron
James et à mon Père le Baron Henri.

Philippe de Rothschild

Château
Mouton Rothschild

APPELLATION PAUILLAC CONTRÔLÉE

MIS EN BOUTEILLE AU CHATEAU

BARON PHILIPPE DE ROTHSCHILD PROPRIÉTAIRE A PAUILLAC

GRAND VIN

CHATEAU
LYNCH ✠ BAGES
GRAND CRU CLASSÉ
PAUILLAC
MÉDOC
1967   APPELLATION PAUILLAC CONTROLÉE

MISE EN BOUTEILLE AU CHATEAU

J.C. CAZES, PROPRE

BERTHON - LIBOURNE

Château GRAND-PUY-LACOSTE
SAINT-GUIRONS
MIS EN BOUTEILLE AU CHATEAU
AU
Pauillac
(MÉDOC)
Appellation PAUILLAC contrôlée
ANNÉE 1967

SYNDICAT
DES GRANDS CRÛS CLASSÉS DU MÉDOC
MARQUE DE GARANTIE

MARQUE DÉPOSÉE

Société du Château Grand-Puy-Lacoste, Propriétaire

Grand Cru Classé en 1855

1972

Registered   Trade mark

CHÂTEAU
PONTET CANET
APPELLATION PAUILLAC CONTRÔLÉE

PRODUCT OF FRANCE

Cruse & Fils Frères

PROPRIÉTAIRES A PAUILLAC (GIRONDE)   73 cl

MIS EN BOUTEILLES AU CHATEAU

Château Ducru-Beaucaillou

A change in management followed a family division of vineyard properties in the early 1950s. Since then Beaucaillou, by dint of unbroken successes in all good and nearly all poor vintages, has progressed to a pinnacle of St.-Julien prestige commanding price premiums above its neighbors and above other second growths. Not only has it made exceptional wines in shabby years such as 1965 and 1968 and lively ones in dull vintages such as 1955 and 1964; it has risen regularly to the heights expected of balanced harvests such as 1953, 1961, and 1966. It combines a glossy texture with abundant bouquet exhilarating in youth and age alike. A superb finish in which the scent of Cabernet mingles wonderfully completes a catalogue of virtues abbreviated by lack of space.

M. Borie, the proprietor, also owns the elegant Pauillac Haut Batailley, a fragrant, forward, balanced wine omitted only for lack of space.

VINTAGE   DATE   PRICE

GUESTS

MENU   COMMENTS

Château Gruaud-Larose

This vineyard, once divided following a scandalous family quarrel, was reunited by the present owners, the Cordier family (see Château Talbot, page 62). Gruaud has expanded by acquiring lands once belonging to Langoa Barton and has become a large estate producing 30,000 cases annually, all marketed through Cordier shippers. If the wines have declined slightly during the last 15 years, they remain fine, subtle, perfumed, and loyal to St.-Julien standards. The aroma and bouquet are discreet; some tasters fancy a comparison with violets. The wines are delicate, maturing fairly rapidly into soft St.-Juliens of Beychevelle-type with a natural, easy series of tasting impressions with a complex finish.

The wines of Château Gloria, a lesser neighboring growth, resemble those of Gruaud in some vintages, but the comparison should not be stretched.

VINTAGE   DATE   PRICE

GUESTS

MENU   COMMENTS

Château Branaire (Duluc-Ducru)

This wine is unusual. It is certainly a very fine claret with dark, brilliant color, a heady bouquet, and great reserves of fruit and body that carry it well into maturity. But, like Château Talbot, it sits uneasily among the tasting qualities associated with St.-Julien wines. Its normal style is to show a purplish color, a flushed and spicy smell, tasting impressions dominated by body quite long on the palate and delicious in themselves but not showing the more scintillating, elusive, and delicate combinations habitually assembled in this appellation. It does give that depth of taste the French call *fond,* and so the wine is harmonious in its own way. It is a survivor; the 1934 was probably the best of the Médoc, and since 1962 it has equaled or surpassed vintage standards, with the possible exception of 1970. With more fruit than Talbot and less elegance than Langoa Barton, it nevertheless makes sense to group these wines as a little clan within St.-Julien.

VINTAGE   DATE   PRICE

GUESTS

MENU   COMMENTS

Château Beychevelle

Beychevelle's magnificent eighteenth-century château overlooks the Gironde and to the north the beginning of the finest stretch of Médoc vineyard. A large vineyard, it produces some 25,000 cases a year of silky, delicious claret, lightest of the major St.-Juliens and one of the most appealing in youth if not in old age. Too much Merlot was set out after World War II; this showed in weak, rapidly drying vintages during the 1950s, a fault since rectified, as the charming and complete series of crops beginning in 1966 show. Beychevelle shares with Léoville-Poyferré an immediate onrush of fruit in the aroma and the promise of something not quite known but surely delicious to follow. And it usually does. Their purity of flavor, perfume, and finesse are irresistible. Across the road descendants of the St.-Pierre family make Bontemps Dubarry, a refined handglass rather than a mirror to Beychevelle.

VINTAGE   DATE   PRICE

GUESTS

MENU   COMMENTS

1962

CHATEAU DUCRU·BEAUCAILLOU

GRAND CRU CLASSÉ DE MÉDOC EN 1855

SAINT·JULIEN·MÉDOC

JEAN-EUGÈNE BORIE, PROPRIÉTAIRE   APPELLATION St.JULIEN CONTROLÉE

CORDIER

GRAND CRU CLASSÉ

RED FRENCH TABLE WINE

1961

CONTENTS 1 Pt. 8 FL. OZ.

CHATEAU GRUAUD·LAROSE

LE ROI DES VINS — LE VIN DES ROIS

Mise en Bouteilles au Château
à Saint-Julien (Haut Médoc)   D. Cordier Propriétaire

APPELLATION SAINT-JULIEN CONTRÔLÉE

PRODUCE OF FRANCE   EXPORTATION STRICTEMENT RÉSERVÉE   IMPRIMÉ EN FRANCE

Grand Cru Classé

1970

Château Branaire

(DULUC-DUCRU)

St-Julien-Médoc

(Appellation Saint-Julien Contrôlée)
PRODUCE OF FRANCE
HtIERS TAPIE, PROPRIÉTAIRES A St-JULIEN (Gde)
MIS EN BOUTEILLE AU CHATEAU

DÉPOSÉE

St. JULIEN   MÉDOC

MIS EN BOUTEILLE AU CHATEAU

CHÂTEAU BEYCHEVELLE

Grand Vin 1967

APPELLATION St.-JULIEN CONTROLÉE

ACHILLE · FOULD

Château Léoville Las Cases

The great eighteenth-century Léoville domaines were dismembered, as it were, by the Revolutionary guillotine, consequences of a celebrated duel and a cowardly murder in the marsh of Beychevelle, a story for which there is no space here. Of the three contemporary Léoville's, Las Cases is the largest, the most popular, and the most attractive to beginners for color and brilliance and, when young, for its heady, spicy aroma. The newly made wines burst with fruit and flavor and have a lush impression that seduces visiting merchants when seen in barrel. The 1970 and 1971 show more natural qualities and should last better than other crops, for the bottle maturation of this wine leaves much to ask, at least between 1953 and 1964 vintages. The much-sung 1959, that darling of the wine reporters, appeals now only to lovers of flabby clarets. That it tastes old is not a quality. But better things appear in store.

VINTAGE   *DATE*   *PRICE*

GUESTS

MENU   *COMMENTS*

Château Léoville Poyferré

Adjacent to Las Cases, Poyferré makes utterly different wines, clarets that answer to descriptions of bygone generations of Bordeaux and to superlatives accorded by the last century to shapers of the finest wine. Léoville Poyferré was wrongly kept (in the view of nineteenth-century critics) in thrall of second-growth classification. That quarrel is now water, and wine, under the bridge. But even today a portrait of an ideal wine of St.-Julien—its qualities countenancing each other and mirrored in its finish—can be found from time to time at this château. It will be compared, by those disposed to appreciate it, to the refinements of the best Château Margaux and Haut Brion and to those alone.

VINTAGE   *DATE*   *PRICE*

GUESTS

MENU   *COMMENTS*

Château Talbot

Like Gruaud Larose, a Cordier property whose wines are unhappily bottled in the unattractive shapes used for Cordier common wines, Talbot comes from a vineyard set back from the main line of properties fronting the estuary. It is matured in very large oak puncheons that I, at least, have not seen elsewhere in the Gironde. Darker in color than the St.-Julien norm, mustier in taste, and thicker in "texture," if one may use that image, it is an individual wine in which characteristic St.-Julien fruit and liveliness are sacrificed to a heavier body. Some appreciate this more powerful style, others find it blunt. Since 1966, whether by accident or design, the wines have tasted thinner and less interesting. Banner years for Talbot were 1949 and 1952, and the present depressed level of its tasting character is a mystery.

VINTAGE   *DATE*   *PRICE*

GUESTS

MENU   *COMMENTS*

Château Léoville Barton

English affection for this elegant claret and its more austere neighbor, Langoa Barton, together with poor distribution in America, have deprived most Americans from experiencing its classic qualities. The bouquet is hesitant in youth, as expected, but develops into a fine, subtle representative of the tasting qualities that follow. Elegant, with a lovely finish, tending slightly toward astringency, the wines begin to come forward after five or six years in bottle and continue to improve steadily. Langoa cedes nothing in finesse, as shown in its remarkable 1952 and 1945 wines, but is often a bit more aloof than Léoville. Yet both succeed remarkably precisely in years where other wines slip into meaner clothing—1945, 1952, 1962, 1967. Both are sophisticated though different wines whose appreciation seems to follow that of more succulent and immediate Médocs. Both endure well in bottle, better than most St.-Juliens.

VINTAGE   *DATE*   *PRICE*

GUESTS

MENU   *COMMENTS*

RÉCOLTE 1970

Grand Vin de Léoville

du Marquis de Las Cases

SAINT-JULIEN-MÉDOC

APPELLATION SAINT-JULIEN CONTROLÉE

PROP⁰ SOCIÉTÉ DU CHATEAU LÉOVILLE LAS CASES A SAINT-JULIEN (Gde)

MIS EN BOUTEILLES AU CHATEAU

IMPRIMÉ EN FRANCE   BERTHON · LIBOURNE

Château
Léoville Poyferré

appellation St-Julien controlée

1967

MIS EN BOUTEILLE AU CHATEAU

Propriét⁻ʳᵉ Stᵉ Cⁱᵉ des Domaines de St-Julien (Gᵈᵉ)

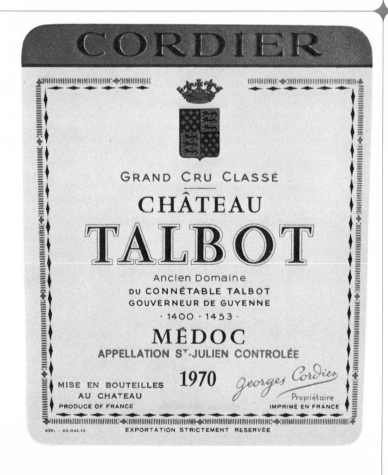

CORDIER

GRAND CRU CLASSÉ

CHÂTEAU

TALBOT

Ancien Domaine
DU CONNÉTABLE TALBOT
GOUVERNEUR DE GUYENNE
· 1400 · 1453 ·

MÉDOC
APPELLATION Sᵗ-JULIEN CONTROLÉE

1970   *Georges Cordier*

MISE EN BOUTEILLES   Propriétaire
AU CHATEAU
PRODUCE OF FRANCE   IMPRIMÉ EN FRANCE

RÉF. 02.042.10   EXPORTATION STRICTEMENT RESERVÉE

Château
LÉOVILLE BARTON

APPELLATION Sᵗ-JULIEN CONTRÔLÉE

H. R. BARTON
PROPRIÉTAIRE Sᵗ JULIEN GIRONDE

MIS EN BOUTEILLE AU CHÂTEAU

1964

Château Margaux

The inadequacy of some few introductory words about wines of high quality is nowhere so clear as in suggesting the qualities of wines from this estate. As in so many clarets that suppress power and astringency in their pursuit of elegant tasting qualities, failed vintages occur. But so do brilliant ones, too many to itemize, for Margaux was considered the first vineyard of Bordeaux from the late eighteenth century through the middle of the nineteenth. The 1948 and 1950 wines, for example, had no betters and, with the 1953, make a trio arguably the most refined of all wines since World War II. Our ideals of finesse in Médoc wines stem in some degree from the model of Margaux. Its emphasis on perfume, harmony, and aftertaste certainly fall short of complete wine from time to time (1962, 1967), but without this model, and that of Latour and Haut-Brion, the elegance of claret would not be expressed completely.

VINTAGE   *DATE*   *PRICE*

GUESTS

MENU   *COMMENTS*

Château Palmer

Palmer's checkered and sometimes hilarious history has entered a period of radically increased prestige based upon a series of distinguished successes since the last world war. Its tasting qualities combine Médoc intensity and Margaux finesse, exemplified in its 1961 and 1966 crops. If a wave of fashion has carried its prices somewhat above its uncontested excellence that is not the fault of its three owners, who continue to make severe selections of their wines, discarding the unworthy lots without benefit of château bottling. There is a bit more variety from vintage to vintage than in some estates, but the features found in good vintages are balance of all elements, steady development in bottle marked by affirmative bouquet followed by a pure succession of tasting qualities. It belongs in any collection of great clarets.

VINTAGE   *DATE*   *PRICE*

GUESTS

MENU   *COMMENTS*

Château d'Issan

Destroyed, then reconstructed during civil wars centuries ago, the castle of Issan is a magnificent landmark and monument whose vineyards are enclosed in stone walls unusual in the Médoc. It belongs to members of the Cruse family, Bordeaux shippers, and since 1972 its wines are regularly château-bottled. Best examples of this wine have unusually dark color for the locale and abundance of flavor and character. Its bouquet is profound, and the general intensity of Issan lends itself to comparisons with Pauillacs as much as with Margaux wines. Yet this is no eccentric wine; it sums up expected and old-fashioned Médoc virtues. Not least among these is a finesse and aftertaste striking enough to come as a climax to a wine of imposing body and, in ripe vintages, spicy flavor.

VINTAGE   *DATE*   *PRICE*

GUESTS

MENU   *COMMENTS*

Château Brane-Cantenac

The subtle, understated wines of Brane Cantenac are deceptive in barrel and during their early years of bottle tasting, causing them to lose praise in comparative tastings. Excellent bouquet, complete and charming tasting qualities, and superior finesse appear at a later day, and those who neglected to buy the 1961, 1962, or 1966 are the losers. It is one of those wines that seem to require really good maturity of crops to make wines with much appeal, though like most such statements, a cunning sniper could ground it, choosing the 1965 Brane as ammunition. Medium-light color, seductive bouquet at maturity, and lovely development on the palate characterize its best offerings.

VINTAGE   *DATE*   *PRICE*

GUESTS

MENU   *COMMENTS*

CHÂTEAU · MARGAUX
GRAND VIN

1970
PREMIER GRAND CRU CLASSÉ
FRANCE
APPELLATION MARGAUX CONTROLÉE
MIS EN BOUTEILLE AU CHATEAU
SOCIÉTÉ CIVILE IMMOBILIÈRE DU DOMAINE DE CHATEAU MARGAUX
Proprietaire à Margaux
DÉPOSÉ

1961

MARGAUX CHATEAU·PALMER MEDOC

APPELLATION MARGAUX CONTROLÉE
SOCIÉTÉ CIVILE DU CHATEAU PALMER, MARGAUX
FRANCE
MIS EN BOUTEILLE AU CHATEAU

Cruse

1967
CHATEAU D'ISSAN
TROISIÈME CRU CLASSÉ EN 1855
APPELLATION MARGAUX CONTROLÉE

RED BORDEAUX WINE

MIS EN BOUTEILLES PAR

Cruse & Fils Frères
NÉGOCIANTS A BORDEAUX (GIRONDE)
PRODUCT OF FRANCE
SOLE DISTRIBUTORS FOR THE UNITED STATES
THE JOS. GARNEAU Co, NEW-YORK N. Y.
CONTENTS 1 PINT 8 1/2 FLUID OUNCES   ALCOHOL 12 % BY VOLUME

GRAND CRU CLASSÉ EN 1855

CHÂTEAU

BRANE·CANTENAC

MARGAUX

1964

APPELLATION MARGAUX CONTROLÉE

L. LURTON. PROPRIETAIRE A CANTENAC·GIRONDE

MIS EN BOUTEILLES AU CHÂTEAU

Château Cantenac Brown

This claret belongs to a family grouping sterner-tasting qualities as distinguished from the blander and more elusive ones occurring so often in the large confines of the southern Médoc. Issan, Palmer, Cantemerle are better comparisons than Prieuré-Lichine, Brane Cantenac, or La Lagune. Its dark color, dry first impressions, and fuller aftertaste can be found in 1961, 1962, and 1966; and like most such wines, awkward vintages (1964) tend to taste thin and mean. Color and body are strong points of this wine and are matched rather than overshadowed by elegance and seductiveness of flavors. It is distributed exclusively by De Luze but administered quite separately from the shipping firm.

VINTAGE   *DATE*   *PRICE*

GUESTS

MENU   *COMMENTS*

Château d'Angludet

Two centuries ago the Angludet estates covered much of what is now Margaux. The solid clean wines now produced are sold through the shipping firm of its owner, Sichel & Co., and in good vintages reflect a basic Médoc style fringed with Margaux benefits—a dash more of breed, a true finish to a long tasting style, and the emphasis on subtlety that sets apart Margaux and Cantenac wines. This is a well-tended vineyard, a carefully made wine loyal to its appellation, and it illustrates the nonsensical aspects of retaining an obsolete classification that omits estates like this one while including others less worthy. The complete style of the wine is not confirmed because of replantings whose influence and maturity remain to be asserted, but the tendency seems to be toward firm wines with forward-tasting features, vigorous body, and a traditional Margaux style.

VINTAGE   *DATE*   *PRICE*

GUESTS

MENU   *COMMENTS*

Château Cantemerle

Cantemerle is a difficult wine to evaluate in youth, when it shows itself blunter and less declarative than the remarkable and elegant bouquet, flavor, and finish exemplified in 1949, 1953, or in the sudden maturing wines of 1955. It belongs to no clear group of clarets; perhaps it might be compared to the dense, tough wines of Malescot St.-Exupéry (omitted for lack of space), but it is not so tannic or austere. It is one of the oldest estates in the Médoc, and like other fine wines sold exclusively through one company (the Barton estates, Cantenac Brown, Issan), it can be irritatingly difficult to find. But its individualistic, firm style is worth experiencing in every ripe vintage.

VINTAGE   *DATE*   *PRICE*

GUESTS

MENU   *COMMENTS*

Château Bel Air-Marquis d'Aligre

Like La Tour de Mons and Château Margaux, this claret exemplifies the particular assembly of Margaux qualities. Subtle, expressive wines of medium light color are reaped in good years and desperately thin ones in crops where ripeness is not fully attained. The wines of 1966 and 1970 serve to show its virtues. In sharp contrast are the plummy, quite fruity wines of Prieuré-Lichine dominated by Merlot style—lush, wonderfully delicious while young, and so often successful in off-years. Space does not allow justice to many other fine wines from Margaux and the southern Médoc, among them Rausan Gassies, a dark conventional claret of erratic success; Château Lascombes, with agreeable fruity and rapidly developing tasting qualities; the austere wines of Malescot; and many others listed in works cited in the brief bibliography. No complete list of fine wines from these locales could be shorter than 40 names.

VINTAGE   *DATE*   *PRICE*

GUESTS

MENU   *COMMENTS*

1970

CHATEAU
CANTENAC BROWN

CRU CLASSÉ EN 1855

MARGAUX

APPELLATION MARGAUX CONTROLÉE

PRODUCE OF FRANCE

Société Civile du Château Cantenac Brown
PROPRIÉTAIRE A CANTENAC-GIRONDE

MISE EN BOUTEILLES AU CHATEAU

CHATEAU D'ANGLUDET

GRAND CRU EXCEPTIONNEL

APPELLATION MARGAUX CONTROLÉE

 1970

Société Civile Viticole du Château d'Angludet • Propriétaire à Cantenac

MIS EN BOUTEILLE AU CHATEAU
Produce of France

APPELLATION HAUT-MÉDOC CONTROLÉE

1966

CHÂTEAU CANTEMERLE

GRAND CRU CLASSÉ DE MÉDOC

Héritiers Pierre J. DUBOS, Propriétaires   Macau-en-Médoc

CHÂTEAU
BEL AIR-MARQUIS D'ALIGRE

GRAND CRU EXCEPTIONNEL

MARGAUX

APPELLATION MARGAUX CONTROLÉE

1967

P. BOYER, PROPRIÉTAIRE

Château La Tour de Mons

Unprepossessing, though long a reputed vineyard, La Tour de Mons hides in a grove behind Soussans, a drab, dirt-floor *chai* (barrel cellar) beside a tacky farmhouse, full of much-used barrels out of which sporadically issues one of the most pristine, pure-bred, and subtle Margaux wines, or indeed Médoc wines, to be made. It is never a big wine, not even in 1961. It attempts, and sometimes achieves, a luxurious combination—genteel bouquet emphasizing the more flowery odors of grape, a body that does nothing to upset this impression, and an aftertaste suggestive and racy rather than technically long. It often fails, in being too dry (1955, 1962), inadequately fruity (1967), or insufficiently vinous (1964). But when it falls into place (1953, 1959, 1966, 1970, and perhaps 1973) there are few more eloquent witnesses to the special class reserved to fine Margaux wines.

VINTAGE   DATE   PRICE

GUESTS

MENU   COMMENTS

Château La Lagune

The introduction to this chapter refers to the recent origin of much land around Ludon and Macau, and La Lagune is situated on this new land created by drainage. It was reconstituted in the 1950s by great effort and expense, having been allowed to slip into grain production between the wars. As a result, its plant is very modern and its management equally excellent. Wine of very regular quality and consistent style is obtained from vines now coming of age. From 1962 onward no good vintage has been allowed to misfire. Both Cabernets and Merlots give luscious grapes in this area, and their abundant fruit is extracted into the wines, whose balance is tipped in favor of an unctuous plumlike style. Inevitably, coming from young vines, La Lagunes of the early 1960s are drying out rather quickly; more recent vintages have more taste and produce wines of generous fruit and youthful charm rather than examples of great finesse.

VINTAGE   DATE   PRICE

GUESTS

MENU   COMMENTS

Château Boyd-Cantenac (Château Pouget)

Apparently twin properties, in reality the two names belong to one vineyard, with the best wines going into Boyd-Cantenac and the less good ones into the less expensive Pouget. The production is small, but Boyd is certainly a rising star among Margaux wines. The 1960s and 1970s have seen a series of traditional clarets, with brilliant color and equally dignified and elegant bouquet. Properly severe and closed in when young, Boyd nevertheless captures excellent Cabernet fruit impressions and finishes with commendable power and elegance of taste. Pouget is thinner and less vibrant in taste and represents an honest division of the crop into better and less good wines. Boyd, in sum, is stylish Margaux claret made lovingly and scrupulously.

VINTAGE   DATE   PRICE

GUESTS

MENU   COMMENTS

Château Giscours

The generation of claret drinkers that began uncorking bottles in the late 1950s and early 1960s conceived a disdain of Giscours that unfairly ignored that thin wines were the inevitable product of young vines; after its acquisition in 1952 the dilapidated vineyard was replanted. Complaints about mean-featured 1959 or 1961 are simply not reasonable. Steady improvement in color, perfume, and above all once lacking unctuosity have since brought it to the front rank of Médocs. A penetrating sensation that the French call *fond*, based on both fruit and body, is one of its ornaments. Balance, great character, a body suitably sinewy for a Labarde claret, and refinement proper to a great Margaux vineyard complete its constitution. The years 1966, 1967, 1969 (good for a meager year), and 1970 left little to be desired; 1965 and 1968 were snatched from *débacle* vintages by the skill and sacrifice of the owners, Messrs. Tari, father and son.

VINTAGE   DATE   PRICE

GUESTS

MENU   COMMENTS

APPELLATION MARGAUX CONTROLÉE

1966

Château LA TOUR DE MONS

GRAND VIN

MARGAUX

Héritiers Pierre J. DUBOS, Propriétaires   Soussans-en-Médoc

GRAND CRU CLASSÉ

CHATEAU LA LAGUNE

HAUT·MÉDOC

APPELLATION HAUT·MÉDOC CONTROLÉE

1970

SOCIÉTÉ CIVILE AGRICOLE DU CHATEAU LA LAGUNE
PROPRIÉTAIRE A LUDON (GIRONDE) FRANCE

MIS EN BOUTEILLE AU CHATEAU

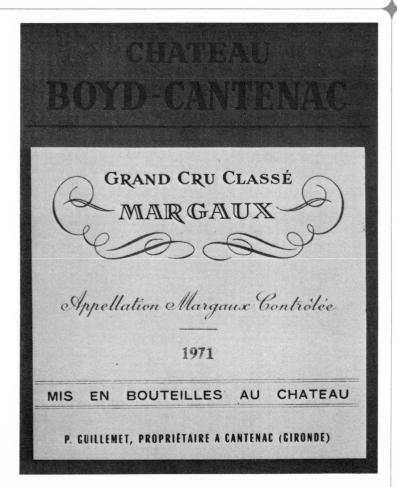

CHATEAU

BOYD-CANTENAC

GRAND CRU CLASSÉ

MARGAUX

Appellation Margaux Contrôlée

1971

MIS EN BOUTEILLES AU CHATEAU

P. GUILLEMET, PROPRIÉTAIRE A CANTENAC (GIRONDE)

Château Giscours

Grand Cru Classé

CLASSEMENT OFFICIEL DE 1855

MARGAUX

1966

APPELLATION MARGAUX CONTROLÉE

NICOLAS TARI, PROPRIÉTAIRE A LABARDE PAR MARGAUX · 33

MIS EN BOUTEILLES AU CHATEAU

Graves

Four centuries ago, the red wines of Graves were preferred over others. The evolution of wine making and its technology has permitted Graves, like other red wines, to be bottled after two years in barrel instead of the five or six years that were standard a century or more ago. But the qualities of red Graves partake of past times and past canons of taste more than do wines from elsewhere in Bordeaux and render many of them inscrutable or at least insufficiently appreciated by today's claret drinker. A few words on a printed page will not rectify this, but difficulties as well as facilities in wine appreciation deserve a little comment.

The Graves district sprawls out in a long fan west and south of Bordeaux. Its complex geography is seconded by a complicated viticulture: it harbors white as well as red wines. Wines are scattered in clusters rather than sectioned off neatly into convenient geographic zones, each with its tasting qualities. Further, since the red wines of Graves struggle along with difficulty, proprietors have intervened in different ways to mold their wines to the prototype they imagine the public might prefer. Thus it is possible to discern one district around Pessac, one around Léognan, and a third in a strip south of Bordeaux itself; but the character of the wines is very individual.

One consequence of this individual variation is a gossip-ridden feud between two neighboring famous properties, a feud as often as not carried on by partisans of either Haut-Brion or La Mission Haut Brion rather than the properties themselves. Having bought and sold wines of both vineyards for years, I can think of few pairs of vineyards so close to each other in place and so distant in immediate tasting qualities. Comparing them is rarely instructive, and choosing between them is downright silly, above all for the beginning claret drinker. With Château Pape Clément, these two great vineyards form a geographical if not a tasting group centered in Talence and Pessac. Around Léognan and to the south, important vineyards include Domaine de Chevalier, Malartic-Lagravière, Haut Bailly, Carbonnieux and some less prestigious but much improved properties such as Haut Bergey. Lastly, scattered just west of Route 113 and the new *autoroute* to the south are a few properties of distinction and many less famous ones. From north to south the important names are Baret, Bouscaut, and Smith-Haut-Lafitte. In Graves there are another score or more properties probably capable of making fine wines but which have not done so regularly or recently. The label section will try to suggest what the wine drinker can expect from good examples of the major growths. But to appreciate the efforts of Graves wine makers, some of their problems should be appreciated as well.

In ripe good vintages, red Graves give wines of irreproachable color, dark and fiery, if macerated for conventional lengths of time. But often they are hardhearted young wines with formidable body, a surplus of dense tasting qualities, and overbearing tannic impressions on the palate. The very long macerations formerly given to fine wines used to make this same statement true of most fine red Bordeaux. But in our lifetimes, in the Médoc, Pomerol, and St.-Émilion, reduced maceration and better understanding of wine acidities have permitted growers to make balanced wines of gentler original constitution and to do so regularly. And such wines conserve quite well the character of their appellations. The same maneuver is frequently less easy to bring off in Graves. Traditional Graves style and Graves finesse often do not seem to take well to abbreviated vinifications. Even if the struggle for adequate fruit and charm to offset the austere body and

tannic strength of many of these wines is not lost, it may be compromised in trying to make them lighter and result in thin clarets. Similar problems occur in Moulis, Listrac, and their environs, where fruit is often short and acerbity prominent. A variety of devices is employed as growers seek to achieve wines with adequate fruit and color without burdening them with such a dense body and such astringency that consumers must wait decades to relish the admittedly often remarkable mature wines that ensue. Cooler, slower fermentations can offer certain advantages. Warming the grapes slightly as they go into the vats confers other qualities and speeds extraction of coloring matter. Alongside old-fashioned reds, more supple and amenable Graves can be found, above all in recent vintages.

Some properties continue to make very traditional red Graves of great power, for which we must simply wait. Wine drinkers should understand, therefore, that the woody, taut, somewhat puckering impression that comes in young wines from conservative vineyards such as Malartic-Lagravière, Domaine de Chevalier, red Carbonnieux, and Bouscaut, to name a few, is not a fault of the terrain or of the vinification but a natural facet of the young wines. These qualities make it more difficult to taste such young wines for balance, masking more than we are normally accustomed their fruit and latent appeal. Vineyards such as Pape Clément and Haut-Brion have developed softer wines in many vintages that are more available to the palate. The extremely fluid style of Pape Clément has caused some speculation about its ability to last well in bottle. And certainly a wine maker may easily be tempted to go too far; many in Bordeaux would agree that vineyards such as Smith-Haut-Lafitte are making wines that are simply too light and small by traditional standards, perhaps in their zeal to market bottles that consumers can attack early on.

This problem of achieving proper balance in red Graves should not be exaggerated. It differs in degree rather than kind from that facing every wine maker who intends to make fine wines that will mature handsomely with time. But the unusual degree of diversity in what is, after all, a single apellation rather than a compartmentalized group such as the Médoc is partly explained by this extra difficulty in making fine red Graves in modern times.

The grape varieties that predominate on the gravel and sandy terrains of Graves are Cabernet Franc, Cabernet Sauvignon, and Merlot. The Petit Verdot, small quantities of which are so very useful to Médoc growers, is not widely considered to give satisfactory results in Graves. While the growing season is slightly more advanced than that of the Médoc, the prospect of early autumn frosts that arrest final maturation of the grapes is a source of anxiety particularly around Léognan. It is a populated region, unlike the Médoc, and while this puts pressure on vineyard land that could otherwise be used for building, it means that harvest labor is typically local and available. Graves properties can thus usually bring in their crops when they desire and quickly—an advantage for any vineyard.

There are not so many truly fine red wine properties in this appellation, and few of them are large. The historic prestige of Graves makes their fine wines more immediately demanded locally than those from the more distant Médoc. Then, too, collectors abroad are frequently inhibited from laying down in their cellars quantities of young wines whose qualities in youth do not appeal to them and whose future is not so apparent. For it is a minority of claret drinkers who have enjoyed very fine old red Graves. But the finesse of these wines at maturity—the ultimate test of quality—is exceeded by no other wine. Their bouquets are less standardized than those of venerable Médocs but just as subtle, if different. Their powerful constitution, a blunting influence in childhood, carries their wealth of savors, some vinous, some spicy, some mineral, into old age in an extraordinary fashion. It is unlikely that the finest red Graves will ever regain the preeminent place that once was theirs; too many efforts are required of the consumer and too much waiting as well. But one may hope that a few fellow voyagers in this twentieth century will not argue very long or hard that popularity is proof of highest quality.

The position of Haut-Brion as one of the oldest and most celebrated vineyards of Bordeaux led to its inclusion in the 1855 Classification of Médoc and Sauternes wines. Earlier classifications had done so as well and included other fine Graves properties. Haut-Brion is also included in contemporary Graves classifications done between 1953 and 1960, both for white and red wines; but its second wine called Bahans-Haut-Brion is not classed.

White wines from Graves are better liked in the Gironde than abroad, and they are an acquired taste. While made from the same noble grapes—Sauvignon, Semillon, and Muscadelle—as the great sweet wines of Bordeaux, their tasting qualities fall along a difficult line imperfectly dividing semisweet from dry and light from heavy wines. Heading the group are a very few vineyards that still produce what might be called classic white Graves. Very full in body and rich in texture, such wines have a wealth of flavor, but it is closed in during youth. White wines they may be, but they require several years of aging to be attractive. Alas, like many lesser white Graves, they are frequently stamped with a smell and taste of sulphur. Exposure to air before drinking and bottle age do much to modify this unpleasant feature; when pronounced, the effects of sulphur kill enjoyment for most drinkers. Nevertheless, the rarer fine wines that have properly aged are noble, impressive, forceful whites superbly marked with rich flavor and long aftertaste. The finest come from no more than half a dozen vineyards.

More common in southern Graves are wines that are virtually semisweet or at least so rich and unctuous as to seem so. There does not seem to be a great international demand for these either, but they are locally appreciated. Finally, in increasing numbers white wine properties are attempting to make crisper, lighter white wines that will serve all the usual purposes of white wine rather than the highly specialized role of heavy, classic white Graves, suitable for rich dishes but overpowering as wines. By picking at less advanced stages of ripeness and by cooler fermentations, white wines are obtained that may not have the unmistakable earthy and "saplike" quality of traditional local wines but are more easily understood and more quickly drinkable than old-fashioned white Graves. White Haut-Brion stands at the head of this class—a generous, well-made white wine but not one intended to exemplify the features of white Graves. The growers who follow these objectives are only doing what the shippers have told them would be desirable to meet contemporary public taste. But since they are competing with all other good white wines, some from quite inexpensive regions, a large economic question mark hangs over the white wine production of the Graves area.

Buying more traditional wines requiring aging presents wine drinkers with perplexing choices. In young Graves a certain amount of sulphur is normal and makes a particularly strong impression immediately after bottling. Wines that will reward cellaring may have a trace of this chemical impression; but they should offer a generous tasting sensation, even when young, in which a certain hardness or earthiness is acceptable provided it is supported by a sense of fruit, richness, and

long aftertaste. Laville-Haut-Brion, Domaine de Chevalier, and Malartic-Lagravière are three properties likely to exemplify classic white Graves, but they are not the only ones. White Graves of highest quality, like Sauternes, are products of exceptional years, and they require and can stand maturity as do few other whites.

The classification of Graves, of which I do not approve at all for reasons already given, represents much effort and discussion by the growers and appellation authorities and it is only fair to present it in conclusion.

CLASSIFIED GRAVES WINES

VINEYARDS MAKING WHITE WINES ONLY
Château Laville-Haut-Brion (Talence)
Château Couhins (Villenave d'Ornon)

VINEYARDS MAKING RED WINES ONLY
Château Haut-Bailly (Léognan)
Château La Mission Haut Brion (Talence)
Château Pape Clément (Pessac)
Château La Tour-Haut-Brion (Talence)
Château Smith-Haut-Lafitte (Martillac)
Château de Fieuzal (Léognan)

VINEYARDS MAKING WHITE AND RED WINES
Château Haut-Brion (Pessac)
Domaine de Chevalier (Léognan)
Château Malartic-Lagravière (Léognan)
Château Bouscaut (Cadaujac)
Château Carbonnieux (Léognan)
Château La Tour-Martillac (Martillac)
Château Olivier (Léognan)

Château Haut-Brion

The bouquet of Haut-Brion is the most distinctive of any great wine in the world and, unlike others, remains so into advanced age. It is the most refined wine of Graves, particularly in its development on the palate (*épanouissement*) and in its finish. Sensory impressions rather than color are its strengths. Unctuousity and character are striking qualities even in thin years (1956, 1958, 1965). It is always a very pure wine to taste. Some enthusiasts like to compare its impressions to coffee or vanilla; I prefer to take the wine itself as an ongoing standard through successive vintages, for its harmonies are original and not found among its neighbors. While the supple and seductive features of Haut-Brion are obvious even to beginning tasters, the winemaking ideals that stress finesse and character are not so obvious. This is exemplary refined red Graves. It is often shy in barrel; casual judgments should be avoided.

VINTAGE   DATE   PRICE

GUESTS

MENU   COMMENTS

Château Pape Clément

Named for a French Pope, the vineyard, shaped like an inverted saucer, lies on a northwest fringe of the town of Pessac. Its wines are very fragrant, and the allure of this aroma and bouquet is quickly followed by delicious tasting impressions that come forward very soon after bottling and are quite like the sensations given in barrel. During the last quarter century Pape Clément has displayed striking attraction in youth but rarely advanced into middle age with a very firm step. It earns best marks for Graves style and a luscious first impression but loses points for its lack of backbone and aftertaste precisely in its mature state when this quality should come forward more. The best available vintage is probably 1964; 1966 and 1967 were lighter but pretty wines, as were recent vintages.

VINTAGE   DATE   PRICE

GUESTS

MENU   COMMENTS

Château Haut Bailly

A beautifully exposed vineyard in Leognan, Haut-Bailly's gravel-covered slopes make a perfect photograph if seen from the road east of the town. Its wines are marvelously fruity and charming in youth; an irresistible silky texture is preceded by aroma and bouquet that are themselves a real treat. The aftertaste is fine in recapturing these qualities, and fruit and body mingle harmoniously. Its ensemble of qualities is better seized at age eight to 12 than in old age. The once exquisite 1952, for example, is now old wine, and the tender and complete 1964 and 1966 are fraying at the edges and drying out; their added bouquet is bought at the price of charm and fruit. Taken at the right time, however, Haut-Bailly offers a singular combination of immediate seductiveness, Graves style, and the scope of a *vin noble*.

VINTAGE   DATE   PRICE

GUESTS

MENU   COMMENTS

Château Bouscaut

Quite a splash of publicity greeted the acquisition of Château Bouscaut by an American group at the turn of the last decade. Its wines are now vinified by Jean Delmas, the manager of Château Haut-Brion. Exquisite clarets were produced here in the 1920s, but thereafter Bouscaut went into a decline, and its wines through the 1960s were either dull or even unpleasant. The improvement since the advent of Mr. Delmas is dramatic. Technical soundness begins the story, but a concept of wine style plays a part too. Graves style is retained; the model is a bit austere but complete with a firm tasting background. If there is emphasis on body and character it is not at the expense of flavor and fruit but rather to support these qualities. The 1970 and 1971 wines are complete and have a future difficult to taste now, as are many Graves wines, but concealing a long flavor under their youthful bluntness.

VINTAGE   DATE   PRICE

GUESTS

MENU   COMMENTS

1961

CHATEAU HAUT-BRION

PREMIER GRAND CRU CLASSÉ

APPELLATION GRAVES CONTRÔLÉE

MIS EN BOUTEILLES AU CHATEAU

DOMAINE CLARENCE DILLON S.A., A PESSAC, GIRONDE

G. CHARLES - BORDEAUX

MARQUE ET BOUTEILLE DÉPOSÉES

BORDEAUX

GRAND CRU CLASSÉ

CHATEAU PAPE CLÉMENT

APPELLATION GRAVES CONTRÔLÉE

1959

Sᵗᵉ MONTAGNE & Cⁱᵉ PROPRIÉTAIRE A PESSAC-GIRONDE

MIS EN BOUTEILLE AU CHATEAU

DÉPOSÉ

ROUSSEAU FRÈRES IMP.

CRU EXCEPTIONNEL

CHATEAU HAUT BAILLY

GRAND CRU CLASSÉ

APPELLATION GRAVES CONTRÔLÉE

1964

Daniel SANDERS · PROPRIÉTAIRE à LÉOGNAN (Gironde)

MIS EN BOUTEILLES AU CHATEAU

DÉPOSÉ

ROUSSEAU FRÈRES IMP.

Mis en Bouteille au Château

1970

Château Bouscaut

GRAND CRU CLASSÉ

1 PT. 8 FL. OZS.

ALCOHOL 12°/. BY VOL.

APPELLATION GRAVES CONTROLÉE

Domaine Wohlstetter - Sloan

Sᵗᵉ Civile du Château Bouscaut

PROPRIÉTAIRE ·

à CADAUJAC près BORDEAUX

RED BORDEAUX WINE

PRODUCT OF FRANCE

Château La Mission Haut Brion

Owned by the family in possession of Laville Haut-Brion, La Mission consistently vinifies wines distinguished by color, power, and emphatic tasting qualities that stand out strikingly in a consistent style. A maximum of these features is intelligently extracted from each crop, and the wines make a great impression on visitors who taste them in barrel. This richness is admirable in weak crops such as 1968, and the property is capable of the greatest heights, witness the 1964. In fact this claret develops fairly quickly in bottle, offering a lush sensation to the taste, including some earth flavors that carry through to the finish. Nearly always a dramatic claret to taste, La Mission lasts well in bottle but does not always acquire with years the elegance and finish to match its corpulent and assertive tasting qualities.

VINTAGE   *DATE*   *PRICE*

GUESTS

MENU   *COMMENTS*

Château Carbonnieux

Carbonnieux is located in Leognan and makes variable red wine sometimes pungent, authoritative, and arresting, such as the 1961. Intense color, tannic impressions, and strong vinosity are what immediately strike a taster in good vintages. Bouquet is slow to develop, and complete vintages show themselves to be traditionally hard and difficult to taste in youth in the classic model of red Graves. Some vintages are outright failures, and there are Bordeaux merchants who would say much more could be made of this ancient vineyard.

While its label does not appear in the white wine section, Carbonnieux is more celebrated for its rich, traditional, and heavy-bodied white wines than for its reds. Its whites too are variable, leaping from extremely typical white Graves maturing well in bottle to batches of wine clearly over sulphured.

VINTAGE   *DATE*   *PRICE*

GUESTS

MENU   *COMMENTS*

Domaine de Chevalier

A flat, unimpressive-looking vineyard in the southwest corner of Graves regularly gives generous and traditional Graves red wines with high technical standards and affirmative character. The output is small, grapes are well selected, the vatting or maceration is longer than most (three weeks), and the powerful wine that results would not prompt a guess that Merlot comprises 50 percent of the vineyard. While a standard for off-vintages in the past was high, and the standard for good ones higher still, accepting that these were classic Graves wines intended for long maturing, following an exclusive contract giving the entire crop to one shipper, prices have rocketed and there has been a dramatic lapse in quality in one good vintage, the 1971. Compare Chevalier to Graves such as La Mission, Carbonnieux, Malartic-Lagravière, drier versions of Bouscaut, and, at a lower level, the strong dark wines of Château Haut-Bergey.

VINTAGE   *DATE*   *PRICE*

GUESTS

MENU   *COMMENTS*

Château Malartic-Lagravière

It was the misfortune of this Leognan vineyard to have replanted during the upswing of interest in fine wine rather than before it, and only in the latter 1960s did finer reds begin to declare themselves. Their dry, powerful sinewy style begins to show in 1966; the 1967 was poorly brought off, but subsequent crops have increased in depth of taste and completeness of features. The style is dense, a bit woody and dry, but promises stately older wines. This is an extreme style that will not attract those who insist upon supple, immediately pleasing wines. Few properties eliminate inferior grapes so ruthlessly from their château wine, with the result that downright poor vintages such as 1968 are attractive here, and dubious ones such as 1972 stand out among their peers. After some experience in lesser Graves such as Smith-Haut-Lafitte, red Pontac Monplaisir, or Baret, return to this traditional model to understand different notions of Graves style.

VINTAGE   *DATE*   *PRICE*

GUESTS

MENU   *COMMENTS*

CHÂTEAU
LA MISSION HAUT BRION

APPELLATION GRAVES CONTRÔLÉE

Grand Cru classé

1968

SOCIÉTÉ CIVILE DES DOMAINES WOLTNER
PROPRIÉTAIRE

BORDEAUX
FRANCE

MIS EN BOUTEILLES AU CHÂTEAU

GRAND VIN DE GRAVES

1966

CHÂTEAU CARBONNIEUX

GRAND CRU CLASSÉ

LÉOGNAN

MISE EN BOUTEILLES
AU CHÂTEAU   PRODUCE OF FRANCE   APPELLATION
"GRAVES" CONTRÔLÉE

Propriétaire : Société des Grandes Graves

DEPOSE   G. MOOLENAAR · BORDEAUX

GRAND VIN DE BORDEAUX

Domaine de Chevalier

GRAND CRU CLASSÉ DE GRAVES

1970

APPELLATION GRAVES CONTROLÉE

JEAN RICARD, PROPRIETAIRE A LÉOGNAN (GIRONDE)

WETTERWALD. BORDEAUX

MIS EN BOUTEILLE AU CHATEAU

CHATEAU
MALARTIC-LAGRAVIÈRE

Grand vin de Bordeaux

CRU CLASSÉ DE GRAVES

APPELLATION GRAVES CONTRÔLÉE

JACQUES MARLY-RIDORET PROPRIÉTAIRE A LÉOGNAN (GIRONDE)

Château Laville Haut Brion

For those who view standards of white Graves in terms of overpowering body, rich texture, and forceful tasting qualities supported on this frame, the better white wines of Laville Haut Brion are something of a model. The most recent stars are 1964, 1966, and 1967, in that order. To reach elsewhere for examples evoking these wines, a taster might think of Corton-Charlemagne in Burgundy, white Hermitage or, at lower levels of finesse, some Spanish white wines. Their concentrated impressions are associated with the texture of sweet wines though they are technically dry. Such wines are today not much in vogue. Château Olivier used to make similar wines, and when Carbonnieux overcomes technical problems its better whites also resemble those of Laville.

VINTAGE   *DATE*   *PRICE*

GUESTS

MENU   *COMMENTS*

Domaine de Chevalier

Born of skillful vinification, white wines of Chevalier are sisters of the reds in following a Graves style, achieving weight without being unbalanced, and developing only slowly with time. Finesse and fruit in particular are not forward in young wines and four or five years' bottle age is desirable for this, as for white Malartic Lagravière. Older vintages of white La Louvière belonged to this same traditional family, and so did an unusually showy white, Pontac Monplaisir, since uprooted and now making red wines. Whether or not it is only accidents of vintage character, the latest crops of Domaine seem to be veering toward more tart, smaller wines in more fashionable, less ponderous Graves style.

VINTAGE   *DATE*   *PRICE*

GUESTS

MENU   *COMMENTS*

Château Malartic-Lagravière

Another member of the small class of conventional Graves with occasional excursions in lighter, more tart wines, Malartic is more often flawed with a bit of sulphur, though usually time and airing (open two hours before serving) will diminish this. Bouquet evolved with bottle age is a strong point in this class of white wine and the nutty and earthy flavors an expected part of tasting style. Contrast this with the elegant but more modern version of white wine consciously striven for at Haut-Brion. Sémillon and Sauvignon are the usual grapes for white Graves as for Sauternes.

VINTAGE   *DATE*   *PRICE*

GUESTS

MENU   *COMMENTS*

Château Couhins

North of Carbonnieux the vineyard of Couhins has promoted itself in the ranks of white Graves by a series of well-vinified vintages that, if lacking the full scope and endurance to the taste of finest Graves, commend themselves highly by fresh fruity flavor, good balance, clean aftertaste, and sometimes distinct Graves style. Château Ferrande, Château Magence, Château Tuquet, and Cantebau-Couhins are roughly in this class, though the last is more tart and less distinctly Graves than its similarly named neighbor. The entire class of white Graves is very much a special taste, but do not decide it is not yours until you have drunk a six- or seven-year-old wine quite free of sulphur whose freshness shows it to be also free of oxidation.

VINTAGE   *DATE*   *PRICE*

GUESTS

MENU   *COMMENTS*

CHÂTEAU
LAVILLE HAUT BRION
APPELLATION GRAVES CONTRÔLÉE
Grand Cru classé
1973
SOCIÉTÉ CIVILE DES DOMAINES WOLTNER
PROPRIÉTAIRE
BORDEAUX
FRANCE
MIS EN BOUTEILLE AU CHÂTEAU   73cl

DOMAINE DE CHEVALIER
GRAND CRU CLASSE DE GRAVES

GRAND VIN DE BORDEAUX

APPELLATION GRAVES CONTROLÉE
JEAN RICARD PROPRIÉTAIRE A LÉOGNAN (GIRONDE)
MIS EN BOUTEILLE AU CHATEAU

CHATEAU
MALARTIC-LAGRAVIÈRE
Grand vin de Bordeaux
1964
GRAND CRU CLASSÉ DE GRAVES
APPELLATION GRAVES CONTRÔLÉE

JACQUES MARLY-RIDORET PROPRIÉTAIRE A LÉOGNAN (GIRONDE)

MISE EN BOUTEILLE AU CHÂTEAU

GRAND CRU CLASSÉ

CHÂTEAU COUHINS
Graves Supérieures
Appellation Graves Supérieures contrôlée

MISE EN BOUTEILLES
DU CHÂTEAU   1961

Sauternes and Barsac

Where else but in France can one find a large district five miles long and two miles wide covered with expensive vines that make salable wine only once every three years, in which every grower dreams of owning one vineyard producing but 500 bottles of wine an acre, when it makes any at all? That a nearly insane pride of ownership and fanatical attachment to prestige of accomplishment find their most extreme expression among the great sweet wines of Barsac and Sauternes seems fitting. This passionate devotion to the quality ideals of Sauternes is surely necessary; without a tinge of dementia on the part of the growers, what once were considered (with some reason) the greatest wines in the world would long since have gone the way of the pagan gods.

To taste Sauternes and understand why a little of the kamikaze spirit must be in every producer of great ones, something must be known about how the wines are made or, rather, how they "happen." Three white grape varieties compose Sauternes: Semillon occupies most of the vineyard; a fifth is in Sauvignon Blanc (called Blanc Fumé in the Loire Valley); and here and there one finds Muscadelle, a fragrant grape thought, but not proven, to add flavor to Sauternes.

Sauternes is possible because these grapes are rotted in a special way by one peculiar fungus called "noble rot." Its scientific name, *Botrytis cinerea,* has passed into wine language; "botrytized" grapes are those affected by this species of gray rot. Elsewhere, in wine or table grapes, it is an awful infection unresponsive to most common spray treatments; but in Sauternes, in Germany, in Hungary, and in the Loire, *Botrytis* is indispensable for fine sweet white wines. In California it refuses to grow wild and has to be imposed on clean grapes. It has a further unpleasant feature: it grows and spreads in weather cool enough to arrest other molds. It can infect grapes during a single autumn night at temperatures as low as 50 degrees F., and even at 35 degrees F. *Botrytis* is still creeping forward slowly rather than dying out—a very persistent infestation indeed. Not only does it settle in moisture on the grape surface caused by rain or broken oozing grapes; very high relative humidity, over 90 percent, suffices to give it a start. It has difficulty starting on berries of low sugar content but does better on richer grapes.

All this would be dreadful news were it not for the accident that this mold tastes good, or rather that, instead of the revolting, retching effect of grape juice tainted with most molds, juice from botrytized grapes has heightened and succulent flavors. Because of this, its effects turn out beneficially. First the mold loosens the skin that normally clings tightly to the juice-containing grape pulp, accelerating evaporation of water. Then the mold spreads, and its filaments penetrate the grapeskin, causing further loss of water. The grape shrivels. This sounds foul, but, in fact, instead of juice containing 20 to 25 percent sugar, the concentration caused by water loss raises sugar to as much as 40 percent. Most will be fermented into alcohol, but a handsome amount remains unfermented and results in white wine with much alcohol and natural residual sugar. If grapes were mechanically shriveled, sugar would be concentrated, but so would acidity, with unpleasant results. Luckily *Botrytis* consumes (metabolizes) acidity. Its rotting process also produces glycerol, thought to heighten the unctuosity of wines. And because the ratio of skin to liquid volume is much higher than in fresh grapes, the aromas and flavors in the skin show prominently in the finished wine.

The propensity of *Botrytis* to carry on its dirty work despite the long, cool autumn evenings and despite cold snaps that would slay or stunt a lesser mold ensures that the shriveling process will go on and on. But it begins in earnest only when sugar accumulates in the grapes. So the stage is set for what is truly *superwine,* whose aroma, taste, and texture are heightened by the concentrating effects of noble rot.

Wines of such high sugar may be awkward to ferment and need more sulphuring than plain white wines. This is a minor drawback; other inconvenient consequences of noble rot weigh far more on the grower. Grapes do not rot conveniently in unison. From late October until early December it may be necessary to comb through the vineyards snipping off properly shriveled grapes, turning bunches this way and that, only to comb through again a week later, and again, and again. . . . As many as nine pickings may be made. This labor cost may escape the attention of those who decide that sweet wines are unfashionable before they have tasted Sauternes of class, but it does not escape the notice of the grower.

The exquisite effects of noble rot are achieved by evaporating the grapes—evaporating, in other words, most of the volume of the harvest. A major St.-Émilion property can get away with 50 hectoliters per hectare (about 535 gallons per acre) and still receive its appellation. For the purely technical reasons we have just reviewed, Château Yquem makes as little as 9 hectoliters per hectare, the equivalent of some 500 bottles per acre. Appellation ceilings on production are set at 25 hectoliters per hectare (268 gallons per acre), just over half that allowed to the greatest red Bordeaux. Yquem's 90 hectares (220 acres), were they situated in the Haut Médoc, say in Pauillac, would give 35,000 cases of expensive château wine three years out of four and a like amount of wine with lower value in the occasional poor vintage. Yquem makes 8,000 to 10,000 cases of fine wine about every third year and perhaps some of a less prestigious vintage. The rest will be sold as generic Sauternes, if that. It is clear that only extremely high prices can justify such an operation as Yquem's. And do they ever; weep not for its owner! Yet when we compare the economies of the twenty superb Sauternes-Barsac vineyards that tread on the heels of Yquem with their red wine counterparts, survival of great Sauternes appears either a miracle or a long flirtation with potential ruin by growers whose determination or perhaps obsession outweighs economic logic. Simply put, the great sweet wine estates produce half as much as red wine properties, spend much more money doing it, and only in unusual years can their wines command prices fetched by known red wines in all but execrated vintages.

These facts, viticultural and economic, apply not only to Sauternes but to Germany, where "peak" wines are made under the designations *Auslese, Berenauslese,* and *Trockenberenauslese,* and to Hungary, where Tokay Aszú is also painstakingly assembled from botrytized grapes, and less significantly elsewhere in Europe.

Barsac is the largest sweet-wine-producing commune and the first met in driving south from Bordeaux; its wines are entitled to their own appellation. Appellation laws wisely give the five major properties in Barsac, as well as seven or eight lesser ones and the smaller growers, the option of calling their wines Sauternes. Technical standards are identical for the two appellations; in fact, the standards of taste by which all sweet wines from this part of the world are judged vary little from place to place. *Liquoreux* is the French word describing their distinctive quality; its usual translation as "luscious" falls short of its full meaning of essence, a medium in which fine things have been dissolved. The wines of Barsac are distinguished from those of the four communes lying south of it across a marshy stream (the Ciron) only by a touch more fruit and a touch less vinosity. Sandy gravel or gravel and clay compose its rather flat vineyards on mixed rock subsoils. This low, flat exposition occasioned immense damage in the 1956 frosts. Most of today's vines date from the late 1950s.

Preignac, Fargues, Sauternes, and Bommes are the other Sauternes communes shaped in a rough triangle of contiguous hilly vineyard south and east of the Ciron. Their soils mix pebble, gravel, calcareous rocks, some sand, and in Preignac some alluvial material, lying on subsoils ranging from clayey to hard, with gravel and freestone alternating. As one approaches the heartland of Bommes and Sauternes itself, the vineyards rise up in beautiful hills covered with pebbles and excellently exposed to ripening sun. There is no significant difference among the best lands of Bommes (the smallest commune), Sauternes, the best of Preignac, or Fargues on its western side, but the eastern sides of Fargues and Preignac drift off toward alluvial edges of the Garonne that yield inferior wines.

The mixture of savors and textures in fine Sauternes and Barsacs is indescribable. Since the wines are both sweet and alcoholic, they tire both palate and brain relatively quickly; enjoyment and common sense suggest attentive drinking of small amounts, either on their own, with a few elaborate rich dishes (either fish or *foie gras*) or with many but not all desserts. (Chocolate is a great assassin of other flavors for most palates.) Growers and merchants whose business is Sauternes are understandably thrown into nervous convulsions by the difficulty of matching such exquisite but overpowering wines with food and wildly insist upon the suitability, even the moral rectitude, of marrying these perfumed wines of lingering taste and magical honeyed texture with all manner of dishes. Certainly enjoyment is the criterion, as always, but it seems to me that one anxious to try these great concentrated wines that age so subtly could best begin to love them by drinking them after a meal, tasting carefully and keeping in mind the tortuous and elaborate story of their birth, harvesting, slow fermentation, and maturation in expensive oak casks. Whether or not your taste liberally links them with *foie gras,* boiled lobster, or other rich seafood dishes, or chooses to drink them with ripe peaches, personal preference will dictate. Once the luxurious, even statuesque

proportions and delicious aftertaste of the wines are appreciated, and their natural sweetness is seen as a quality delicately balanced by body, flavor, and finesse, the appreciative wine buff will find any excuse to drink them and will insist on drinking them cool but not frozen to the point where their aromas and aftertaste never declare themselves to the senses.

The Classification of 1855 placed Yquem at the top of the list as Grand Premier Cru, followed by nine Premiers Crus and 11 Seconds Crus. Property divisions have swelled the number of Premiers Crus to 11 and of Seconds Crus to 15. Raising up a dilapidated red wine vineyard to a position of quality, public esteem, and therefore price is a difficult business; doing the same for a sweet wine property in Sauternes-Barsac is a long, bitter, daunting prospect. The economic vise squeezes harder and more narrowly about the Sauternes grower than on a red wine proprietor. Sweet wine growers invest more—and must have more money to invest—in less wine that sells to a smaller market of connoisseurs than is the case for fine red wine. Properties such as Château de Malle that have grimly and persistently dragged up the quality of their Sauternes deserve exceptional credit, and those such as Nairac in Barsac that are setting out on the same course should get some early attention to encourage them to continue. Many other vineyards are underestimated. None of this detracts, however, from some dozen great properties whose labels represent the best of the sweet wine region in the following pages.

Under these arduous circumstances, several properties have turned to semisweet or dry wines, hoping to recoup expenses, expand markets, and benefit from the renown of their property in selling larger quantities of wine per acre than would be possible within the straitjacket of classic Sauternes specifications. These semisweet and dry whites show Bordeaux or Graves impressions; they sell moderately well in France but compete with a flood of fine white wines available to Anglo-American markets. Semisweet wines appeal little to English-speaking drinkers who know what great Sauternes can be. These maneuvers may help the area's châteaux survive, but such wines, even the Château Y label of Yquem, neither replace great sweet wines nor deserve much attention for their other qualities, at least not at present.

Château d'Yquem

Two vintages in the last generation alone defend Yquem's historic position atop the list of all Sauternes—1962 and 1967. Yet these continue to exemplify the canons of taste to which the whole district aspires: indescribably luscious, perfectly aristocratic and harmonious sweet wines. In other vintages the first dozen Sauternes properties rival Yquem, yet sell at a quarter the price. Its semisweet Château "Y" bears no tasting resemblance to the château's great sweet wines. Well before the specific concentrating action of "noble rot" was scientifically known, late harvest dates at this ancient property suggest that sweet wines were the basis for its historic fame. A little injustice in price today may be forgiven such a monument to the high ideals it continues, if occasionally, to achieve.

VINTAGE DATE PRICE

GUESTS

MENU COMMENTS

Château Climens

Fragrant, balanced, and unusually clean sweet wines of elegant Barsac style successful year after year since World War II elevate Château Climens to uncontested position among the first three or four vineyards of the district, and some would give it first place. Its style varies from full and luscious (1950, 1961, 1962) to delicate and suggestive (1953, 1966, 1970). New ownership may give it badly needed capital but also puts its future style into question. Château Coutet is its chief Barsac rival, a more erratic vineyard capable of making the best wine in a vintage (1950) but also lapsing into sulphurous and awkward wines whose average intensity falls short of that of the first properties.

VINTAGE DATE PRICE

GUESTS

MENU COMMENTS

Château Rieussec

Just to the east of Yquem, in the commune of Fargues, lie the vines of Rieussec. Its style, however, differs from the honeyed, dazzling sweet wines of Yquem, for like Rayne Vigneau, Rieussec tends toward firmer, more restrained impressions. The balance of bouquet, body, fruit, and aftertaste leave nothing to be desired, and good vintages are complete. But archetype Rieussec is more usually found in years such as 1948 or 1961 that stress authority more than overflowing richness. Yet these are mere nuances meant to encourage the reader to his own comparisons, for all great Sauternes have a single main style.

VINTAGE DATE PRICE

GUESTS

MENU COMMENTS

Château Suduiraut

Great vintages of this vineyard, of which the most recent are the classic 1962 and 1967, offer superior finesse, complete Sauternes tasting range firmly grounded on a generous constitution, and intelligent balance of alcohol and sweetness. Bouquet and aftertaste are remarkable and classical, and this marginal superiority may be perceived by contrasting the wines with excellent ones just below it in rank such as Guiraud, Sigalas Rabaud, Rabaud Promis, and the Doisy twins. Château Filhot occasionally rises to this style, as did Lafaurie-Peyraguey, but the last decade's performance encourages use of Suduiraut's label to represent this Sauternes family.

VINTAGE DATE PRICE

GUESTS

MENU COMMENTS

SAUTERNES-APPELLATION CONTRÔLÉE

Château d'Yquem
Lur-Saluces

— • — 1966 — • —

MIS EN BOUTEILLE AU CHÂTEAU

P. CHAMEAU Bᵉ

1970

Château Climens

1ᵉʳ CRU

Haut-Barsac

APPELLATION BARSAC CONTROLÉE

Héritiers H. Gounouilhou, Propriétaires

CHÂTEAU RIEUSSEC

1ᵉʳ Grand Cru

SAUTERNÉS

1955

APPELLATION SAUTERNES CONTROLÉE

Mis en Bouteille au Château   Sté du Château Rieussec, Propre

MIS EN BOUTEILLES AU CHATEAU

SAUTERNES Appellation contrôlée

Château Suduiraut

1962
Sauternes

(Ancien cru du Roy)

Château de Rayne-Vigneau

This is one of a cluster of superior vineyards lying on the Bommes side of Sauternes and sharing some points of style with Rieussec. Its balanced and impressive wines do not lack sweetness or, more exactly, the intangible mingling of qualities the French call *liquoreux*, but authority of flavor predominates, and the character coming through the wines is more memorable than its power or lusciousness. This distinctiveness can be noticed in comparing this wine with balanced and desirable Sauternes such as Romer, Suau, or Caillou that lack precisely this assertive individuality that recommends Rayne-Vigneau. Unfortunately the wine is poorly distributed abroad.

VINTAGE   DATE   PRICE

GUESTS

MENU   COMMENTS

Château La Tour Blanche

A handsome vineyard and a wine that succeeds by being complete rather than unusual, La Tour Blanche is a curiosity in that it was donated to the French State by a former owner and has become an enological school. In consequence much of its wine is sold to French officials. This academic environment has not always restrained the use of sulphur, palpable in many vintages. At the opposite pole in management from this government vineyard is Château de Malle, in Preignac, whose wines rise annually in quality, reflecting the stubborn devotion of the owner, and look shortly to overtake in performance many of the better-known labels appearing on these two pages. Perhaps Sauternes, if not everything, is better left to private enterprise.

VINTAGE   DATE   PRICE

GUESTS

MENU   COMMENTS

Château Guiraud

Beginning in 1961 and continuing through 1962, 1966, 1967, and 1970, the wines of Guiraud have made an increasing impression upon the growing number of wine lovers responsible for reviving appreciation of the extraordinary sweet wines of Bordeaux in English-speaking markets. Guiraud are typically even wines, notably clean to smell and taste, that carry their fruit enveloped in a luscious body. Balanced and forthright, they may lack slightly in delicacy of finish, if one must quibble. The revival of reputation of this vineyard should encourage more recent efforts such as those at Château Nairac in Barsac in their difficult task of rejuvenating high-quality sweet wine vineyards.

VINTAGE   DATE   PRICE

GUESTS

MENU   COMMENTS

Château Doisy-Daëne
Château Doisy-Védrines

As in another Sauternes pair originating in an estate division (Sigalas-Rabaud and Rabaud-Promis), it is a bit cruel to speak in the same breath of the work of two different winegrowers, albeit neighbors. But both properties have achieved success in the last decade in putting forward wines emphasizing fruit, elegance, and a bouquet that characterizes (if marginally) the fine qualities of Barsac as against those of Sauternes. Neither vineyard has yet attained superlative levels, but both have sent out wines complete in constitution and often marked by elegant perfume and clean-tasting qualities. They are well worth collecting and comparing with other Barsacs, and their good vintages surpass inferior ones of far more famous names.

VINTAGE   DATE   PRICE

GUESTS

MENU   COMMENTS

MÉDAILLE D'OR
PARIS 1867

MÉDAILLE D'OR
PARIS 1878

CHATEAU
DE
RAYNE-VIGNEAU

MIS EN BOUTEILLES AU CHATEAU

1966

1er GRAND CRU
SAUTERNES

APPELLATION SAUTERNES CONTROLÉE

PRODUCE OF FRANCE
G. RAOUX · PROPRIÉTAIRE

1967

DONATION OSIRIS

Château
LA TOUR BLANCHE

1er CRU CLASSÉ

SAUTERNES

Appellation Sauternes Contrôlée

MIS EN BOUTEILLE AU CHATEAU

ÉCOLE DE VITICULTURE ET D'ŒNOLOGIE · BOMMES (GIRONDE)

GRAND PRIX   PARIS 1900
EXPOSITION UNIVERSELLE

CHÂTEAU GUIRAUD

1er CRU SAUTERNES

Appellation Sauternes contrôlée

1961

MIS EN BOUTEILLES AU CHÂTEAU

P. RIVAL, PROPRIÉTAIRE   WETTERWALD FRÈRES

GRAND VIN
SEC

du

CHATEAU DOISY-DAËNE

APPELLATION BORDEAUX SUPÉRIEUR CONTROLÉE

· MIS EN BOUTEILLES AU CHATEAU ·

R. DUBOURDIEU · PROPRIÉTAIRE A BARSAC

CHATEAU DOISY-VÉDRINES

GRAND CRU CLASSÉ EN 1855

1967

Ste CIV. IM. CH DOISY-VÉDRINES
CASTÉJA, PROPRIÉTAIRE
BARSAC

APPELLATION SAUTERNES CONTROLÉE

MIS EN BOUTEILLES AU CHATEAU

Saint-Émilion

St.-Émilion is *the* major appellation of the Right Bank of Bordeaux, as the districts east of the Dordogne River are collectively known. It is a huge, fine appellation; and unlike the Médoc, it is not subdivided into smaller, better ones. Satellite appellations hyphenating its distinguished name to their own do hang on its skirts (see page 33), but few are important to English-speaking markets. St.-Émilion violently resists generalizations; an exception to any description lurks over each hill and around each turn.

In rough outline a rising plain with moderate changes of elevation, peppered with clay pockets and sandy soils and alluvial traces, extends from the flat perimeter of Pomerol up to the town of St.-Émilion. Here an abrupt change occurs. Especially on the town's southeast walls, vineyards virtually spill over a cliff on whose limestone descent vines cling bravely. This escarpment varies in pitch, extends irregularly for about half a mile, sloping off at either end. Then, in the southeast corner of the appellation area, a series of high hills come down into a muddy alluvial plain through which the Dordogne weaves and slides, and these hills fade off in the east toward St.-Christophe-des-Bardes into rolling country less good for vines.

Traditionally St.-Émilion wines are divided into those of the plain between Pomerol and the town (Vin de Graves) and those of the steep lands on the other side of the town and on into the hills (Vin des Côtes). Certainly it is possible to distinguish family resemblances in appearance, odor, and taste in properties such as Cheval Blanc, Corbin, Figeac, Fonroque, and others grouped squarely on the plain. Strong resemblances between famous properties of the Côtes—Ausone, Belair, Magdelaine, to name a few—are also not to be denied. But irrepressible variety and paradox leap out of each vintage to upset the usefulness of this simpleminded division. Obscure properties such as Petit-Faurie-de-Soutard northeast of St.-Émilion have produced light-colored, silky wines, perplexing and refined, that, by the rule, should have come from center Côtes. Dark, astringent clarets made at La Gaffelière come from vines that run up the escarpment to intermingle with those producing unctuous, pale, and seductive Belair. Less famous vineyards such as Haut-Sarpe lie nearly cheek by jowl with Balestard-La Tonnelle. Neither the fruity, gentle, velvety Haut-Sarpe nor the eccentric, occasionally dazzling Balestard tastes as the geographic generality would have it. The aristocratic, brilliant Côtes wines of Magdelaine look over their shoulder, as it were, into a pocket containing both loose supple wines from Matras and astringent ones from Tertre-Daugay, and one could go on at length in this disconcerting way. No doubt it is worth the trouble to locate a St.-Émilion when drinking it, and no doubt there is a vague division into plain (Graves) and Côtes. But it will do the adventurer no good to insist upon it or upon its geological foundation when the glass before him contains St.-Émilion of a distinctive style.

It seems more useful to draw attention to a range of wine types of which St.-Émilion is capable. Rarely but regularly, and more regularly in the heart of the Côtes than elsewhere, we find claret whose medium-light color, high perfume unsullied by earthy or vegetal odors, clarity of tasting impressions, and delicate aftertaste remind the palatal memory of fine Médocs. Their more alcoholic composition and slightly grainy texture may hint at their Right Bank origin, but hint only. Such elegant St.-Émilions were made in 1945, 1947, a few in 1949, in 1952, and in 1955. A horrendous break in the chain of St.-Émilion and Pomerol vintages occurred in 1956, when ferocious

frosts in February killed thousands of vines. A carefully evolved age structure of plants was shattered in many vineyards, requiring entire replanting; balances between Merlot and Bouchet (Cabernet Franc) were overthrown, and entire properties were wiped out. While not all the old vines that play a vital role in refined clarets were destroyed, only in 1967 do we meet lighter, more elegant St.Émilion.

The next identifiable style of St.-Émilion clarets finds medium color again but with more vinosity than coloring matter in the balance, much alcohol, an unctuous address to the taste, and often a sweetish sensation in the aftertaste—not quite the same thing as the finesse of the first type of St.-Émilion. Easy to drink, heady, slightly overripe in impression, such clarets are found more often on the plain and in the eastern portion of the appellation. Betimes lacking fixed acidity, their maturation in bottle is rapid. Many such wines appear in the 1964 vintage—ripe, touched with rot, lacking in backbone. They present a curious if not unpleasing combination of high alcohol with insufficient verve to be judged complete.

A third ensemble of tasting qualities specific to St.-Émilion offers a sort of classic model of its wines. Basically rich in all elements, heady in bouquet, dark in color, arresting to the taste in their grainy or, if one prefers, earthy texture, such wines offer broad assertive development in the mouth, invigorating if not surprising taste, hearty and satisfying. While it is understandable that writers have groped to compare such clarets with some rich red wines of Burgundy, this apposition seems to me to hinder rather than help appreciation of either. The better wines of this typical St.-Émilion style hold well with age, improving in bouquet and deepening in flavor. Lesser versions also become attractive early, hold their qualities for several years, and tend to topple from this plateau rather readily, becoming hollow and coarse. But good clarets of this style are most generous and steady performers once recovered from bottle sickness. They appeal to fanciers of classic Bordeaux to the degree to which they attach more finesse to the aftertaste, more gloss to the texture, and less earthiness to the general impressions. From ordinary to excellent, these characteristic St.-Émilion wines are a fundamental resource of the fine wine drinker. Numerous clarets of this stamp are made every good vintage, which on the Right Bank includes the years 1955, 1959, 1961, 1964, 1966, 1967, 1970, 1971, and 1973, all now bottled.

Lastly, in exceptional crops in which grapes ripen excellently yet retain adequate acidity, there occur concentrated fiery clarets marked by intense perfume, abundant vinosity, and forceful backbone—wines that taste remarkable from the day they are made throughout a long life. Here the rougher qualities of the St.Émilion appellation are quite forgotten as one appreciates a virility and scope of body and flavor found in no other wines. Noble St.-Émilion of this rare species were seen in 1945, some in 1947, fewer in 1949, and more in 1961.

These four groupings are not suggested in order to incite the wine drinker to try to cram into them every bottle of St.-Émilion uncorked within his reach. They are offered only to assist him in organizing his experience of an enormous district containing hundreds of individual properties, many small, and hence sporting too much variety for any rigorous description.

Right Bank wines, St.-Émilion among them, have risen in popular appreciation steadily throughout this century, though until shortly after World War I they were not so well considered by the ruling Bordeaux standards that stressed finesse. During the 1950s a classification of St.-Émilion wines was constructed, dividing its clarets into four tiers of aristocracy over and above the appellation St.-Émilion. Cheval Blanc and Ausone were esteemed the finest, followed by ten other properties, nine of which lie in the Côtes (Premiers Grands Crus). Third, 71 other vineyards were ranked Grand Cru Classé; of these 16 are situated in the Graves, or plain, and the rest in the Côtes; but the Côtes in question are far more generously defined than the narrower heartland of thinly covered limestone gullies and bluffs from which come the most elegant wines neighboring the town of St.-Émilion.

The ten properties following Ausone and Cheval Blanc are set out by the Syndicate for the Defense of St.-Émilion as follows, with approval by decree of the Ministry of Agriculture.

> CHÂTEAU BEAUSÉJOUR (Duffau)
> CHÂTEAU BEAUSÉJOUR (Becot)
> CHÂTEAU BELAIR
> CHÂTEAU CANON
> CHÂTEAU-FIGEAC (Vin de Graves)
> CHÂTEAU LA GAFFELIÈRE
> CHÂTEAU MAGDELAINE
> CHÂTEAU PAVIE
> CHÂTEAU TROTTEVIEILLE
> CLOS-FOURTET

St.-Émilion must limit itself to 42 hectoliters per hectare (about 450 gallons per acre) and attain 11 percent alcohol. Wines attaining 11.5 percent alcohol and passing inspection by the tasting board may call themselves Grand Cru, the fourth quality designation, and should rank between the 71 Grands Crus Classés and the ubiquitous St.-Émilion appellation. Having earlier given a negative opinion of the validity of such classifications made by the people whose vineyards the classifications are supposed to rank, I must ask what purpose is served by a system that sets up 71 properties in hereditary possession of a title Grand Cru Classé but admits to a lower classification only those wines attaining 11.5 percent alcohol? Fortunately, the lower reaches of the classification are deservedly disregarded by both the public and the wine trade.

A number of important St.-Émilion properties are openly traded on the Bordeaux market, but many others are either sold to small groups of shippers or monopolized by one shipper. This makes life more difficult, and more expensive, for the wine enthusiast; the unusual and frequently remarkable wines of Château Magdelaine sold through the important firm of J. P. Moueix are difficult to find, whereas the dull and frequently unpleasant wines of Château Ripeau sold through the large firm of Lichine & Cie., now part of Bass-Charrington breweries, can be avoided only by a serious effort. If there is a moral for the consumer, it is to sample the famous wines out of curiosity and to disregard price in adventuring among the lesser ones, within minimum limits of price below which fine wines are unlikely to occur.

As a glance at the map will suggest, St.-Émilion and Pomerol are some 40 minutes by car or bus from the Médoc and Graves districts.

As the following story will suggest, these two Right Bank areas are separated from the vineyards north and southwest of Bordeaux by attitudes far more than distance and are characterized by smaller estates. Also, their marketplace is less organized and less internationally minded than that of the major growths of Médoc, Graves, and Sauternes.

Late one morning I was trying to get into the *chai* of a major St.-Émilion property to taste its current crop of wine. There were urgent business reasons for doing so, for we had to act on an offer by a neighboring property and could not buy and list both wines in that year. As usual, there was no one in the cellars. An agricultural workman turned up and trotted off to find the cellarmaster, who in turn politely rushed to the scene by bicycle with the exciting news that he did not have the keys. The *régisseur* (general manager) had the keys, it was thought. Indeed, pulling up in the usual gray Citroen was the *régisseur*, with keys. He, the cellarmaster, and I tasted and discussed the wine in the cautious, mutually suspicious way more common in the past than today in the Bordeaux district. Finally, satisfied that I was not an utter dunce on the subject of wine, and slowly persuaded that my compelling object in life was not to find fault with their vintage of Château X in order to argue some fraction off the price, they began to exchange actual information. By the time the church bells of St.-Émilion struck noon, the conversation had gotten genuinely animated. Now, both men were near sixty and had spent a lifetime producing a great wine of St.-Émilion; more likely than not, so had their fathers. As I was about to leave, the following exchange took place.

"Tell us something if you please, monsieur."

"Voluntarily, if I am able, monsieur."

"You who travel much, as for the wines of the Médoc, tell us, are they truly good?"

Fortunately I was too stunned to laugh and so lose my new status; I gave a brief description of some signal differences between the finest wines of the Médoc and those of St.-Émilion, such as their own.

Régisseur and cellarmaster, both of them old enough to be my father, stumped off discussing the remarkable news they had just received. Speeding off to Château Troplong Mondot before it closed to taste our parcel of 1964, I did wonder for a moment on the improbability of the wine business and everything else. Had my grandfather's brother not been implicated in the assassination of a czarist minister, the family would never have left Odessa, and on a cold April morning in 1965 I would not be explaining the taste of Médoc to two St.-Émilion wine makers whose ancestors had lived for a millennium with the Médoc on their physical horizon.

The insularity of French fine wine makers is difficult to imagine, and it is either sobering or intoxicating (take your choice) to realize that such remarkable wines are made by people who typically only know their own property. This may explain the often phenomenal individuality of many of the Bordeaux estates' wines, and it may not, but it is a human curiosity nowhere better seen than in St.-Émilion.

Château Ausone

A remarkable small vineyard capable of producing the most refined wines of St.-Émilion, Ausone shares a place with Cheval Blanc at the head of the appellation. Quality declined after the 1956 frost disaster. Recent prices reflect this poor show, but the latest vintages evince substantial recovery in the wines. Superbly vinous yet elegant, Ausone lasts beautifully on the senses; great years such as 1945, 1947, 1952, and 1955 are memorable for the finest points of the wine—fiery color, pure bouquet, and a subtle series of tasting impressions entirely free of earthy overtones that mar so many wines from this region.

VINTAGE   *DATE*   *PRICE*

GUESTS

MENU   *COMMENTS*

Château Belair

Belair belongs to the proprietors of Ausone, and the two wines are aged together in impressive stone cellars carved into the cliff of the town of St.-Émilion. Belair is a confusing wine with special attractions. The pallid color in barrel and bottle gives a perverse introduction. In fact, good vintages show unusual character and finesse, though without any generous surplus of flavor or grapyness. It echoes many qualities of Ausone without attaining the perfect balance and remarkable individuality of which the best Ausone is capable. Some vintages are loose in quality and taste awkwardly. Unripe crops are hopeless, but successful ones such as 1952, 1955, and, one hopes, 1971 offer elegant St.-Émilion wines of uncommon style.

VINTAGE   *DATE*   *PRICE*

GUESTS

MENU   *COMMENTS*

Château Magdelaine

Situated at the edge of the *Côte* around the town of St.-Émilion, this small vineyard, little distributed abroad, varies between wines that fall short of adequate fruit and body and taste hollow and thin and rarer ones that blossom not as generous or powerful wines but as racy and exciting ones that engage the senses in a teasing manner reminiscent of some lighter Margaux wines. The bouquet of fine Magdelaine is restrained and slow to evolve in the glass; to the taste also the wine is hesitant, growing gradually in appeal. The wines on this page are but the most prominent of a collection of *Côte* wines stressing finesse; others include Cadet Piola and Curé Bon La Madeleine. The best Magdelaines are unique clarets.

VINTAGE   *DATE*   *PRICE*

GUESTS

MENU   *COMMENTS*

Château Beauséjour Duffau-Lagarrosse, Château Beauséjour Becot

The Beauséjour twin properties neighbor Châteaux l'Angélus, Canon, and Magdelaine. Their similar wines offer rich body in healthy years, a vinous and complete impression to the senses, flavor less refined than the best and maturing well in bottle up to a point. They stress a broader attack to the taste than others on this page and fall into more conventional models of St.-Émilion wines. The St.-Émilion merchants consider them among the first dozen wines, and they should know, but my experience places them lower than the official classification the locals defend so stoutly.

VINTAGE   *DATE*   *PRICE*

GUESTS

MENU   *COMMENTS*

1973

CHATEAU AUSONE
SAINT·EMILION

APPELLATION
SAINT-ÉMILION 1er GRAND CRU CLASSÉ
CONTROLÉE

Vve C. VAUTHIER & J. DUBOIS-CHALLON
PROPRIÉTAIRES A SAINT-ÉMILION (GIRONDE)

MIS EN BOUTEILLES AU CHATEAU

DÉPOSÉ   GIP - Libourne

CHATEAU BELAIR
SAINT·EMILION

APPELLATION SAINT-EMILION CONTRÔLÉE

1958

EDOUARD DUBOIS-CHALLON
PROPRIÉTAIRE A SAINT-EMILION

MIS EN BOUTEILLES AU CHATEAU

DÉPOSÉ   Offset GIP - Libourne

SAINT-ÉMILION 1er GRAND CRU CLASSÉ

CHÂTEAU MAGDELAINE
1955

Mis en Bouteille au Château

JEAN PIERRE MOUEIX   APPELLATION SAINT-ÉMILION
PROPRIÉTAIRES A St ÉMILION   1er GRAND CRU CLASSÉ CONTRÔLÉE

PREMIER GRAND CRU CLASSE

1971

SAINT-EMILION

La qualité, l'origine et le millésime de ce vin
sont garantis par le certificat d'agréage de
l'Institut National des Appellations d'Origine

Château
Beauséjour

APPELLATION SAINT-ÉMILION 1er GRAND CRU CLASSÉ CONTRÔLÉE

M. BÉCOT - 33330 Saint-Emilion   73 cl

Mis en bouteille au château

Saint-Emilion

CHATEAU BEAUSÉJOUR
PREMIER GRAND CRU CLASSÉ

APPELLATION SAINT-EMILION CONTRÔLÉE

1969

Héritiers Duffau-Lagarrosse
Propres à Saint-Emilion (Gironde)

MIS EN BOUTEILLES AU CHATEAU

DÉPOSÉ   ROUSSEAU IMP

Château Cheval Blanc

Cheval Blanc is paired with Ausone in classifications, now sells above it, but differs completely from it in style. Its chocolate color, hot bouquet, ponderous attack to the taste, grainy texture and pugnacious aftertaste mark it as a wine of the plains (Vin de Graves), and in fact it sidles up to the border of Pomerol. The 1956 frost was particularly murderous in this low-lying vineyard, a veritable saucer designed to hold cold air. Replanted vines are now approaching proper age. In fine years Cheval Blanc is remarkable in bouquet, suggesting vanilla, ripe fruit, and voluminous wine to follow. Its best examples are sweeping, dramatic, and quite exciting to taste; thin vintages are awkward or worse. Comparisons with Burgundy are silly, those with Rhône wines useless. By traditional standards this wine risks being coarse; by popular standards it equals the best.

VINTAGE   DATE   PRICE

GUESTS

MENU   COMMENTS

Château-Figeac

Across the road from Cheval Blanc, the extensive and remarkable vineyard of Figeac unfolds across undulating terrain. Capable of extraordinary successes in hot years such as 1947 and in sound ones such as 1964, among others, it also gave wines of exceptional texture and glossy finish in dull years such as 1955. The years 1962 and 1967 were lapses. The best examples are harmonious, good in hue though not outstanding in brilliance, excellent in bouquet, and follow with subtle tasting impressions sometimes tinged with the earthy or mineral impression usual to wines of this sector. Some neighboring vineyard managers consider the unusually late harvests practiced at Figeac unwise. Like most vineyards of the appellation, Figeac has difficulty making even attractive wines in years of insufficient ripeness.

VINTAGE   DATE   PRICE

GUESTS

MENU   COMMENTS

Clos-Fourtet

Well-exposed slopes west of the town of St.-Émilion and extending toward the plain make up this vineyard. Like Gaffelière, its color and backbone are frequent strong points. To the St.-Émilionnais it is a "hard" wine; its slower development in bottle and sinewy dryish impression prompt comparisons with Médoc wines. At maturity the bouquet of successful crops such as 1947 and 1953 is flowery, memorable, and very fine. Small crops of harder wines such as 1961 and 1971 lend themselves to laying down. Its color is usually brilliant and the total impression of a good ten-year-old claret from this vineyard is dramatic though its precise identity can be elusive. It is bordered by Grand Pontet, among others, also well-colored wine but lacking the refinement of Clos-Fourtet. It ranks near the top, at about the level of Magdelaine, though in a different style.

VINTAGE   DATE   PRICE

GUESTS

MENU   COMMENTS

Château La Gaffelière
(Formerly Gaffelière Naudes)

Not to be confused with the medium-bodied, bland wines of Canon-La-Gaffelière, the vines of this distinguished vineyard nestle into the cliff of the town of St.-Émilion, descend along it, and continue on to flatter terrain, past the handsome stone château. Characteristically dark in color and brilliant, Gaffelière is inherently excellent claret and superior St.-Émilion of a vital yet refined family, but it is often marred by treatment after harvest and during barrel care. Good vintages resemble some Médocs in their color, elegant bouquet, and aftertaste suggesting skin and oak rather than earth and alcohol. More than commonly astringent for this appellation, some vintages have become seamy in bottle with too much volatile acidity. However, distinguished wines such as 1961, 1966, and, when last tasted, 1970 are valuable additions to St.-Émilion appreciation. This is potentially a great wine and one worth tasting in each good vintage.

VINTAGE   DATE   PRICE

GUESTS

MENU   COMMENTS

Château Cheval-Blanc

1971

St.Emilion

1er Grand Cru Classé

HÉRITIERS FOURCAUD-LAUSSAC

PROPRIÉTAIRES

Mis en bouteille au Château   (FRANCE)

APPELLATION SAINT-ÉMILION 1er GRAND CRU CLASSÉ CONTRÔLÉE

PRODUCE OF FRANCE

CHATEAU-FIGEAC

PREMIER GRAND CRÛ CLASSÉ

St ÉMILION

Appellation St-Emilion 1er Grand Crû Classé Contrôlée

1971

MIS EN BOUTEILLES AU CHÂTEAU

A. MANONCOURT PROPre A St ÉMILION (FRANCE)

Bouteille No 061519   PRODUCT OF FRANCE

Clos-Fourtet

PREMIER GRAND CRU

Saint-Emilion

APPELLATION SAINT-ÉMILION CONTROLÉE

François LURTON

PROPRIÉTAIRE

SAINT-ÉMILION

1954

Imp. ARCÉ, Bordeaux

CHÂTEAU

LA GAFFELIÈRE

1er Grand Cru Classé

SAINT-EMILION

1971

Comte de Malet Roquefort

PROPRIÉTAIRE A St EMILION (GIRONDE)

APPELLATION SAINT-ÉMILION 1er GRAND CRU CLASSÉ CONTROLÉE

GIP - Libourne

Château Pavie

Pavie clings to the slopes of a large hill atop which are several vineyards. Troplong Mondot is the largest, and an obscure but often potent dark wine, Larcis Ducasse, is a neighbor. Pavie's vineyards virtually peer out across the Dordogne, and this excellent exposition produces ripe grapes giving a generous, heady wine whose style is squarely St.-Émilion in its combination of vigor, round abundant tasting impressions, rapid development in bottle, and frankness. The vinification is careful, and its clarets are clean and pleasing. I prefer the older-style wines of longer maceration exemplified by the 1950 vintage, but 1964 and 1967 fit the attractive, hearty model suggesting strong alcohol that today's commerce favors. Château Trottevieile is a similar wine in some ways, full, round, and quickly drinkable but touched with a vulgarity from which Pavie is exempt.

VINTAGE   *DATE*   *PRICE*

GUESTS

MENU   *COMMENTS*

Château Fombrauge

This wine is in another and far lower class altogether and is selected to represent a whole collection of lighter-bodied St.-Émilion wines more rapidly produced and intended for immediate consumption. It might be said to have "bourgeois growth" standing. Medium light in color, straightforward and pleasing in taste, such wines should be half the price of Magdelaine or Gaffelière. They come just behind an intermediate class of which Fonroque, Corbin, and Canon-La-Gaffelière are examples, wines differing in assertiveness, more from the plain, less from the slopes. The supple qualities and quick impressions of wines such as Fombrauge make them useful, and yet they retain distinct appellation and even individual character, enough to make them educational and interesting to drink. St.-Émilion and the Fronsac region offer many such bottles.

VINTAGE   *DATE*   *PRICE*

GUESTS

MENU   *COMMENTS*

Château l'Angélus

To one side of the best part of the *Côte,* away from Magdelaine, a little family of generous, mellow, and most agreeable wines make their home around l'Angélus, the best known. This is balanced wine but without the drama of great power or the mystery of great finesse. Its aroma and bouquet represent the tasting qualities well: hearty, of definite appellation character, untroubled by some of the more elusive ups and downs of properties that aim for more complicated results. A medium red color, clear rather than brilliant, announces a sound wine. Fonplégade, Villemaurine, and Soutard are some relatively comparable wines. Individuality is certainly present, but it is not so pronounced as among the top class or the small family of unusual wines represented here by Château Balestard La Tonnelle.

VINTAGE   *DATE*   *PRICE*

GUESTS

MENU   *COMMENTS*

Château Balestard La Tonnelle

I have chosen this label to suggest the wealth and variety of smaller St.-Émilion châteaux of little or no international fame. Others would have served the purpose—Couvent des Jacobins for its unusual 1957, Haut Sarpe for its strangely fruity wines, Larcis Ducasse for its tough classic 1945 and 1961, Grand Corbin Despagne for its 1947. Balestard, in years of small production or great ripeness, comes up with dark wines of glossy finish, curious elegance, and insistent attraction. It is a hermit insofar as international trade is concerned. The 1955, 1961, and 1964 give truffled aromas, delicious tasting qualities.

On the label is a text over the signature of France's greatest poet, François Villon, praising Balestard. The date of his birth given there is wrong by ten years, the date of his death by 30, and Villon never wrote these lines. Everything else about the wine is fine.

VINTAGE   *DATE*   *PRICE*

GUESTS

MENU   *COMMENTS*

Appellation St-Emilion 1er Grand Crû Classé Contrôlée

PREMIER GRAND CRU CLASSÉ

Château Pavie

SAINT-EMILION

1969

MÉDAILLES D'OR
Expositions Universelles
PARIS 1867 - 1889 - 1900
DIPLOMES D'HONNEUR
LIÉGE 1905, LONDRES 1908
HORS-CONCOURS BORDEAUX 1907

VALETTE, PROPRIÉTAIRES A SAINT-ÉMILION (GIRONDE)

Olhat GIP - Libourne

CHATEAU FOMBRAUGE

GRAND CRU

SAINT-EMILION

APPELLATION SAINT-ÉMILION GRAND CRU CONTROLÉE

1969

Sté DE FOMBRAUGE, PROPRIÉTAIRE A St CHRISTOPHE DES BARDES GIRONDE

MISE EN BOUTEILLES AU CHATEAU

SPÉCIM Grand Cru Classé

St EMILION

L'ANGÉLUS

1970

CHÂTEAU L'ANGÉLUS
DE BOÜARD DE LAFOREST & FILS
PROPRIÉTAIRES A SAINT-EMILION - GIRONDE

Appellation St Emilion Contrôlée

J.B.F.Bx

PRODUCE OF FRANCE

MIS EN BOUTEILLE AU CHATEAU

Chau BALESTARD-LA TONNELLE

1955

Vierge Marie, gente déesse,
Garde-moi place en paradis :
Oncque n'aurai joie ni liesse
Ici-bas, puisqu'il n'est permis
De boire ce divin nectar,
Qui porte nom de Balestard ;

Qu'à gens fortunés en ce monde,
Or, suis miséreux et pauvret,
Si donc au Ciel ce vin abonde,
Viens, doulce Mort, point ne m'effraye.
Porte-moi parmi les élus
Qui, là-haut, savourent ce cru.

FRANÇOIS VILLON
(1431-1465)

Extrait de « Saint-Emilion,
son histoire, ses monuments, ses grands vins »,
par le Dr Pierre Bertin-Roulleau.

APPELLATION

St Emilion Grand Crû Classé

CONTRÔLÉE

R. Capdemourlin-Berthon
Propriétaire

MISE EN BOUTEILLES
AU CHATEAU

Pomerol

As its high prices testify, Pomerol is the most demanded appellation in Bordeaux after St.-Julien in the Médoc and is the most expensive appellation of its size. Reasons do not have to be sought for in those second sets of accounts that all French companies (and no others) are said to keep. The usual quality of Pomerol wines is very high; its better wines are not only utterly delicious but display nearly all their attractions early in life. Energetic and faithful demand from northern France, Benelux, and the northern countries underlies this expensive demand "floor." Also, a greater proportion of its wines is sold direct from château to restaurants and private parties than is the case elsewhere in Bordeaux; higher prices can thereby be obtained, as small California wineries have also discovered. And it is not so large a district; approximately 250 harvest declarations are entered each year, but over 100 are from growers owning less than l hectare (2.47 acres), and 200 are from those possessing less than 2 hectares. These account for less than half the vineyard area with the balance in the hands of a collection of middle-size properties.

The appellation is defined as the commune of Pomerol and a bordering parcel of Libourne. It is a rough square of vineyard some 3 miles (5 kilometers) on a side extending from Libourne to the borders of Lalande de Pomerol. The best and biggest properties lie north and east of the village of Catusseau, slightly off the geographic center of the district. Merlot, Cabernet Franc (Bouchet), and some Cabernet Sauvignon make up the vineyards. The undulating plain of topsoil, sandy, gravelly, or clayey, lies over similar lower layers, the best parts of which have an iron-rich sandstone vividly called "iron dross" (translation bowdlerized). The drainage is better and the soil more mineral than the eye might readily lead one to suppose.

Pomerol has some quirks as an appellation. There is no *label*—the tasting board in which representatives of growers, shippers, and brokers sample the wines of the district, unlabeled, to approve each wine's right to the appellation. There is no classification, though Château Pétrus commands First Growth prices and a dozen other *crus* are traded as if they were second growths. It is virtually a closed market; with few important properties whose wines are eagerly demanded, the temptation to enter into "exclusivity arrangements" with shippers is very strong, and the modest quantities produced by Pomerol estates make these arrangements more apparently workable than is the case with larger estates. Since a shipper monopolizing an important Pomerol growth will be less widely represented in foreign markets than the sum of all shippers selling an openly traded wine, consumers have some difficulty in getting their hands on all the major wines. This is especially true in the United States, where the market is geographically dispersed and is victimized by abusive state laws that favor monopolies. While the permitted output per hectare in Pomerol is a low 40 hectoliters (423 gallons per acre), the alcoholic degree demanded, 10.5 percent, is less than St.-Émilion's 11 percent or more frequent 11.5 percent. The total area under vine is in flux but does not reach 2,500 acres (1,000 hectares), giving a legal limit of something less than half a million cases a year, or more when overproduction is sanctioned by the Ministry of Agriculture.

The Bordeaux wine trade often makes a loose distinction between two sorts of Pomerol wines. On the one hand, we have dark, powerful clarets charged with body; archetypes of this genus of Pomerol are Trotanoy and Pétrus. On the other hand, more silky, Médoc-like, seemingly fragile and genteel wines also occur, represented by Vieux Certan, Nenin, and Petit-Village, among others. But it is no service to beginning wine drinkers to insist upon this rough distinction. Above all, the notion that there are "light" Pomerols should be no license to palm off second- and third-rank wines lacking a full range of tasting qualities. Intensity of taste, length on the palate, harmony between bouquet and taste and between the successive impressions, and final finesse remain conventional standards of quality for Pomerol as for all fine wines. Since the district contains a limited number of great names, it lends itself to comparative tastings—efficient schooling in the differences among fine Pomerols of a given vintage.

The general tasting qualities of the wines are not difficult to evoke. Both delicate and luscious fine examples are marked first of all by a rush of fruit and a sense of unctuosity. If the wines are not technically so refined as those of Médoc and Graves, the charm and character lent by these accessible, immediate qualities saves them from vulgarity. It remains for a good constitution with adequate acidity to save them from superficiality; and in good vintages, in good properties, this is the case. Their exceptionally rapid initial development in bottle has obvious practical appeal, but as often as not it is mirrored in a somewhat disappointing old age. Since tender fruity impressions and unctuosity make up so much of the wines' charm, when these dry out with time the remains have little to support them except alcohol. Therefore, in cellaring Pomerols for the future, intensity of taste, balance between acidity and immediate appeal, and length on the palate are cardinal points to look for beyond immediate savor and supple impressions.

Church and monastic names ring through the titles of Pomerol and St.-Émilion vineyards—here a *clos* of a convent, there a Chapelle Hermitage, and so on. Owners tirelessly point to the early establishment of the order of Saint John of Jerusalem and further back to Christian and pagan Roman origins. But in fact Pomerol and St.-Émilion are latecomers to viticultural importance. During the 1700s, as great Médoc estates were taking roughly their present form, Pomerol and St.-Émilion were petty vineyards. Scores of imposing vineyards in the Médoc and Graves figure in the register of properties confiscated from the French nobility during the Revolution of 1789–94, but only one substantial Pomerol estate. Not until the twentieth century did Pomerol and its prices rise above the mass of second-rank regions of Bordeaux. A century earlier, the name Pomerol was hardly known.

This history bears on our understanding and appreciation of Pomerol and St.-Émilion wines today. Two contradictory tendencies support new and strong demand for their wines. First is a vulgarization of taste, at least by old-fashioned standards. Second, technological progress has made it possible for small proprietors and those peripheral to the most favored sites to obtain wines impeccable from a technical point of view. Knowledge, effort, and skill count for more in the final result than they did in the past. To put this another way is to see it better: A century ago no one would have paid premium prices for wines lacking the special finesse of Médoc, Graves, or Sauternes. Equally true, a modest proprietor in Pomerol or St.-Émilion could not have made wine as clean, fruity, generous, and delicious as that which today receives these prices.

Pomerol vineyards and their wines give a healthy shove to some of the superficial and facile generalizations that get slung about freely in English-language writings on Bordeaux wines. I can think of few pundits in New York or London who would identify the dark, vigorous, and assertive clarets of Château Trotanoy or Château Pétrus as coming from Merlot vines. This is another way of saying that California's researchers appear to be on the right track in stressing the adaptation of vines to microclimate and local soil as the factor determining wine style rather than simple equations such as "Merlot makes light, supple wine; Cabernet Sauvignon makes rich, dark wine."

While the area of vineyard in Pomerol has more than doubled in the last 20 years, there remain a number of properties with very old vine structures. The superior, often remarkable clarets they come up with support old French ideas of an ideal vineyard. It is difficult to believe, but a century ago an average vine age of over 40 years was proper, and much older averages could be found in the Médoc.

For the wine drinker beginning to journey among the fine wines of Pomerol, it remains to stress that what you are tasting is claret made principally from Cabernet Franc and Merlot but in a different environment than the Médoc, and claret made with different ideals. By traditional standards of taste, Pomerols are the most elegant wines of the Right Bank; by current market evidence they are the most popular. It is my opinion that understanding and enjoying them is not helped by putting them in direct competition with similarly priced clarets from the Médoc and Graves and even most St.-Émilions. University enologists, whether French or American, would probably pooh-pooh this viewpoint on fine wines; the cellarmasters of Pomerol, St.-Émilion, Graves, and the Médoc would agree with it in the main.

Néac and Lalande de Pomerol used to share Pomerol's eastern border, but Néac was submerged in Lalande de Pomerol a generation ago, the latter being a more commercial designation. Lalande de Pomerol appears infrequently in overseas commerce but is fairly considered a less refined cousin of Pomerol. Often compromised by thinness, a woody attack on the palate, and an aftertaste less than clean, Lalande clarets lack the charm that makes Pomerol in great demand on the continent. However, well-made and well-grown exemplars of this satellite appellation, now swelled to about the size of Pomerol itself, are capable of attaining most of Pomerol's qualities in a lighter model and can be excellent wines in themselves. The full delicacy of the finest wines is lacking but not the essential character. As is often the case, the proclivity of continental markets to accept Lalande for what it can be, a lesser substitute for the more famous appellation, finds little counterpart in English-speaking countries, which care less for confusing nuances.

Fronsac, as the Côtes de Canon Fronsac, Canon Fronsac, and Côtes de Fronsac appellations are collectively known, is a sensationally beautiful fine wine district situated on hills overlooking the sinuses of the Dordogne north of Libourne. Some appreciation of their quality is spreading in England and should spread in America. Well-constituted clarets from a score of bourgeois-rank properties possess the general Right Bank character—a forward, assertive, and vigorous flavor; often generous fruit; even tasting qualities; and proven potential for maturing with finesse. Appellation standards are set at 42 hectoliters per hectare (about 450 gallons per acre) and 11 percent alcohol; and to oversimplify, their tasting qualities stand somewhere between those of Pomerol and St.-Émilion, emphasizing both fruit and a generous, mouth-filling style with some earthy overtones. The finest wines are devoid of faults associated with earthiness and deserve collection more than any other Right Bank red wine except the best of Pomerol and St.-Émilion. A handful of examples, given only by way of introduction, are the following châteaux: La Dauphine, Canon de Brem, Rouet, Canon, du Gaby, La Valade, La Venelle, and Mayne-Vieil.

While the greater part of Bordeaux's vineyards reward a visit, Pomerol offers the foreign tourist little, unless he or she is introduced by someone in the wine trade. Most of the properties are closed to casual visitors or simply not inhabited. The rather flat plain of vineyards does not appear very different from any other vineyard. But one rather undramatic spot has rarely failed to arrest me when scurrying to and fro between cellars—the small ditch just north of Cheval-Blanc on the way from St.-Émilion to Vieux-Certan. Here a few yards separate the vines of Cheval-Blanc, the appellation St.-Émilion, and the "plain" wines (Vin de Graves) of this appellation, on one's right, from Pomerol, particularly vineyard plots of La Conseillante and Vieux-Certan, on one's left. The contrast in style between the wines of Cheval-Blanc and Vieux-Certan is striking. Yet it would be a brave man who would make a comparable difference of the two facing plots of vineyard. When all the talk of soil and subsoil, exposition, grape varieties, and vine age is done with, one may be convinced that these embody necessary conditions for high-quality wines. But just how great is the role of the wine maker, the grower, in determining over and above any basic level of quality the style, the individuality of his wine? That is a humbling thought—both for the wine merchant who clambers back in his automobile and goes on to argue with the grower about bottling dates, delivery terms, and like matters, and for the consumer in some distant city who uncorks a great claret and in one sentence tells himself and his friends what the wine is worth.

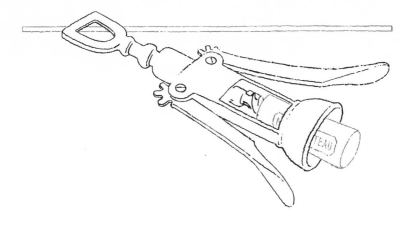

Pétrus

Reigning over other Pomerols, the costly wines of Pétrus show formidable quality steadily maintained. The dark color may sometimes lack a point of brilliance. But, from the first rich bouquet to the last drops of wine charged with flavor, unctuous and flattering the palate without any vulgarity of taste, the resounding qualities of a great wine assert themselves firmly, evenly, and with intensity. Finesse increases with age, but the luscious balance between fruit and vinosity suffers slightly with time. Many tasters will best enjoy light vintages at ages four to eight years and bigger ones between eight and 15 years, rather than waiting decades to drink them. Noble, harmonious Pétrus can be found in 1961, 1964, 1966, 1967, and 1970.

VINTAGE   DATE   PRICE

GUESTS

MENU   COMMENTS

Château Trotanoy

The inky, brilliant, spicy clarets of this small aristocratic property planted entirely in old Merlot vines are favorites of professionals and amateurs alike. They have striking bouquet and expand rapidly on the palate with vigorous taste and unfailing finish suggestive of ripe fruit, the tang of grapeskin, a hint of truffles, and a pleasing muskiness. Color and pure excitement of flavor are strong points; many would rank the vineyard just after Petrus. Trotanoy flourishes in hot years such as 1947, 1961, and 1970. But once at their peak many old vintages have declined rapidly in bottle, and their maturation in bottle should be followed carefully by a prudent drinker, with a slight bias toward appreciation while young. These are authoritative wines, eminently Pomerol through and through, and especially fine in 1961, 1964, 1966, and 1970.

VINTAGE   DATE   PRICE

GUESTS

MENU   COMMENTS

Château La Conseillante

In great ripe years this claret is hard and ungiving in youth, maturing well but slowly. Slightly dry, less flowery to the nose, less unctuous to the palate than some great Pomerols, it offers a very firm flavor and strong body. When successfully mature its superior elegance and aftertaste are striking. Some recent vintages, notably 1969, have been disappointingly weak and thin. New vintages that show deep color and offer some fruit to the taste are sensible speculations for the future; paler mean versions are best avoided. La Conseillante is a refined Pomerol in a somewhat austere style.

VINTAGE   DATE   PRICE

GUESTS

MENU   COMMENTS

Château L'Evangile

Bordering St.-Émilion, this small vineyard produces a wine esteemed among the best-known dozen or so Pomerols for its concentrated style, long development on the palate, and lingering sensation of perfume. The quality is not so regular as could be hoped for, but it is excellent when successful. Its appeal is less obvious and general than that of more supple Pomerols and requires more bottle maturation; young Evangile is frequently blunt and dull. Its favor in Great Britain seems to have fallen off. Just after bottling the elsewhere excellent 1970 tasted vacant and short; conversely, the 1972 shows great attraction. As it is monopolized by a single shipper, access to the wine in barrel is difficult.

VINTAGE   DATE   PRICE

GUESTS

MENU   COMMENTS

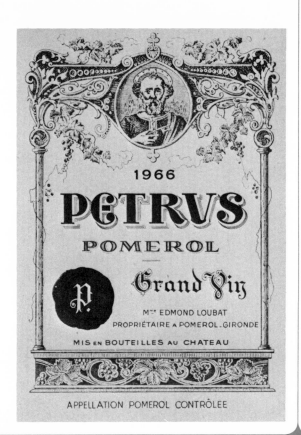

1966

PETRVS

POMEROL

Grand Vin

Mes EDMOND LOUBAT
PROPRIÉTAIRE à POMEROL - GIRONDE

MIS EN BOUTEILLES AU CHATEAU

APPELLATION POMEROL CONTRÔLÉE

APPELLATION POMEROL CONTROLÉE

CHÂTEAU TROTANOY

POMEROL
1966

SOCIÉTÉ CIVILE DU CHATEAU TROTANOY
PROPRIÉTAIRE A POMEROL (GIRONDE)

MIS EN BOUTEILLES AU CHATEAU

CHATEAU

LA CONSEILLANTE

1966

APPELLATION POMEROL CONTROLÉE

HÉRITIERS L. NICOLAS, Propriétaires
A POMEROL (GIRONDE) - FRANCE
MIS EN BOUTEILLES AU CHATEAU

1964

CHATEAU

L'EVANGILE

Grand Cru
POMEROL

Appellation Pomerol contrôlée

SOCIÉTÉ CIVILE DU CHATEAU L'EVANGILE
Héritiers P. DUCASSE
PROPRIÉTAIRES A POMEROL

IMPRIMÉ EN FRANCE

Vieux Château Certan

One of the few Pomerol properties whose history can be traced back as far as the eighteenth century, Vieux Certan is one of the most delicate and refined wines of the commune. When young, off-vintages can be particularly delightful drinking for their silky effect mingled with a perfume suggesting violets. Grander years such as 1967 and 1970 give us intense wines with excellent balance, a complex succession of flavors, and a dazzling finish that captures all the fruit and lusciousness proper to the best Pomerols. In such years its quality ranks with that of Trotanoy, though its style is markedly lighter and more gentle. Strong demand from Belgium and France sets a high basic price on Vieux Certan.

VINTAGE   DATE   PRICE

GUESTS

MENU   COMMENTS

Château Petit-Village

Situated on one of the less imposing-looking sections of the Pomerol plain, Petit-Village in fact has excellent terrain. It occasionally produces exceptionally refined wines the French like to call "tender." The combination of this soft, seductive quality and great finesse in aftertaste reached a peak in 1952, one of the most delicious clarets in the Gironde that year. Other good vintages, such as 1964 and 1967, have much color and come onto the palate with a flushed impact full of fruit. Unctuous and lively when young, Petit-Village ages with distinction; its occasional heights of quality suggest that it could often be still better than it has tasted. The property was recently transferred from one branch of the Ginestet family to another, and the future is therefore up to new management.

VINTAGE   DATE   PRICE

GUESTS

MENU   COMMENTS

Château Lagrange

Not to be confused with the St.-Julien property in the Médoc, Lagrange is on the Pomerol center plain, and its excellent lands yield a rich wine locally considered to have the allure of truffles in deference to its aroma and depth of taste. Some lighter wines with finesse and charm have been made here as well, along with complete if not superlative ones in favored crops such as 1964. Their evolution in bottle is rapid, and most qualities are best captured by drinking young. The label is the least attractive point of the wine.

VINTAGE   DATE   PRICE

GUESTS

MENU   COMMENTS

Château Gazin

Located in the extreme western corner of the appellation, Gazin is a firm wine, with much body, developing well in bottle but characterized by more astringent tasting qualities than more luscious if less good wines such as Nenin. The total harmony is distinguished, the perfume a little restricted; and for these less forward qualities it is often marked down in comparative tastings. While for different reasons Clos l'Église and Certan de May are not now as esteemed as Gazin, they fall into the same class, just below the best wines. Off-years of Gazin tend toward more meanness than is found among the best wines.

VINTAGE   DATE   PRICE

GUESTS

MENU   COMMENTS

Vieux Château Certan
Grand Cru
POMEROL
1970

Appellation Pomerol contrôlée

SOCIÉTÉ CIVILE DU VIEUX CHATEAU CERTAN
(Héritière de Georges Thienpont)
PROPRIÉTAIRE A POMEROL (GIRONDE)

MIS EN BOUTEILLE AU CHÂTEAU

Château Petit-Village
Pomerol

APPELLATION POMEROL CONTROLÉE

1970

SOCIÉTÉ CIVILE DES DOMAINES PRATS
PROPRIÉTAIRE A POMEROL (GIRONDE)

PRODUCE OF FRANCE

CHATEAU LAGRANGE
POMEROL
APPELLATION POMEROL CONTROLÉE

PRODUCE
OF FRANCE

MIS EN BOUTEILLES AU CHATEAU

73 cl

Ets. JEAN-PIERRE MOUEIX
PROPRIÉTAIRES A POMEROL (GIRONDE)

Ancien Domaine des TEMPLIERS

1967
CHATEAU GAZIN
GRAND CRU
POMEROL
APPELLATION POMEROL CONTROLÉE

Mise en bouteilles
du Château

Co-Héritiers SOUALLE, Propriétaires

Château La Fleur-Pétrus

Confusingly named, for there is also a Château Lafleur, this Pomerol falls between the dense and overpowering sensations offered by Trotanoy and the racier, more Médoc-like address that so often characterizes Vieux Certan. Wine of breed, with good color, offering harmony and aftertaste plus a solid representative combination of fruit, body, and even development to the taste, it is a fine Pomerol of the class just behind the very best. Lafleur is often slightly more aromatic but also falls into the general class represented by La Fleur-Pétrus.

VINTAGE   DATE   PRICE

GUESTS

MENU   COMMENTS

Château Latour à Pomerol

In good years this rich, dark-colored wine belongs to the family of Trotanoy, Pétrus, and La Conseillante, emphasizing powerful flavor and imposing body rather than charm, though its finesse is not lacking. It takes a truly mean year such as 1969 to reduce the scope of this vital and robust Pomerol. Even lame vintages such as 1972 nourish at least a fluid, attractive Latour à Pomerol, if not a great one. There is a neat difference between forward, assertive, and immediate impressions and vulgar ones, and this claret stays well within the confines of fine wine. Good vintages such as 1964 and 1970 are harmonious, albeit their "fat" youthful body makes them attractive early on. Good balance carries such wines to middle age well; most Bordeaux connoisseurs would be tempted to drink them between eight and 15 years of age.

VINTAGE   DATE   PRICE

GUESTS

MENU   COMMENTS

Château La Pointe

A relatively large production and proprietors concerned with export markets make this label better known abroad than those of most Pomerols. A range of quality and style has made generalization about the wine difficult if not invidious. There have been unfortunate thin wines (1962), insufficiently intense clarets in years otherwise potent in Pomerol (1967), and dark, generous wines without fault in 1970 and 1971. The best successes offer a fine endowment of fruit and agreeable development on the palate, and if they lack the scintillating and dramatic qualities of Trotanoy on the one hand, or the full charm of Vieux Certan on the other, they are still complete wines representing the accepted merits of the appellation. Château Beauregard has a different style of comparable intensity.

VINTAGE   DATE   PRICE

GUESTS

MENU   COMMENTS

Château Nenin

Like La Pointe, Nenin is a large property exporting energetically and selling directly to individuals and restaurants in France. Its wines, definitely in the second rank of quality, are nonetheless attractive, supple, usually with a violet color and delicious aroma full of fruit; but they lack nerve and vitality and drop off quickly in bottle. It is a pointless wine to put away but a delectable one to drink young. Such wines serve a function at least in the lives of those who have noticed mortality's erratic comings and goings.

VINTAGE   DATE   PRICE

GUESTS

MENU   COMMENTS

CHATEAU LA FLEUR-PÉTRUS

GRAND CRU

POMEROL

APPELLATION POMEROL CONTROLEE

PRODUCE OF FRANCE

1971

Société Civile du Château La Fleur Pétrus

PROPRIÉTAIRE

Mis en Bouteilles au Château

BERTHON - LIBOURNE

CHÂTEAU

LATOUR a POMEROL

PREMIER GRAND CRU

GRAND VIN
1947
APPELLATION CONTRÔLÉE

Mis en Bouteilles
au Château

Château La Pointe

Pomerol

APPELLATION POMEROL CONTROLÉE

Mise en bouteilles au Château

1971

D'ARFEUILLE

PROPRIÉTAIRE A POMEROL

GRAND VIN DE BORDEAUX

CHATEAU NENIN

APPELLATION POMEROL CONTROLÉE

1955

DESPUJOL

Propriétaire

POMEROL

N° 153. deposé

IMP. WETTERWALD FRÈRES. BORDEAUX

Burgundy

Comparisons between the wines of Bordeaux and those of Burgundy, like arguments for the superiority of one or the other, have a philosophical profundity and practical significance best compared to a duel to the death with butter knives over the merits of peaches versus apples. Passionate partisans might actually fight it out, and some of the rest of us might want to watch the action, but no one is likely to be enlightened by the arguments that led up to it. Great wines need no defense, only an acquainted public—enough of a task, as it turns out.

Bordeaux and Burgundy are enormously different. Size of operation and land ownership influence not only the sorts of wine made but also the manner in which it is sold. Fewer than 50,000 vineyards produce some 158 million gallons (6 million hectoliters) of wine in the Gironde Department (Bordeaux), two-thirds of it appellation grade. Some 60,000 vineyards produce in Burgundy about 35 million gallons (1,325,000 hectoliters) of appellation wine and a lesser amount of non-appellation wine. What these numbers spell out is that Burgundy is a vineland of small growers, many of whom produce small amounts of highly esteemed wine. While Bordeaux produces an ocean of appellation wine on some 300,000 acres (120,000 hectares) of vines, Burgundy appellation wine originates in a mere 86,000 acres (35,000 hectares). One major Bordeaux appellation, St.-Émilion, outproduces Burgundy's Côte d'Or, which encompasses every great red wine name in Burgundy. In short, Burgundy is another world, a world of small farmers as contrasted to one of estate managers.

Vineyards entitled to the name of Burgundy lie in clusters across nearly 125 miles (200 kilometers), from Chablis in the north to Beaujolais in the south. Appellations and wine types are strictly organized on geographical bases with clear outlines. The map of Burgundy shows that all the famous, expensive fine wines come from three districts: Chablis, a patch of vineyard quite by itself; the Côte d'Or, a narrow continuous range of hills facing southeast; and the Côte Chalonnaise. Just to the south, the larger Mâconnais flows into Beaujolais, also a large region, which fans out and brings Burgundy to an end just above Lyon, a city famous for its cuisine, infamous for its cupidity, and estimable for the aloof independence that has earned it the jealous hatred of Paris.

Wines made in Burgundy can be simply described and easily remembered. Chablis produces only dry white wines. The Côte d'Or makes rich red and powerful white wines, reds throughout its length, great whites toward its southern end. Red and white Chalonnais resemble Côte d'Or wines but are less rich and less fine. Fine white wines continue into the northern Mâconnais but give way in Beaujolais to very light red wines, famous for their charm, that get ever lighter toward the south.

Burgundy's basic appellations are regional and correspond to these geographical divisions. Chablis of all grades is designated Appellation Chablis. Côte d'Or is split into Côtes de Nuits (red) and Côtes de Beaune (red and white) appellations after its two principal towns. The small Côte Chalonnaise area is carved into four appellations; and wines from Mâcon, red or white, appear either as Pouilly-Fuissé (white) or some sort of Mâcon. Finally, the light red wines of Beaujolais are called just that. Throughout the whole region, both red and white wines made to lower standards may call themselves Burgundy. Some rosé is also produced.

But clear as the general outlines may be, the Burgundy district is so steeped in local traditions and its better wines so specifically associated with special places, communes, villages, hillsides, even little individual vineyards, that as soon as superior qualities of wine attract our attention, and they must, we are immediately drawn into a maze of names by which a thousand years of viticulture have distinguished better sites from the major regional appellations we have just learned. This is understandable but awkward. Fine Burgundy wines are known by their place name. They are identified with specific pieces of land, famous plots. But these famous plots, far from belonging to one grower or carrying one name, as Bordeaux estates do, are jealously divided among many owners. So fine Burgundy wines have identity, exceptional identity, indeed, identity with a vengeance! One climbs the pyramid of quality, narrowing from a regional to a subregional to a local (village) appellation until the highest appellation is reached, a specific vineyard plot considered a great appellation in its own right, a Great Growth, or Grand Cru. Even this plot is divided among many growers, and each grows vines and makes wine differently. The ultimate definition of a great Burgundy is therefore not only its region, subregion, village location, and plot—or, as Burgundians say, its *climat*—but also its grower. We shall have more to say about this person who is responsible for one of the world's two great wines.

Four principal grapes make Burgundy wine; two are noble, two are good. Pinot Noir is the grape parent of all fine red Burgundies. Its white juice allows its use in Champagne and other white wines. Its compact bunches of small berries develop well and ripen early. Because the juice is white, color depends upon maceration with the red skins. Pinot Noir, cultivated throughout Burgundian history, has migrated to vineyards across the world; nevertheless, its flavor at home is finer and different from anywhere else, albeit some of its tasting qualities persist in wines from Switzerland, California, Australia, and elsewhere. Chardonnay bears small golden grapes in longer, looser bunches than Pinot Noir; it is the noble white grape flourishing in marl and chalk soils from which great white wines are made not only in Burgundy's heartland but also to the south in the Chalonnais and to the north in Chablis. In the Mâconnais and Beaujolais the large berries of the Black Gamay of White Juice (*Gamay Noir à Jus Blanc*) ripen well with a special flavor, flowery and fruity, attributed to the districts' granite terrains. Aligoté, a good white grape, is used throughout the same two districts for the tart, lively, abundantly produced wines bearing its name; these large grapes have flavor but little finesse and modest sugar content. No single wine of importance is produced exclusively from the Pinot Blanc grape, but additions of this farflung variety are regularly made to Chardonnay in some appellations.

Chardonnay can be considered the richest grape of the four main strains. It produces a degree more alcohol than any other and as much as 25 percent more total acidity, giving its wines force on the palate. Gamay has the showiest aroma; its usual volatile acidity, which accounts for much of what we smell in a wine, is a third again as high as in the other three varieties. Pinor Noir gives slightly more alcohol than Gamay, but it is its perfume and flavor, both intense, and its finesse that make it superlative.

The finest appellations are built upon single noble grape varieties without exception. General appellations granted to wines originating "somewhere" in Burgundy may be built on single varieties or mixtures and may designate wines declassified from higher appellations. The lowest appellation, Bourgogne Ordinaire or Bourgogne Grand Ordinaire, is unimportant and virtually unknown outside France. Unlike most regions, little wine is made at the bottom of the quality ladder in Burgundy. Gamay and/or Pinot Noir go into red Ordinaire, which must attain 9 percent alcohol. Chardonnay and/or Aligoté and three lesser varieties make white Ordinaire of minimum 9.5 percent alcohol. Red wine may be called Bourgogne Passe-tout-grains if produced from two-thirds Gamay and one-third Pinot Noir with minimum 9.5 percent alcohol; some is hearty enough to export.

The best regional appellation, Bourgogne (Burgundy), is given to Chardonnay, Pinot Blanc, and Aligoté attaining 10.5 percent alcohol and Pinot Noir reaching at least 10 percent alcohol. Gamay Noir à Jus Blanc becomes Bourgogne when made in the Mâconnais or in one of nine superior village areas in Beaujolais. Small amounts of Bourgogne rosé come from red grapes and must be 10.5 percent alcohol. Exported rosé commonly has a village name, the most notable being Rosé de Marsannay. Sparkling (Mousseux) Burgundy must be produced by the same procedures as Champagne, must be one-third noble grape, and must age nine months before sale. The best is good, most is uninspired, the worst is difficult to drink for foreigners conditioned by Champagne. Local and French enthusiasm for the wines keep their prices higher than English-speaking drinkers think appropriate, especially after sparkling wine import taxes are added.

Since 1961 two general subregional appellations have been added: Hautes Côtes de Nuits and Hautes Côtes de Beaune. The intention of the new appellations was to associate wines near the heart of the two Côtes with the more famous, long-respected names. The quiet success of these new designations is due in part to considerable efforts to impose quality through a tasting panel that must approve each wine. Most of these wines come from higher ground west of the best hills of Beaune and Nuits, hence their designation "High Slopes."

Be it Volnay in the Côtes de Beaune, Vougeot in the Côtes de Nuits, Rully in the Côte Chalonnaise, or Fleurie in the Beaujolais, it is the village name that discriminates between plain Burgundy and wine of higher standing. It is easy to visualize how this came to be through the course of time, for we have the same phenomenon in other areas—Venetian cut glass, Smithfield hams, Sheffield cutlery, Colchester (England) or Blue Point (eastern United States) oysters. Prestige is implied and a higher quality earned by decades, perhaps centuries, of superior performance. The *Appellation Contrôlée* laws recognize and codify this past experience, but in Burgundy they go to unusual levels of specificity. The unit of production in highest-quality wines is not just the village but the vineyard site, a definite parcel of vineyard land considered to have its own character and quality. This is the *climat*, often called a *clos* in labeling wines. *Climats* are delineated by the appellation laws and do not change, and Burgundy's best vines form a patchwork map of minuscule detail classing all important *climats* by merit. The seeming anarchy and endless detail of Burgundian wine lore is really the surface appearance of an organization of all *climats* into three orders of quality. The system is easier to understand by starting at the top level.

Some two dozen vineyards in the Côte d'Or have produced wine over the centuries that has made their names famous throughout the wine-drinking world. There are certainly half a million people alive at this moment who do not know what *Appellation Contrôlée* means, that Vougeot is a village in the Côtes de Nuits, still less that it takes its name from a rivulet named the Vouge that drains a pond just outside the village, but who do know that Clos de Vougeot is a famous Burgundy wine. Much the same could be said for Chambertin, Montrachet, Corton, Musigny, Richebourg, Romanée, and more. Their renown has been consecrated by appellation laws that consider such vineyard areas appellations in their own right. And quite rightly, too.

Such is the origin of Burgundy's elite, the Great Growths, or Grand Cru, wines. Generally the appellation name incorporates that of the *climat* or *clos,* and the wretched damnable confusion that plagues Burgundy names begins right here. Many villages throughout Burgundy are allowed to tack on, literally to hyphenate, the name of their most famous *clos* to their village name. Appropriating the name of a more famous wine for one's own is not new, nor is the rationalization that chronically defends it. The famous name is alleged to represent a "type" of wine, and borrowing it for a lesser wine is always done out of generous public-spirited concern that the consumer realize the type of wine he is buying. The argument is as specious in Burgundy as in California or Spain (see pages 211 and 244).

It is not possible, unfortunately, to turn back the clock to rewrite appellation laws. Gevrey-Chambertin illustrates the problem well. This important Côtes de Nuits village produces 250,000 gallons of village wine designated "Gevrey-Chambertin." Chambertin, the famous Grand Cru, finds its name cheerfully riveted onto the village wine. But that is not all. Eight other Grand Cru *climats* adjacent to Chambertin also hyphenate "Chambertin" to their *climat* name, in their case with some justice. One of these, Chapelle-Chambertin, is precisely defined by appellation law on two plots of land totaling exactly 5.39 hectares (about 13 acres), allowing it 1,536 gallons of output. Anyone who can maintain with a straight face that consumers will have an easy time distinguishing Chapelle-Chambertin or any of its Grand Cru cousins from Gevrey-Chambertin as they stare at a rack of Burgundy bottles in a shop or a series of "Chambertin" wines on a wine list has a great career before him as a lobbyist for the farm interest. From a consumer's point of view, then, it is a pity that Burgundy designations append famous *climat* names to larger appellations; this imposes the irksome burden on our memories of recalling which really are the Grand Cru wines and which the village ones. But the adventurer in wine has every compelling interest to learn the pecking order to protect himself. (See the table of Grand Cru and village appellations on page 103 provided for this purpose.)

The second tier of the quality pyramid is that of Premier Cru. Like Grand Cru, *climats* whose land justifies Premier Cru status are scrupulously defined facts of the Burgundian landscape. But as they are less well known, their names are appended to the more familiar ones of major villages. Here lies more confusion, for these are not the mere wines of the village. Premier Cru status can be shown in two ways. First, the *climat* name may follow the appellation but in letters no larger than the appellation name. VOSNE-ROMANÉE LES SUCHOTS or VOSNE-ROMANÉE LES SUCHOTS *Premier Cru* are examples of two accepted formats. Alternatively the grower or shipper may decide that the name of his Premier Cru *climat* is simply not famous enough to help him sell the wine but still wants it known that his wine is of Premier Cru status. Appellation laws allow him to choose the form VOSNE-ROMANÉE PREMIER CRU.

As in all classifications, the division between Grand Cru and Premier Cru wines is imperfect. Actual quality is scattered by many factors, and it is no surprise to find Premier Cru superior to Grand Cru, or unsuccessful Grand Cru wines from various vintages or growers. What is classified is the potential of the *climats*, not the performance of a grower or the fortune of one vintage.

The third tier of quality appears more confusing than it is, for wines are allowed to state their *climat* of origin without being of Premier Cru status. The promiscuous use of Grand Cru vineyard names on village wines may be reprehensible, but the right of a grower or shipper to identify the origin of his wine by a *climat* name is another story. There is simply no other way for a proud grower to raise his wine in public esteem and earn a higher price for his efforts than to identify it. The consumer should understand and even value this right, despite the fact that its exercise adds more names to an already long list.

It is the labeling that tells this third class of wine apart from Premier Cru Burgundies. Two labeling rules must be observed. First, the name of the *climat* or *clos* that follows the village appellation must be written no bigger than half the size of the village name. A grower in the *climat* Les Cras in the village of Aloxe-Corton could label his wine ALOXE-CORTON Les Cras. The second requirement for such wines is that the actual appellation must appear spelled out on the label so that there is no confusing what is really a village wine with a Grand Cru or Premier Cru, whose *climat* name is an integral part of its appellation. Our grower would have to add to his label "Appellation Aloxe-Corton Contrôlée." His may be only a village wine, but if he regularly makes fine Les Cras above the level of village wine, he will obtain renown and better price than other Aloxe-Corton.

The Burgundy wine buyer must look for these distinctions. Some 30 Grand Cru names identify the prestige appellations; at least the most famous should be recognized. Premier Cru wines will show either a large-size type face spelling out the *climat* or *clos* name, or the words "Premier Cru," or both. Village wines always announce village appellations in full, and when stated, the *climat* of origin must be in smaller type than the village name. Below village appellations come subregional ones that take in zones of Burgundy. The long-suffering reader must endure one final complication in understanding these.

Two large village appellations encompass many fine wines, including many Premier Cru. The first is Nuits-St.-Georges, which may also use the appellation Nuits; the second is Côtes de Beaune, which may also use the appellation Beaune. Both pairs of names are village appellations, just like Volnay, Morey-St.-Denis, or Chassagne-Montrachet. Lying slightly outside the Beaune and Nuits village appellations, however, are many vineyards that legitimately claim to have been recognized by the names of the two towns. Two subregional appellations, each incorporating the "Beaune" or "Nuits," were created to take account of these claims: Côtes de Nuits Villages, for the wines of five

communes adjacent to Nuits-St.-Georges; and Côtes de Beaune Villages, for the wines of 16 villages clustered around Beaune. The word "Villages" is accurately and meaningfully used here to tell wine buyers that such wines are subregional, though the region is narrowly defined, and not wines belonging to one village. In the hinterland of both towns two new appellations, Hautes Côtes de Nuits and Hautes Côtes de Beaune, describe still lesser wines that nevertheless are members of the wine families of Nuits and Beaune. These must pass a tasting test to earn the right to association with the two prestigious names.

In summary, three sorts of Nuits and Beaune wines coexist in the Côte d'Or: village appellation wines of high class—Nuits-St.-Georges (: Nuits) and Côtes de Beaune (: Beaune); subregional appellations using the word "Villages"; and peripheral subregional appellations of lower rank distinguished by the words "Hautes Côtes" with the names Nuits and Beaune. Below these come regional appellations defining "Bourgogne."

The bemused and irritated beginning adventurer in wine may certainly be forgiven for suggesting that this whole tangle of appellations was invented in his abundant spare time by a ninety-year-old former jigsaw puzzle manufacturer and rabid teetotaler with the express malignant purpose of making Burgundy too complicated to drink. All that can be rejoined is that the best Burgundies are delicious enough to make it all worth while. The table on the next page may help dispel some of the more flagrant possible confusions in buying important Burgundy wines. It is no disgrace to carry it or similar catalogues of Burgundy appellations in hand when shopping.

The Côte d'Or has exemplary growing conditions. The Côtes de Nuits and Côtes de Beaune form a continuous range of hills facing southeast and dropping to an alluvial plain. These slopes are backed to the west by the higher hills of the Morvan range, which acts as a barrier against prevailing westerlies and their heavy precipitation. Thus the Côte d'Or is a relatively sheltered, hospitable area for vines; while it lies within a temperate zone with winters cold enough to arrest plant activity, its summers and autumns are long and benign enough to give a fine ripening season. Like all great wine districts, however, the weather of the Côte d'Or is marginally favorable—disaster is always a possibility. Only in the lower-quality Mediterranean–North African zone is every year warm enough to achieve full ripeness. In Nuits and Beaune rocky substratum fosters good drainage, especially on the middle slopes where wines are best. Drainage promotes better ripening, drier topsoils being a warmer environment than waterlogged ones, and is a factor in hygiene, as surface water stimulates growth and reproduction of molds. Beaune is distinguished from Nuits by a sharp increase in limestone, ironstone, and marl in the best white wine vineyards. These configurations allow superb results for Pinot Noir and Chardonnay grapes, but the Gamay grape family fares disastrously and is generally forbidden in the Côte d'Or, giving thin, dreary wine.

Vinification is carried out in the Côte d'Or much as in all fine wine regions. Red grapes are destemmed, crushed, and vatted to ferment with their skins, from which the white juice draws pigments and flavoring matter. Today's tendency is to give shorter vattings (four to six days) and to ferment at cooler temperatures (72–86 degrees Fahrenheit) than was the case some fifty years ago. Red wines are then cleaned physically and chemically and begin their maturation in oak casks, a maturation also shorter than in the past. These modifications have the commercial purpose of bringing up wines more supple and

CÔTE D'OR GRAND CRU APPELLATIONS	VILLAGE APPELLATION WITH WHICH CONFUSED
CHAMBERTIN CHAMBERTIN-CLOS DE BÈZE (may call itself Chambertin) LATRICIÈRES-CHAMBERTIN CHARMES-CHAMBERTIN MAZOYÈRES-CHAMBERTIN CHAPELLE-CHAMBERTIN GRIOTTE-CHAMBERTIN MAZIS-CHAMBERTIN RUCHOTTES-CHAMBERTIN	GEVREY-CHAMBERTIN
BONNES MARES CLOS ST.-DENIS CLOS DE LA ROCHE CLOS DE TART	
MUSIGNY	CHAMBOLLE-MUSIGNY
CLOS DE VOUGEOT	VOUGEOT
RICHEBOURG LA TÂCHE GRANDS ECHEZEAUX ECHEZEAUX	
ROMANÉE-CONTI LA ROMANÉE ROMANÉE-ST.-VIVANT	VOSNE-ROMANÉE
LE CORTON CORTON-CHARLEMAGNE	ALOXE-CORTON
LE MONTRACHET CHEVALIER-MONTRACHET BÂTARD-MONTRACHET BIENVENUES-BÂTARD- MONTRACHET CRIOTS-BÂTARD-MONTRACHET	CHASSAGNE-MONTRACHET PULIGNY-MONTRACHET

The following village appellations present themselves in the same hyphenated format that so maddeningly resembles Grand Cru names:

MOREY-ST.-DENIS	AUXEY-DURESSES
NUITS-ST.-GEORGES	ST.-ROMAIN
LADOIX-SERRIGNY	VOLNAY-SANTENOTS
PERNAND-VERGELESSES	DEZIZE-LES-MARANGES
SAVIGNY-LES-BEAUNES	CHEILLY-LES-MARANGES
SAMPIGNY-LES-MARANGES	

Most of these villages contain Premier Cru vineyards whose *climat* name may quite properly appear on the label. These are distinguished from Grand Cru vineyards by the smaller typeface of their names. Some villages may not even be appellations, but their name may appear at the bottom of a label in the address of a shipper or grower. However, "Georges Lecuisinier, proprietaire à Flagey-Echezeaux" at the foot of a label can hardly be mistaken for the Grand Cru appellation Echezeaux.

more forward in tasting qualities and less acerbic than they might otherwise be. It is argued against these measures that less time on the skins allows less coloring matter to infuse into the wine and with it smaller quantities of many compounds believed to make refined contributions to quality and intensity of taste. Matter contributing odors to aroma and bouquet may also fail to find its way into the wine during a shorter vatting. Cooler fermentations are thought partly to rectify these deficiencies and develop a better, more abundant flavor. The residue of material from the vats is pressed to produce an inky, astringent wine called *vin de presse*. This is low in sugar but high in tannin and acidity and can be used in small amounts to invigorate wine lacking in "bite."

Fine white Burgundy grapes are sometimes pressed with their stalks to obtain tannin, for white wine must does not include the skins, which supply this substance to reds. White Burgundies of class receive a longer fermentation than reds, and this is done usually in oak casks. It may sometimes last several weeks. Fermentation temperatures are kept down to lows of 59–64 degrees Fahrenheit and this long, cool process is more and more considered essential for best-quality wine. Addition of sugar to red and white musts is frequent in Burgundy, where lack of ripeness is often a problem during cool weather, and alcoholic degree is more esteemed in itself here than in Bordeaux. The greatest white wines are matured in oak for as long a period as are reds, but most are fit to bottle well before their red counterparts. A whole lower category of white wines and some reds not contending for higher status than regional appellation may never get barrel conditioning at all but are clarified in large storage units from whence they are drawn off for bottling with their fruity and fresh, lively qualities unmodified by slow exposure to air through the oak walls of barrels. For reasons of price or style, it is not judged in the interest of such wines to receive the tannic qualities imparted by wood aging. While good white and red wines from the Mâcon and Beaujolais regions may result from this abbreviated process, the great, powerful, rich white Burgundies of the Côtes de Beaune invariably pass their infancy in oak barrels, as do all superior red wines. For whatever reasons of chemical constitution, it is a well-observed fact that, by comparison with the majority of fine Bordeaux wines, both white and red Burgundy wines, even those of high standing, show more of their qualities sooner after bottling. Thus, while technical processes of production are equally lengthy in both regions, Côte d'Or wines come in quicker reach of the wine consumer; this tasting fact accounts for the rapid sequence in which they are bottled, shipped, and sold. Consumers who wish to drink mature Burgundies are obliged to buy and cellar them promptly, for little backlog of older stock rests with growers or the wine trade.

The Burgundy wine trade typifies the manner in which traditional European vineyard areas made up of many small growers conduct their business. The economic mechanisms that operate here resemble those governing business in Alsace, Germany, the Loire region, and many other quality wine districts where ownership is fragmented and wine type and quality vary incessantly from grower to grower and year to year. Two sets of forces shape this business. On one side are agricultural facts of production, notably small amounts of good wine produced by many growers among a mighty number of confusing appellations. On the other side are commercial needs of importers of fine wines who are wholesale intermediaries with their own problems. If the wine consumer is bewildered by multitudes of Burgundy names, each one in different vintages, the wholesaler is angrily impatient with them. The small, scattered holding of any grower may well cut across commercial divisions of quality, appellation, and even wine type. Consequently one grower's cellar may contain barrels of 3, 11, or 17 different wines in varying amounts. In the Côte d'Or 25 acres (10 hectares) is a big property and its owner an important figure in his appellation. In Bordeaux the same acreage is of dubious economic feasibility to cultivate. A single vineyard of 200 acres (80 hectares) is unthinkable in Burgundy but a good size for a world-famous Bordeaux estate.

The supply of Burgundy begins in the grower's cellar and consists of whatever appellations in whatever qualities he has harvested. But the international business of selling wines requires *quantities* of the *same* wine. Quantities are necessary if consumers are to become widely acquainted with a wine, and this in turn is necessary if the wine trader is to sell it successfully, repeatedly, and in sufficient amount to justify dealing in it. It is easy to see that where highest-quality wines are concerned, a fundamental contradiction exists in the Burgundy marketplace. Little parcels of the best wines are offered by many growers; the merchants, whether shippers (*négociant-éleveurs*) or importers, demand larger quantities of wines of regular, dependable style, quality, and price.

Three sorts of compromises have been adopted, none of which really solves the problem but each workable in its way. Growers may bottle and sell their own wines, whether to shippers or directly to importers. Quality will depend upon the grower's own standards, ability, and land. If he estate-bottles only the best and sells the rest under village appellation, his name will become associated with small amounts of necessarily expensive but very fine, highly individual wine. Conversely, if he maximizes his production and does not discriminate between qualities, there will be more wine to sell but wine of lesser quality. Or a shipper may buy different lots of the same appellation and vintage from different growers, exercising much selection and the blender's craft as well. He ends up assembling a sufficiently commercial quantity of a single appellation in a single year and offers it under his own name. This has been and remains a very typical solution not only in Burgundy but wherever peasant proprietorship dominates a vineyard area. Well done, with integrity and skill, it is the best solution; a sufficient quantity of wine is obtained and the standard of quality can be as high as weather permits in each vintage. Third and last, just as a grower may relax criteria for his estate bottlings and market larger amounts of lesser-quality wine, so may a shipper select cheaper, less-good Burgundies and assemble them into larger lots of any given appellation.

The consumer, or the importer for that matter, cannot distinguish between a shipper doing his job well and one doing it badly by inspecting the label or the list of wines offered, any more than any of us can tell what we are going to receive when we go to dine at a new restaurant. But a closer look at how the market actually works can give us a "feel" or intuition in buying wine and can help evaluate the shippers and growers whose Burgundies appear in export markets.

Dissection of one major village—Gevrey-Chambertin may serve as a model—reveals several tiers of quality as described by appellation laws. Among its Grand Cru appellations is Mazis-Chambertin, whose output of some 6,000 gallons comes from many different growers. Wine of this class is easy to sell profitably and quickly, though growers may not always get the highest prices they feel they deserve. Some sell direct to individuals and restaurants. Others have traditional relationships with one or more shippers. Others offer their wine more openly to shippers who shop through the crop every year looking for the particular quality and price to suit the assembled parcel of Mazis-Chambertin they will sell under their own name. Others estate-bottle their wine and sell it to importers abroad or to merchants in France. Still others may cater to a different class of shippers, who seek the cheapest possible wine with the right to call itself Mazis-Chambertin. And there is such tawdry wine produced every year even among Grand Cru vineyards. For the appellation laws may command growers to make red wine out of Pinot Noir grapes on certain lands in certain maximum amounts with minimum alcohol content of 11.5 percent and less than a certain amount of volatile acidity, but they cannot command them to make wine that tastes delicious.

The market for Mazis-Chambertin may be crisscrossed by buyers from all sides with all sorts of desires and needs, but such a market produces simple results. Higher-priced, high-quality wines sell quickly to buyers, either shippers or buyers of estate bottlings, who want the best and know it will be only part of the crop. A second part of the crop, good but not remarkable, goes to shippers or is estate-bottled and sold at prices less than the best but appropriate for Mazis-Chambertin. Inferior wine sells more slowly to sluggish buyers, but often the very cheapest and worst sells quickly to shippers hungry for this appellation name and at prices that will undercut proper Mazis and/or give them larger profit margins.

The best bottles of Mazis-Chambertin that reach English-speaking markets have some common features. These wines will have been bought by traders, shippers, and importers, each of whom understand quality and believe that his customers will pay more for it. Second, these wines will not come in abundant amounts. Supply and demand conditions make these unavoidable facts of the fine Burgundy wine trade. And these facts have more to do with consumer pleasure, with value for money, and with access to the experience of drinking superb Burgundy than anything except the weather and the grower's desire to make great wine. The best Burgundy was, is, and will be hard to find; such is the agricultural and commercial reality.

Moving down in rank, into Premier Cru grades of Gevrey-Chambertin and finally into the village appellation, there is much more wine available. The *négociant-éleveur* shops among more choices. Prices are lower. But the economic mechanisms are similar. The best wine of Gevrey-Chambertin sells more quickly than the average wine, there is less of it, and its price is higher. The selecting role of the shipper is likely to be more important than in the case of Grand Cru wines. The best Mazis-Chambertin will come either from an estate or a shipper specializing in the finest wines. But like many village wines, the best exported Gevrey-Chambertin is most likely to come from a shipper and to cost a quarter or half again the price of the worst wine with the right to the same appellation.

The consumer, who is the reader of this book, does not have an easy time of it. He waits at the far end of the chain of wine distribution and looks at an array of Gevrey-Chambertin from all manner of sources. His aim should be to acquaint himself with that minority of shippers and growers intent on selling the best wines conditions will allow. Trial and error is his inevitable lot. Price alone cannot guide him, for many wines are sold through multiple intermediaries whose markups bring final prices to high levels. Extremely famous Grand Cru appellations bear a high price based on prestige, scarcity, and glamour. These price components cannot be easily disentangled from a premium price commanded by superior quality.

It should be said that the same logic and the same consequences obtain not only in the Côte d'Or, or in Chablis, or in the rest of Burgundy, but wherever like conditions for growing and selling fine wines exist. When properties are small and the spectrum of quality from best to worst is wide, all trading intermediaries must choose between small amounts of more expensive wine and larger amounts of less-good cheaper wine, all calling itself more or less by the same name. Alsace, Germany, the Rhône, and the Loire are but some of the other regions in a similar situation.

The mechanism separating quality wines into good representatives (and sometimes poor ones) of the region and a few great, individual, memorable wines has two exceptions. In some areas the best lands have gradually been drawn into great estates that dominate quality wine production. Such is true in Bordeaux and partly true in pioneer areas such as Australia and California. Here the best wines are often the most famous ones and are produced in large amounts. The second exception arises when wine quality is determined by systematic blending; in such large operations economy of scale is important and the final product technically difficult to obtain without extensive stocks. Outstanding examples are Champagne and the great fortified wines, Port and Sherry. Small quantities can be made, but in these cases most fine wines are turned out by big firms with the resources to blend well year in and year out.

Burgundy exports over 13 million gallons (500,000 hectoliters) of appellation-grade wine. The amount shipped abroad in barrel is falling to nearly half that figure, though as recently as the early 1960s almost six times as much left France in barrel as in bottle. Switzerland imports by far more Burgundy than the other main customers, the United States, Benelux, Germany, and England. The composition of each trade varies, however. Of Switzerland's imports, approaching 4 million gallons, less than 15 percent is shipped in bottled form. America takes only bottled wines. These facts imply that the average grade of wine shipped to the United States is above that shipped to Switzerland, which is true, but not so dramatically as the figures indicate, for America has no facilities for bottling Burgundy shipped in bulk. Prices at the point of departure and net of intermediary markups are a better guide to quality. In 1969, the average value of a liter of exported Burgundy was approximately the following: United States, 8 francs; England, 5 francs; Benelux, 4 francs; Switzerland, 3.3 francs; Germany, 3.1 francs.

Control of quality is an emotional subject in Burgundy, as elsewhere. Almost alone, the new Hautes Côtes appellations require tasting tests before wines may be sold under their banner. The analyses for alcohol, volatile acidity, and other chemical dimensions that take place in Bordeaux apply to Burgundy appellation wines but not the *label*, or tasting test. Nevertheless, in a very firm tone of voice, the Ministry of Agriculture has announced intentions to institute such a test. Burgundians have replied with a chorus of yodeling protests.

The *label* tasting test (recall the discussion in the introduction to France, page 29) does not impose high quality on each wine passing before it; rather it increases general pressure to make wines to a minimum standard. Underneath Burgundy's outrage lie not only bad reasons for objecting but some reasons that require an answer. How could such a tasting panel effectively operate among thousands of growers making tiny amounts of wine dispersed among some sixscore separate appellations? Remember that no wine could be released commercially—that is to say, loaded onto a truck and taken away to be drunk—until the panel got around to it and all its fellow aspirants to its appellation. For good reasons that have been described in painful

detail, Burgundies are often sold by the barrel, not by a château production of 12,500 cases. How do you guarantee the validity of each sample? Would each barrel be tasted? And what paragon of taste, what all-knowing emissary of Dionysus himself would step forward to taste the difference between two barrels, one of Volnay Clos de la Barre, the other of Volnay Clos des Angles, both claiming Premier Cru grade, and say that la Barre is too "light" for Premier Cru and des Angles just right? The hapless owner of nine-tenths of an acre in la Barre might well shriek that he makes his wine that way because he *likes* it that way, and so do the three restaurants in Brussels that take his whole crop each year and took that of his father before him. The imaginative reader may wish to visualize a fist, grown slightly heavy over a lifetime of rolling oak barrels containing some 502 pounds of wine around a freezing cellar, making appropriate gestures under his nose.

Local color to one side, however, authoritarian tasting standards *do* threaten the individuality of fine Burgundy wines. Yet it might be added by the colder, more logical minds not exactly in short supply in France, if tasting standards are not authoritarian, what purpose do they serve? If they are not impossibly rigorous, then what is the point of paying the crushing price in bureaucracy, appeals, delay, and interference with business efficiency that tasting panels will inevitably bring to Burgundy? The only reply is that too many poor wines from high appellations are getting into commerce, and something must be done about it—not a very coherent answer. Divine Providence has mercifully appointed the author to mention the problem, not to solve it. As it stands, tasting panels are due to be introduced; Burgundians have dropped none of their objections, and they have won wars with authority since the Monks of Cluny began to plow what is now Clos de Vougeot and the Dukes of Burgundy ordered farmers to rip up their vines and plant . . . wheat.

Thus, inevitably in Burgundy, control of quality is a subject that brings us to the grower. Appellation laws have failed to guarantee that wines mirror the highest quality intended for that name. They have given a framework to encourage it. But grower interest in quality, and his ambition for the fame and rewards it brings, must remain the ultimate force behind superior wines. Rewards to high quality, however, can come only from buyers in the trade who want this superiority, and they will pay for it only when sufficient consumers distinguish great Burgundy wines bearing local character and individual style from more ordinary, duller wines. The existence of the finest Burgundy wines thus rests on a web of close relationships binding all parties who care about this delicate product. It is unfashionable to speak of aristocracy; but a pervasive aristocracy of knowledge, taste, and enthusiasm sustains the higher prices that the best wines receive, and must receive, if growers are to make them that way. That is a money price that all of us can understand. But a second price must be paid as well, paid in the effort and attention necessary to taste and compare the admittedly great variety of fine Burgundy appellations and the many names (growers and shippers) responsible for their tasting quality. Not everyone will want to take pains to cultivate enjoyment for what most working tasters consider the greatest of white wines and many think the richest, most impressive and thrilling of reds. The next few pages are dedicated to those who do, with the warning that the variety and quality of Burgundy wine types is vastly greater than I can describe.

CÔTE D'OR

Individual as their refinements may be, the style of fine white wines of the Côte d'Or falls in a more compact range than that of reds. Degrees of tartness may divide different examples of Chassagne-Montrachet or separate the Montrachet family from more succulent whites from Corton-Charlemagne. But still greater stylistic extremes separate fine reds, and more variety flourishes among them, from the dark-colored heady Grand Cru found in the Côtes de Nuits to elusive, perfumed Volnay or Pommard from the Côtes de Beaune. Certainly conventional standards for appraising all fine wines apply in Burgundy—color, aroma, bouquet, intensity of taste, purity, harmonious development to the senses, and fine aftertaste. But Côte d'Or wines are admired for their lush richness of flavor in all its mouth-filling and dramatic nuances no less than for their finesse—a unique combination of attributes. Nuits may emphasize abundance of impression to nose and mouth and Beaune stress finesse, if only by understating shade of color and immediate sensory impact so as to better display aftertaste. Nothing is gained and much is lost by seeking for "favorite" wines or "best" appellations.

Two aberrations plague red Côte d'Or wines. Sadly, both arise from efforts to bully the wines into imagined conformity with public taste. Growers or shippers may convince themselves, or be convinced, to strip their red wines of any feature interfering with immediate drinkability. Burgundies are already forward by inherent style; pushing them ahead further often topples them over the brink into precocity, at the expense of character. Overly short vattings give light, pleasant wines but rather anonymous ones. This is not an effect of sophisticated treatments, such as flash pasteurization (rapid heat stabilization) of wines not truly "finished," but of the goals of vinification itself. The effort to carry a red wine rapidly to a point where it could offend no consumer also carries it to the point where only regional Burgundy style is discernible. On the other hand, producers may be persuaded that bankruptcy if not the gallows awaits any shipper or grower whose Burgundy does not stun the senses with color, body, and other concentrated qualities. Some appear to regard an upper limit of 14 percent alcohol on table wines as an Anglo-Saxon plot to unman France. Often through much expensive trouble, the zealously produced red Burgundies that ensue do make a strong impact on the palate. But they suggest sweetness and lack franker-tasting impressions. Again, general Burgundian qualities are present, but so are less desirable and natural ones.

Both these exaggerations in wine style—lightening or overweighing—end in a result best seen by assembling a collection of different appellations from the same grower or shipper. Whether the wines taste too light or too cloying is less the point than that the Chambolle-Musigny, for example, tastes remarkably like the Vosne-Romanée, which in turn resembles the Pommard, which resembles the Corton. Trying to lighten a naturally dark acerbic wine is more commonly a grower's doing, whereas beefing up a naturally delicate one is a frequent failing of shippers. Appellation character, balance of taste, and certainly individuality suffer from either intervention. Awkward and deficient wines may need special vinification or other treatment. Such correction is not the same operation as imposing one commercial style on many sorts of fine wines. Attempts to standardize Burgundies or anything else are understandable enough. The twentieth century slowly nudges any craftsman toward schizophrenia as it loudly glamorizes quality, originality, and identity, and continues

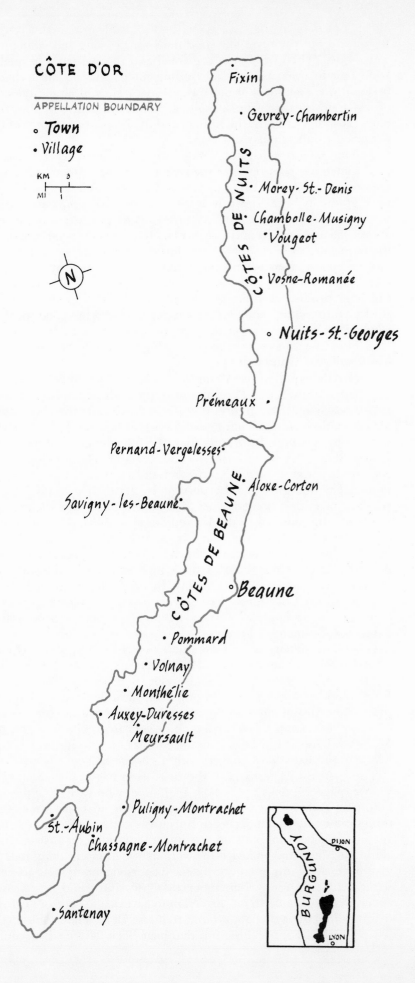

to demonstrate ploddingly how much money can be made from uniform products sold good and hard.

Having armed the reader against some common production practices that blur the distinctive qualities of different Burgundies, it remains to arm him against this book, which could do worse still. To generalize and affirm a single tasting style as being "what to expect" in any Burgundy appellation risks deforming the facts of so many different wines and their understanding and enjoyment. It may be helpful to describe a single ideal Sauternes as what all fine growers in Bordeaux aim at. For Burgundy the equivalent is pompous, silly, wrong. The wines are individual. Certain qualities associate traditionally with certain groupings, now enshrined in appellations or other names by which wines are known collectively. Some, including a few Grands Crus, have more specific attributes than others. Appellations such as Beaune, however, encompass so many delicious styles that any one characterization is dubious and risks interfering with a reader's own appreciation of the wine. To do more than evoke some distinguishing features of each large group of wines would insidiously step over the important line that divides professional description from personal taste, a line that I have strained both to perceive and respect throughout this book; I will not tempt the gods by either repeating the point or pretending to its invariable achievement.

Côtes de Nuits

Fixin is a medium-size appellation producing generous red wines less exported than more famous names immediately to its south. Critics find them less appealing in fruit and aftertaste than the Gevrey family (see below); enthusiasts point to their steady development in bottle. There are at least six First Growth *climats*.

Gevrey-Chambertin, a village appellation in its own right and a very big one, contains Grand Cru Chambertin and a flock of other Grands Crus hyphenating the Chambertin name to their own. The best are intense red wines in which a sense of ripe fruit is introduced by a dark and scintillating color and profound bouquet. Neither to nose or palate is the grapy and vinous style disturbed by earthy, more pungent or mineral impressions sometimes found in the wines of Vosne-Romanée or those of Beaune. This emphasis on pure taste of ripe Pinot Noir at the expense of some more aromatic or flowery impressions runs right through most fine Chambertin, though some tasters find a raspberry suggestion in both the bouquet and aftertaste. These qualities are shared among the more than 20 Premier Cru *climats*, of which Clos St.-Jacques is only the best known. Latricières-Chambertin is frequently distinctive among the Grands Crus for its relative fragrance and subtlety compared to the powerful but frank wines epitomized by the best Chambertin and Clos de Bèze.

Gevrey-Chambertin village wines necessarily vary widely. The best have strong bouquet, less concentration and excitement to the taste than the Grands Crus, but some of the same outlines. Color is often a good prophet, with darker wines showing more intensity of taste and lighter ones alcoholic enough but often short on fruit and flavor.

Morey-St.-Denis contains four Grands Crus: Bonnes Mares, Clos St.-Denis, Clos de la Roche, and Clos de Tart; and one confusion—Bonnes Mares overlaps into neighboring Chambolle-Musigny and may be sold as a Premier Cru of that appellation where it does. Another *climat*, Clos des Lambrays, justifies its indignation at being denied Grand Cru status by producing wines to prove its point. A number of Bonnes Mares growers make wines less intense than the biggest Chambertin, but others of the Grands Crus often if not always share decidedly similar tasting qualities with their Chambertin neighbors, ripe qualities in which body and vinosity make vivid impressions, aftertaste holds closely to initial tasting impressions, which are extremely frank and clean with fruit certainly present and palpable but restrained. Many consider it an error to have separated this village from Gevrey, and in general prices of the village wines of Morey have suffered. Twenty-five Premier Cru vineyards follow the well-known Clos des Lambrays. The village wines, of which some 50,000 gallons (1,895 hectoliters) are produced, broadly resemble Gevrey.

Chambolle-Musigny commences with its share of Bonnes Mares, tending to a gracious style, sometimes elusive, always fine and intriguing when well made. But Chambolle-Musigny is distinguished by fruity impressions and by a wonderful beginning sensation on the palate that the French call *épanouissement*—the opening of a flower or an emotion. Le Musigny, the Grand Cru giving its name to the village, is the exemplar of these qualities—a seductive and delicious first impression of fruit, perhaps the most striking of the whole Côte d'Or, backed by a substantial but not dense body, deceptively supple and silky in texture. All these adjectives suggest delicate wines, and indeed so the best ones of the village taste, but fine ones lack nothing in color and body either and mature well. Yet it is the finesse, nearly ethereal in perfect vintages, and the wonderful first impressions to the senses, which the taster remembers best and to which he or she returns, hoping to find them again. Seventeen Premier Cru *climats* are included in the village appellation, which can yield over 100,000 gallons (3,800 hectoliters) of wine, all red under village name, but a little white under the Musigny designation, an expensive curiosity.

Clos-de-Vougeot occupies a large part of Vougeot village. Its famous red wines are remarkable for an extraordinary glossy or velvety impression to which words cannot do justice. Intense but not aggressive in either bouquet or taste, finest examples of this Grand Cru (symbolic of the monastic origins of Burgundy) seem to have tamed all tasting excesses, whether of fruit, of earthiness, or those evoked by mineral analogies. They are perfect examples of a fine red wine in that the grape variety could not be mistaken for other than the Pinot Noir, nor the regional style confused with another; yet nothing in the bouquet, taste, or aftertaste is excessive or detracts from the whole. Harmonious wines on more modest scale are not uncommon; wines so intense and refined, so heightened in impression yet so balanced are exceptional; its enthusiasts have reason to argue that it is France's greatest red wine. The rest of Vougeot (much smaller than the big Grand Cru *climat*) has four red and one white *climat* designations. Subtle fine wines are made in red; the white tends to heavy styles lacking a vitality and charm. But all are overshadowed by the best of the Clos-de-Vougeot's many growers. The superlative adjectives that have just flowed (more inexpensively than a bottle of it) about the name of Clos-de-Vougeot of necessity apply to finest vintages: where conditions do not allow this great Côte de Nuits such balance, much charm is offered the taster, and much quality of aftertaste, but Clos-de-Vougeot is deified for its peak examples rather than its average product. Disappointing and expensive examples abound.

Vosne-Romanée borders Vougeot in prestige and geographical fact. Its ten Premier Cru *climats* and village appellation wine in the amount of some 125,000 gallons (4,735 hectoliters) necessarily include various qualities and styles. Some of the best-known growers

La Tache

Like its more famous neighbor, Romanée-Conti, La Tache is a monopoly of one shipper; both Grand Cru are mighty expensive, Romanée-Conti ridiculously so. Great vintages of La Tache, particularly those antedating the frosts that badly damaged the vineyard 20 years ago, were remarkable wines in their power, an intensity of flavor that could only be called dramatic, and in their aftertaste suggesting the highest ideals of winemaking, even by the elevated standards of the best Côtes de Nuits Grand Cru. Fine wines were made in dry years such as 1952 and in some thin ones such as 1957. Great crops such as 1949 deserved nearly any price.

VINTAGE   *DATE*   *PRICE*

GUESTS

MENU   *COMMENTS*

Musigny de Vogüé

This famous wine moves in the same rarefied price atmosphere of the others on this page and like them represents a very grand tradition of powerful, elegant wines, standards of taste for their fellows. Occasionally the Musigny de Vogüé is a bit overcharged for an appellation whose hallmarks are fruit, elegance, and silky texture. Those of Louis Latour, for example, show these latter characteristics but fall short of the extreme power and lusciousness achieved in the best wines of this grower. Compare these with Clos des Lambrays or finer members of the Chambertin family.

VINTAGE   *DATE*   *PRICE*

GUESTS

MENU   *COMMENTS*

Chambertin Clos de Bèze

Pierre Gelin's Chambertin Clos de Bèze represents medium-scale fine growers that cannot produce the quantity of any one appellation necessary for a major shipper but are able to hold up a high standard of quality and authenticity with sufficient wine to give enthusiasts occasional access to its taste. There are several score such growers in the Côte d'Or; their wines achieve the highest standards of their appellations and are matched only by the finest selections of dedicated shippers. This Chambertin answers closely to the general description of this Grand Cru appellation—generous, finely colored wine with handsome proportions, elegant bouquet, rich texture, and excellent finesse. Camus and Marey-Monge, Roumier, and Clair Dau are some comparable growers.

VINTAGE   *DATE*   *PRICE*

GUESTS

MENU   *COMMENTS*

Clos-de-Vougeot Liger-Belair

The label shown here is an ancient one and would not now be found; it predates the appellation laws and suggests how even the greatest appellations, and this is one, were once presented to the public with only the guarantee of their seller. This remarkable 1919 vintage showed the extraordinary glossy texture and velvetlike impressions of Clos-de-Vougeot at its best, sensations supported by as delicious a flavor and as exciting a finish as any great wine in Burgundy. Some would argue that its qualities give it the first place. Other firms have shipped fine wines of this great *climat*, and there are many grower-bottled examples, all at expensive prices. The best wines deserve them.

VINTAGE   *DATE*   *PRICE*

GUESTS

MENU   *COMMENTS*

DOMAINE DE LA ROMANÉE-CONTI

LA TACHE

LA TACHE - Appellation Contrôlée

de Villaine & J. Chambon

Petits Fils de J. M. Duvault-Blochet

ANNÉE 1949   Seuls propriétaires

INTERDICTION D'IMPORTER OU DE VENDRE AUX USA ET UK

MUSIGNY

APPELLATION CONTROLÉE

Comte Georges de VOGÜÉ

1945

GRAND VIN DE BOURGOGNE

Mis en bouteilles à la propriété

FILIBER A NUITS.

MIS EN BOUTEILLES A LA PROPRIÉTÉ

Médaille d'Or   Paris 1962

CHAMBERTIN

CLOS DE BÈZE

APPELLATION CONTROLÉE

PIERRE GELIN

PROPRIÉTAIRE A FIXIN ET GEVREY-CHAMBERTIN (CÔTE-D'OR)

1919

C. MAREY & Cie LIGER-BELAIR

LIGER-BELAIR & FILS, Suc^rs

PROPRIÉTAIRES A NUITS & VOSNE (CÔTE-D'OR)

FRANCE

CLOS-DE-VOUGEOT

Gevrey-Chambertin Joseph Drouhin

Drouhin, a large firm carrying a complete line of Burgundy appellations and some branded wines of which the best known is Soleil Blanc, illustrates the issues of the international class of shippers attempting to deal in the finest wines. The company's intentions are excellent, as reflected in this generously bodied red Burgundy with all the force on the palate and lushness expected of well-made village red wines of the Côte d'Or. It is an excellent wine. However, the individuality and appellation style found in the wine from the smaller firm of Thomas-Bassot on this page or elsewhere are lacking. The dilemma resembles that of big shippers everywhere—how to get enough quantity of individual wine. Soleil Blanc is a good value for its tart, clean, and generous tasting qualities. Moillard in Nuits is another large firm with excellent intentions, Faiveley is smaller, and one could name others.

VINTAGE   DATE   PRICE

GUESTS

MENU   COMMENTS

Clos des Lambrays

This is a single vineyard above Morey-St.-Denis that has made extraordinary wines under one owner. Their balance and finesse equal the more famous Grand Cru that surround them. For those fortunate enough to taste it, the 1949 vintage exemplified the startling merits of this property and, in some ways, those of the entire Côtes de Nuits. Brilliant dark color, heady perfume, voluminous and nearly distracting, pure and dignified impressions to the senses, all these balance with each other. Its usual style approaches that of Latricières Chambertin, but ripe years have intensity that do credit to the intentions of the wine makers. There is, still, a continuity of style vintage after vintage, just one more distinction one wishes were found in more famous estates. This brilliant wine represents fine Côtes de Nuits.

VINTAGE   DATE   PRICE

GUESTS

MENU   COMMENTS

Chambolle-Musigny Antonin Guyon

Some harsh remarks have run through these pages about Burgundy wine makers who attempt to build up the body of their wines at the expense of elegance and style. This large grower represents another and contrary tendency, sacrificing the force and color of his wines, even those in appellations associated with richly charged style, to achieve lighter style and more refined aftertaste. The majority of these estates are in Corton and Meursault and were made famous by a former owner, M. Thevenot. Some Bonnes Mares and other Côtes de Nuits growers strive in similar directions. Such wines should be carefully served and tasted, as should all delicate red wines, and offer distinctive combinations of fruit, a soft address to the senses, and a lingering aftertaste.

VINTAGE   DATE   PRICE

GUESTS

MENU   COMMENTS

Clos des Ruchottes-Chambertin Thomas-Bassot

Here a medium-size shipper in Gevrey has bottled the product of a single *climat*. Not only is this a well-made wine in itself, quite fresh yet generous, with a powerful aftertaste untroubled by any defects, but it deserves praise as a fine example of the family of Chambertin wines. The bouquet is particularly lovely with an invigorating aroma of Pinot Noir showing the berrylike odors associated with cassis by Burgundian tasters. On the palate its impressions are firm, the development frank and clean, and the finish very slightly tinged with tannin. It is not a lush version of Chambertin and lacks the full intensity of a Chambertin or Clos de Bèze. Softer, more aromatic features are found in the Griotte-Chambertin of this same shipper, and Thomas-Bassot ships a complete line of lesser Burgundies.

VINTAGE   DATE   PRICE

GUESTS

MENU   COMMENTS

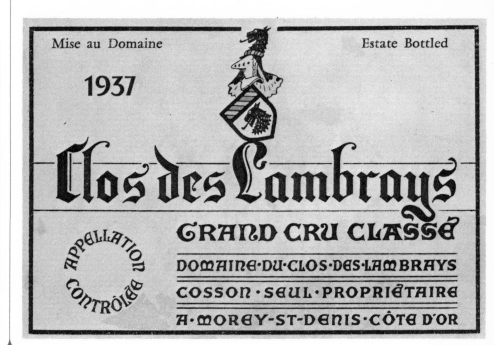

Joseph Drouhin

RÉCOLTE DU DOMAINE

GEVREY-CHAMBERTIN

APPELLATION CONTROLÉE

MIS EN BOUTEILLE PAR

JOSEPH DROUHIN

Maison fondée en 1880

NÉGOCIANT A BEAUNE, CÔTE-D'OR

AUX CELLIERS DES ROIS DE FRANCE ET DES DUCS DE BOURGOGNE

Mise au Domaine   Estate Bottled

1937

Clos des Lambrays

GRAND CRU CLASSÉ

APPELLATION CONTRÔLÉE

DOMAINE·DU·CLOS·DES·LAMBRAYS

COSSON · SEUL · PROPRIÉTAIRE

A·MOREY-ST-DENIS·CÔTE D'OR

TRADE   MARK

Chambolle-Musigny

APPELLATION CONTROLÉE

DOMAINE du VILLAGE

ANTONIN GUYON

PROPRIÉTAIRE A CHAMBOLLE-MUSIGNY (COTE D'OR)

Mis en bouteille au Domaine

MIS EN BOUTEILLES
AU DOMAINE   TRADE   MARK

Clos des
Ruchottes-Chambertin

APPELLATION CONTRÔLÉE

PARIS 1878   PARIS 1889-1900   *Maison Thomas-Bassot*

MEMBRE DU JURY - HORS CONCOURS

Négociant-Eleveur à Gevrey-Chambertin (Côte-d'Or)

Imprimé en France   PRODUCE OF FRANCE   FONDÉE EN 1850
                          DÉPOSÉ   FILUBER A NUITS

Auxey-Duresses
Domaine du Moulin Aux Moines

This appellation reflects merits of red and white Burgundies of the Côte d'Or without possessing the full intensity of the region's greatest wines. Its prices, if not cheap, are restrained in comparison with Grand Cru wines, and it has the virtue of introducing fine Burgundy without bankrupting the wine drinker in the process. Bottled by a proprietor, this 1971 red has excellent Pinot Noir aroma and character traits of the appellation—namely medium light color and a long series of flavors that end well and do not give the artificial impression of wines bolstered to meet expectations of excessive power or sweetness. It is both an excellent and authentic Auxey, deserving of its popularity in England. Auxey-Duresses reds usually mature quickly; the whites may be a little clumsy but contain much flavor and aftertaste. Reds are more generous than the similarly priced reds of Pernand-Vergelesses; the two whites are similar.

VINTAGE   DATE   PRICE

GUESTS

MENU   COMMENTS

Echezeaux Ropiteau Frères

Echezeaux is an appellation that tends to get lost among its glamorous neighbors, Romanée-Conti, La Tache, and Clos-de-Vougeot. Ropiteau is a medium-size shipper sending out good examples of important Burgundy appellations of which Echezeaux is but one. The house style varies. Some wines tend to be overcharged and others lack the particular mark of their appellation, but the level is high and deserves patronage. Echezeaux comes close to the intense, deep-flavored impact of the greatest Nuits, with some of the musty or pungent odors often encountered in Vosne, less fruit on the average than Gevrey-Chambertin, and less delicacy than Chambolle-Musigny. The best are great emphatic wines, impressive in aftertaste and maturing well and long in bottle.

VINTAGE   DATE   PRICE

GUESTS

MENU   COMMENTS

Nuits-St.-Georges
Clos de la Maréchale Faiveley

Clos de la Maréchale may be located at the southern (Beaune) end of the Côtes de Nuits, but the *éleveurs* have finished their wine in a vigorous, dark-colored, firm style representing one type of Nuits wine making. Compared to a more florid style, these drier, more natural-tasting and intense red Burgundies may seem to lack charm, but their development in bottle is usually more assured. Faiveley is a medium-size shipper, a rival of such firms as Bouchard Aine, Coron, Bichot, Ropiteau, Drouhin Laroze, and others whose offerings usually include village appellation wines and individual wines such as this one. At another extreme, Nuits or Nuits-St.-Georges of softer, looser texture and sweeter tasting impressions than this correct and authentic Clos de la Maréchale can easily be found, if less easily admired.

VINTAGE   DATE   PRICE

GUESTS

MENU   COMMENTS

Nuits-St.-Georges Gouges

Not only is the name of Gouges associated with the formation of *Appellation Controlée* laws in Burgundy; it is also prominent among a group of proprietary (estate-bottled) wines from the Côte d'Or that achieved rapid prominence during the 1950s in the American market. This feat is to be credited to a few energetic importer-promoters, among them Robert Haas and Alexis Lichine, and their "stables" of Burgundy growers should be grateful, among them Henri Lamarche, Étienne Sauzet, d'Angerville, Roumier, Trapet, Merodes, Ramonet, and a string of others. Many of these, including Gouges, have subsequently shipped bigger quantities of Côte d'Or wines below the standards that framed their original reputations.

The best Gouges wines are representative Nuits with good flavor and lush qualities. They develop quickly in bottle, at least in recent years.

VINTAGE   DATE   PRICE

GUESTS

MENU   COMMENTS

MIS DU DOMAINE   PRODUCE OF FRANCE

CLOS DU MOULIN AUX MOINES

AUXEY-DURESSES

APPELLATION AUXEY-DURESSES CONTROLÉE
ROLAND THEVENIN
DOMAINE DU MOULIN AUX MOINES

Propriétaire à Auxey-Duresses, Côte-d'Or
Sole Importers : Heyman Brothers Ltd. London, .W. I.

ECHEZEAUX

APPELLATION CONTROLÉE

ROPITEAU FRÈRES

Négociants-Eleveurs à Meursault, Côte-d'Or
depuis 1848

FAIVELEY

TRADE MARK

PRODUCE OF FRANCE   CONTENTS : 1 PINT 8 FL. OZ.
RED BURGUNDY WINE   ALCOHOL 13 % BY VOLUME

Nuits-St-Georges Clos de la Maréchale
Appellation Nuits-Saint-Georges premier cru Contrôlée

JOSEPH FAIVELEY, NÉGOCIANT A NUITS-SAINT-GEORGES (COTE-D'OR)

Dreyfus, Ashby & Co

Imp. Paris, Nuits

MIS EN BOUTEILLE AU DOMAINE

APPELLATION CONTROLÉE
NUITS St GEORGES
La Perrière

Domaine Henri Gouges à Nuits St Georges
(Côte-d'Or)   *Bourgogne*

make lighter, refined wines. When darker, heavier types are vinified, their pungent aroma presages a similar wine often strongly marked by an earthy or mineral taste, agreeably countered by fruit to introduce it and a long finish to smooth its exit, but there nevertheless. This can be criticized as a lack of frankness or enjoyed as part of the *cachet*, or style. The general standard is high and the wines are expensive.

Just west above Vosne-Romanée village lies a cluster of Grand Cru vineyards producing dark, powerful wines with high bouquet, great longevity in bottle, and more address and attack on all the senses than Musigny or Clos-de-Vougeot, their most proximate rivals. By contrast, their aftertaste and finesse, though lacking nothing, are often overshadowed; it is the more dazzling first impressions that are remembered above all in connection with the great names La Tache, Romanée-Conti, and Richebourg. These costly, celebrated red wines are sumptuous; every tasting quality seems abundant, opulent, forceful. Alas, perhaps it is more appropriate to use the past tense in extolling the two most famous Grands Crus, Romanée-Conti and La Tache. They belong to one owner, and their strongest claims to greatness lie rather in the past than in the present, though both remain extravagantly expensive. La Romanée Grands Echezeaux and Echezeaux complete the celebrities among the Vosne Grands Crus. Styles vary from elegant wines tending to thinness to concentrated, dark versions of Côtes de Nuits often closed in and inexpressive until a few years in bottle have brought forward their broad, vital bouquet and flavor, pleasantly musty but soundly rich. Echezeaux wines of much finesse and excitement of flavor are often made but tend to get lost among their illustrious neighbors such as Romanée-Conti, which is wrongly supposed by its wealthy buyers to be superior as a matter of right.

Nuits-St.-Georges (Nuits) is the biggest and most important of the village appellations of the Côtes de Nuits, with 200,000 gallons (7,600 hectoliters) of wine and more Premier Cru than any other village. Its long vineyard, transitional into the Beaune area, is dotted with superb *climats* whose styles vary widely. Fine wines with pungent bouquet, harmony of taste, and great finesse typify the best of red Burgundy. They stress both the odor and "feel" of ripe Pinot Noir and offer long, subtle impressions. Color, a certain immediate pungency of taste, as well as aromatic bouquet and relative mellowness in their development on the palate distinguish them, if sometimes hesitantly, from most Côtes de Beaune red wines. Most tasters would place the best of them on a level with Grands Crus, though no *climats* in Nuits are graded that highly by the appellation authorities.

From this high standard there is a decline in the power of taste on the one hand and, on the other hand, a deviation in style toward subtler wines among many growers. Estate bottling permits consumers to "follow" the style of particular growers. Nuits shippers' wines also have their company styles, some tending to more authority and color, others to blander wines.

Côtes de Beaune

The commune of Ladoix-Serrigny begins the Côtes de Beaune and borders the boundaries of Aloxe-Corton and the different Corton vineyards. Ladoix itself produces a moderate amount of red wine sold well below the prices of its neighbors. The best is quite good, approaching a less intense Nuits, but little exported. Aloxe-Corton,

which is a village appellation in its own right, alone in the Côte d'Or possesses important Grand Cru titles in both red and white wines. From the slopes of a large domelike hill facing east, south, and west come rich red Le Corton and superb white wines designated Corton-Charlemagne. Fine red Corton wines are aromatic; their subtle odors continue into a mixture of unctuous but still spicy tastes. The sense of fruit, of ripe grape, is less emphasized; and some of the grainy or slightly earthy qualities found in Beaune wines can appear. Heady, flattering to the palate, lacking nothing, the usual Corton style offers body and texture, a long taste, and much finesse but less of the volatile immediate rush of flower and fruit whose assault to the senses makes Chambolle-Musigny or some Bonnes Mares so distinct. Some growers make a denser version of Corton with much color and firmness, disclosing itself more slowly in time; others tend to vinify wines that show great delicacy in youth and resemble lighter styles of Beaune wines.

Aloxe-Corton village reds, of which there are nearly 100,000 gallons (3,800 hectoliters) made in good years, do not enjoy abroad the favor that the best of them surely deserve. Their mellow address on the palate, lovely finish, and subtle qualities intermediate between Beaune and Nuits make them extremely attractive individual wines and very useful ones with which to begin an acquaintance with red Burgundies in general, for they include most Côte d'Or virtues in an accessible way. Within Ladoix and Aloxe there are 14 *climats* entitled to First Growth and the Grands Crus Corton-Charlemagne and Le Corton. A third Grand Cru, Charlemagne, was mapped out in this commune, but no grower has used this designation for some time.

The white wines of Corton-Charlemagne are widely considered second only to Le Montrachet. Some members of the wine trade now prefer them, claiming to detect in quality Montrachet the bad effects of a mysterious local disease deforming the vegetation and spacing of grapes on the bunches. Corton-Charlemagne are astoundingly luscious yet rarely cloying or ponderous on the palate—a difficult achievement. They represent one Burgundy extreme of Chardonnay grape character, the driest Chablis or Chassagne-Montrachet standing perhaps for the other. The full bouquet promises a rich wine to follow. Their effect on the senses is overpowering and mouth-filling, yet frank and topped with delicious aftertaste. Few white Burgundies combine so many flavors so well and come in such a rich form, suggesting a liqueur or honeyed beverage yet without actual sweetness. For scope and breadth of taste, they could be compared to Meursault (see below), but their finesse is at a higher level and has none of the eccentricities that plague many Meursault. Both flavor and bouquet mature gracefully for several years in balanced vintages; but the appeal, freshness, and excitement of the wines do not fade easily with time but remain perfumed, vinous, lively. These unctuous and "larger than life" impressions distinguish them in degree rather than kind from the great white wines to the immediate south, but it can be said that succulent, broad-tasting, and long-lived Corton-Charlemagne are more to be met with than like white wines in, say, Chassagne-Montrachet.

Pernand-Vergelesses is hidden behind (west of) the best Corton slopes and extends south of them. Its white wines offer lesser versions of Chardonnay aroma and tasting qualities. They commonly lack peak finesse, the full ripeness, and therefore the power of wines from the best plots; but they are distinguished bottles in their own right. Most tasters seem to share the experience of the author, which is that the whites of this commune are marginally finer and more interesting than the reds, but only a tenth as much white is produced. The reds are flatter, more modest versions of Beaune red wines with firm but shorter impressions. They lack the full finesse of the best Burgundies. Their attractions are the general ones of the Côte d'Or rather than those of a very distinct village style. Prices are relatively low, as in the case of many intermediate regions crushed between famous neighbors, and both whites and reds merit sampling. Ripe vintages alone present major interest, for the wines tend to a thinness of flavor that poor harvest conditions accentuate unpleasantly. Îles de Vergelesses is the best known of the five First Growth *climats*.

Savigny-les-Beaune is a large village appellation that, unlike most of the Côte d'Or, stretches west into the foothills of the ranges backing Burgundy rather than lying neatly north to south along them. Its 24 Premier Cru *climats* intertwine in fact and name with neighboring Vergelesses, and its production divides between some 7,000 gallons (265 hectoliters) of white wine and more than 170,000 gallons (6,440 hectoliters) of red. Appeal, charm, cleanness of taste—features that are now distinctly those of Beaune in most of the better wines—are the attractions of the appellation and its best *climats*. Here and in Vergelesses we begin to find the divorce between color and the tasting qualities associated with it that distinguishes many wines of the Côtes de Beaune from those farther north; wines of irreproachable fruit and intensity can show a light shaded "dress" and yet lack nothing on the palate.

Savigny is too large an appellation to admit of much useful generalization. Its best wines are fine and perfumed. These qualities deteriorate as one crosses the main north-south road linking Beaune and Dijon into the appellation Chorey-les-Beaunes, where light red wines, some attractive, are made on terrains with more alluvium and inferior exposition and drainage.

The town of Beaune is the center for Côte d'Or shippers and the site of their cellars. The famous annual Hospices de Beaune auctions attract tourists and buyers from across the world. Ninety-five percent of the wine produced in the long, sprawling appellation is red, much of it from some 30 Premier Cru vineyards, some as famous as lesser Grands Crus and often producing better wine. Growers who vat their wines longer and achieve ripeness produce wines of great power and impressive appearance, but to characterize the large district is rather to evoke a lighter-colored wine, at least to the eye and first impression. The intense fruit so striking in the heart of Côtes de Nuits—causing tasters to compare Chambertin and Musigny to ripe berries—is less salient here. Drier wines that engage the palate in subtle ways are more the rule, and they impress by their aftertaste and finesse. The very finest capture both qualities, stressing the volume of taste and richness without which a Côte d'Or wine cannot contend for highest honors, and yet following with the exquisite aftertaste, slightly musty, slightly woody, always vinous, which is not found or rarely found outside the best Beaune *climats*. Not to every palate, but to many, Beaune's special style is a more acquired taste than the dramatic sensations of Nuits reds or the flagrant ones of Beaujolais.

Pommard is a large appellation whose name is often taken in vain to suggest dark, dense wines. Its best qualities belong to the family of Beaune wines though it lacks nothing in generosity and breed. Definite-tasting wines with a long finish and a distinct flavor are the ones most admired locally, with reason. The big appellation makes 250,000 gallons (9,470 hectoliters) and offers nearly 30 Premier Cru *climats*. Maximum production limits here as in Beaune are more relaxed than those for Grand Cru wines, but the highest quality can be fairly compared to Grand Cru standards. Some extremely elegant,

flowery versions of this appellation can readily be confounded with Volnay wines, which some southern Côte d'Or growers consider the most elegant of all Burgundy.

Volnay, only two-thirds the size of Pommard but still a large area producing 150,000 gallons (5,700 hectoliters), also contains just short of 30 Premier Cru *climats* and is vastly more appreciated in Burgundy than among wine drinkers abroad. At home, its normally pale color is accepted as a fact of life, and the fire in its hue is as much admired as the subtle bouquet, restrained, flowery, and suggesting the silky but vital wine to follow. Delicacy, balance between vinosity, clarity of taste, and finesse are among its merits. A lovely development on the palate and elusive but exciting aftertaste complete the qualities that local professionals would probably cite to support a reputation for an appellation whose merits are self-evident in the land of its birth. It is easier to find words for more powerful pungent wines than for those that adopt a more refined interpretation of Pinot Noir qualities. Beaune, Pommard, and Volnay all suffer a bit in wine literature from this fact, but the wines suffer much more by any attempt to bolster them up to an image of great lushness, even sweetness. All three are appellations whose greatest excitement resides in their delicacy and style rather than in their corpulence.

Monthélie is a smaller appellation nearly entirely given to red wines of which ten *climats* may be called Premier Cru. The wines are not so much thin as modest, too good to be called small, short on the palate, or incomplete, but restrained and dry, with attraction of flavor and limited finish rather than a memorable or startling tasting impression. Fine wines in that they improve in bottle, but limited in bouquet and aftertaste, they are excellent in their own right or useful as lesser Côte d'Or wines with which to introduce a finer red.

Auxey-Duresses makes one-third white wine and two-thirds red; there are 11 possible Premier Cru *climats* and just over 60,000 gallons (2,273 hectoliters) of total appellation wine. Whites have good features of Côtes de Beaune Chardonnay wines; they are complete in bouquet and balance, but sometimes cede a point of liveliness and show too much alcohol for the flavor or finish. It is rare to find a white Auxey with notable finesse comparable to that of the greater appellations, but by no means rare to find one more worthy of its reasonable price than disappointing whites from the great expensive appellations. Like the reds of Pernand-Vergelesses, those of Auxey, while fresh and appetizing, do not normally embody more than the better general features of Côtes de Beaune. That is high praise, however; and they can surpass in all points inferior examples of greater appellations.

The 18 Premiers Crus of Meursault lie straight between Volnay to the north and Puligny-Montrachet to the south, and beside them in rank are nearly 250,000 gallons (9,470 hectoliters) of village Meursault. No Grand Cru appellation is assigned to this village, whose wines impress by rich texture abounding in earthy, firm flavors carried on a generous body. It could be argued, however, that it is the most rewarding of the great village white wines, for much quality shippers' Meursault, true to its appellation style, is exported at relatively reasonable prices. These do not usually attain the crisp attack on the palate found often in Chassagne and Puligny-Montrachet village appellations, and even at best, Meursault finesse and aftertaste do not surpass those of their southern neighbors. Provided one accepts as a part of the appellation style fairly assertive texture and grainy impression (though these qualities should not be exaggerated), and an occasional hint of musk or smoky flavors, it is easy to develop a

Santenay Les Gravières Prosper Maufoux

Maufoux is a medium-size shipper with an excellent record for quality and unusual talent in selecting and bottling superior wines from the southern part of the Côte d'Or, such as this first-class Santenay. Such wines rarely show the darkest hue of color, but they can be generous Burgundies in ripe years and subtle wines at their best. The correct and distinctive bouquet reflects moderate but not excessive maturation in oak. Three or four years in bottle is normally sufficient for such wine to show its full range of qualities.

VINTAGE   *DATE*   *PRICE*

GUESTS

MENU   *COMMENTS*

Chassagne-Montrachet Claude Ramonet

Alexis Lichine and Co. has made this label familiar in American markets. The red wines of Chassagne-Montrachet rarely achieve the full distinction of the best whites but are supple and flavorful, tending to lightness and with generous rather than overwhelming bouquet. Ramonet's wines vary widely and are typically at the lighter end of this spectrum but show expected bland and attractive tasting features common to most reds from this locale.

VINTAGE   *DATE*   *PRICE*

GUESTS

MENU   *COMMENTS*

Chassagne-Montrachet Pierre Bourée

This plain-looking label from a small *éleveur* specializing in Côte d'Or wines is chosen to contrast with the well-distributed estate-bottled Ramonet Chassagne red wine on this page and so make a point. It is a better representative of its type in every way than the other, more famous wine and shows that competence and integrity in Burgundy can be independent of estate bottling; in fact, an *éleveur* may often be more rigorous than a grower, for he can choose from among more wines.

This 1971 example has harmonious bouquet that overshadows its aroma, but both are subtle and elegant. A beautiful example of the best the appellation can offer, its style is carried on a long series of full tasting impressions ending with racy finish.

VINTAGE   *DATE*   *PRICE*

GUESTS

MENU   *COMMENTS*

Chassagne-Montrachet Marquis de Laguiche

This is a famous label, and a famous name, in the Côte d'Or, for its owner is a proprietor in Le Montrachet, the most expensive white wine in Burgundy and traditionally regarded in a class by itself. While both successful and disappointing examples of white Chassagne-Montrachet are shipped under this label, its general style could be called fuller and sometimes less lively than tarter examples of the appellation. When successful, it emphasizes flavor and body and is a distinctive wine. Quite a variety of estate-bottled Chassagne wines are exported to America. The major shippers normally bottle this appellation under their own labels.

VINTAGE   *DATE*   *PRICE*

GUESTS

MENU   *COMMENTS*

SANTENAY 1er CRU

FONDÉE EN 1860

LES GRAVIÈRES

APPELLATION SANTENAY 1er CRU CONTROLÉE

BURGUNDY TABLE WINE

Prosper Maufoux

NÉGOCIANT A SANTENAY (COTE-D'OR)

· o ·

Imported by **THE HOUSE OF BURGUNDY** NEW YORK N.Y.

PRODUCT OF FRANCE   Net Contents : 12 Fl. Oz.

GRAND VIN   ESTATE BOTTLED
DE

Chassagne-Montrachet

Clos Saint-Jean

APPELLATION CONTROLÉE

PRODUCED AND BOTTLED BY

Claude Ramonet
Propriétaire-Récoltant
à Chassagne-Montrachet
(Côte-d'Or)

Mise au Domaine

STILL RED BURGUNDY WINE

CHASSAGNE-MONTRACHET

APPELLATION CONTROLÉE

PIERRE BOURÉE FILS

NÉGOCIANT - ELEVEUR A GEVREY-CHAMBERTIN

IMPRIMÉ EN FRANCE   IMP JOBARD · DIJON

Joseph Drouhin

Chassagne-Montrachet

APPELLATION CONTROLÉE

Marquis de Laguiche
Propriétaire

Meursault Pierre Olivier

Since it is a large appellation, Meursault provides much opportunity to shippers to blend successfully wines from different growers in the area and maintain a good level of "shipper's" wine under this title. Olivier has regularly exported Meursault with the smoky or slightly aromatic bouquet, heavy texture, and abundant flavor touched with earthy impressions that characterize white wines from the area. It is a particular accomplishment to maintain this rich, flavorful style in a vintage such as 1972 with inadequate ripeness and excessive acidity. Most Olivier wines, even those from the Beaune area, are finished in a rather heavy style giving a generous impression to the palate.

VINTAGE　　　　　DATE　　　　　PRICE

GUESTS

MENU　　　　　COMMENTS

Volnay Clos des Ducs Marquis d'Angerville

An effective job of public relations has brought renown to the elegant, light, and handsomely labeled wines from this large grower. The racy, subtle style of the wines is appropriate to this appellation, admired for its finesse rather than its color or power. Shipper's wines tend to fail to represent these qualities of Volnay as they do of neighboring Pommard, putting out wines too heavy and coarse to give drinkers much intuition of the best and individualistic style of wines such as the one represented here.

VINTAGE　　　　　DATE　　　　　PRICE

GUESTS

MENU　　　　　COMMENTS

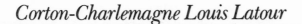

Corton-Charlemagne Louis Latour

Latour is among the best-regarded shippers in the Côte d'Or. Its high appellation wines such as Romanée-St.-Vivant, Corton, and this one command high prices. Latour's reputation for reliability is justified, but the style of some wines is too heavy for the true character of the appellation; in this they resemble Drouhin and some other shippers. This imposing white wine from 1960, an off-vintage, was made with skill and selectivity, commendably full and flavorful, and with the power and rather dramatic development to the senses that alone justify the high prices of this rare and very grand appellàtion. Latour bottles some other estate wines, notably a Corton at their property of Château Grancey.

VINTAGE　　　　　DATE　　　　　PRICE

GUESTS

MENU　　　　　COMMENTS

Bienvenues Bâtard-Montrachet Leflaive

At a mere six acres in extent this is among the smallest and dearest of the great Côte d'Or appellations. Its best qualities combine to make unforgettable white wines such as this splendid version. Chardonnay aroma mingles with remarkable bouquet impossible without cask age but not aggressively woody. It is rare to find white wines tasting so purely of their grape varieties and with such abundant flavor and complex development to the senses; its finesse lingers into a delicious aftertaste completely true to its first impressions to the nose. Wines of comparable elegance, power, and individuality can be found in the appellations of Bâtard-Montrachet, in slightly denser, less lively form in Corton-Charlemagne, and used to be found in the great Le Montrachet appellation. The conceptions of the wine maker come through clearly to make a wine in which grape varietal quality is expressed along with a definite appellation style.

VINTAGE　　　　　DATE　　　　　PRICE

GUESTS

MENU　　　　　COMMENTS

MEURSAULT

APPELLATION CONTROLÉE

•

PIERRE OLIVIER

NÉGOCIANT A NUITS-SAINT-GEORGES (COTE D'OR)

IMP. FILIBER & NUIT'S

MIS EN BOUTEILLE AU DOMAINE

APPELLATION VOLNAY CONTROLÉE

MONOPOLE

VOLNAY

CLOS DES DUCS

1971

MARQUIS D'ANGERVILLE, SEUL PROPRIÉTAIRE
PROPRIÉTAIRE-RÉCOLTANT, VOLNAY, COTE-D'OR, FRANCE

1960

Corton-Charlemagne

APPELLATION CONTROLÉE

Ancien Domaine des Comtes de Grancey

Mis en bouteilles à la propriété

LOUIS LATOUR, Négociant à Beaune (Côte-d'Or)

*Mis en bouteilles
à la Propriété*

Bienvenues Bâtard-Montrachet

APPELLATION CONTROLÉE

DOMAINE LEFLAIVE
PROPRIÉTAIRE A PULIGNY-MONTRACHET (COTE-D'OR)

Jouffroy & Cie, Beaune

Pommard Les Chaponnières Parent

Among the many growers in Pommard this one appears to have found favor in America and deserves credit for frequent vintages of elegant wines that yield little or not at all to the temptation to arrange their natural lightness into purple, sweet, cloying wines that some large shippers fancy the public requires of Pommard. Few names are so abused in the overseas wine trade as this appellation, and hardly a shipper feels that its line of offerings is complete without a wine of this name regardless of its quality. Some of the largest houses are the worst offenders. A bright medium-red color, fragrant aroma, sound but restrained development to the taste culminating in finesse and some complexity are the excellent qualities of the best Pommards. Their family resemblance to neighboring Volnay and subtle Beaune wines is strong.

VINTAGE   DATE   PRICE

GUESTS

MENU   COMMENTS

Hautes Côtes de Beaune Jean Joliot

Selected by the late Frank Schoonmaker to represent one of the two new Burgundy appellations, satellites to the famous towns of Beaune and Nuit, this Pinot Noir represents the authentic and enjoyable qualities hoped for in designating neighboring vineyards by the town names. It certainly could not be taken for a Vosne-Romanée or other Pinot Noir wine from the very best areas but is loyal in its firm, slightly musty bouquet, frank and full development on the palate, and definite varietal character in its aroma; and it reflects the sensible intentions of a grower making wines to be consumed young. It is balanced, drinks well while asserting appellation character, and classes itself as fine wine in Beaune style without full scope. It is correctly priced near $4.00.

VINTAGE   DATE   PRICE

GUESTS

MENU   COMMENTS

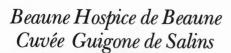

Beaune Hospice de Beaune
Cuvée Guigone de Salins

The history of the Hospice's famous auctions is well described in various books on Burgundy and French wines, and they are if anything increasingly attended. However, they are also increasingly meaningless as an index of Burgundy prices, for buyers, foreign ones above all, consider the publicity received for their expensive purchases of individual *cuvées* at these auctions compensation for the exaggerated prices. Some of the wines are superb and many *cuvée* of Guigone de Salins, one of the most famous, have reflected an extraordinary attack on the senses full of spice, the peculiar mixture the French insist is "truffles," deep flavor, and very exciting aftertaste. The year 1934 was such a vintage. This 1959 was excellent also, and if the style is a bit heavy for Beaune, the wines are certainly noble and instructive Burgundies to experience. The Hospice owns vineyards as well. Auctions are normally in November following the vintage.

VINTAGE   DATE   PRICE

GUESTS

MENU   COMMENTS

Beaune des Chevaliers de L'Arquebuse

This is an elite label of the firm Remoissenet, one of a half dozen superior shippers who, within the limits of the commercially possible, ship wines of authentic appellation style and good quality. This label with its fanciful name, unusual also in omitting the name of the shipper, is their best red Beaune, and the firm claims it is composed nearly entirely of selected Premier Cru Beaune wines. Its brilliant dark color; intense, rather spicy bouquet; and harmonious, characteristic flavor support this claim well. A slight astringency is acceptable in such a powerful and rather young wine, as is a faintly woody taste that, combined with the typical intensity of flavor common to better Beaune reds, might be termed earthy or pungent. The aftertaste is long and firm, showing more vinosity and tannin than fruit. This example from the 1969 crop is only now entering its period of maturity and can be kept safely for many years.

VINTAGE   DATE   PRICE

GUESTS

MENU   COMMENTS

1959

POMMARD

APPELLATION D'ORIGINE CONTROLÉE

Les Chaponnières

ESTATE BOTTLED

Domaine PARENT, PROPRIÉTAIRE A POMMARD, COTE-D'OR
FRANCE

MIS EN BOUTEILLES AU DOMAINE

RÉCOLTE
1971

MISE AU
DOMAINE
ALC. 12,7 % BY VOL.

PINOT NOIR
BOURGOGNE
HAUTES COTES DE BEAUNE

APPELLATION BOURGOGNE CONTROLÉE

Jean Joliot & Fils, PROPRIÉTAIRES A NANTOUX, COTE-D'OR

PRODUCT OF FRANCE
TABLE WINE
CONTENTS 3/4 QUART

BOUTEILLE № 002612

Grand Vin
des
Hospices de Beaune
Beaune

Cuvée Guigone de Salins
APPELLATION BEAUNE CONTROLÉE

HOSPICES DE BEAUNE

1959

ESPECIALLY SELECTED AND PURCHASED FOR
CHARLES L. RICHARDSON & CO., INC
BOSTON, MASS.
AUCTION NOVEMBER 1959.

BOUTEILLE
000915

RÉCOLTE
1969

BEAUNE
DES
CHEVALIERS DE L'ARQUEBUSE

APPELLATION BEAUNE CONTROLÉE

*Chancellerie des Chevaliers de l'Arquebuse
à Beaune, en Côte-d'Or.*

liking for Meursault, helped by their more accessible prices. They are intermediate in style between the very grand, luscious wines of Corton-Charlemagne and the equally grand but more lively and showy whites of Chassagne and Puligny. Exceptions in every direction can be found among growers and shippers alike.

Puligny-Montrachet's 11 Premiers Crus and 100,000 gallons of esteemed white village wine are crowned with a portion of the Le Montrachet Grand Cru vineyard and four other Grand Cru *climats* hyphenating Montrachet to their appellation names: Chevalier-Montrachet, Bâtard-Montrachet, Bienvenues-Bâtard-Montrachet and Criots-Bâtard-Montrachet. The last is so tiny as to be a curiosity. The finest examples of these great whites are marked by intense flavor in which Chardonnay style reaches heights of finesse unsurpassed elsewhere and rivaled only in Corton-Charlemagne. Tart impressions indispensable to any classical dry white wines alternate with the richness and expansive flavors that the noble Chardonnay grape conjures to mind. The best wines are powerful yet fresh and delicious with a particular flavor and expressiveness of aftertaste attributed to marl, sandstone, ironstone, and limestone soils, though this is not proved. If local brokers and shippers were to be asked to distinguish the finest qualities of Puligny as opposed to Chassagne, many might point to a superior balance favoring richness and fullness of both flavor and body; a French term, *sève* (literally "sap," as in a plant), might well be used. Certainly the wines are both delicate and powerful, refreshing and stimulating, and yet bring a taster's attention instantly to their profound savor and long development on the palate. Montrachet is by far the most expensive, much as Romanée-Conti is solicited across the world by consumers who feel obliged to serve "the best," whatever that may mean. Few professionals, of my own acquaintance at least, would be willing automatically to cede it first place among the current vintages of great white Côte d'Or wines. For all the Grands Crus and Premiers Crus of this appellation, it is a tedious truism to notice that there are as many unworthy and therefore overpriced wines as there are exemplary bottles that will introduce the wine adventurer to the best that this great appellation has to offer. The general standard of Puligny village appellation wines may be called lower than Meursaults in that the former embody less regularly (and at higher prices) the best tasting qualities of the appellation.

Chassagne-Montrachet contains a portion of Montrachet itself, as well as the Bâtard and Criots-Bâtard-Montrachet *climats*. Fourteen Premier Cru *climats* are classed. The finest white wines of some Premier Cru cannot be denied equal rank with Grands Crus from neighboring Puligny. A personal taste that prefers an accent on liveliness, an *immediate* impression of refinement, and a less powerful body may enjoy them more. Finesse is hardly lacking in the finest white Chassagne, but this point is achieved more systematically in Puligny. Chassagne may be less unctuous and a little shorter on the palate than the finest Puligny, if a distinction must be made, but higher levels of both communes nevertheless form a single family of white wines of superb quality. Differences should not be exaggerated and certainly not insisted upon in the case of individual wines.

Some 100,000 gallons (3,800 hectoliters) of red Chassagne wine is produced, some of the best by growers who also make white wines. Broad variety of style can be found among the reds. The richest versions are delicious wines that have occasioned comparisons with Côtes de Nuits. Others, drier, less affirmative, but finer finishing, have been compared to Savigny, but generalizing village style of Chassagne red wines is a form of racism.

The appellation St.-Aubin has eight Premiers Crus, mostly red, some white wines. Like St.-Romain, Auxey, and other starlet villages, much of this crop is finally sold as Côtes de Beaune Villages (see page 102) for the reasons cited therein.

Santenay is the last big commune among Beaune villages; its 160,000 gallons (6,060 hectoliters) of red wine have firm tasting qualities that combine vinosity, fruit, and finish. Rarely reaching peak levels, these are nevertheless excellent reds of the Beaune family. Santenay is normally sold as Côtes de Beaune Villages. They fall short of the maximum finesse and sharply defined appellation styles found farther north but typically unite the qualities for which Côtes de Beaune are esteemed.

Côte Chalonnaise

While soil types and grape varieties of the Côte d'Or continue south into the four appellations that make up the Côte Chalonnaise, a new vineyard scene replaces the continuous slopes of the Côte d'Or. Vineyards are clustered around favored locations rather than following uninterrupted topographical features, a pattern continuing into Mâconnais and Beaujolais. Laws are relaxed slightly, allowing, for example, 15 percent mixtures of white grapes into red wines. We are now in southern France and begin to meet a species of delusion of grandeur; many red wine growers make their wines as if they were better than they are. Reds suitable for production into fresh wines full of fruit and charm are often vinified by glory-hungry men determined to compete with the great growths of Beaune. If they are conditioned in barrel like Beaunes, the result frequently falls between two

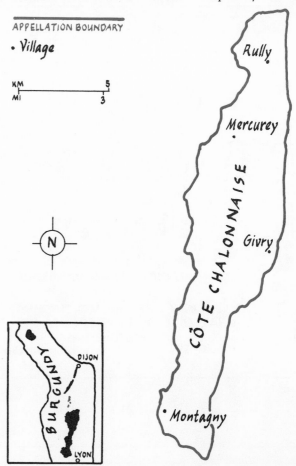

chairs, worn, flat, and dry from age, and yet not robust or intense enough to live up to their grower's image of power or elegance. Nonetheless, this is also a dynamic region with a strong interprofessional association, much planting, a developed technological consciousness, and improved wine quality over the last generation.

The Côte Chalonnaise makes half a million gallons (18,940 hectoliters), three-fourths red Mercurey. Since this appellation is well regarded at home, its best wines command prices that export markets are not willing to pay for a wine wrongly considered abroad a species of Beaujolais or worse, a sort of nonentity. Consequently cheaper, inferior Mercurey are shipped, reinforcing the bad image. In geographical order, Chalonnais style can be suggested as follows.

Rully red wines, a quarter of the appellation's 35,000 gallons (1,325 hectoliters), vary from thin, pleasant Pinot Noirs to extremely attractive, forward wines addressing themselves to nose and mouth with fruit and charm if not with authority. They can be supple, fragrant, and truly fine in aftertaste. The larger production of white is split among several claims. A quantity of dry white wine goes into sparkling production; others are sold as light, rather tart white wine for local or French consumption. Some Chardonnay made for oak-cask maturation can be impressive in body and emphatic in flavor but less so in finesse, compared to the very high standards set by great white Burgundies. Some 20 *climats* have Premier Cru rank.

A portion of Mercurey's huge red wine crop is distinguished by balance, flavor, and some power. A second tier is attractive, dryish in style with the merits of Pinot Noir, and should be consumed young. A quantity, potentially of like description, is slowly and expensively strangled into duller and even oxidized form in the barrels of growers who dream nightly of the Hospices de Beaune auction but whose circumstances, skills, or both are not up to the task of producing finished wine of noble intensity and balance. Six Premier Cru designations are permitted.

Givry, nearly opposite the city of Chalon, which gives its name to the district, by now produces nearly 50,000 gallons (1,890 hectoliters) of red and 6,000 to 7,000 gallons (227–265 hectoliters) of white wines. Though it has no Premier Cru *climats* as of the early 1970s, its reds are the most distinguished of the Côte. The best will have extracted much pigment under conditions permitting very ripe grapes. Other versions of Givry may offer extremely charming and forward wines with appeal, an excellent perfume suggesting violets or other flowery images, and harmonious development to the taste. When kept in balance, they are delightful, but efforts to make them more powerful must be based on grapes fit for intense wine and vatting suitable to its objective, and such are less common than wishful thinking.

Montagny is devoted entirely to white wines, 60,000 gallons (2,270 hectoliters) worth, and all its *climats* are Premiers Crus. Style runs the gamut from quite tart wines to full ones; the best, like those of Rully, are strongly marked by Chardonnay character. Lively, fresh, and clean, they introduce well many of the tasting qualities much and justly admired in Chardonnay wines from farther south, such as the more famous Pouilly-Fuissé. However, they rarely attain the tangy character identifiably special to this appellation.

For both Montagny and Rully, the tendency to overweight, overly alcoholic, and therefore unbalanced whites lacking charm is abetted by appellation laws insisting that Premier Cru wines attain 11.5 percent alcohol. In rich crops such as 1971 and 1969 many growers could well have picked a portion early with more vitalizing acidity and less sugar had they worked under a tolerance of 11 percent. The difference may seem small, but the higher alcohol standard inhibits certain balancing acts of this sort, since a grower cannot know beforehand that brilliant weather (and enough sugar) is to follow. Burgundians, raised to believe that more alcohol is better, will surely disagree with this last remark, and perhaps they know best in the end.

Mâconnais

With the Côte Chalonnaise, the grape monoculture characterizing the Côte d'Or is left behind and replaced by the polyculture of eastern France. In the Mâconnais and Beaujolais vines compete for space with important crops made no less valuable by France's artful bullying for itself the best share of Common Market agricultural price supports. Vines are planted in large islands upon the most favorable terrain, yet the total is substantial; Beaujolais accounts for nearly half the wine having the right to Burgundy's name. Soils favor granite and marl; limestone and ironstone thin out as one progresses south.

At this frontier of what was once another people, language, and civilization, changes occur in the wine world. Barrel size shrinks; vines are pruned globular, upright, not parallel to the ground; grape varieties are mixed; and canons of taste differ from those of the Côte d'Or. Chardonnay persists as the noble grape; the finest whites, for which Mâcon is most esteemed, issue from it. But the ground is shared with the lesser Aligoté, whose dry, lively, but almost sour whites are sold as Bourgogne Aligoté or flow into Beaujolais Blanc. Pinot Noir loses its majestic qualities abruptly, like a Paris tragedian thrust on the stage of a Marseilles farce. The White Juice Gamay, cultivated differently and vinified, often as not, without passing through a crusher-destemmer, replaces it. There are a few big properties, and for smaller growers local *Caves Coopératives* assume a role vastly more important than among rich cultivators of small plots of expensive Côte d'Or wines. Walking into one of these vast government Coops, vats towering several stories overhead, one could be in the lower Rhône, in Nîmes' cheap-wine outskirts, in Viseu, Portugal—anywhere where peasant proprietors produce WINE, in quantity. Higher appellations take village names, but these no longer fawn upon a few prestigious Grands Crus graciously consenting to sell a few cases of their nectar to deferential buyers. Individual growers are well known to the *négociants* and Cooperatives that together dominate the Mâconnais and Beaujolais, for superior wine is always scarce, but to overseas consumers the grower is pretty well lost from view. Wines so quickly consumed as these do not lend themselves to loving collection and study abroad.

The most important appellations among the 4 million gallons (152,000 hectoliters) of wine annually issuing from the Mâconnais are for whites. Pouilly-Fuissé, Pouilly-Loché, and Pouilly-Vinzelles use the same village name, whether with consummate cleverness or stupidity is hard to say. Fuissé is far and away the biggest and best known. All are Chardonnay wines, and the best have long been enormously attractive whites. Their color tends to a greenish gold in lesser years, darker and more strawlike in riper ones. Tart, perky, and stimulating to the taste buds in lighter crops, richer and more imposing in finer years, they not only carry the marks of Chardonnay but exemplify a delightful class of wines of genuine quality and character that nevertheless drink easily and are somehow accessible or casual. The popularity that they enjoy, quite extraordinary in America, has made their prices less than casual, however, and these have risen faster than senatorial ambitions among the hereditary rich.

APPELLATION BOUNDARY

• Village

KM 3
MI 1

MÂCONNAIS

• Solutré-Pouilly
• Fuissé
• Loché
• Vinzelles
• St.-Vérand

BURGUNDY

DIJON

LYON

brated towns may opt for the designation Mâcon Villages rather than pin the village name onto the word Mâcon. The border between Pouilly and Mâcon Villages is one of concept as well as geography, for the single-grape-variety principle that dominates wine appellation to the north is relaxed. Mâcon Villages may be a mixture of Chardonnay and Pinot Blanc, and for such wines an alternative appellation, Pinot Chardonnay Mâcon, is available. A much more sweeping freedom is accorded in crossing from *Appellation Mâcon Villages* to plain Mâcon, for Aligoté is then permitted.

Quality variations in white Mâcon are staggering; the best and worst wines hardly taste like the same appellation. Small amounts of elegant Chardonnay-style wine approach Côte d'Or standards of finesse and balance and are worth paying for. Typically they come from individual growers who have found ways to market wine well, obtaining higher prices and incomes. Receiving more money per volume, able to expend more on producing less, they have sprung out of a vicious circle of low-grade, high-volume production that habitually locks low-price appellations in its thrall. Most Mâcon are good. Their tasting qualities are short of complete but offer both body and flavor, if in a somewhat heavy, inadequately fruity, and not truly refined way. These imbalances persistently nag white wines of the whole region, it is only fair to add. A further quantity of Mâcon is acceptable quaffing wine but coarse. And there is always some to fit the dunce cap—dirty-flavored, bitter, unripe, and a powerful argument for either continuing adult education in the countryside or corporal punishment.

The appellation Mâcon Supérieur, a grade between Mâcon Villages and plain Mâcon, is a nuance for white wines. Mâcon reds are either Mâcon Supérieur or Mâcon; the appellation Mâcon Villages is allowed only for white wines. A few villages are allowed to append their names to Mâcon both for red and white wines, not quite the same thing. Gamay, Pinot Gris, and Pinot Noir are used in Mâcon. Its red wines therefore include some rather flat, modest versions of Pinot red wines, a quantity of mixed wines of various descriptions, and finally Gamay wines that can only be compared to Beaujolais in tasting qualities. On their native ground these are mainly surpassed by Beaujolais' forward and immediate sensations of fruit and appeal, but abroad, better Mâcon reds match more evenly with Beaujolais Supérieur and offer similar virtues. Production of reds includes some 200,000 gallons (7,575 hectoliters) of wine adopting a village name, some 800,000 gallons (30,300 hectoliters) of Mâcon Supérieur, and about 400,000 gallons (15,150 hectoliters) of plain Mâcon red. Large production per area and low alcoholic standards (9 percent) make wines of average or lesser quality in this appellation uninteresting.

Beaujolais

The Côte d'Or and Côte Chalonnaise differ from Mâcon and Beaujolais in viticultural methods but, more important, in the contrast between the Pinot Noir and Gamay grapes and the soils in which they flourish, or fail to flourish. The difference between Beaujolais wines and great red wines from Burgundy and elsewhere is best understood as one of intention. Fine red wines, those we call great, aim to achieve much scope, intensity of taste, finesse; these qualities undergo a process of maturation through which they are revealed and enhanced. Qualities of the grape, locality, and even the vineyard that gave them birth are also apparent. In Beaujolais, while some of the same adjectives may be used, the main intention in wine making is different and

As often, inappropriate, rapid price inflations stimulate not better quality but rising output and a struggle to market it; Pouilly-Fuissé seems to have suffered this fate. Quarreling with public taste is a dangerous habit, at least so far before retirement age as this writer may be, but it should be said somewhere that the logical price for Fuissé is that of any excellent white wine cropped generously. This is the level of good but unknown red Bordeaux property-bottled wine, which is to say the price of a pound of the best sirloin steak that might accompany the latter.

A new appellation, St.-Vérand (sometimes spelled St.-Véran), has been created with the express aim of catapulting it into the Pouilly trinity. Whether burdened by the wines' heavy style and lack of charm, or the ponderous pretensions of the effort itself, the promotion has thudded down short of its mark. St.-Vérand must be entirely a Chardonnay wine by decree of the Ministry of Agriculture. Unfortunately, the same edict neglected to instruct the wine to stop tasting the way it always has—possibly one reason why it was omitted, in September 1936, from the definition of the Pouilly appellation.

Following the three Pouilly wines come a drove of white Mâcon Villages. These are the logical substitutes for Pouilly wines, should the latter make a permanent institution of overpricing. Villages wines must have at least 11 percent alcohol and the best known abroad are Mâcon-Clessé, Mâcon-Lugny, and Mâcon-Viré. Wines from less-cele-

directed to other goals. The accent falls on odors, tastes, and a collection of sensations closer to a bunch of ripe grapes—in a word, to what we call "fruit" in its simplest wine sense.

All wines are made with a desire to keep them clean and fresh and to conserve their fruit. This concern is seen everywhere in wine making; but in Beaujolais these fresh qualities, elsewhere but one dimension of fine wines, become master goals of the grower. And to this goal are sacrificed other constituents, elsewhere considered indispensable. This difference is one in kind, in genus. Beaujolais, more than any other wine, offers the taster the most appetizing and delicious qualities of freshly fermented red grape juice. Beaujolais may be light in color, fragile in its high proportion of volatile acidity, and weak in alcohol; but it readily surrenders to the senses an ebullient, fervent rush of fruit, stimulating grapy and spicy flavors of all sorts, and leaves behind it an aftertaste or impression that has been compared to that of cold crisp cherries or to other happy images.

Many elements sacrificed or underplayed in order to make such remarkable and delicious wines are precisely the ones that conserve a wine's tasting qualities and even its chemical integrity against the passage of time (which is to say, internal changes that cannot be stopped) and against changes abetted by physical disturbance (transportation) and temperature variations incurred in bringing wines to consumers' tables. Not surprisingly, then, Beaujolais shipped abroad is readily debilitated; the fresh bloom, which distinguishes and endears it to everyone who has quaffed it on the spot, is not always entirely gone but is certainly much faded. And for Beaujolais "of the year" or Beaujolais Nouveau, all this and more is true. This wine, much publicized in America and England, and in France for that matter, is nothing more than the current crop rushed from the vats to the consumer. As long as it is drunk quickly, whether or not it is chemically finished matters little. But when it is exported this question is no trivial one. Incompleted chemical transformations take place in the bottle, releasing gases and infusing the wine with by-products that normally would have escaped from the vats or barrels. In a word, all hell breaks loose.

Rather than dwell on the technical details or torment the reader with evocations of how good the stuff is when it is *not* shipped, in effect, where he cannot get at it, it is enough to underline some consequences of this provocative situation. Exporters are legally responsible for wines that subsequently go wrong chemically and as a practical matter are commercially responsible for those that fall apart in bottle after shipment, in the short run or in the medium run. The pressure is enormous to take steps (different vatting and vinification techniques, even pasteurization before bottling) to prevent such occurrences. A catalogue of measures, varying from subtle to gross and from legal to criminal, describes the technical and craft arsenal available to accomplish this task. It is not so much that a good, balanced Beaujolais or Mâcon red cannot be shipped. It is, rather, that to ship these wines is to live dangerously. Since the pursuit of glory more often than not stops at a respectful distance from the bankruptcy court, readers will not be surprised at the outcome; most export Beaujolais has been well or badly treated to prevent or postpone its deterioration. This treatment can be done with the utmost integrity. A grower may pick his grapes as ripe as possible, give his wines a longer vatting, and achieve a red wine of 12 percent alcohol, safely low volatile acidity, bottled after 15 months in wood, and entirely fit to ship. This wine may be excellent red wine. Why should it not be? But it cannot reflect the qualities for which Beaujolais is so much and so justly appreciated. If there are mottos for the consumer abroad, they

are to drink promptly those examples of the wine that have been shipped in virgin condition and show it by their abundant fruit; to appreciate the bigger, well-made wines that conscientious growers and shippers have vinified, aware of export delays and hazards; and to visit the Beaujolais region often in person. For it is there that the consumer can best compare his tasting experiences with the brief characterizations of various species of Beaujolais that follow.

Nine village appellations, considered the finest Beaujolais, are scattered in vineyards west of the Saône River and south of the Mâconnais. Like most superior Beaujolais vineyards, these fall on schist and, above all, granite soils and are planted in the Gamay Noir à

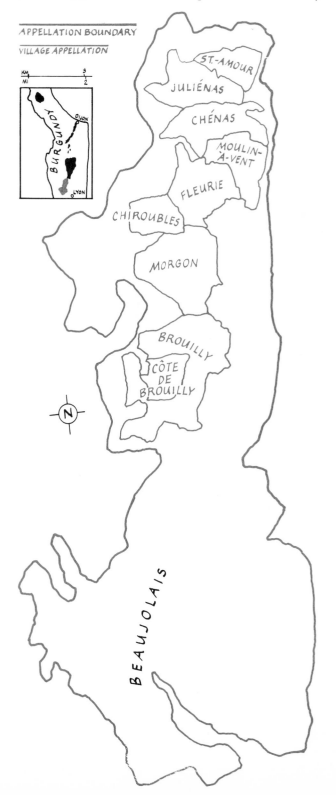

Jus Blanc grape. Beaujolais place names are restricted to red wines of 10 to 11 percent alcohol. Considerable Bourgogne Aligoté white wine is made, and white wine made anywhere here from Chardonnay and Pinot Blanc vines may be sold as Bourgogne Blanc or lower regional appellations; red wine, however, is the region's main product. Beaujolais Supérieur is made in most of the district; from the southern sector large volumes of plain Beaujolais gurgle off into French consumption, much of it taking place between 10 A.M. and 10 P.M. in nearby Lyon.

The wines of Beaujolais are divided into five categories, of which four are explicitly Beaujolais. The nine village appellations, called *Cru,* comprise about 10,000 acres (4,000 hectares) and are entitled the same output per area as the Côte Chalonnaise (more than the Côte d'Or). Roughly from north to south they are St.-Amour, Juliénas, Chénas, Moulin-à-Vent, Fleurie, Chiroubles, Morgon, Côte de Brouilly, and Brouilly. While it is not often done, all the higher appellations except Côte de Brouilly and Brouilly may append to their Cru name that of a *climat* from whence comes the wine. After these privileged areas comes a stream of some 40 villages whose wine may be called Beaujolais Villages in two senses. Either the village name may be tacked to the word Beaujolais, as in Beaujolais-Lantignié or Beaujolais-Quincié, or the wines may be called simply Beaujolais Villages. Wines from the region that achieve 10 percent alcohol (some 600,000 to 750,000 gallons, or 22,730–28,410 hectoliters) may be called Beaujolais Supérieur, and wines with no distinctions but origin, and 9 percent alcohol, still own the name Beaujolais; nearly 7 million gallons (265,150 hectoliters) are vinified. For commercial reasons, it may be desirable to call even some of the best wines something other than Beaujolais, and the fifth channel by which Beaujolais reaches the market is under other subregional names. The most important are Bourgogne Passe-tout-grains and Bourgogne. Any Cru wine may call itself Bourgogne. Any Beaujolais-produced wine (except those from the extreme south) that contains a minimum of one-third Pinot Noir grape may call itself Bourgogne Passe-tout-grains. Beaujolais white wine made from Chardonnay may also call itself Bourgogne (Blanc).

There are differences between the young Cru wines, and a few words can begin to suggest them. St.-Amour, Fleurie, and Chiroubles tend to a more flowery, paler style than Moulin-à-Vent, which is commonly the darkest, most vinous and solid of the Crus. Its character is approached by Morgon, though most wines from this Cru are flatter in taste, without the intensity of Moulin-à-Vent or the ethereal style of the lightest Chiroubles at another extreme. Chénas is a tiny Cru, of which I have drunk too little to say. Juliénas, Côtes de Brouilly, and Brouilly vary; but they accent the delightfully overpowering Gamay fruit—Juliénas more regularly and frequently in a darker red version, Brouilly and Côtes de Brouilly with a finesse of their own. In the latter two Cru regions (which are not interchangeable in designating wines) many producers for the French market make lighter wines than would be suggested by some successful (and very good) export properties.

There is no necessary distinction between styles of different Beaujolais Villages wines and of the Cru regions into which the villages fall or with which they may be interlaced. Prices are higher for the more alcoholic Supérieur grades, so it can be inferred that these are more generous in taste than plain Beaujolais and travel marginally better, or less badly; but none of these nuances, or others that could be drawn, have much interest for the wine buyer abroad.

In Beaujolais, as elsewhere in France, declassification used to allow wine from a more tightly drawn area to call itself by the name of a looser-quality definition or a larger, less restrictive area containing the original higher appellation. This allowance has been ended for most purposes and replaced by rules reiterating restrictions on overproduction and aiming at reducing the flood of cheaper appellations.

Chablis

Chablis, a compact district well north of the main Burgundy vineyard, makes unusual white wines under difficult circumstances and suffers the indignity of seeing its name filched by white wines from California to Australia. Grapegrowing here is (literally) an uphill battle, precarious and costly, with many misfortunes hovering over the grower. The vineyard hills that ring the town of Chablis are painfully steep, though regular enough to permit agricultural machinery to move about. But the soil is hard, marly, easily leached of vital elements, and must lie fallow often. To this naturally obstinate viticulture is added the expensive burden of devices that protect the tender spring vegetation from sudden and horrendous frosts. Chablis viticulture is a tough business; not surprisingly, many growers rolled over and gave up when phylloxera attacked the area in the late 1800s.

Obtaining successful wines depends upon obtaining successful grapes in economic quantities. Chablis labors with other handicaps than the pervasive cold spells. Without a good finale to the growing season, excessive acidities and insufficient sugar give unpleasant, cut-

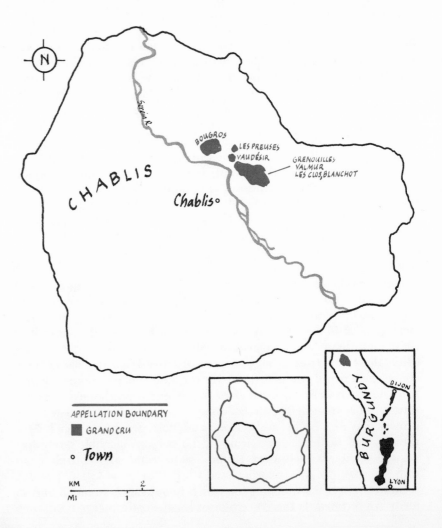

ting wines astringent to the taste. Not only are semiripe Chablis hard, even sour, but without adequate ripeness their flavor also vanishes, like a rainbow clouded off from sunlight. There are similarly cold districts, the Saar, for example; but in these the fruit obtained seems to redeem the wines more readily. Also, in years of exceptional ripeness, many Chablis lose their character and become good, heavy white wines but no longer whites distinguished by that lively acidity so prettily topped with fruit and character that is the district's hallmark. The years 1959 and 1969 afforded examples of such clumsy whites.

Chablis is therefore a special wine whose particular balance is inherently difficult to achieve. Once achieved, authentic versions are not to everyone's taste. Standards for its appreciation are clear enough, however. Green-gold is the appropriate image used to evoke its special color. Bouquet and taste share a certain vitality, a tang, a liveliness difficult to describe as it impresses the nose, mouth, and aftertaste, but quite unforgettable. The grape is the same Chardonnay used to make the celebrated white wines of the Côte d'Or, here called the *Beaunois,* but the resulting wine is a far cry from mellow, unctuous Meursault or the earthy whites of Rully. Many fanciful comparisons have been found by tasters—flint, limestone, lemon, lime, pebbles, or various salts are evoked to express its style, which is dominated by tart successions of taste.

It is a fine wine whose color, bouquet, and flavors deepen with age. Truly venerable bottles can be found in excellent condition in the icy cellars of growers and shippers clustered in the small, quiet town that names the district. The aftertaste of mature wines is very fine and keeps the senses aware of all preceding odors and flavors. Fine Chablis are subtle but make such a vivid impression on the palate as to mask their more delicate qualities. Perhaps this explains why blander, more modified versions of the wine meet greater acceptance than the starker, rarer, more authentic sorts. Just as a few drops of lemon juice or vinegar are used to heighten the delicate flavors of shellfish, so, too, a glass of Chablis, its acidity tingling the taste buds, is rightly considered a perfect accompaniment to fresh- and saltwater fish and mollusks.

A simple hierarchy divides the wines into four groups. Overlooking the town from the east some 250 acres (100 hectares) of privileged slopes rate the highest appellation, Chablis Grand Cru. This band of hills, nearly 1.5 miles (2.5 kilometers) across at its widest point, is divided into seven *climats,* or vineyard groupings: Blanchot, Bougros, Les Clos, Grenouilles, Les Preuses, Valmur, and Vaudésir. Grand Cru must obtain 11 percent alcohol.

Next, east and west of the town, other plots enclaved among the slopes have the right to *Appellation Chablis Premier Cru Contrôlée,* whose longer list of *climat* names includes Vaillon, Fourchaume, Montée de Tonnerre, and other famous sites. Premiers Crus must obtain 10.5 percent alcohol; their total vineyard area is more than five times that of Grands Crus. As usual, classification creates paradoxes. Higher prestige and the price that goes with it incite Grand Cru owners to make all they can and market all they may. But a grower on the west side of the town, for example, whose best wines may only be Premier Cru, may be more selective. It is no surprise to find west-slope Premiers Crus such as Vaillon or Les Forêts that surpass Grands Crus in any given vintage. Superior wines occur often in Fourchaume, a long, elevated stip north of Chablis whose orientation replicates the Grand Cru slopes below it.

Third, and produced in quantities about equal to those of Premier Cru, is *Appellation Chablis Contrôlée,* whose minimum alcohol content is 10 percent. Terrains permitted for this designation are scattered mainly to the south of Chablis; elevation is an important criterion. Finally, *Petit Chablis,* originating on vineyards of varying elevation to the west and north, is made in much smaller amounts, less than half of either of the preceding two classes. As elsewhere in the French appellation system, this hierarchy has traditionally made declassification possible, and a Grand Cru grower may sell off all (but no longer only part) of his crop as Premier Cru or just Chablis or, for that matter, as Bourgogne; similarly, a Premier Cru may be sold as Chablis or Bourgogne, but a Chablis or Petit Chablis may only step down to Bourgogne Grand Ordinaire, a lower animal than Bourgogne. While quality is reasonably separated into these four grades, standards of judgment for all Chablis are pretty well grouped around the same considerations of balance among lively acidity, fruit, and appellation style, with more expected of a Grand Cru and less of a Petit Chablis.

As with many fine Burgundies and wines from elsewhere, most Chablis is vinified in cask, normally either the traditional small *feuillette* (140 quarts, or 132 liters) or the Burgundian *pièce* (241 quarts, or 228 liters). A vintage may be sold barrel by barrel, or all barrels may be pooled to make one wine. Since vineyards are parceled among growers, one may find, in a single cellar, wines of several appellations coming from different *climats* along with amounts of declassified wine. Each barrel or each receptacle may be different. This has certain implications for consumers abroad. A grower may equalize and estate-bottle several barrels of his Premier Cru Beauroy, for example, and such bottles may find their way to Leeds or Chicago. But equally, a shipper may buy selected parcels of Beauroy from several growers and assemble a wine that may be as good, better, or worse, depending upon his skills and judgment.

This pattern is repeated throughout Burgundy, often with admirable results. Thus, direct relationships between a grower and importer are not determinants of quality. There are excellent growers, but equally there are excellent *négociant-éleveurs* whose judgment of what to buy and skill in caring for wine in cask and during bottling are part of the same skills and judgment that make one grower better than another.

Under these rigorous circumstances, and with a total Chablis growing area of only about 3,000 acres (1,200 hectares), it is not surprising that good Chablis is expensive. The permitted amounts of wine per hectare are set at about the same levels as for fine Burgundies. The difficult style of the wines is such that consumers are advised to follow a shipper or grower whose wine-making suits their taste, rather than pursue great *climats* names, regardless of the pleasure these offer, or fail to offer, to individual palates.

Since the Premiers Crus occasionally intermingle in quality with the Grands Crus, it is of interest to reproduce the list of Premier Cru *climats* the Syndicate of Defense of the Wines of Chablis has made. Growers may name their plots in addition.

These are on the Right Bank of the Serein stream, with the Grands Crus: Mont de Milieu, Montée de Tonnerre, Chapelot, Vaulorent, Vaucoupin, Côte de Fontenay, Fourchaume, Pied d'Aloup, Vaupulent.

On the Left Bank are Vaillon, Chatain, Séché, Montmain, Les Forêts, Butteaux, Mélinots, Beugnon, Les Lys, Côtes de Léchet, Beauroy, Troême (Troesme), Vosgros, Vogiros, Roncières, Vaugiraud.

Ten other *climats* are cited for quality but are not Premiers Crus.

Givry Clos Saint-Pierre Baron Thénard

This grower is well known as the owner of a portion of Le Montrachet. The Givry wine is typical of moderately characterful wine and tends to be a commercial example of the appellation. Its color is medium light, the bouquet suggests Pinot Noir without the full richness and mixture of flower and spice obtainable in this appellation. Its flavor is agreeable and shows something of the dryish but complete wine qualities of the area. Givry is normally bigger and finer than Mercurey and less elegant than the best Rully red and can be darker and intense instead of slightly bland like this one. J. F. Delorme, for example, the grower of the Rully white figuring on this page, makes a very traditional, powerful Givry, and many other growers offer wines that are less well distributed and less expensive than this one.

VINTAGE   DATE   PRICE

GUESTS

MENU   COMMENTS

Montagny Louis Latour

While this shipper is considered among the best in Burgundy, and while his wines are generally made to a high standard and are authentic, the reputation somewhat exceeds the average merit of the wines. The Montagny, from an appellation devoted to spritely white wines of Chardonnay character, is excellent, however. The aroma is still young and lively with an exciting mixture of grape and more vinous odors. On the palate a very lively white follows, quite in keeping with the bouquet. Its body is sufficiently generous to make it emphatically Burgundian, but the delicious and rather tangy flavor, slightly tart with much fruit, identifies it as a Montagny rather than a more unctuous Côte d'Or wine. These white wines substitute well for any purpose normally requiring the more expensive Meursault or other Côte d'Or appellations, though Montagny has less finish and weight.

VINTAGE   DATE   PRICE

GUESTS

MENU   COMMENTS

Mercurey Paul Bouchard

This wine represents red Mercurey well and shows itself well on more general ground as a light red Burgundy. Medium to medium light color is normal in Mercurey, and, as here, a hint of violet or purple is acceptable. The bouquet is firm and clear without great volume and hints of oaken or richer sensations come through to the nose. Mercurey tends toward flatter, drier Chalonnais wines rather than the fruity Rully or more complete Givry reds that receive longer vattings. So with this one, a 1972 example giving a good impression of Pinot Noir, a slightly earthy sensation to the taste with a generous body but not stressing fruit or lush qualities. The finish is correctly dry and slightly woody, a trifle too dry for such a young wine with the impression of much alcohol.

VINTAGE   DATE   PRICE

GUESTS

MENU   COMMENTS

Rully Domaine de La Renarde J. F. Delorme

Monsieur Delorme's careful vinifications effectively bring out all the finesse of the noble grapes, Pinot Noir and Chardonnay, used in the Côte Chalonnaise. The red Rully is light and fragrant with a character between a generous Beaujolais and a subtle Beaune wine. His whites give vigorous varietal impressions. Rully also produces much sparkling Champagne-method white wine from the same grapes. The powerful white style of this Rully is much admired in France but may surprise buyers abroad expecting a tarter, smaller wine along the lines of the Montagny on this page. Delorme's Givry is sold with the name Clos Marceau and is a rich purple wine with abundant flavor.

VINTAGE   DATE   PRICE

GUESTS

MENU   COMMENTS

BOUTEILLE
000608

HORS-CONCOURS
MEMBRE DU JURY
MÉDAILLES
AUX EXPOSITIONS

LE PRÉFÉRÉ DU ROI HENRI IV

GIVRY
CLOS SAINT-PIERRE

du Domaine Baron Thénard

APPELLATION GIVRY CONTROLÉE

UNE EXCLUSIVITÉ REMOISSENET PÈRE & FILS
NÉGOCIANTS-ÉLEVEURS A BEAUNE, COTE-D'OR, FRANCE

Montagny

APPELLATION CONTROLÉE

Louis Latour

MAISON FONDÉE EN 1797

NÉGOCIANT A BEAUNE (COTE-D'OR)

ROUALET. BEAUNE.

Contents 1 Pint 8 Fl. Oz.

Red Burgundy Table Wine

Produce of France

Alcohol 13% by Volume

Produce of France

MERCUREY

APPELLATION CONTROLÉE

Shipped by :

Paul Bouchard & Cie.

NÉGOCIANTS À BEAUNE (Côte-D'Or)

Imported by : CAROLINA WINE COMPANY - CAMBRIDGE MASS, 02138

GRANDS VINS DE BOURGOGNE

Domaine de la Renarde

APPELLATION RULLY CONTROLÉE

Jean-François DELORME

PROPRIÉTAIRE A RULLY (SAONE-&-LOIRE)

DISTRIBUÉ PAR :

André Delorme

NÉGOCIANT A RULLY (SAONE-&-LOIRE)

Pouilly-Fuissé
Cave Coopérative de Chaintre

This simple dry Burgundy from one of the main Maconnais villages tastes good but sells for too much money, as do most wines with the title of this appellation. It is limited in power and flavor, made with only average care to suggest rather than emphasize the fruity yet tart and forward tasting qualities that good Pouilly-Fuissé should deliver and has nearly ceased to do. However, it is the sort of wine that can be expected at the mass distribution level.

VINTAGE   *DATE*   *PRICE*

GUESTS

MENU   *COMMENTS*

Pouilly-Fuissé Moillard

This giant shipper at Nuits-St.-Georges has the competence to deliver good wine in any appellation it chooses; this rather rich, generous, and flavorful Pouilly-Fuissé is but one example. Moillard uses new flash heat techniques to stabilize wines in their modern plant. The wine cannot be reproached at any tasting point and certainly shows Chardonnay virtues. But its character as representative of the appellations of Pouilly-Fuissé and Pouilly-Loché leaves much to be desired. It is rather a good white Burgundy with a good house style, one natural to shippers whose stock in trade is ample, well-flavored Burgundy-type wines rather than nuances of delicacy or even those of appellation. Drinkers abroad had better give up on these appellations until the absurd wave of their popularity subsides and it becomes worthwhile to look for correct, dry, rather arresting wines from producers who remember what Pouilly is supposed to taste like.

VINTAGE   *DATE*   *PRICE*

GUESTS

MENU   *COMMENTS*

Mâcon-Clessé Émile Thevenet

At an opposite extreme from the abundantly produced, sound, and drinkable wines represented by the white wine of the Macon Lugny cooperative, a number of private estates make and bottle their own wines with ambitions as high as the temperaments of their owners dictate. This is a superlative example but only one of this class of white wine. It has fine aroma and bouquet. It emphasizes Chardonnay tasting qualities and has a long aftertaste marked by none of the coarseness or earthiness typical of lesser wines or the assembled large lots made by the cooperatives, valid as these last may be. This is an outstanding grower achievement repeated several times during the 1970s.

VINTAGE   *DATE*   *PRICE*

GUESTS

MENU   *COMMENTS*

Mâcon Lugny Cave Coopérative de Lugny

For several years the distinguished name of Frank Schoonmaker has been associated with shipments to America of generous white wines from this village cooperative. The 1973 is typical of their forward tasting qualities commencing with strong aroma, a vinous bouquet, and full strong flavor touched at the end by a slight coarseness expected in inexpensive white wines from a lesser region. Blending of Pinot Blanc and Chardonnay grapes is permitted in the Maconnais, an unusual tolerance for Burgundy appellations. But compare this wine with the lesser Aligoté white to appreciate the distinction conferred by better grape varieties. Variable quality and ripeness marked the 1973 Burgundy harvest; the Lugny cooperative has succeeded in bringing out a white wine of more than average character and firm tasting qualities.

VINTAGE   *DATE*   *PRICE*

GUESTS

MENU   *COMMENTS*

ESTATE BOTTLED **MISE A LA PROPRIÉTÉ**

POUILLY-FUISSÉ

APPELLATION POUILLY-FUISSÉ CONTROLÉE

⚜ 1971 ⚜

73cl

CAVE COOPÉRATIVE DE CHAINTRE A CHAINTRE – 71

WHITE BURGUNDY WINE
PRODUCT OF FRANCE

CONTENTS 1 Pt 8 Fl. Oz.
ALCOHOL 12,5% BY VOLUME

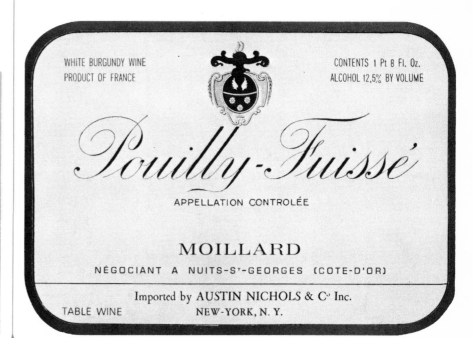

Pouilly-Fuissé

APPELLATION CONTROLÉE

MOILLARD

NÉGOCIANT A NUITS-ST-GEORGES (COTE-D'OR)

Imported by AUSTIN NICHOLS & Cᵒ Inc.
NEW-YORK, N.Y.

TABLE WINE

PRODUCT OF FRANCE
MACON-CLESSÉ

Appellation Mâcon Contrôlée

Des siècles de   *tradition vigneronne*

" Quintaine "

MIS EN BOUTEILLE A LA PROPRIÉTÉ

ÉMILE THEVENET

Propriétaire-Viticulteur à Quintaine-Clessé, par Lugny (S.-&-L.)

ALC. 13 % BY VOL.

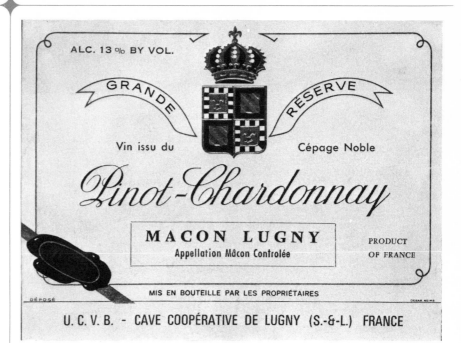

GRANDE   RÉSERVE

Vin issu du   Cépage Noble

Pinot-Chardonnay

MACON LUGNY
Appellation Mâcon Contrôlée

PRODUCT
OF FRANCE

MIS EN BOUTEILLE PAR LES PROPRIÉTAIRES

U.C.V.B. - CAVE COOPÉRATIVE DE LUGNY (S.-&-L.) FRANCE

Brouilly Château de la Chaize

One of the biggest estates in Beaujolais, if not the biggest, Château de la Chaize markets its wines in Britain and America with energy and competence. The medium-colored, very fragrant wines represent a very good standard of export Beaujolais and suggest something of the extra fruit and delicious impressions of Brouilly. It is unfair and pointless to criticize the wine for being made in a heavier style than the best of its neighbors, for it is made by a vineyard whose intentions are to export its wines, and more powerful Beaujolais stands up better to shipping.

VINTAGE *DATE* *PRICE*

GUESTS

MENU *COMMENTS*

Beaujolais-Villages Cave de Juliénas

The cooperatives in the Mâcon and Beaujolais areas play a significant role in the economies of each appellation. This one at Juliénas is very large and makes a range of qualities from grapes of varying ripeness brought from the surrounding countryside. A shipper can find different vats for sale ranging from excellent to quite poor. All wines from cooperatives must name the coop on their label, a concession the French government requires in exchange for the assistance it renders them. This wine is in fact a Juliénas sold as Beaujolais-Villages and shows the forward fruit and elegant aftertaste of wines from the best villages.

VINTAGE *DATE* *PRICE*

GUESTS

MENU *COMMENTS*

Beaujolais-Villages Jadot

This is the most common presentation of Beaujolais wines in France and abroad, bearing the name of the large shipping house that distributes this plain but good wine, identified only by its rank in the hierarchy of Beaujolais appellations. Jadot are very big shippers whose quality is standard and sound. Their wines could be reasonably compared to those of the different Bouchard houses—Jaboulet-Vercherre, Drouhin, Coron, and some other substantial shippers.

VINTAGE *DATE* *PRICE*

GUESTS

MENU *COMMENTS*

Fleurie Georges Duboeuf

This excellent example of a shipper's Beaujolais comes from a former grower who developed a shipping business from the ground up, in Beaujolais.

The deep crimson color is darker than normal for straight Beaujolais but appropriate to this higher classed Cru wine, one of nine village appellations within Beaujolais. Its aroma is properly Gamay from start to finish and to the taste is slightly more assertive and generous than the lighter Cru wines, such as Chiroubles and some Brouilly, and less flat and dry than Morgon, for example.

The 1973 Duboeuf shows less of the forward fruity impressions that characterized that crop and more acidity and depth of flavor, being altogether a bigger wine. Export Beaujolais must be more robust than local ideals would have this Fleurie be.

VINTAGE *DATE* *PRICE*

GUESTS

MENU *COMMENTS*

APPELLATION **BROUILLY** CONTROLÉE
Imported by CHATEAU & ESTATE WINES COMPANY
NEW YORK N.Y.

1 PT. 8 FL. OZ.

ALC. 13 % by VOL.

CHATEAU de LA CHAIZE
- 1676 -

Grand Vin du Beaujolais

RED TABLE WINE

PRODUCE of FRANCE
Estate Bottled

Shipped by:
Marquise de ROUSSY de SALES
Propriétaire à Odenas (Rhône)

MISE EN BOUTEILLE AU CHATEAU

GRAND VIN DU BEAUJOLAIS

BEAUJOLAIS-VILLAGES

APPELLATION CONTRÔLÉE

CAVE DES PRODUCTEURS AU CHATEAU DU BOIS DE LA SALLE
S.I.C.A. - 69 JULIÉNAS-EN-BEAUJOLAIS

MIS EN BOUTEILLE A LA PROPRIÉTÉ

IMP. GOUGENHEIM. LYON

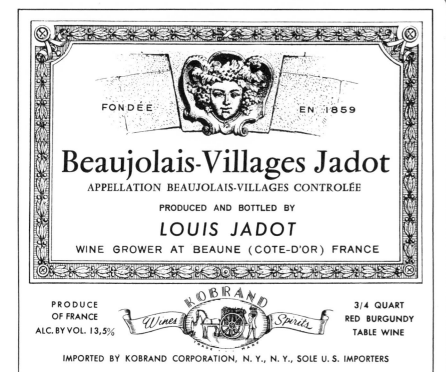

FONDÉE EN 1859

Beaujolais-Villages Jadot

APPELLATION BEAUJOLAIS-VILLAGES CONTROLÉE

PRODUCED AND BOTTLED BY

LOUIS JADOT

WINE GROWER AT BEAUNE (COTE-D'OR) FRANCE

PRODUCE
OF FRANCE
ALC. BY VOL. 13,5%

KOBRAND
Wines Spirits

3/4 QUART
RED BURGUNDY
TABLE WINE

IMPORTED BY KOBRAND CORPORATION, N.Y., N.Y., SOLE U.S. IMPORTERS

GEORGES DUBŒUF

FLEURIE

APPELLATION CONTROLÉE

LES VINS GEORGES DUBŒUF À ROMANÈCHE-THORINS-71

Produce
of France

Volume Net
72 cl

Chablis Les Clos Moreau

An outstanding proprietor but mainly an *éleveur* and shipper, Moreau makes finely bred wines in a generous model with unusual *sève* (sap or unctuosity). This firm is export-oriented, which may explain why Moreau finishes its wines in a slightly less tart fashion, quite deliciously fine in aftertaste but less typical of the appellation than some others. The level is high and reliable. The 1969s were a bit heavy, as were others, but 1970, 1971, and 1973 produced Les Clos, Vaillon, and plain Chablis wines of fine breed and delightful appeal.

VINTAGE   *DATE*   *PRICE*

GUESTS

MENU   *COMMENTS*

Chablis Les Preuses Domaine de la Maladière

This is among the most widely distributed labels, with Premier Cru vineyards in Vaulorent. The fact of estate bottling is less significant than its very regular style and quality. Like the wines of Moreau, Domaine de la Maladière has even tasting qualities, and most of its wines are even less typical of extreme Chablis style than Moreau's. Their development in bottle is slightly erratic in time, and whether or not the wines are intended for immediate consumption after shipping, it is best to drink them that way.

VINTAGE   *DATE*   *PRICE*

GUESTS

MENU   *COMMENTS*

Chablis Vaillon William Bolter

Whether the shipper is one of the large Burgundy houses or a small firm such as the one represented here, the problem is obtaining enough good wine to offer in a style that is not too astringent for the tastes of English-speaking markets, is sufficiently full to travel well, and yet has enough character to be distinctively Chablis. This one strikes something of that balance and in fact comes from an assembly of wines of one producer, bought by the shipper and commercialized to the world under the shipper's label. As in all such cases—and they are general throughout Burgundy (and elsewhere)—the consumer has little but the shipper's name and the designation of the wine to guide him in making his choices. This 1970 Vaillon leans to the mellow side of the range of style available in Chablis. The same grower produced unbearably acid wine two years later.

VINTAGE   *DATE*   *PRICE*

GUESTS

MENU   *COMMENTS*

Chablis Valmur Guy Robin

The wines of Robin have a reputation in the town of Chablis, directly above which his Grand Cru Valmur parcel is perched. This particular wine represents Chablis character well in several vintages, with the finesse expected of its high appellation. Valmur and its neighboring *crus* of Vaudésir, Les Preuses, Grenouilles, and Les Clos are more often seen abroad than their peers Blanchot and Bougros, but without wishing to submerge the individuality of growers' wines, such as that of this cultivator, it may be said that canons of taste for fine Chablis do not differ dramatically among the main parcels. A producer's determination to make fine wines depends for success on his location, but his selectivity and determination are what connoisseurs are best advised to remember when buying wines abroad.

VINTAGE   *DATE*   *PRICE*

GUESTS

MENU   *COMMENTS*

Mise au Domaine

MAISON FONDÉE EN 1814'

Récolte 1973

Chablis Grand Cru

LES CLOS

APPELLATION CHABLIS GRAND CRU CONTROLÉE

J. Moreau & Fils

NÉGOCIANTS À CHABLIS (YONNE)

DOMAINE DE LA MALADIÈRE

Mise en bouteille à la Propriété

Chablis Grand Cru

Les Preuses

St Martin

APPELLATION CHABLIS GRAND CRU CONTRÔLÉE

VARNIER - EPERNAY

CHABLIS

Vaillon

APPELLATION CHABLIS PREMIER CRU CONTROLÉE

1970

WILLIAM BOLTER & Co., NÉGOCIANTS, BORDEAUX, FRANCE

DEVEVEY · BEAUNE

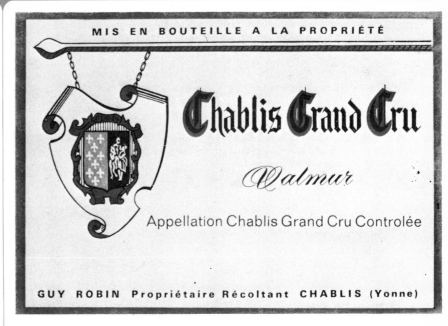

MIS EN BOUTEILLE A LA PROPRIÉTÉ

Chablis Grand Cru

Valmur

Appellation Chablis Grand Cru Controlée

GUY ROBIN Propriétaire Récoltant CHABLIS (Yonne)

Loire

The merits of Loire Valley wines, white, red and rosé, are freshness and delicacy, liveliness and charm, cleanness of bouquet and taste. The wine drinker who fails to approach Loire wines disposed toward these merits risks confusing his own standards. As for those who petulantly and systematically dismiss Loire wines as little wines worth no money, may they grunt all the way home to New York State "sherry," or whatever home may be. Whatever they have magnified in their self-esteem by disdaining Loire wines may be catered to by their mothers or even their wine merchants, but a fine wine region as old as Charlemagne need not follow suit. Their indifference also leaves more Loire for the rest of us to drink. But it is also true and must be said that Loire wines do not normally exemplify finesse in the great sense given meaning by Burgundy, Bordeaux, Champagne, and vintage Port.

It is the unifying points of Loire wines that best introduce them. As elsewhere in France, superior white wines come from subsoils with chalky matter or other calcareous components such as shell lime and usually from slopes whose exposition is favorable and which aid in drainage. Low pruning, resembling that of Bordeaux, is general. So is a problem: balance. Grapes destined for light wines tend to blowzy, dull results when submitted to excessively hot autumns. Loire is meant to be vivacious and, usually, tart. Yet light wines can turn unbearably mean, literally bitter, in wet, cold years when acidity is not reduced at summer's end. Delicacy disappears; aroma, too. Rot, which accompanies wet weather, stands out starkly in this grim background of defects. Red appellations, like whites esteemed for their light, clean qualities, may not fear excess ripeness but do miserably in poor weather as well. Another Loire feature is small-scale peasant viticulture; keen local pride in small differences is jealously maintained. This may be delightful on the spot, where wines of many proprietors each produced in small quantity may be compared. Buying Loire in Dallas, Texas, or Edinburgh, Scotland, is something else. Realizing that large producers or shippers of Loire appellations make excellent wines, but wines necessarily averaged or showing narrower ranges of taste, one should look for unknown rather than familiar labels when information and experience are the object of a wine-sampling purchase.

Loire wines are typically of a single grape. This is instructive for American and English buyers, who meet various other varietal wines in their markets. Last and most laudable of qualities, and one that endears Loire white wines to exhausted wine merchants, is the restraint most growers show in the use of sulphur, which is necessary to clean wines and protect them from oxidation. This temperate sulphuring is odd for several reasons. For ages, Loire wines were thought too fragile to travel; Parisian interest finally coaxed them out of central France and thence abroad. Loire growers, small provincial farmers that they are, might well worry about the condition of such light wines

in the unknown barbarian terrain beyond the sea and sulphur all the more in fear. Ignorance or incredible avarice might explain it all, but it is more pleasant to think that clean Loire bouquet and aftertaste arise from the tact and craft of their wine makers. If an occasional white does oxidize, well, certainly most will find this a lower price to pay than pervasive sulphur dioxide.

Pouilly

The long Loire River begins to interest overseas wine drinkers near its eastern source at Pouilly-sur-Loire, approximately dead center on a map of France. In the environs of this river town two distinct wines are made on different soils from different grapes; local pride blazons "Pouilly" on both appellations. The more valuable but smaller of the two is Pouilly Fumé Blanc, or Blanc Fumé de Pouilly as it may also call itself. Sauvignon Blanc, here called Blanc Fumé, the first of several Loire names for familiar grapes, is the sole grape variety. Grown on elevated slopes with calcareous subsoils, Sauvignon Blanc gives a balanced white wine that must attain 11 percent alcohol for the appellation—a normal standard for white Loire wines. Sauvignon aroma is among the more distinctive in a white wine taster's experience; Blanc Fumé embodies it well. The color is normally a greenish yellow but blanches pallid in unripe years, like all Loire wines; like all others too, it suffers acutely from acidity when grapes fail to mature. When ripe, however, this acidity combines with fresh, fruity impressions to give Pouilly Fumé Blanc the charm, lively yet complete, which most would agree promote it to the head of the list of white Loire wines.

Most producers give wines some barrel age; larger ones such as the *Cave Coopérative* at Pouilly ferment in large vats, not barrels, and bottle directly. With its medium alcohol content, Pouilly is a balanced white wine maturing in bottle in solid years such as 1970. But drinking Loire young is a good rule defied only by a few sweet wines. With its delicate but definite nose, its vinosity, its tartness tempered by a graceful ending on the palate, Pouilly Fumé Blanc is an excellent introduction to Loire white virtues. The small growing area makes good Blanc Fumé necessarily expensive. Loire wines are often bottled in the year after vintage; there is nothing suspicious about Pouilly found in retail stores the summer after its labeled vintage year.

A larger amount of land, lower and flatter and based on clay and siliceous subsoils, is planted in Chasselas grape; from it comes the appellation Pouilly-sur-Loire. Throughout Western Europe, Chasselas is ambiguously regarded; its style veers toward the common. It attains alcohol with difficulty and easily swells with water; hence its popularity as a table grape. But in Pouilly it succeeds well, although only 9 percent alcohol is demanded of it for the appellation. Like

Blanc Fumé, its color tinges green but looks watery in bad years. The aroma, less full, less evident, and less vinous, is more flowery, a characteristic of the grape. Its flavor too is blander; acidity is weak in Chasselas here. Pouilly-sur-Loire is pleasant but simply less expressive and long to the taste than its town fellow. It should be cheaper wherever the two are found.

Sancerre

The town of Sancerre sits across the river from Pouilly atop a large hill commanding a view of some dozen wine villages that make up the appellation. Its soils, limestone and chalk with marly surface, resemble those of Chablis. Appellations are granted for red, white, and rosé wines, but white only finds its way abroad in quantity. Blanc Fumé (Sauvignon) is the sole grape to produce Sancerre—a fragrant, rather delicate white wine with extreme freshness, more perishable and with more elusive tasting qualities than flourish at Pouilly. Red Sancerre and Sancerre rosé are curiosities vinified entirely from Pinot Noir. Paris drinks a large amount of the white wines, and this constant demand firms up prices. In any case, just under 750 acres (300 hectares) are cultivated, so total supply is small. By the time a Sancerre white is assembled into exportable lots and arrives abroad, consumers should drink it immediately; the wine is lighter than that of Pouilly, with 10.5 percent minimum alcohol (10 percent minimum for red and rosé). Tart often as not, lighter in bouquet and less emphatic in taste than Pouilly, Sancerre marks a step in the direction of more distinctly Loire wines in body and style.

Quincy and Reuilly

West of Pouilly are two towns known for their white wines, the last appellation-grade wine made from Sauvignon (Blanc Fumé). Quincy contains tiny properties whose scattered vineyards lie on chalky outcroppings. Its pale dry wines run to extreme styles in which the delicate virtues and acid faults of Loire whites are exaggerated by vintage hazards. Reuilly is a still lighter wine, smaller and drier. Of the two,

Quincy, though hardly rich, has more flavor and is exported abroad. Many tasters find a "flinty" savor to these hesitant, rather teasingly sour but agreeable whites; my own impressions relate to tart tastes of the pulp of slightly unripe white grapes, but then I have never eaten much flint. The reader will find his own images without more assistance. Fragile even when unpleasantly acid, as in 1972, Quincy is certainly a wine to drink young and also one in which cooling, not chilling, is a rule; there is little enough aroma and forwardness of taste without blunting it entirely by freezing. Reuilly makes Pinot Noir red and rosé wines as well as white. The area is small, some 570 acres (230 hectares), and wines are not cheap; but they should be sampled to experience a light extreme of Sauvignon. Ponderous, heavy Quincy has probably been bolstered in body and alcohol by an (understandably) anxious exporter who fears for its durability when buffeted about during shipment.

Vouvray and Montlouis

The considerable area separating Quincy from the solid block of appellation vineyards beginning around Tours and continuing west to the Atlantic at Nantes is not devoid of vines, but no important export appellation exists. Here and throughout the Touraine and Anjou regions that follow, however, lesser wines of all colors are produced, some still, some sparkling. As befits France's heartland, Loire viticulture dates from the Franks and Romans; wine is part of its rich culture, landscape, and history.

Just east of Tours, in a countryside of broken low hills and riverine chalk bluffs rising into rolling plateau country, are the appellations Vouvray and its subordinate, Montlouis. Its chalky soil is easily excavated into wonderful natural cellars as well as forming a vineyard base. Entrances to natural *chais* and grottoes of the Loire dot the façade of vine-covered river banks all around the Tours area. The vines, trimmed low in the Bordeaux fashion, are no longer Sauvignon but Chenin Blanc, a grape familiar to Americans through its wide planting in California. The *goût de coing* (taste of quince) that Tours winegrowers find in their whites is attributed by them to a combination of the aromatic Chenin and the area's chalky subsoil, called *tufa*.

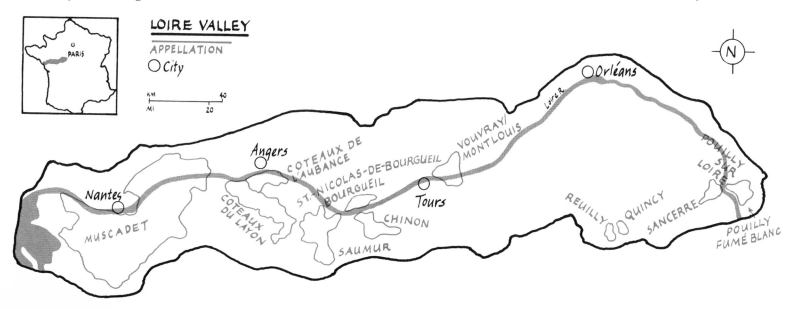

Chenin and the climate may suffice for some of us as an explanation.

Chenin Blanc naturally attains more sugar than Sauvignon, and in consequence Vouvray comes in many styles. Exceptional autumns present the conditions for noble rot; sweet fine wines ensue, with flowery nose, more aroma than aftertaste, but delicious and subtle. Sheltered, balmy areas such as Vallée Coquette are prized for such ripe wines. Frequently attaining great age, with freshness intact, these wines are the pride of local growers. Admire them loudly if you expect to be asked back to the cellar. More normally, ripe Vouvray is a fragrant, mellow white wine, distinctly Chenin in its smoky first impression and developing a pleasing series of flavors, none very intense. Dry extremes, such as those in Quincy or Sancerre, are rare. Alcohol must attain 11 percent for the appellation, and 10 percent potential alcohol is required in the grape before harvest. Montlouis needs be a half degree less. Vouvray drinkers should retain their urbanity in meeting quite dry versions of the wine, slightly cutting, bitter, or acid, in dreary years such as 1972.

Montlouis is in general a more narrow, less suave, less interesting version of Vouvray. But the best wines from the lesser district are preferable to such curt-tasting, charmless wines as do occasionally get away with the appellation Vouvray.

Mousseux (sparkling) Vouvray and Montlouis must be made by the Champagne process but need contain only 9 percent alcohol. Sunless vintages find this a convenient door through which to leave the stage still wearing appellation costume. This gives occasion to a curious feature of the Touraine business—traveling teams of sparkling wine makers who visit peasant growers unable or unequipped to degorge, introduce dosages, or otherwise carry out Champagne-method processes, and perform these services much as mobile bottling teams do elsewhere in the world.

Another vehicle for polite dismissal of weak Vouvray wines is the large appellation Touraine or Coteaux de Touraine, for whites need only be 9.5 percent alcohol in this appellation. Touraine red must reach 9 percent. While these are required to come from Cabernet Franc (or Cabernet Sauvignon) vines, Touraine rosé may derive from coarse varieties such as Cot, Gamay, and Groslot. At best, Touraine rosé faintly traces on the imagination the idea of red grapes. The grayish, watery, acid rosé also found by this name is implausible as appellation-grade wine. Wine fit not for the gods but to hammer contrition home to fallen angels, it would seem.

Bourgueil, St.-Nicolas-de-Bourgueil, Chinon

Twenty-five miles (40 kilometers) downstream (west) on the Loire are two red wine districts much reputed locally, enthused over by their admirers, but little displayed to the overseas wine consumer. If they are esoteric, they did not ask to be and were not always. Bourgueil's appellation area fronts the Loire on its north bank and spreads north behind it; Chinon lies south of the river on a parallel little tributary called Le Loir. St.-Nicolas-de-Bourgueil, the best of several Bourgueil Villages, receives its own appellation. Bourgueil is made only of red grapes. Rosé is permitted but is required to come from the same Cabernet Franc grape as red. Red is worth more, and by logic not lost on the growers, red is produced. Cabernet Sauvignon, technically permitted, is hardly planted. Pruned low in the Bordeaux fashion, Cabernet Franc is set out on gravelly or sandy topsoil, some alluvial, lying on rocky substratum; the vine is known as the Breton. Six

communes of importance are divided into three zones according to soil differences. Rivalry and dispute over the merits of their wines mark village life; the appellation extends for miles, and local pride, as in Chinon under like circumstances, is intense. For all three appellations red wines must make 9.5 percent alcohol and are the lightest fine red wines in France, perhaps in the world.

Vinification and conditioning follow Bordeaux practice, with barrel age somewhat abbreviated and few growers rich enough to afford new oak. Since red wines spend more time in barrel than whites, the preoccupation of Loire peasant growers with relations between the weather and their wooden cooperage is more visible in Bourgueil and Chinon. Growers theorize and worry about phases of the moon and their effect on racking or bottling wines. Once you have bought the crop this seems less like superstition and is now called tradition. If you are not in the wine trade, the sentiment is called fear.

To the south, in Chinon, 11 villages of note make red wines from Breton (Cabernet Franc) in the same way under the same rules, but chalky soils prevail. Chinon is also allowed white and rosé appellations, but little is made. Village and grower pride are intense; the region is large, and a great variety of wines can be found throughout the appellation. Bourgueil is usually more generous than Chinon, with more perfume and a point more body. Neither red wine offers, as most reds do, a sense of power or unctuosity, or is roundly spicy or richly tannic. What they display is a delightful raciness difficult to evoke—a fresh sense of grape taste, beginning and ending on the palate with delicacy. They tread a dangerous ground risking always to topple over into acidity and meanness. But this same precarious constitution allows wonderfully clean-tasting qualities to come forward immediately. Craft and sensitivity are required to make viable red wines at all of such light material, and more so still to capture and balance their merits, particularly if the bouquet is not to be sacrificed, yet color and body obtained. It is the bouquet, flowery and compared to violets or fine berries, of which growers are most proud.

For those who appreciate Bourgueil and Chinon, among them obviously this writer, it is discouraging to find the wines drunk against weighty, powerful reds, compared to which they must taste thin and limited. Tasted comparatively with one another, Loire reds are endlessly fascinating, with their shades of purple color suggesting youth and race and their clean, fragrant effect on the palate. But certainly even partisans would agree that a taster must go more than halfway to meet the qualities that these wines offer.

Cooling your Chinon or Bourgueil is allowed and quite in order, for all qualities except bouquet are enhanced. Like Beaujolais, and for like reasons, they will be enjoyed more if drunk at 50–60 degrees F. St.-Nicolas-de-Bourgueil and more robust wines from the other appellations age respectably for a few years, but it is questionable if they gain as much as they lose with time.

Saumur

Midway between Tours and Angers, along a bend of the Loire, is the town of Saumur, which gives name to a region known in France for sparkling white wines of rather acid style. Still white wines, dry and very clean, if reflecting Chenin Blanc virtues less plainly, are popular in Paris and shipped abroad. These slight, fresh white wines with only 10 percent alcohol fade quickly in bottle, with neither fruit nor body to preserve their attraction. Drinking them young is too weak a suggestion; infanticide is the better notion. Below Saumur, around the town of Champigny, is the Loire's other renowned red wine appellation, Saumur-Champigny. Like Bourgueil, Cabernet Franc is used for a small production of 10 percent alcohol red wine, light and fragrant as the wines of Chinon, with more apparent fruit. This quality reflects bottling in the year after vintage, as is done for white wines; consume Champigny quickly, for the superficial but delightful qualities decline rapidly in bottle.

A rosé exclusively from Cabernet bears the name Cabernet de Saumur, and with it begins an intricate game of names with various species of Anjou rosé wines, most famous of the many wines made by 30,000 growers over some 72,000 acres (29,000 hectares) of vineyard in the region. That the famous battle of Crécy (1346) was lost to the English through confusion has been lost in turn on the Anjou growers, who have asked for, and as punishment received, no fewer than six rosé appellations. No simplification can be too gross for such a muddle; let this one try to serve. Rosé wines are made from red grapes, and Cabernet Franc is the preferred red grape of the Loire. Whenever a rosé may do so it will call itself Cabernet, however buried that word may be amid place names forming the full appellation title. When "Cabernet" is not in the name of an Anjou rosé, it is for the good cruel reason that the wine comes from poor varieties such as Cot, Gamay, or Groslot. Cabernet rosé must attain a respectable 11 to 12 percent alcohol. Failing this distinction, lesser rosés, which do not say Cabernet, are automatically relegated to Rosé d'Anjou. This is an *Appellation d'Origine Contrôlée* of France, guaranteeing that the wine in the bottle is at least 9 percent alcohol and comes from somewhere in the 37,000 acres (15,000-odd hectares) of Anjou appellation vineyard. The logic of this rosé appellation structure is crystal clear; the position of the consumer is somewhat less so.

Like Touraine, Anjou is a large producing region with red and white wines, but rosé is its staple. Its soils are of a shelly, sandy type, called Feluns, to which some importance is locally attached. Rosé wines of the central Loire fall into two sorts: clean and balanced, with color and fruit; and the rest. *Mousseux* wines are made from at least 40 percent Chenin Blanc juice to which up to 60 percent white (or pink) juice from red grapes may be added.

Coteaux du Layon and Coteaux de L'Aubance

South of Angers, on the Loire, a lush agricultural countryside contains a sheltered bucolic pocket of vineyard enjoying exceptionally favorable climate. Its vines are in Chenin Blanc, here called Pineau de la Loire. When occasionally attacked by noble rot, they produce Quarts de Chaume, the best of a small family of sweet Loire wines, named after a village near the Layon River. The best come from schist ground, affirm the French authorities; heavier, less good wines come from clay. Bonnezeaux, south of Chaume, is similarly reputed for sweet white wines and, like Chaume, has its own appellation. Superripe Chenin grapes can give unique wine different from Sauternes. Dominated by a flowery bouquet, very fresh and forceful, the sensation to the taster is as immediate as a handful of crushed grapes. The flavor continues in a honeyed style and successions of tastes more usual to generous Loire whites. Drier Chenin wines come from the northern sector of this area just under the Loire; called the Coteaux de l'Aubance, this area includes Savennières, a village with its own appellation, producing a semisweet or semidry elite wine.

Muscadet

A collossal viticultural district fans out in great plains about the city of Nantes, Atlantic mouth of the Loire. Most of the area here and to the south is planted in wide-rowed tracts of Folle Blanche grape, a common acidic variety used in distilling Cognac. When made around the Nantes region and turned into table wine it is called Gros Plant du Pays Nantais—an acid but sound dry white wine.

Just to the south and east of Nantes, a small portion of this big district is cut into three appellations giving agreeable light wines, all white and all called Muscadet. Muscadet is a grape name, another Loire localism for a Burgundian common variety known as Melon de Bourgogne; in this desolate terrain it offers pleasing qualities.

Muscadet itself is a large appellation area from which extend smaller appellations, the larger, better known Muscadet de Sèvre et Maine and the smaller Muscadet Côteaux de La Loire; the first appellation requires 9.5 percent alcohol, the latter two half a percent more. Distinctions are really a matter of fruit, liveliness, and length of taste; good wines are found in all three districts, albeit more often in Sèvre et Maine.

Muscadet must be gathered early, for it suffers quickly and severely from supermaturation when all its tart, lively qualities are submerged into a watery, uninteresting white wine. This explains the preference given here to northern slopes whose limited exposure fosters more acidity, a critical quality factor in this appellation.

Grapes are picked quickly and fermented in barrel to produce the pale, whitish but fresh wine that will be bottled the following Easter, offering a technically short flavor but one harmonious with fruit in its initial impressions. Characteristically fragile in time more than in shipment, the wines of lighter style must be drunk quickly if any charm is to be recovered from their limited qualities. Crisp in impression, an effect coming from much chilling and little taste, they are paired with shellfish and are avidly consumed in Paris, where Muscadet's superficiality has made it a favorite for decades.

Muscadet *sur lie,* or Muscadet *tiré sur lie,* is a variant of Muscadet whose character is suggested by the French phrases cited, meaning "on the lees" or "drawn [off] the lees." Wines, in fermenting and after, deposit dead or not-so-dead yeasts and other detritus; racking or decanting wine off these into a clean barrel is a standard cellar operation. Muscadet *sur lie* is not racked or often even filtered but rather bottled off the lees from the barrel in which it has fermented. Carbon dioxide produced in fermentation is bottled with it, and such wines are slightly effervescent. Flavor is more intense, more tart; more fruit, much appreciated in this rather bland wine, is achieved by this process. A quantity of wine is sacrificed each time, remaining with the lees, and more labor is involved, making Muscadet *sur lie* a more expensive wine. But the tricky side of the process is not only the physical care required to avoid stirring a sediment film into the wine toward the end. Extended contact with lees also risks fouling the wine (the reason for racking in the first place), and matter drifting into bottles can contain yeasts carrying forward a secondary fermentation of unpleasant proportions after bottling is over. From a consumer's point of view it should be expected that Muscadet *sur lie* will have extra tang and flavor, may have effervescence, and will cost more than regular Muscadet. But a foul-tasting version comes from fouled wine, not part of the bargain and cause for return of the bottle.

Pouilly Blanc Fumé Georges Gaudry

This first-rate grower's wine excellently represents the distinctive varietal aroma of Sauvignon Blanc as it is cultivated around the Loire town of Pouilly. Its flavor is simply delicious and represents the best such wines have to offer. It is imported into America and is unusual in making no compromises to that fact. Flavor and freshness are values in Loire whites as in few other wines, and this is short in neither. Its body reflects a little more ripeness than usual in the eastern Loire, and it is perhaps too full and generous a wine to be called average, but it excels in qualities difficult to combine. The virtue of a young wine is closely allied with its expression of grape variety, and the Sauvignon, here called the Fumé, is done honor to in M. Gaudry's wine. Congratulations to competitor and friend Robert Haas for turning up this Pouilly Blanc Fumé of character.

VINTAGE   DATE   PRICE

GUESTS

MENU   COMMENTS

Sancerre of Chavignol H. Bourgeois

The slopes of the hamlet of Chavignol are one of the preferred sites for Sauvignon Blanc grapes, which make this pale straw-yellow wine sometimes tinged with green. Typically slightly less tart than neighboring Pouilly Fumé wines made from the same grape, Sancerre are nevertheless distinctly dry wines that tend to bitterness in unripe years. They lack aftertaste more than any other quality and rarely achieve concentrated flavor, but they do offer a lively white wine that presents itself very energetically to the palate, has a firm, clean aroma and is useful as an extra-dry wine rather than distinguished as a fine one. These are all qualities better drunk young. This label comes from the commendable 1972 version, which shows the effect of unripe grapes but also the more extreme qualities of this appellation in the central Loire Valley. St.-Satur and Bué are other Sancerre villages whose names appear on exported labels.

VINTAGE   DATE   PRICE

GUESTS

MENU   COMMENTS

Bourgueil Couly-Dutheil

While the finest, lightest, most seductive, and therefore best representatives of Bourgueil come from individual growers, it is nearly impossible to expect their limited supply and variable style to answer needs of international commerce. This wine is from a *négociant* and is authentic, sufficiently generous and rich to stand export treatment, yet gives a good suggestion of what Bourgueil and its classic zone, Saint-Nicolas-de-Bourgueil, have to offer. The striking aroma and fruit are muted—there is no getting away from it—and for much the same reasons as can be seen in muted exported Beaujolais; but the quality and aftertaste are valid, and the style is acceptable and identifiable. Compare this with Chinon and Saumur de Champigny, its red Loire cousins.

VINTAGE   DATE   PRICE

GUESTS

MENU   COMMENTS

Chinon Paul Zéja

This single label will have to represent the myriad small growers of the Loire who work vineyards often too small to merit export efforts. This fruity, fragrant, and delicious light red Cabernet Franc wine is found in England. Its acidity is apparent in its bright ruby color, vital aroma, and refreshing tasting qualities exemplifying the neglected wines of this appellation and its neighbor, Bourgueil. Matured in oak casks two years, it is nevertheless completely fresh and cannot help but evoke the sensation of biting into the ripe grapes from which it was made. Its maker would insist that good Chinon be aged in bottle. Others would prefer it young and cool for its fruitlike qualities carried in a well-made but light wine. In any event, full marks for appellation character!

VINTAGE   DATE   PRICE

GUESTS

MENU   COMMENTS

MIS EN BOUTEILLES   A LA PROPRIÉTÉ

Pouilly Blanc Fumé

APPELLATION CONTROLÉE

Vol. net 73 cl

POUILLY-SUR-LOIRE

GEORGES GAUDRY

PROPRIÉTAIRE-VITICULTEUR

BOISGIBAULT-TRACY (Nièvre) FRANCE

FILIBER NUITS - Reprod Interd

APPELLATION **Sancerre** CONTROLÉE

CHAVIGNOL

MISE EN BOUTEILLES A LA PROPRIÉTÉ

Médaille d'Or

H. BOURGEOIS

Propriétaire-Viticulteur

à Chavignol (Cher)

Concours de Paris

1952 - 1954

1956 - 1962

C.P. - St-Satur

Bourgueil

APPELLATION CONTROLÉE

73 cl

COULY-DUTHEIL-NÉGOCIANT A CHINON (I&L)

L. RUEL. POITIERS

Paul ZÉJA, Prop.-Vitic., LIGRÉ 37, Tél. (47) 93-18-48

IMP. F. MOTION - CHINON

Muscadet Sur Lie de Sèvre et Maine
Clos de la Sablette Marcel Martin

Mouzillon is nearly in the center of Sèvre et Maine, the preferred Muscadet appellation priced higher than Muscadet or Muscadet Côteaux de la Loire. Bottling from a barrel without racking (*tiré sur lie*) is a specialty of this region, which uses Melon (Muscadet) grapes to make light white wines best drunk young; *sur lie* versions are costlier and tarter and can be effervescent. A tinge of acidity in the aroma suggests quality in this wine, for poorly harvested grapes lack the vitality acidity gives. The pleasant but bland flavor reflects qualities of the average and agreeable 1973 Loire crop. This appellation is never generous in fruit and accepts a slight bitterness in aftertaste as the price paid for the acidity gained by early picking. While light in body, it accompanies fish dishes well and should not be expected to show refined aftertaste. It should be priced between $3.00 and $4.50.

VINTAGE   DATE   PRICE

GUESTS

MENU   COMMENTS

Quarts de Chaume Baumard

Part of the unique Côteaux de Layon section of the Loire, a lovely agricultural district nurturing Chenin Blanc grapes to super-maturation with the aid of "noble rot," Quarts de Chaume is the best reputed of a family of wines including Bonnezeaux and Côteaux de Layon Supérieur. Bouquet is flowery above all and will be recognizable to Americans who have drunk California Chenin. Richly textured and giving lush tactile impressions, it develops with finesse and charm to the taste, definitely sweet but never losing Chenin flavor. The effect is honeyed, and both sensation and varietal flavor linger on with finesse. Only moderately expensive for wine produced in paltry amounts, it should be tasted once at least to complete a picture of Chenin white wine styles. Slight hints of sulphur are normal, and airing will remove them; aggressive sulphur smell and taste show indiscreet wine making, and a different grower should be sought.

VINTAGE   DATE   PRICE

GUESTS

MENU   COMMENTS

Vouvray Demi-Sec A. de Marconnay

Chenin Blanc is the most elegant white grape grown along the Loire, and Vouvray is probably its most important appellation area. A ripe year was 1971, and in such harvests wide choice of styles between dry and sweet are available to Chenin grape growers. This wine from a *négociant* rather than a proprietor is a good illustration of a drier version of Vouvray and its sister appellation, Montlouis. The aroma of good Chenin wines is distinctive and flowery, the palatal impressions less rich than the aroma would suggest, and the finish varies from slightly tart, as in this case, to mellow or even quite unctuous and sweet when very ripe grapes have been used. Preferred sites are known as "valleys," the best being Vallée de Coquette, de Nouys, and Chartier. It is preferable to sample wines from growers, but these are difficult to find. Unusual in Loire wines, this Vouvray is flawed by excess use of sulphur to protect it from oxidization.

VINTAGE   DATE   PRICE

GUESTS

MENU   COMMENTS

Vouvray Ackerman-Laurance

This is the Vouvray label most frequently seen in America, and it illustrates the conflict between mass distribution, which for the consumer means availability, and authentic representation of the tasting qualities of fine wines. The bland white wines shipped under this label evoke something of the flavors and, when young, the freshness that endears Vouvray to travelers in the Loire, but they do so only faintly. In England, the wines of Marc Brédif occupy a similar niche but are more interesting. Criteria for Vouvray are freshness, good statement of Chenin Blanc character, and harmony between aroma and aftertaste, the absence of which suggests misguided tampering with the wine. This is as true of sweeter versions as it is of dry ones.

VINTAGE   DATE   PRICE

GUESTS

MENU   COMMENTS

Mise en bouteille sur lie à la Propriété

CLOS DE LA SABLETTE

PRODUCT OF FRANCE — TABLE WINE 3/4 QUART

MUSCADET

APPELLATION MUSCADET DE SÈVRE & MAINE CONTRÔLÉE

Imported by : CLASSIC WINE IMPORTS LTD, Boston, Mass

MARCEL MARTIN, PROPRIÉTAIRE A LA SABLETTE. MOUZILLON (L. ATLANT.)

DOMAINE DES BAUMARD

PRODUCE OF FRANCE — 1969

MISE AU DOMAINE — 1969

QUARTS DE CHAUME

APPELLATION QUARTS DE CHAUME CONTRÔLÉE

Toute la récolte 1969 a été mise en bouteilles au Domaine

BAUMARD — VITICULTEUR AU LOGIS DE LA GIRAUDIÈRE — ROCHEFORT-SUR-LOIRE — M. & L. — FRANCE

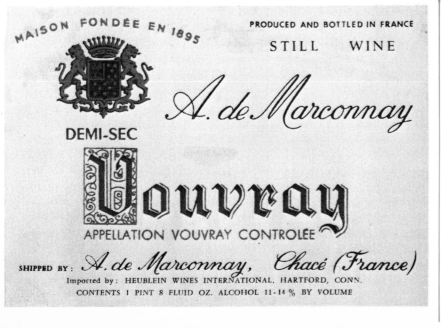

MAISON FONDÉE EN 1895

PRODUCED AND BOTTLED IN FRANCE

STILL WINE

A. de Marconnay

DEMI-SEC

Vouvray

APPELLATION VOUVRAY CONTROLEE

SHIPPED BY : *A. de Marconnay, Chacé (France)*

Imported by : HEUBLEIN WINES INTERNATIONAL, HARTFORD, CONN.

CONTENTS 1 PINT 8 FLUID OZ. ALCOHOL 11-14 % BY VOLUME

ACKERMAN

VOUVRAY

Cuvée St Paul

APPELLATION VOUVRAY CONTROLÉE

ACKERMAN-LAURANCE - Saint-HILAIRE - Saint-FLORENT (M. & L.) FRANCE

IMPORTED BY

SCHENLEY IMPORT Co - NEW-YORK. N.Y.

WHITE WINE · PRODUCE OF FRANCE

CONTENTS 1 PINT 9 FLUID OUNCES · ALCOHOL 12 % BY VOLUME

Alsace

The popularity that good Alsatian wines should logically enjoy by reason of their diversity, elegance, and pronounced grape varietal character has been forestalled by different causes. The export of cheap, poor wines tarnished the region's reputation. Also, German wines seem to cast some kind of evil spell over consumer interest in Alsatian wines. Is it because the bottles look alike yet the wines taste entirely different? Alsatian wines are regarded as poor relations of German wines, while other French wines are rarely compared with wines across the Rhine. Inexpensive, lesser Alsatian wines decline as rapidly in bottle as similar white wines from elsewhere, but importers abroad are especially reluctant to stock them. But probably most telling, a handful of large Alsatian exporters have done an excellent job of placing their well-advertised, correct, but dull wines in all markets. With little or no room for individual wines from many producers, wines whose quality and character would make for consumer interest, it is no wonder that Alsatian wines plod feebly along.

Alsace is a single appellation, and its wines are frank to the taste, easy to recognize, and readily enjoyed. Their theme is grape varietal character, for fine wines from these hills are grown, vinified, and labeled to express qualities of the grape variety used.

The vineyard runs along the foothills of the Vosges Mountains for some 60 miles (100 kilometers) from north to south. It is protected from prevailing westerly winds by the Vosges and exposed eastward to the morning sun much as the best slopes of Burgundy's Côte d'Or. Sinused hills nuzzle and wind into the Vosges from the beautiful city of Colmar north to St.-Hippolyte, forming a sort of heartland. Premium sites scatter north and south of this central section, while the appellation ends with the northern foothills slumping down into the plain opening onto Strasbourg. The Rhine parallels the vineyards; at the end of the long growing season its moist influence favors noble rot. Picking begins in October.

Alsace is an excellent vineyard, and in spots it is superlative. The appellation area of 37,000 acres (15,000 hectares) averages 20 million gallons (750,000 hectoliters) of wine, nearly all white. Not all the land within Alsace's borders has appellation rights, however; low-lying plots are condemned to mere consumption-wine production.

Wide rows permitting the use of tractors are becoming popular. Pruning is high. Wires support yard-tall vines that throw up a further yard of foliage along the two shoots, which are pruned to give eight to ten "eyes," or buds, from which fruit and foliage emerge in summer. The generous appellation allows 100 hectoliters per hectare (about 1,050 gallons per acre), but 70 to 80 hectoliters (say, 800 gallons per acre) are the actual amounts averaged in well-pruned parcels. Vinification is rapid and simple, with centrifuge presses used where affordable; cool fermentations are preferred, emphasizing the fruit and flavor that distinguish these wines. Bottling is normally done in the year following the harvest. Unlike many other appellations, *Appel-* *lation Alsace Contrôlée* must be bottled in Alsace in the traditional tall green fluted bottles.

Most properties are small. Forty-five thousand growers cultivate between 1.2 acres (0.5 hectare) and 6.1 acres (2.5 hectares). Growers owning more than 10 acres (4 hectares) may also be shippers, buying wine and/or grapes. Of the important cooperatives, the oldest are at Eguisheim and Dambach-la-Ville; others are at Sigolsheim, Bennwihr, and Ingersheim. Few big estates exist—the best-known is Schlumberger, near Guebwiller—but in English-speaking markets the labels of four big commercial shippers predominate—Dopff, Hugel, and Dopff-Irion at Riquewihr, and Trimbach. These Big Four ship clean but by and large standardized, muted, and unexciting representatives of the grapes of Alsace. To appreciate Alsatian wine fully, one must hunt for the labels of small shippers and growers.

Appellation laws liberally allow grower-*négociants* to buy wines and grapes throughout Alsace but jealously restrict the use of place, site, or *clos* names. Exceptions must be hallowed by long and continuous use. These range from the minuscule Rangen plot in Thann, to Riquewihr's Schoenenberg, Ammerschwihr's Kaefferkopf, and the larger Clos Ste.-Odile in Obernai, home of the convent named for Alsace's patron saint. The firm responsible for the wine's quality is on the label; the town name only signifies its place of business. Three of the Big Four shippers may be in prestigious Riquewihr, but their wines come from all over.

The authenticity and underappreciated charm of Alsatian grape varieties offer the wine taster, especially the beginner, a ready education in appreciating varietal distinctions. This prepares a person to discern the wine maker's hand in distinguishing wines of the same variety. There is no more convenient and inexpensive school in which to begin to study and appreciate white wines.

Riesling, Gewürztraminer (Traminer), Tokay d'Alsace, Muscat, Pinot Blanc, and Sylvaner are the important varieties to remember in approximately that order. Sylvaner flourishes in the northern zone. The best Rieslings come from the center strip around Ribeauvillé, Riquewihr, Mittelwihr, and Ammerschwihr. Gewürztraminer is another central zone grape. In exceptional vintages Riesling and Gewürztraminer are attacked by noble rot, producing rich, locally prized wines with residual unfermented sugar. Tasters abroad may find them too assertive in flavor and texture. Sylvaner, sometimes classed as a noble grape, only rarely yields very fine wine.

Wine collectors abroad will find Riesling, Gewürztraminer, and Sylvaner and little else among noble grapes. In Alsace, wines mixing varieties must be called Zwicker, and a great deal is drunk on the spot, some still fermenting. A mix of noble grapes is called Edelzwicker; much is exported. It should be dry and clean, offer fruit, and give general impressions of Alsatian spice and aroma. The distinction between Edelzwicker and noble varietal wines is insufficiently appreciated; Edelzwicker mixtures are typically made also from second pressings of grapes, and so are destined for blending. The first pressing is called *tête de cuvée* and is superior. A scrupulous grower would therefore call a second pressing of even a single variety of noble grapes "Edelzwicker."

The label terms *Réserve, Réservée,* or *Grand,* as in *Grand Réserve,* distinguish superior wine of 11 percent alcohol. *Appellation Alsace* normally requires 8 percent alcohol. With ripe harvests this low minimum may and has been raised. Réserve, Grand Cru or Grand Réserve wines must be entirely from noble grapes, as must wines bearing a site name.

Vintage quality can vary greatly. Alsatian whites depend upon fruit, charm, and elegance in addition to mere alcoholic strength and adequate acidity. Unripe years produce mean wines whose low prices do not meet production costs. Weather patterns tend to follow those of Germany and Burgundy. The year 1970 was of pleasant quality without great concentration; 1971 made superb intense wines, very rich and ripe; 1972 was unripe, acidities were excessive and fruit lacking; 1973 made charming wines whose flavor was reduced a bit by the abundant crop; and 1974 showed variety, appealing wines alternating with thin ones.

Edelzwicker, Sylvaner, Pinot Auxerrois, and all the lesser grape varieties are types whose merits show in youth, fresh wines with aroma, fruit and allure; the younger the better. Durability in bottle, flavor, and above all bouquet increase as one climbs the quality ladder through Pinot, Tokay d'Alsace, Muscat, and finally Gewürztraminer and Riesling, especially of Réserve grade. As in German and all fine white wines, some personal tastes will sacrifice freshness for the increased depth and complexity more mature wines achieve; others prefer to catch all the pungency, fruit, and vitality of white wines at their youngest.

MAJOR ALSATIAN GRAPE VARIETIES

RIESLING
: Late ripening, high in alcohol (often 12 to 13 percent), intense flavor, bouquet evolving strongly with age, delicate, vinous, and the most harmonious of Alsatian wines.

GEWÜRZTRAMINER (TRAMINER)
: The distinction between these two is now generally considered invalid. Superbly spicy aromatic wines high in alcohol and of intense character, they are initially startling to the nose and taste; some experience of vulgar versions is necessary to appreciate the finesse and aftertaste of the finest examples.

TOKAY D'ALSACE (PINOT GRIS)
: This has no connection with Hungarian Tokay. At best a luscious, intense flavored white standing well on its own without food. Subtle, refreshing, normally fermented dry.

MUSCAT
: Rarely exported, good versions have distinctive smoky bouquet, much fruit, immediate attraction, and completely escape the vulgarity common to wines from Muscat grapes. Muscat Ottonel is the usual subvariety.

SYLVANER
: The best are lively, aromatic, and stimulating; very fresh to taste, clean to swallow, with less spice and elegance than Gewürztraminer but bearing a resemblance to it on a lighter scale.

Alsace is an exceptionally rewarding region to visit. Its overtly rich cuisine, landscaped villages and hills, and omnipresent small winegrower and his craftmanship are best experienced in person. I cannot evaluate the claim that one local dialect, Walsch, is an outpost of Celtic, but German scholars study Alsatian dialect for clues to modern German and Dutch. However, the slurred effect of Alsatian local speech is not historically explained by the delectable if fiery local *eau-de-vie* (fruit brandy), pear, raspberry, plum, or otherwise, and the very suggestion is a dirty rotten Paris rumor. But what else can be expected of Parisians, who, like the rest of the world, neglect the distinctive, elegant, and inexpensive white wines of Alsace?

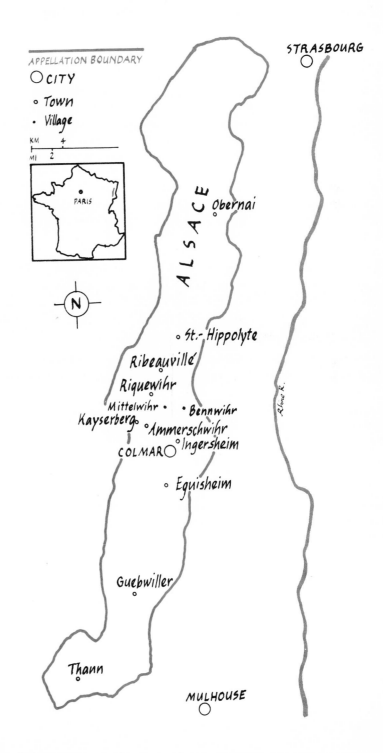

Gewürztraminer Schlumberger

The heady wines of this large and famous estate are unique among the typically lighter wines of Alsace's fine grape varieties. Their assertive, heavy impressions to the senses are attributed to small production per area and excellent ripening exposition on the relatively steep hillsides of their vineyards near Guebwiller. Perhaps it would be reasonable to compare their style to the charged, earthy, vigorous attack of rich German wines from the Palatinate region. Their only rivals are a few wines of Riesling and Gewürztraminer grapes from the best sites elsewhere in Alsace that are deliberately allowed to shrivel and concentrate in favorable long autumns. Alsatian vintages tend to follow weather patterns in nearby Germany. Favored by Europeans, good vintages of Schlumberger fine wines are expensive but fascinating.

VINTAGE   *DATE*   *PRICE*

GUESTS

MENU   *COMMENTS*

Sylvaner Hugel

Hugel is one of the giant firms whose standard wines dominate most markets for Alsatian wines. They are clean and correct and serve as a reasonable introduction to the general tasting qualities of the different major grape varieties, but they show little individuality. Since they pass through national distributing systems, they are more expensive, and an advertising component is to be reckoned with in the price of each bottle. This is a typical example of branded wine with its merits and defects.

VINTAGE   *DATE*   *PRICE*

GUESTS

MENU   *COMMENTS*

Riesling Kaefferkopf Albert Schoech

This single elite label will serve to represent the scores of small independent growers and producers that make various fine Alsatian wines. It is among these that some of the more original tasting qualities of these single-variety whites are to be found. The use of place names such as Kaefferkopf is highly restricted in Alsace, for the whole region is one appellation. Riesling, the noble grape used for the finest German wines, achieves a different style here, but its aroma is still recognizable. Its tasting qualities are a bit more musky, fruit is less pronounced, and body is somewhat more evident on the average, though exceptions abound. There are many fine producers, some of them also shippers, but unfortunately space allows only one label. Some more unusual Alsatian wines are Tokay d'Alsace and a delicate Muscat wine delicious as an aperitif. The region is celebrated for its *eau-de-vie* as well, fragrant and potent.

VINTAGE   *DATE*   *PRICE*

GUESTS

MENU   *COMMENTS*

Gewürztraminer Dopff

This is another of the large firms that dominate the market for Alsatian wines at the expense of the variety obtained from more individual producers. Dopff wines are regular in quality but tend to thinness and lack of expression. Their distribution, as that of Trimbach, Hugel, and Dopff Irion, is excellent both in France and abroad. Gewürztraminer is perhaps the most singular Alsatian wine with its extreme of spice and character in the aroma. It can be heady and forceful to the tasting senses in ripe years and indeed requires a good vintage to give wine of value. Formerly a wine called Traminer used to be shipped, but the two varieties are now considered to be the same. If you find this grape variety and Sylvaner too spicy and curious in flavor, experiment with the blander Pinot or a plain Edelzwicker, good useful white wines with a touch rather than an onrush of Alsatian character.

VINTAGE   *DATE*   *PRICE*

GUESTS

MENU   *COMMENTS*

SCHLUMBERGER

GEWURZTRAMINER

APPELLATION ALSACE CONTROLÉE

MISE EN BOUTEILLE AUX
DOMAINES SCHLUMBERGER VITICULTEUR A GUEBWILLER (HAUT-RHIN)
PRINTED IN FRANCE

APPELLATION ALSACE CONTROLÉE

Vin d'Alsace

HVH

DEPUIS 1639

SYLVANER "HUGEL" ®

ESTATE BOTTLED

HUGEL ET FILS NÉGOCIANTS A RIQUEWIHR (Ht-RHIN)

PRODUCE OF FRANCE · BOTTLED IN FRANCE

SOLE AGENTS : DREYFUS, ASHBY & Cº,
NEW-YORK N. Y.

ALCOHOL BY VOL. : 12 % - NET CONTENTS : 1 PINT 8 FL. OZ.

PRODUCE OF FRANCE

MARQUE DÉPOSÉE

MAISON FONDÉE EN 1840

Appellation Alsace Contrôlée

Riesling Kaefferkopf

Albert Schoech, Négociant à Ammerschwihr Ht Rhin

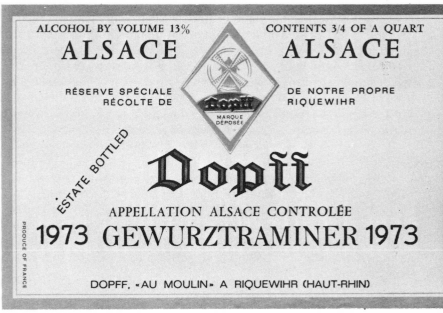

ALCOHOL BY VOLUME 13%   CONTENTS 3/4 OF A QUART

ALSACE   ALSACE

RÉSERVE SPÉCIALE
RÉCOLTE DE

dopff
MARQUE
DÉPOSÉE

DE NOTRE PROPRE
RIQUEWIHR

ESTATE BOTTLED

Dopff

APPELLATION ALSACE CONTROLÉE

1973 GEWURZTRAMINER 1973

PRODUCE OF FRANCE

DOPFF, «AU MOULIN» A RIQUEWIHR (HAUT-RHIN)

Rhône

The Rhône region has as large a quality vineyard area as does Burgundy; average wine quality is also as high as in Burgundy, though of different style. The Rhône's interest to wine consumers abroad grows steadily, for its good wines are cheap, its great wines are remarkable, and improved production methods have raised and regularized quality. Vineyards follow the Rhône River from Lyon to Avignon about 100 miles from north to south. A hot summer climate causes vintage character to differ from those found elsewhere in France. Most of the nearly 200,000 acres (80,000 hectares) of vineyard registered in departments touching the Rhône is given over to common, *vin de table* wines. But two quality zones neatly divide themselves, one around Tain l'Hermitage, the other well below it in the environs of Avignon. The north's small appellations are heady individualistic (and expensive) wines painfully coaxed in small amounts per acre from tortuous vineyards. The sprawling southern area yields abundantly; its moderately priced reds, whites, and rosés show the high alcohol and firm constitutions obtained in Provence summers.

Northern *(Septentrional)* appellations—Côte-Rôtie, Condrieu, and Hermitage—are steep vineyards. Granite substratum is barely covered by meager sandy soils precariously retained by elaborate terraces and, as in other precipitous European vineyards, replenished, recuperated, and retained by much expense of money and labor. The southern *(Méridional)* area is a land of large vineyard expanses varied by broken country, much of it carpeted by alluvial rounded stones. Châteauneuf-du-Pape is its celebrated appellation. Areas excluded from Châteauneuf form the Côtes du Rhône regional appellation, with the better villages allowed to fasten their names to the wines. Tavel, France's best rosé wine, has its appellation here.

Grape varieties used in the north are powerful and pungent white Viognier and red Syrah. The latter, identified with elite Rhône wines, is richly pigmented, attains much sugar, and contributes aromatic, spicy, and vigorous qualities to odor and taste. It fares well in hot climates that bake other grapes to insipidity and has been adapted to regions such as Corsica, Australia, and California. Among the southern Rhône's ancient and traditional grape varieties, the dominant grape is Grenache, a fat, abundantly producing fruit easily turned to rosé and mellow red wine.

In the north, growers work tiny plots for large shippers who are often owners themselves. These powerful, numbing wines require much wood age; cask conditioning is traditional and elaborate. In the south, in Châteauneuf-du-Pape, standards of wine intensity have declined, and a Union of Growers representing big estates is battling against the tide. Among lesser Rhône wines, which are often vinified in the *Cave Coopérative*, different trends are elevating their quality and modernizing their tasting style and economics. Heightened fruit and freshness in simple reds and recognition of consumer preference for fresh whites reflect more alert management.

Côte-Rôtie

Red Syrah wines are made in this small appellation atop the Rhône's west bank. Côte-Rôtie is powerful in taste and the most subtle of famous reds made from Syrah, though the appellation requires only 10 percent alcohol. Côte Blonde and Côte Brune are its two steep slopes, to which cling tiny terraced plots, often only a few rows of vines the height of a man. Côte Blonde is planted with more white Viognier than Côte Brune, and its topsoil is chalkier. Grapes from the two areas may be mixed or vinified separately; traditionally barreling lasts four years. As elsewhere in the Rhône, white grapes (normally less than 10 percent) are vatted in red wines for brilliance, freshness, and perfume. Vatted less than two weeks, the wines attain much color, and during barrel aging traditional growers or *éleveurs* rack them rarely.

As in other big Syrah wines, Côte-Rôtie aroma suggests less alcohol than the mouth suddenly encounters; this burst of volatile alcoholic sensation, a warm, brandylike impact, is well described as "hot." Nevertheless, Côte-Rôtie gives less mouth-coating impression than Hermitage or classic Châteauneuf-du-Pape, and its development in the mouth is drier and less earthy in flavor. A fiery style balances flavor and alcohol but offers little taste or smell of fruit. Spicy impressions abound and invite images of cinnamon or pepper. Côte-Rôtie matures steadily and indefinitely, though growers contrast the more forward tendency of Côte Blonde to the sterner stuff of Côte Brune. Both are subtle wines marked by long aftertaste.

Condrieu and Château Grillet

The slightly more than 17 acres (7 hectares) of Condrieu, including the miniature 4-acre (1.65-hectare) toy appellation of Château Grillet, are a continuation of Côte-Rôtie along the granite slopes of the Rhône. Laborious viticulture turns nightmarish: soils lost to erosion are carted back up the slopes, weed killers are spread around offending grass lest uprooting cost more soil. The law permits only Viognier. Small yields of dense white must are vinified in barrel by a few growers and landowning shippers and at Château Grillet by its sole owner. If some Syrah still grows, its influence is discreet. While the 11 percent minimum alcohol is readily achieved in all but the dankest years, full Viognier bouquet is not. Color is standard yellow and brilliance rarely a strong point. But, beginning with the bouquet, a novel set of sensations impresses the taster. The aroma may evoke almonds and raisins; the bouquet is vinous and strong, one of the more exotic and yet "serious" (as the French say) among white wine bouquets. Young or old Condrieu gives a tactile sensation of concentrated wine, one with glycerine and unctuosity, yet this physical lusciousness is not matched by any rush of flavors. Aromatic suggestions, sometimes fresh, sometimes bitter (almonds), are repeated in the mouth. Dense and odd, Condrieu makes me think of the sap of plants. Like other northern Rhônes, it is a special taste; like all such rare wines, it is dear and Château Grillet a luxury.

Hermitage, Crozes-Hermitage

At Tain, on the Rhône's east bank, a granitic hillside backs the town. From this extension of rocky terrain come the great red and white wines of Hermitage and the lesser ones of Crozes-Hermitage. Chalky and limestone topsoils are thought to establish the superiority of Hermitage over its namesake. Terraces planted in white Marsanne, Roussanne, and a Marsanne stepchild vine called La Roussette produce white Hermitage; sand soils thinly cover the granite platforms on which grow Syrah, for red. Red Hermitage surely vies with Tokay as the oldest world-famous wine. Connoisseurship lavished on Hermitage in past ages when power (in wines) was respected for its own sake lives on in site names such as Les Bessards, Le Méal, and Greffieux; these occur in early nineteenth-century English records as individual wines and still appear on labels. The potent qualities of red Hermitage suggested a verb: "hermitaged" claret was Bordeaux strengthened with bigger wine, usually Malaga, however. Hermitage would hardly have been sacrificed for blending.

Twice as much red Hermitage as white is made. It is aged up to six years in wood, despite the expense, and even table-thumping enemies of long barrel aging such as this writer are grateful for the results. As in Côte-Rôtie, red wines are touched up with white; arguments for this practice neglect to mention the greater price obtained for red wine. A number of important shippers, some from Burgundy, are growers. A few wines are bottled under the equivalent of *clos* names, but most are blended into appellation Hermitage. Crozes-Hermitage uses the same grape varieties but less barrel age.

Hermitage is the richer, fuller, denser uncle of Côte-Rôtie. Both are formidable Syrah wines from which fruit has been wood-aged away, leaving vinosity, great character, and pungency to nose and taste. Once it is tasted, it is easy to imagine men in a past age of magnificence getting magnificently drunk on Hermitage; it is heady stuff indeed. In fact, its actual flavors are less obvious than their alcoholic power, which distracts attention from their long development in the mouth. The spice, the tastes, are subtle; and they linger.

White Hermitage is also alcoholic but shows more fruity impressions. Its strong body skirts the "hot" or burned taste so characteristic of Hermitage reds. Chante-Alouette, the best known site, is the monopoly of a large shipper, Chapoutier, whose Rhône wines are widely available abroad. White Hermitage develops sluggishly in the mouth. The sensational, unforgettable impact of its red counterpart is absent, and it lacks charm, but it has character and vigor.

Crozes-Hermitage is a subdued and less emphatically Syrah wine. Some versions no more evoke Hermitage than other Côtes du Rhône wines. The best are rich and dry but dominated by alcohol, with warmth of flavor and understated grape taste.

The color of old Syrah wines becomes fiery and orange; their bouquet develops remarkably, though it hardly can be called delicate. Longevity among these unusual reds is proverbial. Powerful, alcoholic, and wood-aged for so long, they do not often show the vagaries in tasting quality that lighter wines with more fruit, such as clarets,

evince so distressingly in youth. Their maturing is slow but inexorable. Age is essential for traditionally made Hermitage, and two hours is none too long to air a bottle before pouring.

St.-Joseph, Cornas, St.-Péray

In the long patch of vineyard north and south of Tournon, red and white wines are grouped in the St.-Joseph appellation; darker, denser reds are found in Cornas; and Clairette, a white grape, is added to Roussanne to make sparkling St.-Péray, bravely drunk locally. This grape also goes into sparkling Clairette-de-Die, about which similar unkind remarks are hard to suppress.

Tough growing conditions continue along granitic hillsides, but Syrah is left behind, and red grapes appear whose merits are fully exploited in the southern Rhône—Grenache, Carignan, Gros Noir, and Cinsault. Large shippers, owners as well, dominate the market for small growers' wine. Appellation requires a low 10 percent alcohol, and in St.-Joseph this figure is just met. Vatted and barreled briefly, bottled to offer perfume, pleasantly round body, and good aftertaste without much drive or distinctiveness, St.-Joseph is the only northern red wine that could be called charming. Cornas is a darker, denser, and more aggressive red wine, but it is also within reach of early drinking.

Baumes-de-Venise

France contains many small areas producing what are called *vins doux naturels,* or natural sweet wines, that suit French taste as an aperitif. By universal agreement, or, if the universe will not agree, by my personal conviction, the best of these is a luscious, amber drink made from Muscat grapes in Baumes-de-Venise, northeast of Avignon. Natural sugar content of as much as 16 percent alcohol is reached in its terraced vineyards and most of the best wine comes from the *Cave Coopérative.* Friends who deal in this sweet wine say it is fortified with alcohol despite its *naturel* designation; no one who drinks it cares. It is slightly vulgar, irresistibly pretty, and delicious to all senses—the usually boring sexy metaphors for wine, habitual to French and Italian declaimers, come alive for this one. A neighboring appellation, Rasteau, tries to do the same thing.

Tavel

If red color, a taste of wine as opposed to sugar and alcohol, good bouquet, and varietal aroma are standards of quality, then Tavel is the best rosé in France. It comes from west of Avignon, where red rock outcroppings, little plains covered with the red alluvial stones of the region, and sandy soils eroded from the rock harbor Grenache vines. Eleven percent alcohol is required; more is attained. The appellation is unusual in being reserved for rosé. Cooperatives and big properties make wines quickly in large vats, extracting the amenable Grenache color and bottling speedily. Smaller vineyards often do not take care, and dawdling permits the fragile Grenache juice to oxidize.

Good examples of Tavel are red and bright. Guidebooks (mostly French), and the wine writers who translate them, may describe the color as "onion skin" orange or tawny, but defective, oxidized wine is the picturesque model they are praising. The flavor is fruity, body is generous, and taste is properly vinous. Tavel is full but dry, one of the few rosés whose fundamentally winey character allows it to be drunk with almost anything. This claim is made maddeningly often for pink wines more commonly drinkable with nothing that has a taste; hence, the popularity of rosé in so many restaurants.

Lirac comes from a similar landscape immediately north, but makes red and white wines as well as rosé. Conceived as an appellation in the 1960s, inspired by the then expensive Tavel, Lirac rosé is drier, has less flavor and fruit. But it can be excellent. Prices are down for both rosés, and Lirac growers now see greater profitability in making red wine. It is too early to characterize the first reds beyond noting clean, light impressions.

Châteauneuf-du-Pape

For as long as local wines have commanded prestige in France, Châteauneuf-du-Pape has been the stellar wine of the Rhône. Its large growing area lies between Avignon and Orange, where every January a wine fair displays Rhône wine to the praise, and criticism, of professionals and the public. It was the first appellation created in France. Great estates and smaller farms are set in a hot landscape typical of Provence. Vines are in wide rows. The surface is covered with startlingly large red stones smoothed by the action of the river that has also formed the pebbly and alluvial soils hidden below. The stones have three influences on Châteauneuf-du-Pape. First, they attract photographers and other tourists. Next, this incredibly difficult surface takes an atrocious toll on farm machinery; blades grind, rattle, and shriek through its stubborn irregular layers—plowshares being beaten into swords, as it were. The third function alone explains why the stone cover is still there: heat is retained by them; and not only are the sun's rays reflected up into the vine, but during the night the soil and grapes are also warmed and dried by the hot surface. Remarkable degrees of ripeness are achieved and a clean, dry ripening environment fostered.

Châteauneuf is a botanical antiquary's paradise. Many ancient grape varieties are preserved, producing a wine whose character is unimaginable in connection with any single variety. Syrah, with which the Rhône is associated by many writers, does not figure so greatly among them. Pure Syrah from this superripe vineyard would resemble grape pudding or Syrah syrup, as experimental vats have shown. But grape mixture is at the heart of a controversy much aired in the region. Some 13 varieties have been used traditionally in Châteauneuf. A classic blend would include some 20 percent of Grenache and Cinsault, mellow grapes giving warmth and unctuosity; a third of Mourvèdre, Syrah, Muscadin, and Vaccarèse, for pigment, solidity, aging qualities, and authority of taste; some 40 percent of Picpoul and Counoise, contributing more volatile elements of bouquet, charm, and fresher flavors to offset the others; and 10 percent white grapes, Clairette and Bourboulenc, giving brilliance and lighter texture in what is otherwise a ponderous chocolate-dark wine. Mixtures have been quarreled over and fiddled with for decades, Carignan here rather than Grenache, or Oeillette instead of Clairette, or Terret Noir instead of Cinsault, and so on. Local quibbles matter little to the larger picture. But lately Grenache, a fat, convenient, and attractive grape whose color is quickly extracted and whose wines develop rapidly, thereby sparing growers long, expensive barrel con-

ditioning, has swept much of Châteauneuf before it. Parts are planted up to 80 percent in Grenache; some say the percentage is even higher. The virtues of this versatile grape are not disputed, but radical decline in quality and vitiation of character is the accusation made at the Orange fair and elsewhere against new-style Châteauneuf in which Grenache is two-thirds or more, Syrah and a few others (with luck) are added for backbone, and the whole topped off by white grapes. Simplification, argue the growers who do it, is better and more rational. The Union of Traditional Growers (*Reflêts de Châteauneuf-du-Pape*) does not agree.

This controversy exposes the limits of appellation laws. It also relates to proposals for drawing them tighter around the neck of Burgundian growers, for example (see page 105). By law Châteauneuf must be 12.5 percent alcohol, come from the region, be made from permitted grapes only, and pass a tasting test, a *label* like that of Bordeaux. Wines exceeding the permitted yield per acre are supposed to be declassified entirely. These were traditional standards that the law incorporated. Grenache *is* a permitted variety. Who is to reject a grower's wine should he prefer a Grenache style to one dominated by Mourvèdre and Muscadin? His neighbors who form the tasting panel? A man in a gray suit sent from Paris?

The source of the debasement is not even in France. It is in London, Chicago, Brussels, and Los Angeles, or wherever overseas buyers demand a famous wine but ask that it cost less and taste the same every year. This demand for a depersonalized, unvarying wine is not a criminal plot but an instinct of large marketing organizations. Not astonishingly, such a demand is answered, and character is eroded from popular appellations such as Pommard, Pouilly-Fuissé, and Châteauneuf-du-Pape.

Back in Avignon, the *Reflêts de Châteauneuf-du-Pape* continues its war on Grenache wines. Tasting independently of the appellation tests, it accords wines considered proper special neck-embossed bottle markings or back labels saying, in effect, this is the real thing.

Gigondas, Côtes du Rhône, Côtes du Rhône Villages

East of the Rhône, in the Valley of the Cèze, and west, in the Valley of the Aygues, and behind each of these flat avenues, is an enormous vineyard of plains and terraced hillside. Soils vary from stony hillside to alluvial bottomland. No single wine type prevails, and the wines are loosely designated as Gard (west) or Vaucluse (east).

Red grapes include those of Châteauneuf, above all Grenache, Cinsault, and Carignan. White grapes are the Clairette and the Ugni Blanc (Trebbiano in Italy, St.-Émilion in Cognac).

Lighter reds, more forward and fruity, are generally from the Gard side, with denser, darker, and more powerful wines from the Vaucluse. The best whites, those escaping the sodden tasting impressions of hot-climate wine heavy in alcohol, come from the Gard, for example Laudun. Climate is typically benign, but the region has its own chills and thrills. The mistral, a cold Alpine autumn wind, combined with rainfall, can bring both cold weather and rising atmospheric pressure. One highly unpleasant consequence is that fermentations in progress can slump mulishly to a halt. In the case of a giant cooperative, where hundreds of vats of several different grape varieties are fermenting 1.5 million gallons (60,000 hectoliters) of three colors and

40 styles, the general manager awakened at 3 A.M. with this exciting news is temporarily not to be envied.

Alcoholic degrees required for red, white, and rosé wines vary between 10 percent and 12.5 percent. Like the appellations of Beaujolais, all proper wines within a defined area may be *Appellation Côtes du Rhône.* Then come some 14 superior village areas. If wines from these areas meet higher technical standards, they become Côtes du Rhône Villages and may use their village name. The best-known are Cairanne, Vacqueyras, Vinsobres (a curious image for a wine village), Laudun, and Chusclan. Until January 1971, Gigondas headed this

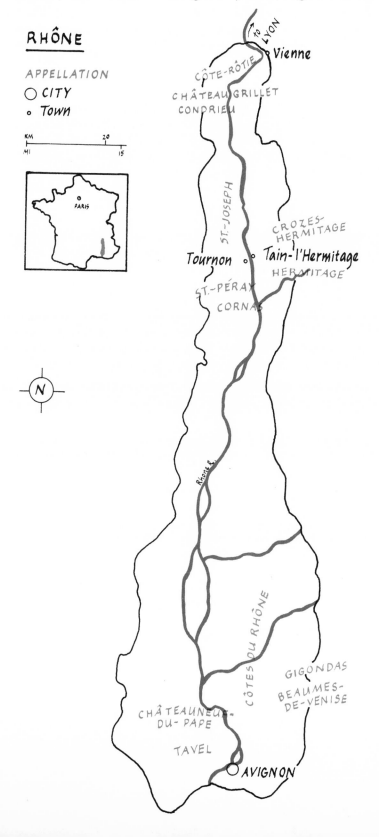

RHÔNE

APPELLATION

○ CITY

○ Town

list, but at that time it was promoted into its own appellation for red and rosé. Others may follow, Chusclan for red and rosé and perhaps Laudun for white.

Steady wine drinkers who care for good minimal quality know that a great amount of generous, sound Rhône red, white, and rosé can be had at fair prices. With its rich color, heady perfume, a cheerful attack on the palate, and clean aftertaste, Gigondas and other Vaucluse Department red wines can be suitable for laying down. Gigondas achieves lovely purple color and delicious fruit in lighter versions for young drinking, and powerful ones are more interesting than bad commercial Châteauneuf-du-Pape.

An increasing quantity of Rhône red wine is made either by the carbonic-maceration process or with a mixture of carbonic-maceration wine and standard fermentation wines. The fruity, forward, often delicious character that results is economical and convenient to buy, for it is ready to drink immediately after production. The process suits many Rhône reds. In the Gard, whites are being made with cooler fermentations, giving better fruit and flavor. Changed attitudes about alcohol inspire harvesting that offers better acidity and more lively white wines.

The *Caves Coopératives,* to which multitudes of growers bring their grapes, are delivering fresher, better wines in less time and therefore for less money. Two instances will illustrate the variety of these changes. Grenache rosé wines formerly required several steps to achieve a clarified state fit for bottling. These involved aging and filtering to clear the wine. Young wine is now clarified completely in a giant centrifuge. Physically clean yet biologically alive and unsubjected to air exposure or clarifying products, such wine has delightful freshness, and it can be centrifuged and bottled virtually as soon as it is fermented. Consumers can do their part by drinking it. This is not a joke; pressures to revert to traditional methods will follow complaints about color deterioration or staleness, which result from keeping the wine too long.

Less dramatic than giant centrifuges is small-vat fermentation of red wines using one or at most two grape varieties. Longer, cooler fermentation in smaller units extracts more flavor. Grenache is much enhanced, Carignan less so, but the experiments show that some cooperatives do not suffer delusions of grandeur and realize that better, younger, inexpensive wine is a worthy goal. The use of carbonic maceration in Châteauneuf-du-Pape seems more questionable, but I have seen no samples.

The tasting features of Rhône and Rhône Village wines vary from village to village, method to method, and grape variety to variety. Longer-vatted reds with much flavor, darker, more full and chewy, contrast with "modern" wines using mixtures of lighter varieties, which offer deliciously clean light reds with enough alcohol for a full taste but without the "hot" impression of Châteauneuf or the denseness of old-fashioned wines from Vaucluse. The best rosés show the perfume and healthy taste of young Grenache, if not the full vinosity and taste of the best Tavel. Southern Rhône white wines with vitality deserve praise; unfortunately, many remain coarsely Ugni Blanc in address or hopelessly heavy for their limited fruit.

Better wines of Rhône *Méridional* are outstripping the structure of appellation laws and are changing in response to demand. Meanwhile, appellation laws seem powerless to maintain traditional wine styles in the face of demand enticing growers and shippers to simplify, hasten, and lighten Châteauneuf-du-Pape. As usual, people make the wine and grasp opportunities to make it better or worse.

Côte-Rôtie Côtes Brune et Blonde E. Guigal

Larger shippers such as Jaboulet or Chapoutier receive better distribution and the designations Côte Brune and Côte Blonde are lapsing, but this mixture of grapes from both slopes excellently displays the best features of Côte-Rôtie wines. A medium-sized shipper of proven ability and stubborn adherence to slow methods has cask-aged a powerful vintage four years. Two hours or longer in air should be given any bottle of northern Rhône Syrah grape wine such as this. The fiery color is backed by aromatic and heady bouquet in which chocolate and cinnamon sensations flit. The "hot" impression given by much alcohol reveals firmer flavors, necessarily woody at times but rich and authoritative, promising longevity and more subtle evolution in time. Strong-tasting as it is, Côte-Rôtie is the most refined Syrah red (with a touch of white grape) of the northern Rhône's granite terraces.

VINTAGE   DATE   PRICE

GUESTS

MENU   COMMENTS

Condrieu G. Vernay

South of Côte-Rôtie and its dazzling wines, rocky terraces continue planted in Viognier, the rich white grape of Condrieu and its four-acre toy appellation Château Grillet. Meager yields give concentrated juice fermented in barrel and wood-aged. These intense wines should receive airing before drinking to allow flowery and spicy aromas to emerge. Their body is remarkable for its weight, nearly that of syrup, but far from cloying. Condrieu are complex, firm wines of original style. The slightly bitter but pleasing scent of almonds sometimes found in the nose is repeated in the mouth and joined by herbal impressions. Fruit, tartness, and lightness are notably absent, leaving an unusual powerful wine that should be tasted at least once to appreciate the Viognier grape qualities that are blended in small amounts into neighboring great Syrah-based reds. Expensive, as all rare wines must be.

VINTAGE   DATE   PRICE

GUESTS

MENU   COMMENTS

Hermitage Chapoutier

Chapoutier is a large exporting shipper whose various Rhône appellations achieve good distribution. Their general level is clean and tasty though often short in character. Some wines have been distinguished. This one is a respectable Hermitage, certainly authentic, of dark, typical color and with the characteristic spicy aroma and bouquet suggesting pitch wood or tar. The body is powerful and clean; emphatic flavors follow each other in good succession, ending well. Certainly it has been carefully wood-aged and suggests the fuller, more overpowering qualities the very best wines achieve.

It is a rotten commentary on the wine trade in America that individual wines from what is, after all, one of the great historic red wine districts of the world are virtually unobtainable. One is grateful to Chapoutier for offering a wine representing the appellation, if not an individual Hermitage.

VINTAGE   DATE   PRICE

GUESTS

MENU   COMMENTS

St.-Joseph Delas

Delas is another important shipping firm in the Rhône region. This particular version of St.-Joseph, an appellation adjacent to Cornas and across the river from Hermitage, making firm red wines, is dominated by the Syrah grape. This feature is reflected in a remarkably spicy and intriguing aroma. The bouquet infers a firm wine. Less ponderous than its surrounding appellations, it represents well the highly drinkable yet individual wines of St.-Joseph, whose full character is suggestive of high alcohol but whose flavor is not deficient, as is often the case with wines from hot localities. It could hardly be called an elegant wine, and no one would spend many adjectives on its fruity qualities, for these are few, but it is generous and good and offers excellent drinking in a hearty style. Such are the desired and expected features of the appellation.

VINTAGE   DATE   PRICE

GUESTS

MENU   COMMENTS

Côte-Rôtie

Côtes Brune et Blonde

APPELLATION "CÔTE-RÔTIE" CONTRÔLÉE

E. GUIGAL

AMPUIS (Rhône)

CONDRIEU VIOGNIER

APPELLATION CONDRIEU CONTRÔLÉE

Mise en bouteilles à la Propriété

Georges VERNAY, Viticulteur - CONDRIEU (Rhône)

GOUGENHEIM IMP PUBLICITÉ - LYON

RED RHÔNE WINE
ALCOHOL 13% BY VOL.

U.S. REPRESENTATIVES
FREDERICK WILDMAN AND SONS
NEW YORK CITY

CONTENTS 1 PT. 9 FL. OZ.
PRODUCE OF FRANCE

MIS EN BOUTEILLES DANS LES CAVES CHAPOUTIER

HERMITAGE

M. DE LA SIZERANNE

APPELLATION HERMITAGE CONTRÔLÉE

M. CHAPOUTIER S.A.

NÉGOCIANTS-ÉLEVEURS, WINE SHIPPER, A TAIN-L'HERMITAGE (DRÔME) FRANCE

DESAR. REIMS

MISE EN BOUTEILLES
DANS NOS CHAIS

PRODUCE OF FRANCE

FAIS BIEN LAISSE DIRE

DELAS

St. Joseph

APPELLATION CONTRÔLÉE

DELAS FRÈRES _ TOURNON-s/-RHÔNE (Ardèche)

Sole Agents: RUTHERFORD, OSBORNE & PERKIN Ltd. LONDON E.C. 3

Châteauneuf-du-Pape Nicolet

There are bigger shippers exporting lighter versions of this famous blend of grapes from Avignon, but this 1967 exemplifies general tasting features of a high-level shipper's Châteauneuf rather than a supple anonymous red technically of the appellation. A dark color without sensational brilliance and slightly burnt nose are acceptable prices to pay for the rich-tasting qualities. Sensations of earth, extremely ripe grapes, fragrant skins, spice, a tannic background, and a long, dry but generous finish are among these. Very round in texture but with vitality and an authoritative progression of tastes, Châteauneuf is among the most assertive and distinctive of the world's highly blended red wines. It should be opened hours before drinking and demands years of bottle age to acquire luster.

VINTAGE   *DATE*   *PRICE*

GUESTS

MENU   *COMMENTS*

Châteauneuf-du-Pape Domaine de Mont-Redon

This is but one representative of a cluster of great estates in this ancient district; some rivals are Château de Fortia, Clos de L'Oratoire, and Château de La Gardine, whose wines lately have often seemed thinner than the highest standard would expect. The values represented by these vineyards—overpowering, pungent, powerful, spicy, slow-maturing wine—are today being challenged by lighter, rapidly maturing wines issuing from Grenache grapes in a heated debate over what style of wine this renowned region should make. It is not unreasonable to ask consumers to pay for concentrated dark wines aged many years in barrel the prices expected of all fine wines so produced, over $4.00 or $5.00 per bottle retail. The understandable anger of the traditional growers is caused by Grenache wines technically entitled to this appellation, the oldest in France, that ask for like prices.

VINTAGE   *DATE*   *PRICE*

GUESTS

MENU   *COMMENTS*

Tavel Sté des Vignerons Producteurs Tavel

There seems to be some natural law dictating that as a wine's popularity increases, its quality goes the other way. Finding good examples of this firm rosé wine with some authority of taste has become more difficult than it was 20 years ago. This sample has the vigorous taste and good color expected of the appellation but lacks the full fruit and charm that are easily extracted from the Grenache grapes from which rosé wines are made throughout the southern Rhône valley. A Tavel from the shipper Bellicard deserves mention in the same breath, and a grower, Maby, is seen in America as well. The wines should have character, a real impression of wine, and a good forward aroma to precede it rather than the insipid, sweetish qualities usually associated with rosé.

VINTAGE   *DATE*   *PRICE*

GUESTS

MENU   *COMMENTS*

Gigondas Paul Jaboulet

Jaboulet is an important shipper of Rhône wines. One of the several villages whose better wines were formerly grouped in the appellation Côtes du Rhône Villages, Gigondas has been elevated to an appellation of its own. This label is from 1969 and does not show the Gigondas designation. Such a variety of grapes are permitted for these appellations that wines bearing the same name necessarily run to different tasting styles. This one, reflecting the intentions of the shipper, is a generous red with a high bouquet showing the influence of Syrah grapes used for more famous appellations (Hermitage, Côte-Rôtie) to the north. Its effect is mouth-filling, and age has made it rather dry and severe. But Gigondas can also offer more luscious wines with impressive fruity effects quite suitable for drinking young, and many other Côtes du Rhône and Côtes du Rhône Villages wines offer immediate appeal and excellent value.

VINTAGE   *DATE*   *PRICE*

GUESTS

MENU   *COMMENTS*

APPELLATION CHATEAUNEUF DU PAPE CONTROLÉE

CHANTE PERDRIX

Châteauneuf du Pape

NICOLET FRERES RECOLTANTS-CHATEAUNEUF DU PAPE

MISE AU DOMAINE

1952

Châteauneuf-du-Pape

S. C. A. PROP. PLANTIN

APPELLATION CHATEAUNEUF-DU-PAPE CONTROLÉE

DOMAINE DE MONT-REDON

HENRI PLANTIN, PROPRIÉTAIRE-RÉCOLTANT A CHATEAUNEUF-DU-PAPE (Vse)

Product of France
Contents : 3/4 Quart

Table Wine

Mellins France

PRODUCE OF FRANCE

ESTATE

BOTTLED

En le testant,
dit Philippe le Bel
il n'est bon vin
que de Tavel

"There is
good wine only
in Tavel"
King Philippe le Bel

ALCOHOL 12,7%
BY VOLUME

CONTENTS
1 PT 7 FL OZS

Tavel

TABLE

WINE

APPELLATION TAVEL CONTRÔLÉE
MISE EN BOUTEILLE A LA PROPRIÉTÉ

Sté DES VIGNERONS PRODUCTEURS TAVEL (GARD) FRANCE
SOLE AGENTS USA : CRISPIN WINES HOUSTON TEXAS

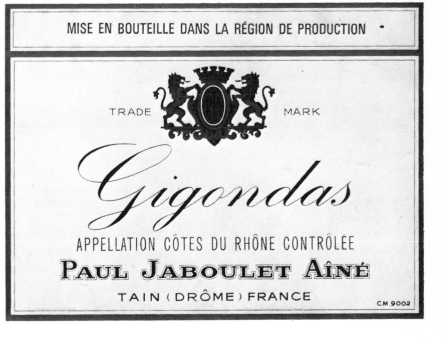

MISE EN BOUTEILLE DANS LA RÉGION DE PRODUCTION

TRADE MARK

Gigondas

APPELLATION CÔTES DU RHÔNE CONTRÔLÉE

PAUL JABOULET AÎNÉ

TAIN (DRÔME) FRANCE

CM.9002

Champagne

Champagne was a primal region of the French Kingdom; its prized red and white still wines bore the names of important towns, such as Sillery, Bouzy, Cramant, and Ay. Three centuries ago the cellar master of the Benedictine Hautevillers Abbey on the Marne River, Dom Perignon, discovered that gas from secondary fermentation could be captured in the bottle and that the acidic and variable wines of this northern zone could be improved by blending. So modern-day Champagne was born.

The Champagne region centers around Reims and Épernay, but its outposts extend south and west. Its three main regions are the Montagne de Reims, just north of the Marne River; the Vallée de la Marne, just south of the river, which merges into what used to be called the Côte de Bouzy; and the Côte des Blancs, a district running north to south around Épernay. Red Pinot Noir grapes are preferred in the first two districts, Chardonnay in the last. The Reims area is divided into eight cantons, Épernay into four, and within these are nearly all the high-quality villages. The present total area under cultivation is said to be 43,000 acres (17,000 hectares), but sources disagree. Vines are planted on chalk, clay, and other siliceous soils that are well drained, porous, and largely covered with pebbles. In this cold climate, drainage and hilly exposition are vital to the hygiene of the late-ripening Chardonnay in particular.

Classification is logical. Best villages are rated as worth 100 percent of whatever price is agreed upon each year, and lesser ones are rated point by point downward from these. Three pressings of the grapes are made, the first pressing being the best. A grower in an 88 percent rated village will receive 88 percent of the price received by the best villages for his first pressing and less for successive pressings. Champagne commerce is a sweeping bargain struck annually between the many growers and the large firms that quantitatively dominate the business. A precise agreement made before the harvest is vital to rapid and orderly harvesting. In addition to the famous firms there are cooperatives and an increasing number of grower-producers (*manipulants*).

While the major firms own vineyards, most grapes are bought village by village and pressed out in the region. Wine is vinified in batches whose origin is carefully noted and preserved. Each firm will end up with hundreds of batches of dry white wine that constitute its resources in the elaborate blending it must do. For not only does Champagne require balancing strengths and weaknesses of different batches to obtain a good wine; a company's reputation rests on its tasting style, and recognizable qualities must be achieved and maintained by artful blending. Roederer must taste like Roederer, Veuve Clicquot should be recognizable as its own style. The ideals of Champagne cannot be easily compared to those of other French wines, in which variety is an accepted fact of life. The best analogy are the great fortified wines of Iberia, Port and Sherry, where large firms also struggle to produce a brand style as well as the best wine possible for the price.

The fermented dry wine, usually between 10 and 11 percent alcohol, reposes some six months in cask or vat. It is then bottled with an addition of yeast and a liquor made of cane sugar dissolved in old wine. During the next period a strong secondary fermentation goes on in the bottle as yeasts work on this newly available sugar. Deposits form, and gas builds up until all the sugar is consumed. Alcohol content rises another degree. Some bottles, 2 or 3 percent of them, are lost through explosions. Finally the bottles are inserted, cork down, at an angle of some 45 degrees in specially designed racks called *pulpits*. All this takes place in the vast cold stone cellars of the companies in Reims or Épernay. For two or three months, the bottles are daily rotated by an expert foreman (*rémueur*), who passes row after row, giving each bottle a little wriggle of some one-eighth turn, shaking the sediment toward the neck and cork. At the same time, the angle of the whole rack of bottles is raised a tiny bit. Eventually the bottles are standing on their heads with all the sediment lying on the cork surface. The bottles pass through a line process in which the necks are frozen. Then they are uncorked (disgorged). Out flies the cork and a lump of slushy ice containing all the sediment.

After disgorging, the final wine style is determined. Some *Brut* (natural) wines are topped up with sparkling wine and given their final dressy corking with no addition of sugar. Sweeter grades get a dosage of sugar in the form of a liquor. *Brut* receives zero to 1.5 percent sugar, *Sec* 2–4 percent, *demi-Sec* 4–6 percent, and Sweet 8–10 percent. Dosage affects not merely sweetness but general tasting style as well. A batch of Champagne may employ 70 or 80 different wines, and different blends demand different dosages.

This is the Champagne Method (Mèthode Champenoise). Sparkling wine can be made in bulk by the Charmat process. The fermented wine is put into pressurized sealed tanks along with yeasts and the liquor; its secondary fermentation takes place there within three or four weeks. It is racked off its deposits under pressure, frozen to precipitate out much matter, and, still very cold, it is filtered and bottled. Cheaper and less subtle, Charmat sparkling wine loses its coarser bubbles quickly after opening.

Champagne is a region, an appellation, and a method, and its name should be reserved for its authentic wines. In addition to a rosé appellation (Rosé de Riceys), rosé Champagne is made from Pinot Noir and shows heavier body. Still wines once called Vin Nature de la Champagne now have their appellation, Côteaux de Champagne. These are elegant but very tart white wines. Still red wines, also fine but quite acid, are sold in France and usually named after their towns of origin. Bouzy and Sillery are the most common. Champagne made under less pressure, gently frothy rather than fully sparkling, is called Crémant. Most Champagne is a mixture of red and white grapes, but particularly around Épernay in the Côte des Blancs, Chardonnay alone is used and called Blanc des Blancs, a phrase (white from white) that makes sense here but is ridiculously applied to white wines all over the world. One of the famous Épernay towns is Cramant; its wines are easy to confuse with the lighter wine type, Crémant.

Vintage Champagne is also blended wine but from grapes nearly entirely of the year stated. It is superior to nonvintage only if the company producing it has chosen superior batches of wine. This is also true of fancy elite Champagne, such as Roederer Crystal and Moët & Chandon's Dom Perignon.

Champagne is inherently expensive, more so than any wine. Its elaborate production, stretching out over three or even six or seven years and involving many steps, makes its high cost inevitable. Governments seem to connect it with sin and tax it more heavily. The advertising of large firms adds to the cost. While drinkers abroad can choose from only a score of large-firm products, in France growing numbers of individual producers market their wines. Some of the most delicious and some of the worst Champagnes come from these *manipulants.* The big firms pretend quality Champagne cannot be made without vast stocks of blending wine. This is not so. What is true is that a regular stream of wine of consistent taste, in amounts justifying world export, can be made only by a big firm with big resources.

Appreciation of Champagne seems to come later in life and later in drinking experience than for other wines. The wines often give an acid underripe impression; their odors and tastes are nuanced and understated and build up to a finesse easily ignored. Good Champagne should emit fine bubbles that persist a long time and rise in thin streams from the bottom of the glass. This froth is intrinsic to Champagne appreciation, and slashing away bubbles with a swizzle stick is silly. One might as well drink still wine.

Champagne commonly arrives in the glass oxidized, stale, frozen to death. Yet hardly any wine suggests itself more to serious comparative tasting among friends sharing the expense of so many dear bottles. House styles can be contrasted. At one extreme some firms stress light, frothy styles that live dangerously near a line separating tart qualities from downright sour ones. Mumm, Piper Heidsieck, Mercier, Charles Heidsieck, and more recently Moët & Chandon frequently tend to this direction. Bollinger, Pommery & Greno, Ayala, Taittinger, Laurent Perrier, Ruinart, Perrier Jouet, and Pol Roger are some famous "Grandes Marques," as the big firms are known, that hold a middle ground. These more solidly affirm the virtues of lighter wines but escape their faults. Progressing toward weightier wines, emphatic in body, maturing with more sensations and aftertaste than many casual consumers expect or even notice, one finds Deutz, Roederer, Veuve Clicquot, and Krug. These and some better blends (often vintaged wines) from the two brigades just mentioned move in a direction of power, body, and elegance requiring time and expense to achieve.

Different batches of Champagne vary, different styles are shipped (intelligently) to different markets, firms get into trouble with stocks, forcing alterations in style, and, in the case of vintaged wines, nearly anything can happen, depending on the year and the cynicism or sincerity of the firm shipping a dated bottle. This all makes predictions of what you will find in the bottle very difficult. Another problem for users of this book is that Champagne labels do not soak off, or should not, according to the producers' intention. The following four pages feature the labels of some prominent Champagne houses and provide space for your notes.

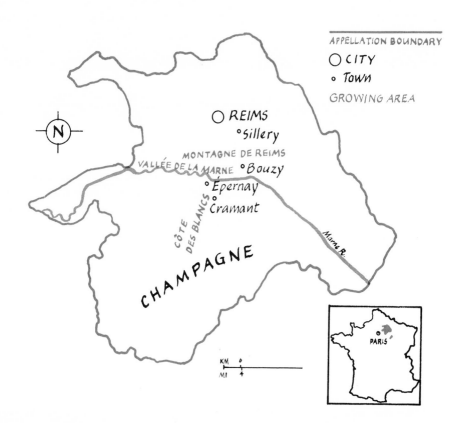

Charles Heidsieck Champagne

VINTAGE   DATE   PRICE

GUESTS

MENU   COMMENTS

Mumm Cordon Rouge Champagne

VINTAGE   DATE   PRICE

GUESTS

MENU   COMMENTS

Deutz Champagne

VINTAGE   DATE   PRICE

GUESTS

MENU   COMMENTS

Ayala Champagne

VINTAGE   DATE   PRICE

GUESTS

MENU   COMMENTS

Piper-Heidsieck Champagne

VINTAGE   DATE   PRICE

GUESTS

MENU   COMMENTS

Laurent Perrier Champagne

VINTAGE   DATE   PRICE

GUESTS

MENU   COMMENTS

By Appointment

1969   1969

Purveyors of Champagne to   His late Majesty King George VI

CHAMPAGNE
Charles Heidsieck
REIMS
FRANCE
N.M. 3.027.452

FINEST EXTRA Q^ty   BRUT

77cl   PRODUCE OF FRANCE

CONTENTS 1 PINT 10 FLUID OUNCES

G.H.MUMM & Co.
Ste VINICOLE DE CHAMPAGNE SUCC^rs
REIMS.
FRANCE

CORDON ROUGE.

1969

CHAMPAGNE BRUT
PRODUCE OF FRANCE
TRADE MARK REGISTERED IN U. S. PATENT OFFICE

ALCOHOL 12% BY VOLUME   N. M. 3.921.422

Champagne Deutz
Maison Deutz & Geldermann
FONDÉE·EN·1838

Brut 1966   Ay·Champagne

CONTENTS 1 PINT 10 FLUID OZS · ALCOHOL 12 % BY VOLUME
PRODUCE OF FRANCE   N.M. 2.736.392

1969   1969

FOURNISSEURS DE
LA COUR D'ANGLETERRE

AYALA & Co.
CHÂTEAU D'AY.
France

CHAMPAGNE
EXTRA QUALITY BRUT   DÉPOSÉ
N.M 2.424.242

CHAMPAGNE
PIPER-HEIDSIECK
Ancienne Maison HEIDSIECK fondée en 1785

BRUT

PRODUCE OF FRANCE   REIMS, FRANCE

ALCOHOL 12% BY VOLUME
CONTENTS 1 PINT & 10 FLUID OUNCES

CHAMPAGNE
Laurent Perrier

Tours-sur-Marne
PRÈS REIMS (FRANCE)

ESTABLISHED 1812

N·M 3048242   PRODUCE OF FRANCE

Taittinger Champagne

VINTAGE   *DATE*   *PRICE*

GUESTS

MENU   *COMMENTS*

Veuve Clicquot Champagne

VINTAGE   *DATE*   *PRICE*

GUESTS

MENU   *COMMENTS*

Moët & Chandon Dom Pérignon Champagne

VINTAGE   *DATE*   *PRICE*

GUESTS

MENU   *COMMENTS*

Moët & Chandon Imperial Champagne

VINTAGE   *DATE*   *PRICE*

GUESTS

MENU   *COMMENTS*

TAITTINGER

ANCIENNE MAISON FOURNEAUX, FOREST ET SUCCᴿˢ

Fondée en 1734

REIMS

CHAMPAGNE **FRANCE** BRUT RÉSERVE
1969

TM* N. M. 3.924.392 PRODUCE OF FRANCE

PRODUCED AND BOTTLED BY : CHAMPAGNE TAITTINGER
IMPORTED BY KOBRAND CORPORATION NEW YORK, N.Y.
SOLE UNITED STATES IMPORTERS

ALCOHOL 12 % BY VOLUME 13/16 QUART

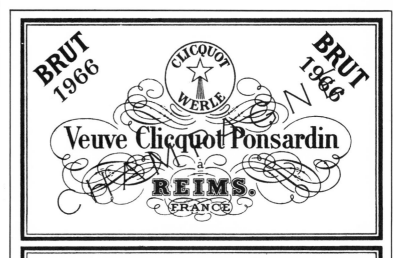

BRUT
1966 *Veuve Clicquot Ponsardin* à **REIMS.** FRANCE BRUT
1966

PRODUCE OF FRANCE
CONTENTS 1 PINT 10 FLUID OUNCES - ALCOHOL 12 % BY VOLUME

N.M. 3.348.392

MOËT et CHANDON à Epernay
Established 1743

Champagne
Cuvée Dom Pérignon
Vintage 1969

PRODUCE OF FRANCE
N M 3 342 272

L. Deletain.

CONTENTS 1 QUART 1 PINT 4 FLUID OUNCES

BRUT IMPÉRIAL
1964

Maison fondée ★ en 1743

MOËT & CHANDON

CHAMPAGNE

ÉPERNAY - FRANCE

N.M. 3 342.272

ALCOHOL 12,3% BY VOLUME

Schieffelin & Cᵒ – New York

IMPORTERS SINCE 1794 SOLE U.S. DISTRIBUTORS

GERMANY

With characteristic fervor, accuracy, and persistence, German enologists have not only pressed their battle to make excellent wines in Europe's most difficult vineyard zone but have created a voluminous literature in so doing. The soils, grape varieties, microclimates, growing, harvesting, and vinifying techniques that contribute to fine Rhine, Moselle, Saar, Ruwer, Nahe, and Palatinate and other wines are studied and described at length, and Germany is a veritable theatre of vine experimentation. Despite this swollen technical bibliography, the task of a basic introduction to fine German wines is an easy and short one. However arduous the job of making wine in these steep, northerly vineyards, their appreciation is delightfully facile, and standards of taste are closely grouped about a few basic points of quality. Ripeness, with the sugar it provides, is one major theme. Nearly all the great wines issue from one grape variety, the Rhine Riesling. The wines are relatively weak in alcohol. Body is not a main point of quality; balance is. Acidity, with its lively taste, is balanced by fragrance, flavor, and bouquet intensity—all the elusive features we sum up as finesse and authenticity—contributed by ripe Riesling grapes grown on their native ground. This precarious but enchanting balance between nearly opposite tasting elements raises the quality of the best German wines to unsurpassed heights. A beginner in the adventure of wine can find no better realm in which to meet and appreciate the idea of finesse, of quality, in wine. This is particularly true because, as many observers have noted well, fine German wines can be enjoyed on their own, without food, as few other wines can.

There are innumerable nuances among the families of German wines, but one standard unifies nearly all the best wine and might quite usefully be kept in mind. This is the rare achievement of ripe Riesling elegance and flavor, whether in the form of a dry but spicy and scintillating Moselle, or in that of a richer Rheingau, with natural sweetness or residual unfermented sugar adding to the excitement.

Germany is a paradoxical consumer, drinking as much coffee as beer(!) and importing ten times as much ordinary wine as it exports fine wine. The enormous overhaul of the wine trade made by the new German wine law that came into effect in 1971 dealt with two distinct sorts of wine. Its first task was to regulate the terms on which 119 million gallons (4.5 million hectoliters) imported annually could be designated and traded alongside domestic ordinary wine. Its second task was to regulate the substantial production of Germany's fine wines in such a way as to guarantee their quality, facilitate their commerce, and protect their future hold on foreign markets while taking account of the interest of thousands of small growers. While the first task is of interest for the Common Market, it is the second that concerns this book. How is the quality sector of the 207,500 acres (84,000 hectares) of vineyard in Germany regulated?

The first dimension of the new wine law concerns the designation of origin. The quality vineyards are divided into eleven Designated Regions (*bestimmten Anbaugebiete*). Each of these is chopped into sub-regions (*Bereiche*). Within a *Bereich* there are further divisions into vineyard groupings, or *Grosslagen*. The *Grosslage* name is typically that of a viticulturally important village, followed by the name of a famous vineyard site in the same locale. For example, in the Designated Region of the Rheingau, the main *Bereich* is called Johannisberg. One typical *Grosslage* for this area, previously called simply Winkeler (from Winkel), is now Winkeler Honigberg. A wine merchant may buy wines from different growers within this defined area and ship it as Winkeler Honigberg, and this type of designation is and will remain very common. But within the *Grosslage* there are individual vineyard sites of special repute and minimal size (5 hectares, or slightly more than 12 acres) that may be specified on the label in addition to other information, and these are called *Einzellagen*. One of these is Gutenberg. It does not follow that all Gutenberg is owned by one person; indeed, this is hardly possible. But wines from this site, whether those of an individual proprietor or a mixed parcel pieced together by a merchant, may call themselves Gutenberg. This system represents a simplification of traditional designating practice. By restricting the *Einzellagen* to those of reasonable size and proven repute, the new wine law reduces the number of wines whose designation suggests quality to a more manageable variety and prunes them to wines from vineyard sites that have proved themselves over time. Most of the *Grosslagen* are familiar names long associated with wines from the area, but the new law attempts to make things more precise and explicit. So much for designation of origin. What about control of quality?

The second dimension of the law concerns the quality of the wine. Wines are divided into common wine (*Tafelwein*) and quality wine. Three sorts of *Tafelwein* are allowed. German "table" wine must be just that, 100 percent German. Wine from the Common Market countries may be blended with German wine up to certain amounts but must say it is *"Tafelwein der EWG."* Wine from outside the community may not be mixed with German wine.

Quality wine begins with German wine from a Designated Region—*Qualitätswein bestimmter Anbaugebiete* (QbA for short). It must indicate the bottler (*Abfüllung*) on the label and show its official certification number, the *Amtliche Prüfnummer* or A.P. Nr.

Wine of QbA grade must be 7 percent alcohol and have a combined alcohol and potential alcohol (in the shape of unfermented sugar) content of 9 percent. But to harvest the grape varieties, the juice must attain minimum sugar contents that vary from region to region and are set out in an elaborate table. The criterion used is the weight of the juice, or must, which is measured in terms of degrees *Oechsle*. This frightening word is neither Swabian dialect for a sick heifer nor the grandson of Count Dracula but rather a measurement of how much heavier a liter of grape juice may be than a liter of water. Since the difference of weight is nearly all accounted for by sugar, it is a handy indication of the sugar content of a must, which is to say the degree of ripeness of the grape. An *Oechsle* of 40 is so bad that the wine should be put in a private bin for grown men who only sit down 40 minutes after they have said "unaccustomed as I am to public speaking. . . ." An *Oechsle* of 95 promises potentially excellent wine. One of 150 is considered sensational and promises wine for connoisseurs. *Oechsle* 150 is the minimum for the highest class of German wines, *Trockenbeerenauslese*. *Oechsle* 57 is the QbA minimum for Riesling grapes grown in the Nahe Nord and is about the lowest sugar content acceptable for harvesting. Higher grades of *Oechsle* are obtained when favorable growing conditions continue late into autumn and growers risk waiting for such optimum conditions to occur.

Local examination boards inspect the wine for color, clarity, bouquet, and flavor. Flavor counts for 60 percent of the total potential score, bouquet for 20 percent. Unless the wine receives at least one-half the maximum score for each of the four points of quality it may not have a number and cannot be QbA wine.

Traditional quality designations such as *Kabinett* and *Auslese* have been given precise meaning by the new law and are still in use. Eleven points out of a potential 20 are required for the QbA designation awarded by the examining board. The next stage up are five grades of *Qualitätswein mit Prädikat* (Quality wines with Attribute, abbreviated QmP). The first is *Kabinett,* and 13 points must be awarded. For each of the four following grades a further point must be gained, in this order: *Spätlese, Auslese, Beerenauslese* and *Trockenbeerenauslese.* It has been possible, and occasionally necessary, to gather grapes in frozen condition. The concentrated juice that results used to be called *Eiswein* (ice wine). The climate has not changed, and frozen grapes are still gathered, but to have the term *Eiswein* it must now also gain one of the grades of QmP.

There are certain tolerances for blending, though blends must be kept within the Designated Region for QbA wines and within the subregion for QmP wines, with 75 percent coming from the wine bearing the name. As is true throughout the Common Market, a vintage must be 85 percent of the year named to be traded abroad. Regulations for blending wines for sale within Germany are more complicated and generous, but the trouble with these blending tolerances, and all others, is that they are too strict for the honest people who want to blend to improve the wine and too wide for the shifty few to whom any blending tolerance is an invitation to cut costs with an inferior product.

The new German wine law represents a remarkable attempt to control each branch of wine production and is the most complete control system among major wine-producing countries. Yet, while it introduces many commendable simplifications, it does away with a few admirable traditions. Formerly, a grower was permitted to label his wine with the barrel number from which it came. Wine collectors obtained highly individual wines. The A.P. number comes closest to replacing this identification but does not really do so at the same level of discrimination. There is the misapprehension that the fourth of the five codes composing the A.P.Nr. signifies a better wine when it is a lower number, whereas in reality it reflects only the number of applications the bottler has made to the board. If the application is the seventh or ninth granted, it does not mean that lot number 7 is better or worse than lot number 9.

Growers used to be able to discriminate between different batches of wine by qualifying terms used with *Spätlese* and *Auslese.* An especially good lot might be called *feinste* (finest) *Auslese* and a superb one *hochfeinste* (very finest). But questionable use of these terms led to their elimination.

READING THE LABEL

In addition to the key terms of the German Wine Law described on these pages, the following expressions will interest consumers:

DIABETEKERWEIN	Dry, more precisely not containing more than 4 grams per liter of unfermented sugar. Not a very useful term.
SCHAUMWEIN	Sparkling. See French *Mousseux.*
SEKT	A traditional sparkling dry wine with nine months' maturation. To bear the label *Deutscher Prädikats Sekt,* it must be 60 percent German wine with nine months' maturation.
WEISSWEIN	White wine.
ROTWEIN	Red wine.
ROSÉE-WEIN	Rosé from red grapes made by short fermentation.
WEISSHERBST	Like *Rosée-Wein,* but of QbA standard and showing the grape variety used.
PERLWEIN	Red or white table wine with CO_2 added.
ROTLING	Blended wine from grapes of different color.
SCHILLERWEIN	Same, but of QbA quality, from Württemberg.
WINZERGENOSSEN-SCHAFT or WINZERVEREIN	Growers' cooperatives.
ERZEUGERAB-FÜLLUNG or AUS EIGENEM LESEGUT	Bottled by the grower; estate-bottled.
AUS DEM LESEGUT VON . . .	A phrase meaning "from the estate of . . ." whereby the bottler (who is not the grower) is giving assurance that the wine is of the property named.

Bottles older than 1971 may display a veritable dictionary of terms condemned to extinction by the new laws that began operating after that year. An expert and lucid authority on the wines of Germany, which have changed far less than the laws, is the late Frank Schoonmaker, author of *The Wines of Germany.*

While Germany is the scene of great activity and experimentation in grape-variety development, the major varieties are few in number.

German red vine plantings have increased in area, as have those of Switzerland. The Blauburgunder is scattered in small amounts through nearly every region, and Baden has a quantity. A like amount of Trollinger is in Württemburg. This region also has Portugieser, as do the Palatinate and Rheinhesse. Portugieser is of lesser quality, is not Portuguese, and gives wines of loose, vaguely Burgundian type. The relatively small amount of red wine produced in the Ahr region comes from Blauburgunder (here called Spätburgunder), which is Pinot Noir.

German sparkling wines may sometimes identify themselves by grape varieties and are often the unsuccessful crops or poor years of quite good estates or regions. More typically they are strongly acidic wines from fringe areas of the better still-wine districts, Moselle, Saar, and Ruwer above all. These are quite properly sold under the manufacturer's trademark, for here it is the blender's art that counts.

In the heartland of the quality regions the Rhine Riesling reigns undisputed. In the Moselle and Rheingau it accounts for about three-quarters of plantings, and the best estates are given over to it entirely. No one could seriously argue that excellent wines are not made from the Sylvaner, also widely used, but no one could pretend that this grape rivals the best Riesling. The very productive Müller-Thurgau crossbreed white grape does not account for the best wines but is quantitatively the most important grape in Germany, especially in peripheral regions of the Palatinate, Franconia, Baden, and elsewhere. Several minor varieties, among them the Elbling and Ruländer, are favored in particular locales, and some Weissburgunder (Pinot Blanc) is found, notably in the Baden district. Often, if not invariably, the minimum sugar content for less esteemed varieties is pegged higher than for Riesling. For example, in Baden you may harvest Riesling at *Oechsle* 63 with alcohol minimum 8.0 percent, but new experimental white varieties cannot be brought in with *Oechsle* inferior to 72 and alcohol of 9.4 percent. This is a laconic but eloquent way of expressing judgment on the merits of the two grape varieties.

THE WINE REGIONS OF GERMANY

The premium vineyards are massed along river banks of two systems, the Moselle and the Rhine, with their tributaries. Peripheral to these centers of quality lie other scattered vineyards. The natural geography of these river systems sometimes defies administrative borders, but the most logical introduction is by Designated Regions, starting with the least noble and working toward the center. The eleven Designated Regions (*bestimmten Anbaugebiete*) are Ahr, Baden, Württemberg, Franken (Franconia), Hessische Bergstrasse, Mittelrhein, Rheinhesse, Rheinpfalz (Palatinate), Rheingau, Nahe, Mosel-Saar-Ruwer.

Ahr

Just south of Bonn, along the small river Ahr, is a nearly 1,250-acre (500-hectare) vineyard, 60 percent of which produces red wines. It has a single *Bereich*—Walprozheim/Ahrtal—with one important *Grosslage*, Walprozheimer Klosterberg. Most authorities insist that the red grape plantings are all Pinot Noir, but the German Wine Academy statistics register only a quarter of the land in this grape (called Spätburgunder here) and show a third in Portugieser. These light red wines, grown farther north than nearly any vine, red or white, are soft, even luscious on occasion, but little exported.

Baden

A big but unexciting vineyard area consisting of some easterly outlying areas such as Bodensee on the Swiss border, Baden is mainly a long strip of flattish country facing Alsace across the Rhine. Bodensee is notable for its pink wines made from Spätburgunder, but over three-quarters of Baden's almost 29,000 acres (11,600 hectares) is planted in white grapes. There are seven *Bereiche*, among which Kaiserstuhl is generally considered the best of the regions along the Rhine. It consists of a roughly circular raised area of volcanic origin planted in Ruländer (Pinot Gris), Sylvaner, and Müller-Thurgau. The famous Australian Kaiserstuhl Cooperative is named after this vineyard site. All up and down the vineyard strip from Baden to Basel are found lesser grape varieties than the Riesling, including some Gutedel, which is the French Chasselas and Swiss Fendant. The Riesling is often called the Klingelberger in this area, though loud demands for Klingelberger in San Francisco or Bristol shops may well elicit sympathetic suggestions about taking a long rest. The Ortenau *Bereiche* north of Kaiserstuhl, and Markgräflerland south of it, are other important regions. German demand for the best Baden wines raises their German prices above those foreigners are willing to pay, so the fine ones remain at home.

Württemberg

Just east of the Baden Rhine vineyard strips is a more compact vineyard area in the Neckar Valley between Stuttgart and Heilbronn, planted roughly 60 percent in red, 40 percent in white grapes. Chief among the reds is the Trollinger grape. Württemberg gushes out a mighty amount of wine, and nearly as mighty an amount is consumed locally. The three *Bereiche* are Remstal-Stuttgart, Wurthemburgisch-Unterland and Kocher-Jagst-Tauber. The Neckar Valley, albeit in the south of Germany, is an extremely cold pocket with a continental winter and generally difficult growing conditions; peak quality wines are very rare. Stuttgart is the home of a giant wine cooperative.

Franken (FRANCONIA)

Something of an oddity in more respects than one are the wines of the more than 7,230 acres (2,893 hectares) of the Main Valley vineyard. While the quality of Franconia wines can be high and the general level is good, the white wines have an address on the palate, savor and style quite different from Rhine and Moselle whites—heavier, earthier, flatter. They are based on Sylvaner and Müller-Thurgau, with but a dribble of Riesling, some 4 percent of the vineyard. The soils are partly of shell lime rather than the surface rock found in the main river valleys to the west. The standard traditional bottle is a plump, dark green flask called a *Bocksbeutel*, which has been imitated in Chile and Portugal. Franconia wines were better regarded (by non-Franconians) in the past than they are now. There are three *Bereiche*, Mainviereck, Maindreieck, and Staigerwald, and the present *Grosslagen* names echo generic names prized in the nineteenth century: Randersacker Ewig Leben, Casteller Herrenberg, and Escherndorfer Kirchberg. There are several famous estates in Franconia, and a still more famous vineyard hill on the north side of Würzburg called Stein. This has caused all Franconian wine to be wrongly called *Steinwein,* which is admittedly easier on the memory than Escherndorfer, but it is technically only applicable to wines from a few sites of which Stein is the most reputed. Yields are small, and many vineyards are extremely steep.

Just as in all historic vineyard areas, and this is one *par excellence,* the Würzburgers defend their wines loyally and prefer them, but it is still fair to remark to foreigners that what comes out of a *Bocksbeutel* is perhaps the least German of fine white wines, not so much because it is not a Riesling but because its style incorporates a heavy body, diminished fruit, and no residual sugar. Even *Kabinett*-grade wines are dry. Top-grade wines command enormous prices on their native ground. On the one hand, I am relieved to notice that Frank Schoonmaker's vast experience confirms my slight one of late-gathered Franconia wines: unsatisfactory overpriced cousins of the great Rheingau peak wines. On the other hand, Peter M. F. Sichel, an equal authority and a German one, considers *Trockenbeerenauslese* Franconian wines the greatest in Germany.

The best vineyards are in Würzburg and so are the three most celebrated producers: the German government (*Staatsweingut*) Hofkellerei and two institutions, the Juliusspital and Burgerspital zum Heiligen Geist. We meet for the first time here the long-standing interest of religious orders, the state, and municipalities in German vineyards, often the last taking over from the first following revolutionary expropriations of church property early in the nineteenth century. We meet too the problem of many estates, sites (of past importance and now reconstructed by the new law), towns, and growers in each important area, an unwieldy list of names too lengthy to tackle. The bibliography directs interested readers to those works that do take up the challenge.

Hessische Bergstrasse

A relatively warm climate bathes this very small district on the eastern edge of the main vineyard areas, containing a mere 680 acres (272 hectares). Half is in Riesling. The exposition is not optimal, for the sites are on the western edge of a small mountain range (the Odenwald), but the greatest Riesling wines display a fine character comparable to those of the Rheingau. The *Bereiche* are Starkenberg and Umstadt, and the important *Grosslage,* Heppenheimer Schlossberg, contains the famous Heppenheimer Steinkopf. Most of the rest of the vineyard is in Sylvaner and Müller-Thurgau, which give plump wines that have less race and distinction but are pleasant enough.

Mittelrhein

Rather unimportant both for quality and quantity, the long stretch of the Rhine running roughly north between Bingen and Bonn is bracketed by some 2,245 acres (898 hectares) of vineyard, mainly in Riesling. It is grouped in two *Bereiche,* Rheinburgengau and Bacharach; Schloss Stahleck and Loreleyfelsen are the major *Grosslagen.* Local consumption and sparkling wine manufacturers account for nearly all the product. Slate and quartzite soils give wines that are technically balanced but without the elegance and race of those of the Rheingau. A very beautiful stretch of river, it is rather for touring than drinking.

Rheinhesse

The second largest *bestimmte Anbaugebiet* of Germany lies in a hook of the Rhine as it runs north from the Palatinate through Worms, Oppenheim, and Nierstein and curves around west to Bingen, where it meets the River Nahe. A wide variety of terrain is contained here, whose 52,500 acres (21,000 hectares) of vineyard produce nearly 40 million gallons (1.5 million hectoliters) of wine annually, 90 percent of it white. Inland throughout the Rheinhesse, ordinary wines are produced on rolling vineyards planted in Sylvaner, Müller-Thurgau, and other varieties. There is a straight "winefront" of riverbank vineyard starting at Guntersblum, continuing through Oppenheim, through Nierstein (above all), and on to Nackenheim. These slopes are distinguished by good exposure, slate surface material, and substantial outcroppings of red sandstone called Red-lier. The small proportion (6 percent) of Rheinhesse's Riesling plantings are concentrated in these premium vineyards, with a little quality outpost around Bingen, facing the Rheingau across the river.

Of the three big Rheinhesse *Bereiche,* Nierstein is the important one to Anglo-Americans. Bingen encompasses a few exported wines, and Wonnegau includes the rest. The important *Grosslagen* perpetuate town names along the Rhine once used to identify generically wines of their respective locales.

The best light, fragrant, and soft wines that have made authentic Niersteiner justly famous are contained in two new *Grosslagen,* Niersteiner Auflangen and Niersteiner Rehbach, both echoes of past

Würzburger Stein Kabinett
Juliusspital

Dry, firm, and balanced, if a trifle anonymous in taste, the wine hailing from one of the best sites of a Würzburg religious hospital bears the name of one of the city's seven permitted *Einzellagen* and displays the tasting qualities of Franconia's good, dry, vinous white wines. Unlike past impersonators, in theory banished offstage by the new wine law, this is proper Steinwein from the Stein hill in Würzburg. Under the same label are other, exotic (for Germany) whites such as Traminers, with spice and metallic finish, and remarkable Sylvaners, some of them condensed peak wines with orange color, deliciously rich and different. Peer carefully at the center of the text to see what you are buying; labels and typical Franconian *Bocksbeutel* are identical, but the wines are poles apart in taste.

VINTAGE　　　　　　DATE　　　　　　PRICE

GUESTS

MENU　　　　　　COMMENTS

Niersteiner Oberer Rehbach Riesling
Feinste Spätlese Gustav Gessert

Rehbach is the finest site of Nierstein, and Nierstein is the preferred village of the Rheinhesse. Nierstein Rieslings such as this (and those of Nackenheim and Oppenheim) combine a good bouquet, more subdued than Moselle or Rheingau, balance of taste (the best smooth and delightful, the less good ones bland), and a clean finish. Gessert makes fine wines at Oelberg as well. In past times, the best Liebfraumilch claimed origin in Nierstein. *Einzellagen* are of unusual interest in the Rheinhesse; much Sylvaner is planted, and superior sites are found cheek by jowl with humdrum vineyards. This is an old label with the now forbidden *feinste Spätlese* term telling us—truthfully—that the bottle is a superior one to *Kabinett* and *Spätlese* grades.

VINTAGE　　　　　　DATE　　　　　　PRICE

GUESTS

MENU　　　　　　COMMENTS

Winzenheim Rosenheck Riesling Kabinett
Reichsgraf von Plettenberg

From Schloss Böckelheim at the southwest edge of the Nahe to Winzenheimer at the north are found vineyards of this owner, who, like so many Nahe growers and merchants, has headquarters in Bad Kreuznach. Riesling bouquet is tempered by the generally subdued style of Nahe wines; richer wines from Plettenberg's Kreuznacher Kallenberg or Schloss Böckelheimer Kupfergrube have more bouquet and a darker, more golden color. Balance between body, fruit, and the "feel" of acidity favors body; and, like many Nahe wines, these are soft and unctuous rather than full of verve and dashing flavors. Labels from different Plettenberg sites come banded vertically in different colors.

VINTAGE　　　　　　DATE　　　　　　PRICE

GUESTS

MENU　　　　　　COMMENTS

Blue Nun Sichel Söhne

German wine shippers, like those of Bordeaux, produce branded wines from various appellations with which they hope to capture popular markets. Blue Nun is certainly the most successful of these in English-speaking markets. Its popularity has been built up steadily during this century. The merits of this wine are its clean regular taste that represents a generalized version of what German wine is like; indeed, a shipper's wine should do this and little more. Its quality has improved after a dip in the 1950s. Its price reflects markups in distribution and advertising costs, as do all wines of this stamp. Deinhard is a principal rival; there are others. It is the most popular and best representative of its kind.

VINTAGE　　　　　　DATE　　　　　　PRICE

GUESTS

MENU　　　　　　COMMENTS

1576

1973er Würzburger Stein
Kabinett
Produce of Germany

3000-038-75
A.P.Nr.

PRODUCE OF GERMANY

RHEINHESSEN

SEIT 1655 WEINBAU
IN NIERSTEIN

Qualitätswein

1970er
Niersteiner Oberer Rehbach
Riesling feinste Spätlese
Original-Abfüllung

Weingut Gustav Gessert / Nierstein a. Rhein

Reichsgraf
VON
Plettenberg

NAHE   WEIN

Qualitätswein   Amtliche
mit Prädikat   Prüfungsnummer

1 710 069 / 24 / 75

Winzenheimer Rosenheck
Riesling Kabinett

REICHSGRÄFLICH v. PLETTENBERG'SCHE VERWALTUNG BAD KREUZNACH / NAHE

PRODUCE OF GERMANY

1971
BLUE NUN ®
WHITE WINE
Shipped by
H. SICHEL SÖHNE, MAINZ ESTD. 1857

CONTENTS:
1 PINT 7 FL. OZS.   A. P. Nr. 4907189/006/73   ALCOHOL
10 % BY VOL
LIEBFRAUMILCH QUALITÄTSWEIN

Schieffelin & Co. — New York
IMPORTERS SINCE 1794   SOLE U.S. DISTRIBUTORS

G J 78667

designations. The fine stretch of Red-lier hills that progresses up to Nackenheim is capable of nourishing Rieslings of great purity and charm, less intense in flavor and less abundant in bouquet than the finest Rheingau, less flowery than the most perfumed Moselle, but with balance and appeal that in themselves leave little to be desired. Alsheimer Rheinblick and Dienheimer Guldenmorgen are the *Grosslagen* south of Oppenheim on the "front," or straight, stretch of the Rhine. The *Grosslage* Oppenheimer Krötenbrunnen contains other important sites. The Bingen wines at the top of the curve of the Rhine are grouped in the *Grosslage* Bingen St. Rochuskapelle and are less esteemed than Niersteiner wines, being heavier, lacking a point in race, and with an earthiness not to everyone's taste. Good but also less regarded are the Mainz area wines now in the *Grosslage* Mainzer St. Albans. Inland are lesser wines from non-Riesling stock and some red wines, notably at Ingelheim. Between Nierstein, Oppenheim, Dienheim, and adjacent sites are some 40 good vineyards whose names may be found on older bottles and many of whom are attached to the new *Einzellagen*. There is a government estate (*Staatsweingut*) in Nierstein and several celebrated growers too, among them F. K. Schmitt, Senfter, and Heyl zu Herrnsheim, all of whose labels are seen abroad. But they are not alone in shipping quantities of valuable wine from this west bank section of the Rhine.

Rheinpfalz (PALATINATE)

The principal configuration of the biggest and hottest of Germany's wine regions is that of a long swath of vineyard with its southern gateway at Alsace, its northern end at the Rheinhesse, and its high-quality sector roughly in the center. The differences in quality within this stretch of vines are very marked; long before the new wine law created the northern *Bereich* now called the Deutscher Weinstrasse (German Wine Road), the *Bereich* Mittelhaardt, and the Südliche Weinstrasse (Southern Wine Road), the inferior quality of the first and last, and superlative quality of the Mittelhaardt, were affirmed by connoisseurs within and outside Germany. The quality factors that promote the wines of the center section, associated with the town names of Forst and Deidesheim, to price levels not surpassed elsewhere are not those of dramatic changes in elevation and exposition but progressive improvement of soils and microclimates.

The Palatinate contains about 48,930 acres (19,570 hectares) of vineyard, averaging nearly 53 million gallons (over 2 million hectoliters) of wine output annually. A quarter is Sylvaner, just under a quarter is Müller-Thurgau; there is over 10 percent red Portugieser and nearly an equal amount of Riesling. Müller-Thurgau, planted in light, soft loess soils, is favored in the southern plains area, where its produce is drunk young as carafe wine (*Schoppenwein*) or even incompletely fermented as *Federweisser* (feather-white). Formerly this area was planted with Traminer, a grape widely cultivated in neighboring Alsace. Sylvaner is mixed in, and there is some Ruländer and a small amount of Muscat variety. Better wines are made along the spine of the Haardt Hills running north than in the alluvial soils of the plain or basin. Maikammerer Mandelhohe is the *Grosslage* of the Südliche Weinstrasse's better sites. This warmest region of Germany has an early spring, little rainfall, and hot summers; consequently wine acidity is lower, alcohol content higher, and the looser, blander taste that ensues mainly yields a *Schoppenwein*-quality wine. Refinement and verve are rarities in this *Bereich*.

From Neustadt on begins the Mittelhaardt, the heartland of the Palatinate, and as the loess and clay give way to basalt and limestone, quality and concentration virtually rise up and pull themselves together in the wines issuing from Ruppertsberg, Bad Dürkheim, Deidesheim, and, above all, Forst and continuing north. The basalt debris is deliberately spread about the vineyards, much as slate is in the Moselle, for the heat it conserves, magnifies and reflects against the ripening grapes. Gimmeldinger Meerspinne, Dürkheimer Feuerberg, Deidesheimer Hofstuck, and Forster Schnepfenflug are the major *Grosslagen*. Of the many sites in these enclosures, Forster Jesuitengarten is the most famous. A great quantity of this prime Mittelhaardt vineyard is in the hands of three celebrated grower families: von Bassermann-Jordan, von Buhl, and Bürklin-Wolf. Still in the premium-quality belt but farther north are the *Grosslagen* Ungsteiner Honigsäckel and Kallstadter Kobnert, evolved from Ungstein and Kallstadt and their respective top-quality sites.

The richest wines of the Mittelhaardt are very great, if not so elegant and ethereal as those of the Rheingau and Moselle. An adventure in German wine would be incomplete without a great estate wine in a fine year from one of the superb vineyards of Forst such as those in Pechstein, Kirchenstück, or Jesuitengarten. They own great authority and maintain great staying power on the palate; they age gracefully and surely. The hot, dry, long maturing season confers residual sugar frequently and abundantly. *Beerenauslese* or *Trockenbeerenauslese* are met with here more often than elsewhere. The earthiness so pronounced in the southern Pfalz fades away substantially, but if a fault is to be laid at the cellar doors of the Palatinate, it is this tinge of mineral or earth savor at the expense of purest Riesling aftertaste. Riesling is cultivated in the best sites to be sure, with up to three-quarters of some areas of Mittelhaardt in this grape.

The old Unterhaardt, now the Deutscher Weinstrasse, continues into the Rheinhesse, but clay, loess, and sand assert themselves to the detriment of finesse in the wines produced up through Gruenstadt. Plenty of good white wine is to be had, however, both here and in an arm of vineyard area extending into the Zell Valley where firmer, more astringent style is obtainable, but these are not bottles that will be much revered abroad.

Rheingau

Between Hochheim to the east and Lorch to the west lies the incomparable Rheingau. Labels from the most famous estates have been chosen for this book, yet it would be unfair to repeat their names in this text and not to mention those of the scores of smaller growers whose wines lack nothing but abundance or past distribution. Anyone who cares for Rheingau will want to make a hobby of acquaintance with both the small and great growers, in writings about them and, above all, in the glass.

The circumstances that combine to produce elite wines from Riesling grapes on this long, steep river bank are easy to appreciate. That the Rhine turns abruptly between Mainz and Wiesbaden and now runs southwest instead of north means that the north bank of the river not only faces south but does so over a large, moving body of water. Therefore, sunshine and humidity mingle to produce extraordinarily favorable conditions during the final autumn ripening, when nuances of highest quality are determined. Also important, this well-disposed stretch of vineyard along the river is protected at its back by the mass of the Taunas Hills, which blocks the north winds. This basic topography fosters a microclimate that, in good years, can make the most of the calcareous soils and bring noble Riesling grapes to rare perfection.

The Riesling is a slow-maturing bearer that requires a long growing season to bring its small berries to full ripeness. Furthermore, it is a grape readily attacked by noble rot, and the resulting super-maturation offers berries condensed by one of the rare molds that does not offend but rather flatters the human palate in its aftereffects. Lastly, all these circumstances find themselves at a very northerly latitude. The cold winters, completely arresting sap flow, which most viticulturalists believe essential to very fine wines, are virtually guaranteed annually. While fine growing seasons, summers and autumns, may occur only once every three or four years, whenever they do, the vines are prepared to yield grapes supremely apt for delicious wines.

The great vineyard names of the Rheingau are appendages of the following locales, listed from east to west: Hochheim, Eltville, Rauenthal, Kiedrich, Erbach, Hattenheim, Hallgarten, Winkel, Johannisberg, Geisenheim, Rüdesheim. The 7,150 acres (2,860 hectares) of the Rheingau, planted 80 percent in Riesling with the balance in Müller-Thurgau and lesser amounts of Sylvaner, with a droplet (two percent) of red grapes, produce about 5.5 million gallons (210,000 hectoliters) of white wine in an average year. Most Rhine wine in shops and in restaurants has by now conformed to the new wine law and reflects its alterations from the old village names.

There is a main *Bereich,* Johannisberg, and a lesser one, Hochheim. The new *Grosslagen,* not the same as the main villages, are from east to west Daubhaus, Steinmächer, Heiligenstock, Mehrhölzchen, Deutelsberg, Gottesthal, Honigberg, Erntebringer, Burgweg, and Steil. That the same village may appear in two *Grosslagen* merely testifies to geographical proximity and that ferocious jealousy of name that this writer, as a petty vineyard manager, is well placed to proclaim a sign of good character in anyone who grows wine grapes. Four *Einzellagen* are so famous that they may use their own names on the label. They may be found simply as Rheingau, with the names Schloss Johannisberg, Schloss Vollrads, Schloss Reichthartshausen, Steinberger.

The economy of the Rheingau is mixed, with numerous small holdings that take distinction from the locale of the vineyard and the proven ability of the grower, a number of large estates in the hands of prestigious families whose wines are revered by connoisseurs, and perhaps most respected of all, the very large German State holdings. The most famous of these is the Steinberg, but on all of them the cultivation, vinification, and care of wine in cask is exemplary.

Worthy of a very few words are the red wines of Assmannshausen from Spätburgunder (Pinot Noir) grapes. Although these are good red wines, sometimes with excellent fruit for such a northern vineyard of red grapes, they are mainly a curiosity. There exists an extremely rare Assmannshausen white wine produced from concentrated Pinot Noir grapes for which, in the phrase of Luigi Veronelli, I would be indebted to any reader for information. Even more so for a bottle of it.

To evoke the tasting qualities of Rhine wines is to invite a boring parade of superlatives, but a few features need mention. Some districts, Rüdesheim for example, have different patterns of success in each vintage than the main body of the Rheingau; but generally vintage merits get reflected across the whole of the slopes. There are three types of vintages: underripe, ripe, and extraripe. Underripe years may produce a few pleasant experiences. Of course they interest professionals and bear witness to the integrity, or lack of it, of many growers. Ripe years provide wines with verve, excellent Riesling character, and occasional excitement and finesse. But it is in great years that Rheingau wines take on the grand balance, harmony, and luscious impressions that set them apart from all other white wines.

Nahe

Outlying areas of the 10,500 acres (4,200 hectares) of Nahe vineyard nudge the inland sections of the Rheinhesse and Palatinate, but the best wines come from a relatively small area of riverine vineyards on the red sandstone bends of the River Nahe. One-quarter of the vineyard is in Riesling, planted in quite narrow borders beside the river, where high mineral content and rocky topography give natural nourishment and preferred exposition to the vines. Some of the finest Nahe therefore come from dramatic landscapes such as the Rotenfelser Bastei, virtually carved out of sandstone on a sharp curve of the stream between Bad Munster and Norheim. Another picturesque domain is the German state "copper mine"—Schloss Böckelheimer Kupfergrube—on another bend between Niederhausen and Schloss Böckelheim. In addition to Riesling, Sylvaner accounts for a third of the area and Müller-Thurgau for about another third.

The main *Bereiche* are Kreuznach and Schloss Böckelheim, for the northern and southern sectors respectively. Kreuznacher Kronenberg and Rüdesheimer Rosengarten are important *Grosslagen.* This Rüdesheimer is not to be confused with the town on the Rhine, though it would be interesting to know how to prevent this from occurring. In addition to the State Domain, there are a number of major exporters; Anheusers (two firms of the name) are certainly the best known abroad. It is puzzling that in a land where ancient viticulture has long since overcome rugged terrain, in Nahe many vineyards date only from this century. Kreuznach is the center of this district for commercial purposes, though as usual the big growers have plots scattered in other sites, among which Norheimer and Niederhauser are important. Many Niederhausen sites are in the *Grosslage* Burgweg.

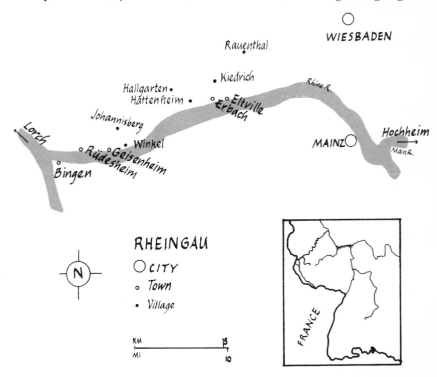

RHEINGAU

○ CITY
○ Town
• Village

N

KM   15
MI   10

Wachenheimer Gerümpel Riesling
Auslese Dr. Bürklin-Wolf

The Mittlelhaardt strip between Deidesheim and Wachenheim contains most of the great sites of the Palatinate, among them Gerümpel, bordering Pechstein and across the "Wine Road" from Jesuitengarten, the most famous. Like two other big growers, von Buhl and von Bassermann-Jordan, Bürklin-Wolf has holdings in many plots; among those exported are Forster Jesuitengarten, Wachenheimer Mandelgarten, and various Deidesheimers such as Hohenmorgen. This 1971 Gerümpel, with its rich earthy texture, limited bouquet, excellent technical balance, and imposing ensemble, is a solid example of Palatinate wines.

VINTAGE   *DATE*   *PRICE*

GUESTS

MENU   *COMMENTS*

Ungsteiner Honigsäckel Silvaner Spätlese
Winzergenossenschaft Herrenberg-Honigsackel

While great growers may own much of the Palatinate, and Riesling may predominate in the very best sites, the Rheinpfalz is huge, and most of it is under other varieties of grapes. Here is a modern label from a growers' cooperative, introducing a pleasant, slightly heavy Sylvaner wine with a bit too much alcohol for the fruit, but very "Pfalz." Ungsteiner Honigsäckel is the *Grosslage* for an area near the north of the Mittelhaardt. The label on this honestly presented subregional wine, which names its grape variety, gives the assurance that it comes from this *Grosslage*, though from more than one grower. Following the new German wine law, it also assures that if there is Sylvaner other than Ungsteiner in it (and there probably is not), it must be less than 25 percent of the total and must come from the same *Bereiche*, Mittelhaardt.

VINTAGE   *DATE*   *PRICE*

GUESTS

MENU   *COMMENTS*

Forster Jesuitengarten Riesling
Trockenbeerenauslese von Bassermann-Jordan

The third of the Palatinate triumvirate, with Bürklin-Wolf and von Bassermann-Jordan, is von Buhl, the biggest private landholder in the Pfalz and a producer of rich, assertive wines from Riesling grapes grown in the hottest German vineyard—the basalt-studded hills of the Mittelhaardt. The label chosen is an old one; the Forster family includes Jesuitengarten, Kirchenstück, and Pechstein. The wines are ponderous and dense, becoming ultra-concentrated in peak grades such as this one.

VINTAGE   *DATE*   *PRICE*

GUESTS

MENU   *COMMENTS*

Forster Ungeheuer Riesling
Trockenbeerenauslese Reichsrat von Buhl

This is a world-famous German wine label. Combining the essential Palatinate qualities, a distinctive, slightly musky bouquet in which Riesling is somewhat submerged in regional style, intense taste attacking across a broad front rather than settling on fruit and spice, and finishing with great authority in a heavy style, the best Rieslings of this grower occasionally display an original quality, difficult to verbalize, in which vinous strength mingles with mineral and aromatic impressions to produce an unusual finish. Perhaps this is but a personal delusion, yet others have also noticed something answering to this description.

VINTAGE   *DATE*   *PRICE*

GUESTS

MENU   *COMMENTS*

RHEIN PFALZ

Weingut Dr. Bürklin-Wolf

WACHENHEIM/WEINSTRASSE

Wachenheimer Gerümpel
Riesling Auslese

Erzeugerabfüllung · A. P. Nr. 5 142 043 14 72

QUALITÄTSWEIN MIT PRÄDIKAT

RHEINBERGER

WINZERGENOSSENSCHAFT HERRENBERG-HONIGSÄCKEL
E·G·M·B·H

Ungstein

1971 RHEIN PFALZ 1971

Amtliche Prüfungsnummer: 5 141 169 20 72

Ungsteiner Honigsäckel
Silvaner Spätlese

Qualitätswein mit Prädikat   Erzeugerabfüllung

Aus dem Rheinpfalz
Weingüte Deidesheim
Geh. Rat Dr. v. Basser- mann-Jordan

IN VITE VITA

Forster Jesuitengarten 1971
Riesling Trockenbeerenauslese

QUALITÄTSWEIN MIT PRÄDIKAT, ERZEUGERABFÜLLUNG
A. P. Nr. 5 106 064 17 73

Rhein pfalz

Weingut   Deidesheim

Reichsrat v. Buhl   Originalabfüllung

Forster Ungeheuer Riesling Trockenbeerenauslese

Rüdesheimer Berg Rottland Riesling
Auslese Staatsweingüter

The black eagle of the German State Domains is certainly the single greatest and most reliable white wine label in the world. Of the famous and less famous sites over which it presides, Steinberger, overlooking Hattenheim and the Kloster Ebebrach, is the most prestigious. Steinbergers are powerful, intense classic Rheingau made to the highest standards of cultivation and vinification. Similar are the rich, honeyed, unctuous wines of Rottland, one of Rüdesheim's best sites, whose State Domain label is reproduced here.

VINTAGE   DATE   PRICE

GUESTS

MENU   COMMENTS

Rauenthaler Baiken Riesling Spätlese
Schloss Eltz

A connoisseur's vineyard, the Baiken plot in Rauenthaler is prized over all other sites in Germany; and its wines, while not treated to superlatives abroad, receive the highest prices paid by German enthusiasts. Favorable years give Rauenthalers from the State Domain and from private properties such as this a prestige based on their heights of fruit, delicacy, intensity, and rare finesse. This old landed family also grows and ships wines from Eltville and Kiedrich.

VINTAGE   DATE   PRICE

GUESTS

MENU   COMMENTS

Erbacher Marcobrunn Riesling
Trockenbeerenauslese Schloss Schönborn

A patrician Rheingau family with important vineyards in Rüdesheim, Johannisberg, and Erbach, and cellar headquarters in Hattenheim, produces excellent *Kabinett* wines and remarkable peak wines of dazzling concentration, such as that illustrated by this label. They are the second largest vineyard owners in the Rheingau. The variety of their holdings and quality grades, albeit covering a multitude of virtues, require careful reading by wine shoppers to ascertain the pedigree of the wine in question. It may amuse predatory shoppers to realize that shops and restaurants alike frequently muddle their pricing between sites and grades, with occasional bonuses to the well-informed buyer.

VINTAGE   DATE   PRICE

GUESTS

MENU   COMMENTS

Eltviller Sonnenberg Riesling
Langwerth von Simmern

These unforgettable, eminently Teutonic labels herald the various estate wines of another distinguished land-owning family whose most famous vineyards are at Marcobrunn. It has been my misfortune to find very variable wines under this label, many with loose-tasting qualities lacking in concentration and finesse; but they have an excellent reputation the world over. Eltville is a relatively large village, producing quantities of excellent wines in good vintages; its other *Einzellagen* are Taubenberg, Sandgrub, Rheinberg, and Langenstück. Sandgrub straddles Eltville's border with Kiedrich.

VINTAGE   DATE   PRICE

GUESTS

MENU   COMMENTS

RHEINGAU
Qualitätswein mit Prädikat

1971er
Rüdesheimer
Berg Rottlend
Riesling

AUSLESE

Erzeuger-Abfüllung - Amtl. Prüf-Nr. 33050 004 72
Verwaltung der Staatsweingüter, Eltville

SCHLOSS ELTZ

Gräflich Eltz'sche Güterverwaltung Eltville a/Rh.

AMTLICHE 33010- 013 -72 PRÜFUNGSNUMMER

DEUTSCHER MIT PRÄDI- KAT QUALITÄTSWEIN

Erzeuger-   Abfüllung

1971er Schloss Eltz
Spätlese
Rauenthaler Baiken Riesling

RHEINGAU

RHEINGAU
Schloss Schönborn

1971er

Erbacher Marcobrunn
Riesling
TROCKENBEERENAUSLESE

Domänenrat

A. P. Nr. 31 052 024.72

Erzeugerabfüllung der Gräflich von Schönborn'schen Kellerei Hattenheim
QUALITÄTSWEIN MIT PRÄDIKAT

QUALITÄTSWEIN · RHEINGAU

Freiherrlich Langwerth von Simmern'sche
Kellerei Eltville
Eltviller Sonnenberg
Riesling   1970er   Riesling

GESETZLICH GESCHÜTZT

Erbacher Marcobrunn Riesling Auslese
Schloss Reinhartshausener

On this page appear labels of four celebrated *Schloss* (castle) estates belonging to patrician families, some with more than one vineyard site. The ready reverence paid to such properties, whether in the Rheingau, Bordeaux, or Burgundy, naturally provokes controversy over the true quality of the wines; but all four are certainly distinguished Rhine Rieslings, and their acquaintance should be made. This Marcobrunn (which is not their Schloss wine) belongs to the Prince of Prussia and is one of two famous holdings in that Erbach *Einzellage*. At best spicy refined wines lingering long on the palate, fine Marcobrunn vintages such as this 1971 should be sampled by serious tasters.

VINTAGE   *DATE*   *PRICE*

GUESTS

MENU   *COMMENTS*

Schloss Vollrads

A legendary estate belonging to the Graf Matuschka-Greiffenclau and situated back and above the town of Winkel, its 80 acres (32 hectares) constitute a very large vineyard by Rheingau standards. The best wines are powerful, harmonious, and live to a great age in bottle; they lack nothing in any point of character. Labeling is confusing, with a starting class of *Qualitatswein* marked by various green and red (better) capsules, QbA *Kabinett* coded by blue and blue and gold capsules, *Spatlëse* grade with pink and pink and gold capsules, white and white and gold capsules for *Auslese*, and finally a gold capsule for *Beerenauslese* and gold with a neck label showing the Schloss tower for *Trockenbeerenauslese*. Winkel has half a dozen or more superlative vineyards in addition to this one.

VINTAGE   *DATE*   *PRICE*

GUESTS

MENU   *COMMENTS*

Kiedricher Gräfenberg Riesling
Kabinett Schloss Groenesteyn

The von Ritter zu Groenesteyn estates, like those of von Schönborn, comprise holdings in several premium communes that bear important labels for Rheingau drinkers. The headquarters of these properties is at Rüdesheim, but this label illustrates one of the two best sites in the village of Kiedrich (Wasseros is the other). As is true of the neighboring village of Rauenthal, Kiedrich wines have more prestige in Germany than abroad. Their intense body, great class in both bouquet and finish, and delicious savor command highest prices in good years. These qualities deepen with age, but the wines are so luscious that it is difficult to resist drinking them young.

VINTAGE   *DATE*   *PRICE*

GUESTS

MENU   *COMMENTS*

Rotlack Kabinett Furst von Metternich
Schloss Johannisberger

A world-famous titled estate, it has been in von Metternich hands since the early nineteenth century. Its vines form one vast descent below the village and castle of Johannisberg. The peak wines are heady and charged with flavor and cast up a powerful bouquet. The castle dominating the 65-acre (26-hectare) vineyard is a Rhineland landmark. A second label, showing the Schloss, is distributed in Germany and exported by a major shipper.

VINTAGE   *DATE*   *PRICE*

GUESTS

MENU   *COMMENTS*

ERBACH   RHEINGAU

Schloss Reinhartshausener

A. P. Nr. 3207102372

Erbacher Marcobrunn Riesling 1971

Qualitätswein mit Prädikat Auslese

ERZEUGER-ABFÜLLUNG

ADMINISTRATION DES PRINZEN FRIEDRICH VON PREUSSEN

VERBAND DEUTSCHER NATURWEIN-VERSTEIGERER E. V.

Unsere Mitglieder besitzen Lagen von Weltruf!

Dieses Zeichen in Verbindung mit dem Korkbrand verbürgt naturreinen Wein!

VEREINIGUNG RHEINGAUER NATURWEIN-VERSTEIGERER E. V.

RHEINGAU

KORKBRAND GES. GESCHÜTZT

GOLD. MED. ST. LOUIS 1904

1970er SCHLOSSABZUG

SCHLOSS VOLLRADS

WINKEL IM RHEINGAU

Graf Matuschka-Greiffenclau'sche Originalabfüllung

REICHSFREIHERR VON RITTER ZU GROENESTEYN

SCHLOSS GROENESTEYN

1971er

Kiedricher Gräfenberg Riesling Kabinett

Qualitätswein mit Prädikat - Amtliche Prüfungsnummer 34016·007·73

Weingut des Freiherr von Ritter'schen Rentamtes Rüdesheim/Rhein

Erzeuger-   RHEINGAU   Abfüllung

QUALITÄTSWEIN MIT PRÄDIKAT

RHEINGAU

A. P. Nr. 26026 001 73

1972er

Schloss Johannisberger.

Rotlack

KABINETT

Erzeuger-Abfüllung

Fürst von Metternich

Domäne Schloß Johannisberg

Kreuznacher Hofgarten Riesling Kabinett Anheuser & Fehrs

Two Anheuser firms, Anheuser & Fehrs and Paul Anheuser, whose familiar red script on white labels are found in England and America, are the best-known Nahe exporters. Each owns individual vineyards, but this particular example, a clean, useful Riesling, toned down to expected Nahe smoothness, simply comes from vines within the limits of the Hofgarten *Einzellage,* one of nearly 40 permitted site names in the Kreuznach Kronenberg *Bereich.* With their softer character, and without the extreme spice and fruit of Moselle wines, Nahe Rieslings can be readily drunk with food at no expense to enjoyment of the wine.

VINTAGE   DATE   PRICE

GUESTS

MENU   COMMENTS

Kupfergrube Kabinett Schloss Böckelheimer Staatlichen Weinbaudomänen

Perched between this famous vineyard and Niederhäuser Hermannsberg, the State Domain makes a variety of fine wines, some pure Riesling, some using Sylvaner, that bear the designations of these two sites and others as well. The Rieslings are more yellow in color, more pronounced in bouquet, and resemble Rheinhesse wines, albeit marked by the mineral or earthy flavors typical of Nahe wines. The Sylvaner or mixed-variety wines, which simply bear the site name and *Kabinett, Auslese,* or other grades, are usually paler, spicy or perfumed in bouquet, with contrasting but harmonious flavors, more originality, and less finesse than the Rieslings. All are well made and interesting.

VINTAGE   DATE   PRICE

GUESTS

MENU   COMMENTS

Zeltinger Sonnenuhr Auslese Friedrich-Wilhelm-Gymnasium

Next to the German state, this private secondary school is the largest vineyard holder in the Moselle district. Look closely at these labels when you buy, for the same design adorns wines from the school's sites at Graach and Trittenheim (less good) and excellent Saar wines from Ockfen and Oberemmel. Zeltingen, largest village of the Mittelmosel, has a less glamorous image than Wehlen or Bernkastel, but its best wines are fragrant and delicious, exemplifying Moselle virtues. Sonnenuhr is one of four new *Einzellagen.* The others are Deutschherrenberg, Himmelreich, and Schlossberg. This is a racy, scintillating wine, with just enough sweetness to match its fruit.

VINTAGE   DATE   PRICE

GUESTS

MENU   COMMENTS

Dhronhofberger Auslese Bischöfliches Priesterseminar

This Trier seminary, which owns vineyards throughout the Moselle, has joined its administration with that of other Catholic institutions, such as the Hohe Domkirche, though the sites remain separate and respected. Grouped in the Michelsberg *Grosslage,* the high vineyards of Dhron overlook the village and little river of the same name. Along with Neumagen and Trittenheim, the township borders the finest Moselle production, though its appetizing and attractive wines have good style if not ultimate finesse. Like many 1971s, this example is sweet and supple but lacks a point of acidity.

VINTAGE   DATE   PRICE

GUESTS

MENU   COMMENTS

Anheuser & Fehrs
Bad-Kreuznach

Deutsche Qualitätsweine

PRODUCE OF GERMANY
STILL NAHE WINE

1971 Kreuznacher Hofgarten

Riesling Kabinett

Qualitätswein mit Prädikat A.P.Nr. 1 710 008 92 72

produced and bottled by Estate August Anheuser

0517/149   REG.

Produce of Germany

NAHE
1973er
Schloßböckelheimer
Kupfergrube
Kabinett

QUALITÄTSWEIN MIT PRÄDIKAT

Amtliche Prüfungsnummer 1 750 053/04/74

Verwaltung der Staatlichen Weinbaudomänen
Niederhausen-Schloßböckelheim
Erzeuger-Abfüllung

Mosel-Saar-Ruwer

Produce of Germany

Amtl. Prüfungs-Nr.
3 561 024 40 72

Qualitätswein mit Prädikat
1971er

Zeltinger Sonnenuhr Auslese

Erzeugerabfüllung

Friedrich-Wilhelm-Gymnasium, Trier

Produce of Germany

MOSEL-SAAR-RUWER
QUALITÄTSWEIN MIT PRÄDIKAT
A. P. Nr. 3 561 012 1 27 72

BISCHÖFLICHES PRIESTERSEMINAR, TRIER
1773

1971er

Dhronhofberger

Auslese

ERZEUGERABFÜLLUNG

BISCHÖFLICHES PRIESTERSEMINAR · TRIER

Most authorities describe the tasting qualities of Nahe as lying between those of the Rheingau and of the Moselle wines, just as the district lies roughly between the two. This does not correspond to my impressions. The best Nahe wines seem rather to be on a Rheingau model but do not emphasize fruit and lusciousness so much as a classic Rheingau will do. The bouquet is less opulent, and the tasting impressions certainly include breed, finish, and a firmness of impression. The term "fiery" seems bound to confuse consumers with its implications of high alcoholic content, but some Nahe Rieslings do have intensity, which is something else, if not the richness of Rheingau or the spice of Moselle. Frequently their blandness suggests Rheinhesse.

MOSEL-SAAR-RUWER

The geographical convenience that causes vineyards of the Moselle proper to be grouped with those of its tributaries finds some echo in the nature of the wines, but it is by no means a single family. Indeed, within very short distances, great differences in terms of tasting qualities arise. The austere, aristocratic wines of Scharzhof in the Saar are a far cry from some nearby Piesporters, in which verve and backbone are not always strengths. The districts are best taken separately.

The Saar

Saar vines commence in earnest at Serrig, in the south, and follow the river through Saarburg, Ockfen, and Wiltingen, with an eastward extension into Oberemmel, past Kanzem, and finally end at Konz, where the Saar meets the Moselle. Wiltinger Scharzberg is the important *Grosslage*. The soil changes at Saarburg; to the south it is marked by shell lime, while northern soils contain shale and surface slate and include the more famous districts. The State Domain at Serrig, whose site is Vogelsang, is the best-known producer in the south, whereas the Scharzhofberg wines of Egon Müller and other sites have earned the best reputation of the main body of wines in the north. Several vineyard sites to the east of the actual river course have reputations—Altenberg, Sonnenberg, and Karlsberg. Religious orders and other institutions, some in Trier, have holdings and are represented in the label section.

The predominant problem of this valley is cold weather, plain and simple. Sufficiently warm growing seasons are rarer here than elsewhere. When the Rieslings, planted at approximately 650 feet (200 meters) elevation, get enough sun, the results are peak wines that unite exquisite flavor with vivacity and a mysterious strength of impression on the palate. When the weather is inadequate the wines are particularly unpleasant and astringent; they dig at the taste and digestive system alike. These wines are either drunk by devoted locals or sold to be blended for sparkling wine. The term "steely" is incessantly applied to Saar wines; I think it an unusually poor tasting term. Put a piece of unwashed flint in your mouth, and you will taste such salts associated with this stone formation as one is able to register; try "tasting" a piece of steel. If the term is meant to convey features of the vinosity or acidity of the wine, it is a rotten precedent, though I am sure to have committed equal crimes at witless moments. It is difficult enough for beginners to segregate out acidity, alcohol, aromatic elements, tannin, and alkaloids without dragging a steel herring

under their nose and across their imagination. This is not to dispute the remarkable vitality of the tasting impressions of fine Saar wines; theirs is a special genus of finesse—inimitable Rieslings with a vibrant effect that lingers long—and longer in fond memory.

SAAR and RUWER

○ TOWN
• Village
VINEYARD SITE (EINZELLAGE)

The Ruwer

The Ruwer vineyards follow the large stream of that name through a district shorter than that of the Saar and through conditions less arduous. The Saar Valley is raked by cold winds and haphazard frosts. The Ruwer is more sheltered, and its wines are lighter in alcohol and have less acid. In all but the finest years Ruwers are more agreeable and reliable than Saar wines.

The wine district progresses north along a band of vineyards varying in width and no more than six miles (ten kilometers) in length. From Waldrach, through Kasel, Grünhaus, and Eitelsbach, the stream joins the Moselle at Pfalzel, just north of the village of Ruwer. The finest vineyards extend in "arms" northwest and southeast of the river as well as lie along it, unlike the configuration of the Nahe, for example, or the Mittelmosel, with the result that some of the great vineyard sites such as Avelsbach are quite far from the stream itself. Avelsbach is legally Moselle but vinously considered Ruwer.

The best-known wine abroad is Maximin Grünhaus, just west of Mertesdorf, though Karthäuserhofberg and the estates of von Kesselstatt enjoy equal reputations among connoisseurs. As with many vineyard estates in this area, the first and second named have their origins in monastic orders, Benedictine and Carthusian respectively. The Trier religious order, important in the Saar, also clings to holdings in the Ruwer.

Ruwer wines at their best are exquisitely flowery, light, and utterly delicious. Commonly the lightest of all wines in alcohol, their tasting qualities are summed up in wonderfully delicate bouquet, followed by a rush of fruit on the palate and finishing refined and uplifting. Naturally, in inadequate years, quite thin wines are made, in which fruit and charm fail to compensate for the inherently limited vinosity of this family of white wines.

While one must admire the technical efforts and financial sacrifice that go into producing small quantities of selected peak wines, *Beerenauslese,* for example, many tasters prefer Ruwer wines in their younger, less concentrated styles. These fragile perfumed wines can serve as excellent introductions to more complete vinous examples of Mittelmosel winemaking, preparing the palate to appreciate the richer wines to follow, and introducing some features of fine Riesling as it is shaped in the Mosel-Saar-Ruwer district as a whole.

The Moselle

The whole of the Mosel-Saar-Ruwer, containing some 26,400 acres (10,700 hectares) of vines and producing about 23.8 million gallons (900,000 hectoliters) annually, is divided into four *Bereiche.* The Saar-Ruwer is one, and the remaining length of the main river, between the Roman center of Trier and Coblenz where the Moselle joins the Rhine, is carved into three: Zell takes in the former Lower Moselle from around Zell to Coblenz, and the Obermosel encompasses the thinner wines from east of Trier to Luxembourg. In the center is the fine-wine course of the river, formerly the Mittelmosel, now the *Bereich* Bernkastel. The Mosel-Saar-Ruwer is planted three-quarters in Riesling, 13 percent in Müller-Thurgau, and 11 percent in Elbling, a lesser vine of ancient origins now being replaced by specially cultivated breeds designed for these particular terrains found unfit for Riesling. But in the Moselle itself, Riesling is nearly 90 percent of the vineyard, and in the best vineyards it is virtually the only grape.

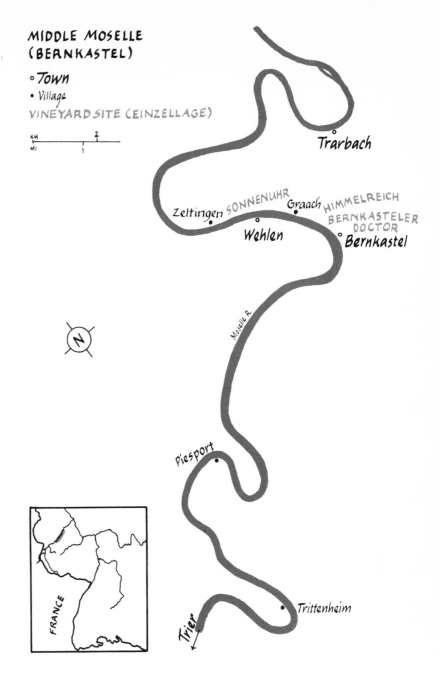

MIDDLE MOSELLE (BERNKASTEL)

○ Town
● Village
VINEYARD SITE (EINZELLAGE)

This cultivation is no mean feat. The Moselle vineyards rise in ramparts with grades of one (height) to three (distance). Terracing is not only advantageous but frequently indispensable for soil retention. It is an agonizing vineyard to work and harvest. Fine-wine cultivation is labor-intensive even in evenly divided rolling landscapes, but the required man-hours per land unit in the Moselle can rise to staggering multiples of labor requirements elsewhere; not surprisingly, labor availability both for cultivation and harvest is an immense problem. The slopes are covered with slate fragments that are regularly replenished by hand for the heat-reflecting and stabilizing properties they contribute to the surface and for the mineral advantages they offer the soils. The steep pitch, rocky ground, and soil type resemble the rigorous growing conditions of the Douro Valley in Portugal. A. Massel has forcefully cited this similarity to underline the dominant influence of climate on wine type in implied rebuttal of those who insist on the semimagical features of certain vines on certain soils.

Bernkasteler Doctor Auslese Dr. Thanisch

The most famous label in the Moselle, though experts no longer consider it the best wine, comes from a town giving its name to the Mittelmosel *Bereich*, a town whose borders have been so expanded by the new law as to provoke criticism within and outside Germany. The three Doctor owners—Thanisch, Deinhard, and Lauerburg—can well be indignant at this dilution of their name; and Thanisch now uses the designation Doctor und Graben, stressing the locale of their orginal Bernkasteler Doctor parcel. Always an expensive bottle, at its best the wine is wonderfully flowery in bouquet, develops on the palate with great style and excitement, and lingers on with a sensation of fruit and delicacy.

VINTAGE   *DATE*   *PRICE*

GUESTS

MENU   *COMMENTS*

Wehlener Sonnenuhr Kabinett Joh. Jos. Prüm

There are several related Prüm families in the heartland of the Mittelmosel. This is the best-known Prüm abroad, and the Sonnenuhr site nurtures their most expensive wines. To experts, this label, in various grades of sweetness, represents wine as good as any in Germany. Other Sonnenuhr sites are in the Moselle. To me, one of the impressive feats of this grower is his ability to make transitions from excellently balanced, delicate wines of *Kabinett* grade to equally superlative, more concentrated wines, *Auslese* grade and above, each wonderfully proportioned. The much abused adjective "classic" finds its home in this Moselle wine, a useful benchmark of quality for its neighbors and a fine introduction to quality German wines in general.

VINTAGE   *DATE*   *PRICE*

GUESTS

MENU   *COMMENTS*

Graacher Himmelreich Dr. Thanisch

With southwest exposures like those of Wehlener Sonnenuhr, the Graach village *Einzellagen*, whose best vineyards are Himmelreich, Josephshofer, and Domprobst, also produce delectable fine wines full of fruit with lovely finesse. The green Thanisch Himmelreich label announces the best known and one of the best of these wines, all markedly Moselle in character, and wines which many prefer to drink young. Bergweiler, von Kesselstatt, and the Friedrich-Wilhelm-Gymnasium are other Graach growers of prestige.

VINTAGE   *DATE*   *PRICE*

GUESTS

MENU   *COMMENTS*

Serriger Vogelsang Auslese

At the end of the nineteenth century the German state vineyards took the lead in developing forest-covered slopes at the south of the Saar Valley, where the climate is the worst of all and the frequency of successful vintages low. This 1973 is an extreme Saar wine, very tart, yet quite delicious, if not to everyone's taste. Vogelsang is the site of the State Domain. While the main vineyards face south, they are still exposed to winter cold, to wind, and to spring and fall frost.

VINTAGE   *DATE*   *PRICE*

GUESTS

MENU   *COMMENTS*

MOSEL · SAAR · RUWER

Berncasteler Doctor
u. Graben
1971er Auslese
Qualitätswein mit Prädikat

A. P. Nr. 2576242-15-72

Original-Kellerabzug

Wachstum Wwe. Dr. H. Thanisch

GESETZLICH GESCHÜTZT

H. DALKWEILER & CO. TRIER

Verband Deutscher
Prädikatswein-
Versteigerer e. V.

Erzeugerabfüllung
Weingut
Joh. Jos. Prüm
Wehlen/Mosel

Mosel — Saar — Ruwer
Qualitätswein
mit Prädikat

Amtliche Prüfungs-Nr.
2 576 511 - 1274

Produce of Germany

Joh. Jos. Prüm

1973er
Wehlener Sonnenuhr
Kabinett

Seit über 400 Jahren
Weinbau-Tradition
Weingut
Wwe. Dr. H. Thanisch
Weinbergslagen

URALTES THANISCH HAUSZEICHEN

Berncasteler Doctor
Graben
Lay
Badstube
Schloßberg
Graacher Himmelreich
Wehlener Sonnenuhr

MOSEL-SAAR-RUWER

1971er
Graacher Himmelreich
Spätlese

WEINGUT Wwe. Dr. H. THANISCH
BERNKASTEL-KUES

MOSEL-SAAR-RUWER

1973er
Serriger Vogelsang
Riesling - Auslese - Eiswein

Qualitätswein mit Prädikat

Amtliche Prüfungsnummer
3 561 107 27 74

Erzeugerabfüllung
Verwaltung der Staatlichen Weinbaudomänen
Trier

Lutz & Co. Trier

Ockfener Bockstein Auslese Gasthauer

Wiltingen and Oberemmel are fine village names in the Saar, but this superior Ockfen 1971 wine from the Bockstein vineyard exemplifies the wines of many private growers struggling to make fine wines in a difficult region. This wine resembles that of the Oberemmel sites. Like its neighbors, it is an elegant wine, not assertive or overpowering in any dimension but immensely attractive and subtle to nose and palate. It does not normally possess qualities that encourage keeping for improvement. Even this 1971 seemed mature at four years of age.

VINTAGE   *DATE*   *PRICE*

GUESTS

MENU   *COMMENTS*

Kanzemer Altenberg Kabinett Maximilian von Othegraven

Kanzem is in the northerly, somewhat less exposed section of the Saar Valley. This elegant, firm wine with a hint of mountain flowers in the bouquet and a decisive flavor stimulating the taste buds comes from the Altenberg *Einzellage* facing south on a river bend. The plot belongs to one of Kanzem's foremost private growers; the Trier Priesterseminar vineyard is its immediate neighbor. Horecker, Schlossberg, and Sonnenberg are the other Kanzem *Einzellagen,* and parts of them run into those of Wiltingen, finest of the Saar villages.

VINTAGE   *DATE*   *PRICE*

GUESTS

MENU   *COMMENTS*

Scharzhofberger Kabinett Deinhard

Bearing the label of one of the largest exporters to England, and seen much in America too, this 1971 Scharzhofberger illustrates the difficulties of shipping commercial quantities of racy, austere Saar wines, even from the greatest sites, as is the case here. While it shows the dry, cutting effect of Saar wines, it lacks just the points of fruit and aftertaste to offset them pleasantly.

VINTAGE   *DATE*   *PRICE*

GUESTS

MENU   *COMMENTS*

Scharzhofberger Kabinett Egon Müller

From one of several estates of the Saar's best-known grower, this 1973 has the inherently sharp initial impression of Saar wines, but dressed in elegant bouquet, moderated by firm and invigorating development on the palate, and ending with a fine and subtle aftertaste. True, it lacks full ripeness, but one does not notice this in the presence of its other qualities. Scharzhofberg lies between Wiltingen and Oberemmel, considered the best Saar villages, and should logically carry "Wiltingen" before its name; but the wines are famous enough to be simply called "Scharzhofberger."

VINTAGE   *DATE*   *PRICE*

GUESTS

MENU   *COMMENTS*

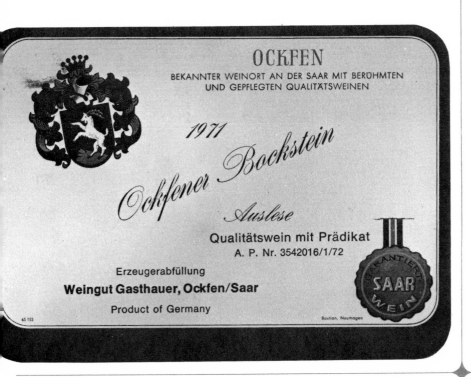

OCKFEN
BEKANNTER WEINORT AN DER SAAR MIT BERÜHMTEN
UND GEPFLEGTEN QUALITÄTSWEINEN

1971

Ockfener Bockstein

Auslese
Qualitätswein mit Prädikat
A. P. Nr. 3542016/1/72

Erzeugerabfüllung
Weingut Gasthauer, Ockfen/Saar

Product of Germany

Seit 1500
Weinbau-Tradition
am Kanzemer Berg

Trierer Verein von
Weingutsbesitzern der
Mosel, Saar
und Ruwer e. V.
(Großer Ring)

QUALITÄTSWEIN MIT PRÄDIKAT
1973er Kanzemer Altenberg Kabinett
Erzeugerabfüllung   A. P. Nr. 3 518 034-15-74

Weingut Kanzemer Berg
Maximilian v. Othegraven
Kanzem a. d. Saar

M O S E L - S A A R - R U W E R

KOBLENZ   AN RHEIN & MOSEL

MOSEL – SAAR – RUWER
QUALITÄTSWEIN MIT PRÄDIKAT – A. P. Nr. 35258561172
SCHARZHOFBERGER
KABINETT
Erzeuger-Abfüllung van Volxem

Deinhard®
Specially selected and shipped by
DEINHARD & CO. KOBLENZ AN RHEIN UND MOSEL

PRODUCE OF GERMANY   REGISTERED TRADE MARK

MOSEL - SAAR - RUWER

1973r

Scharzhofberger Kabinett

Grand Prix Paris 1900
Grand Prix St. Louis 1904

Erzeugerabfüllung Egon Müller zu Scharzhof

*Abgefüllt im Keller
zu Scharzhof*

Qualitätswein mit Prädikat   A.-P. Nr. 3567142 3-74

Maximin Grünhäuser
Abtsberg von Schubert

The nearly 50 acres (20 hectares) of the Ruwer's most famous vineyard hill are divided according to qualities named by the Benedictines who originally cultivated vines here, only to have them expropriated by French revolutionary invaders early in the nineteenth century. This is the best, the *Abtsberg*, or Abbot's, wine. It is easy to class intellectually these racy, ultralight aromatic wines, which seem nothing more (or less) than a burst of pure fruit and scent, in a rank below great Rheingau, Palatinate, or Mittelmosel whites; but in fact they have a place no other can usurp. Elusive the tasting qualities may be, but the Grünhäuser bottle risks being emptied while the debate is going on.

VINTAGE   *DATE*   *PRICE*

GUESTS

MENU   *COMMENTS*

Kaseler Hitzlay Kabinett
Reichsgraf von Kesselstatt

Kasel is the center of the Ruwer attaching its name to seven new *Einzellagen* all grouped under the *Bereich* Romerlay. Typically spicy both in bouquet and taste, this Hitzlay gives all the freshness, ease of drinking, and zestful aftertaste of Ruwer wines such as its Kaseler neighbors Timpert, Paulinsberg, Nies'chen, and Kernagel. In addition to the excellent 1971, the 1973 vintage was a very pretty success in the Ruwer, though its wines should be drunk young. Some fancy to find an aroma of peach or cherry in Ruwers, and it is true that the first palatal impressions, however delicious, do not instantly suggest grape.

VINTAGE   *DATE*   *PRICE*

GUESTS

MENU   *COMMENTS*

Eitelsbacher Karthäuser Hofberger
Rautenstrauch/Tyrell

Across the Ruwer in Eitelsbach, a former Carthusian vineyard faces the Benedictine hill of Maximin Grünhäuser. Its wines are slightly firmer, touched a bit more with a mineral savor, often less ethereal and slightly more vinous than fine Ruwers; but they conform to the same light, sprightly style. The two labels show the impact of the new wine law, though they come from the same owner and from adjacent plots facing south, overlooking Eitelsbach. The 1959 Sang *feine* (now a forbidden term) *Auslese* label appeared alone on its bottle of golden, slightly honeyed wine. The 1973 Kronenberg, which like Sang is a new *Einzellage*, had to add a strip label bearing the certification (A.P. Nr.), as shown.

VINTAGE   *DATE*   *PRICE*

GUESTS

MENU   *COMMENTS*

(Dom) Avelsbacher Altenberg Kabinett
Hohe Domkirche

All the fine wines of this Trier church used to carry the word "Dom" before the site name, a practice forbidden now but insinuated by a faint, large washprinted "DOM" behind the label text. The 1973 shows Avelsbacher qualities well: Ruwer in style, with flowery approach to nose and palate; delicious flavor; and excellent acidity to excite the palate without searing the stomach. The best Kasel, Eitelsbach, or Maximin Grünhäus may fetch better prices than this Avelsbach or those of its neighbor *Einzellagen*, Hammerstein and Herrenberg Rotlei, but all are Ruwer of high class, worth sampling.

VINTAGE   *DATE*   *PRICE*

GUESTS

MENU   *COMMENTS*

Maximin Grünhäuser Abtsberg
1973er · 1973er
Produce of Germany
QUALITÄTSWEIN mit PRÄDIKAT
der C. von Schubert'schen SCHLOSSKELLEREI - GRÜNHAUS
vormals Freiherr von Stumm-Halberg
MOSEL — SAAR — RUWER
A. P. Nr. 3 536 014-27-74

MOSEL-SAAR-RUWER
WEINGUT „ST. IRMINENHOF"

1971er
Kaseler Hitzlay Kabinett
Qualitätswein mit Prädikat - A. P. Nr. 3 561 077-42-72
Reichsgraf von Kesselstatt, Trier

Produce of Germany
MOSEL-SAAR-RUWER
QUALITÄTSWEIN MIT PRÄDIKAT
A. P. Nr. 3 561 012 2 1 74
CAPITULUM CATHEDRALIS ECCL. TREVERENSIS
1973er
Avelsbacher Altenberg
Kabinett
ERZEUGERABFÜLLUNG
HOHE DOMKIRCHE · TRIER

Eitelsbacher Karthäuser Hofberger
Wachstum
1959er Sang
feine Auslese
Hans Wilhelm Rautenstrauch
Original-Kellerabzug
LINTZ-TRIER

Eitelsbacher Karthäuser Hofberger
Kronenberg
1973er Kabinett
Produce of Germany
Erzeugerabfüllung
Werner Tyrell, vorm. H.W. Rautenstrauch
LINTZ-TRIER

In addition to problems posed by topography, the Moselle is one of the last great European vineyards locked in battle with the phylloxera louse, and the expensive substitution of grafted vines for native stocks continues. Also, the incidence of frost at the end of the growing season is high and the physical protection of the vines costly. Frost at this point arrests final maturation of grapes to the great detriment of the resulting wine. Spring frosts are not uncommon, and occasional devastating hailstorms lurk in the background of the possible. It is not an easy region for grapegrowers, and there is a strong tendency for smaller vineyards and those on the fringes of the Upper and Lower Moselle to band together into cooperatives that offer economies of scale in the use of expensive equipment and advantages in marketing.

The Lower Moselle is a less favored vineyard than the middle slopes. The soils are rich in iron but very steeply pitched, and vines grow less well. Winningen Weinhex is one important *Grosslage;* the *Bereich*, Zell, also contains the Schwarze Katz *Grosslage*. These "black cat" labels have been widely spread about in the past, without respect to a few growers in a region originally using this name, but they will henceforth be under the discipline of the new laws of origin.

The *Bereich* Bernkastel covers the Middle Moselle roughly between Zell and Trittenheim nearly to Trier, and most of the famous vineyards are found on both banks of the river in a series of roughly five loops. The effect of this convoluted path is that vineyards on both sides of the river face the same points of the compass at various stages, and unlike the Rheingau with its single aspect, the Moselle heartland offers a patchwork of vineyard sites with the most favored scattered about in accordance with exposition and microclimate. The harsh effects of a straight river valley on wind conditions can be seen in parts of the Saar. The Moselle's configuration is more fortunate, its twisting course providing a baffle to cold winds.

Riesling dominates the best sites to virtual exclusion of other grapes. While there are nuances along the length of the Middle Moselle—with full, heavy but less lively wines at Piesport, drier ones at Zeltingen, finer and more intense wines at Wehlen, Graach, and Bernkastel—there is a close family resemblance among the best wines of this district. Light in alcohol but clean and arresting in flavor, they proffer a bouquet pronounced in its style but elusive and stimulating. The tasting impressions are spicy, lively, and harmonious, with a sensation of fruit giving way to one of balance and breed, with fruit finishing and lingering long after the wine is swallowed. Like many fine white wines that stress delicacy, they must be very good; unsuccessful vintages may be respected for their struggle against the elements but are rarely enjoyable to drink. In fortunate years, however, the great wines of the new *Grosslagen*—Badstube, Kurfürstlay, Michelsberg, Münzlay—and some from sites in Sankt Michael, Schwarzlay, and Vom Heissen Stein, have few rivals for elegance, dash of flavor, and finesse.

Most famous among the vineyard sites is that of Bernkasteler Doctor, held by three owners; but most connoisseurs, if they had to name a single group of wines that exemplified Moselle virtues, would probably select those of Wehlen. Its most esteemed site is Sonnenuhr, a fine riverine vineyard between Zeltingen and Graach, across the river from the town of Wehlen. Graach wines are close to the latter two in style, and Himmelreich, virtually next door to Sonnenuhr, is the best-known Graach site for the export trade. Piesport wines have their partisans, who appreciate a more "feminine" style of the wine, the most famous of which are from Goldtröpfchen. Fine wines in similar style are made all the way down into the environs of Trier, though

bottles bearing this name are technically in the *Bereich* of Saar-Ruwer, from its *Grosslage* Romerlay. Most experts agree, however, that with the villages of Dhron Neumagen and Trittenheim on the southernmost bend of the Moselle, the premium qualities begin to fade out.

The *Bereich* Obermosel stretches through two *Grosslagen,* Gipfel and Königsberg, toward the Luxembourg border. Many of these thinner, more astringent, and less distinguished wines, which are produced from soils now dominated by shell lime rather than the heat-reflecting slate debris of the Middle Moselle, are used for blending in sparkling wines. There are plantings in lesser grapes that, as elsewhere, go into ordinary wine (*Tafelwein*).

Blended Wines

The label section of this introduction to German wines exhibits mainly estates; these bottle the finest wines of Germany much as single Bordeaux châteaux bottle the most exciting wines of that huge area. But, like Burgundy, German quality areas are much divided among growers, and this fragmented tenure allows opportunities for high-quality blended wines. Blends lead readily to confusion; a few words should be deployed on this subject.

There are five main sorts of blended wine to be found in Germany. Last in interest to foreigners is German *Tafelwein* (table wine). This domestic ordinary wine comes from one of five big regions—Mosel, Rhein, Oberrhein, Main, and Neckar. While the names of most sound familiar, their boundaries have little to do with those of the 11 Designated Regions for *Qualitätswein*. Trademarked names, or brand names, however fanciful or sonorous, that do not state that they are QbA or QmP are *Tafelwein* and are unlikely to be worth the retail price necessitated by expenses of export and distribution abroad.

Second, and commercially important abroad, are designations such as Moselblumchen and, above all, the ubiquitous Liebfraumilch. The latter term, once milked indeed for all it was worth, is now restricted to at least QbA grade wines from the Palatinate, Rheinhesse, Rheingau, or Nahe. Trademarked Liebfraumilch, and for that matter all table wine sold as a brand, poses different wine-making and wine-marketing problems than obtain for fine wines. The producers must determine which style, quality, and price can hope to appeal to the widest, or at least a very wide, market and yet be maintained by blending, given vintage and market variations. Then they must achieve this style, quality, and price, maintain the first two year in and year out, and keep price changes within bounds of consumer tolerance. There is no intention, nor could it be sustained if there were, to reflect regional or vintage differences. Such wines can and should be pleasant, can and should be reliably consistent, and because of the intense marketing effort that is only possible with a uniform product, can be found in markets too small to justify stocking fine individual wines. So much for the virtues of branded wines. Against them it must be said that the retail price includes advertising costs as well as higher (and often more) markups in distribution than fine individual wines that may be traded openly. Provided a consumer is willing to educate himself and take risks in so doing, better wines for the price can be found where wide selections are offered. It is fair to admit to relief in finding good blended brand wines where once only beer and spirits were sold, or expected to be found. And if it is maddening to find only blended wines on a restaurant list in some metropolis where scores of finer things are sold wholesale, it is the restaurateur's laziness and not brand-wine salesman's energy that deserves rebuff.

A third kind of blend commences to be of interest to fine wine drinkers: QbA grades from different Designated Regions or important *Bereiche,* Johannisberg Riesling, for example. Large production and interesting quality are both possible within these broad areas. Such wines bear a shipper's name, or that of a cooperative; they may be vintaged and may be of one grape variety. They can offer very generalized types of various quality wines. Whether they are sound authentic plain drinking or dismal, boring thin wine depends on the competence and motives of the blender. At least the new laws give a framework in which such wines can be put forward honestly, with less chance of fatal competition from unscrupulous shippers whose competing trash of the same place name used to be marketed at one-half or two-thirds the price that correct regional wine needed to fetch.

The last two categories of blended wine are assembled lots from within the confines of a single *Grosslage,* or similar lots from within the smaller limits of one *Einzellage.* Either a merchant (shipper) or cooperative (*Winzergenossenschaft*) may tackle the task. A fair number of both seem increasingly inclined to do so, and the new law offers them a sudden respectability which it is in their interest to match with performance. In human terms it is easier for one person, shipper or grower, to pursue a policy of highest quality than to get a cooperative of thirty growers to agree on what should be thrown out and what should be put in; but this much said, there is no reason why a shipper's *Einzellage* selection or that of a cooperative should not be better than many an individual's wine from within the same site. While my experience leads me to suspect that the ratio of good shippers' wines to bad ones is a bigger fraction—*nota bene*—than the ratio of good cooperative wines to bad ones, the same experience convinces me that the task of weeding out good wine from bad is no different in any fine wine region, be it grower, cooperative, or shipper who is doing the sorting.

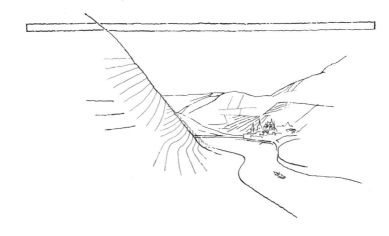

ITALY

There is a mixed relationship between the individuality of different wines and the pleasure to be had in knowing their particular tasting qualities. Common, monotonous wines produced in industrial fashion soon become a bore, however sound and clean they may be. Boredom with a pleasant, reliable article of consumption is hardly the worst that can befall us, but, as the saying insists, variety is the spice of life. Yet, there is a point at which variety becomes so befuddling that not knowing what to expect, we do not know what to appreciate. It is as if an unknown Latin comedy were being played in which all the actors spoke different dialects, none of which was quite understandable. A chapter on Italian wines risks becoming something of that sort.

Introductions to wines of other major producing countries have at least a hope, in the confines of a few pages, of doing just that—introducing. With Italy, not only the world's largest wine producer but also its most diverse, that hope fades. Any complete summary would soon become a prattling catalogue of hundreds of local names for local wines.

At least two excellent books in English truly guide the enthusiast through the maze of Italian wines. Cyril Ray has rewritten *The Wines of Italy* in a paperback edition. This handbook from the pen of a cosmopolitan and professional wine writer details significant features of every sort of Italian wine. Philip Dallas has made a labor of love of his *The Great Wines of Italy*—a personal but scrupulous guide to the location and tasting qualities of all important wines—and he has bravely named his favorite growers in each major region. If you care to learn that Ottonese is made from Buonvino grapes grown in Palestrina or that Capri red is not only Aglianico but also contains Guarnaccia grapes, it is to these authorities that you should turn, supplemented by Luigi Veronelli's *Catalogo Bolaffi dei Vini d'Italia*.

It remains to reduce confusion rather than pretend to create order by mentioning a few generalities, none of which is perfectly true. Until its unification little more than a century ago, Italy was a land of compartments—political, linguistic, economic, viticultural. Wines, like everything else except national despair, sat behind local political and tax walls. Nomenclature, grape varieties, standards of taste, all were prisoners of local tradition and local markets. The sudden unification of the country opened a national market, but it opened as well chaos and downright fraud in designating wines. Slowly, starting with local growers' associations (*consorzi*), abuse of wine names was attacked. At last, spurred on by Common Market definitions and regulations of wine, a system of controls was devised; promulgated in 1963, it began to bite into actual practice in 1965. A stream of decrees defining *Denominazione di Origine Controllata* (Designation of Controlled Areas of Origin, henceforth called D.O.C.) is still flowing from the Ministry of Agriculture and Forestry in Rome, spelling out minimum alcoholic degrees, territorial limits of production, methods, aging in barrel and bottle, units of sale, grape varieties, and other determinants of quality.

Originally the control system envisaged four grades of wine: (1) wine with no title; (2) wine of "simple origin" for which the locale of production would be specified and no more; (3) D.O.C., as sketched out above; and finally (4) D.O.C. "with Guaranty," a supercategory wherein growers would have to submit to extra controls and inspection by their association.

In fact the system has veered in a more simple direction. Wines without title, used for blending or sold as wheat or potatoes are sold, are made in profusion. A second class of wines bearing approval by local private associations of growers, the *consorzi*, is also traded. And finally there are D.O.C. wines. So far there are no "simple appellations" and no "guaranteed wines." D.O.C. wines satisfy the broad Common Market standard known as VQPRD, quality wines from delimited regions. Bluntly put, it is for each country to define quality as it jolly well pleases, publish its standards, and be sure that the resulting wine comes from some place you can point your finger at and document as a zone of delimited origin. No more, no less.

Italian growers and merchants are justly loud in praising both the strictness and speed of the reforms. But it needs to be said that the past is with us still.

Certainly the list of D.O.C. grows and grows. In 1974, 18 D.O.C. were added, making the total about 150, depending on how one tallies up the various names. As good as the laws may be, they cannot do much more than codify what exists, giving a push toward improvement here and a shove toward standardization there. Designation of wines remains a confusing variety of fanciful titles hallowed by long practice, such as Est! Est! Est! of Montefiascone, traditional district names of which Chianti is the best known, and more modern grape varietal designations, such as Riesling Trentino or Barbera d'Alba. The new laws do make sure that wines from a specified district get sold only as Chianti, for example, but they cannot guarantee that consumers are informed that there are two sorts of Chianti produced, one for drinking young and one destined to mature slowly. It is praiseworthy to create a D.O.C. designation Nebbiolo Piemontese, a lucid and straightforward way of describing a wine made from the Nebbiolo grape grown in Piedmont. But then one has to remember that Nebbiolo is called Spanna in the northeast of Piedmont, and that too must, in fairness, be recognized by another D.O.C., Spanna, quite as honest a name, but not quite so lucid. Barolo, Barbaresco, and Gattinara have always been called by those names and are fine red wines also made from Nebbiolo grapes. The result is that fanciful names of long standing, regional names based on tradition, and grape variety names all mingle, bewildering and individual, in the Italian wine bin. Those sufficiently interested will master the subject; the rest will be content to drink it. It is unfortunate but harmless.

Far from harmless is another consequence of the variety of Italian wines and of the chaos and chicanery that so long reigned in their commerce. Italian wines in export commerce are miserably dominated by a few names. These have become familiar by name and often by brand and have occupied the "Italian Wines" niche in restaurants and stores alike. An enterprising restaurant may offer forty Italian dishes, but the wine list will still be short reading: Chianti, Bardolino, Valpolicella, Soave, and Asti Spumante. With luck Barolo and Frascati may join the list. Whose mass-produced but reliable Chianti, whose technically sound but boring Soave will depend on the bargaining power of the wholesaler that supplies the harassed restaurant owner. Neither he nor the public is to blame for this state of affairs. Faced with 700 different wines, most unknown and any one of which might therefore be dreadful, it is natural that restaurants and retail shops prefer to be safe rather than sorry. So the unfortunate legacy of the Italian wine mess has been to create a situation in which the better, individual, more local wines have a bitter uphill battle to fight before they can even hope for public sampling, much less wide appreciation. The stubborn curiosity of a minority of the wine-drinking public and occasional initiative from the wine trade are doing much to improve this picture in England and in parts of the United States. The D.O.C. laws help give this minority more confidence to experiment with new names, which is what they were intended to do, among other things.

There is no immaculately fair way to introduce a few of the better, little-known wines of Italy and mention the tasting qualities of the very popular names. But not to offer a few original, more authentic wines produced in smaller quantity would fail to introduce precisely the kind of wines of most interest to the consumer. The major D.O.C. of each region will be referred to and should be sampled whenever they can be found.

The terminology of Italian labels presents few novelties, though not every country offers the tippler "cooked" wines (*vino cotto*). The glossary covers most terms.

Tasting Italian Wines

Most Italian wines, when young, bear a family resemblance, sometimes elusive, sometimes pronounced, in tasting qualities. Exceptions are wines made of French and German grape varieties in northern Italy. Young white wines have a strong sense of what the French call "sap." This impression resulting from alcoholic strength, abundant flavor, and unctuosity is quite different from very light white wines that slip past the palate pleasantly but hardly draw attention to themselves. While not precise, it serves to make a summary distinction between "strong-flavored" whites and blander ones. Also, the aftertaste of Italian whites is more often than not quite pronounced. Various adjectives apply: nutty (some say a taste of almonds), woody, slightly bitter, or frequently dominated by savors of one or more grape varieties. Character more than refinement is what they offer.

Young red wines have a generous taste of grapes, as young wines should. Tastes include sweetness for incompletely fermented wines such as Lambrusco, vegetal impressions for coarse country wines, musty or woody sensations including some bitterness for others. The range of dryness to sweetness extends further than commonly found in red wines intended for drinking with food. As they offer character and charm, there is little to be gained by criticizing the whites and young reds against standards borrowed from the best French and German wines. They have little relation to these quality wines. They should be bought and drunk to suit the buyer's personal pleasure.

The grander appellations, or D.O.C., usually come with barrel age and are a more serious matter. Frequently, more aging in oak or

READING THE LABEL

COLOR

Bianco	White.
Rosato	Rosé.
Chiaretto, Cerasuolo	Light red, analogous to Spanish *clarete*.
Rosso	Red.
Nero	Dark red, literally black.

STYLE

Amaro	Very dry, literally bitter.
Secco	Dry.
Amabile, Abboccato	Sweet, mellow, semisweet.
Dolce	Sweet.
Liquoroso	Very sweet; may also be fortified with addition of spirits.
Vino santo or vino passito	Wines concentrated by drying the grapes, usually in the sun. The result—more alcohol per volume—is obtained without adding sugar, which is not allowed.
Vino cotto	Wines concentrated by heating. Cooking reduces the volume, concentrates the sugar, and thereby raises the alcohol percentage. Acidity may be lost in the process.
Frizzante	Fizzy. No distinction is made between wines containing gas because of interruption of alcoholic fermentation and those that have gas because they were bottled before termination of the malolactic fermentation (e.g., Portuguese *vinho verde*).
Spumante, Mussante	Sparkling, *mousseux*, including wines made by Champagne method (secondary fermentation in the bottle) and those from bulk or *charmat* process (secondary fermentation in vats).

ORIGIN, BOTTLING

Cantina	Cellar, winery; occasionally means a bar and, in certain contexts, something worse.
Cantina Sociale	Growers' Cooperative Winery.
Tenementi	Holdings—i.e., a property, estate.
Fattoria	Producer, in this case a winery.
Casa vinicola	Wine company.
Consorzio	Local association of growers, typically granting approbation to wine in form of its own seal, set on the neck of the bottle. The *consorzio* designation was originally intended to authorize these associations to make inspections leading to a higher form of appellation, the D.O.C. "guaranteed," but this has not yet been implemented.

QUALITY

Denominazione di Origine Controllata	The fundamental quality-control system. It is official, armed with sanctions, and specifies all the requirements for each "name" that the Ministry of Agriculture deems sufficiently important to the eventual quality of the wine to be worth prescribing. The addition of the *consorzio* is also a quality designation, but a private one rather than a direct control of government.
Superiore	A term added to a D.O.C. wine to connote a better grade, normally based on further age in cask, bottle, or both.
Riserva	Similarly, a step up in age, and therefore quality, from *superiore*. Usually signifies an additional year in wood cask, bottle, or both.
Classico	Special inner zone of a D.O.C.; presumed better.

chestnut goes into Italian red wine of note than into those we normally drink from elsewhere. The kind of maturity that results is not to everyone's taste. Odor, attack on the palate, and aftertaste, marked by wood age at the expense of qualities usually summarized as "fruit," also come in a more alcoholic form than usual. The result, exemplified by old Barolo as well as anything else, is distinctive.

Long storage in cask causes oxidation, or "browning," of the original color and often produces more acetic acid than met with elsewhere. In moderation these symptoms of age are accepted qualities to friends of mature Italian fine red wines, and noticing them is only preparation for appreciating the other features offered by mature Chianti, representatives of the Nebbiolo grape family such as Barolo, Gattinara, old Spanna, and some of the local rarities such as Grumello or Frecciarossa. But excesses in maturing red and, more to the point, white wines are not so easy to accept. The destiny of wine is to spoil and become vinegar; and there is a point where oxidation, breakdown of alcohol, and formation of acetic acid must simply be called spoilage or decay. There is no moral issue in preferring rotten peaches to what the world calls ripe ones or spoiled wine to mature wine, but the preference should be admitted for what it is.

My old friend Alfio Moriconi, born and bred to Italian wines, waxes apoplectic if eloquent when he inveighs against the massacre of delicious young white wines left to pine and fade away in used oak vats, often of dubious cleanliness. As he says, they emerge from long imprisonment in wood with prestige of age stamped on the label but as debilitated and stale white wine in the glass, all delight lost. I agree.

The particular adventure of Italian wines is their variety and character. To experience it fully, one must wade through many, noticing the value of the dull commercial wines that are readily available and figuratively clambering over these to get at, and taste, both the fine individual wines produced in small quantities and the delightful young refreshing wines that offer such inexpensive pleasure.

THE WINE REGIONS OF ITALY

Bisect Italy at the level of Rome and you will swiftly notice that, with the exception of Marsala, Frascati, and one or two others, the well-known wines come from north of that line. This fact has been marched out to support the generalization that very warm climates, such as that of Italy's south, do not produce fine wines. The finest wines have always come from temperate climates, but the question grows as to whether technology, different techniques and/or vines may yield good wines in localities now considered too hot.

The best-known wines of southern Italy are Marsala, a dessert wine from Sicily; red Cannonau from Sardinia; Lacrima Christi of Mount Vesuvius; and a plain white, Greco di Tufo, from Campania Province. Puglia Province at the heel of the peninsula produces much of the ordinary wine for the vermouth industry of northern Italy.

Lazio

South of Rome lies the Castelli Romani (Roman castles) region famous for Frascati, a balanced, rich white wine both refreshing and flavorful. It is produced from Malvasia di Candia, Trebbiano, and lesser varieties. Within Italy this widely distributed white comes in three degrees of sweetness, but dry versions are mainly seen abroad rather than the *amabile* or the Cannellino, as sweet Frascati is otherwise known. For a long time a *consorzio*-controlled region, it is now a D.O.C. The current tendency to light Frascati for export is at the expense of character.

The Castelli Romani include mostly white wines much appreciated in Rome, such as the Colli Albani, Colli Lanuvini, Velletri, and Montecompatri/Colonna, in addition to Frascati. Malvasia, Buonvino, and Trebbiano are the popular white varieties used, but there are also a few generous red wines made from the Cesanese grape, such as Cesanese del Piglio (a D.O.C.). However well regarded in Rome, Castelli Romani wines are little more than good, pleasant wines without much export future. Of interest to tourists is a quantity of undesignated red wine, some of it very good carafe wine, made in the outer environs of Rome, according to the various *trattoria* that serve it.

A newer vineyard around Aprilia, south of Rome, lies on land reclaimed by the draining of the Pontine Marshes in the nineteenth century. Three D.O.C. are Trebbiano, Merlot, and Sangiovese di Aprilia.

North of Rome is Montefiascone, whose white Est! Est! Est! wines have an enormous distribution despite the eccentric shape of the bottle, which seems to have been carefully designed to prevent the wine from being properly binned on its side, at least not in a three-dimensional universe. It is impossible to escape the story of Bishop Johann Fugger and Est! Est! Est! Traveling from Augsburg to Rome for the coronation of Emperor Henry V, he sent his servant ahead that he might chalk *est* ("is," i.e., "is good") on inns whose wines merited dismounting and staying the night. Arriving at Montefiascone, the Bishop found Est! Est! Est! chalked all over the door. Naturally he dismounted, continues the story, and stayed and stayed and stayed, unable to leave the wines. He died of a surfeit of them and willed all his property to Montefiascone.

No student of the Fugger family history could believe any of their lot could be such a clod as that! A different tale was scribbled by a monk on a piece of Italian mongoose parchment dated April 1, 1132, twenty-two years after the event. This relic, dropped or concealed in a stone vat of slivovitz, is all that survives the ruins of the once great Greek Orthodox monastery of Karvadici, Macedonia; petrified by plum brandy, it testifies to past wrongs.

Secret sources revealed that German enemies of the Fugger conspired with willing tools among the "hosts" of Montefiascone. They bribed the servant, so goes the account, to chalk his treacherous Est! Est! Est! on the inn door. Johann Fugger, hot, tired, and thirsty, stopped and tossed off a glass of the local wine. He fell down paralyzed on the spot and was quickly hid in the inn. On the third day he died. The agony and delirium produced by this sort of wine allowed the traitors to get his signature on the will, leaving them everything. This was the reward promised by the rascals back in Augsburg, who knew Johann had to pass Montefiascone on the way to Rome.

At this point the Karvadici monk narrator breaks angrily from Greek into Old Church Slavonic. "God punished the Montefiascone," he continues wrathfully. "He ordained that until the end of time the white wines of Montefiascone could never become any better than on the very afternoon in A.D. 1110 when poor Johann Fugger downed the fatal glass before the inn door."

The story accounts for the present state of affairs and therefore, according to some Marxist schools of history, must be true. The

Italian wine authority Luigi Veronelli is apparently unaware of all this, because he limits himself to politely remarking that he has never found Est! Est! Est! of quality or consistency to merit description.

Umbria

The hills of this small, central, very beautiful province produce the usual variety of country whites made from Trebbiano, reds from Sangiovese, and humbler wines too. Its vinous star is Orvieto, the name of a town, of a small classic region around it, and of the larger D.O.C., the wines of which are normally marketed in wickered *fiaschi* shaped differently from those of Chianti. There is disagreement about the grapes composing this refined, sometimes luscious white wine, but certainly Trebbiano dominates with about two-thirds. Verdello and Malvasia follow, and two minor varieties may be added in small proportion. Orvieto wines are aged two years in cask, the best, it is said, kept in the stone caves that riddle the hill on which the town sits. There are supposed to be two distinct styles, a dry and an *abbocato,* or semisweet; but all the wines I have tasted range over a sliding scale of dryness, some rather dry, others not really sweet, still others palpably sweet. Certainly the best Orvieto is a wine deliberately made to have weight and much aftertaste. Dried or, it is said, rotten grapes are added to the must as it completes fermentation, bringing ripe impression to the finished wine. Extremely dry versions of this wine seem less successful, though all Orvieto is meant to be table wine; character and appeal suffer. The lingering and mellow aftertaste of good Orvieto, even if it is given by adding rotted grapes, is more than acceptable and can be delicious.

Torgiano is a relatively new, small red wine D.O.C. mixing the same Sangiovese, Canaiolo, and white Trebbiano grapes used for Chianti. The Torgiano Rubesco of Lungarotti is seen in both Great Britain and the United States. It varies considerably by vintages, evoking Chianti in its first address to the senses, but with age tasting more plummy and thicker than mature Chianti, with more charm "up front." Color and body are sometimes too light, but older Torgiano can ship well, as the 1966 proved. There is a Torgiano white, but outside Italy no one seems to notice—or care.

Marches

The Marches borders the Adriatic from the Republic of San Marino south to Ascoli Piceno, partially isolated by the Apennine Mountains. Verdicchio, a grape and a wine famous since Roman times, comprises half of the province's large annual production. A small classic zone is defined for Verdicchio dei Castelli di Jesi, the best-known wine. Shipped abroad in ornate green vase-shaped bottles with tiny labels, this plain, clean white wine with a slightly bitter aftertaste sells very well. D.O.C. laws allow sparkling "Verdicchio," but this is seen less frequently. Verdicchio di Matelica, also a useful dry white, is Verdicchio with 20 percent Trebbiano and Malvasia. Production limits are generous, and the resulting wine is neither intense nor, in fairness, expensive.

Along the Metauro River from Urbino to the Adriatic, white wines are vinified from the Bianchello grape and called Bianchello del Metauro (a D.O.C.). This wine is meant to be drunk young, but it takes time to circulate through the channels of export trade, and Bianchello

appears to stand this quite well. Generous, a little clumsy on the palate, with a ripe impression usual to Italian whites, dry but not nasty, it offers distinct character. A curious sparkling red made by provoking secondary fermentation and using Vernaccia grapes is produced at Serrapetrona. But the abundant red wine of the Marches is Rosso Piceno, 60 percent Sangiovese, 40 percent Montepulciano—dry, light, and allowed to call itself *superiore* if a year old. In the other D.O.C. for light red wines, Montepulciano grapes dominate to make Rosso Conero.

Marches is the object of a development plan. Whether the aim is to raise further production and export of Verdicchio, or to improve conditions of viticulturists generally, is not clear.

Emilia-Romagna

This rich region, bordered on the north by the Po River basin, is exceptionally favored in its agriculture. Its capital, Bologna, is also the seat of Italian *grande cuisine.* Rich Bolognese cooking invites comparison with that of eastern France, but the analogy is not helpful for wine. Romagna's interesting local wines are hardly similar to the florid, powerful, varied, and exquisite ones of Burgundy.

As Philip Dallas points out, the Trebbia River gives Romagna claims to being the homeland of the Trebbiano grape, a staple in Italian viticulture. There is a D.O.C. Trebbiano di Romagna. In Romagna, the noble Sangiovese grape may use its name only when produced under D.O.C. limitations and controls, unlike other districts; a *consorzio* of Romagna wants this stricture extended to all Italy. A heavy white wine based on local Albana grapes and made dry or *amabile* has its D.O.C. around Ravenna and Bologna.

In Piacenza we first encounter the Barbera and Bonarda grapes widely cultivated to the north and mixed here to make the red Gutturnio dei Colli Picentini. Italians find Barbera agreeably dry, bright-colored, and attractive. To many outsiders bred on French wines, however, it seems hollow, charmless, and even mean.

The red wine of Lambrusco grapes is the great specialty of Romagna. Several are made depending on location and the Lambrusco varieties used; vinification varies. They are typically fizzy but should be so naturally (adding CO_2 gas is forbidden). The bubbliness comes from early bottling before fermentations have finished. Scented, fruity, sometimes sensationally aromatic, Lambrusco wines range from dry to sweeter than English-speaking drinkers, finding them cloying, are able to enjoy.

Grasparossa, Salamino, and Sorbara are the three principal varieties of Lambrusco and give their names to respective D.O.C. Modena, just south of Sorbara, is considered the homeland of the best Lambrusco. The wine is permitted to be sold as light as 10.5 percent alcohol, light indeed for Italian red wine.

Lambrusco has made enormous progress in export markets, particularly in America. Its modest price cannot be the only consideration; its success seems to point to a consumer's taste for fruity, light wines easy to quaff. Yet the wine is disparaged frequently by gastronomes and parts of the wine trade, as are the palates that enjoy it. This often makes the novice wine drinker feel awkward and is worth a comment.

From Attica to Dijon, two ways of accompanying heavy, rich, luxurious dishes have evolved. One is to match sumptuous food with sumptuous rich wine. The second way is to drink light beverage

Frascati Superiore Vigneti di Colle Fumone M. Magistri

Product of a small grower in the famous vineyard area south of Rome, this dry Frascati has more than 12 percent alcohol and may call itself *superiore*. Others from big firms such as Orfevi or the Cantina Produttore Frascati are easier to find. This dry but full-bodied type, the sweeter *amabile* sort and the sugary-sweet grade (Cannellino) are all made from two Malvasia varieties mixed with Greco and Trebbiano. Pale amber but bright in color, it has a fragrant aroma that suggests almonds to some fanciers of the wine. Strong vinous and woody impressions dominate fruit on the palate. The plush, round texture is characteristic of Frascati and is of course accentuated in the sweeter types.

VINTAGE   DATE   PRICE

GUESTS

MENU   COMMENTS

Orvieto Classico Castello della Sala Antinori

This *secco* rather than sweetish *(abbocato)* Orvieto is an excellent example of the richness, depth of flavor, and finesse of these white wines from the Umbrian hill town after which they are named. Antinori ships its wines in traditional squat, wickered bottles; its rival, Melini, has gone to standard white Bordeaux shapes. Trebbiano and Malvasia are mixed to make Orvieto, but the special mellow taste found even in *secco* is due to the addition of overripe grapes late in the fermentation. The best Orvieto are aged in cask in stone cellars under the town. Compare the excellent Antinori to the Orvieto of smaller growers such as Barberani & Cortoni or to Muzi-Felici's Le Velete estate wine.

VINTAGE   DATE   PRICE

GUESTS

MENU   COMMENTS

Verdicchio dei Castelli di Jesi Tombolini

This light-colored, useful white wine from the Adriatic side of Italy, in Ancona Province in the Marches region, is vinified from Verdicchio grapes. Permitted production per vineyard area is generous (twice as much as Barolo, for example); Verdicchio is light-bodied in consequence, albeit reasonably balanced. Its slightly bitter aftertaste may not please all palates. Verdicchio di Matelica is a neighboring, similar wine in which 20 percent Trebbiano and Malvasia can be mixed. These popular whites offer fragrance and dry clean taste very suitable for fish dishes of all sorts.

VINTAGE   DATE   PRICE

GUESTS

MENU   COMMENTS

Bianchello del Metauro Anzilotti Solazzi

Less famous than the white Verdicchio from the same Marches region of Adriatic Italy, the Bianchello grape cultivated along the Metauro River gives a plain white wine with an interesting aftertaste—nutty, metallic, and somewhat bitter. The color of this light wine is normally medium yellow; brownish wines mean oxidization and should not be accepted. The aroma is full, slightly coarse, and suggests stalk and wood as well as grape. Technically dry, its generous body creates a full impression on the palate. A thinner wine made from the same grapes is Bianchetto, or Bianchetto Pesarese, after the city of Pesaro.

VINTAGE   DATE   PRICE

GUESTS

MENU   COMMENTS

ESTATE BOTTLED

SELECTED BY
COUNT R PANDOLFINI

SELECRU ®

Vigneti di Colle Fumone

DRY WHITE | TABLE WINE

FRASCATI

DENOMINAZIONE DI ORIGINE CONTROLLATA

SUPERIORE

NET CONT 1 PT 8 FL OZ

ALCOHOL 13% BY VOL

PRODUCED BY AZ. AGRICOLA M. MAGISTRI · BOTTLED BY VINADES VIA S. MATTEO · VERMICINO (ROMA)

PRODUCT OF ITALY

IMPORTED BY

Wines, LTD. WASHINGTON D.C.

Castello della Sala

ORVIETO CLASSICO

DENOMINAZIONE DI ORIGINE CONTROLLATA

SECCO

1974

Fattorie dei
Marchesi L. e P. Antinori

Imbottigliato nella zona di origine alle Cantine Antinori
Ponte Giulio - Orvieto (199 TR)

Vino a gradi alcool 12   PRODUCE OF ITALY   Cont. netto litri 0,720

Tombolini
VERDICCHIO

DEI CASTELLI DI JESI CLASSICO

DENOMINAZIONE D'ORIGINE CONTROLLATA

CLASSICAL WHITE DRY WINE

PRODUCED BY CASA VINICOLA G.P.T. S.p.A. TOMBOLINI · LORETO · BOTTLED AND SHIPPED FROM ITALY

Net content 1 Pt. 8 fl. oz.
Al. By Vol. 12%
R.I. 368/An.

1972

DRY WHITE TABLE WINE

BIANCHELLO
DEL
METAURO

DENOMINAZIONE DI ORIGINE CONTROLLATA

AUGUSTUS

ESTATE BOTTLED
AZIENDA AGRICOLA

ANZILOTTI · SOLAZZI

FANO · PESARO

REG. IMB. 0107 PS

IMBOTTIGLIATO ALL'ORIGINE DAL PRODUTTORE NELLA
PROPRIA CANTINA IN LOCALITA' BONTA' DI SALTARA

NET CONT. 1 PINT 8 FLOZ   ALCOHOL BY VOL. 11,5%

Cont. netto lt. 0,720   PRODUCT OF ITALY   Gradi alcool 11,5

PRODUCER SELECTED BY   IMPORTED BY

® ITALCRU   The HOUSE of BURGUNDY
New York, N.Y.

wines frankly subordinated to the food and ease of digestion. For the middle-class townsman or well-off peasant who eats rich cuisine at midday every day of his life and goes on to an afternoon's work, the second way will be preferred, whether it takes the form of a tin cup of retsina with roast kid in the Piraeus or a foaming glass of Lambrusco knocked back with veal in cream sauce with white truffles in Bologna. Foreign visitors who take the trouble and expense to tour the homelands of great cuisine and great wines understandably want to enjoy the finest and richest in both food and wine. Indeed, why not? One does not dine every day in Lyon or Modena. But it is superfluous to make an issue of connoisseurship or taste about a habit of drinking beverage wines that have evolved to meet human needs, within a daily culture, a daily way of living, eating, and drinking. Lambrusco belongs to this family of wines. The same ease of drinking and digesting that recommends it to the gourmets (and gourmands) of Bologna may explain its rampant success among the not very sophisticated populations that consume it so generously in North America. But why denigrate that?

Tuscany

Tuscan wines divide themselves into Chianti and everything else. Official recognition of the place name Chianti to describe local wines retreats three centuries into the past, and surely wines have gushed from those hills since primitive agriculture settled on them. But the blend of as many as five grape varieties, red and white, that we drink as Chianti today is a result of deliberate experimentation a century and a quarter ago. The immediate success of these experiments imposed itself by example on the large viticultural region surrounding the queenly, once tempestuous city of Florence. Chianti's red wines are made with one of two disparate intentions, over and above the usual aim that one's own wine be better and more expensive than one's neighbor's and that he shall be made to understand that fact.

First, there are light red wines into which white varieties are mixed with a heavy hand, with the proportion of strong, stubborn red Sangiovese grape juice now reduced in favor of the more florid red Canaiolo. This juice is fermented rapidly. As the fermentation dies away, a concentrated juice made from drying and crushing the best grapes is added. The fermentation takes off, renewed, and is now allowed to continue until most sugar is converted to alcohol. Then the wine is bottled while some gas is still being released from both alcoholic and malolactic fermentations. The result is a fizzy wine. This is called the *governo* method. Whether or not we are solely indebted for this procedure to Baron Bettino Ricasoli, whose descendants still make Chianti at Brolio Castle, is a matter of dispute; but certainly to him is owed the now traditional Chianti combination of red Sangiovese with white Malvasia grapes. Today red Canaiolo is added to this original blend, and white Trebbiano joins Malvasia, with a bit of red Colorino too. Both *governo* and non-*governo* Chianti are put into the familiar wickered bottles (*fiaschi*), now so expensive they risk extinction. While *governo* wine can age, provided it encounters no problems from continuing activity in the bottle, it is intended to be drunk young.

Not so with classic Chianti, the still red wine exported in Bordeaux-shaped bottles usually tinted brown. The same grape varieties are used, but Sangiovese is emphasized. There is no messing about with second fermentations, and as for any respectable red wine, this

Chianti is aged in wood approximately two years. There is a tradition of connoisseurship in mature Chianti in which the amusing and informative mingle with the boring and pompous, the erudite with the ignorant, the generous with the self-interested—which, in a word, is quite like schools of connoisseurship in anything the world over. That it exists proves that people regard Chianti as a great wine.

The Ministry of Agriculture permits not one but several growers' associations (*consorzi*) to make wine called Chianti. There is a *classico* region between Florence and Siena whose producers argue that the soils of its unique and superior zone, based on clay and schist overlaid with limestone and flint debris and topped with sand, alone entitle it to use the designation Chianti. Modern viticultural ideas emphasize microclimate at the expense of soil, but these older regions still consider that soil contributes most to the elusive differences that distinguish great wines from good ones. In any event, the consumer abroad should recognize the Chianti *consorzio* seal, a black rooster appearing on the bottle neck. If the background of the black cock is red, the wine is *classico*. A silver background testifies to two years in wood (*vecchio*); and a gold, three (*riserva*).

At least eight other associations protect the different subregions of the Chianti district, the best known of which uses the cherub (*putto*) seal to designate Chianti from the Florentine Hills, a symbol also used by the *consorzio* of Rufina, north of Florence. Nearly as well known is

CENTRAL ITALY

PROVINCE
○ CITY
  ○ Town
  • VILLAGE
WINE

the hills of Siena *consorzio* south of the classic zone. As in all wine-growing areas, there are arguments for designating a superior zone, but highest quality Chianti seems rather to be a result of exceptionally favorable microclimate and unusual care given both vines and wines. The Italian authority Veronelli, for example, gives his highest rating to two wines, of which one, the Villa de Capezzana, is not inside the *classico* region. Wherever produced, the D.O.C. requirements for Chianti specify the same grapes and their proportions: Sangiovese, 50–80 percent; Canaiolo, 10–30 percent; Trebbiano and Malvasia, 10–30 percent; Colorino and others, not more than 5 percent.

Having tasted Chianti since childhood and drunk it generously thereafter—somewhere between one and two thousand bottles—this writer is aligned on the side of those who conclude that Chianti even at its best is not a refined wine in the same sense that exemplary Rhine, Bordeaux, Burgundy, Port, Tokay, and occasionally others can be said to be refined. The wines do mature in bottle and acquire bouquet and longer aftertaste in so doing. In time they become notably dry wines with much authority, body, and taste and with a strong impact. Therefore they particularly please those who seek such tasting qualities. This is said not to demean any pleasure that Chianti enthusiasts may take in their excellent wines but to reassure those who find old Chianti austere, lacking fruit and charm, that they are tasting the wines as they in fact are. Exceptions to this generality occur and are memorable. And of course the young wines have an attraction and savor that appeal to all wine drinkers, as their enormous popularity testifies.

Two Tuscan white wines with D.O.C. and modern vinification methods are locally called "virgin wines": Vernaccia di San Gimignamo from the antique many-towered town of that name and the Bianco Vergine of the Val di Chiana. Made from the same Vernaccia grape used for potent aperitif wine in Sardinia, white Vernaccia is exported to England. It has character and good attack to the senses, but sometimes the virginity of its aftertaste would need family pride to defend. The usual Trebbiano/Malvasia marriage gives the Val di Chiana wine. Both wines are fermented from juice pressed and run off without presence of the skins in the fermenting vat; hence the "white virgin" designation. Less astringency, body, and flavor typically result. White D.O.C. wines from Trebbiano and other grapes are sold under their names of origin, Pitigliano and Montecarlo. Red wines from Lucca, blended like Chianti, have their own D.O.C. (Rosso Delle Colline Lucchesi). The Vino Nobile de Montepulciano from the town of that name south of Siena is also a Chianti-style blend. The *nobile* is not just a boast but distinguishes wine of D.O.C. grade from plain Montepulciano red wine.

In the Siena periphery at Montalcino, a variety of Sangiovese locally called Brunello is used to produce one of Italy's rarest and most prized wines, Brunello di Montalcino, with its own D.O.C. Aged as long as five years in wood, it has the right to the designation Chianti but prefers the prestige of its own name, for which it commands the highest of prices and thanks to which it can barely be found in export markets. Two growers at least ship to England. At their best the wines have great bouquet and a mature flavor.

The island of Elba produces white and red D.O.C. wines of commercial importance in Italy, white from Trebbiano and red from Sangiovese vines, but these have not made important inroads into commerce abroad. Cyril Ray thinks well of the Elban Aleatico. Considering Tuscany as a whole, travelers should be reminded that vineyards spread over most of its hills, annually producing close to 80 million gallons (3 million hectoliters) of local wine (wine made without controls and sold in the area of production). A wealth of undesignated, often delightful wines are available to those willing to venture among the carafes of local restaurants.

Liguria

The Italian Riviera between Genoa and France is as unimportant a region for export wines as it is important for tourism. Three D.O.C. regions enjoy local esteem. Cinqueterre Bianco, a dry white wine based on Vernaccia grapes, finds its way in small amounts to America. Cinqueterre Sciacchetrà is its sweet sister, also a Vernaccia wine but now concentrated by the *passito* process, sometimes reaching aperitif strength. The local red is two-thirds Rossese grapes, and its D.O.C. is Rossese di Dolceacqua.

Piedmont

Approximately 35 D.O.C. regions, most of them red, make Piedmont the fine-wine leader of Italy. Extremes in Italian wine production meet here in sharp contrast. Giant firms produce vermouth and Spumante wines for mass markets the world over. Alongside them, small growers produce tiny amounts of expensive wine, aged for years in cask and bottle before it is even presented to the public.

In Piedmont vineyards, which vary from marshy moors to mountains, a few white wines are made. In south Piedmont are dry and semisweet Cortese varieties (Gavi Cortese). Near Turin, both a dry table wine and a strengthened *passito*-process dessert wine are made from Erbaluce; the sweet is called Caluso and must be aged before sale. But it is the Muscat grape, taking the form of sparkling wine, that is certainly the best-known and best-distributed Italian white wine in the world—Asti Spumante and Moscato d'Asti Spumante. Nineteenth-century experiments applied the champagne method to Italian Muscat grapes with uninspiring results and many technical problems caused by the Muscat's high sugar content. A little Champagne-method Muscat is still made, along with a great deal of Champagne method *mousseux* (sparkling) wine from Italian-grown Pinot and other grapes. But the bulk, or *charmat*, process has entrenched itself for making Asti Spumante. Ninety percent of Piedmont's impressive crop of Muscat goes into this type of wine, and there is a well-organized D.O.C. system to supervise and protect what is by now a very big wine business.

Bigness is no obstacle to quality in making *charmat*-process wines. The huge vermouth firms, whose home terrain is Turin, all market excellent Spumante under their familiar labels—Martini & Rossi, Cinzano, and Gancia. Only a few small producers surpass their quality.

Wines from Muscat grapes occupy an extreme position in the range of wine-tasting qualities, but it is one not easy to describe. When professional wine dealers speak of vulgarity in a wine, usually they are referring to sensations peculiar to the grape variety that overwhelm other qualities—vinous aspects of the bouquet, vinosity sensed in the mouth, progress of the wine to the senses, mature flavors, balance, and the like. The grape variety figures right up in front from first sniff to last aftertaste. Americans who have drunk wines from pungent Concord or Catawba grapes will easily recognize this syndrome.

Chianti Classico Vignamaggio Sanminiatelli

This is one of many examples of premium Chianti made by growers rather than large shipping firms. The style is pronounced, with a firm impression on the palate following a fragrant bouquet. While the label does not say, one suspects the presence of more Sangiovese grape than usual. Good balance finishes in an excellent aftertaste. Vignamaggio has the reputation of being one of the very best wines from the Firenze (northern) section of the *classico* region.

VINTAGE   DATE   PRICE

GUESTS

MENU   COMMENTS

Chianti Classico Ruffino Riserva Ducale

Ruffino are large exporters of commercial Chianti of good quality; Riserva Ducale is their premium wine. Fifteen years ago this was a richer, fuller red than it is today and boasted darker color. Now the quality is rather standard, and it is not difficult to find bottles of thinner and drier wine than most connoisseurs would want to praise. Widely and successfully distributed, it is a useful introduction to good-grade commercial Chianti but a slightly costly one.

VINTAGE   DATE   PRICE

GUESTS

MENU   COMMENTS

Chianti Classico Brolio Riserva Barone Ricasoli

Brolio is a famous name in Tuscany, for at this property over a century ago an ancestor of the present Ricasoli proprietors devised a version of the present blend of grapes—Sangiovese, Canaiolo, Trebbiano, Malvasia, and Colorino— that contributes to Chianti's distinctive character. Like all *riserva*-grade Chianti, Brolio's must age three years in wood. It is a full, strong wine with better, brighter ruby color than many of its neighbors and a more balanced aroma. It is justifiably expensive. Brolio and Ruffino ordinary-grade Chiantis are of more equal quality, and both are reliable.

VINTAGE   DATE   PRICE

GUESTS

MENU   COMMENTS

Chianti Frescobaldi Nipozzano

Like Melini, Ruffino, Brolio, Antinori, Bertolli, and several more, this reliable Florence firm ships quantities of good, sound Chianti with something of its own style. It is worth tasting Chiantis comparatively, not only to single out the wine preferred by one's own palate, but also to reinforce the overall qualities of the standard wines as preparation for appreciating the better ones.

VINTAGE   DATE   PRICE

GUESTS

MENU   COMMENTS

Chianti Classico
DENOMINAZIONE DI ORIGINE CONTROLLATA

VIGNAMAGGIO
DRY RED WINE

RISERVA MONA LISA

CANTINE DEI
CONTI SANMINIATELLI
GREVE (FIRENZE) ITALY

PRODUCT OF ITALY

Net. contents 24 fl. ozs. Alcohol 12,5% by volume
Vino imbottigliato nella zona di produzione alle cantine di Vignamaggio - Greve (Firenze)
Cont. Litri 0,720 **PRODOTTO IN ITALIA** Gradi Alcool 12,5

Sole USA Agent de Romeo Brands, Inc., Union, New Jersey
Basic Permit N. J. I-259

RUFFINO

NET CONTENTS 1 PINT 8 FL OZ   ALCOHOL BY VOL. 13%

RISERVA DUCALE
Chianti Classico
DENOMINAZIONE D'ORIGINE CONTROLLATA

Wine produced and bottled in Italy by **I. L. RUFFINO**
IN PONTASSIEVE (FIRENZE). 326/FI

ESTATE BOTTLED   APPELLATION OF ORIGIN
GAIOLE, CHIANTI

MARCA DEPOS. RIEN SANS PEINE

BROLIO RISERVA
CHIANTI CLASSICO
DENOMINAZIONE DI ORIGINE CONTROLLATA

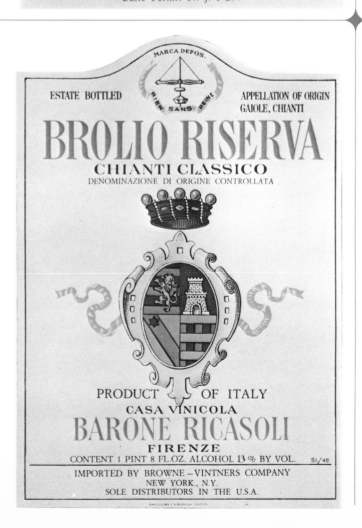

PRODUCT OF ITALY
CASA VINICOLA
BARONE RICASOLI
FIRENZE

CONTENT 1 PINT 8 FL.OZ. ALCOHOL 13% BY VOL. SI/46

IMPORTED BY BROWNE—VINTNERS COMPANY
NEW YORK., N.Y.
SOLE DISTRIBUTORS IN THE U.S.A.

FRESCOBALDI®
IMPORTED FROM ITALY

CASTELLO DI
NIPOZZANO
CHIANTI
DENOMINAZIONE DI ORIGINE CONTROLLATA
DRY RED WINE PRODUCED AND BOTTLED IN ITALY IN THE ORIGINAL ZONE BY
MARCHESI DE' FRESCOBALDI - FIRENZE

NET CONTENTS 1 PT 8 FL. OZS - ALCOHOL 13% BY VOLUME
SOLE DISTRIBUTORS FOR THE U.S.A.-THE JOS. GARNEAU CO.- NEW YORK, N.Y.

Brunello di Montalcino Costanti

The elite Brunello wines that spurn the Chianti *classico* designation to which they are entitled are commonly represented by Biondi-Santi; Costanti is an underdog, shipping to England. The grape varieties used are those of Chianti, and it is to Chianti enthusiasts that the wines will appeal. With fiery color and ripe aroma, Brunello's mature flavor, typical of barrel-aged Sangiovese-type wines, finishes in a dry, individual aftertaste. The wines command the price of classed Bordeaux châteaux.

VINTAGE   DATE   PRICE

GUESTS

MENU   COMMENTS

Torgiano Rubesco Lungarotti

Made from the same Sangiovese, Canaiolo, and Trebbiano grapes used in Chianti, the red wine of this new Umbria D.O.C. is exported to England and America. Better, aged vintages such as 1966 are quite rich in taste, medium dark in color, and boast generous bouquet evidencing wood aging. Dry but not astringent, the wines give a supple but intense impression on the palate that some tasters describe as having a hint of pitch or tar. In light vintages Torgiano can be thin, even dull. While less expensive than premium Chianti, they deserve comparison with them, accepting, however, that Torgiano has more fruit and less power. An interesting and attractive wine.

VINTAGE   DATE   PRICE

GUESTS

MENU   COMMENTS

Lambrusco Castel Ruboun

No one can mistake the distinctive taste and sensation of this beverage wine from the Bologna area. Gases trapped by early bottling before all fermentations are completed account for the fizzy, frothy sensation, which eases away soon after uncorking. Different designations of Lambrusco—Grasparossa, Salamino, Sorbara—arise from subvarieties of the Lambrusco vine planted at different locales, but these nuances matter less than the relative sweetness or dryness of the wine. High scent, a truly gushing sensation of fruit and freshness are accepted qualities of this popular wine. The dark red, clean Castel Ruboun is a delicious Lambrusco. Its immediate fruity charm is clean of the suspicious flavors that mar other Lambruschi. Most tasters prefer to drink these wines cool. If you do not like this wine, correctly priced between $2.00 and $3.00, you do not like Lambrusco.

VINTAGE   DATE   PRICE

GUESTS

MENU   COMMENTS

Barbera d'Asti Bersano

Distinctive Barbera wines emphasize flavors with more delicacy and less earthiness than are often found among the great wines of Piedmont, a family to which Barbera belongs as a cousin rather than an oldest son. Its astringency and clean impressions recommend it to Italians and lovers of Italian food in overseas markets, but good examples such as this one are not easy to come by. It is rarely if ever a wine offering lush fruity impressions; rather it is dominated by body, vigor, and nearly tart sensations and so differs dramatically from some California wines confusingly sold under the same name. While fanciful descriptions are usually to be avoided, the words *taut* or *wiry* convey something of good Barbera's characteristics. This particular wine, a 1971, is distributed in America at reasonable prices, approximately $3.00 retail. Barbera from Asti has the most prestige in Italy.

VINTAGE   DATE   PRICE

GUESTS

MENU   COMMENTS

PODERI
EMILIO COSTANTI
VITICULTORE

BRUNELLO
DI MONTALCINO

Vino a denominazione d'origine controllata
Imbottigliato alla produzione
CANTINA DEL COLLE AL MATRICHESE
MONTALCINO

cont. cl. 72   Reg. 425 SI   grad. alc. 13,5

LUNGAROTTI
ESTATE BOTTLED

RUBESCO®

VINO A DENOMINAZIONE D'ORIGINE CONTROLLATA
TORGIANO
RED TABLE WINE

Produced & Bottled by CANTINE LUNGAROTTI at TORGIANO (PERUGIA)
ALCOHOL 12% by vol.   Net Cont. 3/4 QUART
PRODUCT OF ITALY

TIPO E

ager trixinariae veteris (XIV sec.)

Castel Ruboun
MARCA   DEPOSITATA
Terre del vecchio Tresincro
Lambrusco
VINO AMABILE
~ mellowed in the quiet of the origin zone ~
~ messo in bottiglia nella cantina del castello ~
Luigi Cavalli

SG CL. 385   PRODUCT OF ITALY   Scandiano (Italy)

RED MELLOW TABLE WINE - PRODUCED AND BOTTLED BY: CAVALLI LUIGI - SCANDIANO - ITALY
NET CONTENTS: 13½ FL. OUNCES - ALCOHOL BY VOLUME: 9%
IMPORTED BY: PASTENE WINE & SPIRITS CO. INC. SOMERVILLE - MASS. 02143

CONTENTS
1 PINT 8 1/3 FLUID OUNCES

ALCOHOL BY
VOLUME 12.5%

BARBERA D'ASTI
DENOMINAZIONE DI ORIGINE CONTROLLATA
Da Vigneti di Terre attorno a Nizza
ZONA PREGIATA

PRODUCT
OF ITALY

PIEDMONT
RED WINE

ANTICO PODERE CONTI DELLA CREMOSINA
AMMINISTRAZIONE IN NIZZA MONFERRATO

Riserva numerata
bottiglia № 50080   (ASTI-ITALIA)

BERSANO
IMBOTTIGLIATO NELLA
ZONA DI PRODUZIONE

DEPOSITATA

Barolo Pio Cesare

The Boffa family at Alba buy their Nebbiolo grapes from favorite growers to make wines that follow strict traditional methods: musts stay vatted on skins two months; alcohol reaches 14 percent; the wine is cask-aged in small 70- to 80-year-old barrels for six to nine years without filtering but with careful barrel aging, using oxygen traps to prevent oxidization. The result is an aroma earthy, vegetal, and vinous; medium-dark colored Barolo tinged with amber and savoring of the grape and wood; chewy, with no faults of astringency; unctuous; and with a fine aftertaste. This rare but exemplary Barolo is a standard of comparison for all Nebbiolo wines.

VINTAGE   DATE   PRICE

GUESTS

MENU   COMMENTS

Spanna A. Vallana Cantina Campi Raudii

Spanna is the local northern Piedmont name for the same red Nebbiolo grape that gives us the more famous Barolo and a family of premium red wines. Typically dark in color, with a rich aroma to match, Spanna makes a strong impression in which unctuosity, alcoholic strength, and forceful aftertaste all mingle. Some amateurs prize Spanna aged many years in cask; others think that the resulting astringency and woody overtones detract from the fruit and charm of these fine red wines, which are increasingly seen overseas. Vallana is but one of many fine producers.

VINTAGE   DATE   PRICE

GUESTS

MENU   COMMENTS

Dolcetto di Fontanafredda

Dolcetto and Freisa, like Barbera, are the common red grapes of Piedmont, whereas Nebbiolo and Grignolino go to make the finest wines. Fontanafredda and its rival, Kiola, are the big shippers of this area. Dolcetto sounds sweet, and some slightly *amabile* wines are made; normally, however, it is a dry wine with medium color and a dry, slightly austere attack on the palate. Its qualities—taut, firm, a nearly bitter aftertaste—commend it to admirers of austere reds.

VINTAGE   DATE   PRICE

GUESTS

MENU   COMMENTS

Grignolino del Monferrato Castello di Gabiano

Another celebrated Piedmont red wine, from the delicate but troublesome Grignolino variety that grows best at Asti and Monferrato, it is aged less in wood than more potent Nebbiolo-based wines. The color should be clear, brilliant, medium in shade, tending to purple in hue. The aroma is typically racy and spicy and suggests grape skin and a special perfume. Not a mouth-filling, powerful wine but rather suggestive, a bit pungent, with varietal character, vigorous enough but stressing charm and aftertaste. Bruno, Biggio, and Cantina Govone are among the many Grignolino growers at Asti whose wines merit comparison with this Monferrato.

VINTAGE   DATE   PRICE

GUESTS

MENU   COMMENTS

PIO CESARE

MED. D'ORO · MED. D'ORO · MED. D'ARG.TO · MED. D'ARG.TO · MED. D'ORO

TORINO 1902 · ALBA 1903 · ASTI 1898 · TORINO · BRUXELLES 1910

Barolo

VINO A DENOMINAZIONE DI ORIGINE CONTROLLATA

PRODOTTO E IMBOTTIGLIATO DA

Pio Cesare

NELLA ZONA DI PRODUZIONE

ALBA
ITALIA

39 CN

CASA FONDATA NEL 1881

CONT. LITRI 0,720 - GR. 13,5

VINO SPANNA

ANTONIO VALLANA
E FIGLIO
PIEMONTE · MAGGIORA · ITALIA

CANTINA

CAMPI RAVDII

CATULI ARA

FONTANAFREDDA

VINO

DOLCETTO

DI FONTANAFREDDA

TENIMENTI DI BAROLO E DI FONTANAFREDDA
ALBA

CANTINE IN SERRALUNGA D'ALBA

CONTEN. NETTO LT. 0,72   136/CN   GRADI ALCOOL 12

VINO

GRIGNOLINO
DEL
MONFERRATO

PRODOTTO CON LE UVE DEI VIGNETI DI PROPRIETÀ
IN GABIANO ED IMBOTTIGLIATO NELLE CANTINE DEL

CASTELLO DI GABIANO

CATTANEO ADORNO GIUSTINIANI
GABIANO MONFERRATO
(ITALIA)

GRADI ALC. 12   IMB. AL 648   CONT. Lt. 0,720

MANZONI · TORINO

By these standards Spumante wines from Asti can be reproached as having a vulgar side or tendency.

Some palates will not tolerate Muscat and should not be forced to it. But it would be silly to dismiss these refreshing wines simply because they have that strong grape varietal smell and taste. Many are beautifully made wines that charm the senses and suit a variety of desserts and fruits as few other wines can. Comparison with Champagne is useless and only distracts from the qualities offered by Asti Spumante. The excellence of these wines consists in bringing to the drinker a frankly Muscat aroma and flavor but in a balanced form, supported by a remarkably clean, unobtrusive sparkling body, not too acid and not too flabby, with the finesse and aftertaste of a well-finished wine as well as the special savor of the Muscat grape. There is nothing quite like it.

Barbera is the predominant red grape of Piedmont, and one of its many offspring is usually found wherever a catholic assembly of Italian wines is marketed. For the English or American buyer who speaks no Latin language, it is desperately easy to muddle in mind some of the principal reds—Barbera, Barbaresco, Barolo, Bardolino, Barolino, Bonarda, and so on. Since the Barbera name and vine has been transplanted to California, Americans must read labels twice to be sure what they are drinking.

The range of Barberas is wide. In Piedmont it appears in young, even effervescent form. Both dry and *amabile* are made from it by small farmers and large cooperative wineries. For the D.O.C. Barbera these may be mixed with a maximum 25 percent of other grape musts, usually Dolcetto and Freisa. *Riserva*-class wines rest as long as four years in oak or chestnut barrels. There is a hierarchy of names: Barbera di Monferrato must be made at least 85 percent from the grape named and must reach 12 percent alcohol; Barbera d'Alba, considered better, gets one year in cask and one year of bottle age. Most esteemed is Barbera d'Asti, which has the same requirements. The zones overlap. The wines are enthusiastically described as deep garnet and brilliant and are supposed to age well. Those who do not fancy them find Barbera acid and dry to a fault.

There is less disagreement about Barolo, considered Italy's best D.O.C. and one of its most strict. Production is severely limited. Nebbiolo grapes alone may be used, and Barolo must stand a minimum two years of cask and one of bottle age before being sold. Up to five years of age are required for *riserva*-class wines. The red wines of this name are alcoholic, tannic, and dry, with a powerful attack on the palate in which the sensation of wood and vigor are palpable. Most connoisseurs praise Barolo as the grandest and most imposing red wine in Italy. The intense demand, both from Italy and abroad, permits the wines to afford attaining an elevated and consistent level of quality that a larger, less desired appellation could not do. Comparisons with Burgundy wines are misplaced; the style and flavor are not readily comparable, though they do have in common high alcoholic content. Wine buffs who enjoy these forceful, mature wines will best find points of comparison among the many competing growers who submit to the exigent D.O.C. standards of Barolo.

There is considerably more wine called Nebbiolo than Barolo, but even the better grades that have a town name suffixed to the grape designation are of less standing. Nebbiolo d'Alba commands a premium over the others. One year in cask is the minimum required; and less exposure to wood may account for the lighter, more yielding taste qualities of the resulting wines, as contrasted with dry, powerful, often amber-colored Barolo.

These three red wines of Piedmont are the only ones abundant enough to be commercially important and prominent, but there are considerably more of equal interest to the wine enthusiast. The Nebbiolo grape family includes Barbaresco, a fragrant version of wine, produced in small amounts east of Alba. There is also Gattinara, lighter in color than Barolo but with 90 percent Nebbiolo (called Spanna in North Piedmont). Both can be extremely rich and full both in color and flavor, with a slight impression of tar and a more luscious texture than wines that have stood through years of barrel age. From the hills of Novara comes Ghemme, 60–85 percent Nebbiolo. This popular grape family also includes Boca, Fara, and Sizzano appellations, all with different minimum Nebbiolo proportions and all nearly unknown outside Italy. Last of all, in the Aosta Valley two small D.O.C. use Nebbiolo to make some 26,000 gallons (1,000 hectoliters) each of red Carema and Donnaz D.O.C. These are subtle wines with less power and often less alcohol than those of central Piedmont. In its variety the Nebbiolo family offers its own world of connoisseurship, varying in style and in availability. Barolo is the archetype but not necessarily everyone's favorite.

The Grignolino is a sensitive grape, more difficult to cultivate than the Nebbiolo, and produces a red wine lighter in color and texture, quite dry but at its best perfumed, genteel, and interesting. Grignolino d'Asti is preferred, seconded by that of Monferrato Calese. Two other grapes are used to make abundant quantities of quality D.O.C. red wines. Freisa is grown in two superior grades at Asti and Chieri and throughout central Piedmont; it yields a relatively light red wine, sometimes wandering over the border separating dry from sweet. Dolcetto, the other widely cultivated grape, is not at all sweet as its name suggests but rather a dry, sometimes cutting red wine of lighter texture than Barolo or Barbaresco. Alba, Dogliani, and the Langhe Monrealesi are centers of Dolcetto production.

While Piedmont wines do not taste like those of Burgundy, the range offered is comparable. There are powerful wines of special character (Barolo, Barbaresco, Gattinara, Spanna); wine of middle weight and attack on the palate (Carema, Donnaz, Ghemme); and Dolcetto. Young Nebbiolo, Freisa, and different Barberas are lighter and are followed by the usual formidable array of local country wines, without D.O.C.

Vermouth may not be wine, but nearly three-quarters of anything that calls itself vermouth must be wine. Local Moscato wine has been priced out of the vermouth-base class by the demand for Asti Spumante. Therefore, the immense quantities required in vermouth production must be bought elsewhere, typically from southern Italy. This industrial demand has a powerful effect on the floor price of plain white Italian wine of adequate alcoholic degree.

Lombardy

Like Piedmont, Lombardy borders Italy's northern neighbors but has borrowed more French and German grape varieties than the homeland of Barolo and Asti Spumante. At one extreme of terrain is the Valtelline district, a strip of high-altitude vineyards running along the shore of Lake Como and centered in Sondrio. As with some Swiss vineyards, difficulties in cultivating nearly Alpine vineyards are offset by important advantages in the exposition of the ripening grapes. Of the seven or eight traditional wines from this corner of Italy, four are important enough to find their way abroad: Sassella (considered the

best), Grumello, Inferno, and Valgella. Nebbiolo is the principal grape used to produce these oak-aged, bright-colored, light red wines; not abundantly produced, they are much appreciated for their refinement, eagerly sought locally, and therefore difficult to find in overseas markets.

Between Brescia and Lake Iseo in central Lombardy are several small D.O.C. regions in which mixtures of French and Italian grapes, mainly Pinot, make white wines. Light, pleasant red wines (both are called Franciacorta) are made from Cabernet Franc, Barbera, and other varieties.

Oltrepò Pavese, a low-lying region south of the Po and Milan, is the big Lombard vineyard and the scene of active development. Cooperative wineries process quantities of table wines for domestic consumption, and a few D.O.C. link varietal names to Oltrepò Pavese. The basic dry red Oltrepò Pavese must be two-thirds Barbera, one-quarter Croattina, and the rest Uva Rara; the right to a specific grape variety designation requires 90 percent to be of the grape in question. The important varieties are Barbera, Bonarda, Cortese, Moscato, and Riesling. Pinot Gris and Noir make white wines. Bonarda and Barbera grapes are widely planted to make the lesser wines that fill the carafes of nearby Milan restaurants.

The Frecciarossa label of Dr. Giorgio Odero is well known in Italy and abroad and aggressively invites comparison with French wines. The dry white "Vigne Blanche" is made from Pinot Noir; a second white wine (Sillery), earthy to some tastes and original, mixes this grape with Riesling and Moscato; but it is the red wine, aged four years in cask, that is labeled "Grand Cru." In case anyone should miss the point, we are also told it is "Château-bottled vintage claret." Made from three Italian varieties, it is not like claret; rather it is an extremely

dark, brilliant wine, beautifully aged in wood, with a powerful odor. It is well worth hunting down and tasting.

Lombardy offers a big supply of varied wines, but the prosperous and populous region consumes the greater part of what it grows and looks to continue doing so.

Veneto–Lake Garda

The good wines of eastern Lombardy around Lake Garda join a family of vineyards collectively reviewed as Veneto wines. In Riviera del Garda, the D.O.C. for the west shore, Gropello, Sangiovese, Barbera, and Marsemino combine in dark rosé or light red wines. They are similar in appeal and style to the famous Bardolino from the opposite, east, shore. Under the designation Lugana, Trebbiano white, balanced and pleasant, is cultivated just to the south. A bit of Italian Tocai is grown alongside.

The Veneto proper is a very large region, 10 percent of which is D.O.C., but wines without controlled origin are better here than in southern Italy. Running up and behind the east shore of Lake Garda extensive vineyards annually pour out a vast amount of Bardolino— the light, bland, pinkish-red wine sold wherever Italian wines are available. Half of it must be from the Corvina grape, with Rondinella, Molinara, and Negrara, in that order, finishing the blend. Minimum alcohol level is a low 10.5 percent.

In its homeland Bardolino is often drunk cool, as are many such light red wines. Neither powerful nor profound, it offers a version of charm, but one that travels dangerously. Perhaps because of its fragility, most Bardolino shipped overseas appears to be temperature-stabilized. This guarantees that it will vary little if exposed to heat and cold, but most winemakers consider that such treatment diminishes the immediate appeal of delicate reds (and whites for that matter). Standardized commercial brands of Bardolino have shoved to the sidelines more interesting but less dependable ambassadors of this widely sold D.O.C., and it is more difficult to find truly representative Bardolino abroad than more powerful Italian reds from much smaller zones.

Valpolicella is the second important export wine of the Veneto. Its grapes are those of Bardolino, but soils differ, and the climate of its producing region, east of Lake Garda, is different too. Darker, more alcoholic (11–12 percent) wine results; it has more backbone. Enthusiasts prefer Valpolicella from the environs of Valpantena, whose name is often hyphenated onto that of the wine, but the classic zone is mapped out west of this town. Bardolino makes more wine and exports it more profusely, but Valpolicella is better by conventional red-wine standards; it is superior in color, aroma, vinosity, and aftertaste.

Recioto della Valpolicella is but one of various *recioto* wines. The name refers to the "ears," or tops, of grape bunches that receive more sunlight and are consequently riper than average. These are picked separately and dried, and their concentrated juice is added to the musts. The still fermenting wine is bottled to capture gas and sometimes unfermented sugar. The frothy red wine that results can be dryish or sweet; it varies in weight and intensity between *governo* Chianti and Lambrusco and rich Port. Lighter versions of *recioto* are reminiscent of Lambrusco (see page 191).

Soave is the most important still white wine in Italian export, with a D.O.C. around the town of Soave and 12 other communes in Verona. Its tasting qualities are agreeable and reliable. At best it is dry, clean, and fragrant, with a bland, attractive aftertaste. Permitted yields per vineyard area are generous, and so the wines rarely offer concentrated body or intense taste. A slightly bitter impression, not unpleasant in a dry wine, may linger on. Production is enormous, an estimated 13 million gallons (half a million hectoliters) annually. Seventy to 90 percent of Garganega grapes are blended with 10–30 percent Trebbiano di Soave (also called Nostrano). A small classic zone, defined since 1931, sets a minimum of 10.5 percent alcohol for its Soave; another degree of alcohol entitles the wine to be sold as Soave Superiore. Bolla and Secco-Bertani are the main exporters to English-speaking markets, as they are of other popular Veneto wines. Smaller growers offer less standardized but often more interesting wines.

Soave is a useful dry white that pleases most palates. One can rarely taste a definitive character, but the wines are uniformly pleasant and the best have fragrance and balance. There is a selected *recioto* version, stronger in alcohol and taste, made in still and sparkling form. Soave ranks with Chianti and Asti Spumante in export volume.

Among lesser Veneto wines are dry Mount Berici whites from Sauvignon and Pinot grapes and red from Merlot and native grapes. Farther south is a D.O.C. for the Euganean Hills, whose lesser white and red wines supply Padua and Venice.

This is the home also of Venegazzù, whose admirers include Philip Dallas, a resident Italian and wine expert. A red is made from Bordeaux varieties (Cabernet Franc, Sauvignon, and Merlot). White Venegazzù blends Pinot and Riesling; it is made both still and sparkling. Still without a D.O.C., its reputation among Italian connoisseurs, the red above all, is high. I have not found this wine abroad.

From Lake Garda through the Veneto east into the Piave River area, the Prosecco grape is cultivated for various wines, one of which has a D.O.C. around the towns Conegliano and Valdobbiadene. There are light *frizzante* versions, stronger dry sorts of Prosecco, and sweet dessert or even aperitif-strength wines. Red D.O.C. wines at Breganze using native Italian varieties are not, to my knowledge, shipped abroad.

One D.O.C. zone is so mysterious that even the indefatigable Philip Dallas cannot find it. This is the Bianco di Costoza, created by a decree published Saturday, June 5, 1971. Is this a Rumanian plot or the long arm of the CIA, or did the linotype operators and proofreaders of the official gazette that prints these decrees attend an unusually merry party the evening before? If Dallas cannot find Costoza, should the rest of us try?

Trentino–Alto Adige

The Trentino is an Italian-speaking district producing good and very good wines mainly for domestic consumption. Two-thirds are of D.O.C. grade. Alto Adige is a German-speaking district whose wines are generally so good that D.O.C. is practically irrelevant, and of these an incredibly high proportion, 90 percent, are exported. No other Italian region is so integrated into international wine commerce. Both areas are dominated by foreign vines.

Trentino is itself a D.O.C. for several grape varieties. The most important export is Merlot, but there is Cabernet, Pinot of both colors, Riesling, and Traminer, plus red native grapes—Lagrein and Marzemino. The Merlot is generous, with plenty of alcohol to carry it through the hazards of transoceanic shipping. German and Anglo-American markets both import it. The northern Italian Schiava red grape is extensively grown for non-D.O.C. wines, but there is a small controlled region called Casteller, near Trento. The usual version of Schiava is called Sorni and is sold as such in Italy. Between Trento and the Alto Adige is Teroldego Rotaliano, a D.O.C. making powerful, rather chewy red wines from Teroldego grapes. These are good but not particularly elegant wines whose growing area follows the Noce River. Sparkling wines are made from Pinot Blanc, and typically wherever a white D.O.C. exists, *mousseux* wines are allowed the same name when produced from the same grape varieties.

The viticultural standards of Alto Adige are unsurpassed in Italy. Its large production, based mainly on foreign vines, is eagerly sought by Germany, Austria, and Switzerland. England and America dabble in them. But it is easy to visualize a changed situation; production costs, tariff considerations, or some disaster could suddenly promote Alto Adige wines to a much larger place in international trade. Making their acquaintance is a matter of special interest, as self-interest is politely called. This region is disputed between Austria and Italy, but it is Germanic in language and culture, and Teutonic wine names predominate. Abundant amounts of various whites come from high-ground vineyards between Bolzano and Merano. Terlano (Terlaner to German speakers), a blend of Rhine and Italian (Wälsch) Rieslings, is dry and fresh but unexciting in its finish. Terlano "Pinot Bianco" (white Pinot) is more individual, but Rhine Riesling (Riesling Renano) comes out duller than in Germany or Alsace. French Sauvignon and Sylvaner both make clean but thin white wines in this locale.

Farther north the Schiava is preferred for the finer wines; two names stand out to overseas wine buffs. Select grapes grown north of Bolzano along tracts of the Isarco River may be used for Santa Maddalena, a D.O.C. There is a *classico superiore* grade called Magdalener

Klassischer by the German *vignerons* who produce it. Some British diehards will want to drink them older (they have a red color, you see), but the temptation to consume these red wines young when their fruit is delicious should be resisted only as a penance. Kettmeir is the exporter most frequently met abroad. The high-altitude area around Lake Caldaro is the site of another small classic zone making fine clean reds from Schiava grapes. Caldaro (Kalterer) are light-bodied but elegant and supple and not at all mean or thin as one might fear of Alpine wine. Lago di Caldaro, or Kalterersee, is a better D.O.C. than plain Caldaro, according to Cyril Ray, but it is hard enough to find any of these wines abroad. Local Lagrein and the familiar Alsatian Gewürztraminer grape are also used up here; the Lagrein, either pink or red, is nearly all guzzled up by neighboring Swiss.

In both Trentino and Alto Adige variety is matched by fine quality, and all the varieties are well worth testing. The export figures are no accident.

Friuli–Venezia–Giulia

Vineyards in this northeast corner of Italy run from the River Piave around the top of the Adriatic and down to Trieste. The province has shuttled back and forth between rival nations and was the scene of destructive warfare—and for its cellars, no less destructive occupation—during the two world wars. In defiance of geography, French rather than German or Austrian vines settled here. Its many small growers are either northern Italians or of Slavic origin. Three D.O.C. regions span a broad arc of viticulture in which grape variety classes wines. There is little to choose in quality between the Collio Goriziano inland of Trieste, the Grave del Friuli in the west, or the Colli Orientali del Friuli, as the "eastern hills" D.O.C. is called. A large number of important firms ship their wines from Udine, a central inland city.

Among local specialties, the most *récherché* (and saddest) is Picolit, a dessert wine made from a variety of the same name. Once considered a superb wine, and still revered by nostalgic Italians who either remember or simply believe in its past glories, the Picolit vine has been blasted by an irremediable deformation during its propagation phase. The result is a sort of *coulure*—the flowers will not pollinate properly and "set." Barren queens could be divorced, years ago at least; barren vines, if humbler, are harder to dismiss. A handful of growers struggle on either with old vines or hybrid experiments that they hope will fertilize successfully.

At another extreme, a coarse red, rather astringent Refosco wine is widely produced in Friuli. The small part that growers bother to bottle is exported from Udine. Another Udine specialty is white Verduzzo, normally semisweet but also in a dessert version called Ramandolo. Around Trieste, Italian Tocai is considered the best of whites. This is not a relative of the Hungarian Tokay but rather a yellow-to-amber dry wine with a cutting or bitter finish. Small Trieste producers are permitted to sell wines directly to the public for a fortnight each year, and these are eagerly consumed.

Nearly the same grape varieties are cultivated in all three D.O.C. areas and, except for the native white, Ribolla, are familiar. One should note that, mercifully, whites are usually drunk and bottled young here. Among important reds the Merlot makes thinner, lighter wines than this variety gives in Alto Adige, and the Cabernets are rather more generous, darker, and coarser wines than produced on higher ground in the Trentino-Adige area. The French white Sauvig-

non much in vogue among growers does result in a French style of white wine whose aroma and aftertaste are identifiably and agreeably characteristic of the grape. The following are cultivated in the three D.O.C. and usually sold under their varietal name—a helpful practice for the consumer.

WHITE

Collio blend (Ribolla, Malvasia, Tocai)	Pinot Bianco
Riesling Italico (Wälschriesling)	Pinot Grigio
Riesling Renano (Rhine Riesling)	Sauvignon
Tocai	Traminer
Malvasia	Ribolla
	Verduzzo (Ramandolo)

RED

Cabernet Sauvignon	
Merlot	Pinot Nero
Cabernet Franc	Gamay (being introduced)

Any reader who has patiently worked his or her way this far, to the end of this review of the more important wines and vines of the Italian districts, deserves, without question, to taste all of them as reward for his tenacity. But, like all moral judgments, this one is far easier to make than to carry out.

NORTHEAST ITALY

PROVINCE
○CITY
∘ Town
WINE

Bardolino Classico Superiore Masi

Bolla and Secco-Bertani are the Bardolino brands seen everywhere, and their rosé-colored red wines are bland and pleasant. But this firm shows what can be made of these pinkish-colored wines when something more than inoffensive light wine is expected. Fruit, attraction, and lovely aftertaste are all that should be expected of this D.O.C., and Masi delivers these well. Corvina Veronese, Rondinella, and Molinara are the principal Bardolino grapes. Fifteen percent non-Bardolino wine is tolerated, but this delightful fruity example does not evidence any of it. The aroma is faint but fresh and firm, with some spring fruit such as cherries in its charm. There are many such lesser-known wines from this Lake Garda D.O.C., but they have an uphill battle against the big two.

VINTAGE   *DATE*   *PRICE*

GUESTS

MENU   *COMMENTS*

Valpolicella Valpantena Secco-Bertani

Since it comes from one of the two major wine exporters of the Veneto region, it is no surprise to find this Valpolicella an absolutely reliable, balanced, rather plain red wine with general characteristics of the D.O.C. It is less fruity and attractive than more individual wines, more difficult to find, of smaller producers. Illustrating the light, agreeable, and drinkable style of Valpolicella and unmarked by strong aroma, the Bertani wine serves as a standard against which to rate other examples—that of Mirafiore, for instance, or Bolla. Valpantena's vineyards are preferred by Italians, but there is an official *classico* district as well.

VINTAGE   *DATE*   *PRICE*

GUESTS

MENU   *COMMENTS*

Soave Classico Bolla and Mirafiore

Soave is found wherever Italian wines are sold and must rank with Chianti as Italy's most popular wine export. Bolla is found everywhere as well. It is reliable, highly standardized wine against which nothing can be said except that it is dull and does not show what Soave can do in the way of fruit and appeal. Soave is light wine, just over 10 percent alcohol, made from Garganega grapes with some Trebbiano di Soave. A touch of bitterness in the aftertaste is acceptable. Mirafiore, another important Verona firm, is fighting for a place in the Verona wine market in America with its sound Soave, Valpolicella, and Bardolino. Compare these wines with lesser growers and shippers such as Masi and appreciate them, and all large volume shippers' wines, as representatives of major districts with a commercial job to do.

VINTAGE   *DATE*   *PRICE*

GUESTS

MENU   *COMMENTS*

Asti Spumante Martini & Rossi

Representative Asti Spumante, clean-flavored with a good balance of alcohol and fruit, it is meant to be dominated in smell and taste by the Muscat grape from which it is made. Martini's vermouth rivals, Cinzano and Gancia, also ship fine examples of this sparkling wine that goes so well with light desserts or stands on its own. If it seems expensive, especially in America, that is not vendor's greed but the tax man insisting that whatever sparkles shall pay more duty and excise. The best Spumante are from private growers, but if the correct, well-made type from Martini really displeases your palate, it is not small refinements in flavor or aftertaste that will convert you—Muscat is simply not for you!

VINTAGE   *DATE*   *PRICE*

GUESTS

MENU   *COMMENTS*

Nectar
angelorum
hominibus

MASI

LIGHT RED WINE

BARDOLINO

classico superiore

DENOMINAZIONE DI ORIGINE CONTROLLATA
PRODUCED AND BOTTLED IN ITALY BY
AGRICOLA MASI S.A.S.
S. AMBROGIO VALPOLICELLA
VERONA

DEPOSITATA   (5193-VR)

SOLE AGENTS FOR THE U.K.

R. Trestini Ltd.

CL. 72   LONDON   GR. 12

IMPORTED

PRODUCED AND
BOTTLED IN ITALY

NET. CONT. 1 PT. & 8 FL. OZS.
ALCO. 12% BY VOLUME

ITALIAN LIGHT   DRY RED WINE

SECCO-BERTANI ®

VALPOLICELLA VALPANTENA

DENOMINAZIONE DI ORIGINE CONTROLLATA

PRODOTTO, INVECCHIATO ED IMBOTTIGLIATO ALL' ORIGINE
DALLA CASA VINICOLA

Cav. Giov. Batt. Bertani

VERONA - ITALIA

SOLE U.S.A. DISTRIBUTOR: CARILLON IMPORTERS, LTD. - NEW YORK, N.Y. #0022

NET CONTENTS
PINT 8 FL. OZS.

ALCOHOL 12%
BY VOLUME

SOAVE

CLASSICO - DENOMINAZIONE DI ORIGINE CONTROLLATA

BOLLA

ITALIAN DRY WHITE WINE

PRODUCED AND BOTTLED IN THE CLASSIC ZONE OF
SOAVE - ITALY

BY

FRATELLI BOLLA - PRODUTTORI

VERONA - ITALY

SOLE DISTRIBUTORS FOR THE U.S.A. THE JOS. GARNEAU CO. - NEW YORK, N.Y.

MIRAFIORE ®

NET CONTENTS
1 PINT 8 FL. OZS.

ALCOHOL 12%
BY VOLUME

SOAVE

DENOMINAZIONE DI ORIGINE CONTROLLATA

Classico Superiore

BOTTLED IN ZONE OF PRODUCTION
BY A.V.F.F. S.n.c. Sona—VERONA

SOLE AGENTS: **PATERNO IMPORTS LTD** - CHICAGO - ILL.

PRODUCT OF ITALY

5060 VR

Asti Spumante

DENOMINAZIONE DI ORIGINE CONTROLLATA

MARTINI

PRINTED IN ITALY

PRODUCED FOR THE PROPRIETORS
BY MARTINI & ROSSI - TORINO
(STAB. PESSIONE - CHIERI)

IMPORTED THROUGH
Martini & Rossi Ltd.
LONDON
(REGD. USERS OF TRADE MARK MARTINI)

PRODOTTO ED IMBOTTIGLIATO IN ZONA DI PRODUZIONE

PRODUCT OF ITALY

Lit. D.M. Torino

Merlot Kettmeir

The Merlot grape variety has made a successful voyage from Bordeaux to northern Italy, and its unctuosity, flowery bouquet, and vinous but delicate qualities are captured in this wine from the prominent Trentino-Alto Adige exporter, Kettmeir. Merlots from smaller growers such as Foradori or the C.A.V.I.T. Cooperative at Ravina are worthy rivals. Merlot is but one of many varietal wines made to high wine standards in the far north. Cabernet, Pinot Noir, white Riesling, and Lago di Caldaro (a blend of red Schiava grapes) are all worth sampling. Growers are extremely competent; D.O.C. has little importance, for the producers' standards surpass official ones.

VINTAGE   DATE   PRICE

GUESTS

MENU   COMMENTS

Santa Maddalena (St. Magdalener) Morandell

The most northerly of premium red Italian wines, this version is shipped by an Austrian firm, showing the close international links of Alto Adige with neighboring countries. The best Schiava red grapes are selected for this elite D.O.C. Fresh, fruity, light in body but with enough alcohol to travel, it gives a remarkably charming sensation of freshly crushed fruit. Kettmeir's version is more easily found abroad, and there are several lesser growers. This most Italian, and some would say best, of a family of formidable Alto Adige wines is shipped with Italian and German labels.

VINTAGE   DATE   PRICE

GUESTS

MENU   COMMENTS

Collio Riesling Italico Eno Julia

Italian and foreign vines are skillfully cultivated throughout the top of the Adriatic to make varietal wines of fine character. This example and the Collio Tocai should be compared with like wines from other good producers such as Felluga, Formentini, and Codelli. In German-speaking countries and the Balkans the same grape is known as Wälschriesling. While it offers refreshing and appetizing tasting qualities, in slightly *frizzante* form when young, it does not show the finesse and strength of fine Rhine Riesling. Its merits are fruit, lightness, and ease of drinking.

VINTAGE   DATE   PRICE

GUESTS

MENU   COMMENTS

Collio Tocai Eno Julia

Not to be confused with Hungarian Tokay, this white wine is a specialty of northeast Italy and the preferred table wine of the fish-devouring Trieste population. There are other shippers, such as Pighin in Udine, but the Julia example illustrates the subtle bouquet with a hint of lemon, the rich body and lingering distinctive aftertaste of Italian Tocai. It is not a light wine; its strength of body compares more with whites of central Italy than with French and Teutonic varietals grown by the *vignerons* of Friuli—Venezia—Giulia.

VINTAGE   DATE   PRICE

GUESTS

MENU   COMMENTS

ESTATE BOTTLED
KETTMEIR

MERLOT
DELL'ALTO ADIGE

FINE RED ITALIAN WINE
PRODUCED IN ITALY FROM THE ESTATES OF
G. KETTMEIR, BOLZANO/CALDARO 95 BZ

ALC. 12,5 BY VOL. US. AGENTS BANFI PRODUCTS CORP. NEW YORK CONT. ¾ QT.

MORANDELL
Kaltern-Südtirol

ITALIEN ITALY ITALIA ITALIË

ST. MAGDALENER

Kontrollierte Ursprungsbezeichnung — D.O.C.
Vino a denominazione d'origine controllata
Abgefüllt im Produktionsgebiet

Wein netto Inhalt Lt. 0,72 Reg. imb. 229 BZ Vino 12° ALK

ALOIS MORANDELL & SOHN KALTERN/SÜDTIROL

COLLIO
Denominazione di origine controllata

LIGHT WHITE WINE
VINO

Riesling Italico

Imbottigliato dal produttore all'origine

PRODUCED AND BOTTLED IN ITALY BY

Eno Julia
b.r.l

REG. IMB. N° 8006/GO.

Capriva (Gorizia) Italia

ALCOOL GRADI 12 CONTENUTO NETTO LITRI 0,720

SOLE AGENTS FOR THE U.K. R. TRESTINI Ltd. - LONDON

COLLIO
Denominazione di origine controllata

LIGHT WHITE WINE
VINO

Tocai

Imbottigliato dal produttore all'origine

PRODUCED AND BOTTLED IN ITALY BY

Eno Julia
b.r.l

REG. IMB. N° 8006/GO.

Capriva (Gorizia) Italia

ALCOOL GRADI 12,5 CONTENUTO NETTO LITRI 0,720

SOLE AGENTS FOR THE U.K. R. TRESTINI Ltd. - LONDON

SPAIN

Like her neighbor Portugal, Spain's best-known wine is fortified and created by traditional relationships with England. Sherry, and its little-known cousin, Montilla, are aperitif wines and thus are not discussed in this book. Of the table-wine districts, the Rioja stands out. But in the last decade other Spanish wines have begun filtering into English-speaking markets. Rising prices elsewhere and Spanish export efforts may bring still more.

The so-called Statute of the Vine, of Wine and Spirits, dating from 1970, is complete and good, having had the opportunity to base itself on Common Market experiences. It distinguishes dry, semidry, semisweet, and sweet wines by sugar content per liter, sets minimal alcoholic degrees for wine, creates a class of "noble" or fine wines based upon grape varieties used, and defines fortified wines with an eye to natural qualities, all very sensibly. A National Institute of Denominations of Origin works through local administrations (*Consejos Reguladores*). Two dozen appellations range from about 500 acres of vines (200 hectares) to over 625,000 acres (250,000 hectares). More than half a billion gallons (20 million hectoliters) of ordinary wine, over 13 million gallons (half a million hectoliters) of better table wine, including *vinos nobles* and other wines of export quality, and over 50 million gallons (2 million hectoliters) of fortified wines are made annually.

Labels of Spanish wines normally indicate place of origin, which often is also an appellation, the company responsible for the wine (producer or shipper), often the vintage, and a few indications described below. Twenty years ago, labels were a joke, though not a very funny one. Things have improved radically; labels now usually mean what they say.

Catalonia and Aragón

If you do not want your book banned in Spain, you must remember to say that Catalonia is just another Spanish province. It happens to have its own history, its own language, its own music, its own sense of humor, and its own wines, but do not draw the silly conclusion that it is a different country.

Alella, a small appellation north of Barcelona, is best known for its white wines from the cooperative, Alella Marfil Blanco (sweetish) and Seco. Both can be pleasant. Local pride wistfully insists on comparing Alella to fine Rhine wines.

South of Barcelona, in the Panadés region, is the important firm of Miguel Torres, which exports good, plain, clean wines in large quantity. Spain's sparkling wines come mainly from Panadés. In 1960 a British lawsuit enjoined the use of "Champagne" for Spanish sparkling wines shipped to Britain.

Tarragona Province is a large producer of ordinary blending wines and trashy, cheap so-called Sangria concoctions, forcefully advertised in the United States. Even the very modest Common Market definitions forbid these the term "wine." Priorato, a strong, once famous red, comes from mountains west of the city of Tarragona. Cariñena, from Aragón, is another powerful dry red wine.

Valdepeñas

The south-center of Spain is occupied by a vast high plateau, La Mancha, an austere semiarid landscape that produces wheat, olives, and a staggering quantity of wine for consumption and distillation. The Valdepeñas district, with nearly 1.25 million acres (500,000 hectares) of vines, pours out some 200 million gallons (7.5 million hectoliters) of wine annually. The four appellations are Valdepeñas, Mancha, Mentrida, and Almansa y Manchuela.

Tintorera is the principal red grape, giving wines above average in degree and color. Cencibel and Monastrel are other native red grapes; white wines come from the native white Lairén. Enormous jars of cooked clay, some 10 feet high, replace wooden receptacles for fermenting and storage. While much demanded for consumption the year it is made, Valdepeñas can stand storage for five years. Its merits are good color and natural vinosity. When acidity is sufficient, they have export possibilities. But much of the wine is flabby, due to the burning summers of the Castilian plain. Whites occasionally find their way into Rioja blends. Little is now exported as Valdepeñas, but this vast supply of cheap wine forces lower prices on better wines. Valdepeñas could suddenly become important as production costs rise in other countries.

Spain abounds in wine curiosities. The most esteemed dry red wine in Spain, Vega Sicilia, made on the Duero River east of Salamanca, is hard to come by and expensive. A lighter red called Valbuena is produced in the same *bodega,* both partly from descendants of nineteenth-century Bordeaux grapes.

Rioja

This region in the Ebro River valley enjoys proper rainfall and long autumns propitious to the best-quality grapes. One of Europe's natural vineyards, it is by far the most important premium-wine-producing region in Spain (leaving aside the Jerez fortified-wine district). One stimulus came from contact with Bordeaux immigrants vainly fleeing phylloxera in the late 1800s. Wood aging, and the Bordeaux 225-liter barrel, became fixtures of Rioja wineries. Bordeaux grapes were introduced, but they bore miserably in Rioja soils.

By 1900 Rioja wine types took form. Today quality varies drastically with vintage years. White wines range widely in style. Some are rich, sweetish, overweight for their fruit, with a dark yellow or gold color. Others have "sap," as the French call it—a sensation of volume and

READING THE LABEL

COLOR

Blanco	White.
Rosado	Rosé.
Clarete	Red but light, can approach rosé.
Tinto	Red.
Negro	Black is used in spoken Spanish to emphasize much color and, by implication, strength. Along with *rojo* (red), *negro* may have pejorative connotations and suggest a harsh wine. Neither is a label term, however.

TYPE

Espumoso	Sparkling; *Champaña* (Champagne) is often used in spoken Spanish.
Abocado	Semisweet.
Dulce	Sweet.
Seco	Dry.
Aloque	A mixture of red and white grapes.
Vino de Mesa	Table wine, better than *común* or ordinary *corriente* wine.
Vino de Pasto	Lighter, by implication less good.
Vino de Lágrima	Rare; wine from unpressed grapes, usually sweet.
Vino de Agujas	Used in Galicia for wine bubbly due to gases released by secondary and/or malolactic fermentation in the bottle.
Cepa	Grape variety.

ORIGIN

Denominación de Origen	An appellation defined by law.
Embotellado de (or en) Origen	Safely means estate-bottled. Four nuances qualify origin:
Criado por	Grown by; literally, raised by.
Elaborado por	Made by; therefore probably a winery, not a grower.
Añejado por	Aged by; probably a shipper.
Embotellado por	Bottled by.
Vino de cosecha propria	Wine from someone's own crop or estate.
Viña	Means "vineyard," as does *viñeda*.

QUALITY Quality is implied in the terms above, but *Reserva* denotes the best aged wine. The number of years a wine has been aged in wood is indicated by a number with a degree sign, e.g., 4°, with or without the suffix *Año*, as in 3° *Año*.
Bodega is not only a wine shop; it also means a *chai* (winery) and wine company.

body—but are drier; and still others are pale, crisp, quite dry, with a slightly mineral finishing taste called "stony" by the fanciful. Omnipresent rosé wines vary in degree of sweetness or dryness. Not one but two reds coexist. The biggest, blackest *tinto* Riojas are too chewy and dark for everyone's taste. Hence a lighter *clarete* is vinified from the same grapes.

Commentators tirelessly repeat that *clarete* resembles Bordeaux and *tinto* Burgundy. As the French poet Villon wrote, "Yell 'Christmas' long enough and it will come." We now have *tinto* shipped as "Rioja-Burgundy." The comparison at best is inaccurate, at worst stupid or deceitful. It only encourages production of soupy, bland *tinto,* the producers of which occasionally fail to realize that there is a world sugar shortage. Powerful, nervy, astringent but long-lived *tinto* is Rioja's proper native character. *Clarete* is a compromise toward a blander wine; more compromises are not needed.

The Rioja *Consejo Regulador,* organized in 1925 and now armed with the comprehensive Statute of 1970, permits four grape varieties: the native Temparillo, Rhône Grenache (long naturalized here), and native Graciano and Mazuelo. For white wines, the native Viura and the Malvasia grape are used. Maximum yields per hectare are 6,000 kilos (13,200 pounds) of red and 9,000 kilos (19,800 pounds) of white grapes or approximately 1,300 gallons (50 hectoliters) of red and 1,850–2,000 gallons (70–75 hectoliters) of white wines per hectare. In better land, only 650 gallons (25 hectoliters) per hectare are achieved, a very small yield. The Rioja's total output, one million hectoliters (26.4 million gallons), is small considering the area under vine (45,000 hectares or 100,000 acres).

The law demarcates three regions. The best is Rioja Alta (Upper Rioja), where cooler temperatures result in more acid and refinement and less alcohol. Rioja Alavesa continues southeast, to Logroño; eastward into Navarra Province lies Rioja Baja. Appellation standards vary; red Alta is 10 percent alcohol, Alavesa 9 percent, but red Baja must pass 12.5 percent. White and rosé standards follow suit except for Rosé Alavesa (12.5 percent).

While there are hundreds of *bodegas* in Rioja, only those with capacities approaching a million bottles a year may export wine. Vinification resembles standard Bordeaux practice, but barrel age is longer, often four years. White wines are never vinified with their skins, and lower acidity results. Haro, Cenicero, Fuenmayor, and Logroño house the *bodegas* that supply fine wine to the Spanish-speaking world and increasingly to new markets; America takes half of Rioja's export, all of it bottled. Switzerland imports wine in bulk, followed by France, Sweden, Britain, and Germany.

Fine red Riojas stand, indeed require, age. Their coloring matter and backbone give them power to mature gracefully. Each wine is stamped with a firm's style; Rioja is a *bodega* product, not that of one vineyard. Blending, aging, and selecting are the skills that make a winery's reputation. Taste many brands and search out those whose style pleases your palate. Less delicate than the finest French wines, Riojas nevertheless offer distinctive savor, bouquet, and assertive character—and aftertaste when they mature.

Rioja Lopez de Heredia Viña Tondonia Viña Bosconia

This is a less inky Rioja than some traditional dark wines. Its powerful, spicy, and Burgundian aroma differs from that of more tannic and less sumptuous Rioja reds. Its tasting qualities, however, are more typical of the astringent finish and full flavor that so often combine in Spain's best district. It appears to have a small amount of unfermented sugar, giving a pleasantly sweet hint to its alcoholic body and vigorous development on the palate. Very old bottlings of Rioja by this firm, second to none in the region, can achieve remarkable finesse, albeit in a dry and rather firm style. A Bordeaux-style white wine and a lighter red are labeled simply Viña Tondonia.

VINTAGE   DATE   PRICE

GUESTS

MENU   COMMENTS

Cuné Rioja Clarete Compañía Vinícola del Norte de España

Clarete-type Rioja suggests wine light in color and body and facile in drinking qualities. Too often this is an excuse for shipping trash with no constitution and with dreadful flavor. This is a commendable if commercial example of how this inexpensive genre of wine should taste. Its color is medium red, the aroma is forthright, and the bouquet suggests the plain, astringent but agreeable taste that follows. It is simple in flavor without being vulgar, and it has the mouth-filling vigor and tannic effect on the tongue and palate associated with sound Spanish wines from Rioja and the still less expensive Valdepenas area. CVNE is one of the large wine *bodegas* and exporters, and this wine should sell, if efficiently distributed, for between $2.00 and $3.00 per bottle retail. It vaguely suggests some Bordeaux tasting qualities and recalls the Bordeaux influence in nineteenth-century Rioja wine making.

VINTAGE   DATE   PRICE

GUESTS

MENU   COMMENTS

Marqués de Murrieta

This firm, clean Rioja is increasingly distributed throughout the world and has become chief commercial rival to the longer established Marqués de Riscal. Both are plain but good wines outstripped in density of flavor and local style by the wines of many smaller houses. The Lopez Heredia label reproduced here must carry the flag for these other wines. Murrieta is a complete red wine without faults; it is dry, has a direct attack on the palate, and suggests rather than confirms the range of astringent but vigorous tasting qualities traditional to Spain's best red wine area.

VINTAGE   DATE   PRICE

GUESTS

MENU   COMMENTS

Brillante Bodegas Bilbainas

Exported Spanish white wines vary from the exceptionally well-made, full-bodied, and attractive white shipped by Torres to light, nearly German-style wines from Catalonia exported in hock bottles and include wines from the north of Spain, such as this one, with plain, dry, and agreeable tasting qualities. Many professionals would agree that white wines from the quality areas for red are often too much treated as are the reds—that is, aged too long, and their freshness suffers. There is no space for some of the rarer, more distinguished Spanish wines such as Vega Sicilia, but Spain ships a great variety of red wine worth sampling, the better going to America and much ordinary drinking wine going to England.

VINTAGE   DATE   PRICE

GUESTS

MENU   COMMENTS

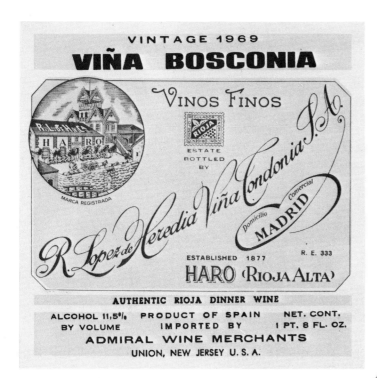

VINTAGE 1969
VIÑA BOSCONIA

Vinos Finos

ESTATE
BOTTLED
BY

R. López de Heredia Viña Condonia P.A.

Domicilio Comercial
MADRID

ESTABLISHED 1877
R. E. 333

HARO (RIOJA ALTA)

AUTHENTIC RIOJA DINNER WINE

ALCOHOL 11,5% PRODUCT OF SPAIN NET. CONT.
BY VOLUME IMPORTED BY 1 PT. 8 FL. OZ.

ADMIRAL WINE MERCHANTS

UNION, NEW JERSEY U.S.A.

U.S. REPRESENTATIVES
FREDERICK WILDMAN AND SONS
NEW YORK CITY

PRODUCE OF SPAIN
RED RIOJA TABLE WINE

CONTENTS 1 PT. 8 FL. OZS.
ALCOHOL 12 % BY VOLUME

CASA FUNDADA EN 1879

C.V.N.E.

Cune

RIOJA CLARETE

1972

Compañia Vinicola del Norte de España

EMBOTELLADO EN BODEGA **HARO, RIOJA**

1885-AMBERES-MEDALLA PLATA ·1894-AMBERES-GRAND PRIX -
1888-BARCELONA-MEDALLA ORO 1900-PARIS-GRAND PRIX -
1889-PARIS-MEDALLA ORO - 1930-BARCELONA GRAN PREMIO

BORDEAUX 1895 (Hors Concours) MEMBRE DU JURY

MARQUÉS DE MURRIETA

Vinos de Rioja

YGAY

(SPAIN)

MARCA REGISTRADA
VINTAGE 1961

LÓPEZ HILERAS 7 MADRID

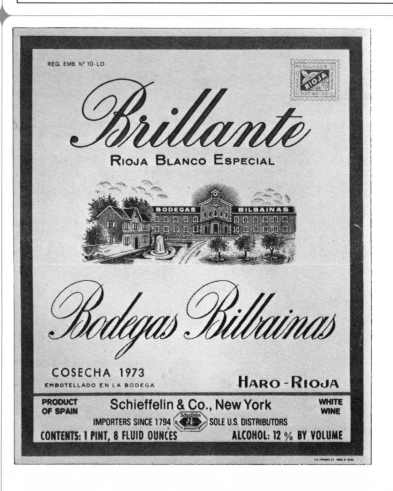

REG. EMB. N° 10-LO.

Brillante

RIOJA BLANCO ESPECIAL

BODEGAS BILBAINAS

Bodegas Bilbainas

COSECHA 1973
EMBOTELLADO EN LA BODEGA

HARO-RIOJA

PRODUCT
OF SPAIN

Schieffelin & Co., New York
IMPORTERS SINCE 1794 SOLE U.S. DISTRIBUTORS

WHITE
WINE

CONTENTS: 1 PINT, 8 FLUID OUNCES ALCOHOL: 12 % BY VOLUME

PORTUGAL

Port may be the best known of Portugal's vineyard products, and certainly it is a wine, and a world, unto itself. But Europe's fourth-largest wine producer offers many wares. Some are mere curiosities, some popular, some undeveloped; all are interesting and nearly all are unique in style. Not equaling the finest vineyards of France, impoverished Portugal nevertheless broods over some of the most remarkable and unrealized quality-grape regions in Europe and indeed the world. At one extreme she spews out a flood of cheap rosé wines, produced industrially, whose low cost and popular style are so advantageous to them that Portuguese rosé dominates our markets for this class of wine. At another extreme she nurses tiny, historic vineyards environing Lisbon whose minute outputs of nearly forgotten, once precious wines are clearly an endangered species. In the Dão region she has unquestioned potential for fine red wines, and the potential for quality Douro red table wine is just beginning to be tapped.

Laws guaranteeing authenticity of origin are fanatically enforced; if a red wine says Dão on the bottle, you may swear upon a stack of police chiefs that Dão is in the bottle. Vintage year has never been as much a subject of concern. But note that even in the Common Market countries, 85 percent of a vintage is the preferred level at which one has the right to put that year on the bottle, although in practice 75 percent is tolerated. A Portuguese wine marked *Colheita 1970* (vintage 1970) is mostly if not entirely 1970 wine. *Vindimia* is another term for vintage. The chart on the next page gives the important facts.

Lisbon Region

Wines of Carcavelos, a demarcated region on the coast northwest of Lisbon, are dark yellow and strong, with a special aroma. A famous district during the early 1800s, Carcavelos was ravaged by the oidium mold in mid-century. Its vines are being displaced by coastal resort development between Estoril and Lisbon, and the wine has become unobtainable.

Some 15 miles (25 kilometers) northeast of Lisbon, in the Trançao River Valley, is Bucelas, a demarcated wine area since 1911. The vineyard is commercially insignificant; only 285 acres (115 hectares) are planted. White Arinto grapes give a light, perfumed white wine with a surprising aftertaste. It is locally esteemed, but foreigners are unlikely to consider Bucelas refined. Sixty-five percent of the grape musts need to be Arinto for the wine to bear this label.

Colares red wines are produced in sand dunes on the coast of Estremadura Province, north of Lisbon. Demarcated since 1907, this curious dry red wine saw halcyon days in the period 1875 to 1900, when Europe's vineyards were throttled by phylloxera. Planting requires digging a trench 10 to 30 feet down through the sand to reach the clay subsoil into which the vine must be bedded (hence its immu-

nity to phylloxera). The native Ramisco grape is used exclusively. Protected from the sea wind by laboriously constructed fences or stone walls, the vines propagate by runner, over the dunes. A short initial vat fermentation is finished in wood receptacles; a further mandatory two years of wood-cask aging result in a light wine (11.5 percent alcohol), delicate and dry, yet usually quite tannic.

Setúbal, southeast of Lisbon, is demarcated for its Muscat, Moscatel de Setúbal. Both red and white grapes go into a must the fermentation of which is arrested by adding spirits when the natural alcoholic degree reaches between 15 and 20 percent. Maturation continues, followed by aging in wood. Dark yellow when young, the mature wines are quite brown. Effectively monopolized by one firm, J. M. da Fonseca, Moscatel de Setúbal comes in a two-year-old version and a Superior, 20 years old.

Two red wines, not of appellation standard, come also from Setúbal: Palmela is little seen, but Periquita is shipped in quantity, also by Fonseca. Firm, clean, slightly astringent, with a lot of coloring matter, it is pleasantly free of the dullness that often taints red wines from hot climates. Paradoxically, the grape used is now called by the brand name of the wine.

Just off the road from Lisbon north to Coimbra rise the striking walls of Obidos, crowned by a mountaintop castle that houses an elegant restaurant. There you will be proudly served the local red Gaeiras. That this agreeable, light, and nicely scented red has such a reputation is perhaps due to the dense, astringent, overpowering qualities of most other Portuguese red wines, compared to which the softness of Gaeiras is notable. Foreigners will enjoy rather than revere this wine, which is produced in small quantity. Lately a local white wine, produced from the Vital variety, has won greater fame and is now the most sought-after white in Lisbon.

Central Portugal

Lying between Coimbra and Aveiro to the north is the puzzling Bairrada district, whose inky, stalky reds and heavy, musty whites are beginning to be exported. Walking the vineyards and tasting the young wines, one cannot help wondering whether equally virile wines of higher quality could not be made if Bairrada red grapes were vinified differently and if a white grape stressing fruit were used. Bairrada white grapes are much in demand for sparkling wines.

The Dão area is the source of the best-matured wines and is the most exciting unfortified wine area of Portugal. Well-drained, well-exposed slopes of granite and schist soils, at good elevations 650 to 1,650 feet above sea level, are planted in old vines severely pruned. The best plots yield only 40 hectoliters per hectare (425 gallons per acre), equivalent to strict French red wine limits. And 35,000 acres

READING THE LABEL

COLOR

Branco	White.
Rosado	Rosé.
Clarete	Light red.
Tinto	Dark red.

TYPE

Espumante	Sparkling.
Adamador *or* **Dôce**	Sweet.
Seco	Dry.
Maduro	Matured white wine.
Verde	Young wine, e.g. *Vinho Verde*.
Velho	Matured red wine, e.g. *Dão Velho*.

ORIGIN   Wines from a *Região demarcada* (demarcated region) have a *Denominação de origem* (denomination of origin— i.e., an appellation). Rarely, unfortified wines will come from a *quinta* (estate), a right difficult to obtain from the Lisbon bureaucracy. Typically they come from an *adega*, best translated as "winery" rather than "cellar." The *adega* may be that of a *négociant-éleveur* (a firm both maturing and blending finished wine from new wine and shipping and distributing wine), or a government cooperative. If bottled at the place of production, the label may so state (*Engarrafado na origem*).

QUALITY   *Vinho de consumo* (consumption wine) is not bottled or labeled. *Vinho de mesa* (table wines) may have an appellation or place of origin. Wines from demarcated regions may be of *Riserva* (reserve) class—that is, aged, typically at least four years. *Garrafeira* is an extra boast that the wine comes from a cellar of bottle stock, the implication being a private cellar, and higher quality wine, but in fact it is commercial stock. This is no different from a California winery that labels certain wines "Private Reserve."

(14,000 hectares) of vines, nearly entirely red, are divided among 16 demarcated districts. Several larger groupings are sufficiently distinct from one another to justify appellations of their own in the future. Demarcated since 1908, the Dão farmers are supervised and assisted by the Federação dos Viticultores do Dão, administered from the government *adega* at Viseu. Government cooperatives ferment 40 percent of the grapes, brought there by the individual farmers. The rich red wines, high in body, glycerine, and aftertaste, are then sold largely to private *négociant-éleveurs*, who care for and mature them.

By 1971 nearly 400,000 gallons (15,000 hectoliters) were exported; export permits are granted only to wines of more than 13 percent alcohol. Grão Vasco is probably the best-known brand sold abroad, but there are scores of producers and numbers of important firms. The quality of the grapes brought to the vats is truly remarkable, though their subsequent treatment leaves much to be desired. Six varieties are urged on the farmers by the Federação. Old red wines from good vintages have depth of flavor, refinement, and balance that rival fine French wines; with proper vinification and maturation, the prospects for the future are unknown but exciting.

Very recently a substantial effort has been put into producing and marketing unfortified white and more red wines from the Douro. The large firms that own several major Port shippers are at the head of this movement. Initially the wines were too Port-like—too sweet and thick for export wines destined to be drunk at table. But the latest crops shipped to America show improvement and the means and determination to create Douro unfortified dry wines.

Vinho Verde

One-quarter of Portuguese light wine is produced in the rich region between the Minho and Douro rivers, in northwestern Portugal. Demarcated as the Vinho Verde, six regions are distinguished. From north to south they are Monçao, Lima, Braga, Peñafiel, Basto, and Amarante. Important red-grape varieties are Vinhao (grown widely), Borrocal, Espadeiro (Espadel), Azal Tinto, and Dourado. Azal Branco, Dourado, and Alvarinho are the major white grapes.

Granite soils combine with a climate that produces acidic wines. Once trained high on trees, the vines are now run up granite posts or onto wires suspended from steel supports. Terracing follows the de-

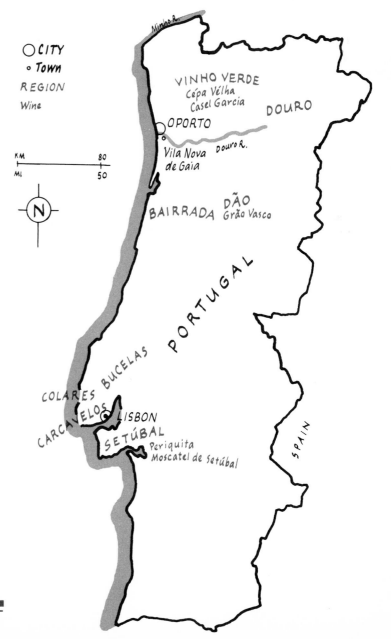

mands of the landscape. Three-quarters of the wines are red, but it is the whites that have been successful outside of Portugal.

Fermentations are cold and slow. These wines have a remarkable amount of malic acid that must be eliminated, but their peculiarity is that the second chemical process after alcoholic fermentation—the so-called malolactic fermentation—is timed to take place in bottle the year following the vintage. The carbon dioxide gas released by the process is captured in the bottle, and the wine is therefore fizzy. If you shipped Beaujolais in this condition it would be returned with howls of indignation, but Vinho Verde enthusiasts delight in the prickly, gaseous effect and the very high acidity of the wines. Red wines are vatted with their stalks, giving more acidity still; whites are made from the pulp only, without the skins. In Lima and Amarante red wine is made from pure Vinhao grapes; in Monçao, richer, more alcoholic white wines are produced from pure Alvarinho musts and are considered the best Vinho Verdes. Cépa Vélha is the best known of these. White Casal Garcia (Aveleda in Britain) is certainly the example from this district most widely known in English-speaking markets. It is shipped by the Sociedade Commercial dos Vinhos de Mesa de Portugal (SOGRAPE), which also owns Mateus.

Commercial Rosé

Nearly half of Portuguese wine exports are ordinary rosés, and the bulk of these are shipped by two large firms. Lancer's rosé is from J. M. da Fonseca, and Mateus is sold by the SOGRAPE group. Black grapes are used, fermentation is arrested artificially, extra sweetness is added, and carbon dioxide is pumped in under pressure to give a slight bubbly effect. Mateus leads with something over 10,500,000 gallons (roughly 400,000 hectoliters) exported per year. The wines have wide acceptance nearly entirely in the consuming sector that does not drink fine wines.

Port

Wine traders would agree that Port stands in the same rank as the great Bordeaux, Burgundy, and German wines. It originated in a special relationship with England cemented by a treaty signed in 1703 giving Portuguese wines preference in English imports. Britain was already locked in its long struggle with France, and French wines were the target of the accord. Enterprising British merchants coming to the valley of the Douro found the wines strong enough for their approval but too dry. They hit upon the solution of stopping fermentation with an addition of brandy; the result was wine that was stronger still in alcohol but sweet, to suit tastes of that time. Port is still made this way. Its intense color comes from long maceration of juice with the skins, traditionally mashed by treading, now done by machine. Many grape varieties are used. When about half the sugar has fermented to alcohol, the unfinished wine is run into barrels a quarter filled with spirits. This immediately kills the fermenting yeasts and arrests the processs. The raw, fiery young wine is then aged—the best of it in oak, the rest in chestnut.

Port is measured in "pipes" of 564 quarts (534 liters). Some 200,000 pipes of wine are produced in the strictly delimited Douro districts, but less than half of this amount gains the appellation Port. A compli-cated system of authorizations each year sorts out the wines produced on the steep rocky slopes and terraces, taking into account quantity produced, the situation of the vineyard and its type of soil, vine prunings, grape varieties, and other factors. A farmer may have four-fifths of his best plot's yield authorized as Port and only one-fifth or none of his least-good vineyard.

The new wines are sold to the Port shippers whose cellars, or lodges, are congregated in Vila Nova de Gaia, across the Douro from Oporto. In addition to restrictions at the point of production, rigorous blind tastings by government experts must be passed before wine may be sent out as Port; and to ensure minimum age, draconian laws oblige shippers to limit what they export in any year to a small portion of their total stock. From the consumer's point of view, six types of Port result from the selection and blending that are the functions of Port shippers.

White Port: Either sweet or dry, an aperitif wine that is not much esteemed outside Portugal.

Ruby Port: Red blends that are mixed painstakingly by each shipping house and aged at least two years with the aim of achieving a constant style and quality that can be recognized and depended upon.

Vintage Style, or Vintage Character, Port: Red blends that are aged longer than Ruby Port and selected to approach the greater aftertaste, intensity, and finish of Vintage Port rather than the simpler, lighter Ruby style.

Tawny Port: Matured in wood, frequently containing proportions of very old wines, Tawny Port varies from simple lighter wines to very fine, elegant, highly perfumed blends in the case of 20- to 40-year-old mixtures. Until recently, mixtures containing some old ports were sold, for example, as "Port of the Vintage 1943"—Tawny Port effectively, but lending themselves to being mistaken for Vintage Port.

Crusted Port and Late Bottled Vintage Port: Technically two different wines, these have the common aim of economically providing ready-to-drink Port of high quality. Crusted Port blends excellent wines from different years or from one year not quite good enough for declaration as Vintage. The name derives from the fact that it "crusts" or forms a deposit like that of Vintage Port. It is given an extra year's wood age to speed maturation, then bottled and sold to consumers. Late Bottled Port is wine of a single year declared to the authorities and aged between four and six years in wood. The authorities must approve it in its fourth year. At this time it is bottled, marketed, and ready, or nearly ready, to drink.

Vintage Port: Inimitable, superb, long-lived, slow-maturing wines made only when shipping firms deem the year outstanding and "declare" it a Vintage. Since 1960 only four years have been widely declared by the shippers. Dense, raw, of nearly choking intensity when young, Vintage Port matures beautifully after bottling, which takes place two years after harvest. Ten years is considered minimum age; most connoisseurs prefer Vintage Ports between 20 and 40 years old. The wines are scented, still intense, but harmonious with indescribable aftertaste. Long cellaring is imperative. Heavy sediments form a crust in the bottle; the wines *must* be decanted (see page 25). Mostly blends of different properties, a few Vintage Ports (and some Late Bottled) are from individual vineyards (*quintas*). Now shipped labeled, formerly found in blank bottles splashed at the foot with white paint to show which side should face up, Vintage Ports are always identified by the shipper and year branded on the superb long corks. Any Vintage Port from a major shipper is infallibly a great wine. The differences are in house styles and, of course, in the vintages.

TAYLOR'S

REGISTERED TRADE MARK

1970

VINTAGE PORT

BOTTLED IN OPORTO 1972
BY
TAYLOR, FLADGATE & YEATMAN
Vinhos S. A. R. L.
ESTABLISHED 1692

PRODUCE OF PORTUGAL

FONSECA'S

FINEST 1960

VINTAGE

PORT

BOTTLED IN
OPORTO IN 1963

BOTTLED BY
GUIMARAENS - VINHOS, S. A. R. L.
OPORTO

PRODUCE OF PORTUGAL

QUINTA DO
NOVAL
1963
VINTAGE PORT

This wine has been produced on the 150th anniversary
of the Shipper ANTÓNIO JOSÉ DA SILVA
VINHOS, S. A. R. L.
VILA NOVA DE GAIA — PORTUGAL
and bottled in 1965, 250 years after the first known
records of the Quinta do Noval - 1715

GRAHAMS
1970
VINTAGE
PORT

BOTTLED 1972

BOTTLED AND SHIPPED BY

OPORTO

REGISTERED BRAND

GRAHAM
OPORTO

PRODUCE OF PORTUGAL

PURVEYOR TO HIS MAJESTY   THE KING OF DENMARK'S HOUSEHOLD

WARRE'S

1966
VINTAGE
PORT

Warre Co
OPORTO

PRODUCE OF PORTUGAL

ESTABLISHED
1670

CROFT

1970

Porto Vintage Port

Bottled 1972

PRODUCE OF PORTUGAL

SHIPPED & BOTTLED BY CROFT & CA.LDA.

VILA NOVA DE GAIA

ALC. BY VOL
20 8/...   ESTABLISHED 1678   CONTENTS
4/5 QUART

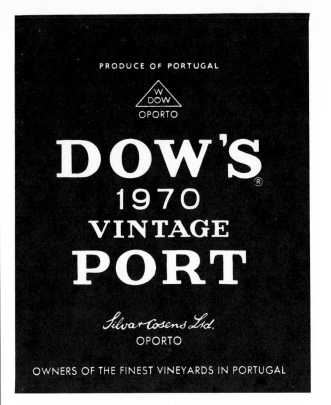

PRODUCE OF PORTUGAL

W DOW — OPORTO

DOW'S

1970

VINTAGE

PORT

Silva Cosens Ltd.

OPORTO

OWNERS OF THE FINEST VINEYARDS IN PORTUGAL

COCKBURN'S

REGISTERED TRADE MARK

1955

VINTAGE PORT

COCKBURN SMITHES & CO

25 ST. JAMES'S SQUARE, LONDON S.W.1

ALCOHOL 20% BY VOL.   CONTENTS 25/32 QUART

SHIPPED BY COCKBURN SMITHES & CIA LDA OPORTO

PRODUCE OF PORTUGAL

SOLE DISTRIBUTORS FOR THE UNITED STATES OF AMERICA

MUNSON SHAW CO   NEW YORK   NEW YORK

Lagosta Vinho Verde Real Companhia Vinicola do Norte de Portugal

Packaged in a squat juglike bottle with metal and plastic caps to retain the slight gas pressure, this dry, clean, and moderately piquant version of Vinho Verde comes from one of Portugal's large exporters. It is not as tart or bitter as local wines found on the spot but shows some basic features of this type of wine, which is unusual in that it is deliberately bottled with a second, malolactic fermentation still active to give a particular taste and bubbles of carbon dioxide gas. Imagine a wine more pungent still, with more fruit and freshness, and you will be approaching the authentic style of these white wines. Reds made in the same way are extremely flat and taste harsh, with a powerful bitter impression.

VINTAGE   *DATE*   *PRICE*

GUESTS

MENU   *COMMENTS*

Periquita J.M. da Fonseca

This lively red wine from a district south of Lisbon is made entirely from a native Portuguese grape bearing the same name as the wine. Honest and lively on the palate, it is astringent but has much flavor. Unlike many inexpensive wines shipped in quantity from hot climates, it is neither dull nor flabby, nor has it been subjected to brutal stabilizing treatment in its production. A satisfying inexpensive red wine with distinct character, ideal for frequent informal drinking.

VINTAGE   *DATE*   *PRICE*

GUESTS

MENU   *COMMENTS*

Dão Porta Dos Cavaleiros

Grao Vasco is the branded Dão red widely seen in England and America, but this red wine from a medium-size firm located between the Dão and Bairrada districts better represents the emphatic, astringent, and generous tasting qualities of Portugal's main quality red table wine. Compare it with similarly full-bodied dark-colored reds from Rioja in Spain, and, not altogether different, some of the rougher California red wines sold young. It is drier than red Douro table wine. Caves São João ship a variety of table wines strong in taste and with considerable body. These include white Dão, whose lack of fruit will not endear it to English-speaking drinkers but whose full alcoholic style is favored in Portugal's domestic market, quite astringent red wines and tangy whites from Bairrada, and the usual collection of sparkling white wines.

VINTAGE   *DATE*   *PRICE*

GUESTS

MENU   *COMMENTS*

Mateus

This is the grandfather of the flock of sheep that followed upon the dubious byways of its success. These generally dull-tasting branded Portuguese pink wines in squat-shaped bottles are arranged with enough sugar to appeal to a very general taste, if not one for wine. The initial success of Mateus was based on excellent marketing, handsome packaging, and an intelligent approach to finding popular taste that may be compared with the efforts of firms such as Gallo in California. That much deserves credit. The vicious side of Mateus, as of all branded wines sold hard, it that it becomes a facile if expensive substitute for better wines. Wholesalers and retailers become dependent on such brands and give them the attention more authentic items badly need. When you see this and similar wines, remember that something better could be in their place.

VINTAGE   *DATE*   *PRICE*

GUESTS

MENU   *COMMENTS*

REAL COMPANHIA VINICOLA
DO NORTE DE PORTUGAL
VILA NOVA DE GAIA

BRANCO — WHITE

Lagosta

VINHO VERDE

(REGIÃO DEMARCADA)
ENGARRAFADO EM V.N DE GAIA
EM 1971
PRODUCE OF PORTUGAL

PERIQUITA

MARCA — REGISTADA

J. M. da Fonseca, Succs.

AZEITÃO-SETUBAL   FUNDADA EM 1834   PORTUGAL

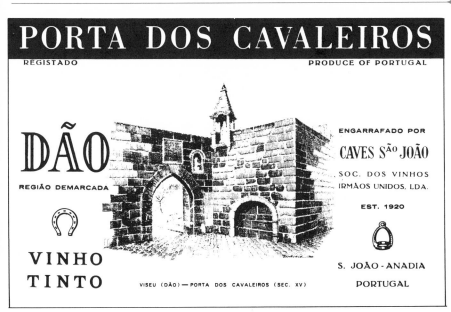

PORTA DOS CAVALEIROS

REGISTADO — PRODUCE OF PORTUGAL

DÃO

REGIÃO DEMARCADA

ENGARRAFADO POR

CAVES SÃO JOÃO

SOC. DOS VINHOS
IRMÃOS UNIDOS, LDA.

EST. 1920

VINHO
TINTO

VISEU (DÃO) — PORTA DOS CAVALEIROS (SEC. XV)

S. JOÃO - ANADIA

PORTUGAL

MATEUS

PRODUCE OF PORTUGAL

ROSÉ
STILL WINE

YUGOSLAVIA

Two alphabets, 12 ethnic groups, four languages (all censored), five recognized religions, and six republics coexist in this Balkan state. So do a score of white and nearly as many red wines, scattered throughout more than 600,000 acres (250,000 hectares) of vineyard. Along the Austrian and Italian borders light wines arise from European varieties. Along the Adriatic coast native vines make white and red wines heavier in alcohol, more concentrated, and sweeter than English-speaking consumers normally drink with meals. State organizations and their local cooperatives are responsible for the somewhat anonymous presentation of exported wines. Viticulture remains in the hands of small proprietors officially limited to 10 hectares each.

Labels usually indicate grape variety, place of origin, vintage, and the following terms.

READING THE LABEL

COLOR		SWEETNESS	
Bijelo	White.	**Deserto vino**	Dessert wine.
Crno	Red.	**Slatko**	Sweet.
Ruzica	Rosé.	**Polsuho**	Semidry.
		Suho	Dry.

TYPE		ORIGIN	
Pirodno	Natural.	**Poizvedeno**	Provenance of —
Stolno vino	Table wine.		followed by place
Biser	Sparkling. Yugoslavia		and/or cooper-
	rejects the Common		ative name.
	Market's definition of		
	sparkling wine. *Biser*		
	means only that the		
	wine is bubbly.		

Only a few wines have legally delimited production zones. European white vines include Sauvignon, Semillon, Pinot Blanc, Chardonnay, Rhine Riesling and Wälschriesling, Traminer, Müller-Thurgau, Pinot Gris (the Italian "Tokay"), Grüner, and Muscat Ottonel. Plavac Beli (white) and Zuli (yellow) are native vines with local variations. Cabernet Franc, Cabernet Sauvignon, Merlot, Pinot Noir, Gamay, Barbera, Refosco, red Portugieser and "Blue" Portugieser European vines join native black (Mali) Plavac, Balkan Kadarka, the strong-tasting Prokupac, and the blander Plovdina.

In western Slovenia, near Italy, a "Tokay" is made from Pinot Gris. Bland pale Merlot and Cabernet are exported to America, neither much resembling their Bordeaux namesakes. Austrian vines produce other reds. Cvicek, a light red, is consumed at home. Northeast Slovenia contains Yugoslavia's best-known wines. Lutomer Riesling, foremost among them, is often seen in Britain. Clean, dull, correct, occasionally lively with Riesling taste, its popularity arises from reliable minimal quality, novelty, and cheap price. The Lutomer/Ormoz district includes the celebrated "Jerusalem" vineyards, named for passing Crusaders. Rhine Riesling dulled by hot weather, sweet Traminers, white Pinot, and Sauvignon are shipped from here, as is Sipon, a fragrant white based on Furmint grapes. Mediocre sparkling wines are made from Gorna Radgona on the Hungarian border.

Cabernet Sauvignon, Merlot, and Gamay are made around Porec, on the Istrian Peninsula, for home consumption and export. Merlot and Cabernet are pleasant light reds here and little more. The by now well-traveled Adriatic (Dalmatian) coast has introduced foreigners to native wines—Opol rosé, sweet rich Prosek from desiccated grapes, Plavac reds, and heavy wines from the islands north of Dubrovnik, Vugava, Grk, Posip, and Marastina. Postup and Dingac are rich reds from the coast that, like Posip, a white, have legal delimited production regions. Overpowering by Western European standards, these all suit the ingredients and cooking of their homeland.

From the western sea-facing slopes native white Zilavka, not exported, is esteemed at home. Like red Blatina, tasting it requires a pilgrimage to Mostar, a Moslem city.

Slovenia, formerly Croatia, battleground for Balkan dominance and seat of Serb-Croat feuding, offers Welschriesling and Traminer from Zagreb and red Portugieser, none exciting in quality. God himself, says the Slavonian story, addressed a Croat mountain peasant, offering him fulfillment of one wish. "But remember," He said, "whatever I do for you, twice will that be done for Oleg the Slav who keeps sheep near you at Kutjevo." The Croat thought long and darkly and muttered, "O God, take out one of my eyes!" One hopes that new Chardonnay plantings north of Kutjevo will be less ungrateful.

The Fruska Gora district fronting Romania and Hungary has been planted in Wälschriesling, Semillon, Sauvignon, Pinot, and Sylvaner, replacing a celebrated red wine vineyard at Carlowitz (Sremski Kalovic). Farther north a sand desert has been put to vine in a land-reclamation project using Veltliner, Muscat Ottonel, and Kadarka, as has the sandy Banat Plain bordering Romania where mediocre Rieslings are made.

Half of Yugoslavia's vineyards are in the south, French varieties and Wälschriesling around Kosovo, native varieties elsewhere. Serbian white Smedervka makes Zupa, red Prokupac makes Krajina red, rosé, and the Vlasotinci rosé as well as heavy red wines in Macedonia. These are sometimes blended with milder Plovdina. Wild Montenegro has rough red Vranac and Kratosiza; few if any are exported. Throughout the south attempts to tame red Prokupac with Gamay or other European varieties are under way; all appear destined for Eastern markets.

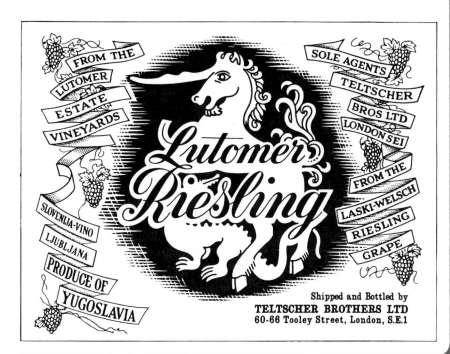

Lutomer Riesling

In the excruciatingly price-conscious British market for inexpensive wines, cheap whites from Yugoslavia have found a spacious home, aided by the familiar name Riesling. This is not noble Rhine Riesling, of course, but at £1 a bottle no one cares. Clean-tasting in the main, bland, neither tart nor sweet, as much manufactured as vinified, Lutomer Rieslings have become a supermarket staple and offer common qualities but acceptable ones for the price. They successfully compete with cheap wines from South America and Italy and, if often less interesting, are less eccentric and more reliable in tasting qualities. More than half the retail price is taken up in taxes and import costs, leaving little money disposable for wine, but as everywhere, the logical conclusion (to spend twice as much for something five times as good) is not drawn by the general public.

VINTAGE   *DATE*   *PRICE*

GUESTS

MENU   *COMMENTS*

Cabernet Istria Adriatica

As in southern-central Europe and into northern Italy, the modern tendency to present wines under varietal labeling has spread to Yugoslavia and in itself is desirable. This medium-colored inexpensive Cabernet is typical of correct red wines with vinous bouquet, good balance of acidity and fruit, and clean if not distinguished tasting qualities. It might not be immediately recognizable as Yugoslav, and its Cabernet character is faint rather than pronounced, but it is well made and agreeable at a low price (about $2.50). It could be sensibly compared to California or South American wines in its price range and is made for immediate drinking.

VINTAGE   *DATE*   *PRICE*

GUESTS

MENU   *COMMENTS*

GREECE

From 420,000 acres (170,000 hectares) of vines, Greece exports a small quantity of wine little esteemed in world trade, and that thanks to the energy of a few large export firms. Resin is put into half the wines produced in Greece. Resinated wines, called *Retsina,* are as old as the oldest amphora used for storing wines, which is to say, as old as classical antiquity. Retsina varies in style and in quality. Both white and rosé wines are so treated, but even the fondest supporters of this drink would be hard pressed to maintain that much remains of local character or varietal grape style after a wine is resinated. Attica, the long peninsula ornamented at its southern end by Athens, is the home of Retsina, made from the white Savatiano grape and others. But resinated wines are found throughout Greece and the islands.

Despite loud sniggers from the Western European fine wine trade, there *are* criteria of quality in judging Retsina. The wine should have a refreshing taste that is clean from start to finish (accepting the resin flavor as part of the wine's style). Neither the vinosity or, above all, the fruit of the wine should be drowned in resin, which is to say that a balance must be struck between the natural qualities of the wine and those of the additive. The wine itself must be properly fermented out to dry, to avoid a sweet taste. Wines of high alcoholic strength are frowned upon by Retsina lovers; 13 percent is the limit, and lighter wines are preferred.

The purpose of resinating wine is disputed. Sandarac resin is used. Most often one reads the claim that resin preserves wine. Others insist that the purpose was to give resin flavor to the wine, plain and simple. These partisans argue that resinated wines do not age and hence would not have been the object of an effort to preserve them. The last statement is wrong. Retsina does age. It just does not age nicely. Ten-year-old wine gives an unpleasant palatal impression of resin on one side and of a rather stale if technically mature peculiar white wine on the other. The virtues of freshness that recommend the wine to be drunk with pungent, often oily Greek food are lost, and the harmony between the wine and its resin flavor goes to pieces.

The freshest, lightest, and most innocent Retsina is found locally in Greece. The best guide to buying the wine abroad is the firm exporting it. Metaxas (mainly supplying the British market) ships the most refined, Cambas is usually the most resinated, and Achaia-Clauss falls between the two. Different palates prefer different versions.

The island of Samos, a Turkish possession until just before World War I, is the legendary source of sweet Muscat wines bearing its name and one of the few appellations seriously protected by Greek law. Other regional wines may include up to a third of wine from elsewhere, but no alien wine may be brought into Samos. Also much exported, and as famous, is sweet white Mavrodaphne. This is not a place name but rather a fanciful name for a wine type, made now in northern Peloponnesus and the nearby island, Cephalonia. Monemvasia is the grape used, which to confuse matters further is not properly a grape name but a place from which sweet wines were traditionally exported; the wines were grown at Naxos and other islands in the Cyclades. The grape is believed to be the progenitor of Malmsey (known to English speakers) and similar traditional sweet wine grapes in Europe—Malvagia (Spain), Malvoisie (France), and Malvasia (Italy). Sweet wine, also of Muscat type, called Malvasia comes from Rhodes. Dry white Lindos wines are also found there.

Macedonia produces mostly red wines, strong in color and texture. Naoussa vinified from a native grape called Popolka is the best known. Central Greece has little interest for foreigners. Thessalia produces Ambelakia, and Ipiros makes Ropa at Corfu and Ipiros Zitsa, which reportedly find their way into German markets.

Next to the Peloponnesus, Attica makes the most wine, notably white Retsina; a dry light red shipped to the United States by Cambas called Pendeli; and, in the north, sweet Mavroudi, a rather sticky red wine with little appeal to our markets.

Peloponnesian wines constitute a quarter of all Greek wines and span a variety of types. Very dry, very strong "black" (Mavro) wine takes the name of its township, Nemea. Patras, in the far north, boasts a large production of Mavrodaphne, called Aghiorghitico, that Greeks both esteem and can pronounce, as well as white Phileri and a boring white called Santa Helena. Sweet Muscat wines are made in many locations and suit local tastes. Rosé wines are vinified throughout Greece from the Rhoditis grape, and a quantity is exported to the overseas restaurant trade. They are typically strong in alcohol but, like most rosé wines, offer little flavor or distinction.

The Age of Reason and the Age of Enlightenment have given way to the Age of Anxiety and Adolescence, which is too busy with itself to bother learning the language of its parent culture, Greek. Those who read Greek will not need the following short glossary of wine label terms; those who don't may have trouble recognizing them.

READING THE LABEL

Οινος	Wine. Ask for it in a *taverna* and you may get a puzzled look, followed by "Ah, Retsina" (Ρετσινα), which is what will arrive at the table.
Οινος Ερυθρος, Μαυρος	Red wine but Μαυρος is normally darker.
Οινος Λευκος	White wine.
Κοκκινελι	Rosé.
Ξηρος	Dry (Greek wine is normally sweetish).
Επιτραπεζιο κρασι	Ordinary ("on-the-table") wine.
Ενδικως διατηρημενον	Quality wine.
Παλαιον	Very old wine.
Παραγωγη και Εμφιαλωσις	Produced and bottled by . . .
Αφρωδες κρασι	Sparkling wine.

Naoussa Boutari

Coming from northern Greece (Thessaloniki), this native wine is well regarded if rarely encountered. Its vintage style varies. The aroma suggests some lighter versions of Pinot Noir from California, but in fact the tasting impressions are more astringent and individual. Dominated by body, it is nevertheless not so flushed out with alcohol and sugary impressions as some chocolate-colored wines from Cyprus, and it has more character than the usual Pendeli or Kokkineli commonly found in shops under the names of the three or four main shippers. It will have to stand for a flock of individual local wines that one hopes will appear more in export than they have to date. It certainly proves that balanced red wine of character can be made in this temperate locale.

VINTAGE   *DATE*   *PRICE*

GUESTS

MENU   *COMMENTS*

Samos Muscat

The Muscat grape in its different varieties is cultivated for wine and table use throughout the Mediterranean, and in both classical and present times the sweet-scented wines of Samos have been esteemed. This example is still within the realm of table wine, lighter, fresher, more moderate in both aroma and flavor than overpowering Commandaria, for example, the famous Cyprus dessert wine, but Samos can also serve as an aperitif. It could be compared to sweet natural wines made in other parts of the Mediterranean, southern France's Baume de Venise for example. It is certainly Greek, as Greek as Retsina, if far less widely seen.

VINTAGE   *DATE*   *PRICE*

GUESTS

MENU   *COMMENTS*

HUNGARY

Hungarian vine culture traces its origins to Asian invaders who first traversed, then settled this fertile corridor south of the Carpathians during Roman times. Magyar tribes are supposed to have brought with them vineyard workers of Bulgar origin (the Kaliz) and vines from Asia and India. In the fourteenth or fifteenth century settlers from the Low Countries brought the Furmint grape from which the famous Tokay wine is made. The effect on the Furmint of noble rot (*Botrytis cinerea*) is said to have been discovered in Hungary as early as the mid-1600s. The same mold desiccates fine white grapes in Sauternes, concentrating the juice, but it was not identified in the Bordeaux region until much later.

The remarkable wines that take their name from the town of Tokaj deserve separate discussion from the more normally produced wines grown beside Lake Balaton and in a dozen other districts. Within Hungary, approximately 420,000 acres (170,000 hectares) of wine grapes are cultivated by large state-run farms, collectives that group the efforts of numerous viticulturists, and individual peasant growers. As in other socialist countries, state organizations control commercialization of all wines; exports are totally managed by Monimpex, a government marketing board. Ancient viticultural traditions and a distinguished recent history of enterprising oenological work have thus been brought into the framework of a nationally controlled economy. The results for lesser wines produced *en masse* is bound to be favorable; the future of the very finest wines, particularly special varietal wines and Tokay, is, according to Heublein, the American distributor, increasingly in the hands of small independent farmers.

Hungarian wine labels are scarcely easy to read or, rather, decipher. Labels typically state grape variety, place of origin, the cooperative or organization responsible for producing the wine, and include a sort of seal of origin in the form of a government stamp. To add greater bewilderment, not only do native vine varieties play a large role in Hungarian wine making, but quite familiar Western European varieties are, naturally, designated by their Hungarian names. The following table illustrates the point, as well as the range of grapes grown in the country.

Ordinary wines are *Kimert Bor,* table wines *Asztali Bor,* and better wines *Minosëgi Bor*. If it is *Fehér* it is white, *Vörös* will be red. Sparkling wines are *Habzó,* sweet wines (other than Tokay) *Édes,* and *Šráraz* indicates relatively dry wine. Most Hungarian wines are identified principally by grape variety and the place from which they came, which will have a final possessive "i" added to it. For example, Ezerjó grapes are cultivated near the town of Mór. The wine is labeled *Móri Ezerjó,* Ezerjó-from-Mór.

While more than half the planted vines lie in a great southeast plain or gravelly depression between the Danube and Tisza rivers, the wines they produce are ordinary reds and whites of little interest to English-speaking markets. In the extreme southwest, a fine wine dis-

WHITE VARIETIES

Hungarian Name	European name
Olaszrizling	Wälschriesling
Szilváni, Zoldszilváni	Sylvaner
Piros, Tramini	Traminer
Szürkebarát	Pinot Gris
Fehér	Pinot Blanc
Sárgamuskotály (Tokay grape)	Yellow Muscat
Furmint (Tokay grape)	
Hárslevelü ("lime-tree leaf")	
Ezerjó	No Western European
Leányka	equivalent
Mézesfehér	
Kéknyelü ("blue-stalked")	

RED VARIETIES

Hungarian Name	European name
Nágyburgundi	Pinot Noir
Kékfrankos	Gamay
Kadarka (red and rosé wines)	Kadarka
Médoc Noir	Merlot
Cabernet	Cabernet (Franc and Sauvignon)

trict on the Yugoslav frontier, formerly called Pécs-Villány, now the Mecsek, makes red wines of repute from Pinot Noir grapes. They are exported as Villányi-Burgundi, and the same town exports a fine Kadarka wine. Furmint, Wälschriesling, and Pinot all give dry white wines in this area. Northeast of Villány, on the Danube, Szekszárd vineyards produce an equally celebrated Kadarka red wine. The remaining Hungarian fine grapes are grown either along Lake Balaton or along the northern border.

Lake Balaton stretches approximately 50 miles in length, roughly on an east-west axis. Thus its northern shore, made up of low hills, faces south. This disposition, with excellent soils of volcanic origin based often on basalt subsoils, constitutes a fine natural vineyard. North of the lake is Somló, a tiny district producing deep-flavored, long-lived white wines, at one time more prized than they are today. The best Somló is made from Furmint, followed by Wälschriesling; both varieties turn out sweet in this district.

But it is along Lake Balaton that the more famous white wines are made and in greater quantity—16,000 acres (6,500 hectares) of vines compared to 1,100 acres (450 hectares) at Somló. Balaton wines existed in Roman times, and what the Romans initiated, medieval monastic orders carried on and improved. Today the vineyards are divided into three officially defined appellations: Badacsony, Balatonfüred-Csopak, and Balaton. Unlike vines growing in sand, Balaton vines, by dint of soil, low elevation (less than 1,700 feet, or about 500 meters), and, of course, botanical type, were fully exposed to attack from the phylloxera louse. European stocks were wiped out but were rapidly replanted on American roots at the end of the last century. Badacsony's best whites are made from Riesling, Furmint, Pinot Gris, and, in smaller quantity, the native Kéknyelü vine, expensive because of its low yield per area.

Just east, enjoying a slightly warmer microclimate, is Balatonfüred-Csopak. Riesling is the higher-rated variety here, but Furmint and Sylvaner also grow well. Farther northeast, in Balaton, Wälschriesling predominates, seconded by native Mézesfehér, Ezerjó, and new plantings in Sylvaner. Balaton makes thinner wines than the first two appellations; part of its vineyard is formed of clay rather than the superior basalt substratum topped with loess that distinguishes the western part of the lakefront.

The homeland of the Ezerjó grape is north of Balaton in Mór and Bársonyos-Császár. Here sandy soils with a high content of fragmented rock protected European vines from phylloxera; in consequence, an unusual amount of ungrafted original vine types persists. Normally dry white wines are made from Ezerjó in Mór, but in very good rich years higher sugar content in the grape pushes the wines toward a sweet dessert style.

To the far west on the Austrian border a very small vineyard around Sopron makes white wines from Austrian varieties and from Gamay grapes a red wine of top Hungarian classification—the Soproni Kékfrankos. The foothills of the Matras range in north-central Hungary are the site of her best-known red wine, Egri Bikavér. It is made in Eger, mainly from Kadarka grapes, with about one-fifth of Pinot Noir juice and about one-tenth of Merlot juice. Nearby, at Debrö, the native Hárslevelü is cultivated, to make a white wine of vigorous aroma that is highly rated by Hungarian standards.

Tokay

At last, in the extreme northeast, at the Russian border, we come to the legendary and unique wines of Hungary, the great white Tokay. Nearly 30 villages of the Tokaj-Hegyala hill district have the right to use the name Tokay for their wines. The combination of fine volcanic-origin soils at moderate elevations (650 feet, or about 200 meters), the beneficial influence of the Bodrog River draining the slopes, and hot summers and cold winters offer an excellent setting for the Furmint, Hárslevelü, and Sárgamuskotály grapes that make the precious Tokay wines. Barrels come from nearby Gönc. The excellent stone cellars offer shelter under fine conditions for the long barrel fermentation of Tokay.

Harvesting traditionally begins on the feast day of Saints Simon and Jude, in late October. In successful years the grapes, notably the Furmint, are attacked by noble rot, shrivel, and concentrate their juice. This condition is called Aszu. The grape musts, 70 percent Furmint, 25 percent Hárslevelü, and 5 percent yellow Muscat, are vatted and begin a slow fermentation. In a procedure peculiar to Tokaji Aszu, a portion of Aszu grapes is then mashed into a paste by foot

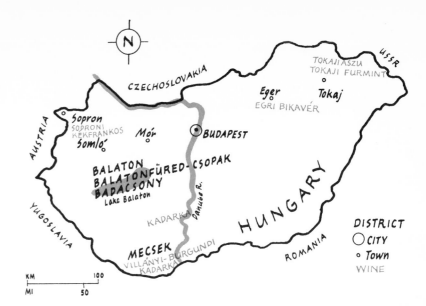

or by machine. This paste is measured out in the same 30- to 35-liter (about 9 gallon) wooden baskets (*puttonyos*) that are used to bring in the grapes. For every barrel (130 liters, or about 137 quarts) of wine in the vats, a certain number of *puttonyos* of sweet paste is added to the fermenting young wine. In theory one to six *puttonyos* can be added; in practice it is three to five. The more paste added, the sweeter the result. Wine that has macerated with this sugar-rich and fruit-rich mush will absorb sweetness, body, and taste in the process. The musts are filtered after a few days and the wine run off into barrels (*gönci*) to be stored in the remarkable stone cellars for its long period of fermentation in cask. Unlike most wines, Tokay is not topped up in cask; from this exposure to air a type of vegetation forms on top of the liquid, contributing a distinctive flavor to the wine. This surface life is not the same as the *flor* of sherry, but the results are not altogether dissimilar.

Before all these steps are taken, however, a species of cream-of-the-crop is drawn off the grapes. Aszu grapes lying in the *puttonyos* or on the sorting tables exude a small amount of the ripest juices. This unpressed finest juice of the finest grapes is carefully collected and made into an exquisite concentrated wine, high in sugar and flavor and low in alcohol. This is the fabled Tokaji Eszencia or Tokay essence.

The different designations of Tokay become more comprehensible with this background:

Tokay essence (Tokaji Eszencia), still made and used to improve the Aszu wines, but rarely exported.

Tokaji Aszu, bottled as three, four, or five *puttonyos* wines, of increasing sweetness and concentration.

Tokaji Szamorodni. Sweetish or dry depending on harvest conditions, this is wine made from the same grape varieties as Aszu but picked "as is," shriveled or unshriveled.

Tokaji Furmint, wine from the Tokaj region made of Furmint grape must only.

Tokaji Forditás. By putting new wine on the old lees of Aszu wines that have been run off into barrels, it is possible to get a second, lesser wine, nevertheless enriched by maceration with the lees, which still contain sugar and flavor. A sort of secondhand Tokaji Aszu.

Old Eszencia is, naturally, priceless. Tokaji Aszu is bound to be expensive, the other grades less so. Eszencia and Aszu age gracefully over enormous numbers of years; century-old wines in superb condition are not unusual.

Egri Bikavér

This handsome label and engagingly named red wine is among the most widely distributed of all labels coming from southeastern Europe. Present versions are well made with a moderate bouquet showing clean character. It develops well on the palate with a generous series of impressions and is satisfying. My criticism stems from memories of this wine 20 years ago when, if it showed a little less expertise in wine making, it showed a darker color, firmer and more exciting flavor, and generally was a more original wine. One cannot fault the Hungarians for making wines with more universal appeal than in the past, but compare this with a Nemes Kadarka, for example, and you may observe some difference in individuality. Hungarian wines have not lost their character; rather this leader has become standardized if still pleasant drinking.

VINTAGE *DATE* *PRICE*

GUESTS

MENU *COMMENTS*

Badacsonyi Szürkebarát
Hungarian Grayfriar

Balaton, or Balatoni Pinot Gris, is what this wine might logically be called in English, for that is the grape used for its production in the preferred growing area on the north shore of Lake Balaton. It is rather bland wine compared to some more unusual Hungarian whites from the same area, and it offers a limited but clean bouquet. This is followed by ample body, about the density of a Pinot Blanc-type Burgundy, only more unctuous, and a fairly short impression with some fruit and character. It may be that the method of production averages all crops into a single blend.

VINTAGE *DATE* *PRICE*

GUESTS

MENU *COMMENTS*

Tokaji Aszu 5 Puttonos

The wines of Hungary own no more fabled or famous name than this coveted, expensive, and unique Tokay produced from a traditional blend of grapes and aged in oak barrels. Most tasters would agree that Tokay is a wine to drink on its own rather than one that marries well with food. Its qualities are richness, a natural sweetness derived from concentrated grapes, as in Sauternes, though production methods differ. There is no other wine quite like Tokaji Aszu, but there is an elite version called Eszencia, or essence, made from the first freely run juice. Tokay is expected to be aromatic; the mature flavor and darker color are caused by deliberate aging and form part of the style of the wine. It is necessarily costly.

VINTAGE *DATE* *PRICE*

GUESTS

MENU *COMMENTS*

Villányi Burgundi

Bright red, clean-tasting wine of medium to medium-heavy body with a good approach and a good finish to the taste, the "Burgundi" is of course no more Burgundy than California Chablis is Chablis, but it is an excellent bottle of sound red wine, correctly priced and with reliable tasting features. There are more individual and distinctive wines from Hungary, some mentioned in the text and mostly distributed in the United States by Heublein; but this example shows what Hungary can do in the way of a firm, balanced, modern red wine. Contrast this with the lively Kadarka.

VINTAGE *DATE* *PRICE*

GUESTS

MENU *COMMENTS*

PRODUCED AND BOTTLED IN HUNGARY

NET CONTENTS 1 PT. 7 FL. OZS.

ALCOHOL 12.5% BY VOLUME

EGRI BIKAVÉR

BULLS BLOOD OF EGER — HUNGARIAN RED WINE

EXPORT MONIMPEX – HUNGARY

Imported by Heublein Wines International, Hartford, Connecticut

PRODUCED AND BOTTLED IN HUNGARY

NET CONTENTS 1 PT. 7 FL. OZS.

Badacsonyi Szürkebarát

Badacsony

BALATON

Grayfriar of Badacsony

HUNGARIAN LIGHT WINE

ALCOHOL 12.5% BY VOLUME

EXPORT MONIMPEX, HUNGARY

IMPORTED BY HEUBLEIN WINES INTERNATIONAL, HARTFORD, CONNECTICUT

PRODUCED AND BOTTLED IN HUNGARY

ALCOHOL 13,8 % BY VOLUME

NET CONTENTS, 1 PT 7 FL OZS

Kb. 0.5 l

5 PUTTONOS

TOKAJI ASZU

HUNGARIAN LIGHT SWEET WINE

EXPORT MONIMPEX – HUNGARY

Imported by Heublein Wines International, Hartford, Connecticut

PRODUCED AND BOTTLED IN HUNGARY

NET CONTENTS 1 PT. 7 FL. OZS.

ALCOHOL 12,5% BY VOLUME

VILLÁNYI

HUNGARIAN RED WINE

BURGUNDI

EXPORT MONIMPEX, HUNGARY

Imported by Heublein Wines International, Hartford, Connecticut

ARGENTINA

Argentina's present position as a mass producer of good wines arises from an old viticulture expanding in haphazard circumstances; coincidences do much to explain why this ethnically mixed nation should be Latin America's largest wine producer. The earliest Criolla vines migrated from Mexico to Chile and into southern Argentina in the mid-sixteenth century. Immigrants, mainly Italians, expanded their domestic plots into commercial ones during the nineteenth century, when population growth and world trade stimulated a native wine industry. Today's three zones emerged at this time: San Juan Province, along the Andes; Mendoza, just below it; and Río Negro, a cooler outpost in the south.

While Chile's nineteenth-century viticultural development was consciously drawn from French models, Argentina's was more cosmopolitan, if less selective: Pedro Ximenez, Trebbiano, Riesling, Sauvignon Blanc, and Sémillon white grapes, Barbera, Merlot, Malbec, and Cabernet Sauvignon for reds. Currently, 741,000 acres (300,000 hectares) give 580 million gallons (22 million hectoliters) of wine. The distribution of vines has changed little; as of 1971, Mendoza still has the 70 percent share of vineyard area she boasted half a century ago, but now half the province is under vines—as much as all the rest of Latin America. San Juan contains a quarter of Argentina's production; Río Negro, a small fraction. Malbec grapes account for two-thirds of the red wine produced. Criollas still produces rosé and a major share of common whites. Better varietal wines include Pinot Blanc, Merlot, Cabernet Sauvignon, and Sauvignon Blanc, but Argentina's vineyard is built on grapes destined for common wines, vermouths, and distilled products. Sweet and fortified wines are made in hotter areas of San Juan. Some sparkling wine is made by the Champagne process, but 80 percent of Argentina's production goes into the daily *vino común* with as little as 8 percent alcohol. Large vat fermentation, rapid turnover, bulk shipment for local bottling or retail sale from bulk all signify a sophisticated mass-market industry. Fewer than a dozen firms produce a fifth of the national total; many, notably in Mendoza, are also important vineyard owners who do everything from planting vines to delivering packaged inexpensive bottles to retail outlets.

Mendoza dominates Argentina's wine business. Vast mechanized, irrigated properties cover semiarid plains beside the Andes, source of the essential water supply. Outputs per area are enormous and costs minimal. Although latitude approximates that of Algeria, the Mendoza–San Juan plateau is 2,000 to 2,500 feet above sea level. Wines are generous in alcohol, deficient in acidity and flavor. Wide-ditch irrigation swells and dilutes production; the hot climate does the rest. Quality wines struggle for concentrated tasting qualities rather than for ripeness. Phylloxera-infested vineyards are periodically flooded to drown the pests, much as was done in the primitive days of France's battle against phylloxera in the late 1800s. More precise, costly surface irrigation, earlier picking, and lower yields might result in better wines. It is easy to criticize from the sidelines, but Mendoza growers are probably wise in aiming at low-cost wines that are competitive abroad and cheap at home.

Argentina's better wines, those found in English-speaking markets, are wholesome and authentic rather than distinguished. The Ministry of Agriculture regulates an elaborate quality-control system. Growers must file complete harvest declarations, varietal wines must be entirely as labeled, blends must also be stated, as in "Cabernet-Malbec." The place of origin, vintage, and grape variety must all be stated. Inspectors of the Ministry of Agriculture take measures to validate the authenticity of a crop at the point of production, and large firms supervise vineyards from which their product will eventually come. A certificate of authenticity is required for export wines.

Argentine wines derive their style from the grape variety, are modeled after European wine types, or emanate from a wine maker's endeavor to satisfy local or international tastes. As in Australia or California, these diversities cut right across varietal names. The wines can be faulted for awkwardness, excess alcohol (as in other hot climates), lack of flavor and vitality (attributable to their large production per area), excess aging (especially for white wines), and for coarseness. On the other side, both red and white wines have generous, clean-tasting qualities, frank development to the taste, and generally healthy sensation. The best wines show good vinous constitution and announce their varietal character, whatever it may be. Lower-class wine—good nonvarietal drinking—is usually fairly priced and should be drunk young. It competes with cheap California wine in America and with inexpensive Mediterranean wine in England.

Among white wines, successful Pinot Blancs have recognizable aroma and full body but fresh and wholesome taste. Sauvignon Blanc and German varieties seem less successful; light and lively Argentine whites may be made, but I have not tasted them. Among the reds are strong-flavored, aggressively full wines that seem to be made on a Rioja model, with a healthy but rough impact appealing to Hispanic taste. These are described by Spaniards as "having punch" (*tener golpe*). Other reds answer more to California and Australian types, with very abundant flavor, much alcohol or at least a sensation of it, and pervasive aftertaste. At least one firm, Norton, ships Barbera that evokes its Italian namesake—clean, strong in alcohol, and with varietal aroma. Better Malbec and Cabernet reds are clean wines without enough flavor to carry off their alcohol, but mellow. For both, as for Merlot, older vintages seem to fare worse than young ones, lacking the finesse that age is imagined to confer. Success seems to fall most on wines whose intentions appear modest—generous, clean reds and young whites. Since wine making in Argentina is directed toward sound, inexpensive wines for daily drinking, these results are hardly surprising. The label section represents such wines—and more power to them.

Norton Mendoza Pinot Blanc

One of the large modern wineries adding export product to their ordinary Argentine table wines, Norton's range includes white Sauvignon, Malbec, and Barbera. The agreeable Pinot Blanc wine offers a clean bouquet with good points of varietal character, followed by a wholesome first impression on the palate. High alcoholic content is correctly set off by good flavor and impressions of fruit. While the wine is far from tart, being rather mellow, it is balanced and offers the characteristics associated with the grape. It is direct in tasting style and a better example of Argentine varietal wine than most.

VINTAGE   DATE   PRICE

GUESTS

MENU   COMMENTS

Viña San Felipe

This label is a well-distributed national brand in Argentina and one found in North American markets. It shows some of the illusions (some would say pretensions) of South American wine making in labeling itself "Burgundy type" wine. In fact, its virile, generous aroma introduces a vigorous, alcoholic, and chewy, or slightly acerbic, red table wine distinctly South American in its ensemble of qualities. It has little or no elegance and much drinkability, sells at modest prices (under $3.00) and deserves them. While its producers are unlikely to have sacrificed quantity for quality, they have succeeded in making a vigorous-tasting red table wine with abundant flavor.

San Felipe competes logically and well with lower-priced California wines as well as with others from Argentina and Chile. Its defect is a slightly medicinal impression.

VINTAGE   DATE   PRICE

GUESTS

MENU   COMMENTS

CHILE

Two generations ago, Chile had more vineyards than California. In 1971, from 314,000 acres (127,000 hectares), 105 million gallons (4 million hectoliters) were vinified. But during the first nine months of 1975 the United States imported a scant 11,000 gallons, less than 5 percent of what it had taken three years earlier. These figures say only what newspaper readers already know: economic disruption and civil war dominate Chile's life in the 1970s and, whether above or below ground, look to do so for some time.

The sluggish development of Latin America's best vineyards reflects three interrelated problems: imposing high (expensive) technical standards on viticulture, arriving at a landholding of economic size, and marketing quality wines persistently viewed as cheap substitutes for more famous European wines. The first two points are politically explosive: investments and larger size conflict with the desire for peasant ownership of the land. The third point pits rising production costs against expectations abroad that wines such as Chilean Riesling remain cheap.

Wine grapes came to Chile with the Spanish conquerors of the 1500s. Muscat varieties are still grown in Chile's northern zone. As in Argentina, economic expansion during the nineteenth century gave growers incentive to plant vines. Under a concerted program, French vines and technicians arrived in the mid-1800s. Chilean vineyards took a French direction, with government aid as well.

Today red Merlot and white Sémillon, both of Bordeaux provenance, flourish widely. Other familiar red varieties introduced mostly in the central zone of Chile were Malbec, Pinot Noir, and Cabernet. Among white grapes were Sauvignon Blanc, Sylvaner, Pinot Blanc, and Riesling. Wines from native varieties, among them the Torrentes, Albilla, and Uba, are still made in southern Chile.

Chilean vineyards are in latitudes comparable to those of Cyprus and North Africa rather than the cooler zones of Europe's famous vineyards. The northerly and hottest zone lies below the Atacama Desert. Like the Mendoza vineyard of Argentina, it is irrigated with water from the Andes.

The far southern zone, from Valdivia to the Maule River, is mostly rocky and muddy. Native varieties, notably the País, predominate, and common wines result.

Chile's most famous vineyards and best varietals are grouped around major river systems in the central zone. The Aconcagua River area north of Santiago and the Maipo south of it are considered Chile's finest. This region is less arid than the north but still irrigated. The O'Higgins district borders the Cachapoal River, and other areas lie to the south.

Early importation of European varieties and geographical isolation spared Chile from phylloxera. Strenuous border supervision has so far prevented infestation. Chile is also free of oidium. But phylloxera is now in Argentina, too close for much optimism.

Chile, like France, is between 2 and 3 percent under vine, but most of her 30,000 vineyards are poor affairs with a hectare or less of vines. As elsewhere, the government funds cooperatives, but they leave unanswered problems of vineyard development, enterprise, and quality. There are, or were, or are again (depending on what has happened) fewer than 200 estates with sufficient production to justify marketing a vineyard wine internationally.

Government policy in Chile has a split personality. Aid and controls spur planting and production of quality wine. Yet wines produced too abundantly face penalties. Quality of export wines is respectable by international comparison. Whites must be 11 percent alcohol and reds 10.5 percent. Exports pass a physical inspection for clarity and cleanness. They must be aged one year. But in its understandable campaign against rural alcoholism the government discourages individual or collective enterprise. Each vineyard's annual quota is based on the percentage its wine production forms of the national production that year. When the property or cooperative exceeds this quota, the surplus (if that is the word) is "declassified" and must be disposed of. This quota is based on a "safety" notion of 60 liters of wine per Chilean per year, and jettison the rest. Such a clumsy ax of a program keeps wine consumption down at home but hardly encourages growth of export-oriented agricultural business or the building up of more efficient units.

Government quality designations foolishly upgrade older wine, disregarding aging potential. *Courant* (ordinary) wines must be one year old; *Special*, two years old; *Reserve*, four years old; and *Gran Vino*, six years old. This entices growers and merchants to keep white wines particularly too long, resulting in brown, stale dull whites. Some red Cabernets can withstand *Gran Vino* age, frequently Merlot and Malbec fare less well, and Pinot Noir produced in warm climates ages dubiously. Costs arise with keeping; cost increases partly account for the recent Chilean Riesling export debacle.

During the 1950s and 1960s Chilean wines, led by her Rieslings, made considerable inroads on export markets. Whites, varying from fresh to mellow, and generous reds were understandably successful. Then as now, most were shipped in dark, squat Franconian flasks (*Bocksbeutel*). Cabernet and Merlot wines vary; only a few have distinct varietal character, most are clean and attractive, some astringent but fuller, some to a point of being dull. "Burgundy" and/or Pinot Noir seem less successful, or at least transport poorly.

Among whites, substitution of Pinot Blanc for Riesling has given wines veering clumsily toward 13 percent alcohol. This has not aided the success of these wines, which are becoming more expensive. The rising world flow of light, commercial white wines more quickly and cheaply produced has created strong competition. A generous, balanced clean red from the central zone can be produced and shipped competitively; one label shown here exemplifies this class of wine. Past performance of Chilean Riesling shows that it can be excellent. The rest is speculation about the future.

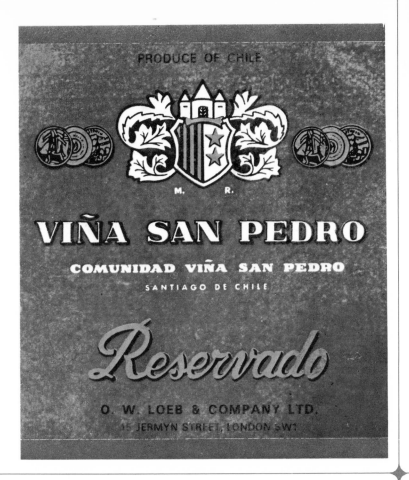

Viña San Pedro Reservado

Imported in bulk into England, where it is bottled and sold at prices as reasonable as high duties allow, San Pedro represents the type of healthy, generous red wine with vitality that Chile is able to produce mainly from Cabernet and other Bordeaux grapes. It is dark-colored, full, yet with enough firmness and acerbity to achieve a Bordeaux-type style. Its merits are in constitution and correct flavor and value. A younger version might find wide acceptance in America, for its tasting qualities are also those that make so many California Cabernets popular there. Viña San Pedro is appropriately sold in Bordeaux bottles.

VINTAGE   DATE   PRICE

GUESTS

MENU   COMMENTS

Viñã Tarapacá Ex Zavala

Produced in Chile's best-regarded river valley, the Maipo plain (Llano de Maipo), this is an aged Cabernet Sauvignon with good hue and a bouquet reflecting a definite Bordeaux Cabernet style but on the unctuous side. No California Cabernet could more easily be taken for claret by its clean and distinguished aroma.

This tastes like a well-vinified wine whose woody, slightly dry finish and flavor distract from its delicacy and good varietal taste. Perhaps it is excessively aged in cask. It strongly resembles fine California Cabernet Sauvignon in its address on the palate, with fruit not very evident and lacking lusciousness, but one is praising with faint damns, for the wine is technically perfect and will appeal to Western Hemisphere drinkers who accept its dry style and faintly alcoholic ending as natural.

VINTAGE   DATE   PRICE

GUESTS

MENU   COMMENTS

AUSTRALIA

Vines were first planted in Australia in the late 1700s, and her wines have been sent to London for a century, but only in the last decade have energetic promotion and rising interest in fine wines brought Australian wines of high quality to markets far afield.

Like California, Australia is a pioneer vineyard area including industrial-scale-beverage wine makers and a minority of quality wine operations. Wine regulations reflect these extremes. Like the United States and South America, Australia accepts that such famous names as Burgundy describe wine types, not places of origin. Happily, many growers label fine wine informatively and candidly, noting grape variety, vintage year, and vineyard site. Sections of the wine code take the consumer's point of view. Australian wine blends from different regions must declare their origin on the label in order of importance in the blend. At least 80 percent of a grape variety is needed to call the wine by that varietal name. When a description implies one origin but the wine is of another (Australian or foreign), its true origin must precede the name. However, wineries may use (or abuse) 12 great European names as if they were wine types: for red wines, Burgundy and Claret; for white wines, Champagne, Chablis, Graves, Sauternes, Moselle, and Hock; for fortified and dessert wines, Sherry, Port, Madeira, and Marsala. These rules allow, for example, a Hunter River red to be sold as "Burgundy," but to market the same wine as "St.-Émilion," a subregion of Bordeaux, the label would have to say "Australian St.-Émilion."

"Champagne" must be fermented in bottles not exceeding five liters' capacity and aged on its lees at least six months. This affords some protection of quality, for it is aging on the lees that contributes to the flavor and fineness of sparkling wines.

Australia's advanced wine technology has been commendably spurred by government and industry interest and investment. Technical regulations are fairly relaxed, however. Unhealthy substances, such as sulphur dioxide and volatile acidity, have legal limits. Others forbidden in Western Europe are allowed, including several acids, activated carbon, and concentrated grape juice. Fermenting with cultured yeasts rather than those occurring naturally on the grape surface is common; in France this is looked upon with disapproval. On the other hand, some gruesome misuses of the word "wine" permitted in the United States are forbidden; Australia accepts Europe's definition that wine results from complete or partial fermentation of fresh grapes or fresh grape must. Exceptions (Meat Wine, Quinine Tonic Wine, and Malt Wine) are rigorously defined.

A government board inspects wine exports. This may not eliminate mediocre or even downright unpleasant wines, but neither do European systems, Port regulations possibly excepted. I have never met technically unsound Australian wine, though some suggest grape concentrate. The same cannot be said for the five main European exporter countries.

Australia is hardly crowded with sizable wineries; fewer than 200 vineyards crush more than ten tons of grapes each harvest. The best lie in patches across southeast Australia, but viticulture spots the subcontinent from the warm extremes of the 34th parallel to the colder climates of the 38th and even farther south in Tasmania. Favorable regions cross state boundaries, but wines are labeled by state. Three states predominate: New South Wales, whose vineyards lie inland of Sydney; Victoria, whose vineyards are along her borders; and South Australia, whose grape culture centers around Adelaide.

New South Wales

In New South Wales, the Hunter Valley district and the Sydney area can reasonably call themselves the cradle of the Australian wine industry. A number of pioneer family wine enterprises survive into the fourth and fifth generation. Kirkton, the first important Hunter Valley commercial vineyard, was founded in the 1830s by James Busby in foothills of the Broken Back Mountains. No longer a vineyard, the name remains as a widely distributed white wine of the large Lindemans Wines Pty. Company founded by Henry J. Lindeman of Sydney in 1840. Lindemans owns the Ben Ean Vineyard in Hunter Valley and others at Cawarra, Corona, and Coolalta. One of Lindemans's largest rivals is Penfolds Pty., which began in the Barossa Valley near Adelaide and spread through the Murray River area to Hunter Valley. In 1960 Penfolds took the old vineyard name "Dalwood" for their new plantings 40 miles (66 kilometers) from the original site. Today this red wine is one of the best known in Australia.

Vineyards around the town of Pokolbin possess superior exposition. Seppelt and McWilliam's are important growers here, and Tullock is a quality name. The Rothbury Estate's excellent white Sémillon can compete with fine French white Burgundy in quality and price.

The northerly, warm Hunter Valley climate leads growers to rely upon Shiraz (red Hermitage), but Cabernet Sauvignon and Pinot Noir for red wines and Ugni Blanc, Sémillon, and Blanquette for white are grown, with Shiraz and Sémillon preponderant. Sandy to heavy topsoils lie on limestone and shale base. Rainfall is annoyingly concentrated around harvest time, varying vintage quality. Less important New South Wales vineyard districts are Rooty Hill and Parramatta, near Sydney; Muswellbrook and Mudgee, northwest of Hunter Valley; and Corowa, Swan Hill, and Robindale, in the south. But it is Hunter Valley that earns New South Wales's reputation.

Victoria

Planted in the early 1800s, expanded in mid-century, Victoria was by far the largest vineyard state in Australia until the arrival of phylloxera in the 1890s. Tokay, Cabernet Sauvignon, and red and white Hermitage were introduced in Melbourne's Lilydale district around 1840, and areas north and west of Melbourne were planted late in the century. Phylloxera put Lilydale under, and Melbourne's urban expansion finished off what the louse had begun. Vineyard acreage in Victoria shrank dramatically.

Great Western Township, which produces much of Australia's sparkling wine, was saved from the scourge by its isolation. Seppelt is the main grower, and Bests's winery is on the Wimmera River, north of the town. Château Tahbilk, built in the 1860s, produces red and white wines on the Coulburn River; some are bottled in London. Major vineyards north of Melbourne are Rutherglen, Glenrowan, Milawa, and Merbein. Mildura, an important vineyard in northwest Victoria, is the oldest of these, founded in the 1880s by two California brothers, W. B. and George Chaffey.

South Australia

The Murray River district near the Victoria border crosses Renmark, Paringa, and Waikerie. Rainfall is stingy, consequently vines are irrigated. Sandy soils on clay subsoil contain much lime. Sweet wine and brandy production predominate. Renmark was the site of Australia's first cooperative winery.

South of Adelaide lies the Southern Vales region, planted in 1838 by a settler named John Reynell, founder of Walter Reynell & Sons. A tough and canny pioneer (among many) named Thomas Hardy, who had made a modest stake in driving beef cattle to feed gold miners, bought the bankrupt Tintara Vineyard Company in the 1870s, and the fourth Hardy generation today runs Thomas Hardy & Sons. Tintara is among the best-known vineyards; its label boasts a sketch of the original buildings.

Vineyards established around Adelaide by the first settlers have been engulfed by the city, but their names persist. Christopher R. Penfolds's original (1844) vineyard at Glenelg in the McLaren Vale is within Adelaide's suburbs; Hamilton's Ewell vineyard (1840) is nearby. Only three miles from the cooling breezes of the Gulf of St. Vincent is Seaview, built on the site of George Manning's plantings

and owned since 1948 by Edwards & Chaffey Ltd. The Australian Wine Institute makes its home among these Southern Vales wineries. The hot climate is tempered by the nearby ocean; soils are dry and unfertile, but they allow light table wine of character.

The most important quality district of South Australia begins at Lyndoch, a short drive north from Adelaide. The Barossa Valley unfolds along the Para River north to Nuriootpa, then turns east toward Angaston. Hamilton's famous Springton vineyard and Penfolds at Eden Valley are its eastern outposts. The Barossa district had German origins: B. Seppelt & Sons, descendants of a Silesian refugee, and G. Gramp & Sons are important vineyard owners. Soils vary, but the best slopes are on the eastern side of the Barossa range. Annual rainfall is moderate. Barossa and the Southern Vales account for the most interesting Australian wines.

Roughly equidistant from Adelaide and Melbourne, the remote Coonawarra region is unusual and remains small. Frosts occur, and vintage variation is marked. A narrow strip of red earth called Terra Rosa lies above limestone, and this purports to give the region's Cabernet and Shiraz wines subtle, light, and often less clumsy qualities than other Australian wines. Wynns Coonawarra Estate Cabernet Sauvignon is esteemed among the "red earth" wines. The Rouge Homme Estate, pioneered by the Redman family, among others, and owned by Lindemans since 1965, is the largest "red earth" grower, with nearly 1,000 acres (410 hectares). Penfolds and Mildara grow red and white grapes here, and private growers include a surviving Redman.

At present Australian wines are not as good as most Australians understandably wish to believe. Most are dull and lack finesse by the highest European standards. The high technical level of export wines, rapid progress, and the presence of truly fine wines forecast a dramatic Australian challenge, certainly to middle-level table wines and possibly to all but the most favored European vineyards. The human effort invested in this achievement deserves nothing less than unstinting and unqualified admiration and respect.

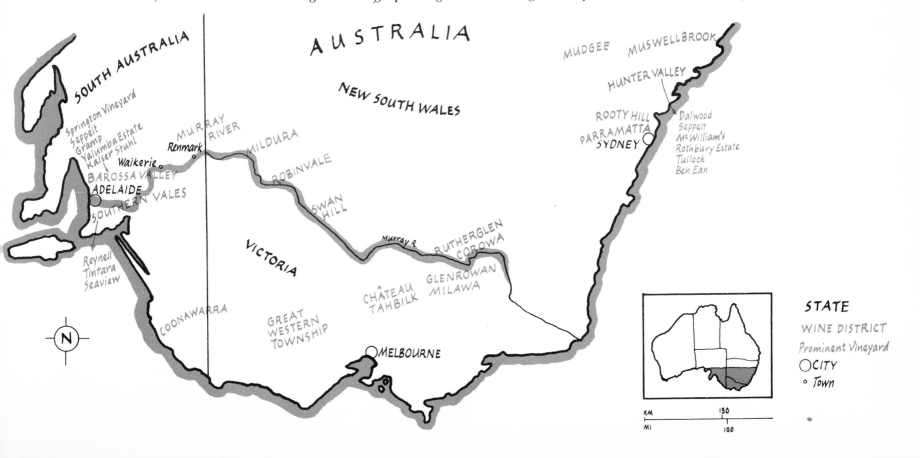

The Rothbury Estate

Made in the Hunter Valley completely from Sémillon grapes, exported in handsomely packaged Burgundy bottles, this superb white wine is brilliant and yellow gold in color, with a firm aroma suggesting ripeness and a bouquet hinting at elegance. Many Australian white wines are powerful, as is this rich and memorable example, but few have its long refined aftertaste matching the style of rich Burgundy white wines of high breeding, the distinguished development on the palate, and the excellent balance between fruit and body, easy to achieve in light white wines but far less so in heady rich wines destined for slow maturing. It is one of the rare Australian wines to rival the finest European whites in subtlety and elegance.

VINTAGE   DATE   PRICE

GUESTS

MENU   COMMENTS

Kaiser Stuhl Late Picking Rhine Riesling

Grown at Wyncroft Vineyards, Eden Valley, in the Barossa district, this fine Riesling is fermented at the Barossa Kaiser Stuhl Cooperative. Its fermentation is arrested by refrigeration to result in wines with residual unfermented sugar. Its vinification deserves praise for capturing tasting qualities of the Rhine Riesling grape and achieving the desired balance of sweetness and fruit, though it is less rich a wine than its model—the best German late-gathered designations. The fresh aroma is followed on the palate by a long, refined series of taste impressions, nicely balanced and finishing with commendable elegance. It is a superior Riesling by any standard and a remarkably faithful one, considering the difficulty of using this grape in hot climates.

VINTAGE   DATE   PRICE

GUESTS

MENU   COMMENTS

Wynns Coonawarra Estate
Cabernet Sauvignon

This is a rich red wine from the unique "red earth" vineyards in South Australia, nicely presented in Bordeaux bottles. Deeply colored, the wines show a generous youthful aroma. To the taste, youthful firmness and astringency are supported by a wholesome texture and fruit in the background. Natural and clean in attack on the palate, they suggest very good Zinfandel from California rather than Cabernet Sauvignon but do show their qualities obtained from oak cask. These are distinctive and honest red wines whose potential for bottle age remains unknown.

VINTAGE   DATE   PRICE

GUESTS

MENU   COMMENTS

Hardy's Nottage Hill Claret

Made from Hermitage (Shiraz) grapes in the McLaren Vale south of Adelaide, on the site of the century-old Tintara Winery, these dark red wines are aged in small oak barrels two years before bottling. Their aroma is notably powerful and spicy. Capturing the pungent, vigorous tasting qualities of the red Hermitage grape, the wine has intense flavor, heady yet balanced by delicious fruit and distinguished as well by its clean aftertaste. An outstanding success in wine making, it presents handsomely the natural dash and lusciousness of the grape variety skillfully matured into a harmonious wine.

VINTAGE   DATE   PRICE

GUESTS

MENU   COMMENTS

The Rothbury Estate

HUNTER VALLEY

PRODUCE OF AUSTRALIA 750ml

Kaiser Stuhl
Individual Vineyard Wines
1973 Late Picking
RHINE RIESLING

THE BAROSSA VALLEY

A PRODUCT OF AUSTRALIA F 81

VINTAGED BY
BAROSSA
CO~OP
WINERY LTD

CLASSIFICATION %
738 Ml

GRAPES GROWN ON
WYNCROFT Eden Valley

BOTTLED BY WYNN WINEGROWERS LTD COONAWARRA ESTATE

WYNNS

COONAWARRA ESTATE

CABERNET
SAUVIGNON

VINTAGE 1971

AUSTRALIAN CLARET 738 ML

E2003   J04-1-71

ESTATE BOTTLED

The ORIGINAL 'TINTARA' CELLARS —1853

HARDY'S
Nottage Hill Claret
AUSTRALIAN
DRY RED TABLE WINE

BOTTLED BY THE MAKERS
THOMAS HARDY & SONS PTY LTD
OF SOUTH AUSTRALIA F 38

ALCOHOL 12% BY VOLUME
NET 1 PINT 9 FLUID OZ
PRODUCT OF AUSTRALIA

Hamilton's Springton Claret

These are among the best-known wines of South Australia, apparently made from a mixture of varieties, among which Shiraz seems prominent from the odor and flavor. A pretty, medium-colored appearance and a nose suggesting wine made under hot conditions are followed on the palate by a mature flavor that shows its two years of age in oak cask. It develops on the palate with a strong sensation of alcohol and a slightly sweet style, earthy and mouth-filling, and finishes with a grainy texture. All in all, a wine with corpulent and fleshy rather than firm tasting qualities, but pleasant in its way.

VINTAGE   DATE   PRICE

GUESTS

MENU   COMMENTS

Barossa Rhine Riesling G. Gramp & Sons

This is a dry, appetizing wine from a famous winery, one of several Barossa vineyards planted by nineteenth-century German settlers. The Riesling grapes are picked early with the intention of producing the bright greenish-yellow color and the aroma that herald a tart, dry, and lively wine. The suggestion of healthy grapes is borne out in the display of Riesling spice to the taste. Attractive rather than subtle, and not powerful, these Barossa whites drink well and preserve their zest in export conditions. They strongly suggest Riesling wines from Alsace rather than from the German vineyards and indeed could pass as such in a blind tasting.

VINTAGE   DATE   PRICE

GUESTS

MENU   COMMENTS

Yalumba Carte d'Or Riesling

This widely distributed Riesling from Angaston in the Barossa district has typical greenish-yellow cast and a full but rather plain aroma. This winery appears to emphasize body and alcohol at the expense of fruit and finish; its wines give a somewhat heavy, even sweetish impression, though presumably they are technically dry. Charm and vivacity are the losers for this, and while sound and clean, they give a somewhat dull impression common to Riesling wines from warm climates and suffer from bluntness.

VINTAGE   DATE   PRICE

GUESTS

MENU   COMMENTS

McWilliam's Mount Pleasant Philip Hermitage

Product of the favored Pokolbin district of the Hunter Valley, aged in very large oak casks, this Hermitage varietal contrasts interestingly with Hermitage grape wines from other Australian vineyard districts. Light color and a firm, natural, but restrained aroma introduce the wine, rather than the flushed, heady odors typical of Hermitage wines. Its tasting qualities are also drier in attack, though balanced. A metallic savor and a taut impression in the finish of the wines evoke austere reds from northern Italy rather than the sumptuous, intoxicating Rhône wines with which the Hermitage grape is associated. Made and packaged with integrity, these are clear, clean, light, slightly woody red wines quite different from their cousins near Adelaide.

VINTAGE   DATE   PRICE

GUESTS

MENU   COMMENTS

PRODUCE OF AUSTRALIA   EST. 1837

AUSTRALIAN   AUSTRALIAN

HAMILTON'S
SPRINGTON
CLARET

"This fine wine was made in our cellars at the township of Springton, South Australia, from selected vines. It has won numerous prizes and was matured in oak casks for two years, and then bottled and binned."

GROWN AND BOTTLED BY HAMILTON'S EWELL VINEYARDS PTY. LTD.
SOUTH AUSTRALIA · F234

26 FL OZ

ORLANDO
Barossa Rhine Riesling
PRODUCT OF AUSTRALIA

VINTAGED BY
G. GRAMP & SONS PTY. LTD.
ORLANDO VINEYARDS, Sᵗʰ AUSTRALIA
738 ml

YALUMBA
Carte D'or
RIESLING

BOTTLED BY
S. Smith Son Pty. Ltd.

YALUMBA VINEYARDS. ANGASTON. S.A. F/13011

PRODUCE OF AUSTRALIA   NET 750 ml

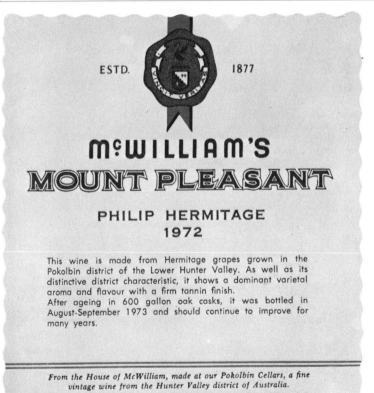

ESTD.   1877

McWILLIAM'S
MOUNT PLEASANT

PHILIP HERMITAGE
1972

This wine is made from Hermitage grapes grown in the Pokolbin district of the Lower Hunter Valley. As well as its distinctive district characteristic, it shows a dominant varietal aroma and flavour with a firm tannin finish.
After ageing in 600 gallon oak casks, it was bottled in August-September 1973 and should continue to improve for many years.

From the House of McWilliam, made at our Pokolbin Cellars, a fine vintage wine from the Hunter Valley district of Australia.

A PRODUCT OF AUSTRALIA   26 FL OZ
McWILLIAM'S WINES PTY. LTD.   N.S.W.   D 3177

Seaview Burgundy Edwards & Chaffey

Produced in the McLaren Vale by a firm of partly American ancestry, this "Burgundy" is but one of a line of good table wines widely distributed in Australia. Less deep in color than some of its neighbors, it has a pleasing bouquet of mature nuances and delicacy. Full and harmonious to the taste, lasting well in the mouth, the wines deserve good marks for balance of flavors and clean aftertaste and are free of the blowzy, "cooked" impression of many Australian reds. The style is less sure; it would be difficult to identify grape variety or origin. The tacky label belies the quality of the contents as well. But Seaview has shown that the Southern Vales district can make clean, light red wines that mature well and are free of the cloying or "overstuffed" traits of some of its neighbors.

VINTAGE   *DATE*   *PRICE*

GUESTS

MENU   *COMMENTS*

Seppelt Moyston Claret

One of Australia's largest producers and distributors ships this "claret" showing reliable, good color with generous aroma typical of red wines from hot climates. Taken simply as good, strong red wines, they are without serious faults, having fruit and plenty of body. Resemblance to tasting qualities of Bordeaux is hard to find; use of the word "claret" is strained. The tasting style is thick, chewy, persistent, and vulgar, but sound body and acceptable finish round off a fleshy red wine widely appreciated in its native land. Its style is not unlike some commercial wines from California or southeastern Europe.

VINTAGE   *DATE*   *PRICE*

GUESTS

MENU   *COMMENTS*

Penfolds Dalwood Australian Hermitage

The name of this famous old estate has been transferred to a new large vineyard by one of Australia's largest table wine producers, and Dalwood is met virtually wherever Australian wines are marketed. It would be difficult to identify these wines as Hermitage grape wines by color, smell, or taste. They offer clean aroma and body dominated by a sensation of alcohol with some fruit in the background. Well made and heady, but coarse, without impressions of much intensity, they suggest any good red table wine from a warm climate, yet have a wide acceptance in their native country.

VINTAGE   *DATE*   *PRICE*

GUESTS

MENU   *COMMENTS*

Lindemans's Kirkton Australian Chablis

This is another of the very successful, widely distributed wines from a major Australian producer and distributor. Named after a nineteenth-century pioneer vineyard in New South Wales, it is sold nonvintage. The color is bright, with a tint of greenish yellow; the aroma is brisk, shows verve, and hints at a pleasantly acidic white wine. The flavor suggests a conscientious effort to produce a wine of Chablis style, tart, quite dry, with a touch of fruit in the background. Fault can be found with the sulphurous finish. In sum, it is a white table wine without delicacy, made for the general market, but without much distinction. Lindemans is owned, since 1971, by Philip Morris, the American tobacco manufacturer.

VINTAGE   *DATE*   *PRICE*

GUESTS

MENU   *COMMENTS*

SEAVIEW

BURGUNDY

PRODUCE OF AUSTRALIA

GROWN AND BOTTLED BY

EDWARDS & CHAFFEY PTY. LIMITED

Seaview Winery

MCLAREN VALE   SOUTH AUSTRALIA

NET 1 PINT 6 FL OZ

F 13001

SEPPELT

MOYSTON
CLARET

AUSTRALIAN STILL RED WINE

Moyston is a small village a few miles south of the Great Western cellars. The vineyards in this district produce the wines that have made dry reds from this region famous and eagerly sought after by wine lovers.

ALCOHOL CONTENTS 13% BY VOLUME

BOTTLED BY B. SEPPELT & SONS LIMITED, SEPPELTSFIELD, S.A.

PRODUCE OF AUSTRALIA · 1 PT. 9 FL. OZ. CONTENTS

IMPORTED BY: SEPPELT WINES LIMITED, LOS ANGELES, CALIF.

PENFOLDS

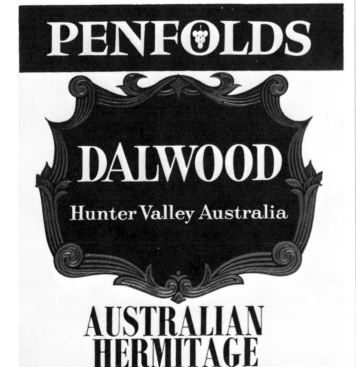

DALWOOD

Hunter Valley Australia

AUSTRALIAN HERMITAGE

PRODUCED AND BOTTLED BY PENFOLDS WINES PTY. LTD.

SYDNEY AND ADELAIDE PRODUCE OF AUSTRALIA

26 FL OZ

SELECTED   BOTTLING

KIRKTON
AUSTRALIAN CHABLIS

PRODUCE OF AUSTRALIA

LINDEMANS WINES PTY. LTD.

SYDNEY, AUSTRALIA

ALCOHOL 10%   NET CONTENTS

BY VOLUME   1 PT 9 FL OZ

CALIFORNIA

by DARRELL CORTI and STEVEN J. SCHNEIDER

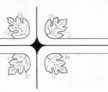

California presents both a fascinating and bewildering offering of wines. California wines are the cleanest in the world and are made with technical knowledge unsurpassed, on the average, by that of wine producers in any other country. Yet their diverse history and circumstances and the different intentions of many different wine makers result in such a variety of tasting qualites and wine styles that no generalizations can communicate to wine drinkers any features common even to the best wines. Some wine makers shape their wines to fit preconceived ideals that may or may not be based on European traditions. Others produce wines whose excellence is defined in more scientific terms and consider they have succeeded when a wine of irreproachable technical quality is produced; its character can be given only by the manner in which the grape variety used matures in the microclimate where these vines are grown.

While California's low-quality wine is better than ordinary wines elsewhere, the region's wines are habitually marketed to consumers with suggestions, adjectives, and packaging that present them in superlative terms, whether they be common, good, or fine. Information about growing areas and vines is excellent, but no comprehensive law controls names of origin, as it does in many other countries. Wines are marketed as the produce of certain districts, but different grape varieties are grown with varying success in zones within these large districts. Legislation protecting names of origin and linking these to high-quality growing and production methods may be on its way, but it is not here yet. In such an anarchic picture generalizations may be unfair to some individual wineries.

Earliest winegrowing came, naturally, to earliest settlement centers around what is now the Los Angeles area. Spanish Franciscans brought grapes here from Mexico in about 1770. Grape culture for the next 60 years spread north with the missions and the populations they served. In 1833 a Bordeaux winegrower named Jean-Louis Vignes settled in the Los Angeles area and founded a vineyard. His contributions included the importation of French varieties into grape nurseries, from which French vines spread across California; the introduction of European aging methods in wood casks; and his inducements to other Frenchmen to migrate to California. Between 1860 and 1880 a Hungarian, Agoston Haraszthy, founded both a vineyard and the Buena Vista Viticultural Society in Sonoma. Haraszthy traveled to Europe, importing vine cuttings from Germany, France, and Italy; he influenced California's winegrowing strongly, particularly in the North Coast areas. The list of vineyard pioneers grows swiftly from the mid-nineteenth century. They came from many lands, but it is fair to characterize most wine production in California from the late nineteenth through the early twentieth centuries, until Prohibition, as having an Italian influence. Wines were fermented in large wood vats, reached high alcoholic degree, and were made abundantly to satisfy a growing population. Most of today's production centers were planted

and defined: vineyards in Napa, Sonoma, and Mendocino counties north of San Francisco; to the south, the Bay Area of five counties surrounding that of Santa Clara; and mass-produced wines in the Central Valley running from San Joaquin County through Merced, Fresno, and into King. The growth of Los Angeles infringed on older vineyards, presenting a choice between viticulture and urban expansion that was to be repeated, often dramatically, as both California wines and Californians expanded in this century.

After Prohibition, two influences seem to have marked California wines and the people making them. Long association with the Beaulieu vineyards in the Napa Valley gave the enologist André Tchelistcheff opportunities to impress current generations of wine makers with modern European wine-making techniques; these aimed at small amounts of finer wine made and aged in better equipment. More sweeping has been the influence of university scholars. Three generations of wine makers have issued from a growing tradition of scientific viticulture and vinification. Albert Winkler and Maynard Amerine are but the best known of a group of modern researcher-teachers whose students are found everywhere in responsible positions in the California wine industry. This technological tradition can be seen in many California wines.

If there has been a rising tide of knowledge about wine production, it has certainly been matched by a rising tide of enthusiasm. Numbers of Californians have settled in established winegrowing areas (and elsewhere) not to make large commercial quantities of wine but to cultivate smaller crops aimed at high-priced markets and superior quality, however each grower may define "quality." The 1970s has witnessed an enormous expansion of plantings. The supply of grapes is rising rapidly, and grape prices are falling. To the excitement of pioneering has been added the less desirable excitement of a potential crisis of agricultural overexpansion.

CALIFORNIA VINEYARDS

Most of the vineyards in California, including some of the most famous names, are set on valley floors; but both historically and today the best wines come from vineyards in the hills. The slopes of areas such as Santa Maria and parts of Monterey County resemble those of Burgundy, and settlers planted on such steep land long ago. Nevertheless, agriculturalists today are intent on caring for vineyards quickly and thoroughly. In many great growing areas, such as the Central Valley, the land gives the appearance of an industrial-scale orchard set on flat irrigated plains. Sadly, many older vine plots have been abandoned or ripped out because of the effort required to work them; one of California's oldest Cabernet vineyards, at Los Gatos in

Santa Clara County, was turned into sheep pasture because it could only be cultivated by animal labor and not by tractors. Terracing or anything resembling it is unthinkable in America's economic environment. Many excellent sites may remain unplanted, and the appearance of its vineyards is less varied than other fine wine areas.

Vines are trained higher, trained bigger, spaced farther apart, and grow more vigorously than their counterparts in Europe. Wineries tend to be set in the midst of vineyards, not shunted off into towns. Wine land has grown expensive, but this casual use of vineyard area for production and storage building reflects an older America. Also California's strict waste-water regulations tend to keep wineries away from towns.

Fine grape varieties are expanding rapidly in California. The state's climate zones have been extensively studied and classed according to average temperatures. Irrigation is a fact of life, not only in the less favored zones but also in quality areas. This contrasts sharply with practices in quality regions of France and Germany. Yet California growers striving for quality wines end up with a volume of wine per land area closely resembling that of Europe's best vineyards. A California vineyard cropping and crushing three tons of grapes per acre is operating much as quality-control laws in France, Germany, or Italy require their growers to do. Approximately 150 gallons (570 liters) of wine are obtained from a ton of grapes.

While California growers now know much about their grape varieties and their possibilities, in the past vineyards were laid out with less selectivity than in the older, more evolved sites of Europe. Important contributions to improving this casual attitude have been made in the last 50 years. Some other contrasts between winegrowing in Europe and California are these:

While Californians may not chaptalize wines (i.e., add cane sugar to musts to raise alcoholic degree), they generally have far more freedom to make wines as they please. This can be seen vividly in the area of cheap table-wine production. A California winery can virtually "strip" the wine it is about to make of many of its natural constituents such as tannin and then replace them in the amount desired to achieve a certain taste it deems will appeal to a mass market. This is the case with many big brands of wine, typified by the most successful, Gallo. In the case of quality wines, California wine makers tend to suppress the wild and other natural yeasts coming in on the grape skins by killing them with sulphur dioxide as grapes are crushed, then inducing fermentations with selected strains of added yeasts. Fermentations go forward more quickly and more completely in many cases.

Fearing loss of acidity, natural secondary fermentations reducing acidity are less encouraged than in Europe. The presence of volatile acid is keenly discouraged. Balanced pure wines result from all these careful interventions in natural fermentation, but they tend to have a less voluminous aroma and bouquet. Californians more readily filter their wines and consider as "dirty" many odors and flavors that Europeans not only accept but even consider expected parts of a wine's style. For this and other reasons, California varietals can contrast starkly with traditional European wine made from identical varieties. A fair statement might be that California wines have had an easier, cleaner fermentation under more human control than European wines; they are technically cleaner but have less smell and sometimes less taste than European fine wines. All these statements are relative, however: no California fine wine producer aims to make tasteless wine just as no fine wine producer in Europe aims to make sick or foul-tasting wine.

WINE-PRODUCING ZONES OF CALIFORNIA

A characteristic of California's vineyard might be said to be lack of discrimination in settling one variety in its best locale; a franker phrase would say that vines have been quickly planted where money was thought to be made. For example, Cabernet Sauvignon, whose price was noticeably high, has been slapped into any land that could be bought instead of adapting this excellent grape to optimal sites.

Much like Italy, and unlike France and Germany, wine grapes can be grown throughout California. But superior locales can be suggested. One of the first descriptions is that of A. J. Winkler—a zoning system based on "heat summation," the average amount of sun-generated heat a growing grape would receive. This general zoning has been refined by attention to soil conditions and microclimate; not least in these reconsiderations has figured the same Dr. Winkler. California producers, however, think of their land, or more pointedly that of other growers, as belonging in Region I, II, III, IV, or V, classed on a statistical basis of average "heat summation."

California vineyards begin in the so-called North Coast region, the counties of Mendocino, Sonoma, and Napa. This is reputed the finest California area. In fact it includes zones ranging from Region I to Region IV, and its best grapes seem to be Cabernet Sauvignon, Pinot Noir, Chardonnay, Zinfandel, Petite Sirah, Sauvignon Blanc, and Gewürztraminer.

Going east and south we meet the northern end of San Joaquin Valley comprising Sacramento, Lodi, and the Sierra foothills. The valley is divided into the Amador and Clements growing areas. This is Zinfandel country. Back toward the coast, five counties (Alameda, Santa Clara, Santa Cruz, San Benito, Monterey) make up the southern Bay Area. High population density is displacing vineyards toward the south. Virtually every grape type grown in the state is cultivated here.

Two recently cultivated areas are San Luis Obispo and Santa Barbara counties, with concentrations of plantings at Paso Robles/Shandon, San Luis Obispo township, Santa Inez Valley, and Santa Maria district. This area ripens somewhat earlier than Monterey and includes terrain of Regions I and II. The Central Valley, bordered by the Sierra Nevadas on the east and the Gabilan range on the west, is the vast vineyard terrain of which it could be said, as Frank Schoonmaker has aptly put it, that men planted grapes not knowing whether their living lay in wine or raisins. This land includes Regions III, IV, and V, and from its hot climate come California dessert, fortified, and common-grade wines.

The oldest vineyard area has been uprooted by Los Angeles, and air pollution and urban development have virtually put an end to wine-grape growing in nearby San Bernadino County. Mission grapes persist in San Bernadino as do old Italian plantings (Grignolino) but in Rancho California, just to the south in Riverside, a whole new heterogenous vineyard that could be likened to the Monterey plantings in variety and enterprise has been created. The economy of this new district is dominated by Brookside, however, a large West Coast company owned by Beatrice Foods and producing wine sold only in their own outlets.

At the north end of San Diego County, careful study has pioneered selected varieties in favored ground with more scruple than characterized vineyard development in the late 1960s.

WINE REGULATION AND QUALITY CONTROL

Laws attempting to regulate wine quality and authenticity turn out to offer a study of national character: German laws go into immense detail regulating such things as grape sugar content; French laws are logical but complex and based on persistent principles; and American laws are freewheeling, helter-skelter, and slightly anarchic. It is paradoxical that California wines, technically the best in the world, are sold to a public nearly totally unprotected by law, and it is doubly paradoxical that such laws as exist often prohibit specific information about the real authenticity of a wine. Many grower-producers of absolutely authentic wine are forbidden to use the name of their locality, for instance, because it is "insufficiently well known." You may own a vineyard in St. Helena, for example, and grow Cabernet Sauvignon grapes on it; you may make them into a wine you are proud of, and yet not be allowed to label your wine St. Helena Cabernet Sauvignon. But this same set of laws allows anyone to call his wine Cabernet even if it is half or, more exactly, 51 percent of that grape variety. One is tempted to throw up both hands in despair and stop with that paradoxical example; but something of a system does exist.

Two government bodies regulate California wines and their descrip-

tions on labels: the Alcohol, Tobacco and Firearms Division of the Internal Revenue Service, and the State of California. ATF must approve every label on alcoholic beverages sold in America. The State of California has its own ideas, for example forbidding the addition of sugar to grape juice or the use of water to lower excess acidity, both practices allowed in other states. But in typically American fashion, ATF consults the industry it is regulating, and the voice it listens to is that of the California Wine Institute, founded in 1934 to promote California wine. The Wine Institute is a club of wine producers funded by the one-half cent per gallon of wine sold that are the club's "dues." Therefore it is dominated by the big mass producers, and it is not too much to say that the Institute is Gallo and then everyone else, since United Vintners, California's second largest producer, has quit the club. At the moment there is a debate running on whether or not wine should be regulated by the Federal Food and Drug Administration, since it is a product Americans consume.

While Europe defines wine as fermented juice of fresh grapes, America is by no means so narrow-minded. There is such a thing as light wine made with "natural" or "special natural" flavors. Consumers will not be amused to learn that this may mean damned near anything. An "apple wine" may be flavored by such "natural" substances as essential oils from petroleum rather than apples.

Table wine, however, is from grapes. In California it is wine between 10.5 and 14 percent alcohol. Since in America alcoholic content is stated within 1.5 percent of actual strength, a wine labeled as 12.5 percent alcohol fits the 10.5 to 14 percent limits. Not only may alcoholic degree be bolstered by adding grape concentrate; once 10.5 percent is achieved, alcoholic degree may be brought up to 14 percent by adding alcohol. Examples of this are "Robusto" or "Fortissimo" wine types usually sold in bulk. In Europe this procedure would class a wine as "fortified." There is no technical distinction in America between natural or "fortified" table wines. ATF cares that it gets higher taxes on wines over 14 percent alcohol, and that is all.

"Mountain" wine was used to denote wine from higher slopes, therefore presumed better. Today "mountain" wines come from vineyards above sea level. There are three sorts of superior designations for wines: one steals European place names and considers them "wine types," such as Chablis; a second designates grape varieties and insists that their production locale be specified, however generally, such as "American Cabernet Sauvignon" or "California Chardonnay"; a third exists for grape varieties presumed local to California, such as Zinfandel, Emerald Riesling or White Riesling, Ruby Cabernet, Muscat, Carnelian, and Carmine. Wine types such as Chablis or Burgundy are described in such broad terms by the Wine Institute as to become meaningless.

When we turn to European varietals, a most puzzling situation exists. The broadest designation is American. Then comes California. Finally, ATF recognizes certain regions as having identity, Napa Valley for example. It recognizes counties such as Alexander Valley, which is in both Napa and Sonoma counties. Sometimes a town name is allowed; Livermore is one example, and wines made from grapes vaguely surrounding this locale can so call themselves. Grapes grown in Napa Valley may be carted off to Monterey to be made into wine calling itself Napa Valley Cabernet. Worst of all, a mere 51 percent of one grape variety suffices for the varietal designation. There is nothing wrong and a great deal right with blending grape varieties, but something is wrong about a system that allows two wines to be sold as Pinot Noir from Sonoma when one of them is 100 percent Pinot Noir and the other is 51 percent Pinot Noir, 30 percent Alicante Bouchet, and 19 percent "other." The law is stricter in designating such regions as it chooses to recognize: Monterey wine is 75 percent from grapes grown in Monterey County. If it is a vintage wine, it must be 95 percent from wine of the place stated on the label. And if it presents itself as 1971 Monterey Zinfandel, then it must be 95 percent of 1971 crop grapes. This was sensibly reduced from 100 percent to allow wine makers to top up barrels aging in their wineries.

Turning to the authenticity of the producer, a hierarchy of terms decreases in truthfulness. "Grown, produced, and bottled by" means what it says. "Produced and bottled by" means that the company selling the wine has crushed and fermented 75 percent of the grapes making up that wine. "Made and bottled by" is totally misleading. Any winery may say this provided that it crushes, ferments, and bottles no less than 10 percent of the wine it sells. "Vinted by" or "Perfected by" means only that some part of the wine in that bottle was treated (barrel aged, for example) by the firm selling it. "Bottled by" merely means what it says. The European concept of estate bottling is exemplified only by wines saying "Grown, produced, and bottled by." "Estate Bottled" is a California wine label term but means only that the seller of that wine either grew the grapes that made it or bought them under contract; thus it is a less strong guarantee than "Grown, produced, and bottled by."

As usual, legislation permits mass producers of inexpensive wine to dress themselves, by implication, in finer terms than the truth would allow. And, as usual, legislation is irrelevant at the top end of quality where ambitious wine makers are battling for high prices and for glory by making the best wines possible. However, a few things obviously could be tightened up. It is unseemly that mass-produced wines can confusingly masquerade under the same distinguished names as fine ones. For Americans, certain grape varietal names connote quality. Yet "Cabernet Sauvignon" priced from $2.00 to $18.00 a bottle stares at you in the wine shop, and only past experience of the brand helps you to choose. Can label laws make a cheap industrial product readily distinguishable from a wine made by a craftsman's care and pride? Maybe not. But should American wine be allowed to call itself Champagne, Chablis, or Burgundy? And can someone explain why it should not be 100 percent Chardonnay or Pinot Noir if that is what it so enticingly claims to be?

EUROPEAN RED VARIETIES

The swing from marketing wines under a brand name or European type to featuring wines of a single grape variety has been a dominant fact of recent California wine history. Producers of ordinary mass-produced wines have recently joined this trend. It may not be possible to say precisely what should be the tasting qualities of a Cabernet Sauvignon. But it is appropriate to say firmly that wines presented as Cabernet Sauvignon without any distinctive characteristics and intensity of flavor can be attacked as misleading. Unfortunately the California Wine Institute in its published *Type Specifications* has announced that ". . . heavier-bodied and darker-colored wines should be on an equal footing with the lighter-bodied and lighter-colored wines." In other words, anything goes. We disagree. We think this poor, sleazy advice and a policy not serving the public interest. Not only in fine wine-producing regions throughout the world but even among makers of ordinary wines, generous color, body, and taste have been

and remain positive points of quality. One need not define a precise style in order to class wines roughly as ordinary as against good.

Mission Grape

The Spaniards called the early plantings *Criolla*. This word (like *Creole*) means a child born in the New World but of European ancestry—Spain in this case. *Criolla* or Mission grape has been likened to Sardinia's Monica variety or France's Grenache. Unlike European varietals imported in the nineteenth century, Mission has evolved freely during its four centuries in the New World. It is used for fortified wines, and today interest in its cultivation is nonexistent. Its pallid wines, poorly pigmented, notoriously low in acid, and easily oxidized, have played their part in California history and are on their way out. Nevertheless, it is America's oldest wine grape. The last plantings were in 1972. In 1974 just over 6,000 acres (2,400 hectares) of these vines were standing.

Cabernet Sauvignon

Cabernet Sauvignon was not the first European varietal vine introduced, but it is now the most important quality wine grape. The plant grows well in suitable California regions. Its acidity is desirably high. It yields less than five tons per acre under best conditions but can make six or seven tons. It produces wine of more alcoholic degree here than in its native Bordeaux—a fact influencing wine style. During the 1970s more has been planted than was previously in acreage. In 1974, of some 25,000 acres (10,000 hectares) standing, 16,000 (6,400 hectares) were in young vines not yet bearing.

Cabernet wine style varies by winery and locale, even among the large sellers. Those of Almadén contrast with those of Beaulieu. Grower-producers have their own ideas. Good examples of wine from this grape show dark color, tannin and astringency, and abundant flavor, though the nature of this flavor is much influenced by production methods, cask age, and of course conditions under which grapes are vintaged. Bordeaux wine makers might dislike the style most California quality wine makers aim for in good Cabernet wine, but they would recognize it as Cabernet; California wines of this variety remain within a family showing varietal character. Cabernet styles most admired in California have in common a vigorous effect on the palate with much tannin and astringency, often combined with a "hot" impression arising in part from generous alcohol degrees. Such rich, intense wines command prices comparable to better French wines. Local demand is very strong, and many of the most esteemed wines never leave California. This is true of many of the state's better wines.

Mass-produced wines bearing the name Cabernet may be clean but bland and give no definite tasting impression. Designating such wines "Cabernet" is misleading. Growing or vinification techniques are not to blame as much as the blending in of other wines up to the limit of 49 percent within which a wine may still be called Cabernet. Wines showing Cabernet character need not be 100 percent Cabernet, but a solid majority of this grape is necessary to obtain varietal attributes. Large new Cabernet plantings in unproven areas raise questions about future wine style; from 1970 to 1974 some 5,000 acres (2,000 hectares) have been planted in Monterey County, for example. A decade ago, Napa County had about half the Cabernet standing in

California, approximately 950 out of 1,950 acres (380 of 780 hectares). Clearly many changes of uncertain success are in store for the latter part of this decade.

Zinfandel

Until recently, the fiction that Pinot Noir was the second important quality red grape of California was stubbornly maintained. Now most fine growers consider Zinfandel, once little esteemed, clearly to be next in importance to Cabernet; and some think it better. This change, the most rapid, dramatic, and important event in California, is interesting. Zinfandel was easy to cultivate; it made sound red wine and was taken for granted. Not until the care reserved for finest wines was lavished on its production did Zinfandel reveal its full powers.

The precise European origins of Zinfandel are not known historically but are nearly proved experimentally; it seems to be the Primativo di Gioia, a grape from southern Italy. Plantings from Italy compared with those of Zinfandel seem to show exact correspondences. It is an easy grape to grow, the bush tidy and fairly vigorous. Its color is fine and dark, its yield in alcohol good, and volume is high even in very old vines; 40-year-old plants can give four to five tons per acre. More old Zinfandel exists in California than old Cabernet or Chardonnay. It fares badly in wet ground, however; tight bunches are vulnerable to bunch rot. Hence its traditional growing areas are best, such as Amador, Sonoma, and Mendocino counties. Napa Valley Zinfandels of quality are rare. Regrettably, as with other old interesting vines, much Zinfandel area was ripped up and replanted in Cabernet due to higher prices for this more fashionable grape.

Since it is a sound grape that ripens well, a range of wine styles can result from Zinfandel. Its aroma is not dramatic, but it is characteristic. Its wines have complete qualities and balance, with varietal character. Strong-colored, very full balanced wines with assertive flavor are regularly made from it. These can be chewy and astringent, very mouth-filling. It is possible deliberately to make lighter, fresher red wines; since 1973 Zinfandel made by carbonic maceration method and intended, like Beaujolais, to be consumed within weeks of its production has been marketed. (Monteviña Zinfandel Nuevo is one of several such wines.) Zinfandel is above all a sound, wholesome, flavorful, generous, complete, and clean red wine. To market as Zinfandel wine not natural in taste or complete in qualities is inexcusable, for that sort of wine is easy to produce from this grape.

In 1974 of California's 30,000 acres (12,000 hectares) of Zinfandel, one-third were immature vines. This dramatizes recent appreciation for the grape. Much new planting has occurred in Monterey, San Joaquin, and Stanislaus counties. A decade ago San Joaquin, San Bernardino, and Sonoma counties accounted for some 75 percent of California's 16,500 acres (6,600 hectares) of this vine. Among red wines, California can point to quality Zinfandel as virtually its unique contribution to the world's family of fine wines. Present costs place good quality Zinfandel at retail prices between $2.00 and $3.00 per bottle and even less in California. So far it is not the large wineries that have shown either initiative or performance in developing this excellent wine.

Pinot Noir

This famous European variety makes red Burgundy wines and most Champagne. There are three types of this vine, however, and many subvarieties. While some plantings from Burgundy were made in California, most of the vines used come from the Swiss version of Pinot Noir that promised to bear better in California. It is widely cultivated and still being planted, but it cannot be said that its results resemble those tasting qualities obtained in France. This contrasts sharply with the Burgundian Chardonnay vine, whose California white wines resemble those obtained in Burgundy. It is now thought that some new regions—e.g., Monterey, Santa Maria, and Carneros—may give more exciting results for Pinot Noir for climatic reasons. Certainly it has done poorly in California's hot regions.

Not only is Pinot Noir a meager bearer in California, but it is also unstable in that its behavior in different terrains and under different cultivation methods varies too much. These changes affect not simply the amount of fruit produced each year but also the taste, or lack of it, of the wine that results. Still, its better wines are strongly appreciated in California and elsewhere. Their aroma is restricted compared to some other red varieties, but what is there is subtle and grapy; aging in small oak barrels or other wood of course adds various odors. California wine makers are avid students and experimenters in the different influences of diverse wood casks.

Pinot Noir sharply reflects growing condition, vinification, and aging more than any other major California grape. Burgundian oak imparts "Burgundian" odors to California Pinot Noir, causing them to resemble red Burgundy to that degree. When a malolactic fermentation is pressed forward in a California Pinot Noir, other resemblances with its French cousin may arise. When cask aging promotes increased volatility, California Pinot Noirs also come to resemble familiar Burgundy impressions. Pinot Noir not made in these ways will resemble similar ones in France—light, hard wines lacking aroma such as Pinot Noir in Champagne (Bouzy, Sillery).

Much Pinot Noir under commercial labels has been made from vines planted in disregard of the best conditions for this difficult vine and shows the following character: lack of definition in varietal aroma, awkwardness in balance, flatness (lack of acidity), coarseness disappointing to those familiar with the fame of Pinot Noir classic qualities. The fact that in a small area in Europe's northern zone great red (Burgundy) and white (Champagne) wines can be produced from this grape has led to overly high expectations of what Pinot Noir can do in California or, more precisely, what it has done so far. There may be areas in which far superior quality can be extracted. In 1974 10,098 acres (4,040 hectares) of vines included 6,375 (2,550) in nonbearing young vines.

Gamay Beaujolais

This is Pinot Noir that was originally planted as "Gamay Beaujolais." The law allows both names.

Petite Sirah

This variety is known to old California growers, who have some doubts about the pronunciation, as "Pets." Here is another mistake. Most plantings are not real Syrah—the Rhône Valley plant—but another Rhône variety, called Duriff, with less intense flavor, color, and acidity than Syrah. Introduced for color and other contributions to

"Burgundy" wines, it is now grown throughout the state and sold as a varietal. Adapting well to warm climate, it is extensive in San Joaquin and used there for standard red table wine, coarse wines by whatever name, dull but appreciated by consumers favoring "hot" burned flavors. In colder areas with well-drained soil, intense purple color, fragrant perfume, tannin, and body result. Such wines, hailing from Mendocino and Sonoma counties and from the area of Livermore, age with some distinction. Newer vineyard areas in the southern part of California, around Paso Robles and San Diego County, have normally obtained not the Duriff but the Rhône-type Syrah (used for Hermitage and Côte-Rotie). Both varieties are and probably will be sold as Petite Sirah, though California growers distinguish between "French Syrah" and Petite Sirah. As in the Rhône, true Syrah gives dense, dark, powerful wines of distinct character. In 1974 there were 13,074 acres (5,230 hectares), of which 7,714 acres (3,086 hectares) were planted in young vines.

Gamay (or Napa Valley Gamay)

This is the true Gamay Noir à Jus Blanc of Beaujolais. California conditions result in heavier-bodied wines than in Beaujolais. They are less perfumed (though this may be due to California's fermentation with its determination to reduce volatility) but well-colored, balanced, medium red wines with flavor appropriate to good red wine though not the more overpowering varietal flavor found, for example, in good Cabernet. Good acidity recommends Gamay to moderately warm areas such as the northern Napa Valley or Sacramento County. Sometimes it is used in blended wines. The popularity of Gamay Beaujolais, really Pinot Noir as we have seen, has led to addition of true Gamay to "Gamay Beaujolais" wines, and the combination may be, and is, legally sold as Gamay Beaujolais. Christian Brothers sell a variety properly called Gamay Noir. In 1974 there were 4,760 acres (1,900 hectares) of vines, of which 3,128 acres (1,251 hectares) were young vines.

Merlot

Until 1969 Merlot was not bottled as a varietal wine. It had been used only for blending. For the same reasons as in its native Bordeaux, Californians are turning to this generously yielding, easily harvested grape, whose wines mature rapidly, becoming soft, pleasing reds. Its adaptability to some new areas is exciting; in Monterey County it ripens earlier and better than Cabernet. Unblended, the wine is highly distinctive, with aroma and color closely resembling that of Cabernet but with less tannin and therefore rounder characteristics to the taste. In 1974 there were 20,244 acres (8,098 hectares), of which 6,897 acres (2,759 hectares) were in young vines.

Grenache

Prevalent in mass-production areas of the Central Valley, this variety makes as many different wines as growing locations permit. The ubiquitous Grenache rosé so familiar to Americans comes from the Central Valley, where Grenache combined with other red grapes also yield common red wine. It produces California Port as well. In cooler growing areas, such as Napa and Monterey, Grenache gives better colored rosé and red wines that, if lacking in color, have distinctive tasting qualities identifiable with this grape. The Almadén Grenoir Original is one of these. Grenache needs considerable heat to ripen.

Barbera

This Italian variety was brought to California for its high total acidity, intense color, and ability to produce well-balanced juice in warm regions. In the Central Valley, Barbera gives wines without distinction that have high acidity but lack the intensity of Barbera varietal taste.

In northern California it faintly approaches its Italian prototype. Acidity is higher still, a quality prized in this varietal. Intensely colored red-black or red-purple, its aroma may be neutral, but its tasting characteristics account for its popularity. Barbera is unusual in that its limited tannin avoids mouth-coating astringency, yet it is acid enough to give extremely lively wines. It is always sold as Barbera since it is much demanded for its drinkability and its image as ideal for Italian food. In fact, California Barbera is much blander than its forceful Italian counterpart. In 1974 there were 20,576 acres (8,230 hectares) of vines, 11,824 (4,730) in young vines.

Grignolino

Little of this is produced and sold, though before Prohibition it was an important California variety producing characteristically light-bodied orange red wine achieving some success as red and more as rosé. It is still grown as a relic by a handful of producers who turn it into red or rosé: Heitz, Beringer, Cresta Blanca, San Martin, and the California Wine Association among them. A few smaller producers also make Grignolino for local sale.

Carignane

Used as a blending red variety in the Central Valley, it yields much and softens early. American consumers will see its name on bottles from a few small producers, Fetzer for example, in Mendocino County, where old vines in cooler zones produce light, attractive red wine. In 1974 there were 30,710 acres (12,284 hectares) planted, of which 4,181 acres (1,672 hectares) were young vines.

Alicante Bouchet

A varietal of this name is about to be sold by Angelo Papagni from his old vineyards in Madera. Properly cultivated, this variety gives very flavorful wine with the darkest color possible in any red wine. A hybrid developed for its color, it is one of the few red grapes with red juice. It resembles California Petite Sirah in tasting qualities. In 1974 there were 6,820 acres (2,608 hectares), of which 519 acres (208 hectares) were in young vines.

EUROPEAN WHITE VARIETIES

Chardonnay

It is the most important quality white wine in California, and its repute in the state is based on its great success in Burgundy plus the happy coincidence that its best tasting qualities in California actually resemble those achieved in Burgundy. Depending on its producing area, its wines are less or more pronounced in body and flavor. Certain Chardonnay types are best grown in heavier soil where rich, ripe Chardonnay grape flavor emerges, as in Burgundy. The Napa Valley floor, Santa Clara mountain areas, and favored Monterey County locations are among these.

Recommended as the white variety suitable for coldest regions, it nevertheless achieves depth of flavor in regions warmer than the coldest. In these last its high acidity is better suited to sparkling wine and generally it does not achieve its full tasting range.

Its yield is low. It responds strongly to fermenting methods, the most common of which is in French oak casks. Aging also gives results summed up as a more "French" taste. These methods seeking to achieve French-style wine mask the innate flavor of Chardonnay well grown in California. A California ideal might be a yellow color with green tints, the lack of which suggests more ponderous or even stale taste. The particular perfume of California Chardonnay is a ripe grape odor and is suggestive of apples rather than the vanilla and oak overtones contributed by cask. It is a wine very generous in body, more than other California whites. Its ripe grape aroma is repeated in the mouth in the sensation of ripe grapes, and its development on the palate is more straightforward and more dominated by a taste of fruit than those seeking French style.

Badly done, too commercial Chardonnay markedly lacks either of the above styles. Such wines are thin and watery, lacking taste, body, or mouth-filling qualities.

Some other preferred appellations are Santa Maria in Santa Barbara County, Sonoma, and the Carneros region of Napa. Mendocino produces interesting but acid examples. Producers specializing in Chardonnay, though by no means alone in producing excellent examples, usually emerge with more interesting wine. It has been discovered that the so-called Pinot Chardonnay grape does not belong to the Pinot family. While its designation is now "Chardonnay," use of the term "Pinot Chardonnay" continues. In 1974 there were 10,037 acres (4,015 hectares), of which 6,429 acres (2,572 hectares) were in young vines.

Johannisberg (White) Riesling

This true Riesling grape, mother of German fine wines, is designated "Rhine Riesling" in Europe.

In California it has not achieved the heights of quality—or the tastes—it attains in Germany. Perhaps better-adapted regions will give better results. Sugar content is adequate, but intensity of flavor is not. Attempts at not merely less dry but decidedly sweet Rieslings that possess "German" flavor are being made. The best examples suggest Riesling odor and flavor, but they are not white wines that offer the direct, continued style that wins highest praise. In 1974 there were 7,194 acres (2,878 hectares) planted, of which 5,141 acres (2,056 hectares) were in young vines.

Grey Riesling

This is not a true Riesling, but its wines resemble them. Its aroma and flavor are delicate, and it is usually designated "medium dry" to "medium sweet." It is medium-bodied and should be inexpensive. In 1974 there were 1,698 acres (679 hectares) planted in Grey Riesling, of which 824 (330) were in young vines.

Sauvignon Blanc

This is also sold as Blanc Fumé or Fumé Blanc. These last two designations commonly offer wine less tart and less strongly Sauvignon Blanc in character. Livermore is the traditional producing ground for Sauvignon Blanc in California; its rocky soils were thought to resemble those in France, where this grape was favored. Cooler areas such as Monterey County and Mendocino tend to emphasize Sauvignon varietal character, and their wines sometimes resemble whites from the Loire. Warmer areas like Napa and Livermore produce Sauvignon with varietal attributes but less startling in general tasting style. In 1974 there were 3,193 acres (1,277 hectares), of which 1,874 (750) were in young vines.

Sémillon

This other Bordeaux variety fits well in Sauvignon growing conditions and, as in Bordeaux, is commonly blended with it. In California the blend is sold as Sauvignon Blanc. Sémillon grows well in the hot Central Valley and makes a full-bodied white wine. When sold as Sémillon, it usually originates in Livermore or Napa Valley and ranges from medium-full to positively sweet with good flavor and fruit. In 1974 there were 3,356 acres (1,342 hectares) planted, of which 1,399 (560) were in young vines.

Gewürztraminer

This famous spicy Alsatian grape gives high alcohol in California. Its full-bodied wine may be left slightly sweet to capture the heady and characteristic perfume of the grape. When fermented completely dry, it rarely offers this opulent perfume, though it retains character. (The wine sold as Traminer in California is not Traminer but Red Veltliner and has no connection with Gewürztraminer.) In 1974 there were 2,175 acres (870 hectares), 1,433 (573) in young vines.

Chenin Blanc

The workhorse of Californian white varietal grapes is grown from north to south and is produced anywhere from bone dry to positively sweet in style. Dry styles offer small aroma, good acid, and therefore tart taste, medium body, and a particular, slightly bitter finish.

Medium-dry to medium-sweet Chenin can give richer perfume, more body and texture, and a generous sensation in the mouth, and as one progresses toward sweeter versions the latent bitter aftertaste drops away; most drinkers prefer this Chenin style. Very dry varieties will be labeled "dry," whereas fuller ones are usually simply sold as Chenin Blanc. As in France, it is sold as Pineau de la Loire, here by Christian Brothers from their mountain vineyards. Their Chenin Blanc is richer.

This grape and Sémillon, the best white producers in the Central Valley and other warm areas, are used there to improve white table wine. In 1974 there were 19,826 acres (7,930 hectares) of vines, 9,816 (3,926) in young vines.

Pinot Blanc

Considered a white mutation of Pinot Noir, this grape is no longer widely grown in California. A bit is sold as Pinot Blanc. Grown in Monterey for blending, it is favored for sparkling wines, with only a few firms (Wente, Chalone, Novitiate, Paul Masson, Almadén, and others) producing it as a varietal. In 1974 there were 1,296 acres (518 hectares), 570 (228) in young vines.

French Colombard

In the Central Valley this grape is widely grown for blended white wines and as the base for cheap white sparkling wines. Cooler regions give a pleasant, balanced white varietal wine that should be slightly sweet. Parducci Ukian, in Mendocino, is among the leaders in varietal marketing of Colombard. In 1974 there were 26,616 acres (10,646 hectares) of vines, 5,693 (2,277) in young vines.

Muscat

Two varieties, differing in origin and use, are grown in California. Moscato Canelli, famous in Europe as Moscato d'Asti, is grown in the Central Valley to make dessert wine sold as Muscat Frontignan and in Napa and Santa Clara to make light table wine. Muscat of Alexandria is basically a Central Valley raisin variety. Dry wine from this second Muscat is also made there, but it loses Muscat perfume and flavor under these conditions.

Green Hungarian

Uninteresting wine despite its jazzy designation, it is Hungarian in name only and is little cultivated.

Folle Blanche

Once a French Cognac grape, Folle Blanche is now produced solely by Louis Martini Winery. The wine is quite dry, light in flavor, high in acid, and fairly widely distributed. In 1974 there were 247 acres (100 hectares) planted.

Sylvaner

This is technically spoken of as Frankenriesling or Sylvaner Riesling. It is a preferred grape in Franconia and the Palatinate in Germany.

Delicate, German-style white wine of good overall quality can be made from this grape in California. The Monterey Vineyard calls its version Grüner Sylvaner. Some sparkling blended wine also uses this grape. In 1974 there were 1,668 acres (667 hectares) planted, 542 (217) in young vines.

Malvasia Bianca

Italian, with Muscat perfume and flavor, the grape is grown in the Central Valley for light table wine and fortified dessert wine. It is used also for blending for its touch of Muscat quality. In 1974 there were 960 acres (384 hectares) of vines, 490 (196) in young vines.

NATIVE CALIFORNIA VARIETIES OR CROSSES

Ruby Cabernet

Developed at the University of California at Davis in the late 1930s and offered for planting in the 1940s, it is a cross of Cabernet and Carignane designed to combine Cabernet flavor and the productivity of Carignane vines in the Central Valley.

Wines sold under varietal designation are recent. "Cabernet" was sufficient, "Cabernet Sauvignon" more specific. The introduction of Ruby Cabernet required legislative distinction from Cabernet Sauvignon. Cabernet Sauvignon must now have a local appellation; Ruby Cabernet need not state its origin within the state.

Ruby Cabernet displays strong flavor, as does Cabernet Sauvignon. The motive for its development was climatic adaptation, but this has been ignored by large wineries who see it as a cheap substitute for Cabernet. No examples on the market reflect its potential. Instead, the consumer finds a harsh, limited imitation of Cabernet Sauvignon. In 1974 there were 17,583 acres of vines (7,033 hectares), 12,644 (5,058) in young, non-bearing vines.

Carnelian and Carmine

These two new varieties of Cabernet parentage will presently be commercialized. They will be lighter-bodied than Ruby Cabernet, with adequate acidity and low alcohol. The first is adapted for warmer, the second for cooler climates. The University of California at Davis has released them. Like Ruby Cabernet, both are hybridizations by Harold Olmo, and both promise to be commercially important.

Emerald Riesling

This is another cross developed by Dr. Olmo. Made from white Riesling and Muscadelle and released in the late 1940s, it was also destined for the Central Valley, because of its good acidity in warm climates. It suggests Riesling flavor, with some Muscadelle bitter finish. It is typically sold as Riesling-type wine, in long green bottles. Paul Masson calls it Emerald Dry. It is usually inexpensive, between $2.00–$3.00. In 1974, 2,846 acres (1,138 hectares) were planted, 1,564 acres (626 hectares) in young vines.

Italian Swiss Colony Rhineskellar Moselle

This wine's name is a merchandiser's delight and a wine maker's nightmare. Imagine trying to make a Moselle wine in a Rhine cellar! In its name, this wine shows the lengths to which advertising will go in attempting to get across a point.

This blandly flavored, medium-dry white wine, made in what California conceives to be a German style, is somewhat successful in its destined market: that which considers Liebfraumilch the last word in wine. Produced from a mixture of white grapes from the North Coast and the Central Valley, its overall taste impression is one of simplicity and rather ordinary grapiness coupled with a sweet overtone. A small amount of carbonic acid gas gives it a liveliness in part reminiscent of its namesake wines. It usually costs under $1.50 a bottle.

VINTAGE   DATE   PRICE

GUESTS

MENU   COMMENTS

Guild Vino da Tavola

The packaging is conceived to appeal to a public image of things Italian, with its distinctive checkerboard label and its pitch as a wine for daily consumption. It originated as a red wine but is now made white and pink as well. Once simply a light wine with fruit, pleasant if slightly sweet, it has evolved in the direction of what might be termed "light Burgundy" type, meaning a light beverage wine with no varietal character at all. This type of brand label and innocuous tasting quality is gradually being pushed aside in favor of more distinctive wines varietally named. Like its rivals, Gallo Vino Paisano and Cribari Vino Rosso, its price is less than $2.00 per bottle.

VINTAGE   DATE   PRICE

GUESTS

MENU   COMMENTS

Gallo Hearty Burgundy

The largest-selling red wine of its kind in America is made with a good proportion of North Coast grapes. It is concocted to attract a taste seeking an immediate impression of smoothness, balance, and body and gives a sensation richer than its 12.5 percent alcohol. The technique is to strip wine of many of its natural substances and then add back some of them under highly sophisticated controls in such a manner as to fit what the manufacturer conceives to be the widest public taste. This has been extremely successful. It is expertly made and more flavorful and less artificial tasting than some of its "Burgundy-type" rivals. Despite its reputation, however, this technically perfect achievement is utterly uninteresting even among wines of the ordinary class. Among its competitors are C. K. Barberone and others producing wines of the "hearty" or "robust" type.

VINTAGE   DATE   PRICE

GUESTS

MENU   COMMENTS

Giumarra Ruby Cabernet Rouge

The law now requires wineries such as this to correct their original designation of Cabernet to read "Ruby Cabernet," a lesser grape. Giumarra is a large Central Valley grower whose wines have been favorably received at the Los Angeles County Fair, though wines sold in commerce do not appear to come from the same bottling lots. The wines are mass produced in stainless-steel tanks and have national distribution. Intensely flavored and somewhat overpowering, they give the peculiar impressions of Ruby Cabernet grown in these hot climates—strong taste but no merits beyond the suggestion of varietal character. The Ruby Cabernet of Conti Royal, Barengo, Almadén, Inglenook, and Paul Masson are competing reds that show similarities with this one.

VINTAGE   DATE   PRICE

GUESTS

MENU   COMMENTS

Italian Swiss Colony ®

Colony *Rhineskeller Moselle is a Semi-Dry, Medium-Bodied, Fruity White Wine. Its Special Character and Fine Taste complements any Meal.*

Rhineskeller Moselle

Serve Chilled.

from California

Produced & bottled by

Italian Swiss Colony, Italian Swiss Colony, Calif. Alc. 11.5% by vol.

GUILD · VINO DA

TAVOLA RED ®

CALIFORNIA TABLE WINE

MADE AND BOTTLED BY GUILD WINE CO., LODI, CALIF., ALC. 12½% BY VOL

GALLO ®

HEARTY BURGUNDY. ®

OF CALIFORNIA

Its rich, full-bodied flavor—from fine varietal grapes—will surprise you. Made and bottled at the Gallo Vineyards in Modesto, California. Alcohol 13.5% by vol.

Giumarra Classic California

Ruby Cabernet Rouge

(1974)

Giumarra Classic Ruby Cabernet Rouge is an eminently pleasing red table wine, with brilliant color, distinctive Cabernet aroma and a velvety taste sensation on the palate. This delightful wine is produced from the Ruby Cabernet grape, which is the offspring of the marriage of two famous grape varieties—Cabernet Sauvignon and Carignane. The Giumarra Family has designated the wine produced from this splendid grape "Ruby Cabernet Rouge." It goes particularly well with beef, lamb, pasta. Serve at cool room temperature.

Produced and bottled by Giumarra Vineyards, Edison, Calif. · Alcohol 12% by vol. · 4/5 quart

Franzia Champagne

Probably the sparkling wine most often poured in America, it is served free on some airlines and has created a demand for sparkling wine where once none existed. Made from grapes such as Tokay, Thompson Seedless, and French Colombard, it is produced by the bulk (Charmat) process and varies a good bit from batch to batch. It has bland, apparently sweet flavors that give little indication of grape and are associated with the *dosage* or addition of grape concentrate and sugar used in making sparkling wines. Gallo Champagne, Almadén Le Domaine, and various labels produced for others by Weibel at their Mission San Jose Fremont plant are its competitors.

VINTAGE   DATE   PRICE

GUESTS

MENU   COMMENTS

Paul Masson Rubion

Paul Masson led in creating proprietary trademark wines showing a house style. Rubion, one of his first, is made mostly from Ruby Cabernet, the California-created cross between California Cabernet and Carignan. Other Masson brands include Baroque, a California Burgundy-style red, Rhinecastle, a German-style white, and Emerald Dry, another faintly German-style wine made from Emerald Riesling, the California cross between Muscadelle and White Riesling.

Rubion is a fleshy red wine suggesting claret, with enough interest for everyday use. Masson's bottle shapes and colors imitate the European wine types on which the wines are modeled, but that is a far cry from misleading the consumer with European place name designations. Masson brands compete successfully with other inexpensive, mass-distribution labels appearing on this and succeeding pages.

VINTAGE   DATE   PRICE

GUESTS

MENU   COMMENTS

Almadén Grenache Rosé

This was the first varietal rosé produced in America. This innovative step was taken before World War II under the direct influence of Frank Schoonmaker. Almadén Grenache Rosé is made to be slightly sweeter than its French counterpart, Tavel, and more resembles the sweet Anjou style of rosé. Its color and balance are aimed at simple quaffing wine, and its sweetness is an adaptation to the American mass market. Almadén has been in the forefront of vineyard expansion and among the first to realize the potential of areas south of the usual growing zones. Until the extensive replantings of the last decade, Almadén was the largest grower of classic varietal grapes in California.

VINTAGE   DATE   PRICE

GUESTS

MENU   COMMENTS

Sebastiani Barbera

This wine is made with some pretensions to quality, and it does achieve a measure of distinction, always being sold with cask and bottle age. It does not replicate Italian Barbera but shows the style of an Italian variety aged in wood; it resembles true Barbera in its astringent, aged tasting qualities. It sells for about $3.30 in nearby markets. Sebastiani is an old Sonoma winery, but until recently it supplied wines in bulk to other bottlers. The firm is among the few selling inexpensive aged wines to the national market. Buena Vista, Kenwood, and a few others also make a Sonoma Barbera. We know of no Barbera plantings in the Napa Valley being turned into Barbera varietal wine at this time.

VINTAGE   DATE   PRICE

GUESTS

MENU   COMMENTS

FRANZIA®

CALIFORNIA

CHAMPAGNE

Naturally fermented. Charmat bulk process. Sparkling wine.

Franzia Champagne has won the approval of experts. Made and bottled by Franzia Brothers Champagne Cellars, Ripon, Calif. Alcohol 12% by vol.

RUBION

PAUL MASSON®

LIGHT SOFT DINNER WINE

A bright ruby-red color and fruity bouquet distinguish this dry table wine. Blended from fine varietal grapes, Rubion is medium-bodied with a soft taste. ℘ *Made and Bottled by Paul Masson Vineyards, Saratoga, Calif. Alcohol 12% by Vol.*

Vineyards Established 1852

Serve   Chilled

ALMADÉN

California

GRENACHE ROSÉ

A fresh, appetizing fragrant rosé wine made from the famous Grenache grape of France, grown in the fine wine vineyards of Northern California.

MADE AND BOTTLED BY
Almadén Vineyards, Los Gatos, California
Alcohol 12½ % by volume

25288   R1-674

VINEYARDS ESTABLISHED 1825

Sebastiani

FOUNDED AT THE END OF EL CAMINO REAL

NORTH COAST COUNTIES

BARBERA

Bold and Robust

PRODUCED AND BOTTLED BY SEBASTIANI VINEYARDS

SONOMA VALLEY, CALIFORNIA

ALC. 12½% BY VOL. BONDED WINERY 876.

Christian Brothers Château La Salle

This is a corporation owned by a lay teaching order of the Roman Catholic church. Château La Salle is a proprietary name given to a light sweet wine mainly of Muscat grapes and named for the order's founder, Saint Jean Baptiste de la Salle. Producing a complete range of both varietal and generic wines, table and fortified, Christian Brothers are also a major brandy maker. Their vineyards extend from Napa Valley down through the Central Valley. Always sold without vintage date, Christian Brothers wines offer standard, sound tasting quality but, as is the case with many large distributors, do not always embody the special varietal characteristics of the grape presented on the label.

VINTAGE   *DATE*   *PRICE*

GUESTS

MENU   *COMMENTS*

Louis Martini Zinfandel

Both a grower and a buyer of grapes, Louis Martini is one of the oldest and best-known names in the Napa Valley wine business. Martini Zinfandel is considered the example of medium-bodied Zinfandel; it is given age in large wood containers so as to achieve a natural-tasting, light, fruity red wine style with mass appeal. Until the recent advent of richer Zinfandels, this was considered the limit of the grape's possibility. Martini is a maker of sound natural wines well worth their modest price. These reliable wines are pitched to reach the general public for regular economical and pleasurable drinking.

VINTAGE   *DATE*   *PRICE*

GUESTS

MENU   *COMMENTS*

Charles Krug Chenin Blanc

Formerly the property of a California pioneer wine maker, this vineyard belongs to the Mondavi family, and, under Robert Mondavi's administration, the company was the first, in 1959, to market a Chenin Blanc varietal wine. It has been a success ever since for its fruity style; it is sold nonvintage. In fact it is a slightly sweet wine, as are so many popular ones. Charles Krug can be fairly compared to both Martini and Sebastiani in producing a range of red and white wines of sound, natural tasting qualities, none exemplary models of its grape variety, but offering good drinking. Krug prices, however, are above those of Martini and Sebastiani.

VINTAGE   *DATE*   *PRICE*

GUESTS

MENU   *COMMENTS*

Brookside Mouvedre

Brookside has pioneered the Rancho California area and makes unusual, even unique wines in California, such as their white St.-Émilion (Trebbiano) and their Mouvedre (French Mourvèdre) red wine, a light creature resembling Rhône tasting qualities. The firm is owned by Beatrice Foods, a Chicago-based firm, and its origins are among the oldest in modern California wine making. The Biane family still manages this winery, which began with its nineteenth-century Cucamonga vineyard.

VINTAGE   *DATE*   *PRICE*

GUESTS

MENU   *COMMENTS*

the
Christian
Brothers®

CHATEAU LA SALLE®
LIGHT WINE
A NATURALLY SWEET LIGHT WINE FROM CALIFORNIA
SERVE CHILLED OR ICED

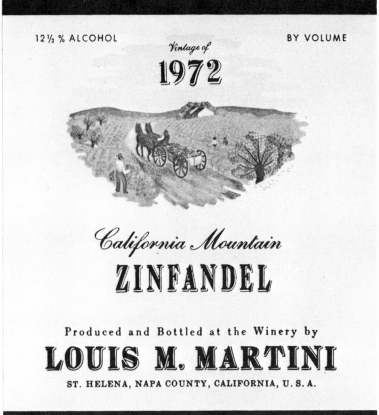

12½ % ALCOHOL   BY VOLUME

Vintage of
1972

California Mountain
ZINFANDEL

Produced and Bottled at the Winery by
LOUIS M. MARTINI
ST. HELENA, NAPA COUNTY, CALIFORNIA, U.S.A.

ESTABLISHED 1861

Charles Krug

NAPA VALLEY
CHENIN BLANC

A MEDIUM DRY WHITE WINE MADE
FROM THE CHENIN BLANC GRAPE

PRODUCED AND BOTTLED BY
Charles Krug Winery
ST. HELENA · CALIFORNIA
ALCOHOL 12% BY VOLUME

BROOKSIDE

CALIFORNIA
MOUVEDRE

DRY ROSÉ WINE

12% ALCOHOL BY VOLUME

PRODUCED AND BOTTLED BY
BROOKSIDE VINEYARDS CO.
GUASTI   CALIFORNIA

Beaulieu Vineyard Cabernet Sauvignon
Private Reserve

Private Reserve, in existence since the 1939 vintage, was created to exemplify the finest Cabernet the firm could make. It is the most highly regarded Cabernet in California, always intensely flavored, dark-colored, dense wine. It is 100 percent Cabernet; grapes are selected right in the vineyard to make this wine. Special care is taken in its production; it is aged both in cask and in bottle before the wine is sold. The finesse is a model for three decades of wine makers; present-day Cabernet Sauvignon style finds it hard to match. The firm's range of wine types is better in red than white. Owned by the giant Heublein company and expanding production in various regions, BV's wines are reliable in quality but sometimes overpriced and usually unexciting.

VINTAGE   *DATE*   *PRICE*

GUESTS

MENU   *COMMENTS*

Inglenook Cabernet Sauvignon Cask

Like BV, Inglenook Vineyards is located in Rutherford, Napa Valley. Founded in 1879, Inglenook's elite vineyard-selected Cabernet Sauvignon Cask has a friendly rivalry with its neighbor's Private Reserve, but Inglenook uses up to one-third Merlot as the wine maker sees fit and is aged in large old oak puncheons rather than new 50-gallon barrels. These two different firms are owned by Heublein. The cask wines are elegant, unusually perfumed, and lighter than 100 percent Cabernet wines. It and BV Reserve are in the same class. Inglenook's estate-bottled varietals show annual improvement, thanks to modern cellaring techniques. They are usually 100 percent of variety named, worth their average $3.00–$5.00 price, and should *not* be confused with Inglenook District Vintage wines coming from other Heublein cellars. These are mere standard inexpensive wines competing with mass-distribution firms.

VINTAGE   *DATE*   *PRICE*

GUESTS

MENU   *COMMENTS*

Sterling Vineyards Cabernet Sauvignon

Among the newest and grandest wineries built in Napa Valley, Sterling owns vineyards in the warm climate of the northern Napa Valley, around Calistoga. Merlot is mixed with their Cabernet and aged exclusively in French barrels. They have proved that rigorous vineyard practice can produce first-class grapes in regions once thought too warm. These practices result in one of the most Bordeaux-like of California red wines. Sterling makes Pinot Noir, Merlot (a 100 percent varietal), Chardonnay, Sauvignon Blanc (with Sémillon blended in, as in Bordeaux), Chenin Blanc, and Gewürztraminer. They have been operating since 1969, definitely using French methods. Their overall style cannot yet be characterized.

VINTAGE   *DATE*   *PRICE*

GUESTS

MENU   *COMMENTS*

Ridge Cabernet Sauvignon

Started in 1959, Ridge was first among a small flock of purist wine makers operating on a tiny scale with high ideals. In addition, this winery, whose first commercial crop appeared in 1962, initiated a style of wine making in which wines are "left alone" as much as possible, whatever past practice may have been. Incredibly full-bodied, colored, and flavorful reds result from long maceration with skins during fermentation and from bottling unfined, unfiltered wine. This Cabernet Sauvignon is an example. Wines from different vineyard sources are segregated and labeled as such. Ridge's own vineyard is on Montebello Ridge in the Santa Cruz Mountains in western Santa Clara. They have attained national distribution and probably produce 50,000 gallons of wine annually. Their whites are decidedly less good than reds.

VINTAGE   *DATE*   *PRICE*

GUESTS

MENU   *COMMENTS*

Beaulieu Vineyard

ESTATE BOTTLED

GEORGES DE LATOUR

PRIVATE RESERVE

NAPA VALLEY CABERNET SAUVIGNON

PRODUCED & BOTTLED BY BEAULIEU VINEYARD
AT RUTHERFORD, NAPA COUNTY, CALIFORNIA

ALCOHOL 12.5% BY VOLUME

Inglenook

ESTATE BOTTLED

CASK G-9

NAPA VALLEY

CABERNET SAUVIGNON

Distinctive flavor and aroma of the famous Cabernet Sauvignon grape variety. A full **1969** bodied dry red table wine made from grapes grown in our Napa Valley vineyards.

Produced and Bottled by Inglenook Vineyards Rutherford, California. Alcohol 12% by Volume.

STERLING VINEYARDS

Napa Valley
CABERNET SAUVIGNON

Grown, Produced and Bottled by Sterling Vineyards.
Calistoga·Napa Valley·California

alcohol 12% by volume

RIDGE CALIFORNIA CABERNET SAUVIGNON 1971

ESTATE GROWN GRAPES, **MONTE BELLO** 2300 FT
BOTTLED OCT 1973 ALCOHOL 12.2% BY VOLUME
PRODUCED AND BOTTLED BY RIDGE VINEYARDS
17100 MONTE BELLO RD, CUPERTINO, CALIFORNIA

Beringer Traubengold

One of Napa Valley's oldest names (bought by Nestlé, itself owned by the Union Bank of Switzerland), Beringer produces the usual Napa range of wines: the label shows its new proprietary brand of Riesling—"Grapegold." Riesling grapes from Santa Maria, Santa Barbara County, 400 miles away, are blended with small quantities of Muscat to obtain a perfumed, slightly sweet German-style white wine. Nestlé is attempting to improve Beringer's image by making and reserving small lots of superior varietal wine. The rest of the line can be compared in quality and style to Krug, Sebastiani, Martini, and the like, though Beringer prices are about those of Krug.

VINTAGE   *DATE*   *PRICE*

GUESTS

MENU   *COMMENTS*

Robert Mondavi Fumé Blanc

When he left Krug to found Robert Mondavi Winery in 1966, Mondavi created the name Fumé Blanc for a dry Sauvignon Blanc wine, inspired by the grape's name in the Loire. It is aged a short time in cask. It does not impress the palate as bone dry but rather is agreeably textured with distinct Sauvignon fruit but without completely expressing 100 percent Sauvignon character. A procession of imitators have rebaptized their Sauvignon-type wines Fumé Blanc or Blanc Fumé, including Almadén, Beringer, and, most recently, Charles Krug. Mondavi wines seem yet to find a definite style. Many experiments have followed one another. The company is owned by Sicks Rainier Brewing Co., Seattle.

VINTAGE   *DATE*   *PRICE*

GUESTS

MENU   *COMMENTS*

Chappellet Chenin Blanc

Coming from one of the highest planted areas in Napa Valley, its eastern slope, the Chappellet vineyard is the expensive expression of the desire of its wealthy founder to produce fine wine. Cabernet, Johannisberg Riesling, Chardonnay, and Chenin Blanc are the grape varieties. This completely dry, even austere, version of Chenin Blanc is somewhat of an anomaly; the more usual, successful Krug style is medium dry. Fruit grown at such high elevations ripens well but not in such a way as to give wine of pronounced flavor; too, the meticulous vinification adds to the impression of delicate but nearly sterile wines. This characterizes all Chappellet varieties except the Cabernet. Chappellet, like Stony Hill on the west slope of Napa, produces white wines having more finesse but less pungency than those grown on the valley floor.

VINTAGE   *DATE*   *PRICE*

GUESTS

MENU   *COMMENTS*

Souverain Mountain Zinfandel

Souverain began to sell wines bearing vintage dates in 1968, but their Napa Valley tradition of high-country Zinfandel wines goes back many years. The original Souverain winery, founded in 1941 by Lee Stewart, is now called Burgess Cellars and is under separate ownership. The name Souverain, once Souverain of Rutherford, since owned by the Pillsbury Flour Company and now by another group, is now to be used only for their Geyserville plant. It continues to make a light-bodied, medium-weight Zinfandel representing an older style of this grape made clean and pleasant for casual quaffing but not one evoking the full intensity that others have proven capable of extracting.

VINTAGE   *DATE*   *PRICE*

GUESTS

MENU   *COMMENTS*

Beringer

Traubengold

A MEDIUM DRY CALIFORNIA RIESLING

Produced and bottled by
Beringer Vineyards, St. Helena, Napa Valley, California
Alcohol 12½% by Volume

1974
Napa Valley
FUMÉ BLANC
Dry Sauvignon Blanc
ALCOHOL 12% BY VOLUME
PRODUCED AND BOTTLED BY
ROBERT MONDAVI WINERY
OAKVILLE, CALIFORNIA

CHAPPELLET

VINEYARD

1973
Napa Valley

CHENIN BLANC

GROWN AND BOTTLED BY CHAPPELLET VINEYARD
PRITCHARD HILL, ST. HELENA, CALIFORNIA   ALCOHOL 13.4% BY VOLUME

Souverain
of Rutherford

Mountain Zinfandel
Napa Valley

produced & bottled at the winery by Souverain   Rutherford, Ca.
Alcohol 13% by volume

Wente Pinot Chardonnay

Wente is among the few remaining family-held vineyard wineries established in California. The winery is still located in Livermore, Alameda County, but this wine mainly comes from pioneer plantings in Monterey County. Until the 1970s, Wente Chardonnay was considered the most prestigious of California white wines. Wente are white wine specialists, and their determined production of a varietal Chardonnay continues to enjoy prestige. This is a California-style Chardonnay, not oak-aged but fermented and matured in stainless steel with lighter, more direct tasting qualities. Wente inherited a Livermore tradition of Bordeaux-style white wines that includes Sauvignon Blanc and Sémillon found in dry and sweet form. Their vineyards include vines from the famous Château d'Yquem in Bordeaux's Sauternes region.

VINTAGE   DATE   PRICE

GUESTS

MENU   COMMENTS

Concannon Petite Sirah

Another family winery of long tradition and a neighbor of Wente, Concannon led the way in marketing Petite Sirah varietal wine. This is probably Duriff rather than "French Syrah," the true Syrah grape as it is called here, and though the landscape suggests Châteauneuf-du-Pape in its stony appearance, neither in color, aroma, or intensity of taste does the wine fully imitate powerful Rhône reds. Concannon wines are occasionally delicate but normally bland. They lack vitality and sometimes are crudely made for what is usually a quality winery. Concannon is the only producer of a Russian grape variety, Rkatsiteli (a white Georgian grape). The firm was established as producers of sacramental wines. The old Hallcrest vineyard at Felton, Santa Cruz County, sells its Cabernet and White Riesling to Concannon. Like Wente, however, Concannon is known for its white wines.

VINTAGE   DATE   PRICE

GUESTS

MENU   COMMENTS

Mirassou Petite Rosé

Petite Rosé is based on Petite Sirah grapes. Its birth was a mistake. In 1968 Grenache, the usual rosé grape, was followed into the vats by gondola loads of Petite Sirah without anyone realizing what had happened. Carrying this mistake to its conclusion, Mirassou made a dry rosé of individuality, unlike the usually sweet California Grenache Rosé pioneered by Almadén. Urban development of Mirassou land in Santa Clara has pressed the firm to drive plantings into Monterey, where they are the principal vineyard owners, and both Santa Clara and Monterey County appellations exist. Producing wines for sale to other wineries for nearly a century, Mirassou launched its own labels in 1967. These include Petite Sirah, Zinfandel of much reputation, Cabernet, Pinot Noir, an interesting Gamay Beaujolais made sparkling, and a Chenin Blanc, the first to be commercialized (in 1970) from machine-picked grapes.

VINTAGE   DATE   PRICE

GUESTS

MENU   COMMENTS

The Monterey Vineyard Del Mar Ranch

The third and newest winery in Monterey (along with Paul Masson and Chalone), The Monterey Vineyard controls the most grape. It is alone in designating its wines "Monterey County." This wine is from a particular vineyard, a "ranch" to Californians. The wine is a blend of Chenin Blanc and Pinot Blanc (40 percent each) and Sylvaner. This is original in that a branded wine is sold based on a deliberate planting of a specific vineyard. Another firm might sell such a blend as "Chablis." A plain, clean wine is what results, free of some of the vegetal taste plaguing Monterey wines and sold cheaply at about $2.50. Monterey experiments with bottling timing and with unusual varieties such as their promising Merlot, and the outlook for Pinot Noir in this cooler area is interesting. The vineyards are owned by a syndicate headed by the farming family M. B. MacFarland and Sons.

VINTAGE   DATE   PRICE

GUESTS

MENU   COMMENTS

WENTE BROS.

1974 VINTAGE

CALIFORNIA
PINOT CHARDONNAY

PRODUCED AND BOTTLED BY WENTE BROS.
LIVERMORE, CALIFORNIA, U.S.A.
ALCOHOL 12% BY VOLUME

VINTAGE 1971

CONN GAN AN

Concannon
vineyard
SINCE 1883

ESTATE
BOTTLED

LIVERMORE VALLEY
PETITE SIRAH

ALCOHOL 12% BY VOLUME
PRODUCED AND BOTTLED BY
CONCANNON VINEYARD
LIVERMORE, CALIFORNIA

Vintaged
Mirassou
Monterey-Santa Clara
Petite Rosé

Produced and Bottled by Mirassou Vineyards
San Jose, California

Alcohol 12%　　　　*By Volume*

THE MONTEREY VINEYARD

MONTEREY COUNTY
Del Mar Ranch
DRY WHITE MONTEREY WINE

Produced and Bottled by
The Monterey Vineyard
Gonzales, California USA

ALCOHOL 11½% BY VOLUME

Korbel Natural Champagne

Korbel Natural Champagne was the first of its type to appear in California. The intention was to effect in America the same association of "dryness" and quality as in expensive French champagne, hence the label and bottle. Korbel, located in Guerneville, Sonoma County, is the oldest continuous sparkling-wine producer in California. The blend is based on Pinot Blanc, Chardonnay, Sylvaner, and Chenin Blanc. Korbel's fame exceeds its quality. Like some of its competitors, Korbel uses true Champagne method for making wine, completing secondary fermentation in the very bottle sold rather than removing wine to vat after bottle fermentation for rebottling under pressure (the so-called transfer process). The quality, however, is often no better than the cheaper method.

VINTAGE   *DATE*   *PRICE*

GUESTS

MENU   *COMMENTS*

Hanns Kornell Champagne

One of two sparkling wine producers in Napa Valley, Kornell calls its wines *California* Champagne; Schramsberg, the other producer, uses only Napa Valley grapes. Kornell's is based on Sylvaner and Riesling, reflecting a German background, whereas Schramsberg is based on Chardonnay and Pinot Blanc. The *dosage* for extra dry is 2.5 percent sugar, so the wine tastes slightly sweet. Kornell produces at Saint Helena sparkling wine marketed by other firms, Oakville, Heitz, and Inglenook among them. The prestige of the firm is carried by their Sehr Trocken sparkling wine made from Riesling and usually matured six years in contact with yeasts. A full range of sparkling wine is produced, including a Muscat type.

VINTAGE   *DATE*   *PRICE*

GUESTS

MENU   *COMMENTS*

Oakville Sauvignon Blanc

An ambitious undertaking that appears to have gotten into difficulties as a result of its elaborate cost structure, Oakville began producing wine in 1968. Its wines are produced in German fashion and include Cabernet, Zinfandel, and Gamay. Oakville innovated in marketing "House Red" and "House White" wines, frankly sold as plain table wines. Its vineyards outside Oakville supply Sauvignon Blanc grapes fermented in stainless steel. The white wine shows the clean, fragrant aroma typical of such a process and is finished slightly sweet. The red wines tend to good color and tannin but do not include press wine and thus do not show the body of such wines. They are distinguished by fruit and drinkability and do not offer complexity.

VINTAGE   *DATE*   *PRICE*

GUESTS

MENU   *COMMENTS*

Sutter Home Zinfandel

Sutter Home is unique among California wineries in having tied its fortunes to one wine and also is singular in Napa Valley for owning no vineyard. It pioneered the use of grapes from distant vineyards and reestablished the fame of Amador County as a viticultural area by buying its grapes there. It has limited its vintages to one or sometimes two vineyards. Dark-colored wines strong in alcohol even by California standards, rich and mouth-filling but mercifully free of raisinlike character are the Zinfandels they have made their hallmark. The winery has moved from a production of 40 different wines sold under two sorts of labels to the one Zinfandel. Sutter Home is the oldest winery building still in use in the Napa Valley.

VINTAGE   *DATE*   *PRICE*

GUESTS

MENU   *COMMENTS*

FOR THE PARTICULAR AND DISCRIMINATING CHAMPAGNE CONNOISSEUR WHO APPRECIATES EXTREME DRYNESS AND DELICATE FLAVOR THIS CHAMPAGNE WAS PRODUCED TO COMMEMORATE OUR 100TH ANNIVERSARY.

KORBEL NATURAL

CALIFORNIA

Champagne

Extremely Dry

PRODUCED AND BOTTLED BY F. KORBEL and BROS. Inc. GUERNEVILLE, SONOMA CO., CALIFORNIA. B.W. No. 74. ALCOHOL 12½% BY VOL. NET CONTENTS 4/5 QUART.

Hanns Kornell

THIRD GENERATION

CALIFORNIA

Champagne

EXTRA DRY

PRODUCED & BOTTLED BY HANNS KORNELL CHAMPAGNE CELLARS ST. HELENA, CALIF.

CONTENTS 4/5 QUART

NATURALLY FERMENTED IN THIS BOTTLE

Oakville Vineyards

NAPA VALLEY

SAUVIGNON BLANC

1973

ALCOHOL 12% BY VOLUME
PRODUCED & BOTTLED BY
OAKVILLE CELLARS
OAKVILLE, CALIFORNIA

"Sutter Home"

~ 1973 ~

ZINFANDEL

Produced and Bottled By
Sutter Home Winery,
St. Helena, California
Alcohol 13% By Volume

This Zinfandel was produced from grapes grown on the K. Deaver and J. Ferrero ranches in the Shenandoah Valley of Amador County.

Located in the foothills of the Sierra Nevada, the climate and temperature of this area make it perfect for growing Zinfandel. Here these grapes produce a superior wine with great depth and fullness and more spicyness and richness than anywhere in California.

Freemark Abbey Edelwein

As of 1973, this was the largest parcel of botrytized Johannisberg Riesling produced in California. When picked, the grapes had the sugar degree of a German Beerenauslese. The wine's aroma, flavor, and sweetness are intense and reflect Riesling character well. The wine has extraordinary sugar for its limited alcohol. Freemark produces Cabernet, Pinot Noir, Petite Sirah, Chardonnay, and White Riesling. All but the White Riesling are aged in Nevers oak and bear a strong family resemblance. Long aging lends oak flavor, but the style is being moved continuously toward more fruity wines. The good reputation of Freemark is based on elegant wines; its critics find them too distinctly shaped by house style.

VINTAGE   *DATE*   *PRICE*

GUESTS

MENU   *COMMENTS*

Simi Rosé of Cabernet Sauvignon

Simi is one of the oldest producing wineries in Sonoma and is now owned by the Scotch distillers Scottish & Newcastle. This is not the only rosé made from Cabernet; Buena Vista, Llords and Elwood, and Mountainside are other producers. The Simi rosé is well colored for its type, distinctly perfumed, and finished slightly sweet in response to demand. Simi makes a full complement of dry wines. Their vineyards are in Sonoma County and in Alexander Valley.

VINTAGE   *DATE*   *PRICE*

GUESTS

MENU   *COMMENTS*

Sonoma Vineyards River East Vineyard Johannisberg Riesling Sonoma County

Sonoma Vineyards has facilities at Windsor and vineyards extending throughout Sonoma County and the Alexander Valley. Recently, it has been in the forefront of sweet White Riesling production. This example is unusual for California in that the precise locale is specified on the label. A creek bordering the vineyard parcel gives it its name. In this humid situation it is possible to promote the growth of noble rot (*Botrytis cinerea*), and wines of sweet character ensue. Sonoma is 51 percent owned by Renfield, distributors of alcoholic beverages. In fact the wines present themselves under three names: Tiburon Vintners, Windsor Vineyards, and Sonoma Vineyards. Private label bottles that show the stamping Windsor, California, are from Sonoma Vineyards. This is a large winery controlling about 5,000 acres of vineyard.

VINTAGE   *DATE*   *PRICE*

GUESTS

MENU   *COMMENTS*

Novitiate Black Muscat

This is a Portlike fortified wine produced from the red variety Muscat Hamburg grown in Novitiate of Los Gatos's Guadeloupe Valley vineyards near Modesto. The Novitiate is owned by the Society of Jesus. Their wine-making activity goes back to the 1880s when sacramental wine was made from their original vineyards in the Santa Cruz Mountains at Los Gatos. Ruby-colored, this wine has the obvious perfume of Muscat grapes but with a pleasant amount of tannin arising from fermentation on the skins, which is intended to extract color from this variety. Fresh-tasting versions will not have been dulled by overaging in small cooperage. The Novitiate makes a large quantity of table wines—Cabernet Sauvignon, Ruby Cabernet, Chenin Blanc, Pinot Blanc, Dry Malvasia, two rosé wines, and a gamut for fortified, aperitif, and dessert wines. Their renown comes from this latter class of wine.

VINTAGE   *DATE*   *PRICE*

GUESTS

MENU   *COMMENTS*

FREEMARK ABBEY

1973
NAPA VALLEY

Sweet Johannisberg Riesling

Edelwein

Produced and Bottled by
FREEMARK ABBEY WINERY, ST. HELENA, CALIFORNIA

Alcohol 11.4% by volume

Residual Sugar 10% by weight

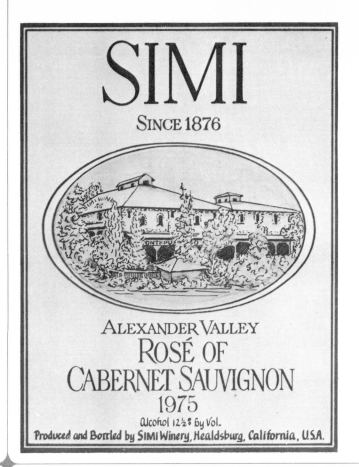

SIMI
SINCE 1876

ALEXANDER VALLEY
ROSÉ OF
CABERNET SAUVIGNON
1975

Alcohol 12½% by Vol.

Produced and Bottled by SIMI Winery, Healdsburg, California, U.S.A.

Sonoma Vineyards
Sonoma County
Johannisberg Riesling
Estate Grown -1974- River East Vineyard
PRODUCED AND BOTTLED AT THE WINERY BY SONOMA VINEYARDS
WINDSOR, SONOMA COUNTY, CALIFORNIA, ALCOHOL 11% BY VOLUME.

Jesuit Wines
Since 1888

Noviliate
CALIFORNIA
BLACK MUSCAT

ALCOHOL 18% BY VOLUME

PRODUCED AND BOTTLED BY
Novitiate of Los Gatos
LOS GATOS, CALIFORNIA

Heitz Cabernet Sauvignon
Martha's Vineyard

Beginning by buying wines of various pioneers, such as James Zellerbach at Hanzell, and intelligently following up on the success these achieved, Heitz winery has gone on to a larger range of wines built on this double role of grower and style maker of other people's grape product. This Cabernet grown near Oakville on the western slope of Napa Valley was the first to pay tribute on its label to the superior source of the grapes grown at another locale not belonging to its maker. Intensely flavored with a strong aroma that Californians image as eucalyptus and an oily texture from expert cool fermentations, this is truly an example of wine *making.* Other reputed wines are Heitz's Pinot Chardonnay (*sic*) from Zinfandel Associates (see Harbor Winery, page 268) on Napa Valley floor land; generic wines, such as Chablis, Burgundy; and his own growings of Grignolino. Heitz wines are expensive but original.

VINTAGE   DATE   PRICE

GUESTS

MENU   COMMENTS

Mayacamas Cabernet Sauvignon

The Mayacamas range divides Napa and Sonoma counties. Astraddle the hill country sits this vineyard that, 25 years ago, began the idea in Napa of grower-made wine. It calls itself Napa Mountain, and such saddleback-located vineyards yield tannic black Cabernet rich in fruit. The winery shares naturalistic ideals with those of Ridge. Mayacamas gives us also a Chardonnay dominated by oak contributions and has impressed California with its "late harvest" Zinfandel, a red distinguished by power. Following the 1959 experiments of Myron Nightingale (now at Beringer), Mayacamas is making a sweet Sémillon/Sauvignon white by inducing botrytis (noble rot). This is difficult and costly.

VINTAGE   DATE   PRICE

GUESTS

MENU   COMMENTS

Joseph Swan Zinfandel

This tiny production has become a cult object in California. Joseph Swan, a retired airline pilot, produced his first wine in the 1950s and commercialized his first vinification only in the 1970s. To the Zinfandel from the Dry Creek sector of Sonoma some 10 percent Petite Sirah is added, resulting in perfumed impressions meticulously produced in small batches. Here the hand of the wine maker overwhelmingly dominates the grape varieties used. Swan has done something extraordinary; he has realized in each of his red wines, Zinfandel and Pinot Noir, a quality the French call *fond*—that power and depth of taste without which no red wine is great. His extreme intentions include a selection by clone of his Pinot Noir grapes. Since plants reproduce asexually, it is possible to select a clone, one individual, and use its cutting to found an entire vineyard. Surely this is exceptional devotion in what most people consider to be a business.

VINTAGE   DATE   PRICE

GUESTS

MENU   COMMENTS

Mount Eden Pinot Noir

This vineyard winery came to its present owners, the Mount Eden Investor Group, after a decade of bitter court struggle with its founder, the irascible Martin Ray. Situated atop the Santa Cruz Mountains at some 2,300 feet, Cabernet, Pinot Noir, and Chardonnay produce wines typified by strong body. The Pinot Noir is fascinating in being the old planting of Paul Masson's importation of this vine variety transplanted from his original estate down the hill. This is dark wine whose tightly knit qualities are associated with the clone type of vine, called in France the Petit Pinot noirien. Mount Eden's Chardonnay is a rich golden wine resembling those made by David Bruce on an extension of the same slope; pungent Cabernets join the family.

VINTAGE   DATE   PRICE

GUESTS

MENU   COMMENTS

VINTAGE 1970   BOTTLED AUGUST, 1974

Bottle ___ of a total of 10,400 bottles

Heitz Cellar

NAPA VALLEY
CABERNET SAUVIGNON

ALCOHOL 13% BY VOLUME

 PRODUCED AND BOTTLED IN OUR CELLAR BY
MARTHA'S VINEYARD
HEITZ WINE CELLARS
ST. HELENA, CALIFORNIA

MAYACAMAS

1971
NAPA MOUNTAIN
CABERNET SAUVIGNON

ALCOHOL 13% BY VOLUME

PRODUCED AND BOTTLED BY

Mayacamas Vineyards
NAPA, CALIFORNIA

1972
Sonoma

Zinfandel Lot 2

Joseph Swan Vineyards

Alcohol 13.0% by volume
Produced and Bottled by Joseph Swan Vineyards, Forestville, California

---

Mount Eden Vineyards

*Made entirely from berries of a selected,
authentic clone of the grape variety named,
this wine is grown, fermented and bottled
2000 feet above the floor of the Santa Clara
Valley, on a peak of the Chaîne d'Or, at*

Saratoga, California

PINOT NOIR
1972
ESTATE BOTTLED

Produced and bottled by Mount Eden Vineyards
Alcohol 13.0 % by volumne   Saratoga, California

Spring Mountain Chardonnay

Until now, Spring Mountain has gained esteem by buying grapes and wine and finishing its production in a distinctive style. Their vineyards joined this stream in 1976, yielding fine wines forceful in their acidity, touched by wood maturing and finishing with an elegance often lacking in California. Chardonnay, Sauvignon Blanc, and Cabernet Sauvignon are what they do. A Bordeaux style marks the Cabernet. The Chardonnay is conceived as a grape-flavored rather than a wood-flavored wine. The Sauvignon Blanc has evolved from the thicker Bordeaux style to the fresher version the grape takes in the Loire Valley. Like Heitz, Spring Mountain sometimes retains the now disproved name of "Pinot Chardonnay" for the Chardonnay grape.

VINTAGE   DATE   PRICE

GUESTS

MENU   COMMENTS

Harbor Winery Mission Del Sol

A tiny winery in western Sacramento makes rich wines from Chardonnay and Zinfandel that emphasize grapy qualities rather than fashionable woody ones. Old wood is favored over new for maturing. The red Zinfandel is drawn from Amador County, affirming that district as a fine grape producer. In aroma, taste, and body, the Zinfandel asserts the qualities of that variety. The Chardonnay (whose grapes come from Zinfandel Associates in Napa Valley) has the immediate and authentic qualities associated with that noble grape. Harbor is unique in making this white dessert wine exclusively from century-old Mission vines in Amador County, the first vines planted there. Grape concentrate is added to the fermenting must, alcohol builds up, and slowly but surely the yeasts die off naturally at about 17 percent alcohol level. This is an example of fine wine making as it was conceived two centuries ago.

VINTAGE   DATE   PRICE

GUESTS

MENU   COMMENTS

Chalone Vineyard Pinot Blanc

Containing California's most ancient fine varietal plantings, Chalone is also the most difficult vineyard in the state to cultivate. Planted in 1916, it was recuperated in 1966 as Chalone by Richard Graff. It is remarkable in being entirely planted in chalk soils resembling those of the white wine areas of France's Côte de Beaune. The tiny output (1,000 cases) will be raised by adjacent land planted in Chardonnay and Pinot Noir; 5,000 cases of each are the target. Fermentation in new oak in the best Burgundian tradition produces golden dark wines. Its aroma couples Pinot Blanc odor with new wood, while its highly acid body carries a rich flavor on a strong alcoholic style. Chalone defends a last outpost of Pinot Blanc production against the Chardonnay wave.

VINTAGE   DATE   PRICE

GUESTS

MENU   COMMENTS

Hanzell Chardonnay

This winery, conceived in French terms even in its architecture, is the starting point for the "French style" counterrevolution emphasizing flavor and finesse against the antiseptic school of California wine making that followed so naturally out of the great contributions of university scholars. Yet this same scientific progress gave the intuition and the means to develop its balanced, elegant Chardonnay and Pinot Noir, the latter made in that most difficult of models, the fine wines of Beaune/Volnay. French oak casks, small stainless-steel vats, steel trays to carry in the grapes—all reflect a wealthy man's desire to prove a point, not the least of monuments the late James Zellerbach left his fellows. He was the first to use French oak casks, and as American Ambassador to Rome it must have been a happy moment to hear European tasters identify his first Chardonnay crop (1956) as a white Burgundy but ask from which Côte d'Or vineyard did it come.

VINTAGE   DATE   PRICE

GUESTS

MENU   COMMENTS

Spring Mountain

1973

Napa Valley

CHARDONNAY

MADE AND BOTTLED BY

Spring Mountain Vineyards • St. Helena, California

ALCOHOL 13.0% BY VOLUME

HARBOR WINERY

1974

Amador County

MISSION DEL SOL

A Sweet White Wine of Mission Grapes

Produced and bottled by Harbor Winery
West Sacramento, California

Alcohol 18% by Volume

1973

CHALONE VINEYARD

CALIFORNIA

PINOT BLANC

ESTATE BOTTLED

This vintage produced 5342 bottles,
of which this is No.

A table wine, grown and bottled on Mount Chalone by Chalone
Vineyard, The Pinnacles, Soledad, Monterey County, California.

1973

Hanzell

SONOMA VALLEY

CHARDONNAY

Grown and Bottled at the Winery by
HANZELL VINEYARDS, SONOMA, CALIFORNIA
BONDED WINERY #4470 · 4/5 QUART · ALCOHOL 13% BY VOLUME

R 5303   KRUGMANN

Your Personal Selections

VINTAGE   DATE   PRICE

COMMENTS

VINTAGE   DATE   PRICE

COMMENTS

VINTAGE   DATE   PRICE

COMMENTS

VINTAGE   DATE   PRICE

COMMENTS

VINTAGE   DATE   PRICE

COMMENTS

VINTAGE   DATE   PRICE

COMMENTS

VINTAGE   *DATE*   *PRICE*

COMMENTS

VINTAGE   *DATE*   *PRICE*

COMMENTS

VINTAGE   *DATE*   *PRICE*

COMMENTS

VINTAGE   *DATE*   *PRICE*

COMMENTS

VINTAGE   *DATE*   *PRICE*

COMMENTS

VINTAGE   *DATE*   *PRICE*

COMMENTS

VINTAGE   DATE   PRICE

COMMENTS

VINTAGE   DATE   PRICE

COMMENTS

VINTAGE   DATE   PRICE

COMMENTS

VINTAGE   DATE   PRICE

COMMENTS

VINTAGE   DATE   PRICE

COMMENTS

VINTAGE   DATE   PRICE

COMMENTS

VINTAGE   *DATE*   *PRICE*

COMMENTS

VINTAGE   *DATE*   *PRICE*

COMMENTS

VINTAGE   *DATE*   *PRICE*

COMMENTS

VINTAGE   *DATE*   *PRICE*

COMMENTS

VINTAGE   *DATE*   *PRICE*

COMMENTS

VINTAGE   *DATE*   *PRICE*

COMMENTS

VINTAGE   DATE   PRICE

COMMENTS

VINTAGE   DATE   PRICE

COMMENTS

VINTAGE   DATE   PRICE

COMMENTS

VINTAGE   DATE   PRICE

COMMENTS

VINTAGE   DATE   PRICE

COMMENTS

VINTAGE   DATE   PRICE

COMMENTS

Vintage Chart

Some vintages are uniform, others diverse. In the first case generalizations can be helpful; the second case offers endless chances for misleading statements. Some wine regions such as Porto and Champagne use vintage designations for their best wines only. The comments below reflect what would be experienced by tasting a large range of wines from each of the areas, and years, in question.

CHAMPAGNE

1955	Balanced, excellent
1959	Very full-bodied, ripe-tasting, heavy and duller as they age
1961	Strong body, balanced
1962	Light, esteemed for elegance
1964	Generous body and flavor, many fine and balanced
1966	Body, flavor good, character complete, some delicious standouts
1967	The best are light, refined; others thin, variable
1969	Elegant, often fruity, some fine and powerful, a few coarse
1970	Large crop of balanced wine, most very good

RHÔNE

1966	Good standard achieved in all regions
1967	Strong-bodied; great appellations very suitable for long maturing
1968	Light
1969	Small crop of good wine, some fine
1970	As elsewhere, a large crop; balanced, good quality
1971	Small crop of good to very good wine
1972	Northern Rhône reds excellent, others less distinguished
1973	Forward, medium-bodied, developing quickly, not enough acidity
1974	General level poor; some good reds in southern Rhône

BURGUNDY

1966	Variable, intensity of taste often lacking, some fine, others dull
1967	Delicate, now fading, a few with breed but little impact survive
1968	Thin, underripe, poor
1969	Distinguished; color, perfume, character, and elegance rival 1971
1970	Moderate in power but flavor and character good, some outstanding
1971	Rivals 1969 as a great year but deeper; more power and flavor; elegance pronounced
1972	A good year, unlike elsewhere; attractive wines of limited power
1973	Large crop, fruit and appeal, developing quickly
1974	Variable, poor results in Beaujolais, difficult to judge, overall not showing well now
1975	Cold year, unripe, much rot, meager wines

BORDEAUX

One gambles on old vintages: storage conditions, luck in individual bottles make for successful versus disastrous very old wines.

1916	Coarse wines; some stand out for flavor and character
1918	Elegant, some exquisite when surviving
1920 1922 1924 1926	Generous individual bottles, a few elegant, survive; most flat and finished
1928	Remarkable year for color, body, tannin; surviving wines are extraordinary in power and impression on the palate; many dried out, lacking charm
1929	Once a supreme year for elegance, only rare bottles preserve bouquet, aftertaste, and finesse, showing superlative quality
1933	Queer wines; some have intensity but few are balanced; poor risk
1934	Dark, rich body; sometimes unctuous, often oily texture; much bouquet when surviving but coarse
1937	Well rated in vintage charts but in fact poor; few Margaux wines show elegance. Very poor risk
1943	Once pretty, well rated, now nearly all decayed
1944	Occasionally surprising and exciting wines but these terribly rare; most poor and mean
1945	Exciting, great, powerful year; dreadfully expensive but a good bet for quality; some thrilling mature wines remain in perfect form
1947	Rich flavor, but often disintegrating; some remarkable St.-Émilion and Pomerol still full in bouquet, strong in style, exciting. Finesse rare, however
1948	Firm vintage, excellent style, conserves well; good bet, especially Médocs
1949	Charming racy vintage dying of acetic acid poisoning; many still delicious and exciting; watch out for storage conditions, fragile. Gamblers only to play

The following characterize good vintages between 1950 and 1962 throughout the Bordeaux area:

1950	Balanced, fruit, charm; many lasting well; underestimated badly in the past
1952	Overrated on charts. Dry, hard, unpleasing. Some excellent exceptions possess fruit
1953	Lovely clarets, harmonious, elegant, subtle, conserved by balance
1955	Full-bodied, dull; some rich exceptions and many excellent ones in St.-Émilion, Pomerol, and Graves
1957	Astringent, a few redeemed by mature bouquet; softened by age
1959	Much overrated; unbalanced, mostly vulgar, loose; exceptions saved by fruit and enough body to conserve
1960	Flawed vintage but includes charmers, most decayed or rotted
1961	Balanced, grand, charming, complete, reliable, finesse too. Many superlative
1962	Complete Médocs, many just below peak quality; misunderstood: balanced wines condemned as light because of big crop. St.-Émilion and Pomerol lack body, flavor

The following are good Bordeaux vintages from 1964 to the present, by district:

MÉDOC

1964 Insufficient acidity, concentration, and ripeness. Rectified into coarse, sugary wines or left as thin, short, drinkable. Some St.-Julien charmers

1966 Charming, balanced; fruit, body, elegance, successful throughout; most properties true to type; delicious now and for the future

1967 Lack fruit of 1966s but firm wines, some with weak flavor, most a bit dry; misunderstood vintage; good ones austere rather than "light," as often claimed

1969 Many thin, nasty; well selected vats attractive for early consumption, nothing more

1970 Balanced, generous, charming, excellent throughout; developing quickly; flavorful, stable, but lack intensity often as not

1971 Dark, severe, variable and hard to judge; intensity apparent, charm less sure

1972 Unripe. Some pleasant and useful for young drinking; variable, none great

1973 Much fruit, forward qualities, immediate charm; could evolve surprisingly well in bottle; remember premature misjudgments of 1950s and 1953s; second thoughts in order

1974 Color, constitution firm; appear to lack fruit and charm; may resemble 1971. Difficult to judge

1975 Certainly exceptional. Inky-dark, very powerful, intense body and texture; potent flavor. Impossible to characterize eventual style at maturity, certainly big

GRAVES

1964 Successful year, deep taste; many balanced, some dark and superb; scope and character pronounced

1966 Charming, complete wines following the Médoc pattern

1967 Good but thinner than Médocs; lack power finish of first-rate clarets; some loose in tasting impressions

1969 Incomplete, light, lacking ripe flavor and body. Drink young

1970 Successful, balanced, most elegant; share general success of Bordeaux reds

1971 Varied, some coarse, others thin, still others solid

1972 With a few exceptions (selected grapes), mean and sorry

1973 Good but variable, dry style in some, lighter in others, average quality a bit below Médoc

1974 Seem to be fine wines but show little fruit at this point; hard to judge

1975 Share success, overpowering impression of 1975 Bordeaux crop

SAUTERNES

1961 Many fine, if lighter than reds, a few intense and grand

1962 Great, powerful year, many superb; stellar crop

1964 Flavorful, fruity without full strength, some elegant, others short

1966 Not as good as reds, many charming but with insufficient power and depth of taste

1967 Like 1962 a superlative year; most rich, a few dazzling; standard very high in all but few accidental cases

1969 Surpass reds, some light and tasty, others short; much selection made

1970 Medium to good body and character, many fruity, too, but variable

1971 Sound, many satisfying, some elegant

SAINT-ÉMILION AND POMEROL

1964 Most are generous and flavorful, few coarse, some powerful Style varies from soupy light to superb dark; classic, complete wines

1966 Less complete and appealing than Médocs; good and tasty, but in most cases lack intensity and extra dash of excitement and finish; few delicious standouts

1967 Broad, assertive with body and flavor, especially St.-Émilions; some Pomerols elegant

1969 Below average in fruit and body; many pleasant for drinking now

1970 Fine crop showing rounder style of Right Bank wines compared to Médocs; balanced, rich wines; excellent flavor, body, and aftertaste

1971 Irregular; some flavorful, some lacking power, some awkward, many hard to judge

1972 Mean and thin; occasional pleasant exceptions for early drinking

1973 Attractive, fast maturing; much fruit, charm and color; tasty crop; useful wines all around but with several disappointments

1974 Body, color, clearly present; like Médocs, hard to judge

1975 High-powered, concentrated, extraordinary but hard to predict for style; lesser Right Bank appellations exciting

GERMANY

1969 Ripe year with many rich wines; varying degrees of finesse

1970 Useful good year lacking full concentration; attractive

1971 Highly regarded at home and abroad as a great year with a full range of tasting qualities and excitement of peak year conditions

1972 Unripe year

1973 Good fruit, appeal; lacks the intensity and scope of best years

1974 Unexciting crop without distinctiveness; many useful wines for current drinking

1975 Promising, ripe crop with hopes for exciting, concentrated wines

CALIFORNIA

1960 Full, typical California style, now aging noticeably

1961 Tendency to lighter wines

1962 Light year

1963 Light year

1964 Classic California-style year; big, intense wines

1965 Generally light wines with some very good Cabernet Sauvignon

1966 Cool year, reds resemble Bordeaux in astringency; good

1967 Lighter than average

1968 Hot, late vintage gave rich Cabernet Sauvignon with cooked flavor

1969 Light year with some exceptions; many excellent Zinfandels

1970 Spectacular Cabernet Sauvignon and generally fine red wines

1971 Resembles 1972 but a small crop as well

1972 Rain diluted harvests; light style the result

1973 Large crop; sound, complete, not dramatic in quality

1974 Cabernet Sauvignon excellent, as were some white wines

1975 Outstanding year for early ripening varieties such as Pinot Noir, variable for others

Bibliography

GENERAL INFORMATION

Bespaloff, Alexis. *The Signet Book of Wines.* New York: New American Library, 1971.

Johnson, Hugh. *The World Atlas of Wine.* New York: Simon and Schuster, 1971.

Lichine, Alexis. *New Encyclopedia of Wines & Spirits.* New York: Alfred A. Knopf, 1974.

Schoonmaker, Frank. *Encyclopedia of Wine.* Revised edition. New York: Hastings House, 1973.

FRANCE

Cocks, Charles, and Feret, Eduard. *Bordeaux et Ses Vins.* 12th edition. Bordeaux: Feret, 1969.

Jacquelin, Louis, and Poulain, René. *The Wines and Vineyards of France.* London: Paul Hamlyn, 1962.

Penning-Rowsell, Edmund. *The Wine and Food Society's Guide to the Wines of Bordeaux.* Revised edition. London: Wine and Food Society, 1971.

Poupon, Pierre, and Forgeot, Pierre. *The Wines of Burgundy.* Revised edition. Paris: Presses Universitaires de France, 1974.

Shand, P. Morton. *A Book of French Wines.* Revised edition. New York: Alfred A. Knopf, 1960.

Yoxall, H. W. *The Wines of Burgundy.* London: Wine and Food Society, 1968.

GERMANY

Hallgarten, S. F. *Rhineland Wineland.* 3rd edition, revised. London: Elek books, 1955.

Schoonmaker, Frank. *The Wines of Germany.* Revised edition. New York: Hastings House, 1966.

SOUTHERN AND SOUTHEASTERN EUROPE

Dallas, Philip. *The Great Wines of Italy.* New York: Doubleday, 1974.

del Castillo, José, and Hallett, D. R. *The Wines of Spain.* Bilbao: Proyección Editorial, 1972.

Gunyon, R. E. H. *The Wines of Central and Southeastern Europe.* London: Duckworth, 1971.

Ray, Cyril. *The Wines of Italy.* New York: McGraw-Hill, 1966.

Read, Jan. *The Wines of Spain and Portugal.* London: Faber and Faber, 1973.

Veronelli, Luigi. *Catalago Bolaffi dei Vini d'Italia.* Turin: Giulio Bolaffi, 1969.

CALIFORNIA

Adams, Leon D. *The Wines of America.* Boston: Houghton Mifflin, 1973.

Blumberg, Robert S., and Hannum, Hurst. *The Fine Wines of California.* Doubleday, 1971.

Chroman, Nathan, and Boss, David. *The Treasury of American Wines.* New York: Crown, 1973.

Melville, John. *Guide to California Wines.* 4th edition. Revised by Jefferson Morgan. San Carlos, California: Nourse Publishing Co., 1972.

AUSTRALIA AND NEW ZEALAND

Evans, Len. *Australia and New Zealand Complete Book of Wine.* Sydney; New York: Paul Hamlyn, 1973.

WINE PRODUCTION AND TECHNICAL INFORMATION

Amerine, M. A., Berg, H. W., and Creuss, W. V. *The Technology of Wine Making.* 3rd edition. Westport, Connecticut: Avi Publishing Co., 1972.

Broadbent, J. M. *Wine Tasting.* London: Christie Wine Publications, 1973.

Frumkin, Lionel. *The Science and Technique of Wine.* 4th edition. Cambridge, England: Patrick Stevens, 1974.

Puisais, J., Chambonon, R. L., *Initiation into the Art of Wine Tasting.* Madison, Wisconsin: Interpublish, 1974.

Winkler, A. J. *General Viticulture.* Berkeley and Los Angeles: University of California Press, 1962.